MILADY'S STANDARD
Nail Technology

6th Edition

ALISHA RIMANDO BOTERO

CATHERINE M. FRANGIE

JIM MCCONNELL

JANET MCCORMICK

JACQUELINE OLIPHANT

VICKI PETERS

DOUGLAS SCHOON

JERYL SPEAR

DEBORAH BEATTY

JEWELL CUNNINGHAM

LIN HALPERN

LACINDA HEADINGS

NANCY KING HEUPEL

TERRI LUNDBERG

GODFREY F. MIX, D.P.M.

LAURA J. MIX

REBECCA MORAN

SUE ELLEN SCHULTES

CENGAGE
Learning™

Australia • Brazil • Japan • Korea • Mexico • Singapore • Spain • United Kingdom • United States

CENGAGE
Learning™

**Milady's Standard: Nail Technology,
Sixth Edition**
Milady

President, Milady: Dawn Gerrain

Publisher: Erin O'Connor

Product Manager: Jessica Mahoney

Editorial Assistant: Elizabeth Edwards

Director of Beauty Industry Relations:
Sandra Bruce

Executive Marketing Manager: Gerard McAvey

Production Director: Wendy Troeger

Senior Content Project Manager:
Nina Tucciarelli

Senior Art Director: Joy Kocsis

Library of Congress Control Number: 2010926978

ISBN-13: 978-1-4354-9768-9

ISBN-10: 1-4354-9768-6

Milady
Executive Woods
5 Maxwell Drive
Clifton Park, NY 12065
USA

Cengage Learning is a leading provider of customized learning solutions with office locations around the globe, including Singapore, the United Kingdom, Australia, Mexico, Brazil, and Japan. Locate your local office at **www.cengage.com/global**

Cengage Learning products are represented in Canada by Nelson Education, Ltd.

To learn more about Milady, visit **milady.cengage.com**

Purchase any of our products at your local college store or at our preferred online store **www.cengagebrain.com**

Notice to the Reader

Publisher does not warrant or guarantee any of the products described herein or perform any independent analysis in connection with any of the product information contained herein. Publisher does not assume, and expressly disclaims, any obligation to obtain and include information other than that provided to it by the manufacturer. The reader is expressly warned to consider and adopt all safety precautions that might be indicated by the activities described herein and to avoid all potential hazards. By following the instructions contained herein, the reader willingly assumes all risks in connection with such instructions. The publisher makes no representations or warranties of any kind, including but not limited to, the warranties of fitness for particular purpose or merchantability, nor are any such representations implied with respect to the material set forth herein, and the publisher takes no responsibility with respect to such material. The publisher shall not be liable for any special, consequential, or exemplary damages resulting, in whole or part, from the readers' use of, or reliance upon, this material.

Printed in the United States of America
8 16 15 14

table of contents

CONTENTS

PART BUSINESS SKILLS / 429

PROCEDURES

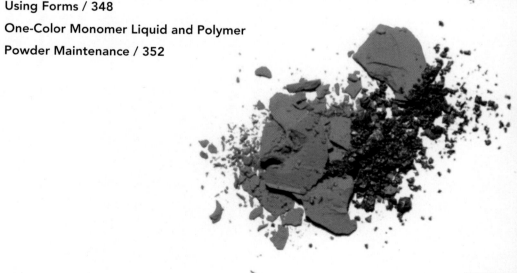

TO THE STUDENT

Congratulations! You have chosen a career filled with unlimited potential, one that can take you in many directions and holds the possibility to make you a confident, successful professional. As a nail professional, you will play a vital role in the lives of your clients. They will come to rely on you to provide them with ongoing service, enabling them to look and feel their best.

Each year professional nail technicians perform more than six billion dollars' worth of manicuring, pedicuring, and nail enhancement services for millions of fashion-conscious clients. The business of nails continues to progress and grow with new breakthroughs in product technologies, application techniques, and business strategy. Thus, the need for educated and competent nail technicians is expanding in the same way. *Milady's Standard: Nail Technology* 6e is the complete first step to basic nail technology that all professional nail technicians need to kick off their career.

You are fortunate because you will learn from gifted instructors who will share their skills and experiences with you. You will meet other industry professionals at seminars, workshops, and conventions where you will learn the latest techniques, specific product knowledge, and management procedures. All of the experiences in which you have the opportunity to participate will provide you with additional insights into the profession you have chosen. You will build a network of professionals to turn to for career advice, opportunity, and direction. Whatever direction you choose, we wish you a successful and enjoyable journey!

TO THE INSTRUCTOR

This sixth edition of *Milady's Standard: Nail Technology* was prepared with the help of many instructors and professionals. Milady surveyed more than 50 instructors, practicing nail professionals, and state board officials, and received in-depth comments from a host of other experts to learn what needed to be changed, added, or deleted from this text.

Milady's Standard: Nail Technology 6e contains new and updated information on many subjects including infection control, product chemistry, manicuring, pedicuring, electric filing, monomer liquid and polymer powder nail enhancements, and UV gels, and a completely new chapter, The Creative Touch, loaded with the latest nail art mediums and techniques.

You asked Milady to make your job easier by aligning overlapping editorial content between *Milady's Standard: Nail Technology* and *Milady's Standard: Cosmetology*, and we listened! This alignment includes the following chapters: History and Opportunities, Life Skills, Your Professional Image,

Communicating for Success, Infection Control: Principles and Practices, General Anatomy and Physiology, Skin Structure Growth, Nail Structure and Growth, Nail Diseases and Disorders, Basics of Chemistry, Basics of Electricity, Seeking Employment, On the Job, Business Skills, Manicuring, Pedicuring, Monomer Liquid and Polymer Powder Nail Enhancements, and UV Gels. We also listened when you asked for photographs and art that depict nail technicians performing their work and serving their clients; we conducted a six-day photo shoot to update more than 400 pieces of art throughout the book, including procedural art.

FEATURES OF THIS EDITION

In response to *your needs*, this exciting new edition of *Milady's Standard: Nail Technology* 6e includes the following features:

- *Chapters and Parts*. The book is divided into twenty-two chapters and four parts so it is very easy to use.

- *Full-Color Art*. All art is in full color, with brand-new photographs to show you step-by-step procedures for manicuring, pedicuring, tips and wraps, electric filing, monomer liquid and polymer powder nail enhancements, UV gels, and a completely new basic nail art.

- *Learning Objectives and Review Questions*. Learning objectives provide goals for the students in each chapter. These objectives are reinforced by review questions that assess how well the student has mastered the goals established in the learning objectives.

- *Actual Photos of Nail Disorders*. Full-color photos are included to help students identify nail disorders more accurately.

- *Client Consultation Guidelines*. A complete chapter focuses on client consultation and gives suggestions for identifying and meeting the needs of each individual client.

- *Chemical Safety Coverage*. A complete chapter is devoted to the important topic of chemical safety in the nail salon. Students will learn to identify the chemicals commonly used in the nail salon, how they can cause harm, how to protect themselves and their clients, and how to read Material Safety Data Sheets (MSDSs).

- *State Licensing Exam Topics*. The topics required for state licensing examinations are presented in a complete, easy-to-read fashion.

- *Safety Cautions*. Highlighted safety cautions alert students to services that include potentially dangerous procedures. These cautions explain how to avoid dangerous situations and how to provide services in a safe, clean environment.

- *Tips*. These tips provide hints on the most efficient and effective ways to complete step-by-step procedures and help students improve their nail technology skills.

- *Regulatory Agency Alerts*. Because state regulations vary, regulatory agency alerts remind students to check with their instructors for specific regulations in their state.

- *Business Tips*. These tips help nail technicians improve their business relations to achieve complete customer satisfaction.

- *Application Tips*. These tips give additional insight to nail technicians as they perform the service procedures.

- *Web Resources*. Throughout the text, the reader will be directed to a variety of useful and informational Web sites that they can use in and out of school.

SUPPLEMENTS FOR THE STUDENT AND INSTRUCTOR

Milady's Standard: Nail Technology, Sixth Edition, features these supplements:

MILADY'S STANDARD: NAIL TECHNOLOGY WORKBOOK

This brand-new, interactive workbook provides students with exercises, problems to solve, ideas to think about, and resolutions to create that will engage their interest and contemplative skills. The four-color workbook includes short-answer, short essay, sentence completion, matching, definition, labeling, crossword puzzles, and word review activities. The workbook also includes tips on preparing for the practical exam.

MILADY'S STANDARD: NAIL TECHNOLOGY COURSE MANAGEMENT GUIDE

This step-by-step, simple-to-use course guide has been designed specifically to help the nail technology instructor set up and operate a successful nail technology training program. It includes:

- guidelines for starting and implementing a nail technology program.

- detailed lesson plans for each chapter in the book.

- learning reinforcement ideas or activities that can be implemented in the nail technology classroom.

- the answers to the review questions at the end of each textbook chapter and *Milady's Standard: Nail Technology Workbook*.

MILADY'S STANDARD: NAIL TECHNOLOGY EXAM REVIEW

This book of exam reviews contains multiple-choice type questions similar to those found on state licensing exams for nail technology. Groups of questions are arranged under major subject areas.

MILADY'S STANDARD: NAIL TECHNOLOGY STUDENT CD-ROM

This interactive student product was designed to reinforce classroom learning, stimulate the imagination, and aid in preparation for board exams.

Featuring video clips and graphic animations to demonstrate practices and procedures, this exciting educational tool also contains a test bank, learning games, and an audio glossary.

MILADY'S STANDARD: NAIL TECHNOLOGY COURSE MANAGEMENT GUIDE—CD-ROM

Includes all the elements of the print version Course Management Guide and includes:

- a computerized test bank for instant creation of review tests with answer keys.

- an Image Library including all images in the text to be used in handouts or PowerPoint® presentations.

MILADY'S STANDARD: NAIL TECHNOLOGY INSTRUCTOR SUPPORT SLIDES

The Instructor Support Slides contain a complete PowerPoint® presentation for every textbook chapter, and even include a new interactive feature of audio pronunciation for difficult terminology.

MILADY'S STANDARD: NAIL TECHNOLOGY DVDS

This DVD series brings to life complete coverage of the practical applications of the textbook. This series will enhance classroom learning and is essential for remedial work and individual learning.

ADVANCED, REFERENCE, AND CONTINUING EDUCATION MATERIAL AVAILABLE FROM CENGAGE LEARNING

- *Nail Structure and Product Chemistry*, *2nd edition*, Douglas D. Schoon—An informational guide for anyone interested in learning more about how and why professional nail products work; how to troubleshoot, understand, and solve most common salon problems; why products sometimes don't work and how to avoid these problems; how to avoid product-related skin allergies; and much more.

- *Guide to Owning and Operating a Nail Salon*, Joanne Wiggins— Includes well-organized, step-by-step tips for starting a salon; business features specific to nail salons; and tips on developing a long-term plan.

- *Nail Q & A Book*, Vicki Peters—This book has over 500 questions and answers for nail technicians, ranging from nail preparation to business practice tips.

- *The Professional's Reflexology Handbook*, Shelley Hess—This handbook offers a full spectrum of treatments using pressure points of the foot, hand, and ear. This guide provides clear, concise instructions and background on how reflexology treatments can be used in selected areas of service.

- *Spa Manicuring for the Salon and Spa*, Janet McCormick—This is the most complete and instructional source of information for any nail technician wishing to treat body, mind, and spirit. Easy to understand, concise, and inspiring, this book takes manicuring—and us as professionals—to a higher level of knowledge. It will change your concept of the spa service.

- *The Salon Professional's Guide to Foot Care*, Godfrey Mix, DPM—A licensed podiatrist offers invaluable information on the human foot and its care. Common foot problems and general diseases that can affect the foot are discussed. Knowing how and when to consult a medical professional or refer a client will help you better serve your clientele and increase loyalty.

ALISHA RIMANDO BOTERO

Alisha is recognized as one of the nail industry's leading experts in training and education. In her first two years as an educator, Alisha taught classes in over 100 beauty schools and vo-techs across the U.S. In her 14 years of experience, her work has been described as "groundbreaking"; she has been a platform artist and motivational speaker for more than 1,500 promotional and educational events, and has competed in over 100 nail competitions around the globe, winning a World Championship in 2005. She has worked with R&D chemists to develop artificial nail enhancement products, nanotechnology skin care and cuticle treatments, polish collections, and natural nail treatments. One of her innovative product lines was awarded an industry ABBIE for best packaging, and several others have been recognized with readers' choice awards for best products.

Alisha's artistic creations have been sought after for numerous ads and campaigns where hands and feet play a pivotal role for product sales. She continues to achieve notoriety as "manicurist to the stars," and recently was featured with Jennifer Hudson in her video "Spotlight." At NYC Fashion Weeks, Alisha has worked with designers Isaac Mizrahi, Diane von Furstenberg, Zac Posen, Tony Cohen, and many others, creating innovative nail looks for their runway shows.

CATHERINE M. FRANGIE, SERIES EDITOR/ CONTRIBUTOR

Catherine M. Frangie is the owner of FrangieConsulting, LLC, a marketing and communications firm that specializes in creating innovative strategies for business. FrangieConsulting's clients include some of the largest and most successful companies in the professional beauty business, and Catherine and her firm are the recipients of seven ABBIE awards, including two Gold ABBIES.

Catherine has been a dedicated and passionate beauty professional for more than 25 years and began her career as a licensed cosmetologist, salon owner, and beauty school instructor. Since then, Catherine has held prominent and dynamic positions throughout many facets of the professional beauty industry, including marketing, communications, and education vice president for a leading product company; communications director; trade magazine editor/publisher; and textbook editor and author.

JIM MCCONNELL, CONTRIBUTOR

Jim McConnell received his B.S. in Chemistry from the University of Oregon in 1986. He has been a chemist in the field of polymers since 1988. After graduating from the University of Oregon, Jim worked as a catalytic chemist in the petroleum industry and as a urethane and epoxy chemist in the wood products, concrete coating, and steel coating industries for 12 years. He and his wife, Lezlie, began McConnell Labs, Inc., in 1998 making Light Elegance Nail Products for their salon in Eugene, Oregon. After making Light Elegance for use in their own salon, they began selling the UV gel products internationally. Jim has contributed to numerous nail technology magazines around the world to answer questions, contribute chemistry, and explain UV light technology. He was on the board for various committees for SSPC (Steel Structures Painting Council) and NACE (National Association of Corrosion Engineers) prior to starting McConnell Labs with his wife.

JANET MCCORMICK, MS, CIDESCO, CONTRIBUTOR

Janet McCormick is a licensed and experienced esthetician and manicurist, a sought-after trainer, a former spa director, and has owned her own successful salons. She has been writing for over 20 years including hundreds of highly respected articles in the beauty industry trade magazines and three books, and she has contributed chapters in the industry's leading textbooks for two specialties.

Janet is co-owner of the Just For Toenails Nail System, a gel system sold only to podiatrists, and the Medinail Learning Center, which provides two certifications, the Advanced Nail Technician certification program for salon-based nail technicians and the Medical Nail Technician certification, a program to prepare nail technicians to work in podiatry offices. She is also owner of Spa Techniques, a consulting and training firm, and writes under that banner.

JACQUELINE OLIPHANT, CONTRIBUTOR

Jacqueline Oliphant is known as the original "Jackie O." in the beauty industry. She is a talented and gifted freelance cosmetologist and barber who specializes in beauty and image consulting. In 1996, she became a licensed nail specialist, a facial specialist in 2002, a cosmetologist in 2008, and a barber in 2010. Her career highlights within the nail business industry include becoming an author for Milady, a beauty expert on nail care for how-to video segments a Nail Specialist Learning Leader for Paul Mitchell The School in 2008, and an award-winning nail artist of the Golden Reel Award in 2001, as well as for a nail art exhibit traveling to art museums in 2006.

Being so well-rounded in the art of beauty has allowed her to land assignments beyond nail care. She has also freelanced as a makeup artist/hair stylist for The Lion King and The Wizard of Oz tours and a skin care consultant for a RoC/More Magazine's event. Merging her B.A. in Broadcasting with her Cosmetology license, she has freelanced with celebrities and high-profile professionals, local film production companies, and fashion shows, and has performed marketing and promotions locally for the Kiss Cosmetics Beauty and Model Search tour. Her advice to future nail professionals is to stay focused, overcome obstacles, be of service to someone, live your dream every day of your life, and keep God first.

VICKI PETERS, CONTRIBUTOR

As a nail technician, Vicki Peters has wowed the industry with her championship nails. As a cover artist and author, her work has been published worldwide, more than any other tech in the history of the nail business. As an educator, she has trained techs from Russia, Germany, Japan, Ireland, the United Kingdom, Canada, Mexico, Africa, Australia, and the United States. As an industry leader, she has mentored thousands. As a world-master nail technician with her own line of products, Vicki will pioneer the industry to new levels.

Vicki Peters is a 28-year veteran nail technician, past competition champion, judge and competition director, technical educator, and featured business speaker. She is also author of the *Milady's Nails Q&A Book, Drilltalk, The Competitive Edge*, and *Novartis' Nail Healthy Guide*. Her nail artistry has been on the covers of *TV Guide, Dayspa, Nails, Nailpro, Nailpro Europe*, and numerous fashion magazines. Her expertise in the nail business ranges from salon work and hands-on technical experience to R&D, education, and lecturing worldwide.

DOUGLAS SCHOON, CONTRIBUTOR

Doug Schoon is the Chief Scientific Advisor for Creative Nail Design (CND). With over 30 years of experience as a research scientist, international lecturer, author, and educator, he has become a recognized authority in the professional beauty industry. He led CND's research and development program for 19 years. Now as president of his own consulting firm, Schoon Scientific, he continues to focus on assisting CND with scientific, technical, and regulatory issues that help shape the industry. He works as a strong advocate for salon safety and represents the professional nail industry on scientific and technical issues in the U.S., Europe, Canada, Australia, and Japan.

Doug is the author of several books and video and audio training programs, as well as dozens of magazine articles about salon chemicals, chemical safety, and disinfection. As a writer and speaker, he is applauded for his ability to make complex chemical theories and concepts seem simple and easy to understand. His latest book, *Nail Structure & Product Chemistry, Second Edition*, Cengage Learning, is also considered an excellent resource for nail professionals. Currently, Doug is a co-chair of the Nail Manufacturers Council (NMC) of the Professional Beauty Association (PBA).

JERYL SPEAR, CONTRIBUTOR

Jeryl E. Spear is a veteran stylist and salon owner who has perfected her craft over a 17-year stint in the beauty business. She has been contributing articles for several years, publishing her work in *Modern Salon, Salon News*, and *DaySpa* magazines, plus writing for magazines such as *Self, Healing Lifestyles and Spas*, and *Spa*. Loving all things beauty and fashion, she is now the executive editor of *Launchpad* magazine and *The Colorist*.

PREVIOUS EDITION CONTRIBUTORS

DEBORAH BEATTY, CONTRIBUTOR

The Publisher would like to honor Deborah Beatty who passed away in December 2008. Deborah developed a wealth of knowledge over 35 years of industry experience, which she shared during her educational seminars as well as in her classrooms. In addition to being a master cosmetologist and licensed instructor, she was a master barber and licensed practical nurse, and was licensed by the Georgia Professional Standards Commission. Deborah was well known at Milady as a textbook and product reviewer for Cengage Learning and as an educator for Milady's Career Institute. She acted as the contributing editor for the revision of *Milady's Standard: Cosmetology* and *Milady's Standard: Nail Technology*. She authored *Preparing for the Practical Exam: Cosmetology* for students and instructors, as well as *Preparing for the Practical Exam: Nail Technology* for students and instructors.

JEWELL CUNNINGHAM, CONTRIBUTOR

Jewell Cunningham has been involved with the beauty industry for over 25 years in many roles, including as a judge for national and international competitions, writing rules and regulations, and now as a nationally recognized consultant to day spas, manufacturers, and salon owners. As a licensed nail technician, she competed in sculptured nail competitions from 1981 through 1986, winning 25 first-place awards, an industry record, including International World Champion and National Champion.

LIN HALPERN, CONTRIBUTOR

A native New Yorker, Lin Halpern has been a nail technician for 46 years. Lin started her professional nail shop business in 1980 and expanded it to a full-service spa salon in 1981. Over the years she has worked as a consultant to nail product manufacturers, contributed to magazine articles, produced marketing design concepts, and judged international nail competitions. She has even developed numerous new and innovative products from fast-drying topcoats and easier-to-use controlled-flow acrylics to a unique pink-and-white application using a three-dimensional nail tip covered by a U.S. patent. In recent years Lin created a company that works exclusively on new and innovative polymer chemistry with top chemists in this field. She and her partners continue to bring the latest techniques and advanced chemistry to both the professional and retail sides of the nail industry.

LACINDA HEADINGS, CONTRIBUTOR

LaCinda's passion for education has influenced her 22 years in the beauty industry as a cosmetologist specializing in nails. Her background includes 10 years in the salon, manufacturer's top trainer and consultant, school nail and cosmetology instructor, distribution, and currently assistant director at Xenon International Academy, one of the top cosmetology schools in the country. LaCinda has helped numerous nail technicians and salons start and grow their nail business. Her varied experience in the industry gives her a unique perspective that allows her to connect with nail technicians in every aspect of the business. LaCinda has inspired nail technicians all over the world with her motto of "Live, Laugh, Love, and Learn."

NANCY KING HEUPEL, CONTRIBUTOR

Nancy King Heupel is an internationally recognized expert on safe salon practices and regulation and is one of the top salon safety educators in the United States today. She began her regulatory experience by serving on the Maryland State Board of Cosmetologists. Since then, she has provided research, support data, and testimony at the state and federal levels on a variety of issues pertaining to the cosmetology industry. Nancy has served as a consultant and industry spokesperson to several television networks for stories about safety in nail salons. Nancy is the foremost expert on pedicure safety and electric filing techniques. She has been retained by prominent law firms throughout the United States to serve as an expert witness in salon malpractice cases in both state and federal courts.

TERRI LUNDBERG, CONTRIBUTOR

Terri Lundberg has been a licensed nail technician since 1982 and a nail technology educator in both the professional arena and the schools since 1990. She spent a large part of her career as the international education director for a nail product manufacturer. She trained nail technicians and educators across the world, and developed a "train the trainer" method that is still used today. Terri also developed a mentoring program, creating a unique curriculum for mentoring nail technicians to a higher skill level, and authored and taught an advanced skills course. Terri still teaches advanced classes in schools and salons and is always excited to see new ways for nail technicians to be successful in the nail industry. She is also on the *Nailpro* magazine advisory board.

GODFREY F. MIX, D.P.M., CONTRIBUTOR

Godfrey "Oscar" Mix is a doctor of podiatric medicine, as well as a member of the American Podiatric Medical Association, the California Podiatric Medical Association, and the Sacramento Valley Podiatric Medical Society, of which he is a past president. He is an associate of the American College of Foot Surgeons and is board certified by the American Board of Podiatric Foot Surgery. Dr. Mix is the author of *The Salon Professional's Guide to Foot Care*, published by Cengage Learning, and currently writes on foot-related subjects for *Nailpro* magazine, continuing to work as a manufacturer's consultant in the professional beauty industry. Dr. Mix is also on the *Nailpro* advisory board.

LAURA J. MIX, CONTRIBUTOR

Laura Mix began her career as a clinical laboratory technician for a major metropolitan hospital in Sacramento, California. After a number of years as a technician, then as a full-time homemaker, Laura returned to work with her husband, Dr. Oscar Mix, in his podiatry practice. The Mixes decided to offer pedicure services to patients, and so Laura began manicuring school in June of 1993. After obtaining her license, Laura continued working with her husband, providing pedicures and nail services. In November of 1998, she and Dr. Mix opened a specialty day spa, Footworks, Inc., and she also worked as a product educator for a fiberglass nail enhancement system. She has consulted as a subject matter expert for the Sacramento Bureau of Barbering and Cosmetology. Laura is now retired, but she continues to keep her manicuring license current.

REBECCA MORAN, CONTRIBUTOR

Rebecca Moran has been a nail technologist, salon owner, licensed cosmetology, nail and esthetic instructor, director of education, and an independent special education facilitator and researcher within our industry for over 18 years now. She has worked as a subject matter expert and expert reviewer and has authored such works as the *Milady's Standard: Nail Technology* CD-ROM for Cengage Learning, as well as being a contributing author.

SUE ELLEN SCHULTES, CONTRIBUTOR

Sue Ellen Schultes is an award-winning nail artist, a licensed nail technician, and a former salon owner whose business was recognized as one of the top 100 nail salons in the country by *Nails* magazine for 10 years in a row. Sue is recognized as one of the leading nail art technology authorities in the United States and has taught extensively throughout the United States, conducting workshops and seminars via Notorious Nails Seminars. Sue serves as competition judge for various trade shows, both nationally and internationally. Besides acting as series editor and contributing author for Cengage Learning, Sue also contributes special interest articles to *Nails* magazine and several other publications. Sue was commissioned by the Smithsonian Institution's National Museum of American History to create a full set of nails commemorating the U.S. Presidential Inauguration of George H. W. Bush in 1989.

The staff of Cengage Learning and the Contributors wish to acknowledge the many individuals and organizations who helped shape the sixth edition of *Milady's Standard: Nail Technology*. Their input enabled us to produce a book that will be a valuable resource for both students and professionals in the field of nail technology. To all those who contributed to this edition we extend our sincere thanks and appreciation.

SPECIAL THANKS TO:

- **Entity 1 Gel Technology** (http://www.entitybeauty.com)

- **Atwood Industries** (http://www.atwoodindustries.net)

- **Medicool, Inc**. (http://www.medicool.com). Special thanks to Steve Wallace for supplying images of electric bits for chapter 15.

- **KUPA, Inc**. (http://www.kupainc.com)

- **Josephine (Pina) More** for her fantastic job on the photo shoot, and for not only her perfect technical skills but also her unwavering energy and professionalism.

- **Amy Elizabeth Smith**, Makeup Artist, for her incredible makeup designs on our models.

- **Debra Windus**, The Burmax Company, Inc., Holtsville, NY. Burmax was a tremendous help in gathering all of the supplies for our photo shoot.

- **Jean Claude and his team from Jean Paul Day Spa and Hair Salons**, Albany, NY. Jean Claude welcomed the Milady staff for a full day of shooting. Special thanks to Kelly, Linette, and Veronica for all of their assistance. For more information, visit www.jeanpaulspa.com.

- **Staff and students at *Austin School of Spa Technology*** in Albany, NY. Thank you for your generous hospitality in letting the Milady staff take over the cosmetology area for an entire week. The results of the shoot were amazing, but they could not have been accomplished without your assistance and energetic group of students who were willing to act as models. Special thanks to Maria Neal, the Director of Marketing and Communications, for arranging all of the details for the shoot.

- **Cheryl Simkins-Anderson**, Spa Manager at CNY Healing Arts Wellness Center & Spa in Latham, NY. Cheryl did a fantastic job of rounding up models and accommodating us for a full day of shooting. Thank you for the opportunity to take photos of such a beautiful location and for assistance from your wonderful team of professionals. For more information, visit http://www.cnyhealingarts.com.

- **Bryan Durocher**, President, Durocher Enterprises Inc.

- ***Nails Magazine***

- **Manx National Heritage**

- **The Rome Nail Academy**
- **Catherine Wong** – Ecsalonce
- **Viv Simmonds** – VIVid Nail & Beaute Salon
- **Cindy Davis**
- **Nails made by Massimiliano Braga**
- **Noble Nails by Louise Callaway**
- **LCN / Wilde Cosmetics GmbH**
- **Emilio** at http://www.emilio-online.com

SIXTH EDITION REVIEWERS

Initial Development Reviewers

Frances Antonopoulos, Viaggio Salon, Grand Junction, CO
LaNita Battle, Kenneth Shuler Schools of Cosmetology, Aiken, SC
Mindy Borrego, Kay Harvey Hairdressing Academy, West Springfield, MA
Debbie Eckstine-Weidner, DeRielle Cosmetology Academy, Mechanicsburg, PA
Lin Halpern, Levittown Beauty Academy, Jenkintown, PA
Jean Harrity, The Salon Professional Academy, Elgin, IL
LaCinda Headings, Xenon International Academy, Wichita, KS
Tina Hjelm, Alabama School of Business and Cosmetology, Moulton, AL
Karen Hodges, Freelance Educator, Key West, FL
Carolyn Kraskey, Central Beauty School, Minneapolis, MN
Rhonda Limbacher, Riverside Community College, Riverside, CA
Kim March, Cameo College of Essential Beauty, Murray, UT
Linda McKew, Academy of Nail Technology, Phoenix, AZ
Gina Morgan, International School of Skin and Nail Care, Atlanta, GA
Crystal Musgrove, Xenon International Academy, Wichita, KS
Kathy Phelps, Moore Norman Technology Center, Norman, OK
Chesley Phillips, Nails, Skin & Hair of America, LLC, Aiken, SC
Glynis Powell, A-1 Beauty & Barber College, Portsmouth, VA
Julie Schilling, Academy of Nail, Skin & Hair, Billings, MT
Angela Sharp, Sharp's Academy of Hairstyling, Inc., Grand Blanc, MI
Madeline Udod, Eastern Suffolk BOCES, Farmingville, NY

First Draft Reviewers

Mindy Borrego, Nail Instructor, Kay Harvey Hairdressing Academy, MA
Suzanne Casabella, Orlo School of Hair Design & Cosmetology, Albany, NY
Carla Collier, Nail Professional, Tehachapi, CA
Patricia Fagan, Nail Technician, Writer, Salon Owner, AR
Tiffany Greco, Hair Addix Salon, Carlsbad, CA
Meg King, Meg & Company Salon, Narberth, PA
Ani Landberg, Capello III Salon & Spa, East Amherst, NY
Maria F. Moffre, NY State, Private School Instructor of Cosmetology, Albany, NY
Andrina R. Monte, Brio Academy, Meriden, CT
Lisa Tihista-Riedmann, Academy of Nail, Skin and Hair, Inc., Billings, MT
Kristina Saindon, Denver, CO
Darlene Sammons, Miller-Motte Technical College, Chattanooga, TN

Lisa Sparhawk, Private Educator, Albany, NY

Desiree L. Tatum, Nail Instructor and Nail Technician, Chicago, IL

Elaine Watson, Global Education Director for Star Nail International, CA

Text Design Reviewers

Allison Murphy, Marketti Academy of Cosmetology, Waterford, MI

Brenda Shcarmn, Cameo College of Essential Beauty, Murray, UT

Yota Batsaras, Sephora, Cypress, CA

Jessica Kimball, Cameo College of Essential Beauty, Murray, UT

Jean Harrity, The Salon Professional Academy, Elgin, IL

Lisa W. Crawford, Bellefonte Academy of Maysville, Maysville, KY

RaNae Barker, Southern Oklahoma Technology Center, Ardmore, OK

Alysia Cornish, Professional Beauty College of Australia, Brisbane, Qld.

Ami Enzweiler, Salon 4 U, Cincinnati, OH

Heather Wiggins, Epic Salon and Day Spa, Sandy, UT

Kimberly Schroeder, Avalon School of Cosmetology, Worthington, MN

Sophia C. Albersman, Avalon School of Cosmetology, Worthington, MN

Gabriela Gagnier, Knoxville Institute of Hair Design, Knoxville, TN

Brenda Baker, Lincoln College of Technology, West Palm Beach, FL

Crystal Sims, Southeastern Beauty/Barber Schools, Columbus, GA

Brian West, Southeastern Beauty/Barber Schools, Columbus, GA

Maria Foust, Southeastern Beauty/Barber Schools, Columbus, GA

Mckeshian Mathews, Southeastern Beauty/Barber Schools, Columbus, GA

Tiffany Bellamy, Southeastern Beauty/Barber Schools, Columbus, GA

Lakiesha Young, Southeastern Beauty/Barber Schools, Columbus, GA

Billie Smith, Smith's Rapid Edge Sharpening, Tyler, TX

Laurie Biagi, Skyline Community College, San Bruno, CA

Betty Ann Woerhman, Raphael's School of Beauty Culture, Brunswick, OH

Yolanda Matthews, The Cosmetology Connection, Houston, TX

PHOTO SHOOT LOCATIONS:

- Austin's School of Spa Technology, Albany, NY

- CNY Healing Arts Wellness Center & Spa, Latham, NY

- Jean Paul Spa & Salons, Albany, NY

- Kimberley's… A Day Spa, Ltd., Latham, NY

- Sue Ellen Schultes, Notorious Nails, Green Brook, NJ

PHOTOGRAPHERS:

- Dino Petrocelli, professional photographer, Albany, NY
  (http://www.dinopetrocelli.com)

- Paul Castle, Castle Photography, Inc., Troy, NY
  (http://www.castlephotographyinc.com)

- Michael Dzaman Photography © Michael Dzaman/Dzaman Photography
  (http://www.dzamanphoto.com)

photo credits

IMAGE CREDITS

■ **PART 1:** inset photo, Castle Photography.

Chapter 1: chapter opener photo, (Spa and wellness); © crolique, 2010; used under license from Shutterstock.com. Figure 1-1 and Figure 1-2, © Milady, a part of Cengage Learning. Photography by Dino Petrocelli.

Chapter 2: chapter opener photo, (Young woman reading book); © S.P., 2010; used under license from Shutterstock.com. Figures 2-1, 2-3, 2-7, and 2-9, © Milady, a part of Cengage Learning. Photography by Dino Petrocelli. Figure 2-2 (Young girl with a digital camera); © Leegudim, 2009; used under license from Shutterstock.com. Figures 2-4 and 2-6, Photodisc. Figure 2-5, Corbis.

Chapter 3: chapter opener photo, (Manicure on female hands); © Sakala, 2010; used under license from Shutterstock.com. Figures 3-1, 3-3, 3-5 to 3-9, © Milady, a part of Cengage Learning. Photography by Dino Petrocelli. Figure 3-2 (A pretty girl gets ready for the day in the mirror); © zulufoto, 2009; used under license from Shutterstock.com. Figure 3-4, © Milady, a part of Cengage Learning.

Chapter 4: chapter opener photo, (nail salon technician); © Rich Legg, 2010; used under license from iStockphoto. Figures 4-1, 4-2, 4-3, 4-7, and 4-10, © Milady, a part of Cengage Learning. Photography by Dino Petrocelli. Figure 4-4, © Milady, a part of Cengage Learning. Figure 4-5 © Full body of an attractive blond woman wearing gray business pant suit with hair tied up and eyeglasses over white); © GeoM, 2009; used under license from Shutterstock.com. Figure 4-6 (Portrait of beautiful woman with brown hat, studio shot); © Aleksandar Todorovic, 2009; used under license from Shutterstock.com. Figures 4-8 and 4-9, Courtesy of Bryan Durocher, President, Durocher Enterprises, Inc. Images rendered by Bill Smith Group.

■ **PART 2:** inset photo, Getty Images.

Chapter 5: chapter opener photo, (streptococcus); © Sebastian Kaulitzki, 2010; used under license from Shutterstock.com. Figure 5-1, © Milady, a part of Cengage Learning. Photography by Paul Castle. Figures 5-2 to 5-9, Tables 5-1 and 5-2, © Milady, a part of Cengage Learning. Figure 5-10, courtesy of Godfrey F. Mix, DPM, Sacramento, CA. Figures 5-11 to 5-16, & Procedure 5-3 photos © Milady, a part of Cengage Learning. Photography by Dino Petrocelli.

Chapter 6: chapter opener photo, (human anatomy) © Sebastian Kaulitzki, 2010; used under license from Shutterstock.com. Figures 6-1 to 6-24, Tables 6-1 and 6-2, © Milady, a part of Cengage Learning.

Chapter 7: chapter opener photo, (portrait of fresh and beautiful woman); © Solovieva Ekaterina, 2010; used under license from Shutterstock.com. Figures 7-1 to 7-5, 7-7, 7-11, © Milady, a part of Cengage Learning. Figure 7-6 (Young female during fitness time and exercising); © Kristian Sekulic, 2009; used under license from Shutterstock.com. Figures 7-8, 7-9, 7-12, 7-14, 7-16, 7-19 to 7-21, Reproduced with permission from American Academy of Dermatology, Copyright© 2010 All rights reserved. Figure 7-10, photo courtesy of Timothy Berger, MD, Associate Clinical Professor, University of California San Francisco. Figure 7-13, courtesy of Centers for Disease Control and Prevention (CDC). Figures 7-15 and 7-17, T. Fitzgerald, *Color Atlas & Synopsis of Clinical Dermatology*; 3 ed., 1996. Reprinted with permission of The McGraw-Hill Companies. Figure 7-18, Michael J. Bond, M.D.

Chapter 8: chapter opener photo, (hands with manicured nails on natural pearly background) © Ivanova Inga, 2010; used under license from Shutterstock.com. Figures 8-1 and 8-2, © Milady, a part of Cengage Learning.

Chapter 9: chapter opener photo,(studio portrait on black background of an expressive woman); © ostill, 2010; used under license from Shutterstock.com. Figures 9-2, 9-4, 9-17, 9-22, courtesy of Robert Baran, MD (France). Figures 9-5, 9-7, 9-8, 9-10, 9-13, 9-15, courtesy of Godfrey F. Mix, DPM, Sacramento, CA. Figure 9-6, © Milady, a part of Cengage Learning. Photography by Paul Castle. Figure 9-12, © Milady, a part of Cengage Learning. Photography by Dino Petrocelli. Figure 9-14, courtesy of Orville J. Stone, M.D., Dermatology Medical Group, CA. Figure 9-21, reproduced with permission from American Academy of Dermatology. Copyright © 2010 All rights reserved. Figures 9-1a &b, 9-3, 9-9, 9-11, 9-16, 9-18, 9-19, 9-20, Tables 9-1 and 9-2, © Milady, a part of Cengage Learning.

Chapter 10: chapter opener photo, (Pipette with drop of liquid over glass test tubes for an experiment in a science research lab) © Olivier Le Queinec, 2010; used under license from Shutterstock.com. Figures 10-1 to 10-12, Tables 10-1 and 10-2, © Milady, a part of Cengage Learning.

Chapter 11: chapter opener photo, © Bork, 2010; used under license from Shutterstock.com. Figures 11-1 and 11-3, © Milady, a part of Cengage Learning. Figure 11-2, © Milady, a part of Cengage Learning. Photography by Michael Dzaman.

Chapter 12: chapter opener photo, (lightbulb) © Dan Brandenburg, 2010; used under license from iStockphoto. Figures 12-1 to 12-8, © Milady, a part of Cengage Learning.

■ **PART 3:** inset photo, Getty Images.

Chapter 13: chapter opener photo, (hand massage)© Tomasz Markowski, 2010; used under license from Shutterstock.

com. Figures 13-1, 13-3, 13-9, European Touch. Figure 13-2, Collins Manufacturing Company. Figures 13-4 to 13-8, 13-10 to 13-17, 13-19 to 13-22, 13-28, and 13-35, © Milady, a part of Cengage Learning. Photography by Dino Petrocelli. Figure 13-18 courtesy of purespadirect.com. Figures 13-23 to 13-26, 13-30 © Milady, a part of Cengage Learning. Photography by Yanik Chauvin. Figures 13-27 (Natural herbal ingredient prepared for the ultimate aromatherapy and spa sessions). © Hywit Dimyadi, 2009; used under license from Shutterstock.com. Figure 13-29 (SPA cosmetics series. cosmetics bottles); © Katarzyna Malecka, 2009; used under license from Shutterstock.com. Figure 13-31, Nails by Massimiliano Brago. Figure 13-32, Emilio's Airbrush Studio at http://www.emilio-online.com. Figure 13-33, Nail Art by Alisha Rimando Botero. Photos in Procedures 13-1 to 13-7, © Milady, a part of Cengage Learning. Photography by Dino Petrocelli. Photos appearing in Procedure 13-8, © Milady, a part of Cengage Learning. Photography by Yanik Chauvin.

Chapter 14: chapter opener photo, © Tomek_Pa, 2010; used under license from Shutterstock.com. Figures 14-2 to 14-5, 14-7, and 14-8: European Touch. Figures 14-1, 14-6, 14-10, 14-11, and all procedure photos © Milady, a part of Cengage Learning. Photography by Dino Petrocelli. Figure 14-9, © Milady, a part of Cengage Learning. Photography by Yanik Chauvin. Figures 14-11 to 14-14, © Milady, a part of Cengage Learning. Photography by Michael Dzaman. Figure 14-15: Noble Nails by Louise Callaway.

Chapter 15: chapter opener photo, courtesy of NAILS magazine. Figures 15-2, 15-3, 15-4, 15-5, 15-8, 15-9, 15-11, 15-14 a, b, 15-15 © Milady, a part of Cengage Learning. Photography by Dino Petrocelli. Figures 15-6, 15-12, 15-20, 15-21, 15-22, and 15-23, Courtesy of Bruce Atwood, Atwood Industries, CA. Figures 15-7, 15-10, 15-13, 15-16, 15-17, 15-18, Courtesy of Medicool. Figures 15-1, 15-24, and 15-25, photos courtesy of Nancy King Heupel. Figure 15-19, courtesy of NAILS magazine. Electric bits supplied by Atwood Industries, KUPA, Inc., and Medicool Inc.

Chapter 16: chapter opener photo, © Milady, a part of Cengage Learning. Photography by Dino Petrocelli. Figures 16-1, 16-2, 16-3, Procedures 16-3 to 16-7, © Milady, a part of Cengage Learning. Photography by Dino Petrocelli. All photos in Procedure 16-8, © Milady, a part of Cengage Learning. Photography by Yanik Chauvin.

Chapter 17: chapter opener photo, © Milady, a part of Cengage Learning. Photography by Dino Petrocelli. Figure 17-1, Procedures 17-3 to 17-7, © Milady, a part of Cengage Learning. Photography by Dino Petrocelli.

Chapter 18: chapter opener photo, © Milady, a part of Cengage Learning. Photography by Dino Petrocelli. Figures 18-1, Procedures 18-3 to 18-9, © Milady, a part of Cengage Learning. Photography by Dino Petrocelli. Figure 18-2, McConnell Labs, Inc.

Chapter 19: chapter opener photo, The Rome Nail Academy. Figure 19-1 (vector color wheel); © Romanova Ekaterina, 2010; used under license from Shutterstock.com. 19-10 © Milady, a part of Cengage Learning. Figures 19-2 to 19-8, 19-18, Nail Art by Alisha Rimando Botero. Figures 19-9, 19-12, 19-19, © Milady, a part of Cengage Learning. Photography by Michael Dzaman. Figures 19-11 and 19-21: courtesy of Nails Magazine. Nail art by Alisha Rimando Botero. Figures 19-13 and 19-14, Procedures 19-1 to 19-5 © Milady, a part of Cengage Learning. Photography by Dino Petrocelli. Nail art by Alisha Rimando Botero. Figure 19-15, Cindy Davis, Studio 1632. Figures 19-16, 19-23, 19-24 Nails by Massimiliano Brago. Figure 19-17, LCN/Wilde Cosmetics GmbH. Figure 19-20 and Procedure 19-6 photos, courtesy of Noble Nails by Louise Callaway. Figure 19-25, Emilio's Airbrush Studio at http://www.emilio-online.com. Figure 19-21, courtesy of NAILS Magazine. Nail art by Vu Nguyen. Figures 19-22 and 19-26, Viv Simmonds from ViVid Nail and Beaute. Figures 19-27 to 19-31: Courtesy of Catherine Wong, Ecsalonce.

■ PART 4: inset photo, Getty Images.

Chapter 20: chapter opener photo, © Milady, a part of Cengage Learning. Photography by Dino Petrocelli. Figures 20-1, 20-5, © Milady, a part of Cengage Learning. Photography by Paul Castle. Figures 20-2, 20-4, 20-7, 20-13, 20-14 © Milady, a part of Cengage Learning. Photography by Dino Petrocelli. Figures 20-3, 20-6, 20-8 to 20-12, © Milady, a part of Cengage Learning.

Chapter 21: chapter opener photo, © Milady, a part of Cengage Learning. Photography by Dino Petrocelli. Figures 21-1 to 21-3, 21-5, 21-7, 21-9, 21-10, and 21-11, © Milady, a part of Cengage Learning. Photography by Dino Petrocelli. Figures 21-4, 21-6, © Milady, a part of Cengage Learning. Figure 21-8, © Milady, a part of Cengage Learning. Photography by Paul Castle.

Chapter 22: chapter opener photo, (Pamper Me CD) Stockbyte at Getty Images. Figure 22-1, Colleen Brescia Photography and MARIPOSA Studio. Figures 22-2, 22-4, 22-5, 22-8 to 22-13, 22-15 © Milady, a part of Cengage Learning. Photography by Dino Petrocelli. Figure 22-3 (Two interracial businesswomen working on laptop computer); © Kristian Sekulic, 2009; used under license from Shutterstock.com. Figures 22-6, 22-14, and Table 22-1, © Milady, a part of Cengage Learning. Figure 22-7, © Milady, a part of Cengage Learning. Photography by Paul Castle.

Chapter 1: Shutterstock 7072345 (female hand): © Liv friis-larsen, 2010; used under license from Shutterstock.com. Shutterstock 3494267 (Venus statue isolated over white): © Philip Lange, 2010; used under license from Shutterstock.com. Shutterstock 7072345 (Female Hand): © Liv Friis-larson, 2010; used under license from Shutterstock.com. Shutterstock 5704735 (Famous bust of Queen Nefertiti isolated on white): © Vladimir Wrangel, 2010; used under license from Shutterstock.com. Shutterstock 17057080 (Oysters): © Pennyimages, 2010; used under license from Shutterstock.com. Shutterstock 2537373 (Blue glass amphora (clipping path included)): © Gordana Sermek, 2010; used under license from Shutterstock.com. Shutterstock 566271 (Statue at Louvre Museum in Paris, France): © Heather L. Jones, 2010; used under license from Shutterstock.com. Shutterstock 29225701 (Served place setting: Hot morning porridge and eggs on white background): © Lisovskaya Natalia, 2010; used under license from Shutterstock.com. Shutterstock 34217392 (nail file isolated): © Arber, 2010; used under license from Shutterstock.com. Shutterstock 34491274 (black mascara): © Kadroff, 2010; used under license from Shutterstock.com. Shutterstock 1339597 (nail polish): © Ewa Walicka, 2010; used under license from Shutterstock.com. Shutterstock 13247134 (Spa and wellness): © crolique, 2010; used under license from Shutterstock.com. Shutterstock 14112487 (fruit therapy items. kiwi, towels, and facial mask): © arteretum, 2010; used under license from Shutterstock.com. Shutterstock 3519056 (Young woman covering her leg with skin crème, isolated over white background with clipping-path): © Philip Lange, 2010; used under license from Shutterstock.com.

Chapter 2: Shutterstock 12200470 (manicure on female hands): © Sakala, 2010; used under license from Shutterstock.com. Shutterstock 10887505 (young student holding folders, diary and paper work): © Dean Mitchell, 2010; used under license from Shutterstock.com. Shutterstock 15106132 (Pencil in woman hand isolated on white background): © Tatiana Popova, 2010; used under license from Shutterstock.com. Shutterstock 7978753 (Excited, happy young family in a joyful huddle): © Junial Enterprises, 2010; used under license from Shutterstock.com. Shutterstock 11920279 (interior hair salon): © Lorraine Kourafas, 2010; used under license from Shutterstock.com. Shutterstock 10376242 (Colorful notebooks with pen): © RoJo Images, 2010; used under license from Shutterstock.com. Shutterstock 13336804 (Gossiping girls): © Lana K, 2010; used under license from Shutterstock.com.

Chapter 3: Shutterstock 4758463 (young attractive Asian woman with freshly manicured hands): © Phil Date, 2010; used under license from Shutterstock.com. Shutterstock 7312327 (Three young successful business women): © Raisa Kanareva, 2010; used under license from Shutterstock.com. Shutterstock 27725599 (portrait of mid adult hairstylist looking at camera): © Diego Cervo, 2010; used under license from Shutterstock.com. Shutterstock 40792279 (Dental care products on bright background): © Colour, 2010; used under license from Shutterstock.com.

Chapter 4: Shutterstock 12388690 (manicure treatment at the spa salon): © Sandra Gligorijevic, 2010; used under license from Shutterstock.com. Shutterstock 1632395 (An Attractive female model sat on a chair looking at the viewer isolated on White): © C Wells Photographic, 2010; used under license from Shutterstock.com. Shutterstock 9257245 (Friendly smiling businesswoman. Isolated over white background) © Kurhan, 2010; used under license from Shutterstock.com. Shutterstock 10906138 (reading a magazine) © Raisa Kanareva, 2010; used under license from Shutterstock.com. Shutterstock 29233633 (Businesswoman signing contract): © wrangler, 2010; used under license from Shutterstock.com. Shutterstock 29277205 (woman's hand with clock over white): © fotobazilio, 2010; used under license from Shutterstock.com. Shutterstock 26665849 (Two businesswomen discussing during a job interview): © Radu Razvan, 2010; used under license from Shutterstock.com.

Chapter 5: Shutterstock 41281036 (Young businesswoman in office with lot of tissues around - flue concept): © Piotr Marcinski, 2010; used under license from Shutterstock.com. Shutterstock 10761817 (Woman about to wash her skin, making foam of soap on her hands): © yummy, 2010; used under license from Shutterstock.com. Shutterstock 7727899 (sterilizer isolated on white): © Patricia Hofmeester, 2010; used under license from Shutterstock.com. Shutterstock 2304985 (massage chair): © Dave Wetzel, 2010; used under license from Shutterstock.com. Shutterstock 25507306 (a cute maid cleaner woman with mop and bucket): © Stephen Coburn, 2010; used under license from Shutterstock.com.

Chapter 6: Shutterstock 22875925 (human heart): © Sebastian Kaulitzki, 2010; used under license from Shutterstock.com. Shutterstock 29257576 (cell structure): © Sebastian Kaulitzki, 2010; used under license from Shutterstock.com. Shutterstock 19834270 (Six of the main human body systems-high detail): © Matthew Cole, 2010; used under license from Shutterstock.com. Shutterstock 22875925 (human heart): © Sebastian Kaulitzki, 2010; used under license from Shutterstock.com. Shutterstock 2349404 (lymphatic system): © Sebastian Kaulitzki, 2010; used under license from Shutterstock.com.

Chapter 7: Shutterstock 32483695 (Portrait of Fresh and Beautiful woman isolated on white): © Solovieva Ekaterina, 2010; used under license from Shutterstock.com. Shutterstock 3128142 (Three colorful bottles for fragrance, body spray and lotion isolated on white background) © Denise Kappa, 2010; used under license from Shutterstock.com. Shutterstock 30220525 (Human skin anatomy. Digital illustration.): © Andrea Danti, 2010; used under license from Shutterstock.com. Shutterstock 15309595 (Hand on back of woman with backache): © Andre Blais, 2010; used under license from Shutterstock.com. Shutterstock 42411610 (Close-up of beautiful wet woman face with water drop. On white background): © Raisa Kanareva, 2010; used under license from Shutterstock.com. Shutterstock 20328388 (spa products): © Khomulo Anna, 2010; used under license from Shutterstock.com. Shutterstock 11167330 (mandarin): © Valentyn Volkov, 2010; used under license from Shutterstock.

Part 1

ORIENTATION

1

history and
opportunities

chapter outline

After completing this chapter, you will be able to:

1 Describe the origins of personal beautification.

2 Name the advancements made in nail technology during the twentieth and early twenty-first centuries.

3 List the career opportunities available to a licensed nail technician.

Key Terms

Page number indicates where in the chapter the term is used.

cosmetology / 4

nail technology / 4

Brief History of Cosmetology and Nail Technology

Cosmetology is a term used to encompass a broad range of beauty specialties, including hairstyling, nail technology, and esthetics. It is the art and science of beautifying and improving the skin, nails, and hair, and the study of cosmetics and their applications. In this text, we will primarily focus on nail technology, which is defined as "the art and science of beautifying and improving the nails and skin of the hands and feet."

> A woman without paint is like food without salt.

THE ICE AGE

Archeological studies reveal that personal beauty was practiced in some form as early as the Ice Age. The simple yet effective grooming implements used at the dawn of history were shaped from sharpened flints, oyster shells, or bone. Animal sinew or strips of hide were used to tie back the hair or as adornment. Ancient people around the world used natural elements to color their hair, skin, and nails, and practiced tattooing. Pigments were made from roots, berries, tree bark, nuts, herbs, leaves, minerals, insects, and other materials. Many of these colorants are still used in beauty products today.

THE EGYPTIANS

The Egyptians were the first to cultivate beauty in an extravagant fashion and to use cosmetics as part of their personal beautification habits, religious ceremonies, and preparing the deceased for burial. In fact, as early as 3000 B.C., Egyptians used minerals, insects, and berries to create makeup for their eyes, lips, and skin, and henna to stain their hair and nails a rich, warm red. In both ancient Egypt and the Roman Empire, military commanders stained their nails and lips in matching colors before important battles.

Queen Nefertiti (1400 B.C.) used a henna paste to stain her nails a deep red, wore lavish makeup designs, and used custom-blended essential oils as signature scents. Queen Cleopatra (50 B.C.), who preferred a rust-red nail hue, took this dedication to beauty to an entirely new level by erecting a personal cosmetics factory next to the Dead Sea.

THE CHINESE

History shows that during the Shang Dynasty (1600 B.C.), Chinese aristocrats rubbed a tinted mixture of gum arabic, gelatin, beeswax, and egg whites onto their nails to turn them crimson or ebony. Throughout the Chou Dynasty (1100 B.C.), gold and silver nails were strictly reserved for royal family members. In fact, during this early period in history, nail tinting was so closely tied to social status that commoners who were caught wearing these royal nail colors faced a punishment of death. Extraordinarily long nails were also status symbols of the ancient Chinese elite. Some even wore gold, jewel-adorned nail guards to protect against damaging their lengthy symbols of wealth and leisure.

THE GREEKS

During the Golden Age of Greece (beginning in 500 B.C.), hairstyling became a highly developed art. The ancient Greeks also made lavish use of perfumes and cosmetics in their religious rites, in grooming, and for medicinal purposes. They built elaborate baths and developed excellent methods of dressing the hair and caring for the skin and nails.

Greek soldiers often painted their lips and nails red when preparing for battle. And Greek women used white lead powder on their faces, kohl on their eyes, and ground cinnabar—a brilliant red mineral that is a chief source of mercury—on their cheeks and lips. Interestingly, these powder and ointment preparations represent the basis of many cosmetic formulations still in use today.

THE ROMANS

Regaling the power of cosmetics to beautify one's appearance, Roman philosopher Plautus (254–184 B.C.) wrote, "A woman without paint is like food without salt." Roman women used a mixture of chalk and white lead to powder their complexions. They also used hair color to indicate their class status:

- Noblewomen colored their hair red;
- Middle-class women colored their hair blond;
- Poor women colored their hair black.

Both men and women used sheep's blood mixed with fat to add color to their nails.

THE MIDDLE AGES

The Middle Ages is the period of European history between classical antiquity and the Renaissance, beginning with the downfall of Rome in A.D. 476 and lasting until about 1450. Many tapestries, sculptures, and other artifacts from this period show towering headdresses, intricate hairstyles, and the use of cosmetics on the skin and hair. Women wore colored makeup on their cheeks and lips, but not on their eyes or nails.

THE RENAISSANCE

During the Renaissance period (A.D. 1450–1600), Western civilization made the transition from medieval to modern history. Paintings and written records tell us a great deal about the grooming practices of the time. Throughout this period, both men and women wore elaborate clothing. Fragrances and cosmetics were used, although highly colored preparations for the lips, cheeks, eyes and nails were discouraged. Despite the avoidance of colored nail cosmetics, people of wealth definitely manicured their nails, as evidenced by archeological digs that have uncovered cosmetic tools from the Renaissance period, including nail cleaners—some doubling as ear scoops—made of bone or metal in a wide variety of designs.

THE VICTORIAN AGE

The reign of Queen Victoria of England (A.D. 1837–1901) was known as the Victorian Age. Fashions in dress and personal grooming were drastically influenced by the social customs of this austere period in history. To preserve the health and beauty of the skin, women used beauty masks and packs made from honey, eggs, milk, oatmeal, fruits, vegetables, and other natural ingredients. Rather than use cosmetics such as rouges or lip stains, Victorian women pinched their cheeks and bit their lips to induce natural color. Nails were sometimes tinted with red oil and then buffed with a chamois cloth.

✔ LO1 Complete

THE TWENTIETH CENTURY

In the early twentieth century, the invention of motion pictures coincided with an abrupt shift in American attitudes. As viewers saw pictures of celebrities with flawless complexions, beautiful hairstyles, and manicured nails, standards of feminine beauty began to change. This era also signaled the onset of industrialization, which brought a new prosperity to the United States, and all forms of beauty began to follow trends.

> ...all forms of beauty began to follow trends.

1901 to 1919

1908: Max Factor began manufacturing and selling makeup to movie stars that wouldn't cake or crack, even under hot studio lights.

1910: Flowery Manicure Products introduced the first emery board that is nearly identical to the emery boards used today.

1917: Women massaged commercial powders, pastes, and creams onto their nails, and then buffed them to a gleaming finish. One such polishing paste was Graf's Hyglo Nail Polish Paste. Some women painted their nails with a clear varnish that was applied with a very small camel hair brush.

1920s

The cosmetics industry grew exponentially. Cosmetic advertising in magazines swelled from $2.5 million in 1915 to $25 million in 1925. The total sales of cosmetics and toiletries mushroomed from $8.6 million in 1909 to $33.5 million in 1920.

1930s

In 1932, inspired by a new, opaque paint that was being produced for the automobile industry, Charles Revson introduced the first mass-market nail lacquers in a variety of colors. This beauty milestone marked a dramatic shift in nail cosmetics, as women literally had an array of nail polish colors at their fingertips. Early screen sirens Jean Harlow and Gloria Swanson glamorized this hip new nail lacquer trend by appearing in films wearing matching polish on their fingers and toes.

1940s

Aerosol cans were invented, which eventually led to the first hair sprays. Shiny lips also came into vogue for the first time when women began applying petroleum jelly over their lipstick. Nail polish applications omitted the moon at the base of the nail and sometimes did not include the tip of the nail.

1950s

The 1950s saw the introduction of tube mascara, improved hair care and nail products, and the boom and then death of the weekly salon appointment. In the early 1950s, red nail lacquer was extremely popular, with nail technicians leaving the moon free of polish. As the decade progressed, full-coverage, frosted pastel colors—especially light coral, silver-white, pink, and apricot-gold—were all the rage. Hot oil manicures were the ultimate luxury in nail and hand care.

1960s

Juliette (paper) nail wraps—the precursor to the now popular silk and fiberglass wraps—were commonly used to protect natural nail tips. (Juliettes are credited with establishing the now familiar biweekly nail maintenance appointments.) Detached nail tips were reaffixed with model airplane glue and reinforced with thin strands of cotton. Human nail clippings were also used to add nail length. Clients brought their separated nail tips to their nail appointments for reattachment. Nail technicians also created "nail banks" that consisted of nails donated by all their clients. Frosted nail shades continued to be extremely popular. Hot oil manicures continued to be the luxury service of choice.

1970s

The first monomer liquid and polymer powder nail services were offered by nail technicians. Plastic nail tips affixed with cyanoacrylate adhesive replaced nail clippings affixed with model airplane glue to instantly extend nail length. Jeff Pink invented the French manicure (clear nail bed with white tips) and Ridgefiller (a product that makes ridged nails appear smooth). Square-shaped nail tips came into vogue.

1980s

Nail art—done with decals, jewels, metallic strips, and hand-drawn images—came into vogue. Monomer liquid and polymer powder nail formulations continued to improve in terms of ease of application and longevity for wearers.

1990s

The day spa business was born, ushering in a huge resurgence in natural nail care and pedicure services. Spray guns were commonly used to apply monomer liquid and polymer powder nail colors, especially the white tip of a French manicure and for nail art. In 1998, Creative Nail Design introduced the first spa pedicure system to the professional beauty industry.

Other notable achievements of the twentieth century include:

- UV gel systems grew in popularity.
- Color UV gel and monomer liquid and polymer powder nail enhancements swept the industry.
- Popularity of natural nail care services reached a high-point.
- Demand for pedicure services was at an all-time high.
- Nail technicians had unprecedented career choices.
- Nail enhancement performance vastly improved.
- Nail polish became safer and longer-lasting.

TWENTY-FIRST CENTURY

Nail grooming reaches an all-time zenith in terms of client demand and product and service choices. It is no longer considered a luxury; it is an expected part of every client's grooming ritual. An unprecedented demand for nail services of all types creates a critical shortage of nail technicians in the beauty industry.

Here are some examples of the exciting changes we've seen so far:

- UV gel enhancements grow by leaps and bounds because of their adhesion capabilities, thinness of application, permanent shine properties, and no-odor formulations. Color and glitter UV gel and monomer liquid and polymer powder products also gain in popularity.
- Nail polish formulations evolve to embody chip-resistant, fade-resistant characteristics that retain a lustrous finish for up to two

weeks. Manufacturers continue to improve their nail polish formulas by incorporating safer ingredients. And manicuring implements improve dramatically by incorporating new ergonomic designs, better materials, and enhanced workmanship.

- A bevy of professional, natural nail care products enter the professional beauty arena, allowing nail technicians to address specific nail concerns.

- Foot-and-hand skin treatment products continue to grow in numbers and popularity, including many scrubs, masks, and serums that specifically address dryness, dullness, and skin-aging issues.

 ✔ **LO2 Complete**

Career Paths for a Nail Technician

To become part of this exciting and growing profession, make the most out of your school experience, eagerly embrace new information, push the limits of your creativity, and explore all of your career options to find the choices that are right for you.

NAIL TECHNICIAN IN A TRADITIONAL SALON

Today, clients are eagerly requesting a variety of nail services that require a combination of skills. Natural nail services—luxurious manicures and pedicures, as well as natural nail-strengthening treatments—monomer liquid and polymer powder nail enhancements, the latest UV gel nail services, and silk and fiberglass nail wraps are all very popular salon and day spa services. You can now specialize in one specific area of your field (e.g., natural nails, pedicures, or nail enhancements) or be a full-service nail technician who offers many different types of nail services (**Figure 1-1**).

Because of the high demand for nail services, you also have the choice of working in a nail salon, full-service hair salon, day spa, resort spa, men's barbershop, or other beauty-related locations.

FIGURE 1-1
A full-service nail salon.

NAIL TECHNICIAN IN A MED SPA

Your school experience will provide a foundation for you to both succeed in your future as a nail technician and prepare you to seek further education in such specialties as reflexology, aromatherapy, and other specialty treatments. Studying additional or advanced information in hand, foot, and nail care will take your current knowledge to a whole new level and propel your success to its highest potential.

After acquiring some good, solid experience as a nail technician, one new opportunity you may want to explore is working in medical settings such

as in podiatry and medical offices, veteran's hospitals, and other medical facilities. The medical industry is awakening to the benefits of using nail technicians to perform safe manicures and pedicures on their at-risk patients. Foot spas, owned by podiatrists, are also developing across the country for nail technicians with the proper training. In these situations medical nail technicians work directly under the supervision of the physician performing services.

While medical career paths require additional education and training, they can be very rewarding work for a nail technician. Courses providing the important information required for working in medical settings are now available to nail technicians. These courses usually include an internship so that nail professionals are able to perfect the technical aspects of working with physicians before working with actual patients. These new possibilities are wonderful opportunities for those who feel the call to expand their nail career into working in a medical setting.

SALON MANAGEMENT

If business is your calling, you will find that management opportunities in the salon and spa environment are quite diverse. They include inventory manager, retail sales manager, department head, special events manager (promotions), assistant manager, and general manager. With experience, you can also add salon owner to your list of career possibilities. To ensure your success, it is wise to enroll in business classes to learn more about managing products, departments, and, above all, people.

ADDITIONAL CAREER CHOICES

While you will most likely begin your career by performing nail services, your career choices do not end there. A few additional career possibilities include:

- Product educator for a manufacturer or distributor
- Distributor sales representative
- Freelance editorial nail technician for photo shoots, films, and more
- Beauty school instructor/supervisor of a cosmetology school
- Product development
- Product marketing and public relations

Beyond defining your area of expertise, you must also decide whether you want to work in one or more of the following environments in your career:

- Nail salon
- Full-service salon (hair, skin, and nail services)
- Day spa (skin, body, nail, and hair services that emphasize beauty and wellness) **(Figure 1-2)**
- Medical spa, medical office, or foot spa

To learn more about all types of salon business models and resources for advanced education see **Chapter 20**.

▲ FIGURE 1-2

Nail services are very popular in the day spa setting.

✓ **LO3 Complete**

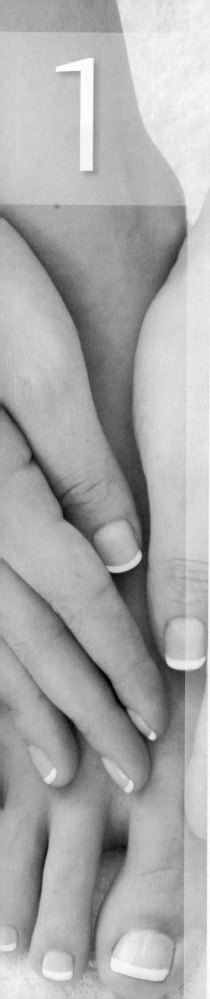

review questions

1. What are the origins of personal beautification?

2. Name the advancements made in nail technology during the twentieth and early twenty-first centuries.

3. List some of the career opportunities available to licensed nail technicians.

2 life skills

chapter outline

- ► The Psychology of Success
- ► Motivation and Self-Management
- ► Managing Your Career
- ► Goal Setting
- ► Time Management
- ► Study Skills
- ► Ethics
- ► Personality Development and Attitude

✓ Learning Objectives

After completing this chapter, you will be able to:

1. List the principles that contribute to personal and professional success.

2. Explain the concept of self-management.

3. Create a mission statement.

4. Explain how to set short-term and long-term goals.

5. Discuss the most effective ways to manage time.

6. Describe good study habits.

7. Define ethics.

8. List the characteristics of a healthy, positive attitude.

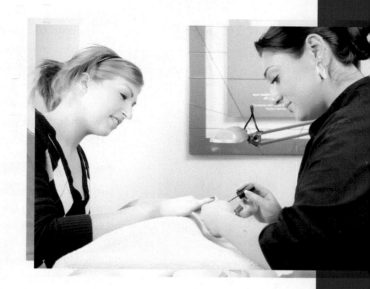

Key Terms

Page number indicates where in the chapter the term is used.

ethics / 22

game plan / 16

goal setting / 18

mission statement / 18

perfectionism / 16

prioritize / 20

procrastination / 16

While going through beauty school has its own set of challenges, staying on course for your entire career can be even more difficult without having good life skills. This is particularly true of cosmetology since the hard-and-fast rules that apply to more structured industries are frequently absent in the salon business. By nature, the salon is a creative workplace where you are expected to exercise your artistic talent. It is also a highly social atmosphere that requires strong self-discipline and excellent people skills. Besides making a solid connection with each client, you must always stay focused and feel both competent and enthusiastic about taking care of every client's needs—no matter how you feel, or how many hours you have already worked. Your livelihood and your personal feeling of success depend on how well you do this.

Practicing good life skills helps to build self-esteem, puts you at greater ease in social and work situations, and allows you to become more tolerant of others. Strong life skills can give you the confidence and freedom to decide what you want to do and who you want to be.

There are a great many life skills that can lead to a more satisfying and productive beauty career. Some of the most important life skills include:

- Being genuinely caring and helpful to others.
- Successfully adapting to different situations.
- Sticking to a goal and seeing a job to completion.
- Being consistent in your work.
- Developing a deep reservoir of common sense.
- Making good friends.
- Feeling good about yourself.
- Maintaining a cooperative attitude.
- Defining your own code of ethics and living within your definition.
- Approaching all your work with a strong sense of responsibility.
- Mastering techniques that will help you become more organized.
- Having a sense of humor to bring you through difficult situations.
- Acquiring one of the greatest virtues: patience.
- Always striving for excellence.

▼ **FIGURE 2-1**
Loving your work is critical to your success.

The Psychology of Success

Are you passionate about studying? Do you see yourself sustaining this passion one year, five years, or even 10 years from now? While beauty school is definitely demanding, it becomes much easier when you put that extra amount of effort, enthusiasm, and excitement into your studies. If your talent is not fueled by the passion necessary to sustain you over the course of your career, you can have all the talent in the world and still not be successful (**Figure 2-1**).

TAKE OWNERSHIP OF YOUR EDUCATION

To be successful, you must take ownership of your education. While your instructors can create motivational circumstances and an environment to assist you in the learning process, the ultimate responsibility for learning is yours. To get the greatest benefits from your education, commit yourself to the following rules that will take you a long way down the road of success:

- Attend all classes.
- Arrive for class early.
- Have all necessary materials ready.
- Listen attentively to your instructor.
- Highlight important points.
- Take notes for later review.
- Pay close attention during summary and review sessions.
- When something is not clear, ask, ask, ask.
- Never stop learning.

The cosmetology industry is continually changing due to a constant influx of new trends, techniques, products, and information. Read industry magazines and books, and attend trade shows and advanced educational classes throughout your career.

GUIDELINES FOR SUCCESS

Defining success is a very personal thing. There are some basic principles, however, that form the foundation of all personal and business success. You can begin your path to success right now by examining and putting these principles into practice:

- • Build self-esteem. Self-esteem is based on inner strength and begins with trusting your ability to reach your goals. It is essential that you begin working on improving your self-esteem while you are still a student.

- Visualize success. Imagine yourself working in your dream salon, competently handling clients, and feeling at ease and happy with your situation. The more you practice visualization, the easier you can turn the possibilities in your life into realities.

- Build on your strengths. Practice doing whatever it is that helps you to maintain a positive self-image. If you are good at doing something (e.g., playing the guitar, taking photographs, running, cooking, gardening, or singing), the time you invest in this activity will allow you to feel good about yourself (**Figure 2-2**). Also remember that there may be things you are good at that you cannot see. You could be a good listener, for instance, or a caring and considerate friend.

- Be kind to yourself. Put a stop to self-critical or negative thoughts that can work against you. If you make a mistake, tell yourself that it is okay and you will do better next time.

▼ **FIGURE 2-2**

Spend time doing things that you enjoy and do well.

- Define success for yourself. Do not depend on other people's definitions of success; be a success in your own eyes. What is right for your father or sister, for instance, may not be right for you.

- Practice new behaviors. Because creating success is a skill, you can help develop it by practicing positive new behaviors such as speaking with confidence, standing tall, or using good grammar.

- Keep your personal life separate from your work. Talking about yourself and others at work is personally counterproductive and causes the whole salon to suffer.

- Keep your energy up. Successful nail technicians do not run themselves ragged, nor do they eat, sleep, and drink beauty. They take care of their personal needs by spending time with family and friends, having hobbies, enjoying recreational activities, and so on.

- Respect others. Make a point of relating to everyone you know with a conscious feeling of respect. Exercise good manners with others by using words such as please, thank you, and excuse me. Do not interrupt people; instead, practice being a good listener.

- Stay productive. There are three bad habits that can keep you from maintaining peak performance: (1) procrastination, (2) perfectionism, and (3) lack of a game plan. You will see a nearly instant improvement in your performance when you work on eliminating these troublesome habits.

- Avoid procrastination. Procrastination is putting off until tomorrow what you can do today. This destructive, yet common habit is a characteristic of poor study habits ("I'll study tomorrow."). It may also be a symptom of taking on too much, which, in turn, is a symptom of faulty organization.

- Don't be a perfectionist. Perfectionism is an unhealthy compulsion to do things perfectly. Success is not measured by always doing things right. In fact, someone who never makes a mistake may not be trying hard enough. A better definition of success is not giving up, even when things get really tough.

- Lacking a game plan. Having a game plan is the conscious act of planning your life, rather than just letting things happen. While an overall game plan is usually organized into large blocks of time (5 to 10 years ahead), it is just as important to set daily, monthly, and yearly goals. (For more in-depth information about short-term and long-term goals, read Goal Setting in this chapter.)

> ...take care of your personal needs by spending time with family and friends...

✓ **LO1 Complete**

Motivation and Self-Management

(12) Motivation propels you to do something; self-management is a well-thought-out process for the long haul. When you are hungry, for example, you are motivated to eat. But it is self-management that helps you to decide how you will get food. A motivated student finds it much easier to learn. **(13)** The best motivation for you to learn comes from an inner desire to grow your skills as a professional—a lifelong pursuit that is motivated by the ever-changing world of professional beauty.

If you are personally drawn to nail technology, then you are likely to be interested in the material you will be studying in school. If your motivation comes from some external source—for instance, your parents, friends, or a vocational counselor—you will have a difficult time finishing school and jump-starting your beauty career. To achieve success, you need more than an external push; you must feel a sense of personal excitement and a good reason for staying the course. You are the one in charge of managing your own life and learning. To do this successfully, you need good self-management skills.

YOUR CREATIVE CAPABILITY

(14) One self-management skill we can draw on is creativity. Creativity means having a talent such as painting, acting, or doing artificial nail enhancements. Creativity is also an unlimited inner resource of ideas and solutions. To enhance your creativity, keep these guidelines in mind:

- Do not be self-critical. **(15)** Criticism blocks the creative mind from exploring ideas and discovering solutions to challenges.

- Do not look to others for motivation. Tapping into your own creativity will be the best way to manage your own success.

- Change your vocabulary. Build a positive **(16)** vocabulary by using active problem-solving words like explore, analyze, and determine.

- Do not try to go it alone. In today's hectic and pressured world, many talented people find that they are more creative in an environment where people work together and share ideas. This is where the value of a strong salon team comes into play (Figure 2-3).

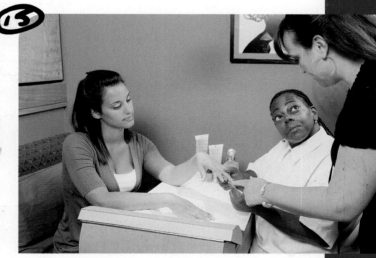

▲ **FIGURE 2-3**
Build strong relationships for support.

✓ **LO2 Complete**

Managing Your Career

No matter how creative, talented, or motivated you are, you will come up against shallow spots, rocks, swift currents, and even an occasional iceberg as you navigate your beauty career. Knowing how to manage your career will make all the difference in staying afloat.

CREATE A MISSION STATEMENT

Every successful business has a business plan. An essential part of this plan is the mission statement. A mission statement establishes the values that a business or an individual lives by and sets up future goals (Figure 2-4). To also succeed in life, you need a well thought-out sense of purpose and a reason for being.

Try to prepare a personal mission statement in one or two sentences that communicates who you are and what you want for your life. One example of a simple, yet thoughtful mission statement is: "I am dedicated to pursuing a successful career with dignity, honesty, and integrity." Whatever you want for your future will be based on the mission statement that you make now. It will point you in a solid direction, and help you to feel secure when things temporarily are not working out as planned. For reinforcement, keep a copy of your mission statement where you can see it and read it every day.

▲ FIGURE 2-4

Example of a personal mission statement.

✔ LO3 Complete

F☀CUS ON... **The Goal**

Determine whether your goal-setting plan is a good one by asking yourself these key questions:

- Are there specific skills I will need to learn in order to meet my goals?
- Is the information I need to reach my goals readily available?
- Would I be willing to seek out a mentor or a coach to enhance my learning?
- What is the best method or approach that will allow me to accomplish my goals?
- Am I always open to finding better ways of putting my plan into practice?

GOAL SETTING

Some people never have a specific goal in mind. They go through life one day at a time without really deciding what they want, where they can find it, or how they are going to live their lives once they get it. They drift from one activity to the next with no firm direction. Does this describe you? Or, do you have drive, desire, and a dream? If so, do you have a reasonable idea of how to go about meeting your goal?

Goal setting is identifying short-term and long-term goals to help you decide what you want to achieve in your life. When you know what you want, you can draw a circle around your destination and chart the best course to get there. By mapping out your goal, you will see where you need to focus your attention, and what you need to learn in order to fulfill your dreams.

How Goal Setting Works

There are two types of goals: short-term and long-term. An example of a short-term goal is to get through a competency exam successfully. Another short-term goal would be your graduation from cosmetology school. Short-term goals are usually those you wish to accomplish in one year or less.

Long-term goals are measured in larger sections of time such as five years, 10 years, or even longer. An example of a long-term goal is telling yourself that in five years you will own your own salon.

Once you have organized your thinking around your goals and written them down in short-term and long-term columns, divide each set of goals into workable segments. In this way, reaching your goals will not seem out of sight or overwhelming. For example, one of your biggest goals at the moment should be getting your license to practice your chosen career path. At first, the prospect of getting this license might seem to require a huge amount of time and effort. When you separate this goal into short-term goals (such as going to class on time, completing homework assignments, and mastering techniques), you begin to see how you can accomplish each one without too much difficulty.

The important thing to remember about goal setting is to have a plan and re-examine it often to make sure that you are staying on track. Even after successful people have accumulated fame, fortune, and respect, they still set goals for themselves. While they may adjust their goals and action plans as they go along, they never lose sight of the fact that their goals are what keep them going.

66 The important thing to remember about goal setting is to have a plan and re-examine it often...

✓ LO**4** Complete

Time Management

Many experts have researched how to make time more manageable. One thing they all agree on is that each of us has an inner organizer. When we pay attention to our natural rhythms, we can learn how to manage our time most efficiently and reach our goals faster and with less frustration. Here are some tips from the experts.

- Learn to prioritize by making a list of tasks that need to be done in the order of most important to least important.

- When designing your own time management system, make sure it will work for you. For example, if you are a person who needs a fair amount of flexibility, schedule in some blocks of unstructured time.

- Never take on more than you can handle. Learn to say, "No," firmly but kindly, and mean it. You will find it easier to complete your tasks if you limit your activities, and do not spread yourself too thin.

- Learn problem-solving techniques that will save you time and needless frustration.

- Give yourself some down time whenever you are frustrated, overwhelmed, worried, or feeling guilty about something. You lose valuable time and energy when you are in a negative state of mind. Unfortunately, there may be situations—like being in the classroom—when you cannot get up and walk away. To handle these difficult times, try practicing the technique of deep breathing. Just fill your lungs as much as you can and then exhale slowly. After about 5 to 10 breaths, you will find that you have calmed down and that your inner balance has been restored.

- Carry a notepad or an organizer with you at all times. You never know when a good idea might strike. Write it down before it slips your mind!

- Make daily, weekly, and monthly schedules for study and exam times, and for any other regular commitments. Plan your leisure time around these commitments, and not the other way around (Figure 2-5).

- Identify the times of day when you are highly energetic, and when you just want to relax. Plan your schedule accordingly.

- Reward yourself with a special treat or activity for work well done and time managed efficiently.

- Do not neglect physical activity. Remember that exercise and recreation stimulate clear thinking and planning.

- Schedule at least one additional block of free time each day. This will be your hedge against events that come up unexpectedly like car trouble, babysitting problems, friends in need, and so on.

- Understand the value of to-do lists for the day and week. They can help you prioritize your tasks and activities, which are key to organizing your time efficiently (Figure 2-6).

- Make time management a habit.

▲ FIGURE 2-5

Keep a schedule for yourself and be sure to refer to it on a frequent basis.

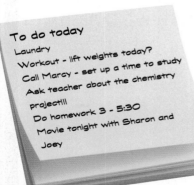

To do today
Laundry
Workout - lift weights today?
Call Marcy - set up a time to study
Ask teacher about the chemistry project!!!
Do homework 3 - 5:30
Movie tonight with Sharon and Joey

▲ FIGURE 2-6

Example of a to-do list.

✓ LO5 Complete

Study Skills

 If you find studying overwhelming, divide your study time into smaller segments. For example, instead of trying to study for three hours at a stretch and suffering a personal defeat when you fold after 40 minutes, set the bar lower by studying in smaller chunks of time. If your mind tends to wander in class, try writing down key words or phrases as your instructor discusses them. Any time you lose your focus, you can stay after class and ask questions based on your notes.

Another way to get a better handle on studying is to find other students who are open to being helpful and supportive. The more you discuss new material with others, the more comfortable you will become with it, and the more successful you will be. If possible, study together (**Figure 2-7**).

◀ FIGURE 2-7
Studying with a friend can be effective and fun.

ESTABLISHING GOOD STUDY HABITS

Part of developing consistently good study habits is to know where, when, and how to study.

Where

- Establish a comfortable, quiet spot where you can study uninterrupted.
- Have everything you need—books, pens, paper, proper lighting, and so on—before you begin studying.
- Remain as alert as possible by sitting upright. Reclining will make you sleepy!

When

- Start out by estimating how much study time you need.
- Study when you feel most energetic and motivated.
- Make good use of your time by planning to study while you are waiting in the doctor's office, taking a bus across town, and so on.

How

- Study a section of a chapter at a time, instead of the entire chapter at once.
- Make a note of key words and phrases as you go along.
- Test yourself on each section to ensure that you understand.

Remember that every effort you make to follow through on your education is an investment in your future. The progress you make with your learning will increase your confidence and self-esteem across the board. In fact, when you have mastered a range of information and techniques, your self-esteem will soar right along with your grades.

 **✓ LO6 Complete**

Ethics

(34) Ethics are the principles of good character, proper conduct and moral judgment expressed through personality, human relations skills and professional image. Ethical people often embody the following qualities:

- *Integrity*. Maintain your integrity by making sure that your behavior and actions match your values. For example, if you believe that it is unethical to sell products just to make money, then do not do so. On the other hand, if you feel that a client needs products and additional services, it would be unethical not to give the client that information.

(35) - *Discretion*. Do not share your personal problems with clients. Likewise, never *breach confidentiality* by repeating personal information that clients have shared with you.

- *Communication*. Your responsibility and ethical behavior extend to your communication with your customers and the other people with whom you work.

F✳CUS ON... Professional Ethics

In cosmetology, each state board sets the ethical standards for disinfection and safety that all nail technicians working in this state must follow. In the salon setting, ethics also entail the role you assume with your clients and fellow employees. When your actions show that you are respectful, courteous, and helpful, you are behaving in an ethical manner.

Here are five ways to show that you are an ethical person:

(36) 1 Provide skilled and competent services.

2 Be honest, courteous, and sincere.

3 Never share what clients have told you privately with others—even your closest friend.

4 Treat all clients fairly; never practice favoritism.

5 Always give correct information to clients about treatments and any products that they may want or need to purchase.

✓ LO7 Complete

Personality Development and Attitude

Some occupations require less interaction with people than others. For example, if you are a computer programmer, you may not be exposed to all different sorts of people every day. As a nail technician however, dealing with people from all walks of life is a major aspect of your work. It is useful, therefore, to have some sense of how different personalities and attitudes can affect your performance.

Refer often to the following ingredients of a healthy, well-developed attitude to see if they match your recipe.

- *Self care.* Many service providers suffer from stress and eventual burnout because they focus most of their energy and time on other people, and very little on themselves. If you are to be truly helpful to others, it is essential to take care of yourself. Try the self-care test to see how you rate (Figure 2-8).

- *Diplomacy.* Being assertive is a good thing because it helps people know where you are coming from. However, it is a short step from being assertive to becoming aggressive, and even bullying. Take your attitude temperature to see how well you practice the art of tact. Being tactful means being straightforward, not critical. This is called diplomacy.

- *Tone of voice.* Your words may not seem harsh, but what about your tone of voice? This is a good example of an inborn personality trait that you can modify by softening the sound of your voice and speaking clearly. Also, if you have a positive attitude, you can deliver your words more pleasantly.

FOCUS ON... The Whole Person

An individual's personality is the sum total of her or his inborn characteristics, attitudes, and behavioral traits. While you may not be able to alter most of your inborn characteristics, you certainly can work on your attitude. This is a process that continues throughout your life. In both your business and personal life, a pleasant attitude gains more associates, clients, and friends.

THE SELF-CARE TEST

Some people know intuitively when they need to stop, take a break, or even take a day off. Other people forget when to eat. You can judge how well you take care of yourself by noting how you feel physically, emotionally, and mentally. Here are some questions to ask yourself to see how you rate of the self-care scale.

1. Do you wait until you are exhausted before you stop working?
2. Do you forget to eat nutritious food and substitute junk food on the fly?
3. Do you say you will exercise and then put off starting a program?
4. Do you have poor sleep habits?
5. Are you constantly nagging yourself about not being good enough?
6. Are your relationships with people filled with conflict?
7. When you think about the future are you unclear about the direction you will take?
8. Do you spend most of your spare time watching TV?
9. Have you been told you are too stressed and yet you ignore these concerns?
10. Do you waste time and then get angry with yourself?

Score 5 points for each yes. A score of 0-15 says that you take pretty good care of yourself, but you would be wise to examine those questions you answered yes to. A score of 15-30 indicates that you need to rethink your priorities. A score of 30-50 is a strong statement that you are neglecting yourself and may be headed for high stress and burnout. Reviewing the suggestions in these chapters will help you get back on track.

▲ **FIGURE 2-8**
Self-care test.

> Receptivity involves taking the time to really listen...

▶ **FIGURE 2-9**
Being receptive is an important personal skill.

- *Emotional stability.* Our emotions are important. Some people, though, have no control over their feelings, and may express themselves excessively or inappropriately. When they are happy, they are almost frantic; when they are angry, they fly into a rage. Learning how to handle a confrontation, as well as sharing how you feel without going overboard, are important indicators of maturity.

- *Sensitivity.* Sensitivity is a combination of understanding, empathy, and acceptance. Being sensitive means being compassionate and responsive to other people.

- *Values and goals.* Neither values nor goals are inborn characteristics; we acquire them as we move through life. They show us how to behave, and what to aim toward.

- *Receptivity.* To be receptive means to be interested in other people, and to be responsive to their opinions, feelings, and ideas. Receptivity involves taking the time to really listen, instead of pretending to do so **(Figure 2-9)**.

- Communication skills. People with a warm, caring personality have an easy time talking about themselves and listening to what others have to say. When they want something, they can ask for it clearly and directly.

✓ **LO8 Complete**

review questions

1. List the basic guidelines for personal and professional success.

2. What are three common habits that can prevent people from being productive?

3. Define a game plan and how it can keep your career on target.

4. List at least three steps that you can take to enhance your creativity.

5. In one to five sentences, write a personal mission statement.

6. List three short-term and three long-term goals you have set for yourself.

7. Why is it so important to learn how to manage your time?

8. List the qualities and characteristics of professional ethics.

9. List the characteristics of a healthy, well-developed attitude.

3 your professional image

chapter outline

- ► Beauty and Wellness
- ► Looking Good
- ► Your Physical Presentation

✓ Learning Objectives

After completing this chapter, you will be able to:

1. Understand professional hygiene.

2. Explain the concept of dressing for success.

3. Demonstrate an understanding of ergonomic principles and ergonomically correct postures and movements.

Key Terms

Page number indicates where in the chapter the term is used.

ergonomics / 32

personal hygiene / 28

physical presentation / 31

professional image / 30

stress / 31

Because you are in the image business, how you look and present yourself has a big influence on whether you will be successful working as a licensed nail technician. If you are talking style, then you need to look stylish; if you are recommending hand care services, it is critical that your hands and nails are well manicured. When your appearance and the way that you conduct yourself is in harmony with the beauty business, your chances of being successful increase by as much as 100 percent! After all, when you look great, your clients will assume that you can make them look great, too (**Figure 3-1**).

> **Being well groomed begins with looking and smelling fresh.**

▶ **FIGURE 3-1**
Project a professional image.

Beauty and Wellness

PERSONAL HYGIENE

Being well groomed begins with looking and smelling fresh. This is especially important in the beauty business where nail technicians are frequently only inches away from their clients during services. It is a given that you should shower or bathe every day, use deodorant before going to work, and generally be neat and clean. Beyond that, though, there are special considerations when working in a salon.

One weak moment of drinking coffee right before performing a service, for instance, or wearing something that needs laundering because you did not plan ahead, could spell disaster. Rather than telling you that you smell offensive, most clients will simply not return for another service. Equally distressing, they will typically tell three of their friends about the bad experience they had while sitting at your station.

Personal hygiene is the daily maintenance of cleanliness by practicing good sanitary habits (**Figure 3-2**). Working as a stylist behind the chair, or doing makeup, nail care, or skin care means that you must be extremely meticulous about your hygiene.

◀ **FIGURE 3-2**
Practice meticulous personal hygiene every day.

One of the best ways to ensure that you always smell fresh and clean is to create a hygiene pack to keep in your station or locker. Your hygiene pack should include:

- Toothbrush and toothpaste.
- Dental floss.
- Mouthwash.
- Deodorant or antiperspirant.
- Liquid soap for hand washing, or sanitizing liquid or wipes if you do not have access to soap and water.

Your hygiene pack will be useful in following these guidelines:

- Wash your hands throughout the day as required, including at the beginning of each service.
- Use deodorant or antiperspirant.
- Brush and floss your teeth, and use mouthwash or breath mints throughout the day as needed.
- Do self-checks periodically to ensure that you smell and look fresh.
- If you smoke cigarettes, do not smoke during work hours. If you cannot wait until after work, make sure to smoke in a well-ventilated area at least 30 minutes before seeing your next client. Always brush your teeth, use mouthwash, and wash your hands after smoking, if you are still servicing clients!

✔ **LO1 Complete**

Looking Good

Naturally, in the line of work that you have chosen, an extremely important element of your image is having well-groomed hair, skin, and nails that serve as an advertisement for your commitment to professional beauty. Make sure that you:

- Put thought into your appearance every day.
- Keep your haircut and color in tip-top shape.
- Keep your skin well groomed.
- Determine the best length and grooming for your nails and meticulously maintain their appearance.
- Change your style frequently to keep up with trends.

CAUTION

Perfume

Many salons have a no-fragrance policy for staff members during work hours because a significant number of people are sensitive or allergic to a variety of chemicals, including perfume oils. Whether or not your salon has a no-fragrance policy, perfume should be saved for after work.

PERSONAL GROOMING

Many salon owners and managers view appearance, personality, and poise as being just as important as technical knowledge and skills. One of the most vital aspects of good personal grooming is the careful maintenance of your wardrobe. First and foremost, your clothes must be clean—not simply free of the dirt that you can see, but stain-free, a feat that is sometimes difficult to achieve in a salon environment. Because you are constantly coming into contact with products and chemicals that can stain fabrics in a nanosecond, it is a good idea to invest in an apron or smock to wear while handling such products. Be mindful about spills and drips when using chemicals, and avoid leaning on counters in the work area—particularly in the dispensary.

DRESS FOR SUCCESS

If you want to go out on the weekend and wear something wild and crazy, that is your choice. But while you are at your place of employment, you will need to consider whether your wardrobe selection expresses a professional image that is consistent with the image of the salon. A professional image is the impression projected by a person engaged in any profession, consisting of her or his outward appearance and conduct exhibited in the workplace. Common sense should also rule when it comes to choosing clothing to wear at work. When shopping for work clothes, you should always visualize how you would look in them while performing professional client services. Is the image you present one that is acceptable to your clients?

To a large degree, your clothing should reflect the fashions of the season by embodying current styles, colors, textures, and so forth. Depending on where you work, you may be encouraged to wear stylish torn jeans and faded tees, or they may be expressly forbidden. Just remember to tune in to your salon's energy and clientele so that you can make the best clothing choices that promote your career as a promising nail technician.

You should always be guided by your salon's dress code with regard to these matters, but the following guidelines are generally appropriate (Figure 3-3).

- Make sure that your clothing is clean, fresh, and in step with fashion.
- Choose clothing that is functional, as well as stylish.
- Accessorize your outfits, but make sure that your jewelry does not clank and jingle while working. This can be irritating to fellow professionals and drive clients to distraction.
- Wear shoes that are comfortable, have a low heel, and good support. Ill-fitting shoes, and any type with high heels, are not the best choices to wear when performing pedicures and portable services within the salon. (Figure 3-4).

▲ FIGURE 3-3
Be guided by your salon's dress code.

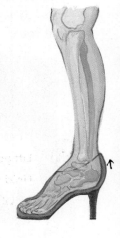

▲ FIGURE 3-4
Working in high heels can throw off the body's balance.

THE ART OF MAKEUP

Makeup is an exciting category for beauty professionals. It helps to promote your professional image, and is an area where some of your most lucrative sales can be made. You should always use makeup to accentuate your best features, and mask your less flattering ones. With that said, it is vital to always wear makeup at work. A freshly scrubbed face may look great for a leisurely day at the beach, but it does nothing to promote your image as a beauty professional while at work. Likewise, unless you are working in a trendy urban salon, things like heavily smoked eyes are generally best left to the club scene. Let the salon's image be your guide on the right makeup choices to wear for work (Figure 3-5).

▲ **FIGURE 3-5**
Expertly applied makeup is part of having a professional image.

 **LO2 Complete**

Your Physical Presentation

▲ **FIGURE 3-6**
Good physical presentation is important.

POSTURE

Good physical posture, walk, and movements are very important parts of your physical presentation. They show off your figure to its best advantage and convey an image of confidence. From a health standpoint, good posture and healthy movements can also prevent fatigue and many other physical problems. When you work within the field of cosmetology, sitting improperly can put a great deal of stress on your neck, shoulders, back, and legs. Stress on the body can result in strain and/or injury. Having good posture, on the other hand, allows you to get through your day feeling good, and doing your best work (Figure 3-6).

Some guidelines for achieving and maintaining good work posture include:

- Keep the neck elongated and balanced directly above the shoulders.
- Lift your upper body so that your chest is out and up (do not slouch).
- Hold your shoulders level and relaxed, not scrunched up.
- Sit with your back straight.
- Pull in your abdomen so that it is flat.

Here's a Tip:

After you have determined how your work posture can be improved following the basic guidelines in this chapter, do a periodic check to determine whether you are still maintaining a good work posture. It's easy to fall back into old habits!

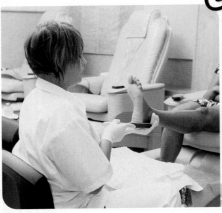

▲ FIGURE 3-7

Be careful not to extend your elbows more than a 60-degree angle away from your body for long periods of time.

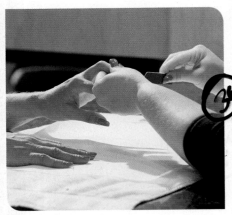

▲ FIGURE 3-8

Be sure to rest your wrists in a straight or neutral position as much as possible.

▲ FIGURE 3-9

Follow proper ergonomic techniques when giving nail services to protect yourself and your client.

ERGONOMICS

Each year, hundreds of cosmetology professionals report musculoskeletal disorders, including carpal tunnel syndrome and back injuries. Beauty professionals expose their bodies to potential injury on a daily basis. Busy nail technicians sit all day and hold their bodies in unnatural positions for long periods of time. They are susceptible to problems of the hands, wrists, shoulders, neck, back, feet, and legs. If not attended to, these problems can become career threatening.

Prevention is the key to alleviating these problems. An awareness of your body posture and movements, coupled with better work habits and proper tools and equipment, will enhance your health and comfort. An understanding of ergonomics is useful as well. Ergonomics is the study of how a workplace and tools should be designed for maximum comfort, safety, efficiency, and productivity. It attempts to fit the job to the person, rather than the other way around. One example is a nail technician's stool that can be raised or lowered to accommodate different heights. Others include ergonomically designed nippers and clippers.

Stressful repetitive motions have a cumulative effect on the muscles and joints. Monitor yourself as you work to see if you are:

- Gripping or squeezing implements too tightly.
- Bending the wrist up or down constantly when using the tools of your profession.
- Holding your arms away from your body as you work.
- Holding your elbows more than a 60-degree angle away from your body for extended periods of time (**Figure 3-7**).
- Bending forward and/or twisting your body to get closer to your client.

Try the following measures to avoid some of the problems discussed above:

- Rest your wrists while working and keep them in a straight or neutral position as much as possible (**Figure 3-8**).
- When giving a manicure, do not reach across the table; have the client extend her hands across the table to you. This is ergonomically correct for you and your client (**Figure 3-9**).
- Use ergonomically designed implements.
- Keep your back and neck straight.
- Break up repetitiveness of the motions you use by including regular stretching exercises in your daily routine.

In every aspect of your work, always put your health first and then the task at hand. It will serve you well in the beauty business and ensure a long, injury-free career.

✓ **LO3 Complete**

review questions

1. List three basic habits of personal hygiene.

2. Define professional image.

3. List the elements of professional image.

4. List the general guidelines of dressing for success.

5. Identify what is included in a hygiene pack. Where is it kept?

6. How often should you freshen up throughout the day?

7. What is the role of posture in good health?

8. Assess your own work posture. How can it be improved?

9. Define the term ergonomics.

10. Give examples of ergonomically beneficial equipment.

11. List steps you can take to prevent potential injury to yourself through ergonomics.

4 communicating for success

After completing this chapter, you will be able to:

1. List the golden rules of human relations.
2. Explain the importance of effective communication.
3. Conduct a successful client consultation.
4. Handle delicate communications with your clients.
5. Build open lines of communication with coworkers and salon managers.

Key Terms

Page number indicates where in the chapter the term is used.

► **FIGURE 4-1**
Communication is part of building
lasting relationships with your clients.

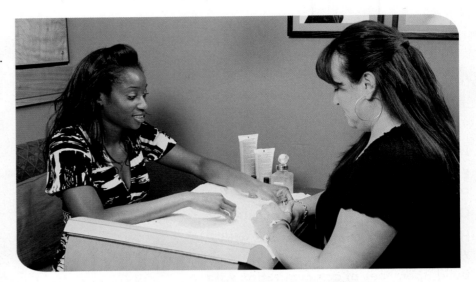

Do you have outstanding technical skills? Artistic talents? If you do, you are definitely on your way to becoming successful in your chosen career path within the field of cosmetology. It is important to realize, though, that technical and artistic skills can only take you so far. In order to have a thriving clientele, you must also master the art of communication **(Figure 4-1)**. Effective human relations and communication skills build lasting client relationships, aid in your growth as a salon practitioner, and help to prevent misunderstandings and unnecessary tension in the workplace.

Human Relations

> The ability to understand people is the key to operating effectively...

No matter where you work, you will not always get along with everyone. It is not possible to always understand what people need, even when you know them well. Even if you do think you understand what people want, you cannot always be sure that you will satisfy them. This can lead to tension and misunderstanding.

The ability to understand people is the key to operating effectively in many professions. It is especially important in cosmetology where customer service is central to success. Most of your interactions will depend on your ability to communicate successfully with a wide range of people: your boss, coworkers, clients, and the different vendors who come into the salon to sell products. When you clearly understand the motives and needs of others, you are in a better position to do your job professionally and easily.

The best way to understand others is to begin with a firm understanding of yourself. When you know what makes you tick, it is easier to appreciate others and to help them get what they need. Basically, we all have the same needs. When we are treated with respect and people listen to us, we feel good about them and ourselves. When we create an atmosphere where customers and staff have confidence in us, we will get the respect we deserve. Good relationships are built on mutual respect and understanding. Here is a brief look at the basics of human relations along with some practical tips for dealing with situations that you are likely to encounter.

- A fundamental factor in human relations has to do with how secure we are feeling. When we feel secure, we are happy, calm, and confident, and we act in a cooperative and trusting manner. When we feel insecure, we become worried, anxious, overwhelmed, perhaps angry and suspicious, and usually do not behave very well. We might be uncooperative, hostile, or withdrawn.

- Human beings are social animals. When we feel secure, we like to interact with other people. We enjoy giving our opinions, take pleasure from having people help us, and take pride in our ability to help others. When people feel secure with us, they are a joy to be with. You can help people feel secure around you by being respectful, trustworthy, and honest.

- No matter how secure you are, there will be times when you will be faced with people and situations that are difficult to handle. You may already have had such experiences. There are always some people who create conflict wherever they go. They can be rude, insensitive, or so full of themselves that being considerate just does not enter their minds. Even though you may wonder how anyone could be so unfeeling, just try to remember that this person, at this particular time, feels insecure or he/she wouldn't be acting this way.

To become skilled in human relations, learn to make the best of situations that could otherwise drain both your time and your energy. Here are some good ways to handle the ups and downs of human relations:

- *Respond instead of reacting.* A fellow was asked why he did not get angry when a driver cut him off. "Why should I let someone else dictate my emotions?" he replied. A wise fellow, don't you think? He might have even saved his own life by not reacting with an eye-for-an-eye mentality.

- *Believe in yourself.* When you believe in yourself, you trust your judgment, uphold your own values, and stick to what you believe is right. It is easy to believe in yourself when you have a strong sense of self-worth. It comes with the knowledge that you are a good person and you deserve to be successful. Believing in yourself makes you feel strong enough to handle almost any situation in a calm, helpful manner.

- *Talk less, listen more.* There is an old saying that we were given two ears and one mouth for a reason. You get a gold star in human relations when you listen more than you talk. When you are a good listener, you are fully attentive to what the other person is saying. If there is something you do not understand, ask a question to gain understanding.

- *Be attentive.* Each client is different. Some are clear about what they want, others are aggressively demanding, while others may be hesitant. If you have an aggressive client, instead of trying to handle it by yourself, ask your manager for advice. You will likely be told that what usually calms down difficult clients is agreeing with them, and then asking what you can do to make the service more to their liking. This approach is virtually guaranteed to work (Figure 4-2).

▼ **FIGURE 4-2**

Be attentive to your client's needs.

- *Take your own temperature.* If you are tired or upset about a personal problem, or have had an argument with a fellow student, you may be feeling down about yourself and wish you were anywhere but in school. If this feeling lasts a short time, you will be able to get back on track easily enough, and there is no cause for alarm. If, however, you begin to notice certain chronic behaviors about yourself once you are in a job, pay careful attention to what is happening. An important part of being in a service profession is taking care of yourself first and resolving whatever conflicts are going on so that you can take care of your clients. Trust can be lost in a second without even knowing it—and, once lost, trust is almost impossible to regain.

THE GOLDEN RULES OF HUMAN RELATIONS

Keep the following guidelines in mind for a crash course in human relations that will always keep you in line and where you should be:

- Communicate from your heart; troubleshoot from your head.
- A smile is worth a million times more than a sneer.
- It is easy to make an enemy; it is harder to keep a friend.
- See what happens when you ask for help instead of just reacting.
- Show people you care by listening to them and trying to understand their point of view.
- Tell people how great they are (even when they are not acting so great).
- Being right is different from acting righteous.
- For every service you do for others, do not forget to do something for yourself.
- Laugh often.
- Show patience with other people's flaws.
- Build shared goals; be a team player and a partner to your clients.
- Always remember that listening is the best relationship builder.

> Always approach a new client with a smile on your face.

✔ **LO1 Complete**

Communication Basics

Communication is the act of successfully sharing information between two people or groups of people so that it is effectively understood. You can communicate through words, voice inflections, facial expressions, body language, and visual tools (e.g., a portfolio of your work). When you and your client are both communicating clearly about an upcoming service, your chances of pleasing that person soar.

▲ FIGURE 4-3

Welcome your client to the salon.

MEETING AND GREETING NEW CLIENTS

One of the most important communications you will have with a client is the first time you meet that person. Be polite, genuinely friendly, and inviting (which you will continue to be in all your encounters), and remember that your clients are coming to you for services for which they are paying hard-earned cash **(Figure 4-3)**. This means you need to court them every time they come to see you; otherwise, you may lose them to another nail technician or salon.

To earn clients' trust and loyalty, you need to:

- Always approach a new client with a smile on your face. If you are having a difficult day or have a problem of some sort, keep it to yourself. The time you are with your client is for her needs, not yours.

- Always introduce yourself. Names are powerful and they are meant to be used frequently. Many clients have had the experience of being greeted by the receptionist, ushered back to the service area, and when the service has been performed and the appointment is over, they have not learned the name of a single person.

- Set aside a few minutes to take new clients on a quick tour of the salon.

- Introduce them to people they may have interactions with while in the salon, including potential service providers for other services such as skin care or makeup.

- Be yourself. Do not try to trick your clients into thinking you are someone or something that you are not. Just be who you are. You will be surprised at how well this will work for you.

✓ **LO2 Complete**

The Client Consultation

The client consultation is the verbal communication with a client to determine the desired result of a service. It is the single most important part of any service and should always be done before beginning any part of the service. Some nail technicians skip the client consultation altogether, or they make time for it only on a client's first visit to the salon. These professionals are making a serious mistake. A consultation should be performed, to some degree, as part of every single service and salon visit. It keeps good communication going, and allows you to keep your clients looking current and feeling satisfied with your services.

CLIENT CONSULTATION FORM

The client consultation form, also called an intake form or client questionnaire, should be filled out by every new client prior to sitting at your nail station. Whether in the salon or in school, this form can prove to be extremely useful **(Figure 4-4)**.

Some salon consultation forms ask for a lot of detailed information, and some do not. In cosmetology school, the consultation form may be accompanied by a release statement in which the client acknowledges that the service is being provided by a student and not a licensed nail technician. This helps to protect the school and the student from any legal action by a client who may be unhappy with the service.

HOW TO USE THE CLIENT CONSULTATION FORM

The client consultation form is a questionnaire used to gather information about a client's needs, history and preferences; it is filled out before the client's first service is performed at the salon and can be used from the moment a new client calls the salon to make an appointment. When scheduling the appointment, let her know that you and the salon will require some information before you can begin the service, and that it is important for her to arrive 15 minutes prior to her appointment time to fill out a brief form. You will also have to allow time in your schedule to do a 5-minute to 20-minute client consultation, depending on the type of service you will be performing and the needs of the client.

PREPARING FOR THE CLIENT CONSULTATION

It is important to be prepared so your time is well spent during the client consultation. To facilitate the consultation process, you should have certain important items on hand. These include clippings from beauty magazines, particularly close-ups of hand/foot models that have beautiful nails. If you are stressing nail enhancements in your future practice, always include clippings from trade magazines that show beautiful silk, UV gel, and monomer liquid and polymer powder enhancements. You should also take before-and-after photos of your best work to use as a communication tool and client confidence builder during client consultations. Equally important, have a chart of different nail shapes that are identified by name: square, round, oval, squoval (square oval), and pointed.

THE CONSULTATION AREA

Presentation counts for a lot in a business that is concerned with style and appearance. Once you have brought the client to your station to begin the consultation process, make sure she is comfortable. You and she are about to begin an important conversation that will clue you in on her needs and preferences. Your work area needs to be freshly cleaned and uncluttered.

CLIENT CONSULTATION FORM

Dear Client,

Our sincerest hope is to serve you with the best nail care services you've ever received! We want you to be happy with today's visit, and we also want to build a long-lasting relationship filled with trust and complete satisfaction with our services. In order for us to do this, we would like to learn more about you, your nail care needs, and your preferences. Please take a moment to answer the questions below as completely and as accurately as possible.

Thank you and we look forward to building a "beautiful" relationship!

Name

Address _____

_____

Phone Numbers: Day _____   Evening _____

Mobile _____

Email Address: _____

What is your preferred method of communication?

_____

Gender: _____Male   _____Female

How did you hear about our salon? _____

If you were referred to our salon, who referred you?

_____

Please answer the following questions in the spaces provided. Thanks!

1. Approximately when was your last nail care service?

_____

2. In the past year, have you had any of the following services done either in or out of a salon?

_____Manicure   _____Pedicure

_____ Nail Enhancements   _____Other

3. It is important that you discuss with your nail technician any chronic condition(s) you may have, so that precautions can be considered. Examples of conditions would be circulatory diseases, diabetes, peripheral artery disease (PAD), arthritis, high blood pressure, and others.

4. How would you characterize your natural nails?

_____Normal   _____Strong

_____Brittle   _____Flexible

_____Other

▲ FIGURE 4-4

Typical client consultation card. (continued)

CLIENT CONSULTATION FORM

5. Do you regularly receive any of the following nail services? (Check all that apply):

______Monomer and Polymer Nail Enhancements

______Monomer and Polymer Nail Enhancements with UV Gel Overlay

______UV Gel Nail Enhancements

______Fabric Wraps (Circle Type: Silk, Linen, or Fiberglass)

______Manicure

______Natural Nail Treatments

______Paraffin Hand Treatments

6. Do you receive any of the following foot services? (Check all that apply):

______Basic Pedicure ______Spa Pedicure

_______Masks or Paraffin Foot Treatments

7. Please share information about your most successful and least successful types of nail services. ____

____

8. What types of frequent activities do you engage in that could cause damage to your nails? ____

____

9. What are you goals for today's nail appointment? ____________________

____

10. Do you have a special occasion coming up in the near future where your nails must look their absolute best? If so, when?

▲ **FIGURE 4-4**

Typical client consultation card. (continued)

Have your photos, magazine clippings, nail shape drawings, and all other appropriate aids for the desired service available. You should read the consultation form carefully, and refer to it often during the consultation process. Throughout the consultation, and especially once a course of action is decided on, make notes on the consultation form. Record any formulations or products that you use and include any specific techniques you follow or goals you are working toward, so that you can remember them for future visits.

10-STEP CONSULTATION METHOD

Every complete consultation needs to be structured in such a way that you cover all key points that consistently lead to a successful conclusion. While this may seem like a lot of information to memorize, it will become second nature as you become more experienced and have many consultations under your belt. Depending on the service requested, the consultation will vary to some degree. For example, a full-set of gel nails with tips will require a more detailed consultation than a basic manicure. To ensure that you always cover your bases, keep a list of the following 10 key points at your station for referral and modify it as needed for the actual service.

This method is highly effective prior to caring for new nail clients, and before every new nail service.

1. *Review.* Review the consultation form your client has filled out and feel free to make comments to break the ice and get the consultation going.

2. *Assess your client's nails.* Are they long, short, or somewhere in between? Are the nails healthy and strong? Brittle and weak? Are the edges peeling?

FOCUS ON... Understanding the Total Look Concept

While the enhancement of your client's image should always be your primary concern, it is important to remember that the nails, skin, and hair adorn the body and are reflective of an entire lifestyle. How can you help a client make choices that reflect a personal sense of style? Start the process by doing a little research. Look for books or articles that describe different fashion styles, and become familiar with them. This exercise is useful for developing a profile of the broad fashion categories to which you can refer when consulting with clients.

For example, a person may be categorized as having a classic style if simple and sophisticated clothing, monochromatic colors, and no bright patterns are preferred. A classic client would likely want a simple, elegant, and sophisticated look with respect to her nails.

Someone who prefers a more dramatic look, on the other hand, will choose nail designs that demand greater attention and allow for more options. These clients are likely to be more willing to try new products and spend more time having additional services, such as nail art, that will help achieve the desired look (**Figure 4-5 and Figure 4-6**).

▶ **FIGURE 4-6**
Dramatic look.

▶ **FIGURE 4-5**
Classic look.

3   *Preference*. Always ask clients what they like or dislike about their nails. Delve into their nail history to learn which nail services they've had in the past (e.g., nail enhancements, etc.) and the outcome of those services.

4   *Analyze*. Analyze and determine the ideal length and shape based on the shape of the fingertips and the nail bed, and personal preferences.

5   *Lifestyle*. Always ask clients about their career and personal lifestyles.

   • Does your client spend a great deal of time outdoors? Does she swim everyday?

   • Is your client an executive in a conservative industry? An artist? A stay-at-home parent?

   • Does your client have a strong personal style that she wishes to project?

   • How much time is she willing to invest on nail and hand grooming?

6   *Show and tell*. Encourage her to flip through your photo collections and point out finished looks that she likes and why. This is a good time to get a real grasp on whether she not only understands but also accepts any personal limitations. Listening to the client and then repeating—in your own words—what you think the client is telling you, is critical to having a clear understanding of what both of you are really saying. This is known as reflective listening. Mastering this listening skill will help you to always be on target with your services and build a deep trust with your clients.

7   *Suggest*. Once you have enough information, you can make valid style suggestions. Narrow your selections to lifestyle and other characteristics applicable to the desired service such as nail characteristics, or face and body shapes.

When making suggestions, clarify them, or make them clear, by referencing the above parameters. Tactfully discuss any unreasonable expectations she may have shared with you by picking out photos that are unrealistic based on her characteristics and personal needs.

8   *Additional services*. Never hesitate to suggest additional services to make the new look complete or better in some way. For example, you may have only provided a nail service; however, recommending the client for another service, such as a pedicure or even a color service from a stylist you trust, could help the client achieve the total desired look.

9   *Upkeep*. Counsel every client on the lifestyle limitations associated with a given style, as well as salon and home maintenance commitments needed to keep her nails looking their best at all times.

10 *Repeat*. Reiterate everything that you have agreed on. Make sure to speak in measured, precise terms and use visual tools to demonstrate the end result. This is the most critical step of the consultation process because it determines the ultimate service(s). Take your time and be thorough.

✓ **LO3 Complete**

CONCLUDING THE SERVICE

Once the service is finished and the client has let you know whether or not she is satisfied, take a few more minutes to record the results on the record card. Ask for her reactions and record them. Note anything you did that you might want to do again, as well as anything that does not bear repeating. Also, make notes of the final results and any retail products that you recommended. Be sure to date your notes and file them in the proper place.

Special Issues in Communication

Although you may do everything in your power to communicate effectively, you will sometimes encounter situations that are beyond your control. The solution is not to try to control the circumstances, but rather to communicate past the issue. Your reactions to situations, and your ability to communicate in the face of problems, are critical to being successful in a people profession such as the beauty industry.

HANDLING TARDY CLIENTS

Tardy clients are a fact of life in every service industry. Because nail technicians are so dependent on appointments and scheduling to maximize working hours, a client who is very late for an appointment, or one who is habitually late, can cause problems. One tardy client can make you late for every other client you service that day, and the pressure involved in making up for that lost time can take its toll. You also risk inconveniencing the rest of your clients who are prompt for their appointments.

Here are a few guidelines for handling late clients:

- Know and abide by the salon's tardy or late policy. Many salons set a limited amount of time that they allow a client to be late before they require them to reschedule. Generally, if clients are more than 15 minutes late, they should be asked to reschedule. Most will accept responsibility and be understanding about the rule, but you may come across a few clients who insist on being serviced immediately. Explain that you have other appointments and are responsible to those clients as well. Also explain that rushing through the service is unacceptable to both of you.

- If your tardy client arrives and you have the time to take her without jeopardizing other clients' appointments, let your client know why you are taking her even though she is late. You can deliver this information and still remain pleasant and upbeat. Say, "Oh, Ms. Lee, we're in luck! Even though you're a bit late, I can still take you because my next appointment isn't for two hours. Isn't it great that it worked out?" This lets her know that even though you are accommodating her, it should be considered an exception and not the rule.

- As you get to know your clients, you will learn who is habitually late. You may want to schedule such clients for the last appointment of the day, or ask them to arrive earlier than their actual appointments. In other words, if a client is always 30-minutes late, schedule her for 2:30 but tell her to arrive at 2:00!

- Imagine this scenario. In spite of your best efforts, you are running late. You realize that no matter what has happened in the salon that day, your clients want and deserve your promptness. If you have your clients' telephone numbers, call them and let them know about the delays. Give them the opportunity to reschedule, or to come in a little later than their scheduled appointments. If you cannot reach them beforehand, be sure to approach them when they come into the salon and let them know that you are delayed. Tell them how long you think the wait will be, and give them the option of changing their appointment. Apologize for the inconvenience and show a little extra attention by personally offering them a beverage. Even if these clients are not happy about the delay, or they need to change their appointment, at least they will feel informed and respected.

HANDLING SCHEDULING MIX-UPS

> **We are all human, and we all make mistakes.**

We are all human, and we all make mistakes. Chances are you have gone to an appointment on a certain day, at a certain time, only to discover that you are in the wrong place, at the wrong time. The way you are treated at that moment will determine if you ever patronize that business again. The number-one thing to remember when you, as a professional, get involved with a scheduling mix-up is to be polite and never argue about who is correct. Being right may sound good, but this kind of situation is not about being right; it is about preserving your relationship with your client. If you handle the matter poorly, you run the risk of never seeing that client again.

(22)

Even if you know for sure that she is mistaken, tell yourself that the client is always right. Assume the blame if it helps keep her happy. Do not, under any circumstances, argue the point with the client.

Once you have the chance to consult your appointment book, you can say, "Oh, Mrs. Montez, I have you in my appointment book for 10:00, and, unfortunately, I have already scheduled other clients for 11:00 and 12:00. I am so sorry about the mix-up. Can I reschedule you for tomorrow at 10:00?" Even though the client may be fuming, you need to stay disengaged. Your focus is to move the conversation away from who is at fault, and squarely in the direction of resolving the confusion. Make another appointment for the client and be sure to get her telephone number so that you can call and confirm the details of the appointment in advance.

▲ FIGURE 4-7
Accommodate an unhappy client promptly and calmly.

HANDLING UNHAPPY CLIENTS

No matter how hard you try to provide excellent service to your clients, once in a while you will encounter a client who is dissatisfied with the service. The way you and the salon handle this difficult situation will have lasting effects on you, the client, and the salon, so you need to know how best to proceed.Once again, it is important to remember the ultimate goal: make the client happy enough to pay for the service and return for more of the same **(Figure 4-7)**.

Here are some guidelines to follow:

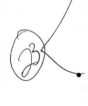

(23)

- Try to find out why the client is unhappy. Ask for specifics. If she has a difficult time expressing herself, break the service down for her piece by piece until you determine exactly what has caused the dissatisfaction.

- If it is possible to change what she dislikes, do so immediately. If that is not possible, look at your schedule to see how soon you can do it. You may need to enlist the help of the receptionist in rescheduling your other appointments. If the client seems open to the suggestion, ask her to return to the salon at a time when you are free. If this is not possible, explain that you will begin her service, but will need to take your next client and will be relying on help from another practitioner. Do whatever you have to do to make her happy, and explain along the way who will be working with her and what the other practitioner will be doing.

(24)

- If you cannot change what the client does not like, or it is simply impossible to change, you must honestly and tactfully explain the reason why you cannot make any changes. The client will not be happy, but you should still offer any options that may be available.

- Again, never argue with the client, or try to force your opinion. Unless you can change what has caused the dissatisfaction, this will just fuel the fire.

- Do not hesitate to call on more experienced nail technicians or your salon manager for help. They have encountered a similar situation at some point in their careers, and have insights that can help you.

- If, after you have tried everything, you are unable to satisfy the client, defer to your manager's advice on how to proceed. The client may be too upset to handle the situation maturely, and it may be easier for her to deal with someone else. This does not mean that you have failed; it simply means that another approach is needed.

- Confer with your salon manager after the experience. A good manager will not hold the event against you, but rather view it as an inevitable fact of life from which you can learn. Follow your manager's advice and move on to your next client. Use whatever you may have learned from the experience to perform future client consultations and services better.

✓ **LO4 Complete**

FCUS ON...
Professionalism

A long-time client reveals to you one day that she and her husband are going through a messy divorce. You care for her and try to be understanding as she reveals increasingly personal details. Other practitioners and their clients are soon listening to every word of this conversation. You want to be helpful and supportive, but this is not the right time or place. What can you do?

Try this: Tell her you understand the situation is very difficult, but while she is in the salon, you want to do everything in your power to give her a break. Let her know that while she is in your care, you should both concentrate on her enjoyment of the services and not on the things that are stressing her. She will appreciate the suggestion, and you will have put her back on the track of her real reason for coming to see you.

GETTING TOO PERSONAL

Sometimes when a client forms a bond of trust with her nail technician, she may have a hard time differentiating between a professional and a personal relationship. That will be her problem, but you must not make it your problem. Your job is to handle your client relationships tactfully and sensitively. You cannot become your clients' counselor, career guide, parental sounding board, or motivational coach. Your job and your relationship with your clients are very specific: The goal is to advise and service clients with their beauty needs, and nothing more.

In-Salon Communication

Behaving in a professional manner is the first step in making this meaningful communication possible. Unfortunately, many beauty professionals act immaturely and get overly involved in the salon rumor mill.

The salon community is usually a close-knit one in which beauty professionals spend long hours working side by side. For this reason, it is important to maintain boundaries around what you will and will not do or say at the salon. Remember, the salon is your place of business and, as such, must be treated respectfully and carefully.

COMMUNICATING WITH COWORKERS

As with all communication, there are basic principles that must guide your interactions. In a work environment, you will not have the opportunity to handpick your colleagues. There will always be people you like or relate to better than others, and people whose behaviors or opinions you find yourself in conflict with. These people can try your patience and your nerves, but they are your colleagues and are deserving of your respect.

Here are some guidelines to keep in mind as you interact and communicate with fellow staffers:

 Treat everyone with respect. Regardless of whether or not you like someone, your colleagues are professionals who service clients who bring revenue into the salon. And, as practicing professionals, they have information they can offer you. Look at these people as having something to teach you, and hone in on their talents and their techniques.

 Remain objective. Different types of personalities working side-by-side over long and intense hours are likely to breed some degree of dissension. In order to learn and grow, you must make every effort to remain objective and resist being pulled into spats and cliques. When one or two people in the salon behave disrespectfully toward one another, the entire team suffers because the atmosphere changes. Not only will this be unpleasant for you, but it will also be felt by the clients who may decide to take their business elsewhere, if they find the atmosphere in your salon too tense.

 Be honest and be sensitive. Many people use the excuse of being honest as a license to say anything to anyone. While honesty is always the best policy, using unkind words or actions with regard to your colleagues is never a good idea. Be sensitive. Put yourself in the other person's place and think through what you want to say before you say it. In that way, any negative or hurtful words can be suppressed.

- *Remain neutral.* Undoubtedly, there will come a time when you are called on to make a statement or pick a side. Do whatever you can to avoid getting drawn into the conflict. If you have a problem with a colleague, the best way to resolve it is to speak with her or him directly and privately.

- *Seek help from someone you respect.* If you find yourself in a position where you are at odds with a coworker, you may want to seek out a third party—someone who is not involved and can remain objective—such as the manager or a more experienced practitioner. Ask for advice about how to proceed and really listen to what this mentor has to say. Since this person is not involved, he or she is more likely to see the situation as it truly is, and can offer you valuable insights.

- *Do not take things personally.* This is often easier said than done. How many times have you had a bad day, or have been thinking about something totally unrelated, when a person asks you what's wrong, or wonders if you are mad at them? Just because someone is behaving in a certain manner, and you happen to be there, do not interpret these words or behaviors as being meant for you. If you are confused or concerned by someone's actions, find a quiet and private place to ask the person about it. The person may not even realize she was giving off any signals.

- *Keep your private life private.* There is a time and a place for everything, but the salon is never the place to discuss your personal life and relationships. It may be tempting to engage in that kind of conversation, especially if others in the salon are doing so, and to solicit advice and opinions, but that is why you have friends. Coworkers can become friends, but those whom you selectively turn into friends are different from the ones whose chairs happen to be next to yours.

FOCUS ON...
Keep it Out of the Salon

Too much time spent on discussing your personal matters in the salon means time away from the task of perfecting your skills and artistry, and building-up the business for yourself and the salon.

COMMUNICATING WITH MANAGERS

Another very important relationship for you within the salon is the one you will build with your manager. The salon manager is generally the person who has the most responsibility for how the salon is run in terms of daily maintenance and operations and client service. The manager's job is a very demanding one. Often, in addition to running a hectic salon, she also has a clientele that she personally services.

Your manager is likely to be the one who hired you, and is responsible for your training and how well you move into the salon culture. Therefore, your manager has a vested interest in your success. As a salon employee, you will see the manager as a powerful and influential person, but it is also important to remember that she is a human being. She isn't perfect, and she will not be able to do everything you think should be done in every instance. Whether or not she personally likes you, her job is to look beyond her personal feelings and make decisions that are best for the salon as a whole. The best thing you can do is to try to understand the decisions and rules that she makes, whether or not you agree with them.

Many salon professionals utilize their salon managers in inappropriate ways by asking them to solve personal issues between staff members. You and your manager must both understand that her job is to make sure the business is running smoothly, and not to baby-sit temperamental practitioners or mediate personal disagreements.

Here are some guidelines for interacting and communicating with your salon manager.

- *Be a problem solver.* When you need to speak with your manager about some issue or problem, think of some possible solutions beforehand. This will indicate that you are working in the salon's best interest and trying to improve the situation.

- *Get the facts straight.* Make sure that all your facts and information are accurate before you speak to your salon manager. In this way, you will avoid wasting time solving a "problem" that really does not exist.

- *Be open and honest.* When you find yourself in a situation you do not understand, or do not have the experience to deal with, tell your salon manager immediately and be willing to learn.

- *Do not gossip or complain about colleagues.* Going to your manager with gossip or to "tattle" on a coworker tells your manager that you are a troublemaker. If you are having a legitimate problem with someone and have tried everything in your power to handle the problem yourself, then it is appropriate to go to your manager. But you must approach her with a true desire to solve the problem, and not just to vent.

- *Check your attitude.* The salon environment, although fun and friendly, can also be stressful, so it is important to take a moment between clients to take your temperature. Ask yourself how you are feeling. Do you need an attitude adjustment? Be honest with yourself.

- *Be open to constructive criticism.* It is never easy to hear that you need improvement in any area, but keep in mind that part of your manager's job is to help you achieve your professional goals. She is supposed to evaluate your skills and offer suggestions on how to increase them. Keep an open mind and do not take her criticism personally.

COMMUNICATING DURING AN EMPLOYEE EVALUATION

Salons that are well run will make it a priority to conduct frequent and thorough employee evaluations, periodic assessments of an employee's skills, attitudes, and behaviors and how they are used and perceived in the salon setting. Sometime in the course of your first few days of work, your salon manager will tell you when you can expect your first evaluation. If she does not mention it, you might ask her about it and request a copy of the form she will use, or the criteria on which you will be evaluated (**Figure 4-8 and Figure 4-9**).

Take some time to look over this document. Be mindful that the behaviors and/or activities most important to the salon are likely to be the ones on which you will be evaluated. This is very useful information. You can begin to watch and rate yourself in the weeks and months ahead so you can assess how you are doing. Remember, everything you are being evaluated on is there for the purpose of helping you to improve. Make the decision to approach these communications positively. As the time draws near for the evaluation, try filling out the form yourself.

Handwritten annotations: 32, 35 Performance evaluation covers • job knowledge • your productivity • challenge solving abilities, 33, 34

PERFORMANCE EVALUATION

Name:_____ _____

Date:_____

Position: _____ _____

Supervisor: _____

	EXCEPTIONAL	SATISFACTORY	OPPORTUNITY	COMMENTS
JOB PERFORMANCE				
JOB KNOWLEDGE				
PRODUCTIVITY				
QUALITY OF WORK				
CHALLENGE SOLVING				
COMMUNICATION				
ADAPTABILITY				
ATTENDANCE				

▲ **FIGURE 4-8**

Example of a simple employee evaluation form.

TECHNICIAN PERFORMANCE EVALUATION FORM

Name:_____

Date:_____

Reviewed by: _____

Employee Start Date:_____ Next Review Date:_____

	POOR	FAIR	GOOD	EXCELLENT	POINTS		
					THIS REVIEW	PREVIOUS REVIEW	COMPARISON
TECHNICAL SKILLS							
RETAIL SALES							
CUSTOMER SERVICE							
CLIENT RETENTION							
TEAM WORK							
Communication							
Efficiency							
Cooperation							
Sets Example							
Supportive							
PERSONNEL							
Attendance							
Tardiness							
Dependable							
Follows Policy							
PROFESSIONALISM							
Attitude							
Dedication							
Follow-through							
Image Projection							
TOTAL POINTS							

Comments: _____

_____

_____

Signature of Employee: _____

Signature of Management: _____

▲ FIGURE 4-9

Example of a thorough employee evaluation form.

► FIGURE 4-10

Your employee evaluation is a good time to discuss your progress with your manager.

In other words, give yourself an evaluation, even if the salon has not asked you to do so. Be objective, and carefully consider your comments. Then, when you meet with the manager, show her your evaluation and tell her you are serious about your improvement and growth. She will appreciate your input and your desire to be the best that you can be. And, if you are being honest with yourself, there should be no surprises (**Figure 4-10**).

Before your evaluation meeting, write down any thoughts or questions you may have so you can share them with your manager. Do not be shy. If you want to know when you can take on more services, when your pay scale will be increased, or when you might be considered for promotion, this meeting is the appropriate time and place to ask. Many beauty professionals never take advantage of this crucial communication opportunity to discuss their future because they are too nervous, intimidated, or unprepared. Do not let that happen to you. Participate proactively in your career and in your success by communicating your desires and interests. At the end of the meeting, thank your manager for taking the time to do an evaluation and for the feedback and guidance she has given you.

> Participate proactively in your career and in your success ...

✓ **LO5 Complete**

review questions

1. List the golden rules of human relations.

2. Define communication.

3. Name some of information that should go on a client consultation card.

4. What is the total look concept?

5. How should you prepare for a client consultation?

6. List and describe the 10 steps of a successful client consultation.

7. How should you handle tardy clients?

8. How should you handle a scheduling mix-up?

9. How should you handle an unhappy client?

10. List at least five things to remember when communicating with your coworkers.

11. List at least four guidelines for communicating with salon managers.

Part 2

GENERAL SCIENCES

5

infection
control:
PRINCIPLES AND PRACTICES

chapter outline

☑ Learning Objectives

After you have completed this chapter, you will be able to:

1 Understand state laws and rules and the difference between them.

2 List the types and classifications of bacteria.

3 Define hepatitis and HIV and explain how they are transmitted.

4 Explain the differences between cleaning, disinfecting, and sterilizing.

5 List the types of disinfectants and how they are used.

6 Discuss Universal Precautions.

7 List your responsibilities as a salon professional.

8 Describe how to safely clean and disinfect salon tools and equipment.

Key Terms

Page number indicates where in the chapter the term is used.

acquired immunity / 70

acquired immunodeficiency syndrome (AIDS) / 69

allergy / 72

antiseptics / 79

asymptomatic / 80

bacilli / 65

bacteria / 63

bactericidal / 63

bloodborne pathogens / 68

chelating soaps (chelating detergents) / 78

cilia (flagella) / 65

clean (cleaning) / 71

cocci / 64

contagious disease / 66

contamination / 67

decontamination / 67

diagnose / 63

diagnosis / 67

diplococci / 65

direct transmission / 64

disease / 61

disinfectants / 71

disinfection / 71

efficacy / 73

exposure incident / 80

flagella (cilia)/ 65

fungi / 69

fungicidal / 63

hepatitis / 68

hospital disinfectants / 61

human immunodeficiency virus (HIV) /69

immunity / 70

indirect transmission / 64

infection / 62

infectious / 64

infectious disease / 62

inflammation / 66

local infection / 66

Material Safety Data Sheet (MSDS) / 60

Methicillin-resistant *Staphylococcus aureus* (MRSA) / 66

microbes (germs) / 63

microorganisms / 63

mildew / 69

mitosis / 65

motility / 65

multi-use (reusable) / 76

mycobacterium fortuitum furunculosis / 62

natural immunity / 70

nonpathogenic / 63

occupational disease / 67

-ology / 64

parasite / 70

parasitic disease / 67

pathogenic / 63

pathogenic disease / 67

phenolic disinfectants / 75

porous / 77

pus / 66

quaternary ammonium compounds (quats) / 74

sanitation (sanitizing) / 60

scabies / 70

single-use (disposable) / 77

sodium hypochlorite / 75

spirilla / 65

staphylococci / 64

sterilization / 72

streptococci / 65

systemic disease / 67

toxins / 70

tuberculocidal disinfectants / 61

tuberculosis / 61

Universal Precautions / 80

virucidal / 63

virus / 68

In previous editions of this chapter the words sanitation, also known as sanitizing, were used interchangeably to mean clean or cleaning. You will also find that many commercially available products used in the cleaning and disinfecting process continue to use the words sanitize and sanitizing. However, the publishers goal is to end any possible confusion about the use and definition of these words by clearly defining them below and within the glossary because:

- There is much confusion and misuse of the terms cleaning, sanitizing, disinfecting, and sterilizing within the beauty industry, including at the state regulatory level. In an effort to do what we can to clarify these critical terms, Milady opted to consistently use cleaning, instead of using cleaning in one sentence and sanitizing in another sentence.
- Professionals in the health care and scientific communities (of disease prevention and epidemiology) and associations like The Association for Professionals in Infection Control and Epidemiology generally do not use the terms interchangeably either. Instead it is more common for infection control professionals to use the term cleaning. Infection Control professionals consider sanitation a layperson's term or a product marketing term (as in hand sanitizers).

The word **cleaning** is defined as: a mechanical process (scrubbing) using soap and water or detergent and water to remove dirt, debris and many disease-causing germs. Cleaning also removes invisible debris that interferes with disinfection.

The word **sanitizing** is defined as: a chemical process for reducing the number of disease-causing germs on cleaned surfaces to a safe level.

The word **disinfecting** is defined as: a chemical process that uses specific products to destroy harmful organisms (except bacterial spores) on environmental surfaces.

To be a knowledgeable, successful, and responsible professional in the field of nail technology, you will be required to learn about the types of infections you may encounter in the salon, the chemistry of the products that you use, and how to use these products to keep yourself, your clients, and your salon environment safe. Understanding the basics of cleaning and disinfecting and following federal and state rules will ensure that you have a long and successful career in the field of nail technology.

Regulation

Many different state and federal agencies regulate the practice of nail technology. Federal agencies set guidelines for the manufacturing, sale, and use of equipment and chemical ingredients, and for safety in the workplace, placing limits on the types of services you can perform in the salon. For example, nail professionals are prohibited from cutting or puncturing the living skin and from removing callused skin, warts, corns, in-grown nails, etc. State agencies regulate licensing, enforcement, and your conduct when you are working in the salon.

FEDERAL AGENCIES
Occupational Safety and Health Administration (OSHA)

The Occupational Safety and Health Administration (OSHA) was created as part of the U.S. Department of Labor to regulate and enforce safety and health standards to protect employees in the workplace. Regulating employee exposure to potentially toxic substances and informing employees about possible hazards of materials used in the workplace are key points of the Occupational Safety and Health Act of 1970. This regulation created the Hazard Communication Act, which requires that chemical manufacturers and importers assess the potential hazards associated with their products. The Material Safety Data Sheet (MSDS) is a result of this law.

The standards set by OSHA are important to the nail industry because of the products used in salons. These standards address issues relating to the handling, mixing, storing, and disposing of products; general safety in the workplace; and, your right to know about any potentially hazardous ingredients contained in the nail products you use and how to avoid these hazards.

Material Safety Data Sheets (MSDS)

Both federal and state laws require that manufacturers supply a Material Safety Data Sheet (MSDS) for each product sold. The Material Safety Data Sheet (MSDS) contains information compiled by a manufacturer about its product, including names of potentially hazardous ingredients, safe use and handling procedures, precautions to reduce the risk of accidental harm or overexposure, flammability warnings, useful disposal guidelines, and medical and first aid information should it ever be needed for any reason. When necessary, the MSDS can be sent to a doctor, so that the situation can be properly treated. OSHA and state regulatory agencies require that MSDSs be kept available in the salon for all products. Either OSHA or state board inspectors can issue fines for the salon not having these available during regular business hours. There are also training requirements. Employers must train workers on how to read and understand the MSDSs and the OSHA regulations.

Federal and state law requires nail salons to obtain a MSDS from the product manufacturers and/or distributors for each professional product that you use. You can often download them from the product manufacturer's or the distributor's Web site. Not having MSDSs may pose a health risk to anyone in a salon who is exposed to hazardous materials and is a violation of federal and state regulations. Take the time to read all of this information to be certain that you are protecting yourself and your clients to the best of your ability.

Environmental Protection Agency (EPA)

The Environmental Protection Agency (EPA) registers all types of disinfectants sold and used in the United States. The two types that are used in salons are hospital and tuberculocidal. Hospital disinfectants (HOS-pih-tal dis-in-FEK-tents) are effective for cleaning blood and body fluids in hospitals and on nonporous surfaces in the salon, thus controlling the spread of disease (dih-ZEEZ), an abnormal condition of all or part of the body, organ, or mind that makes it incapable of carrying on normal function.

Tuberculocidal disinfectants (tuh-bur-kyoo-LOH-sy-dahl dis-in-FEK-tent) are proven to kill the bacteria that causes tuberculosis (tuh-bur-kyoo-LOH-sus), a disease that is caused by bacteria that is only transmitted through coughing, which is more difficult to kill. These products are also hospital products. This does not mean that you should use a tuberculocide; in fact, these products can be harmful to salon tools and equipment, and they require special methods of disposal. Check the rules in your state to be sure that the product you choose complies with requirements.

It is against federal law to use any disinfecting product contrary to its labeling. Before a manufacturer can sell a product for disinfecting surfaces, tools, implements, or equipment, it must obtain approval from the EPA registration number that qualifies that the disinfectant may be used in the manner prescribed by the manufacturer's label for each particular use. For example, pedicure tub disinfectants must be approved for that use or the manufacturer is breaking federal law. This also means that if you do not follow the instructions for mixing, contact time, and the type of surface the disinfecting product can be used on, you have not complied with federal law and can be held to blame, if there is a lawsuit.

Did **You** Know...

A single nail technician can put many clients at risk unless stringent cleaning and disinfection guidelines are performed every day. A case in point was the spread of a bacterium called Mycobacterium fortuitum furunculosis (MY-koh-bak-TIR-ee-um for-TOO-i-tum fur-UNK-yoo-LOH-sis), a microscopic germ that normally exists in tap water in small numbers. Until an incident occurred, health officials considered it to be completely harmless and not infectious. In 2000, over 100 clients from one California salon had serious skin infections on their legs after getting pedicures. The infection caused stubborn, ugly sores that lingered for months, required the use of strong antibiotics, and, in some cases, caused permanently scarred legs. The source of the infection was traced to the salon's whirlpool foot spas. Salon staff did not clean the foot spas properly, resulting in a build-up of hair and debris in the foot spas that created the perfect breeding ground for bacteria.

The outbreak was a catalyst for change in the industry. As a result, the state of California issued specific requirements for pedicure equipment in the hope of preventing another outbreak in the future. In spite of their efforts at that time, there have been other outbreaks affecting hundreds of clients since then, and not only in California. In Texas, the family of a paraplegic woman sued a salon charging that the woman died because of an improperly disinfected pumice stone that caused an infection on her foot that spread and resulted in a fatal heart attack. As a result of media scrutiny, many clients have become more aware of the cleanliness practices of nail salons and the industry has become more enlightened about the importance of cleaning and disinfection practices, especially for pedicure equipment.

STATE REGULATORY AGENCIES

State regulatory agencies exist to protect professional and consumer health, safety, and welfare while receiving nail and pedicure services in the salon. State regulatory agencies include licensing agencies, state boards of cosmetology, commissions, and health departments. These agencies do this by requiring that everyone working in a nail salon or spa follow specific procedures. Enforcement of the rules through inspections and investigations of consumer complaints is also part of an agency's responsibility. The agency can issue penalties against both the salon owner and the operator's license ranging from warnings to fines, probation, and suspension or revocation of licenses. It is vital that you understand and follow the laws and rules in your state at all times—your salon's reputation, your license, and the client's safety depend on it.

LAWS AND RULES— WHAT IS THE DIFFERENCE?

Laws are written by both the federal and state legislatures that determine the scope of practice (what each license allows the holder to do) and establish guidelines for regulatory agencies to make rules. Laws are also called *statutes*. *Rules* or *regulations* are more specific than laws. Rules are written by the regulatory agency or the state board and determine how the law will be applied. Rules establish specific standards of conduct, and can be changed or updated frequently.

✔ **LO1 Complete**

Principles of Infection

Being a salon professional is fun and rewarding, but it is also a great responsibility. One careless action could cause injury or infection (in-FEK-shun), the invasion of body tissues by disease-causing pathogenic bacteria, and you could lose your license or ruin the salon's reputation. Fortunately, preventing the spread of infections is easy if you know what to do and you practice what you have learned at all times. Safety begins and ends with *you* (**Figure 5-1**).

INFECTION CONTROL

There are four types of potentially harmful organisms that are important to practitioners of nail technology. These are bacteria, fungi, viruses and parasites. An infectious disease is caused by harmful organisms that are easily spread from one person to another person.

Remember, nail professionals are not allowed to diagnose, determine the nature of a disease from its symptoms, treat, or recommend treatments for infections, disease or abnormal conditions. Clients should be referred to their physicians. What you will learn in this chapter will teach you how to properly clean and disinfect tools and equipment so they are safe to use on clients. These steps are designed to prevent infection or disease. Disinfectants used in salons must be bactericidal (back-teer-uh-SYD-ul), capable of destroying bacteria, fungicidal (fun-jih-SYD-ul), capable of destroying fungi, and virucidal (vy-rus-SYD-ul), capable of destroying viruses. Be sure to mix and use these disinfectants according to the instructions on the labels so they are effective.

Contaminated salon tools and equipment may spread infections from client to client if the proper disinfection steps are not taken, after every client. You have a professional and legal obligation to protect consumers from harm by using proper infection control procedures. If clients are infected or harmed because a service or an infection control procedure is not performed correctly, you may be found legally responsible for their injuries or infections.

▲ FIGURE 5-1
A sparkling clean salon gains your clients' confidence.

BACTERIA

Bacteria (bak-TEER-ee-ah)—also known as microbes (MY-krohbs) or germs, the nonscientific synonyms for disease-producing bacteria— are one-celled microorganisms (my-kroh-OR-gah-niz-ums), organisms of microscopic or submicroscopic size, with both plant and animal characteristics. Some are harmful, some are harmless. Bacteria can exist almost anywhere: skin, water, air, decayed matter, body secretions, clothing, or under the free edge of nails. Bacteria are so small they can only be seen with a microscope. In fact, 1500 rod-shaped bacteria will fit comfortably on the head of a pin (Figure 5-2)!

Types of Bacteria

There are thousands of different kinds of bacteria that fall into two primary types: pathogenic and nonpathogenic. Most bacteria are nonpathogenic (non-path-uh-JEN-ik), harmless organisms that may perform useful functions and are safe to come in contact with since they do not cause disease or harm. They can perform many helpful functions. For example, bacteria are used to make yogurt, cheese, and some medicines. In the human body, nonpathogenic bacteria help the body break down food, protect against infection, and stimulate the immune system. Pathogenic (path-uh-JEN-ik) bacteria are considered harmful because they may cause disease or infection in humans when they invade the body. Salons and schools must maintain strict standards for cleaning and disinfecting at all times to prevent the spread of pathogenic microorganisms. It is crucial that nail technicians learn proper infection control practices while in school to ensure that you understand the importance of following them throughout your career. Table 5-1, Causes of Disease, presents terms and definitions related to pathogens.

▲ FIGURE 5-2
Some general forms of bacteria.

TABLE 5-1 Causes of Disease

TERM	DEFINITION
Bacteria (singular: bacterium)	One-celled microorganisms having both plant and animal characteristics. Some are harmful while others are harmless. Also known as microbes or germs.
Direct Transmission	Transmission of blood or body fluids from or to the client through touching (including handshaking), kissing, coughing, sneezing, and talking.
Indirect Transmission	Transmission of blood or bodily fluids through contact with an intermediate contaminated object, such as a razor, extractor, nipper, or an environmental surface.
Infectious	Communicable; can be spread from person to person.
Microbes/germs	Nonscientific synonyms for disease-producing bacteria.
Microorganism	Any organism of microscopic or submicroscopic size.
-ology	Suffix meaning "study of" (e.g., microbiology).
Parasite	An organism that grows, feeds, and shelters on or in another organism while contributing nothing to the survival of that organism (referred to as *host*). Parasites must have a host to survive.
Toxins	Various poisonous substances produced by some microorganisms (bacteria and viruses).
Virus (plural: viruses)	A parasitic submicroscopic particle that infects and resides in cells of biological organisms. A virus is capable of replication only through taking over the host cell's reproduction function.

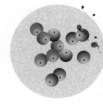

▶ FIGURE 5-3
Cocci.

▶ FIGURE 5-4
Staphylococci.

Classifications of Pathogenic Bacteria

Bacteria have distinct shapes that help to identify them. Pathogenic bacteria are classified as follows:

1 Cocci (KOK-sy) are round-shaped bacteria that appear singly (alone) or in groups (**Figure 5-3**).

- Staphylococci (staf-uh-loh-KOK-sy)—Pus-forming bacteria that grow in clusters like a bunch of grapes. They cause abscesses, pustules, and boils (**Figure 5-4**).

- Streptococci (strep-toh-KOK-eye)—Pus-forming bacteria arranged in curved lines resembling a string of beads. They cause infections such as strep throat and blood poisoning (**Figure 5-5**).
- Diplococci (dip-lo-KOK-sy)—Spherical bacteria that grow in pairs and cause diseases such as pneumonia (**Figure 5-6**).

2 Bacilli (bah-SIL-ee)—Short rod-shaped bacteria. They are the most common bacteria and produce diseases such as tetanus (lockjaw), typhoid fever, tuberculosis, and diphtheria (**Figure 5-7**).

Spirilla (spy-RIL-ah)—Spiral or corkscrew-shaped bacteria. They are subdivided into subgroups, such as *Treponema papillida*, which causes syphilis, a sexually transmitted disease (STD), or *Borrelia burgdorferi*, which causes Lyme disease (**Figure 5-8**).

► **FIGURE 5-5**
Streptococci.

► **FIGURE 5-6**
Diplococci.

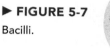
► **FIGURE 5-7**
Bacilli.

► **FIGURE 5-8**
Spirilla.

Movement of Bacteria

Different bacteria move in different ways. Cocci rarely show active motility (moh-TIL-ee-tee), self-movement. They are transmitted in the air, in dust, or within the substance in which they settle. Bacilli and spirilla are both capable of moving and use slender, hairlike extensions, known as flagella (flu-JEL-uh) (singular: flagellum), or cilia (SIL-ee-uh), for locomotion (moving about). A whiplike motion of these hairs moves the bacteria in liquid (**Figure 5-9**).

Bacterial Growth and Reproduction

Bacteria are tiny, microscopic bags generally consisting of an outer cell wall that contains liquid called protoplasm. Cells manufacture their own food from what they can absorb from the surrounding environment. They give off waste products, grow, and reproduce. The life cycle of bacteria consists of two distinct phases: the active stage and the inactive or spore-forming stage.

Active Stage

During the active stage, bacteria grow and reproduce. Bacteria multiply best in warm, dark, damp, or dirty places where food is available. When conditions are favorable, bacteria grow and reproduce. When they reach their largest size, they divide into two new cells. This division is called mitosis (my-TOH-sis). The cells that are formed are called daughter cells and are produced every 20 to 60 minutes, depending on the bacteria. The infectious nail pathogen *Staphylococcus aureus* undergoes mitosis every 27 to 30 minutes. When conditions become unfavorable and difficult for them to thrive, the bacteria either die or become inactive.

Inactive or Spore-forming Stage

Certain bacteria, such as the anthrax and tetanus bacilli, coat themselves with wax outer shells that are able to withstand long periods of famine, dryness, and unsuitable temperatures. In this stage, spores can be blown about and are not harmed by disinfectants, heat, or cold.

When favorable conditions are restored, the spores change into the active form and begin to grow and reproduce. Although spores are dangerous if they enter the body during a surgical procedure and become active, they pose little or no risk to clients in a salon.

► **FIGURE 5-9**
Bacteria with flagellum.

means hunger or starvation [handwritten note]

flagellum

Bacterial Infections

An infection occurs when body tissues are invaded by disease-causing or pathogenic bacteria. There can be no bacterial infection without the presence of pathogenic bacteria. So if they are eliminated, clients cannot become infected. Pus is a fluid created by tissue inflammation (in-fluh-MAY-shun)—a condition in which a part of the body reacts to protect itself from injury, irritation, or infection; characterized by redness, heat, pain, and swelling. It contains white blood cells, bacteria, and dead cells. The presence of pus is a sign of a bacterial infection. A local infection, such as a pimple or abscess, is confined to a particular part of the body and is indicated by a lesion containing pus.

Staphylococci (staph) are among the most common human bacteria, and are normally carried by about a third of the population. Staph can be picked up on doorknobs, countertops, and other surfaces, but are more frequently spread through skin-to-skin contact, such as shaking hands or using unclean files or implements when performing services. If these bacteria get into the wrong place they can be very dangerous. Although rare considering the number of nail services performed, every year there are lawsuits brought against nail salons and nail technicians for allegedly causing staph infections during performance of their services.

Staph is responsible for food poisoning and a wide range of diseases including toxic shock syndrome. Some types of infectious bacteria are highly resistant to certain antibiotics—for example, the staph infection called Methicillin-resistant *Staphylococcus aureus* (MRSA). Historically, MRSA occurred most frequently among persons with weakened immune systems or in people having undergone medical procedures. Today, it has become more common in otherwise healthy people. Clients who appear completely healthy may carry this organism and bring it into the salon to infect the others. They may not even be aware of their infection, while others may show more obvious symptoms. The symptoms usually appear as skin infections, such as pimples and boils that can be difficult to cure and have resulted in death. Because of these highly resistant strains, it is important to clean and disinfect all tools and implements used in the nail salon. You owe it to yourself and your clients!

Also, NEVER perform your services if the client's hands or feet show visible signs of infections. Nail technicians are only allowed to work on healthy nails and skin.

When a disease spreads from one person to another, it is said to be a contagious disease (kon-TAY-jus dih-ZEEZ). Some of the more common contagious diseases that will prevent a salon professional from servicing the client are the common cold, ringworm, conjunctivitis (pinkeye), viral infections, natural nail or toe and foot infections. The chief sources for spreading these infections are dirty hands, especially under the

> ## "
> If these bacteria get into the wrong place they can be very dangerous.

fingernails and on the webs between the fingers. They also may be spread by contaminated implements, cuts, infected nails, open sores, pus, mouth and nose discharges, shared drinking cups, telephone receivers, and towels. Uncovered coughing or sneezing and spitting in public also spread germs. **Table 5-2, Terms Related to Disease**, lists general terms and definitions that are important for an understanding of disease in general.

TABLE 5-2 Terms Related to Disease

TERM	DEFINITION
Allergy	Reaction due to extreme sensitivity to certain foods, chemicals, or other normally harmless substances.
Contagious Disease	Also known as *communicable disease*; disease that is spread by contact from one person to another person.
Contamination	The presence, or the reasonably anticipated presence, of blood or other potentially infectious materials on an item's surface or visible debris or residue such as dust, hair, skin, etc.
Decontamination	The removal of blood or other potentially infectious materials on an item's surface and the removal of visible debris or residues such as dust, hair, and skin.
Diagnosis	Determination of the nature of a disease from its symptoms and/or diagnostic tests.
Disease	Abnormal condition of all or part of the body, organ, or mind that makes it incapable of carrying on normal function.
Exposure Incident	Contact with non-intact (broken) skin, blood, body fluid, or other potentially infectious materials that is the result of the performance of an employee's duties. Previously called blood spill.
Infectious Disease	Disease caused by pathogenic (harmful) microorganisms that enter the body. An infectious disease may or may not be spread from one person to another person.
Inflammation	Condition in which a part of the body reacts to protect itself from injury, irritation, or infection, characterized by redness, heat, pain, and swelling.
Occupational Disease	Illnesses resulting from conditions associated with employment, such as prolonged and repeated overexposure to certain products or ingredients.
Parasitic Disease	Disease caused by parasites, such as lice, mites, and ringworm.
Pathogenic Disease	Disease produced by organisms, including bacteria, viruses, fungi, and parasites.
Systemic Disease	Disease that affects the body as a whole, often due to under- or over-functioning of internal glands or organs. This disease is carried through the blood stream or the lymphatic system.

VIRUSES

A virus (VY-rus) is a parasitic submicroscopic particle that infects the cells of a biological organism. A virus is capable of replication only through taking over the host cell's reproduction machinery. Viruses are so small that they can only be seen under the most sophisticated and powerful microscopes available. They cause common colds and other respiratory and gastrointestinal (digestive tract) infections. Other viruses that plague humans are measles, mumps, chicken pox, smallpox, rabies, yellow fever, hepatitis, polio, influenza, and HIV, which causes AIDS.

Did You Know...

An example of a common viral infection often seen in nail salons is the human papillomavirus (HPV). The virus can infect the bottom of the foot and resembles small black dots, usually in clustered groups. HPV is highly contagious, difficult to kill, and can be passed from pedicure client to pedicure client by dirty implements and foot baths. If the client shows signs of HPV infection, do not perform a pedicure service; instead refer the client to a physician.

One difference between viruses and bacteria is that a virus can live and reproduce only by penetrating other cells and becoming part of them, while bacteria can live and reproduce on their own. Bacterial infections can usually be treated with specific antibiotics while viruses are hard to kill without harming the body in the process. Viruses are not affected by antibiotics. Vaccinations prevent viruses from growing in the body but are not available for all viruses. Vaccines are available for hepatitis B. Health authorities recommend that service providers in industries with direct contact to the public, such as teachers, florists, nail technicians, and bank tellers, should ask their doctor about getting a hepatitis B vaccine.

✓ LO2 Complete

Bloodborne Pathogens

Disease-causing microorganisms that are carried in the body by blood or body fluids, such as hepatitis and HIV, are called bloodborne pathogens. The spread of bloodborne pathogens is possible through shaving, nipping, clipping, facial treatments, waxing, tweezing, or any time the skin is broken. Use great care to avoid cutting or damaging clients' skin during any type of service. Cutting the living skin is considered outside the scope of the nail technician's licensed and approved practices. Federal law allows only qualified medical professionals to cut living skin, since this is considered a medical procedure. This means that nail technicians are not allowed to trim or cut the skin around the nail plate. Cutting hardened tissue and removing a callus are both considered medical procedures. Even if the client insists, nail technicians may not intentionally cut any living skin for any reason.

Hepatitis

A bloodborne virus causes hepatitis (hep-uh-TY-tus), a disease that damages the liver. In general, it is difficult to contract hepatitis, but hepatitis is easier to contract than HIV, because it can be present in all body fluids of those who are infected. Unlike HIV, hepatitis can live on a surface outside the body for long periods of time. It is vital that all surfaces that contact a client are thoroughly cleaned.

There are three types of hepatitis that are of concern within the salon: hepatitis A, hepatitis B, and hepatitis C. Hepatitis B is the most difficult to kill on a surface, so check the label of the disinfectant you use to be sure that the product is effective against it. Hepatitis B and C are spread from person to person through blood and less often through other body fluids, such as semen and vaginal secretions. Those who work closely with the public can be vaccinated against hepatitis B. You may want to check with your doctor to see if this is an option for you.

HIV/AIDS

Human immunodeficiency virus (HIV) (HYOO-mun ih-MYOO-noh-di-FISH-en-see VY-rus) is the virus that causes acquired immunodeficiency syndrome (AIDS) (uh-KWY-erd ih-MYOO-no-di-FISH-en-see sin-drohm). AIDS is a disease that breaks down the body's immune system. HIV is spread from person to person through blood and less often through other body fluids, such as semen and vaginal secretions. A person can be infected with HIV for many years without having symptoms, but testing can determine if a person is infected within six months after exposure to the virus. Sometimes, people who are HIV-positive have never been tested and do not know they are infecting other people.

The HIV virus is spread mainly through the sharing of needles by intravenous (IV) drug users, and less often by unprotected sexual contact or accidents with needles in healthcare settings. The virus is less likely to enter the bloodstream through cuts and sores. It is not spread by holding hands, hugging, kissing, sharing food or using household items such as the telephone or toilet seats. There are no documented cases of the virus being spread by food handlers, insects, casual contact, or hair, skin, nail, and pedicure salon services.

If you accidentally cut a client who is HIV-positive and you continue to use the implement without cleaning and disinfecting it, you risk puncturing your skin or cutting another client with a contaminated tool.

 **LO3 Complete**

FUNGI

Fungi (FUN-jI), microscopic plant parasites, which include molds, mildews, and yeasts, can produce contagious diseases, such as ringworm. Mildew (MIL-doo) affects plants or grows on inanimate objects, but does not cause human infections in the salon. Nail infections can be spread by using dirty implements or by not properly preparing the surface of the natural nail before enhancement products are applied. Nail infections can occur on both hands and feet. Fungal infections are much more common on the feet than hands, but bacterial infections can occur on both. Both bacterial and fungal infections can be spread to other nails, or to other clients, unless everything that touches the client is either properly disposed of (disposable or single-use items) or properly cleaned and disinfected before reuse. The FDA has determined that topical treatments applied directly to the fingernails, skin,

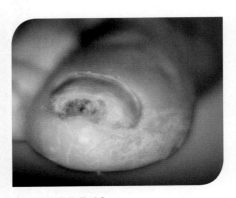

▲ FIGURE 5-10

Nail fungus.

and toenails are not effective in eliminating fungal infections. In short, they don't work. The FDA prohibits sale of antifungal products for fingernails and toenails without a medical prescription **(Figure 5-10)**.

How Pathogens Enter the Body

Pathogenic bacteria, viruses or fungi can enter the body through:

- broken skin, such as a cut or scratch (intact skin is an effective barrier to infection).
- the mouth (contaminated water, food, or fingers).
- the nose (inhaling dusts).
- the eyes or ears (less likely, but possible).
- unprotected sex.

The body prevents and controls infections with:

- healthy, unbroken skin—the body's first line of defense.
- body secretions, such as perspiration and digestive juices.
- white blood cells within the blood that destroy bacteria.
- antitoxins that counteract the toxins (TAHK-sin), any of various poisonous substances produced by some microorganisms (bacteria and viruses).

Parasites

Parasites are organisms that grow, feed, and shelter on or in another organism, while contributing nothing to the survival of that organism (referred to as a host). They must have a host to survive. Parasites can live on or inside of humans and animals. They also can be found in food, on plants and trees, and in water.

Scabies (SKAYbeez) is another contagious skin disease that is caused by the itch mite, which burrows under the skin. Contagious diseases and conditions caused by parasites should only be treated by a doctor. Contaminated countertops, tools, and equipment should be thoroughly cleaned and then disinfected for 10 minutes with an EPA-registered disinfectant or 10% bleach solution.

IMMUNITY

Immunity is the ability of the body to destroy and resist infection. Immunity against disease can be either natural or acquired and is a sign of good health. Natural immunity is partly inherited and partly developed through healthy living. Acquired immunity is immunity that the body develops after overcoming a disease, or through inoculation (such as flu vaccinations), or through exposure to natural allergens, such as pollen, cat dander, and ragweed.

Principles of Prevention

There are two methods of decontamination—Method 1: cleaning and disinfecting and Method 2: cleaning and sterilizing. Because of the low risk of infection compared to medical facilities, salons are only concerned with cleaning and disinfecting.

CLEANING

The first step of decontamination method one is to clean; that is, to remove all visible dirt and debris from tools, implements, and equipment with liquid soap and water. When a surface is properly cleaned, the number of contaminants on the surface is greatly reduced, as is the risk of infection. The vast majority of contaminants and pathogens can be washed from the surfaces of tools and implements through proper cleaning. This is why cleaning is an important part of disinfecting nail tools and equipment. A surface must be properly cleaned before it can be properly disinfected. Using a disinfectant without cleaning first is like using mouthwash without brushing your teeth—it just does not work properly!

Cleaned surfaces can still harbor small amounts of pathogens, but the fewer there are the less likely they can spread infections. Putting antiseptics on your skin or washing your hands is a type of cleaning because this drastically lowers the number of pathogens on your hands, but it will not clean them. The proper cleaning of the hands requires liquid soap, running water, a nail brush, and a clean towel.

Do not underestimate the importance of proper cleaning and hand washing. They are the most powerful and important ways to prevent the spread of infection.

Methods of Cleaning

- Washing with soap and water and scrubbing with a clean and properly disinfected brush.
- Using an ultrasonic unit.
- Using a cleaning solvent (i.e., on metal bits for electric files).

DISINFECTING

The second step of decontamination method one is disinfecting. Disinfection is the process that eliminates most, but not necessarily all, microorganisms on non-living surfaces. This process is not effective against bacterial spores. In the salon setting, disinfection is extremely effective in controlling microorganisms on surfaces such as shears, nippers, and other multi-use tools and equipment.

Disinfectants are chemical products that destroy all bacteria, fungi, and viruses (but not spores) on surfaces. *Disinfectants are not for use on human skin, hair, or nails.* Never use disinfectants as hand cleaners since this can cause skin irritation and allergy, a reaction due to extreme sensitivity to certain foods, chemicals, or other normally harmless substances. *All disinfectants clearly state on the label to avoid skin contact.* This means avoid contact with your skin as well as the client's. Do not put your fingers directly into any disinfecting solution. These are pesticides and can be harmful to the skin if absorbed through the skin. If you mix a disinfectant in a container that is not labeled by the manufacturer, it must be properly labeled with the contents and the date mixed.

STERILIZATION

The second method of decontamination is cleaning and sterilizing. The word sterilize is often used incorrectly. Sterilization is the process that completely destroys all microbial life, including spores, and is necessary only when surgical instruments cut into the vascular layers of the body (this does not mean an accidental cut). The most effective methods of sterilization use high-pressure steam autoclaves. Simply exposing instruments to steam is not enough. To be effective against disease-causing pathogens, the steam must be pressurized in an autoclave. Dry heat forms of sterilization are less efficient and require longer times at higher temperatures and, therefore, are not best for use in the salon.

Most people without medical training do not understand how to properly use an autoclave. For example, dirty implements cannot be properly sterilized without pre-cleaning. Autoclaves need regular maintenance and testing to ensure they are in good working order and performing properly. Color indicator strips on autoclave bags can provide false readings so you should never rely solely on these to ensure proper sterility. These strips are only an indication, not verification that the autoclave is working properly.

The Centers for Disease Control and Prevention (CDC) requires that autoclaves be tested weekly to ensure they are properly sterilizing implements. The accepted method is called a spore test. Sealed packages containing test organisms are subjected to a typical sterilization cycle and then sent to a contract laboratory that specializes in autoclave performance testing. You can find laboratories to perform this type of test by simply doing an Internet search for *autoclave spore testing*. Other regular maintenance is also required to ensure the autoclave reaches the proper temperature and pressure, just as your car requires regular maintenance.

Salons should always follow the manufacturer's recommended schedule for cleaning, changing the water, service visits, replacement parts, etc. Be sure to keep a logbook of all usage, testing, and maintenance for the State Board to inspect. Showing your logbook to clients can provide them with peace of mind and confidence in your ability to protect them from infection.

Did **You** Know...

Nail professionals are not allowed to use needles, lancets, and probes that penetrate the skin, nor are they are allowed to offer any invasive services, such as callus removal.

✓ LO**4** Complete

Read Labels Carefully!

Manufacturers take great care to develop highly effective disinfection systems. However, disinfectants can be dangerous when used improperly. If you do not follow proper guidelines and instructions, any professional salon product can be dangerous. Like all products, disinfectants must always be used exactly as the label instructs.

Choosing a Disinfectant

To use a disinfectant properly, you must read and follow the manufacturer's instructions. Mixing ratios (dilution) and contact time are very important. Not all disinfectants have the same concentration, so be sure to mix the correct amount according to the instructions on the label. If the label does not have the word "concentrated" on it, the product is already mixed and must be used as is. All EPA -registered disinfectants, even those sprayed on large surfaces, require at least 10 minutes of contact on pre-cleaned, hard, non-porous surfaces, unless the manufacturer specifies differently on the label.

Disinfectants must have efficacy claims on the label. Efficacy is the effectiveness with which a disinfecting solution kills specific organisms when used according to the label instructions. Salons pose a very low infection risk when compared to hospitals. In hospitals, cleaning and disinfection standards are much stricter than in salons, and for good reason. Some types of disinfectants are much too dangerous for use in the salon environment, especially since the risk of causing serious infection is low. Even so, there is a risk of spreading certain types of infections to nail clients; therefore, it is important to always clean and disinfect correctly. Fortunately, any EPA-registered liquid hospital disinfectant will be effective enough for salons. Hospital infection control guidelines now include the use of an EPA-registered hospital liquid disinfectant or bleach solution for use in the salon. For this reason, when salon implements accidentally contact blood, body fluids, or unhealthy conditions, they should be cleaned and then completely immersed in an EPA-registered hospital disinfectant solution that shows effectiveness against HIV, hepatitis, or tuberculosis, or a 10 percent bleach solution. Of course, you should wear gloves and follow the proper Universal Precautions protocol for cleaning exposure incidents (described later in this chapter).

Proper Use of Disinfectants

All implements must be thoroughly cleaned of all visible matter or residue before soaking in disinfectant solution because residue can interfere with the disinfectant and prevent proper disinfection. Properly cleaned implements and tools, free from all visible debris, must be completely immersed in disinfectant solution. Complete immersion

Did You Know...

Not all household bleaches are effective as disinfectants. To be effective, the bleach must contain at least 5 percent sodium hypochlorite and must be diluted properly to a 10 percent solution consisting of nine parts water to one part bleach.

CAUTION

Disinfectants must be registered with the EPA. Look for an EPA registration number on the label.

means there is enough liquid in the container to cover all surfaces of the item being disinfected, including the handles, for at least 10 minutes (Figure 5-11).

▲ FIGURE 5-11
Completely immerse tools in disinfectant.

Disinfectant Tips

1 Use only on pre-cleaned, hard, nonporous surfaces—not abrasive files or buffers. May also be used on surfaces such as abrasive files made of metal, glass and ceramic, if indicated in the manufacturers directions for disinfection. Read the manufacturer's directions carefully.

2 Always dilute products according to the instructions on the label.

3 A contact time of 10 minutes is required unless the product label specifies differently.

4 To disinfect large surfaces such as table tops, carefully apply disinfectant onto the pre-cleaned surface and allow it to remain wet for 10 minutes, unless the product label specifies differently.

5 If the product label states, "Complete Immersion," the entire implement must be completely immersed in the solution.

6 Proper disinfection of a whirlpool pedicure spa requires that the disinfecting solution circulate for 10 minutes, unless the product label specifies otherwise.

Types of Disinfectants

Disinfectants are not all the same. Some are appropriate for use in the salon, and some are not. You should be aware of the different types of disinfectants and the ones that are recommended for salon use.

Quats

Quaternary ammonium compounds (quats) (KWAT-ur-nayr-ree uh-MOH-neeum), are disinfectants that are very effective when used properly in the salon. The most advanced type of these formulations are called multiple quats because they contain sophisticated blends of quats that work together to dramatically increase the effectiveness of these disinfectants. Quat solutions disinfect implements usually in 10 minutes. These formulas may contain anti-rust ingredients, but leaving tools in the solution for prolonged periods can cause dulling or damage. They should be removed from the solution after the specified period, rinsed (if required), dried, and stored in a clean, covered container.

> Always dilute products according to the instructions on the label.

[handwritten note: Disinfection is usually a minimum of 10 min. Maximum of 30 min.]

CAUTION

Improperly mixing disinfectants to be weaker or more concentrated than the manufacturer's instructions can dramatically reduce their effectiveness. Always add the disinfectant concentrate to the water when mixing and always follow the manufacturer's instructions for proper dilution. Safety glasses and gloves are recommended to avoid accidental splashes and skin contact.

Phenolics

Phenolic (fi-NOH-lik) disinfectants are powerful tuberculocidal disinfectants. Phenolics have a very high pH, and can cause damage to the skin and eyes. Some can be harmful to the environment if put down the drain. Phenolic disinfectants have been used reliably over the years to disinfect salon tools; however, they do have other drawbacks. Phenol can damage plastic and rubber and can cause certain metals to rust. Phenolic disinfectants should never be used to disinfect pedicure tubs or equipment. Extra care should be taken to avoid skin contact with phenolic disinfectants.

Bleach

Household bleach, 5.25 percent sodium hypochlorite (SOH-dee-um hy-puh-KLOR-ite), is an effective disinfectant for all uses in the salon. Bleach has been used extensively as a disinfectant. Using too much bleach can damage some metals and plastics, so be sure to read the label for safe use. Bleach can be corrosive to metals and plastics, and can cause skin irritation and eye damage. To mix bleach solution, always follow the manufacturer's directions. Disinfectants should be mixed fresh daily, not stored.

Disinfectants Not Appropriate for Salon Use

Fumigants

Years ago, formalin tablets or paraformaldehyde were used as fumigants (a gaseous substance capable of destroying pathogenic bacteria) in dry cabinet sanitizers. This was before EPA-registered disinfectants came on the market and before it was known that paraformaldehyde slowly releases low concentrations of formaldehyde gas , which can potentially cause eye, nose and lung irritation or allergic inhalation sensitivity in nail professionals who constantly breathe this sufficient amounts of these gases. The level of formaldehyde gas produced is not high enough to cause more serious health problems, but, even so, fumigants are no longer used in the salon because the label clearly requires that these be kept in an airtight container for 24 hours, and the gas is potentially dangerous to breathe.

Glutaraldehyde is a dangerous chemical used to sterilize surgical instruments in hospitals. It is not safe for salon use.

✔ LO5 Complete

Disinfectant Safety

Disinfectants are pesticides (poison) and may cause serious skin and eye damage. Some disinfectants appear clear, while others are a little cloudy, especially phenolic disinfectants. Always use caution when handling disinfectants, avoid skin and eye contact, and follow the safety tips below.

Safety Tips for Disinfectants

ALWAYS

- Always keep an MSDS on hand for the disinfectant(s) you use.
- Always wear gloves and safety glasses when mixing disinfectants (Figure 5-12).

CAUTION

Bleach is not a magic potion! All disinfectants, including bleach, are inactivated (made less effective) in the presence of oils, lotions, creams, hair, skin, nail dusts and filings, etc. If bleach is used to disinfect pedicure equipment, it is critical to use a detergent first to clean away residues left by pedicure products.

CAUTION

Fumigant tablets should never be left open in drawers or cabinets in the salon! This is a potentially hazardous practice.

Formaldehyde is known to cause cancer!

▲ **FIGURE 5-12**
Wear gloves and safety goggles while handling disinfectants.

- Always add disinfectant to water (not water to disinfectant) to prevent foaming, which can result in an incorrect mixing ratio. Water should be room temperature or cool water, never hot.
- Always use tongs, gloves, or a draining basket to remove implements from disinfectants.
- Always keep disinfectants out of reach of children.
- Always carefully measure and use disinfectant products according to label instructions.
- Always follow the manufacturer's instructions for mixing, using, and disposing of disinfectants.
- Always change disinfectants every day, or more often if the solution becomes soiled or contaminated.

NEVER

- Pre-mix large amounts of disinfectants, mixing them freshly on a daily basis is best.
- Let pour quats, phenols, formalin or any other disinfectant come into contact with your skin. If you get disinfectants on your skin, immediately wash the area with liquid soap and warm water. Then rinse the area and dry the area thoroughly.
- Place any disinfectant or other product in an unmarked container (Figure 5-13).

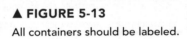

▲ FIGURE 5-13
All containers should be labeled.

Jars or containers used to disinfect implements are often incorrectly called wet sanitizers. The purpose of these containers is to hold a disinfectant solution; not to clean. Disinfectant containers must be covered but not airtight. Remember to clean the container every day and to wear gloves. Always follow the manufacturer's instructions for disinfecting products.

Disinfect or Dispose?

How can you tell which items in the salon can be disinfected and used more than once? There are two types of items used in salons: multi-use, or reusable, and single-use, or disposable items. If the process of cleaning and disinfecting damages the item or changes its condition, it is a single-use item.

Multi-use, or reusable, items can be cleaned, disinfected, and used on more than one person, even if the item is accidentally exposed to blood or body fluid. These items must have a hard, nonporous surface. Examples of multi-use items are nippers, shears, pushers, some nail files, bits, and buffers.

fyi Another word you may see for mulit-use or reusable items, used in marketing and sales copy, is disinfectable, which means these items can be disinfected.

Porous describes an item that is made or constructed of a material that has pores or openings that allow liquids to be absorbed. Some porous items can be safely cleaned, disinfected, and used on more than one client. Examples of these are towels, chamois, and some nail files and buffers.

If a porous item contacts broken skin, blood, body fluid, or any unhealthy condition, it must be discarded immediately. Do not try to disinfect it. If you are not sure whether an item can be safely cleaned, disinfected, and used again, throw it out. Remember: *When in doubt, throw it out!*

 Absorbent nail files must be properly disposed of if the skin is accidentally cut or comes into contact with unhealthy skin or nails.

Single-use, or disposable, items cannot be used more than once, either because they cannot be properly cleaned so that all visible residue is removed—such as pumice stones used for pedicures—or because cleaning and disinfecting damages or contaminates them. Examples of disposable items are wooden sticks, cotton balls, sponges, gauze, tissues, paper towels, and some nail files and buffers. Single-use, or disposable, items must be thrown out after use.

Disinfection Procedures

Tools and Implements. Tools and implements must be cleaned and disinfected after each time they are used and before they may be used on another client. Be certain to dilute and mix disinfectants according to the label on the product that you choose. Mix disinfectants according to manufacturer's directions, always adding disinfectant to the water (**Figure 5-14**).

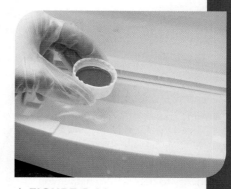
▲ **FIGURE 5-14**
Carefully pour disinfectant into the water when preparing disinfectant solution.

GO TO → **PROCEDURE 5-1 page 83**

Towels and Linens. Clean towels and linens must be used for each client. After a towel or linen has been used on a client, it must not be used again until it has been properly laundered. Store soiled linens and towels separately from clean linens and towels in covered or closed containers. You should store clean towels in covered or closed containers, even if your state regulatory agency does not require it. Whenever possible, use disposable towels, especially in rest rooms.

Work Surfaces. Before beginning a service for each client, all work surfaces must be cleaned and disinfected. It is not necessary to disinfect tables and chairs unless the customers touch them with their skin, but they certainly need to be cleaned regularly (**Figure 5-15**). Clean doorknobs and handles daily to reduce transferring germs to your hands.

▲ **FIGURE 5-15**
Clean manicure tables.

Individual Client Packs for Nail Services

If your state allows, you may save client packs with items such as nail files and buffers. You must, however, follow these steps:

1. Each item must be properly cleaned, disinfected, and dried before being placed in the pack.

2. Do not store single-use items in client packs between services.

3. Never use bags or containers with an airtight seal to store tools and implements. These provide a great environment for the growth of bacteria if the item is not properly cleaned, disinfected, and dried thoroughly before being stored.

4. Setting aside or storing client tools to avoid cleaning and disinfecting them is very risky, not safe, and violates state rules. Remember, state rules require *all* tools and equipment be cleaned and disinfected before each use—even if used on the same person! This also applies to clients who bring their tools with them to the salon. Before you use the client's tools, you must clean and disinfect each item for 10 minutes or as specified by the disinfectant manufacturer's label. For this reason, it is not recommended that clients be allowed to bring their own implements. Home implements could be harboring infectious organisms and contaminate other items in the salon. Remember, *it is your license that is at risk if there is a problem, even if your client brings her tools with her*. This very risky practice should be discouraged.

Disinfecting Foot Spas and Pedicure Equipment

All equipment that contains water for pedicures, including whirlpool spas, pipe-less units, foot baths, basins, tubs, sinks, and bowls must be cleaned and disinfected after every pedicure and the information must be entered into a logbook. Inspectors may issue fines if there is no logbook.

Detergents and Soaps. Chelating soaps or chelating detergents break down stubborn films and are very important for removing the residue of pedicure products such as scrubs, salts, and masks. The chelating agents in these detergents work in all types of water, are low-sudsing, and are specially formulated to work in areas with hard tap water, which reduces the effectiveness of cleaners and disinfectants. Check with your local distributor for pedicure cleaners that are effective in hard water. This will be stated on the label.

Additives, Powders, and Tablets. There is no additive, powder, or tablet that eliminates the need for you to clean and disinfect. You cannot replace proper cleaning and disinfection with a shortcut. These products cannot be used instead of EPA-registered liquid disinfectant solutions. Water sanitizers do not properly clean or disinfect equipment. They are designed for Jacuzzis and hydrotherapy tubs where no oils, lotions, etc. are used, so they don't work well in a salon environment. Never rely solely on water sanitizers to protect your clients.

CAUTION

Electric or bead sterilizers do not disinfect or sterilize implements; in fact, these devices can spread potentially infectious diseases and should never be used in salons. Remember: *State rules require that you use liquid disinfecting solutions!*

CAUTION

Products and equipment that have the word sanitizer on the label are merely cleaners and not disinfectants. Items must be both properly cleaned and disinfected after each and every use and before using them on another client.

CAUTION

Some states require that all procedures for cleaning and disinfecting pedicure equipment be recorded in a salon pedicure logbook. Check with your regulatory agency to determine whether you are required to do so. It is a good practice even if not required and shows clients you're serious about protecting their health.

CAUTION

Most pedicure spas hold five gallons of water; check with the manufacturer so that you use the correct amount of disinfectant.

Remember:
1 gallon = 128 ounces
5 gallons = 640 ounces

So if you are working with a pedicure spa that holds five gallons of water, you will have to measure the correct amount of water needed to cover the jets and then add the correct amount of disinfectant.

Products that contain Chloramine T, for example, are not effective disinfectants for equipment and only treat the water. They have limited value in the salon. These products do not replace proper cleaning and disinfection.

GO TO **PROCEDURE 5-2** page 84

Dispensary. The dispensary must be kept clean and orderly, with the contents of all containers clearly marked. Store products according to manufacturers' instructions, away from heat, and out of direct sunlight. Keep MSDSs for all products used in the salon.

Handling Disposable Supplies. All disposable supplies (single-use), such as wooden sticks, cotton, gauze, nail wipes, porous nail files and paper towels, should be thrown away after one use. Anything exposed to blood must be double-bagged and marked with a biohazard sticker or disposed of according to OSHA standards (separated from other waste and disposed of according to federal, state, and local regulations).

Hand Washing. Washing your hands is one of the most important actions you can use to prevent spreading germs from one person to another. Hand washing removes germs from the folds and grooves of the skin and from under the free edge of the nail plate by lifting and rinsing them from the surface. In the salon, both your hands and your clients' hands should be thoroughly washed with soap and warm water before each service. Never perform a service without asking clients to first wash their hands and be sure to provide them with a clean and disinfected nail brush. Medical studies suggest that antimicrobial and antibacterial soaps are no more effective than regular soaps or detergents. Using a moisturizing hand lotion can help prevent dry skin, which can be caused by repeated hand washing. Avoid using very hot water since this can damage the skin.

For your protection, be sure to wash your hands thoroughly after you have completed the service.

GO TO **PROCEDURE 5-3** page 88

Waterless Hand Sanitizers. Antiseptics (ant-ih-SEP-tiks) are chemical germicides formulated for use on skin that are registered and regulated by the FDA. Antiseptics can contain either alcohol or benzalkonium chloride (less drying to the skin than alcohol). Neither type can clean the hands of dirt and debris; this can only be accomplished with liquid soap, a soft bristle brush, and water. Use hand sanitizers only after properly cleaning your hands, and never use an antiseptic to disinfect instruments or other surfaces, since they are ineffective for that purpose.

CAUTION

Remember this rule for all tools and supplies: *Disinfect or discard.* If you cannot disinfect your tools or supplies, you must discard them.

CAUTION

When washing hands, use liquid soaps in pump containers. Bar soaps can grow bacteria.

It is important that specific procedures are followed if blood or body fluid is present.

Universal Precautions

Universal Precautions are guidelines published by OSHA that require the employer and the employee to assume that all human blood and body fluids are infectious for bloodborne pathogens. Because it is impossible to identify clients with infectious diseases, the same infection control practices should be used with all clients. In most instances, clients who are infected with the hepatitis B virus or other bloodborne pathogens are asymptomatic, which means that they show no symptoms or signs of infection. Bloodborne pathogens are more difficult to kill than germs that live outside the body.

OSHA sets safety standards and precautions that protect employees when they are potentially exposed to bloodborne pathogens. Precautions include washing hands, wearing gloves, and proper handling and disposal of sharp instruments and items that have been contaminated by blood or other body fluids. It is important that specific procedures are followed if blood or body fluid is present.

AN EXPOSURE INCIDENT: CONTACT WITH BLOOD OR BODY FLUID

Accidents happen. An exposure incident (previously called blood spill) is contact with non-intact skin, blood, body fluid, or other potentially infectious materials that results from the performance of an employee's duties. Should this occur, follow these steps for the client's safety, as well as yours:

1. Stop the service.

2. Wear gloves to protect yourself against contact with the client's blood.

3. Clean the injured area with an antiseptic. Every salon must have a first aid kit.

4. Bandage the cut with an adhesive bandage.

5. Clean your workstation, using an EPA-registered disinfectant designed for cleaning blood and body fluids.

6. Discard all contaminated objects. Discard all disposable contaminated objects such as wipes or cotton balls by double-bagging (place the waste in a plastic bag and then in a trash bag). Use a biohazard sticker (red or orange) or a container for contaminated waste. Deposit sharp disposables in a sharps box (**Figure 5-16**).

7. Before removing your gloves, make sure that all tools and implements that have come into contact with blood or other body fluids are thoroughly cleaned and completely immersed in an EPA-registered, tuberculocidal disinfectant solution or 10 percent bleach solution for 10 minutes. Because blood may carry pathogens, you should never touch an open sore or wound.

8. Remove your disposable gloves and seal them in the double bag along with the other contaminated items. Thoroughly wash your

▼ **FIGURE 5-16**

A sharps box.

hands and clean under the free edge of your nails with soap and warm water before returning to the service.

 Recommend that the client see a physician if any signs of redness, swelling, pain, or irritation develop.

 **LO6 Complete**

The Professional Salon Image

Cleanliness should be a part of your normal routine as well as for those who work with you. This way, you and your coworkers can project a steadfast professional image. The following are some simple guidelines that will keep the salon looking its best.

1   Keep floors and workstations dust-free. Mop floors and vacuum carpets every day.

2   Keep trash in a covered waste receptacle to reduce chemical odors and fires.

3   Clean fans, ventilation systems, and humidifiers at least once each week. Keep vents clean and free from dust.

4   Keep all work areas well lit.

5   Keep rest rooms clean, including door handles.

6   Provide toilet tissue, paper towels, liquid soap, properly disinfected soft bristle nail brushes, and a container for used brushes in the restroom.

7   Do not allow the salon to be used for cooking or living quarters.

8   Never place food in the same refrigerators used to store salon products.

9   Prohibit eating, drinking, and smoking in areas where services are performed or where product mixing occurs (i.e., back bar area).

10 Empty waste receptacles regularly throughout the day. A metal waste receptacle with a self-closing lid works best.

11 Make sure all containers are properly marked and properly stored.

12 Never place any tools or implements in your mouth or pockets.

13 Properly clean and disinfect all tools before reuse.

14 Store clean and disinfected tools in a clean, covered container. Clean drawers may be used for storage if only clean items are stored in them. Always isolate used implements away from disinfected implements.

15 Avoid touching your face, mouth, or eye areas during services.

16 Clean and disinfect all work surfaces after every client. This includes manicure tables, workstations, and pedicure foot spas and basins.

17 Have clean, disposable paper towels available for each client.

18 Always properly wash your hands before and after each service.

19 Never provide a nail service to clients who have not properly washed their hands and carefully scrubbed under their nails with a disinfected nail brush.

20 Use effective exhaust systems in the salon. Replacing the air in the salon with fresh air at least four times every hour is recommended. This will help ensure proper air quality in the salon. For more information on proper nail salon ventilation, see *Milady's Nail Structure and Product Chemistry*, second edition, by Douglas Schoon, Cengage Learning.

YOUR PROFESSIONAL RESPONSIBILITY

You have many responsibilities as a salon professional, but none is more important than protecting your clients' health and safety. Never take shortcuts for cleaning and disinfection. You cannot afford to skip steps or save money when it comes to safety.

Remember, *it is your professional and legal responsibility to follow state laws and rules*. Keep your license current and notify the licensing agency if you move or change your name. Check the state Web site weekly for any changes to the rules.

✔ LO7 Complete

Non-electrical tools and implements include items like pushers, nippers, tweezers, nail clippers, and multi-use abrasive nail files.

1. It is important to wear gloves while disinfecting non-electrical tools and implements to prevent possible contamination of the implements by your hands and to protect your hands from the powerful chemicals in the disinfectant solution.

2. Rinse all implements with warm running water, and then thoroughly wash them with soap, a nail brush, and warm water. Brush grooved items, if necessary, and open-hinged implements to scrub the area.

3. Rinse away all traces of soap with warm running water. The presence of soap in most disinfectants can cause them to become inactive. Soap is most easily rinsed off in warm, but not hot, water. Hotter water will not work any better. Dry implements thoroughly with a clean or disposable towel, or allow them to air dry on a clean towel. Your implements are now properly cleaned and ready to be disinfected.

4. It is extremely important that your implements be completely clean before placing them in the disinfectant solution. If they are not, your disinfectant may become contaminated and rendered ineffective. Before immersing cleaned implements open any hinged implements to the open position. Immerse cleansed implements in an appropriate disinfection container holding an EPA-registered disinfectant for the required time (usually 10 minutes). If the disinfection solution is visibly dirty, or if the solution has been contaminated, it must be replaced.

5. After the required disinfection time has passed, remove tools and implements from the disinfection solution with tongs or gloves, rinse them well, and pat them dry.

6. Store disinfected implements in a clean, covered container until needed.

7. Remove gloves and thoroughly wash your hands with liquid soap, then rinse, and dry them with a clean fabric or disposable towel.

 ✓ **LO8 Complete**

DISINFECTION OF WHIRLPOOL FOOT SPAS AND AIR-JET BASINS

After every client:

1. Put on gloves. Drain all water from the basin.

2. Scrub all visible residue from the inside walls of the basin with a brush and liquid soap and water. Use a clean and disinfected brush with a handle. Brushes must be cleaned and disinfected after each use.

3. Rinse the basin with clean water and drain.

4. Refill the basin with clean water to cover the jets and circulate the correct amount (read the product label for mixing instructions) of the EPA-registered hospital disinfectant through the basin for 10 minutes.

5. Drain, rinse, and wipe dry with a clean paper towel.

6. Enter the disinfection information into the salon's logbook, if required by state law or by salon policy.

At the end of every day:

1. Put on gloves. Remove the screen and any other removable parts. (A screwdriver may be necessary.)

2. Clean the screen and other removable parts and the area behind these with a clean, disinfected brush and liquid soap and water to remove all visible residue. Replace properly cleaned screen and other removable parts.

3. Fill the basin with warm water and chelating detergent (cleansers designed for use in hard water) and circulate the chelating detergent through the system for five to ten minutes, following the manufacturer's instructions. If excessive foaming occurs, discontinue circulation and let soak for the remainder of the time, as instructed.

4. Drain the soapy solution and rinse the basin.

5. Refill the basin with clean water and circulate the correct amount (as indicated in mixing instructions on the label) of the EPA-registered hospital disinfectant through the basin for ten minutes.

6. Drain, rinse with clean water, and wipe dry with a clean paper towel.

7. Allow the basin to dry completely.

8. Enter the disinfection information into the salon's logbook, if required by state law or by salon policy.

DISINFECTION OF WHIRLPOOL FOOT SPAS AND AIR-JET BASINS CONT.

At least once each week:

1. Put on gloves. Drain all water from the basin.

2. Remove the screen and any other removable parts. (A screwdriver may be necessary.)

3. Clean the screen and other removable parts and the area behind these with a brush and liquid soap and water to remove all visible residue and replace properly cleaned screen and other removable parts.

4. Scrub all visible residue from the inside walls of the basin with a brush and liquid soap and water. Use a clean and disinfected brush with a handle. Brushes must be cleaned and disinfected after each use.

5. Fill the basin with clean water and circulate the correct amount of the EPA-registered hospital disinfectant (as indicated in mixing instructions on the label) through the basin for 10 minutes or for the time recommended by the manufacturer.

6. Do *not* drain the disinfectant solution. Instead, turn the unit off and leave the disinfecting solution in the unit overnight.

7. In the morning, put on gloves, then drain and rinse the basin with clean water.

8. Refill the basin with clean water and flush the system.

9. Enter the disinfection information into the salon's logbook, if required by state law or by salon policy.

PIPE-LESS FOOT SPAS

For units with footplates, impellers, impeller assemblies, and propellers.

After every client:

1. Put on gloves. Drain all water from the foot basin or tub.

2. Remove impeller, footplate, and any other removable components according to the manufacturer's instructions.

3. Thoroughly scrub impeller, footplate, and/or other components and the areas behind each with a liquid soap and a clean, disinfected brush to remove all visible residue, then reinsert impeller, footplate, and/or other components.

4. Refill the basin with water and circulate the correct amount of the EPA-registered hospital disinfectant (as indicated in mixing instructions on the label) through the basin for 10 minutes or for the time recommended by the manufacturer.

PIPE-LESS FOOT SPAS CONT.

At least once each week:

5. Drain, rinse with clean water, and wipe dry with a clean paper towel.

6. Enter the disinfection information into the salon's logbook, if required by state law or by salon policy.

At the end of every day:

1. Put on gloves. Fill the basin with warm water and chelating detergent and circulate the chelating detergent through the system for five to 10 minutes (follow manufacturer's instructions). If excessive foaming occurs, discontinue circulation and let soak for the remainder of the time, as instructed.

2. Drain the soapy solution and rinse the basin with clean water.

3. Refill the basin with clean water and circulate the correct amount of the EPA-registered hospital disinfectant (as indicated in mixing instructions on the label) through the basin for 10 minutes or for the time recommended by the manufacturer.

4. Drain, rinse with clean water, and wipe dry with a clean paper towel.

5. Enter the disinfection information into the salon's logbook, if required by state law or by salon policy.

At least once each week:

1. Put on gloves. Drain all water from the basin.

2. Remove impeller, footplate, and any other removable components according to the manufacturer's instructions.

3. Thoroughly scrub impeller, footplate, and/or other components, and the areas behind each with a liquid soap and a clean, disinfected brush to remove all visible residue, then reinsert impeller, footplate, and/or other components.

4. Refill the basin with water and circulate the correct amount of the EPA-registered hospital disinfectant (as indicated in mixing instructions on the label) through the basin for 10 minutes or for the time recommended by the manufacturer.

5. Do *not* drain the disinfectant solution. Instead, turn the unit off and leave the disinfecting solution in the unit overnight.

6. In the morning, put on gloves, then drain and rinse the basin with clean water.

7. Refill the basin with clean water and flush the system.

8. Enter the disinfection information into the salon's logbook, if required by state law or by salon policy.

NON-WHIRLPOOL FOOT BASINS OR TUBS

This includes basins, tubs, footbaths, sinks, and bowls—all non-electrical equipment that holds water for a client's feet during a pedicure service.

After every client:

1. Put on gloves. Drain all water from the foot basin or tub.

2. Clean all inside surfaces of the foot basin or tub to remove all visible residue with a clean, disinfected brush and liquid soap and water.

3. Rinse the basin or tub with clean water and drain.

4. Refill the basin with clean water and the correct amount of the EPA registered hospital disinfectant (as indicated in mixing instructions on the label). Leave this disinfecting solution in the basin for 10 minutes or the time recommended by the manufacturer.

Never Less than!

5. Drain, rinse with clean water, and wipe dry with a clean paper towel.

6. Enter the disinfection information into the salon's logbook, if required by state law or by salon policy.

At the end of every day:

1. Put on gloves. Drain all water from the foot basin or tub.

2. Clean all inside surfaces of the foot basin or tub to remove all visible residue with a clean, disinfected brush and liquid soap and water.

3. Fill the basin or tub with water and the correct amount of the EPA-registered hospital disinfectant (as indicated in mixing instructions on the label). Leave this disinfecting solution in the basin for 10 minutes or for the time recommended by the manufacturer.

4. Drain, rinse with clean water, and wipe dry with a clean paper towel.

5. Enter the disinfection information into the salon's logbook, if required by state law or by salon policy.

Proper Hand Washing

Hand washing is one of the most important procedures in your infection control efforts and is required in every state before beginning any service.

1. Turn the water on, wet your hands, then pump soap from a pump container onto the palm of your hand. Rub your hands together, all over and vigorously, until a lather forms. Continue in this manner for a minimum of 20 seconds.

2. Choose a clean nail brush, wet it and pump soap on it, and brush your nails horizontally back and forth under the free edges. Change the direction of the brush to vertical and move the brush up and down along the nail folds of the fingernails. The process for brushing both hands should take about 60 seconds to finish. Rinse hands in running water.

3. Use a clean cloth or paper towel, according to the salon policies, for drying your hands.

4. After drying, turn off the water with the towel and then dispose of the towel.

review questions

1. What is the primary purpose of regulatory agencies?

2. What are MSDSs? Where can you get them?

3. List the four types of organisms that are pertinent to nail technology.

4. What is a contagious disease?

5. Is HIV a risk in the salon? Why or why not?

6. What is the difference between cleaning, disinfecting, and sterilizing?

7. What is complete immersion?

8. List at least six precautions to follow when using disinfectants.

9. How do you know if an item can be disinfected?

10. Can porous items be disinfected?

11. What are Universal Precautions?

12. What is an exposure incident?

13. Describe the procedure for handling an exposure incident in the salon.

14. List the steps for cleaning and disinfecting whirlpool foot spas and air-jet basins after each client.

6 general anatomy and physiology

chapter outline

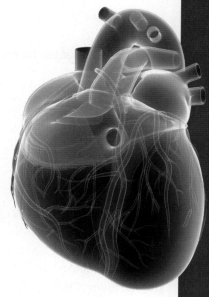

☑ Learning Objectives

After you have completed this chapter, you will be able to:

1 Define and explain the importance of anatomy, physiology, and histology to the nail profession.

2 Describe cells, their structure, and their reproduction.

3 Define tissue and identify the types of tissues found in the body.

4 Name the 11 main body systems and explain their basic functions.

Key Terms

Page number indicates where in the chapter the term is used.

abductors / 101
abductor hallucis / 102
adductors / 101
adipose tissue / 95
adrenal glands / 110
anabolism / 94
anatomy / 93
anterior tibial artery / 104
aorta / 106
arteries / 106
atrium / 105
autonomic nervous system (ANS) / 102
axon (axon terminal) / 103
belly (muscle) / 99
bicep / 100
blood / 107
blood vascular system / 105
body systems / 95
brain / 102
capillaries / 106
cardiac muscle / 99
carpus / 98
catabolism / 94
cell membrane / 93
cells / 93
central nervous system (CNS) / 102
circulatory system (cardiovascular system or vascular system) / 105
common peroneal nerve / 104
connective tissue / 95
cytoplasm / 93

deep peroneal nerve (anterior tibial nerve) / 104
deltoid / 100
dendrites / 103
diaphragm / 111
digestive enzymes / 110
digestive system / 110
digital nerve / 103
dorsal nerve (dorsal cutaneous nerve) / 104
dorsalis pedis artery / 108
endocrine glands (ductless glands) / 109
endocrine system / 109
epithelial tissue / 95
excretory system / 110
exhalation / 111
exocrine glands (duct glands) / 109
extensors / 100
extensor digitorum brevis / 102
extensor digitorum longus / 101
eyes / 96
femur / 98
fibula / 98
flexors / 100
flexor digitorum brevis / 102
gastrocnemius / 101
glands / 109
heart / 105
hemoglobin / 107
histology (microscopic anatomy) / 93

hormone / 109
humerus / 97
inhalation / 111
insertion / 99
integumentary system / 111
interstitial fluids / 108
intestines / 96
joint / 97
kidneys / 96
latissimus dorsi / 100
leukocytes / 107
liver / 96
lungs / 111
lymph / 105
lymphatic/immune system / 108
lymph capillaries / 108
lymph nodes / 105
lymph vascular system (lymphatic system) / 105
median nerve / 104
metabolism / 94
metacarpus / 98
metatarsal / 98
mitral valve (bicuspid valve) / 106
motor nerves (efferent nerves) / 103
muscular system / 98
muscle tissue / 95
myology / 99
nerves / 103
nerve tissue / 95
nervous system / 102

Whether applying a new set of tips, performing a manicure, or giving a foot massage, licensed nail technicians are permitted to touch people as part of their profession. This is true of very few other occupations, and it is an honor to be able to aid others in achieving a greater sense of well-being.

Why Study Anatomy?

As a nail professional, an overview of human anatomy and physiology will enable you to:

- Understand how the human body functions as an integrated whole.
- Recognize changes from the norm.
- Determine a scientific basis for the proper application of services and products.
- Give safe and effective manicure and pedicure services aided by your knowledge of hand/foot nerves, bones, and muscle structure.
- Create personalized nail services that will enhance the shape of your clients' hands or feet.
- Perform manipulations involving the hands, forearms, feet, and lower legs safely and effectively as a result of your understanding of bones, muscles, nerves, and circulation.

Cells are the basic units of all living things... Without cells, life does not exist.

Anatomy is the study of the human body structures that can be seen with the naked eye, and what they are made up of. It is the science of the structure of organisms or of their parts.

Review Q #1

Physiology (fiz-ih-OL-oh-jee) is the study of the functions and activities performed by the body's structures.

Histology (his-TAHL-uh-jee) is the study of tiny structures found in tissue. It is also called microscopic anatomy.

✓ **LO1 Complete**

Cells

Cells are the basic units of all living things, from bacteria to plants and animals, including human beings. Without cells, life does not exist. As a basic functional unit, the cell is responsible for carrying on all life processes. There are trillions of cells in the human body, and they vary widely in size, shape, and purpose.

#1)

Review Q #3.

BASIC STRUCTURE OF THE CELL

The cells of all living things are composed of a substance called protoplasm (PROH-toh-plaz-um), a colorless jelly-like substance found inside cells in which food elements such as proteins, fats, carbohydrates, mineral salts, and water are present. You can visualize the protoplasm of a cell as being similar to the white of a raw egg. In addition to protoplasm, most cells also include the following (**Figure 6-1**):

- The nucleus (NOO-klee-us) is the dense, active protoplasm found in the center of the cell. It plays an important part in cell reproduction and metabolism. You can visualize the nucleus as the yolk of a raw egg.

- The cytoplasm (sy-toh-PLAZ-um) is the protoplasm of a cell, except for the protoplasm that is in the nucleus, that surrounds the nucleus. It is the watery fluid that cells need for growth, reproduction, and self-repair. *#2)*

- The cell membrane (SELL MEM-brayn) is the cell part that encloses the protoplasm and permits soluble substances to enter and leave the cell.

CELL REPRODUCTION AND DIVISION

Cells have the ability to reproduce, thus providing new cells for the growth and replacement of worn or injured ones. The usual process of cell reproduction of human tissues occurs when the cell divides into two identical cells called daughter cells by the process known as mitosis. As long as conditions are favorable, the cell will grow and reproduce. This is true of human cells, plant cells, and single-cell creatures such as bacteria. Favorable conditions include an adequate supply of food, oxygen, and

▼ **FIGURE 6-1**
Anatomy of the cell.

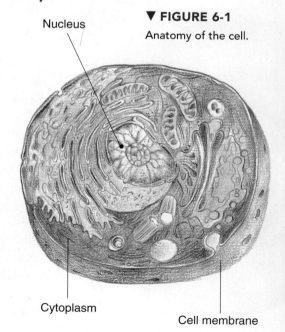

Nucleus

Cytoplasm

Cell membrane

water; suitable temperatures; and the ability to eliminate waste products. If conditions become unfavorable, the cell will become impaired or may die. Unfavorable conditions include toxins (poison), disease and injury. (Figure 6-2).

▶ **FIGURE 6-2**

Phases of mitosis.

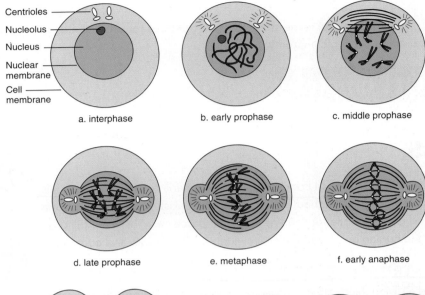

Centrioles
Nucleolus
Nucleus
Nuclear membrane
Cell membrane

a. interphase

b. early prophase

c. middle prophase

d. late prophase

e. metaphase

f. early anaphase

g. late anaphase

h. telophase

i. interphase

✓ LO2 Complete

CELL METABOLISM

Metabolism (muh-TAB-uh-liz-um) is a chemical process that takes place in living organisms, through which the cells are nourished and carry out their activities. Metabolism has two phases.

Anabolism (uh-NAB-uh-liz-um) is constructive metabolism, the process of building up larger molecules from smaller ones. During this process, the body stores water, food, and oxygen for the time when these substances will be needed for cell growth, reproduction, or repair.

Catabolism (kuh-TAB-uh-liz-um) is the phase of metabolism that involves the breaking down of complex compounds within the cells into smaller ones. This process releases energy that has been stored.

Anabolism and catabolism are carried out simultaneously and continually within the cells as part of their normal processes.

Tissues

A tissue (TISH-oo) is a collection of similar cells that perform a particular function. Each tissue has a specific function and can be recognized by its characteristic appearance. Body tissues are composed of large amounts of water, along with various other substances. There are four types of tissue in the body.

- **Connective tissue** is fibrous tissue that binds together, protects, and supports the various parts of the body. Examples of connective tissue are bone, cartilage, ligaments, tendons, and fat or adipose tissue (ADD-ih-pohz TISH-oo) tissue that gives smoothness and contour to the body.

- **Epithelial tissue** (ep-ih-THEE-lee-ul TISH-oo) is a protective covering on body surfaces. Skin, mucous membranes, the tissue inside the mouth, the lining of the heart, digestive and respiratory organs, and glands are all examples of epithelial tissue.

- **Muscle tissue** contracts and moves various parts of the body.

- **Nerve tissue** carries messages to and from the brain and controls and coordinates all bodily functions. Nerve tissue is composed of special cells known as neurons, which make up the nerves, brain, and spinal cord.

[Handwritten annotations: "Liquid tissue is Blood and Lymph", "# 40", "Review Q #3"]

✓ LO3 Complete

Organs and Body Systems

Organs are structures composed of specialized tissues designed to perform specific functions. A system is comprised of a group of body organs acting together to perform one or more functions. **Table 6-1, Some Major Body Organs and Their Functions**, lists some of the most important organs of the body.

Body systems are groups of body organs acting together to perform one or more functions. The human body is composed of 11 major systems as shown in Table 6-2, Eleven Main Body Systems and Their Functions on page 97.

[Handwritten annotations: "Review Q #6", "#5"]

✓ LO4 Complete

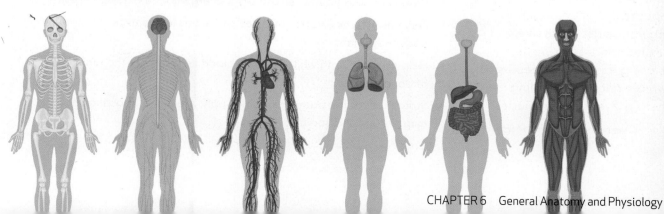

TABLE 6-1 Some Major Body Organs and Their Functions

ORGAN	FUNCTION
Brain	Controls the body
Eyes	Control vision
Heart	Circulates the blood
Kidneys	Excrete water and waste products
Liver	Removes waste created by digestion
Lungs	Supply oxygen to the blood
Skin	External protective coating that covers the body
Stomach and intestines	Digest food

The Skeletal System

Did **You** Know...

People often complain of joint pain, which is usually caused by inflammation of the tissue surrounding the joint.

The skeletal system is the physical foundation of the body. It is composed of 206 bones that vary in size and shape and are connected by movable and immovable joints. Osteology (ahs-tee-AHL-oh-jee) is the study of anatomy, structure, and function of the bones. Os (AHS) means bone, and is used as a prefix in many medical terms, such as osteoarthritis, a joint disease.

Except for the tissue that forms the major part of the teeth, bone is the hardest tissue in the body. It is composed of connective tissue consisting of about one-third organic matter, such as cells and blood, and two-thirds minerals, mainly calcium carbonate and calcium phosphate.

Did **You** Know...

Painful inflammation involving the carpus area can be caused by repetitive motions, such as flexing your wrist excessively or locking it in a bent position while using a nail file. Keeping the wrist straight while filing can help prevent these injuries.

The primary functions of the skeletal system are to:

- Give shape and support to the body.
- Protect various internal structures and organs.
- Serve as attachments for muscles and act as levers to produce body movement.
- Help produce both white and red blood cells (one of the functions of bone marrow).
- Store most of the body's calcium supply, as well as phosphorus, magnesium, and sodium.

Review

11 body Systems #8

SYSTEM	FUNCTION
Circulatory	Controls the steady circulation of the blood through the body by means of the heart and blood vessels
Digestive	Changes food into nutrients and wastes; consists of mouth, stomach, intestines, salivary and gastric glands, and other organs
Endocrine	Affects the growth, development, sexual activities, and health of the entire body; consists of specialized glands
Excretory	Purifies the body by the elimination of waste matter; consists of kidneys, liver, skin, large intestine, and lungs
Integumentary	Serves as a protective covering and helps in regulating the body's temperature; consists of skin, and its accessory organs, such as oil and sweat glands, sensory receptors, hair, and nails
Lymphatic or Immune	Protects the body from disease by developing immunities and destroying disease-causing toxins and bacteria
Muscular	Covers, shapes, and supports the skeleton tissue; muscles contract and move various parts of the body
Nervous	Controls and coordinates all other systems inside and outside of the body and makes them work harmoniously and efficiently; consists of brain, spinal cord, and nerves
Reproductive	Responsible for processes by which plants and animals produce offspring
Respiratory	Enables breathing, supplying the body with oxygen, and eliminating carbon dioxide as a waste product; consists of lungs and air passages
Skeletal	Physical foundation of the body; consists of 206 bones that vary in size and shape and are connected by movable and immovable joints

A joint is the connection between two or more bones of the skeleton. There are two types of joints: movable, such as elbows, knees, and hips; and immovable, such as the pelvis or skull, which allows little or no movement.

BONES OF THE ARMS AND HANDS

The important bones of the arms and hands that you should know include the following:

- Humerus (HYOO-muh-rus). Uppermost and largest bone of the arm, extending from the elbow to the shoulder.
- Ulna (UL-nuh). Inner and larger bone of the forearm (lower arm), attached to the wrist and located on the side of the little finger.
- Radius (RAY-dee-us). Smaller bone in the forearm (lower arm) on the same side as the thumb.

> Did **You** Know...
>
> The fingernails' purpose is to provide protection for the delicate tips of the phalanges in the hand. If a phalange is accidentally broken, the finger loses much of its fine dexterity and has a more difficult time picking up very small objects such as sewing needles and coins.

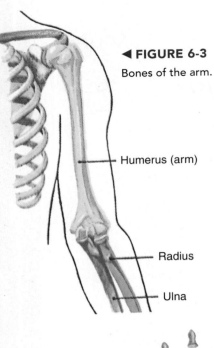

◄ FIGURE 6-3
Bones of the arm.

Humerus (arm)

Radius

Ulna

► FIGURE 6-4
Bones of the hand.

Metacarpus or palm (5 bones)

Phalanges (14 bones)

Carpus or wrist

Ulna

Radius

◄ FIGURE 6-5
Bones of the leg.

Femur

Patella

Tibia

Fibula

- Carpus (KAR-pus). The wrist; flexible joint composed of a group of eight small, irregular bones held together by ligaments.
- Metacarpus (met-uh-KAR-pus). Bones of the palm of the hand; parts of the hand containing five bones between the carpus and phalanges.
- Phalanges (fuh-LAN-jeez). Bones of the fingers or toes, or digits (**Figures 6-3 and 6-4**).

BONES OF THE LEG, ANKLE, AND FOOT

The four bones of the leg are:

- The femur (FEE-mur) is a heavy, long bone that forms the leg above the knee.
- The tibia (TIB-ee-ah) is the larger of the two bones that form the leg below the knee. The tibia may be visualized as a bump on the big-toe side of the ankle.
- The fibula (FIB-ya-lah) is the smaller of the two bones that form the leg below the knee. The fibula may be visualized as a bump on the little-toe side of the ankle.
- The patella (pah-TEL-lah), also called the accessory bone, forms the cap of the knee joint (**Figure 6-5**).
- The ankle joint is made up of three bones:
  - The tibia, which comes down from the leg.
  - The fibula, which comes down from the leg.
  - The talus (TA-lus), or ankle bone, of the foot.

The foot is made up of 26 bones. These can be subdivided into three general categories: seven tarsal (TAHR-sul) bones (talus, calcaneous, navicular, three cuneiform bones, and the cuboid), and five metatarsal (met-ah-TAHR-sul) bones, which are long and slender, like the metacarpal bones of the hand, and 14 bones called phalanges, which compose the toes. The phalanges are similar to the finger bones. There are three phalanges in each toe, except for the big toe, which has only two (**Figure 6-6**).

The Muscular System

The muscular system is the body system that covers, shapes, and supports the skeletal tissue. It contracts and moves various parts of the body.

The nail technician must be concerned with the voluntary muscles that control movements of the arms, hands, lower legs, and feet. It is important to know where these muscles are located and what they control. These muscles become fatigued from excessive work or injury and can benefit greatly from the massaging techniques you can incorporate into your services.

Myology (my-AHL-uh-jee) is the study of the structure, function, and diseases of the muscles. The human body has over 600 muscles, which are responsible for approximately 40 percent of the body's weight. Muscles are fibrous tissues that have the ability to stretch and contract according to demands of the body's movements. There are three types of muscular tissue.

[handwritten notes: # 11, 3 types, Reviewed, # 10]

Striated muscles (STRY-ayt-ed), also called skeletal muscles, are attached to the bones and are voluntary or consciously controlled. Striated (skeletal) muscles assist in maintaining the body's posture and protect some internal organs (Figure 6-7).

Nonstriated muscles, or smooth muscles, are involuntary and function automatically, without conscious will. These muscles are found in the internal organs of the body, such as the digestive or respiratory systems (Figure 6-8).

Cardiac muscle is the involuntary muscle that is the heart. This type of muscle is not found in any other part of the body (Figure 6-9).

[handwritten note: # 45]

A muscle has three parts. The origin is the part that does not move; it is attached to the skeleton and is usually part of a skeletal muscle. The insertion is the part of the muscle at the more movable attachment to the skeleton. The belly is the middle part of the muscle. Pressure in massage is usually directed from the insertion to the origin.

[handwritten notes: # 46, # 12]

Muscular tissue can be stimulated by:
- Massage (hand, electric vibrator, or water jets)
- Electrical current (high frequency or faradic—alternating or interrupted—current).
- Infrared light
- Dry heat (heating lamps or heating caps)
- Moist heat (steamers or moderately warm steam towels)
- Nerve impulses (through the nervous system)

[handwritten note: # 47]

▼ FIGURE 6-6

Bones of the foot and ankle.

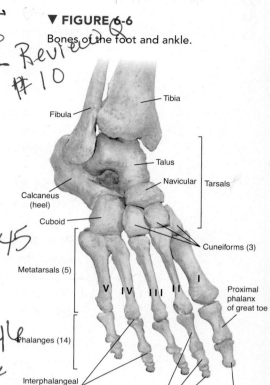

Fibula
Tibia
Talus
Navicular
Calcaneus (heel)
Cuboid
Cuneiforms (3)
Tarsals
Metatarsals (5)
V IV III II I
Proximal phalanx of great toe
Phalanges (14)
Interphalangeal joints
Proximal phalanx
Middle phalanx
Distal phalanx
Distal phalanx of great toe

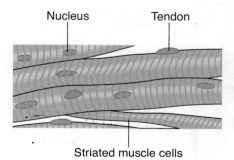

Nucleus
Tendon
Striated muscle cells

▲ FIGURE 6-7

Striated muscle cells.

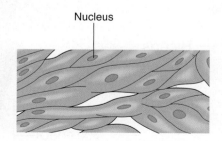

Nucleus

▲ FIGURE 6-8

Nonstriated muscle cells.

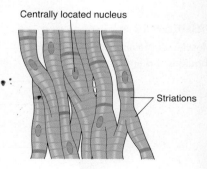

Centrally located nucleus
Striations

▲ FIGURE 6-9

Cardiac muscle cells.

MUSCLES THAT ATTACH THE ARMS TO THE BODY

The muscles that attach the arms to the body are briefly summarized below.

- Latissimus dorsi (lah-TIS-ih-mus DOR-see). A large, flat triangular muscle covering the lower back.
- Pectoralis major (pek-tor-AL-is MAY-jor) and pectoralis minor. Muscles of the chest that assist the swinging movements of the arm.
- Serratus anterior (ser-RAT-us an-TEER-ee-or). Muscle of the chest that assists in breathing and in raising the arm.
- Trapezius (trah-PEE-zee-us). Muscle that covers the back of the neck and upper and middle region of the back; rotates and controls swinging movements of the arm.

MUSCLES OF THE SHOULDER AND ARM

There are three principal muscles of the shoulders and upper arms (**Figure 6-10**):

Bicep (BY-sep). Muscle producing the contour of the front and inner side of the upper arm; they lift the forearm and flex the elbow.

Deltoid (DEL-toyd). Large, triangular muscle covering the shoulder joint that allows the arm to extend outward and to the side of the body.

Tricep (TRY-sep). Large muscle that covers the entire back of the upper arm and extends the forearm.

The forearm is made up of a series of muscles and strong tendons (**Figure 6-11**). As a nail technician, you will be concerned with:

- Extensors (ik-STEN-surs). Muscles that straighten the wrist, hand, and fingers to form a straight line.
- Flexors (FLEK-surs). Extensor muscles of the wrist, involved in bending the wrist.
- Pronators (proh-NAY-tohrs). Muscles that turn the hand inward so that the palm faces downward.

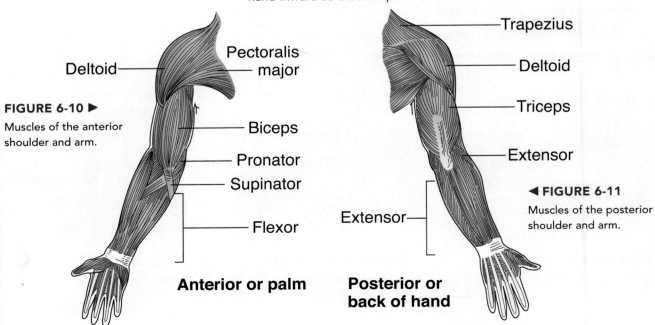

Deltoid

Pectoralis major

FIGURE 6-10 ▶
Muscles of the anterior shoulder and arm.

Biceps

Pronator

Supinator

Flexor

Anterior or palm

Trapezius

Deltoid

Triceps

Extensor

◀ FIGURE 6-11
Muscles of the posterior shoulder and arm.

Extensor

Posterior or back of hand

- Supinator (SOO-puh-nayt-ur). Muscle of the forearm that rotates the radius outward and the palm upward.

MUSCLES OF THE HAND

The hand is one of the most complex parts of the body, with many small muscles that overlap from joint to joint, providing flexibility and strength to open and close the hand and fingers. Important muscles to know include the:

- Abductors (ab-DUK-turz). Muscles that separate the fingers (**Figure 6-12**).
- Adductors (ah-DUK-turz). Muscles at the base of each finger that draw the fingers together (**Figure 6-12**).

MUSCLES OF THE LOWER LEG AND FOOT

As a nail technician, you will use your knowledge of the muscles of the foot and leg during a pedicure. The muscles of the foot are small and provide proper support and cushioning for the foot and leg. (**Figure 6-13**). The muscles of the lower leg include:

- The extensor digitorum longus (eck-STEN-sur dij-it-TOHR-um LONG-us) bends the foot up and extends the toes.
- The tibialis anterior (tib-ee-AHL-is an-TEHR-ee-ohr) covers the front of the shin. It bends the foot upward and inward.
- The peroneus longus (per-oh-NEE-us LONG-us) covers the outer side of the calf and inverts the foot and turns it outward.
- The peroneus brevis (BREV-us) originates on the lower surface of the fibula. It bends the foot down and out.
- The gastrocnemius (gas-truc-NEEM-e-us) is attached to the lower rear surface of the heel and pulls the foot down.
- The soleus (SO-lee-us) originates at the upper portion of the fibula and bends the foot down.

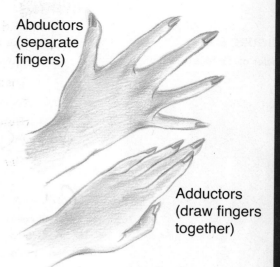

Abductors (separate fingers)

Adductors (draw fingers together)

▲ **FIGURE 6-12**

Muscles of the hand.

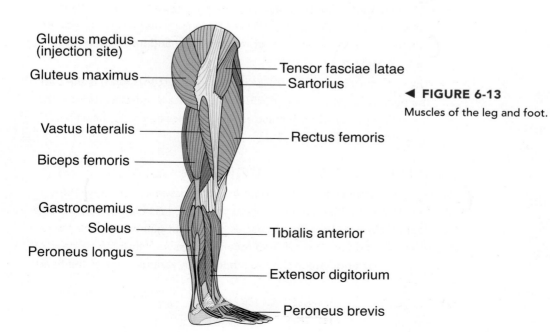

Gluteus medius (injection site)

Gluteus maximus

Tensor fasciae latae

Sartorius

Vastus lateralis

Biceps femoris

Rectus femoris

Gastrocnemius

Soleus

Peroneus longus

Tibialis anterior

Extensor digitorium

Peroneus brevis

◀ **FIGURE 6-13**

Muscles of the leg and foot.

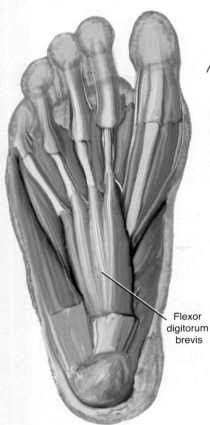

Flexor
digitorum
brevis

The muscles of the feet include:

- The extensor digitorum brevis (ek- STEN-sur dij-it-TOHR-um BREV-uş) moves the toes and helps maintain balance while walking.
- The abductor hallucis (ab-DUK-tohr ha-LU-sis) moves the toes and helps maintain balance while walking and standing.
- The flexor digitorum brevis (FLEKS-or dij-it-TOHR-um BREVus) moves the toes and helps maintain balance while walking.
- The abductor separates the toes (Figure 6-14).

The nervous system is an exceptionally well-organized body system, composed of the brain, spinal cord, and nerves, th at is responsible for controlling and coordinating all other systems inside and outside of the body and makes them work harmoniously and efficiently. Every square inch of the human body is supplied with fine fibers known as nerves; there are over 100 billion nerve cells, known as neurons, in the body. The scientific study of the structure, function, and pathology of the nervous system is known as neurology (nuh-RAHL-uh-jee).

An understanding of how nerves work will help you perform services in a more proficient manner when administering massage techniques during manicures and pedicures. It will also help you understand the effects that these treatments have on the body as a whole.

DIVISIONS OF THE NERVOUS SYSTEM

The nervous system, as a whole, is divided into three main subdivisions.

- The central nervous system (CNS) consists of the brain, spinal cord, spinal nerves, and cranial nerves. It controls consciousness and many mental activities, voluntary functions of the five senses (seeing, hearing, feeling, smelling, and tasting), and voluntary muscle actions, including all body movements and facial expressions.
- The peripheral (puh-RIF-uh-rul) nervous system (PNS) is a system of nerves that connects the peripheral (outer) parts of the body to the central nervous system; it has both sensory and motor nerves. Its function is to carry impulses, or messages, to and from the central nervous system.
- The autonomic (aw-toh-NAHM-ik) nervous system (ANS) is the part of the nervous system that controls the involuntary muscles; it regulates the action of the smooth muscles, glands, blood vessels, heart and even breathing (Figure 6-15).

THE BRAIN AND SPINAL CORD

The brain is the largest and most complex nerve tissue in the body. The brain is contained in the cranium and weighs a little less than three pounds, on average. It controls sensation, muscles, activity of glands, and the power to think, sense, and feel. It sends and receives messages through 12 pairs of cranial nerves that originate in the brain and reach various parts of the head, face, and neck.

The spinal cord is the portion of the central nervous system that originates in the brain, extends down to the lower extremity of the trunk, and is protected by the spinal column. Thirty-one pairs of spinal nerves extending from the spinal cord are distributed to the muscles and skin of the trunk and limbs.

NERVE CELL STRUCTURE AND FUNCTION

A neuron (NOO-rahn), or nerve cell, is the primary structural unit of the nervous system. It is composed of the cell body, nucleus, dendrites, and the axon. Dendrites (DEN-dryts) are tree-like branchings of nerve fibers extending from the nerve cell that carry impulses toward the cell and receive impulses from other neurons. The axon (AK-sahn) and axon terminal send impulses away from the cell body to other neurons, glands, or muscles (Figure 6-16). Nerves are whitish cords made up of bundles of nerve fibers held together by connective tissue through which impulses are transmitted. Nerves have their origin in the brain and spinal cord and send their branches to all parts of the body.

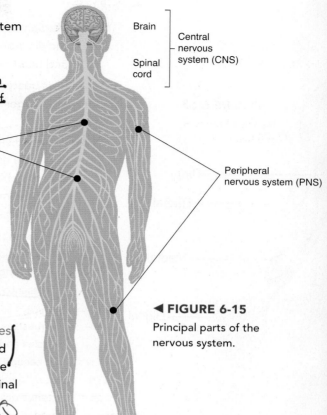

◀ **FIGURE 6-15**

Principal parts of the nervous system.

TYPES OF NERVES

Sensory nerves or afferent nerves (AAF-eer-ent NURVS) carry impulses or messages from the sense organs to the brain, where sensations of touch, cold, heat, sight, hearing, taste, smell, pain, and pressure are experienced. Sensory nerve endings called receptors are located close to the surface of the skin. As impulses pass from the sensory nerves to the brain and back through the motor nerves to the muscles, a complete circuit is established, resulting in movement of the muscles.

Motor nerves, or efferent nerves (EF-uh-rent NURVS), carry impulses from the brain to the muscles or glands. The transmitted impulses produce movement.

A reflex (REE-fleks) is an automatic reaction to a stimulus that involves the movement of an impulse from a sensory receptor along the sensory nerve to the spinal cord. A responsive impulse is sent along a motor neuron to a muscle, causing a reaction (for example, the quick removal of the hand from a hot object). Reflexes do not have to be learned; they are automatic.

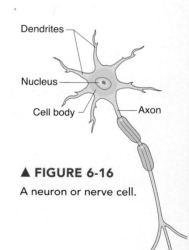

▲ **FIGURE 6-16**

A neuron or nerve cell.

NERVES OF THE ARM AND HAND

The principal nerves supplying the superficial parts of the arm and hand are as follows:

- Digital nerve (DIJ-ut-tul) (sensory-motor), with its branches, supplies the fingers.
- Radial nerve (RAY-dee-ul) (sensory-motor), with its branches, supplies the thumb side of the arm and back of the hand.

" The brain is the largest and most complex nerve tissue in the body.

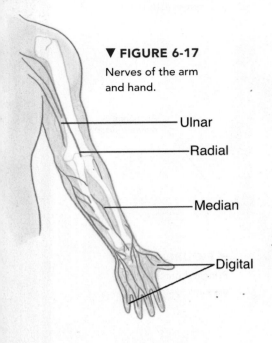

▼ FIGURE 6-17

Nerves of the arm
and hand.

— Ulnar

— Radial

— Median

— Digital

- Median nerve (MEE-dee-un) (sensory-motor), smaller nerve than the ulnar and radial nerves that, withits branches, supplies the arm and hand.
- Ulnar nerve (UL-nur) (sensory-motor), with its branches, affects the little finger side of the arm and palm of the hand (**Figure 6-17**).

NERVES OF THE LOWER LEG AND FOOT

- The tibial nerve (TIB-ee-al NURV), a division of the sciatic nerve, passes behind the knee. It subdivides and supplies impulses to the knee, the muscles of the calf, the skin of the leg, and the sole, heel, and underside of the toes.
- The common peroneal nerve (KAHM-un per-oh-NEE-al NURV), also a division of the sciatic nerve, extends from behind the knee to wind around the head of the fibula to the front of the leg where it divides into two branches. The deep peroneal nerve, also known as the anterior tibial nerve, extends down the front of the leg, behind the muscles. It supplies impulses to these muscles and also to the muscles and skin on the top of the foot and adjacent sides of the first and second toes. The superficial peroneal nerve, also known as the musculo-cutaneous nerve (MUS-kyoo-lo-kyoo-TAY-nee-us NURV), extends down the leg, just under the skin, supplying impulses to the muscles and the skin of the leg, as well as to the skin and toes on the top of the foot, where it is called the dorsal nerve (DOOR-sal NURV) or dorsal cutaneous nerve.
- The saphenous nerve (sa-FEEN-us NURV) supplies impulses to the skin of the inner side of the leg and foot.

► FIGURE 6-18

Nerves of the lower
leg and foot.

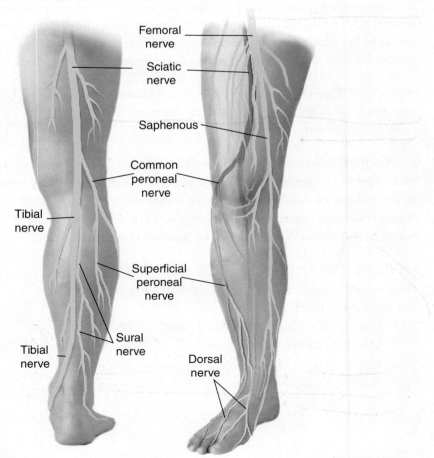

Femoral
nerve

Sciatic
nerve

Saphenous

Common
peroneal
nerve

Tibial
nerve

Superficial
peroneal
nerve

Tibial
nerve

Sural
nerve

Dorsal
nerve

- The sural nerve (SUR-ul NURV) supplies impulses to the skin on the outer side and back of the foot and leg (Figure 6-18).

The Circulatory System

The circulatory system, also referred to as the cardiovascular system (KAHRD-ee-oh-VAS-kyoo-lur SIS-tum) or vascular system, controls the steady circulation of the blood through the body by means of the heart and blood vessels. The circulatory system is made up of two divisions:

The blood vascular system, which consists of the heart, arteries, veins, and capillaries that distribute blood throughout the body.

The lymph vascular system (LIMF VAS-kyoo-lur SIS-tum), or lymphatic system, which acts as an aid to the blood system and consists of the lymph spaces, lymphatics (lymph vessels), lymph nodes (LIMF NOHDS) special structures found inside the lymphatic vessels that filter lymph), and other structures. Lymph is a clear fluid that circulates in the lymphatics of the body, where it helps to carry wastes and impurities away from the cells, and is routed back into the circulatory system.

THE HEART

The heart is often referred to as the body's pump. It is a muscular, cone-shaped organ that keeps the blood moving within the circulatory system. It is enclosed by a double-layered membranous sac known as the pericardium (payr-ih-KAR-deeum), which is made of epithelial tissue.

The heart is the approximate size of a closed fist, weighs approximately nine ounces, and is located in the chest cavity. The heartbeat is regulated by the vagus (tenth cranial) nerve and other nerves in the autonomic nervous system. A normal adult heart beats about 60 to 80 times per minute, but it can beat as high as 100 times per minute.

The interior of the heart contains four chambers and four valves. The upper, thin-walled chambers are the right atrium (AY-tree-um) and left atrium, through which blood is pumped to the ventricles. The two lower, thick-walled chambers are the right ventricle, one of the two lower chambers of the heart, (VEN-truh-kul) and left ventricle. Valves are structures that temporarily close a passage or permit blood flow in only one direction. With each contraction and relaxation of the heart, the blood flows in, travels from the atria (plural of atrium) to the ventricles, and is then driven out, to be distributed all over the body.

The blood is in constant and continuous circulation from the time that it leaves the heart until it returns to the heart. Two systems attend to this circulation. Pulmonary circulation sends the blood from the heart to the lungs to be purified, then back to the heart again. Systemic circulation (PUL-muh-nayr-ee sur-kyoo-LAY-shun) or general circulation carries the blood from the heart throughout the body and back to the heart. The following is an overview of how these systems work.

1. Deoxygenated blood flows from the body into the right atrium.

2. From the right atrium, it flows through the tricuspid valve into the right ventricle.

3. The right ventricle pumps the blood to the pulmonary arteries, which move the deoxygenated blood to the lungs. When the blood reaches the lungs, it releases waste gases (carbon dioxide) and receives oxygen. The blood is then considered to be oxygen- rich.

4. The oxygen-rich blood returns to the heart through the pulmonary veins and enters the left atrium.

5. From the left atrium, the blood flows through the mitral valve (MY-trul VALV), or bicuspid valve (by-KUS-pid VALV), into the left ventricle.

6. The blood then leaves the left ventricle and travels to all parts of the body (Figure 6-19).

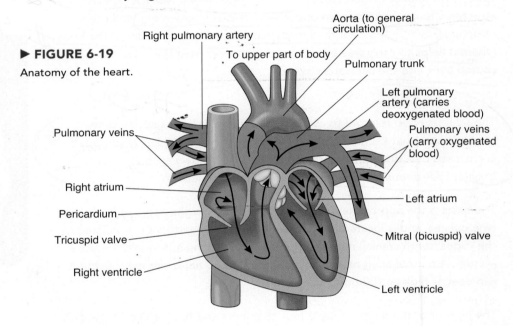

▶ **FIGURE 6-19**
Anatomy of the heart.

Right pulmonary artery
Aorta (to general circulation)
To upper part of body
Pulmonary trunk
Left pulmonary artery (carries deoxygenated blood)
Pulmonary veins (carry oxygenated blood)
Pulmonary veins
Right atrium
Pericardium
Tricuspid valve
Right ventricle
Left atrium
Mitral (bicuspid) valve
Left ventricle

BLOOD VESSELS

The blood vessels are tube-like structures that include the arteries, capillaries, and veins. The function of these vessels is to transport blood to and from the heart and then on to various tissues of the body.

- Arteries (AR-tuh-rees) are thick-walled, muscular, flexible tubes that carry oxygenated blood away from the heart to the capillaries. The largest artery in the body is the aorta (ay-ORT-uh).

- Capillaries are tiny, thin-walled blood vessels that connect the smaller arteries to the veins. They bring nutrients to the cells and carry away waste materials.

- Veins are thin-walled blood vessels that are less elastic than arteries. They contain cup-like valves that prevent backflow and carry blood containing waste products from the capillaries back to the heart and

lungs for cleaning and to pick up oxygen. Veins are located closer to the outer skin surface of the body than arteries (Figure 6-20).

THE BLOOD

Blood is a nutritive fluid circulating through the circulatory system (heart, veins, arteries, and capillaries) to supply oxygen and nutrients to cells and tissues and to remove carbon dioxide and waste from them. There are approximately eight to 10 pints of blood in the human body, which contribute about 1/20th of the body's weight. Blood is approximately 80 percent water. It is sticky and salty, with a normal temperature of 98.6 degrees Fahrenheit (36 degrees Celsius). It is bright red in the arteries (except for the pulmonary artery) and dark red in the veins. The color change occurs with the exchange of carbon dioxide for oxygen as the blood passes through the lungs, and the exchange of oxygen for carbon dioxide as the blood circulates throughout the body. Red blood is oxygen rich; blue blood is oxygen poor.

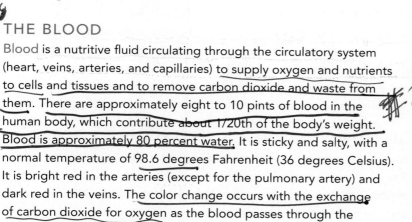

Blood flow toward the heart

Valve open to allow for blood flow

Valve closed to prevent back flow

◄ FIGURE 6-20
Valves in the veins.

Composition of the Blood

Blood is composed of red and white cells, platelets, plasma, and hemoglobin.

Red blood cells are produced in the red bone marrow. They contain hemoglobin (HEE-muh-gloh-bun), a complex iron protein that binds to oxygen. The function of red blood cells is to carry oxygen from the lungs to the body cells and transport carbon dioxide from the cells back to the lungs.

White blood cells, also called white corpuscles or leukocytes (LOO-koh-syts), perform the function of destroying disease-causing microorganisms.

Platelets (PLAYT-lets) are much smaller than red blood cells. They contribute to the blood-clotting process, which stops bleeding.

Plasma (PLAZ-muh) is the fluid part of the blood in which the red and white blood cells and platelets flow. It is about 90 percent water and contains proteins and sugars. The main function of plasma is to carry food and other useful substances to the cells and to take carbon dioxide away from the cells.

Blood is a nutritive fluid circulating through the circulatory system...

Chief Functions of the Blood

Blood performs the following critical functions:

- Carries water, oxygen, and food to all cells and tissues of the body.

- Carries away carbon dioxide and waste products to be eliminated through the lungs, skin, kidneys, and large intestines.

- Helps to equalize the body's temperature, thus protecting the body from extreme heat and cold.

- Works with the immune system to protect the body from harmful toxins and bacteria.

> • Seals leaks found in injured blood vessels by forming clots, thus preventing further blood loss.

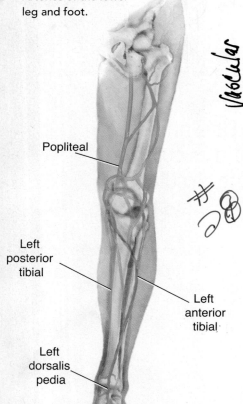

◀ **FIGURE 6-21**

Arteries of the arm and hand.

— Radial artery

— Ulnar artery

BLOOD SUPPLY TO THE ARM AND HAND

The ulnar and radial arteries are the main blood supply of the arms and hands. The ulnar artery and its numerous branches supply the little-finger side of the arm and palm of the hand. The radial artery and its branches supply the thumb side of the arm and the back of the hand. While the arteries are found deep in the tissues, the veins lie nearer to the surface of the arms and hands (**Figure 6-21**).

BLOOD SUPPLY TO THE LOWER LEG AND FOOT

There are several major arteries that supply blood to the lower leg and foot.

- The popliteal (pop-lih-TEE-ul) artery, which supplies blood to the foot, divides into two separate arteries known as the anterior tibial artery and the posterior tibial artery.
- The anterior tibial (TIB-ee-al) artery supplies impulses to the lower leg muscles and to the muscles and skin on the top of the foot and adjacent sides of the first and second toes. This artery goes to the foot and becomes the dorsalis pedis artery.
- The posterior tibial artery supplies blood to the ankles and the back of the lower leg.
- The dorsalis pedis artery supplies the foot with blood.

▼ **FIGURE 6-22**

Arteries of the lower leg and foot.

Popliteal

Left posterior tibial

Left anterior tibial

Left dorsalis pedia

As in the arm and hand, the important veins of the lower leg and foot are almost parallel with the arteries and take the same names (Figure 6-22).

The Lymphatic/ Immune System

The lymphatic system, is made up of lymph, lymph nodes, the thymus gland, the spleen, and lymph vessels that acts as an aid to the blood system. Lymph is a colorless, watery fluid derived from blood plasma as a result of filtration through the capillary walls into the tissue space. Its function is to protect the body from disease by developing immunities and destroying disease-causing microorganisms, as well as to drain the tissue spaces of excess interstitial fluids (in-tur-STISH-al FLOO-id) (blood plasma found in the spaces between tissue cells) to the blood. It then carries waste and impurities away from the cells.

The lymphatic system is closely connected to the blood and the cardiovascular system. They both transport fluids, like rivers throughout the body. The difference is that the lymphatic system transports lymph, which eventually returns to the blood where it originated.

The lymphatic vessels start as tubes that are closed at one end. They can occur individually or in clusters that are called lymph capillaries, blind end tubes that are the origin of lymphatic vessels. The lymph capillaries are distributed throughout most of the body (except the nervous system).

The lymphatic vessels are filtered by the lymph nodes, which are gland-like structures found inside the lymphatic vessels. This filtering process helps to fight infection.

The primary functions of the lymphatic system are to:

- Carry nourishment from the blood to the body cells.
- Act as a defense against toxins and invading bacteria.
- Remove waste material from the body cells to the blood.
- Provide a suitable fluid environment for the cells.

The Endocrine System #29

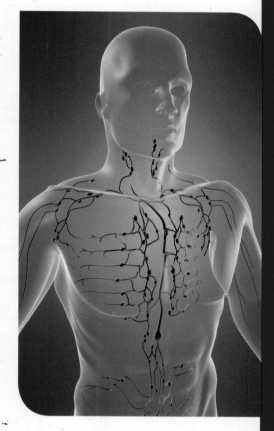

The endocrine (EN-duh-krin) system is a group of specialized glands that affect the growth, development, sexual activities, and health of the entire body. Glands are specialized organs that remove certain elements from the blood to convert them into new compounds. There are two main types of glands.

#30
- Exocrine glands (EK-suh-krin GLANDZ), or duct glands produce a substance that travels through small, tube-like ducts. Sweat and oil glands of the skin belong to this group.

Review Q #14
- Endocrine glands or ductless glands, such as the thyroid and pituitary glands, release secretions called hormone (HOR-mohnz) directly into the bloodstream, which, in turn, influence the welfare of the entire body. Hormones, such as insulin, adrenaline, and estrogen, stimulate functional activity or secretion in other parts of the body.

Here is a list of the endocrine glands and their functions.

- The pineal gland (PY-nee-ul GLAND) plays a major role in sexual development, sleep, and metabolism.
- The pituitary gland (puh-TOO-uh-tair-ee GLAND) is the most complex organ of endocrine system. It affects almost every physiologic process of the body: growth, blood pressure, contractions during childbirth, breast milk production, sex organ functions in both women and men, thyroid gland function, the conversion of food into energy (metabolism).
- The thyroid gland (THY-royd GLAND) controls how #31 quickly the body burns energy (metabolism), makes proteins, and how sensitive the body should be to other hormones.
- The parathyroid glands (payr-uh-THY-royd GLANDZ) regulate blood #32 calcium and phosphorus levels so that the nervous and muscular systems can function properly.
- The pancreas (PANG-kree-us) secretes enzyme-producing cells that are responsible for digesting carbohydrates, proteins, and fats. The islet of Langerhans cells within the pancreas control insulin and glucagon production.

- The adrenal glands (uh-DREEN-ul GLANDZ) secrete about 30 steroid hormones and control metabolic processes of the body, including the fight-or-flight response.
- The ovaries and testes function in sexual reproduction, as well as determining male and female sexual characteristics (Figure 6-23).

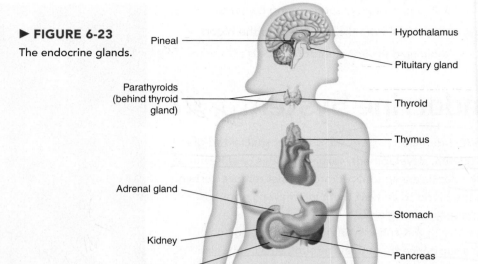

▶ **FIGURE 6-23**

The endocrine glands.

Pineal

Parathyroids (behind thyroid gland)

Adrenal gland

Kidney

Duodenum

Ovary (female)

Hypothalamus

Pituitary gland

Thyroid

Thymus

Stomach

Pancreas

Testicle (male)

The Digestive System

The digestive system (dy-JES-tiv SIS-tum), also called the gastrointestinal (gas-troh-in-TES-tunul) system, is responsible for breaking down food into nutrients and waste.

Digestive enzymes (EN-zymz) are chemicals that change certain kinds of food into a form that can be used by the body. The food, now in soluble form, is transported by the bloodstream and used by the body's cells and tissues. The entire food digestion process takes about nine hours to complete.

The Excretory System

The excretory system (EK-skre-tor-ee) is responsible for purifying the body by eliminating waste matter. The metabolism of body cells forms toxic substances that, if retained, could poison the body.

Each of the following organs plays a crucial role in the excretory system:
- The kidneys excrete waste containing urine.
- The liver discharges waste containing bile.

- The skin eliminates waste containing perspiration.
- The large intestine eliminates decomposed and undigested food.
- The lungs exhale carbon dioxide.

The Respiratory System

The respiratory system (RES-puh-ra-tor-ee SIS-tum) enables breathing (respiration, the exchange of carbon dioxide and oxygen in the lungs and within each cell) and consists of the lungs and air passages. The lungs are spongy tissues composed of microscopic cells in which inhaled air is exchanged for carbon dioxide during one breathing cycle. The respiratory system is located within the chest cavity and is protected on both sides by the ribs. The diaphragm (DY-uh-fram) is a muscular wall that separates the thorax (THOR-aks), the chest, from the abdominal region and helps control breathing (Figure 6-24).

With each breathing cycle, an exchange of gases takes place. During inhalation (in-huh-LAY-shun), or breathing in through the nose or mouth, oxygen is passed into the blood. During exhalation (eks-huh-LAY-shun), or breathing outward, carbon dioxide (collected from the blood) is expelled from the lungs.

Oxygen is more essential than either food or water. Although people may survive for more than 60 days without food, and several days without water, if they are deprived of oxygen, they will die within a few minutes.

Nose

Right lung

Left lung

Diaphragm

Respiratory System

▲ FIGURE 6-24
Respiratory system.

The Integumentary System

The integumentary system (in-TEG-yuh-ment-uh-ree SIS-tum) is made up of the skin and its various accessory organs, such as the oil and sweat glands, sensory receptors, hair, and nails. (Skin structure and growth are discussed in detail in Chapter 7.)

The Reproductive System

The reproductive system (ree-proh-DUK-tiv SIS-tum) performs the function of reproducing and perpetuating the human race. Although important to the perpetuation of the species, it is not of major importance to the nail tech.

> Oxygen is more essential than either food or water.

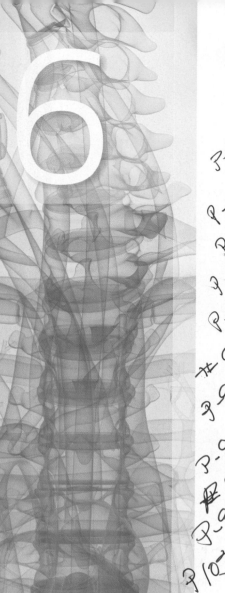

review questions

P-92 1. Why is the study of anatomy, physiology, and histology important to the nail technician?

P-93 2. Define anatomy, physiology, and histology.

P-93 3. Name and describe the basic structures of a cell.

P-94 4. Explain cell metabolism and its purpose.

P-95 5. List and describe the functions of the four types of tissue found in the human body.

P-95 6. What are organs?

P-96 7. List and describe the functions of the main organs found in the body.

P-97 8. Name the 11 body systems and their main functions.

P-96 9. List the primary functions of the skeletal system.

P-99 10. Name and describe the three types of muscular tissue found in the body.

P-103 11. Name and describe the types of nerves found in the body and how they react.

P-196 12. Name and briefly describe the three types of blood vessels found in the body.

P-107 13. List and describe the composition of blood.

P-109 14. Name and discuss the two main types of glands found in the human body.

P-110 15. List the organs of the excretory system and their functions.

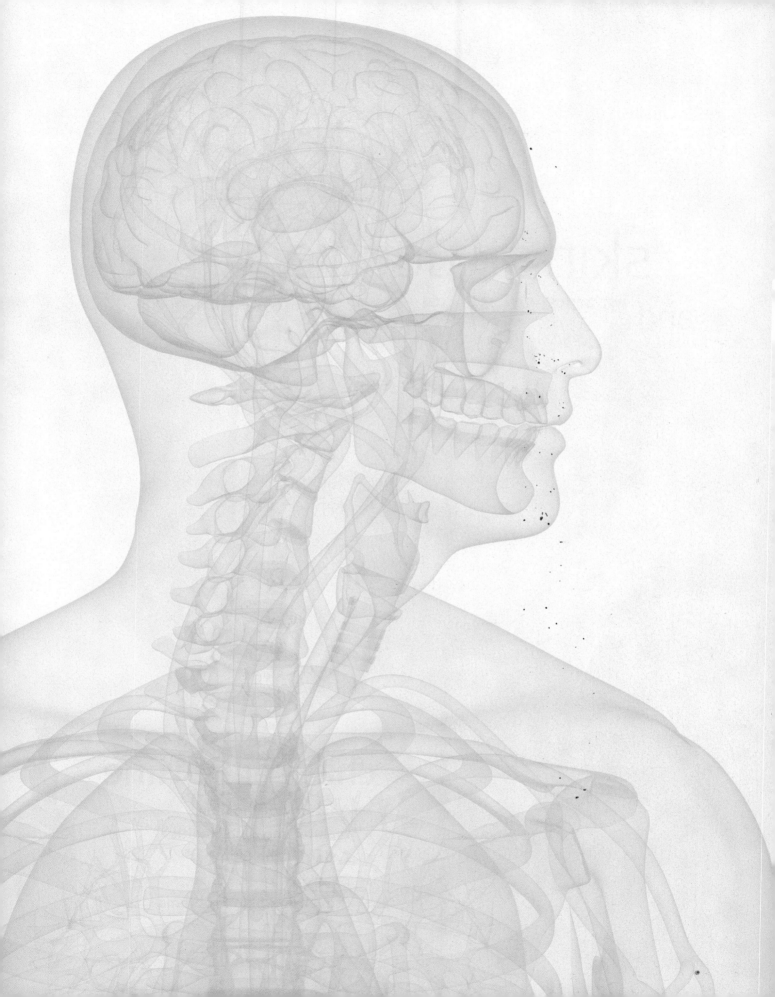

7
skin structure
and growth

chapter outline

- ▶ **Anatomy of the Skin**
- ▶ **Maintaining Skin Health**
- ▶ **Aging of the Skin**
- ▶ **Disorders of the Skin**
- ▶ **Preventing Skin Problems in the Salon**

✓ Learning Objectives

After you have completed this chapter, you will be able to:

1 Describe the structure and composition of the skin.

2 List the functions of the skin.

3 Describe how to maintain skin health and why it is important.

4 Describe the aging process and the factors that influence aging of the skin.

5 Define important terms relating to skin disorders and list which skin disorders may be handled in the salon, and which should be referred to a physician.

6 List ways to prevent skin problems from occurring as a result of visiting the nail salon.

Key Terms

Page number indicates where in the chapter the term is used.

acne papule / 121
adipose tissue / 118
albinism / 130
allergic contact dermatitis / 133
anhidrosis / 129
arrector pili muscles / 119
basal cell carcinoma / 131
basal cell layer / 117
bromhidrosis / 129
bulla (plural: bullae) / 128
callus / 116
chloasma / 130
cicatrix / 129
collagen / 120
comedo (comedones) / 121
contact dermatitis / 133
corium / 117
crust / 129
cutis / 117
cyst / 128
derma / 117
dermatitis / 130
dermatologist / 116
dermatology / 116
dermis / 117
eczema / 130
elastin / 120
epidermis / 117
esthetician / 125
excoriation / 129
fissure / 129

hematoma / 129
histamines / 136
hyperhidrosis / 129
hypertrophy / 131
initiator / 134
irritant contact dermatitis / 133
keloid / 129
keratin / 117
keratoma / 131
lentigenes / 130
lesion / 127
leukoderma / 130
macule (plural: maculae) / 128
malignant melanoma / 132
melanin / 119
melanocytes / 117
miliaria rubra / 130
mole / 131
motor nerve fibers / 119
nevus / 130
overexposure / 133
papillary layer / 118
papule / 128
psoriasis / 130
pustule / 121
reticular layer / 118
scale / 129
scar / 129
sebaceous glands / 120
secretory coil / 121
secretory nerve fibers / 119

sensitization / 134
sensory nerve fibers / 119
skin tag / 131
squamous cell carcinoma / 132
stain / 131
stratum corneum / 117
stratum germinativum / 117
stratum granulosum / 117
stratum lucidum / 117
stratum spinosum / 117
subcutaneous tissue / 118
subcutis tissue / 118
sudoriferous glands / 120
sweat glands / 120
tactile corpuscles / 118
tan / 131
telangiectasias / 127
true skin / 117
tubercle / 128
tumor / 128
ulcer / 129
verruca / 131
vesicle / 128
vitamin A / 123
vitamin C / 123
vitamin D / 123
vitamin E / 123
vitiligo / 131
wheal / 128

Clear glowing skin is one of today's most important hallmarks of beauty. With all the latest high-performance ingredients and state-of-the-art delivery systems, twenty-first century skin care has entered the realm of high technology with products and services that truly help protect and preserve the health and beauty of the skin.

No matter how advanced the latest skin care technology may be, knowing how to care for skin begins with understanding its underlying structure and basic needs. As a licensed nail technician, you also must recognize adverse conditions, including inflamed skin conditions, diseases, and infectious skin disorders so these clients can be referred to a medical professional for treatment, if needed.

Anatomy of the Skin

Did **You** Know...

The skin located under our eyes and around the eyelids is the thinnest skin of the body; the skin on the palms of our hands and soles of our feet is the thickest.

The medical branch of science that deals with the study of skin—its nature, structure, functions, diseases, and treatment—is called dermatology.

A dermatologist is a physician engaged in the practice of treating the skin, its structures, functions, and diseases. Nail technicians can provide cleansing, preservation of health, and beautification of the skin on the hands, arms (below the elbow), feet and legs (below the knee). They are not allowed to prescribe, or provide any type of treatment for abnormal conditions, illnesses, or diseases.

The skin is the largest organ of the body. If the skin of an average adult were stretched out, it would cover over 3,000 square inches and weigh about six to nine pounds. Our skin protects the network of muscles, bones, nerves, blood vessels, and everything else inside our bodies. It is our only barrier against the environment.

Healthy skin is slightly moist, soft, and flexible with a texture (feel and appearance) that ideally is smooth and fine-grained. The surface of healthy skin is slightly acidic and its immune responses react quickly to organisms that touch or try to enter it. Appendages of the skin include hair, nails, and sweat and oil glands.

Continued, repeated pressure on any part of the skin can cause it to thicken and develop into a callus, which is an important and much needed protective layer that prevents damage to the underlying skin.

The skin is composed of two main divisions: epidermis and dermis (**Figure 7-1**).

▼ **FIGURE 7-1**

Layers of the skin.

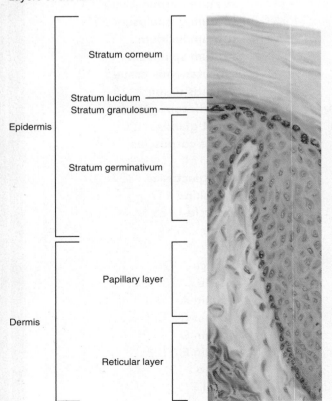

Stratum corneum

Stratum lucidum
Stratum granulosum

Epidermis

Stratum germinativum

Dermis

Papillary layer

Reticular layer

The epidermis (ep-uh-DUR-mis) is the outermost and thinnest layer of the skin. It contains no blood vessels, but has many small nerve endings. The epidermis is made up of the layers discussed below.

- The basal cell layer, also referred to as the stratum germinativum (jer-mih-nah-TIV-um), is the deepest layer of the epidermis. It is composed of several layers of differently shaped cells. It is the live layer of the epidermis, which produces new epidermal skin cells and is responsible for the growth of the epidermis.

- The spiny layer, also referred to as the stratum spinosum, is just above the basal cell layer. The spiny layer is where the process of skin cell shedding begins.

- The stratum granulosum (gran-yoo-LOH-sum), or granular layer, consists of cells that look like distinct granules. These cells are dying as they are pushed to the surface to replace dead cells that are shed from the skin surface layer.

- The stratum lucidum (LOO-sih-dum) is the clear, transparent layer just under the skin surface; it consists of small cells through which light can pass.

- The stratum corneum (STRAT-um KOR-nee-um), or horny layer, is the outer layer of the epidermis. The corneum is the layer we see when we look at the skin, and the layer cared for by salon products and services. Its scale-like cells are continually being shed and replaced by cells coming to the surface from underneath. These cells are made up of keratin, a fibrous protein that is also the principal component of hair and nails. The cells combine with lipids or fats produced by the skin to help make the stratum corneum a protective, water-resistant layer.

- The stratum germinativum has special column-shaped cells that produce other cells called melanocytes (muh-LAN-uh-syts), which produce a dark skin pigment, called melanin, which helps to protect the sensitive cells in the dermis below from the destructive effects of excessive ultraviolet light of the sun or those from an ultraviolet lamp. The type of melanin produced also determines skin color.

The dermis (DUR-mis) is the underlying or inner layer of the skin. It is also called the derma, corium (KOH-ree-um), cutis (KYOO-tis), or true skin. This highly sensitive layer of connective tissue is about 25 times thicker than the epidermis. Within its structure, there are numerous blood vessels, lymph vessels, nerves, sweat glands, oil glands, and hair follicles, as well as arrector pili muscles (small muscles that work in connection with the hair follicles and cause goose pimples) and papillae (small cone-shaped projections of elastic

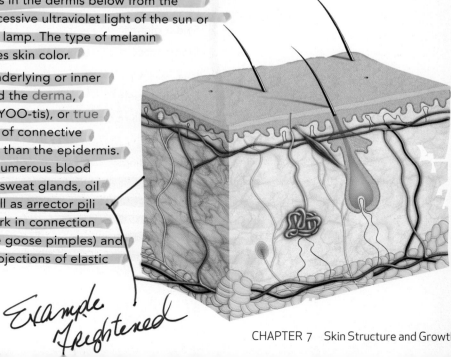

Example
Frightened

tissue that point upward into the epidermis). The dermis is comprised of two layers: the papillary or superficial layer, and the reticular or deeper layer **(Figure 7-2)**.

▶ **FIGURE 7-2**

Structures of the skin.

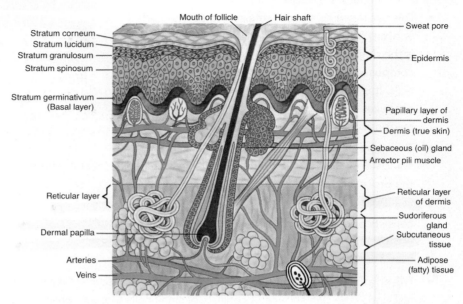

- The papillary layer (PAP-uh-lair-ee) is the outer layer of the dermis, directly beneath the epidermis. Here you will find the dermal papillae (puh-PIL-eye), which are small, cone-shaped elevations at the bottom of the hair follicles. Some papillae contain looped capillaries and others contain small epidermal structures called tactile corpuscles (TAK-tile KOR-pusuls), with nerve endings that are sensitive to touch and pressure. This layer also contains melanocytes, the pigment-producing cells. The top of the papillary layer where it joins the epidermis is called the epidermal–dermal junction.

- The reticular layer (ruh-TIK-yuh-lur) is the deeper layer of the dermis that supplies the skin with all of its oxygen and nutrients. It contains the following structures within its network:

  - Fat cells
  - Sweat glands
  - Blood vessels
  - Hair follicles
  - Lymph vessels
  - Arrector pili muscles
  - Oil glands
  - Nerve endings

The subcutaneous tissue (sub-kyoo-TAY-nee-us) is a fatty layer found below the dermis. This fat tissue is also called adipose or subcutis (sub-KYOO-tis) tissue, and varies in thickness according to the age, gender, and general health of the individual. It gives smoothness and contour to the body, contains fats for use as energy, and also acts as a protective cushion for the skin.

HOW THE SKIN IS NOURISHED

Blood supplies nutrients and oxygen to the skin. Nutrients are molecules from food, such as protein, carbohydrates, and fats. These nutrients are necessary for cell life, repair, and growth.

Lymph, the clear fluids of the body that resemble blood plasma but contain only colorless substances, bathe the skin cells, remove toxins and cellular waste, and have immune functions that help protect the skin and body against disease. Networks of arteries and lymph vessels in the subcutaneous tissue send their smaller branches to hair papillae, hair follicles, and skin glands. The skin cannot be nourished from the outside in; it can only get nourishment from foods that we eat.

NERVES OF THE SKIN

The skin contains the surface endings of the following nerve fibers:

- Motor nerve fibers are distributed to the arrector pili muscles attached to the hair follicles. These muscles can cause goose bumps when a person is frightened or cold.

- Sensory nerve fibers react to heat, cold, touch, pressure, and pain. These sensory receptors send messages to the brain.

- Secretory nerve fibers are distributed to the sweat and oil glands of the skin. Secretory nerves, which are part of the autonomic nervous system, regulate the excretion of perspiration from the sweat glands and control the flow of sebum (a fatty or oily secretion of the sebaceous glands) to the surface of the skin.

SENSE OF TOUCH

The papillary layer of the dermis houses the nerve endings that provide the body with the sense of touch. These nerve endings register basic sensations such as touch, pain, heat, cold, and pressure. Nerve endings are most abundant in the fingertips. Complex sensations, such as vibrations, seem to depend on the sensitivity of a combination of these nerve endings.

SKIN COLOR

The color of the skin—whether fair, medium, or dark—depends primarily on melanin, the tiny grains of pigment (coloring matter) deposited into cells in the basal cell layer of the epidermis and the papillary layers of the dermis. The color of the skin is a hereditary trait and varies among races and nationalities. Genes determine the amount and type of pigment produced in an individual.

The body produces two types of melanin: *pheomelanin*, which is red to yellow in color, and *eumelanin*, which is dark brown to black. People with light-colored skin mostly produce pheomelanin, while those with dark-colored skin mostly produce eumelanin. In addition, individuals differ in the size of melanin particles.

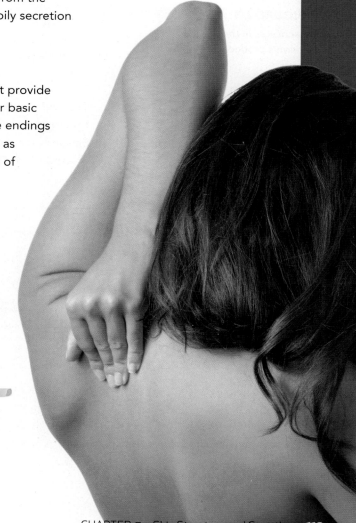

Activity

Next time you're smoothing a callus, pay close attention. You'll come to a point where a thin layer of protective callus skin is all that remains. That's the time to stop removing additional layers of the callus. Check yourself to ensure a thin layer of callus skin remains to prevent blisters and skin damage. If the area feels like soft, new skin, you have removed too much.

Light skin   Dark skin

Melanin
Melanocytes

▲ FIGURE 7-3

Melanocytes in the
epidermis produce melanin.

Melanin helps to protect sensitive cells against UV light,
but that's not all that is needed to prevent skin damage.
Daily use of a sunscreen with a sun protection factor (SPF)
of 15 or higher can help the melanin in the skin protect it
from burning, and from receiving damage that can lead
to skin cancer or premature aging (Figure 7-3).

STRENGTH AND FLEXIBILITY OF THE SKIN

The skin gets its strength, form, and flexibility from two
specific structures composed of flexible protein fibers
found within the dermis. These two structures, which
make up 70 percent of the dermis, are called collagen
and elastin.

Collagen is a fibrous protein that gives the skin form
and strength. This fiber makes up a large portion of the
dermis and helps give structural support to the skin by
holding together all the structures found in this layer.

When collagen fibers are healthy, they allow the skin
to stretch and contract as necessary. If collagen fibers
become weakened due to age, a lack of moisture,
environmental damage such as sun tanning or routine
unprotected sun exposure, or frequent changes
in weight, the skin will begin to lose its tone and
suppleness. Wrinkles and sagging are often the result of collagen fibers
losing their strength.

Collagen fibers are interwoven with elastin a protein base similar to collagen
that forms elastic tissue. This fiber gives the skin its flexibility and elasticity.
Elastin helps the skin regain its shape, even after being repeatedly stretched
or expanded.

Both of these fibers are important to the overall health
and appearance of the skin. As we age, gravity causes
these fibers to weaken, resulting in some degree of
elasticity loss or skin sagging.

A majority of scientists now believe that most signs of
skin aging are caused by sun exposure over a lifetime.
Keeping the skin healthy, protected, moisturized, and
free of disease will slow the weakening process and
help keep the skin looking young longer.

GLANDS OF THE SKIN

The skin contains two types of duct glands that extract
materials from the blood to form new substances: the
sudoriferous glands (sood-uh-RIF-uhrus) or sweat
glands, and the sebaceous glands (sih-BAY-shus) or
oil glands (Figure 7-4).

Hair
Epidermis
Sebaceous
(oil) gland
Veins
Arteries
Sweat pore
Epidermis
Cross section
of sweat gland
Sweat duct
Sudoriferous (sweat)
gland
Fundus

▲ FIGURE 7-4

Sweat gland and oil production.

Sudoriferous (Sweat) Glands

The sudoriferous or sweat glands, which excrete sweat from the skin, consist of a coiled base, or secretory coil, and a tube-like duct that ends at the surface of the skin to form the sweat pore. Practically all parts of the body are supplied with sweat glands, which are more numerous on the palms, soles, and forehead, and in the armpits.

The sweat glands regulate body temperature and help to eliminate waste products from the body. The evaporation of sweat cools the skin surface. Their activity is greatly increased by heat, exercise, emotions, and certain drugs.

The excretion of sweat is controlled by the nervous system. Normally, one to two pints of liquids containing salts are eliminated daily through sweat pores in the skin.

Sebaceous (Oil) Glands

The sebaceous or oil glands of the skin are connected to the hair follicles. They consist of little sacs with ducts that open into the follicles. These glands secrete sebum, a fatty or oily secretion that lubricates the skin and preserves the softness of the hair. With the exception of the palms and soles, these glands are found in all parts of the body, particularly in the face and scalp, where they are larger.

Ordinarily, sebum flows through the oil ducts leading to the mouths of the hair follicles. However, when the sebum hardens and the duct becomes clogged, a pore impaction or comedo, a hair follicle filled with keratin and sebum, is formed, which may lead to an acne papule or pustule. Acne is a skin disorder characterized by chronic inflammation of the sebaceous glands from retained secretions and bacteria.

 ✔ **LO1 Complete**

Day 7 Friday

FUNCTIONS OF THE SKIN

The principal functions of the skin are protection, sensation, heat regulation, excretion, secretion, and absorption.

Protection. The skin protects the body from injury and bacterial invasion. The outermost layer of the epidermis is covered with a thin layer of sebum and fatty lipids between the cells produced through the cell renewal process, which make it water-resistant. This outermost layer is resistant to wide variations in temperature, minor injuries, chemically active substances, and many forms of bacteria.

Sensation. By stimulating different sensory nerve endings, the skin responds to heat, cold, touch, pressure, and pain. When the nerve endings are stimulated, a message is sent to the brain. You respond by saying, "Ouch," if you feel pain, by scratching an itch, or by pulling away when you touch something hot. Some sensory nerve endings are located near hair follicles (Figure 7-5).

▼ **FIGURE 7-5**

Sensory nerve endings in the skin.

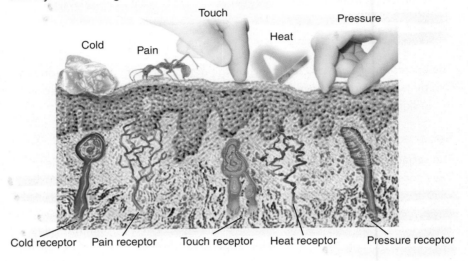

Cold   Pain   Touch   Heat   Pressure

Cold receptor   Pain receptor   Touch receptor   Heat receptor   Pressure receptor

Heat Regulation. This means that the skin protects the body from the environment. A healthy body maintains a constant internal temperature of about 98.6 degrees Fahrenheit (37 degrees Celsius). As changes occur in the outside temperature, the blood and sweat glands of the skin make necessary adjustments to allow the body to be cooled by the evaporation of sweat.

Excretion. Perspiration from the sweat glands is excreted through the skin. Water lost through perspiration takes salt and other chemicals with it.

Secretion. Sebum, or oil, is secreted by the sebaceous glands. This oil lubricates the skin, keeping it soft and pliable. Oil also keeps hair soft. Emotional stress and hormone imbalances can increase the flow of sebum.

Absorption. Absorption is limited to some ingredients, but very few can penetrate past the epidermis. Small amounts of fatty materials, such as those used in many advanced skin care formulations, may be absorbed between the cells, and through the hair follicles and sebaceous gland openings. Cosmetic products are designed to not penetrate past the epidermis.

Cosmetic products are designed to not penetrate past the epidermis.

LO2 Complete

Maintaining Skin Health

For your own benefit, as well as the benefit of your clients, you should have a basic understanding of how best to maintain healthy skin. To keep the skin and the body healthy, the adage "You are what you eat" still holds true. Proper dietary choices help to regulate hydration (maintaining a healthy level of water in the body), oil production, and overall function of the cells. Eating foods found in all three basic food groups—fats, carbohydrates, and proteins—is the best way to support the health of the skin.

VITAMINS AND DIETARY SUPPLEMENTS

always eat healthy

Vitamins play an important role in the skin's health, often aiding in healing, softening, and fighting diseases of the skin. Vitamins such as A, C, D, and E have all been shown to have positive effects on the skin's health when taken internally. Although experts agree that taking vitamins internally is still the best way to support the health of the skin, external applications have only limited value when applied to the skin. Vitamins are nutritional supplements, not cosmetic ingredients. In fact, the law prohibits manufacturers from claiming that any cosmetic has nutritional value. When vitamins in foods are ingested, they can help the skin in significant ways:

Hydration means to keep moisture in

Dehydration means to keep it out

- **Vitamin A** supports the overall health of the skin and aids in the health, function, and repair of skin cells. It has been shown to improve the skin's elasticity and thickness. *Sources → milk, eggs, Chicken & fish*

- **Vitamin C** is an important substance needed for proper repair of the skin and various tissues. This vitamin aids in, and even speeds up, the healing processes of the body. Vitamin C is also vitally important in fighting the aging process and promotes the production of collagen in the skin's dermal tissues, keeping the skin healthy and firm. *Sources → Strawberries oranges peas & Brodeoli*

- **Vitamin D** enables the body to properly absorb and use calcium, the element needed for proper bone development and maintenance. Vitamin D also promotes healthy, rapid healing of the skin. *Sources → oily fish & Dairy products*

- **Vitamin E** helps protect the skin from the harmful effects of the sun's rays. Some claim that vitamin E helps to heal damage to the skin's tissues when taken by mouth. *Tocopherol Sources → Avacodos, tomatoes, Spinach, Salmon & Blackberries*

The nutrients the body needs for proper functioning and survival must come primarily from the foods we eat. If daily food consumption is lacking in nutrients, a person should eat better and not rely on vitamins and mineral supplements. These cannot make up for poor nutrition. They are called supplements, and are not replacements for healthy eating. Clients will occasionally ask you about nutrition and their skin. While it is important that the nail professional know the basics of nutrition, nail technicians are not registered dieticians, and should never give nutritional advice. Instead, refer the client to a registered dietician.

▶ FIGURE 7-6
Water is essential for healthy skin.

WATER AND THE SKIN

There is one essential item that no person can live without, and that is water. To function properly, the body and skin both rely heavily on the benefits of water. Water composes 50 percent to 70 percent of body weight.

Drinking pure water is essential to the health of the skin and body because it sustains the health of the cells, aids in the elimination of toxins and waste, helps regulate the body's temperature, and aids in proper digestion. All these functions, when performing properly, help keep the skin healthy, vital, and attractive.

The amount of water needed by an individual varies, depending on body weight and the level of daily physical activity. There is an easy formula to help you determine how much water you need every day for maximum physical health: take your body weight and divide by 16.

The resulting number approximates how many eight-ounce glasses of water you should drink every day. For instance, if you weigh 160 pounds, you should drink 10 glasses of water a day. If intense physical activity is performed daily, add two extra glasses of water to the final number. This will help replace extra fluids lost while exercising **(Figure 7-6)**.

Did **You** Know...

Research suggests that the benefits of water on human health and functioning are many:

- Even mild dehydration will slow metabolism by as much as three percent.
- Drinking lots of water can help stop hunger pangs for many dieters.
- Cracked skin on the feet and lips are often early warning signs of dehydration.
- Lack of water is the principal cause of daytime fatigue.
- A two-percent drop in body water can trigger fuzzy short-term memory and trouble with basic math, and may cause difficulty focusing on a computer screen or printed page.

Pass the water, please!

✓ LO3 Complete

Aging of the Skin

> " One does not necessarily age as one's parents have.

Aging of the skin is a process that takes many years and can be influenced by many different factors. One does not necessarily age as one's parents have.

Many outside factors such as the sun, environment, health habits, and general lifestyle greatly influence the signs of skin aging to such an extent that it has been estimated that heredity may be responsible for only 15 percent of the factors that determine how skin ages.

THE SUN AND ITS EFFECTS

The sun and its ultraviolet (UV) light have the greatest negative impact on how our skin ages. Approximately 80 to 85 percent of our skin's aging is caused by the sun. As we age, the collagen and elastin fibers of the skin naturally weaken. This weakening happens at a much faster rate when the skin is frequently exposed to ultraviolet light without proper protection. The UV light of the sun reaches the skin in two different forms, as UVA and UVB light.

no longer considered light but Energy

Each of these types of light influences the skin at a different level. UVA light, also called aging rays, is deeper-penetrating light which causes the skin to tan by affecting the melanocytes, the cells of the epidermis that are responsible for producing melanin—the skin pigment. UV light weakens the collagen and elastin fibers, causing wrinkling and sagging in the tissues.

UVB light, also referred to as the burning rays, causes sunburns. Melanin is designed to help protect the skin from UV light, but can be altered or destroyed when large, frequent doses of UV light are allowed to penetrate the skin. Although UVB penetration is not as deep as UVA, both types of light are damaging to the skin and can damage the eyes as well. On a positive note, UVB light contributes to the body's synthesis of vitamin D and other important minerals. However, the amount of sun exposure necessary for vitamin D synthesis is minimal (e.g., ten minutes per day) not to mention the fact that you can get vitamin D from fortified milk or orange juice.

Solar rays Waves

If clients seek additional professional advice on how to protect their skin from the sun, refer them to a physician or a licensed esthetician, a specialist in cleansing, preservation of health, and beautification of the skin and body. However, as a consultant to your clients, you may wish to advise them about the necessary precautions to take when they are exposed to the sun:

- On a daily basis, wear a moisturizer or protective lotion with a sunscreen of at least SPF 15 on all areas of potential exposure.

- Avoid prolonged exposure to the sun during peak hours, when UV exposure is highest. This is usually between 10 AM and 3 PM.

- Sunscreen should be applied at least 30 minutes before sun exposure to allow time for protection to develop. Many people make the mistake of applying sunscreen after they are already in the sun. Therefore, they will have less protection for the first 30 minutes and skin damage may occur.

- Apply sunscreen liberally after swimming or any activities that result in heavy perspiration. If the skin is exposed to hours of sun, such as during a boat trip or a day at the beach, sunscreen should be applied periodically throughout the day as a precaution. Water-resistant sunscreens are more effective under these conditions.

- Ideally, sunscreens should be full or broad spectrum to filter out UVA and UVB light. Check expiration dates printed on the bottle to make sure that the sunscreen has not expired.

- Avoid exposing children younger than six months old directly to the sun.

irritation of certain pollutants.
Adverse skin Reactions

- If prone to burning frequently and easily, wear a hat, protective clothing, and high SPF sunscreens when participating in outdoor activities. Redheads and blue-eyed blondes are particularly susceptible to sun damage.

- In addition to following the above precautions, clients should be advised to regularly see a physician specializing in dermatology for checkups of the skin, especially if any changes in coloration, size, or shape of a mole are detected, or if the skin bleeds unexpectedly or a lesion or scrape does not heal quickly.

- Home self-examinations can also be an effective way to check for signs of potential skin cancer between scheduled doctor visits. When performing a self-care exam, clients should be advised to check for any changes in existing moles and pay attention to any new visible growths on the skin.

SKIN AGING AND THE ENVIRONMENT

While the sun may play the major role in how the skin ages, changes in our environment also greatly influence this aging process. Pollutants in the air from factories, automobile exhaust, and even secondhand smoke can all influence the appearance and overall health of our skin. While these pollutants affect the surface appearance of the skin, they can also change the health of the underlying cells and tissues, thereby speeding up the aging process.

The best defense against these pollutants is the simplest one: follow a good daily skin care routine. Routine washing at night helps to remove the buildup of pollutants that have settled on the skin's surface throughout the day. The application of daily moisturizers, protective lotions, and even foundation products all help to protect the skin from airborne pollutants.

AGING AND LIFESTYLE

Aging of the skin cannot be blamed entirely on the outside influences of the sun or wind. What we choose to put into our bodies also has a profound effect on the overall aging process. The impact of poor choices can be seen most visibly on the skin. Smoking, drinking, drug abuse, and making poor dietary choices all greatly influence the aging process. It is the responsibility of the practitioner to be aware of how these habits affect the skin, tactfully point out the effects to clients, and refer them to a physician or licensed esthetician.

Smoking and tobacco use may not only cause cancer, but have also been linked to premature aging and wrinkling of the skin. Nicotine in tobacco causes contraction and weakening of the blood vessels and small capillaries that supply blood to the tissues. In turn, this contraction and weakening causes decreased circulation to the tissues. Eventually, the tissues are deprived of essential oxygen, and the effect of this becomes evident on the skin's surface. The skin may appear yellowish or gray in color and can have a dull appearance. The smoke can absorb into the nail plate or artificial nail enhancement and cause yellow stains.

The use of illegal drugs affects the skin as much as smoking does. Some drugs have been shown to interfere with the body's intake of oxygen, thus affecting healthy cell growth. Some drugs can even aggravate serious skin conditions, such as acne. Others can cause dryness and allergic reactions on the skin's surface.

The overuse of alcohol has an opposite, yet equally damaging, effect on the skin. Heavy or excessive intake of alcohol over-dilates the blood vessels and capillaries. This constant over-dilation and weakening of the fragile capillary walls will cause them to become distended. These dilated capillaries, called telangiectasias (te-lanj-ec-tay-jas) may also be caused by tobacco use, sun exposure, or other environmental factors. Both smoking and drinking contribute to the aging process on their own, but the combination of the two can be devastating to the tissues. The constant dilation and contraction that occur on the tiny capillaries and blood vessels, as well as the constant deprivation of oxygen and water to the tissues, quickly make the skin appear lifeless and dull. It is very difficult for the skin to adjust and repair itself. Usually, the damage done by these lifestyle habits is hard to reverse or diminish.

Like any other organ of the body, the skin is susceptible to a variety of diseases, disorders, and ailments. In your work as a nail technician you will often see skin disorders, so you must be prepared to recognize certain common skin conditions and know what you can and cannot do with them. Skin disorders should only be treated by a physician. Any healing or medicinal preparations must be prescribed by a physician. Nail technicians must never attempt to diagnose, treat, or prescribe treatment for any abnormal conditions of the skin. Clients with abnormal skin *or nails* must be referred to a physician.

It is very important that a nail salon does not serve a client who is suffering from an open wound or inflamed skin. The nail professional should be able to recognize abnormal conditions, and recommend the client see a physician to avoid more serious consequences.

Disorders of the Skin *start Wed.*

Listed below are a number of important terms relating to skin, scalp, and hair disorders that you should know.

SKIN LESIONS

A lesion (LEE-zhun) is a mark on the skin. Certain lesions could indicate an injury or damage that changes the structure of tissues or organs. There are three types of lesions: primary, secondary, and tertiary. The nail technician is concerned with primary and secondary lesions only. If you are familiar with the principal skin lesions, you will be better equipped to stop abnormal conditions that may not be treated in a salon (Figure 7-7).

The terms for the lesions listed below often indicate differences in the area of the skin layers affected and the size of the lesion. These disorders cannot be diagnosed by a nail technician or treated in the salon. They are presented only so that you can more easily spot abnormal conditions and know that a client with them should be referred to a physician.

► **FIGURE 7-7**

Primary skin lesions.

Bulla:
Same as a vesicle only greater than 0.5 cm
Example:
  Contact dermatitis, large second-degree burns, bulbous impetigo, pemphigus

Macule:
Localized changes in skin color of less than 1 cm in diameter
Example:
  Freckle

Tubercle:
Solid and elevated; however, it extends deeper than papules into the dermis or subcutaneous tissues, 0.5-2 cm
Example:
  Lipoma, erythema, nodosum, cyst

Papule:
Solid, elevated lesion less than 0.5 cm in diameter
Example:
  Warts, elevated nevi

Pustule:
Vesicles or bullae that become filled with pus, usually described as less than 0.5 cm in diameter
Example:
  Acne, impetigo, furuncles, carbuncles, folliculitis

Vesicle:
Accumulation of fluid between the upper layers of the skin; elevated mass containing serous fluid; less than 0.5 cm
Example:
  Herpes simplex, herpes zoster, chickenpox

Nodule/Tumor:
The same as a nodule only greater than 2 cm
Example:
  Carcinoma (such as advanced breast carcinoma); **not** basal cell or squamous cell of the skin

Wheal:
Localized edema in the epidermis causing irregular elevation that may be red or pale
Example:
  Insect bite or a hive

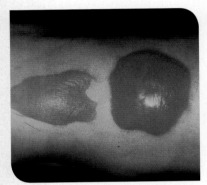

▲ **FIGURE 7-8**

Bullae.

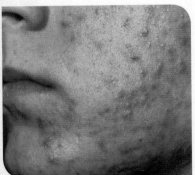

▲ **FIGURE 7-9**

Papules and pustules.

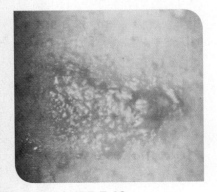

▲ **FIGURE 7-10**

Poison oak vesicles.

Primary Lesions

Primary lesions are briefly summarized below.

- Bulla (BULL-uh) (plural: bullae). A large blister containing a watery fluid; similar to a vesicle but larger (**Figure 7-8**).

- Cyst (SIST). A closed, abnormally developed sac, containing fluid or pus, that is above or below the skin.

- Macule (MAK-yool) (plural: maculae) (MAK-yuh-ly). A spot or discoloration on the skin, such as a freckle. Macules are neither raised nor sunken.

- Papule (PAP-yool). A pimple; small circumscribed elevation on the skin that contains no fluid but may develop pus.

- Pustule (PUS-chool). An inflamed pimple containing pus (**Figure 7-9**).

- Tubercle (TOO-bur-kul). An abnormal rounded, solid lump above, within, or under the skin; larger than a papule.

- Tumor (TOO-mur). A swelling; an abnormal cell mass resulting from excessive multiplication of cells, varying in size, shape, and color. Nodules are also referred to as tumors, but are smaller bumps caused by conditions such as scar tissue, fatty deposits, or infections.

- Vesicle (VES-ih-kel). A small blister or sac containing clear fluid, lying within or just beneath the epidermis. Poison ivy and poison oak, for example, produce vesicles (**Figure 7-10**).

- Wheal (WHEEL). An itchy, swollen lesion that lasts only a few hours; caused by a blow, the bite of an insect, urticaria (skin allergy), or the sting of a nettle. Examples include hives and mosquito bites.

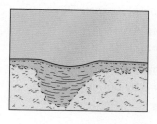
Scar

Crust

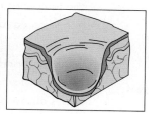
Ulcer

◀ **FIGURE 7-11**
Secondary skin lesions.

Scale

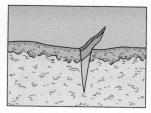
Fissure

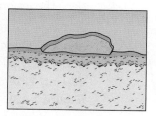
Excoriation

Secondary Lesions

Secondary skin lesions develop in the later stages of disease (**Figure 7-11**). These lesions include the following:

- Crust. Dead cells that form over a wound or blemish while it is healing; an accumulation of sebum and pus, sometimes mixed with epidermal material. An example is the scab on a sore.

- Excoriation (ek-skor-ee-AY-shun). A skin sore or abrasion produced by scratching or scraping.

- Fissure (FISH-ur). A crack in the skin that penetrates the dermis, such as chapped hands or lips.

- Keloid (KEE-loyd). A thick scar resulting from excessive growth of fibrous tissue (**Figure 7-12**).

- Scale. Any thin plate of epidermal flakes, dry, or oily. An example is abnormal or excessive dandruff.

- Scar or cicatrix (SIK-uh-triks). Light-colored, slightly raised mark on the skin formed after an injury or lesion of the skin has healed.

- Ulcer (UL-sur). An open lesion on the skin or mucous membrane of the body, accompanied by pus and loss of skin depth.

- Hematoma (HEE-mah-toh-mah). A collection of blood that is trapped underneath the nail. This blood usually results in pain and pressure that is on the nail bed. This excess blood may need draining by a physician.

DISORDERS OF THE SUDORIFEROUS (SWEAT) GLANDS

- Anhidrosis (an-hih-DROH-sis). Deficiency in perspiration, often a result of fever or certain skin diseases.

- Bromhidrosis (broh-mih-DROH-sis). Foul-smelling perspiration, usually noticeable in the armpits or on the feet.

- Hyperhidrosis (hy-per-hy-DROH-sis). Excessive sweating with unknown causes. People with hyperhidrosis may sweat even when

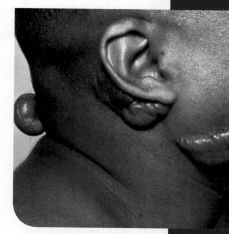

▲ **FIGURE 7-12**
Keloids.

▲ FIGURE 7-13
Eczema.

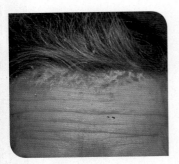

▲ FIGURE 7-14
Psoriasis.

CAUTION

Do not treat or remove hair from moles. Never attempt to treat any mole, skin tag, or other skin growth. These are medical procedures, and their removal is not within the scope of practice for which nail technicians are licensed.

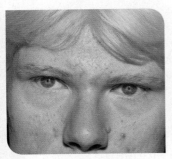

▲ FIGURE 7-15
Albinism.

the temperature is cool or when they are at complete rest. This is a medical condition that is treatable.

- Miliaria rubra (mil-ee-AIR-ee-ah ROOB-rah). Prickly heat; acute inflammatory disorder of the sweat glands, characterized by the eruption of small red vesicles and accompanied by burning, itching skin. Caused by blockage of the sweat glands.

SKIN INFLAMMATIONS

- Dermatitis (dur-muh-TY-tis). Abnormal inflammatory condition of the skin. The lesions come in various forms, such as vesicles or papules.
- Eczema (EG-zuh-muh). An inflammatory, painful itching disease of the skin, acute or chronic in nature, presenting many forms from flakey or dry itchy skin to moist lesions. There are several different types of eczema. Eczema is not contagious and can be treated by a physician. **(Figure 7-13)**.
- Psoriasis (suh-RY-uh-sis). A skin disease characterized by red patches, covered with silver-white scales usually found on the scalp, elbows, knees, chest, and lower back. Psoriasis is caused by the skin cells turning over faster than normal. It rarely occurs on the face. If irritated, bleeding points occur. Psoriasis can also affect the nail plates, causing them to develop surface pits, red spots on the nail bed, or other related symptoms. Psoriasis is not contagious **(Figure 7-14)**.

PIGMENTATION DISORDERS

Pigment can be affected by internal factors such as heredity or hormonal fluctuations, or by outside factors such as prolonged exposure to the sun. Abnormal coloration accompanies every skin disorder and many systemic disorders. A change in pigmentation can also be observed when certain drugs are being taken internally. The following terms relate to changes in the pigmentation of the skin.

- Albinism (AL-bi-niz-em). Congenital leukoderma, or absence of melanin pigment of the body, including the skin, hair, and eyes. Hair is silky white. The skin is pinkish white and will not tan. The eyes are pink, and the skin is sensitive to light and ages more rapidly **(Figure 7-15)**.
- Chloasma (kloh-AZ-mah). Condition characterized by increased pigmentation on the skin or dark spots that are not elevated. Chloasma is also called liver spots. They have nothing to do with the liver. They are generally pools of melanin, caused by cumulative sun exposure.
- Lentigenes (len-TIJ-e-neez) (singular: lentigo) (len-TY-goh). Technical term for freckles. Small yellow- to brown-colored spots on skin exposed to sunlight.
- Leukoderma (loo-koh-DUR-muh). Skin disorder characterized by light abnormal patches; caused by a burn or congenital disease that destroys the pigment-producing cells. It is classified as vitiligo and albinism.
- Nevus (NEE-vus). Small or large malformation of the skin due to abnormal pigmentation or dilated capillaries; commonly known as a birthmark.

- **Stain.** Abnormal brown or wine-colored skin discoloration with a circular and irregular shape. Its permanent color is due to the presence of darker pigment. Stains occur during aging; after certain diseases; and after the disappearance of moles, freckles, and liver spots. The cause is unknown **(Figure 7-16)**.

- **Tan.** Change in pigmentation of skin caused by exposure to ultraviolet light from tanning beds or the sun.

- **Vitiligo** (vih-til-EYE-goh). Milky-white spots (leukoderma) of the skin. Vitiligo is hereditary, and may be related to thyroid conditions. Skin with this condition must be carefully protected from overexposure to any source of UV light **(Figure 7-17)**.

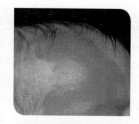

◀ **FIGURE 7-16**
Port wine stain.

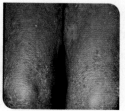

◀ **FIGURE 7-17**
Vitiligo.

HYPERTROPHIES OF THE SKIN

A hypertrophy (hy-PUR-truh-fee) of the skin is an abnormal growth of the skin. Many hypertrophies are benign, or harmless.

- **Keratoma** (kair-uh-TOH-muh). An acquired and protective, superficial, thickened patch of epidermis commonly known as callus, caused by pressure or friction on the hands and feet. If the thickening grows inward, it is called a corn.

- **Mole.** A small, brownish spot or blemish on the skin, ranging in color from pale tan to brown or bluish black. Some moles are small and flat, resembling freckles; others are raised and darker in color. Large dark hairs often occur in moles. Any change in a mole requires medical attention.

- **Skin tag.** Small brown or flesh-colored outgrowth of the skin. Skin tags occur most frequently on the neck of an older person. They can be easily removed by a dermatologist or qualified medical practitioner and should never be removed in the salon **(Figure 7-18)**.

- **Verruca** (vuh-ROO-kuh). Technical term for wart; hypertrophy of the papillae and epidermis. It is caused by a virus and is infectious. It can spread from one location to another, particularly along a scratch in the skin.

SKIN CANCER

Skin cancer—primarily caused from overexposure to the sun—comes in three distinct forms, varying in severity. Each is named for the type of cells that it affects.

- **Basal cell carcinoma** (BAY-zul SEL kar-sin-OH-muh) is the most common type and the least severe. It is often characterized by light or pearly nodules **(Figure 7-19)**.

✕ **Did You Know...**

Clients with the following skin conditions and disorders should be referred to a physician:

- Basal cell carcinoma (a form of skin cancer).
- Squamous cell carcinoma (a form of skin cancer).
- Malignant melanoma (a serious form of skin cancer).
- Anhidrosis (a deficiency in perspiration often resulting from fever or skin disease).
- Hyperhidrosis (excessive sweating caused by heat or general body weakness).
- Eczema (an inflammatory, painful itching disease of the skin).
- Irregular mole (a mole that changes shape, color, or size).
- Verruca (an infectious wart).

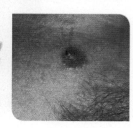

◀ **FIGURE 7-18**
Skin tags.

◀ **FIGURE 7-19**
Basal cell carcinoma.

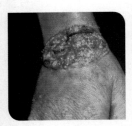

◄ FIGURE 7-20
Squamous cell carcinoma.

◄ FIGURE 7-21
Malignant melanoma.

- Squamous (SKWAY-mus) cell carcinoma is more serious than basal cell carcinoma, and often is characterized by scaly red papules or nodules (Figure 7-20).
- Malignant melanoma (muh-LIG-nent mel-uh-NOH-muh), The third and most serious form of skin cancer, which is often characterized by black or dark brown patches on the skin that may appear uneven in texture, jagged, or raised (Figure 7-21).

Malignant melanomas often appear on individuals who do not receive regular sun exposure, and are most commonly located on areas of the body that are not regularly exposed. They are often nicknamed the city person's cancer. Malignant melanoma is the least common, but most dangerous type of skin cancer.

If detected early, anyone with any of these three forms of skin cancer has a good chance for survival. It is important for a cosmetologist to be able to recognize the appearance of serious skin disorders in order to better serve clients. It also important to remember that a nail technician should not attempt to diagnose a skin disorder, but should sensitively suggest that the client seek the advice of a dermatologist.

✓ **LO5 Complete**

fyi

The American Cancer Society recommends using the ABCDE Cancer Checklist to help make potential skin cancer easier to recognize. When checking existing moles, look for changes in any of the following:

A. **Asymmetry.** One half of the mole does not match the other half.

B. **Border irregularity.** The edges of the mole are ragged or notched.

C. **Color.** The color of the mole is not the same all over. There may be shades of tan, brown, or black and sometimes even patches of red, blue, or white.

D. **Diameter.** The mole is wider than about 1/4" (although doctors are now finding more melanomas that are smaller).

E. **Evolution.** The mole evolves or changes; may include darkening or variations in color, moles that itch or hurt and changes in the shape or growth of the mole.

Changes to any of these should be examined by a physician. For more information, contact the American Cancer Society at www.cancer.org or (800) ACS-2345.

Preventing Skin Problems *Thurs.* in the Salon

Skin problems are common in every facet of the professional salon industry. Nail, skin, and hair services all can cause problems for the sensitive client. Fortunately, the vast majority of fingernail-related problems can be easily avoided—if you understand how!

DERMATITIS

As explained above, dermatitis is a medical term for abnormal skin inflammation. There are many kinds of dermatitis, but only one is important in the salon. Contact dermatitis is the most common skin disease for nail technicians. Contact dermatitis is caused by touching certain substances to the skin. This type of dermatitis can be short-term or long-term. Contact dermatitis can have several causes. When the skin is irritated by a substance, it is called irritant contact dermatitis. It is also possible to become allergic to an ingredient in a product, which is known as allergic contact dermatitis.

PROLONGED OR REPEATED CONTACT

The first most common reason for allergic reactions is prolonged or repeated direct skin contact. This type of skin problem does not occur overnight. Monomer liquid and polymer powder nail wraps, and UV gels are all capable of causing allergic reactions. In general, it takes from four to six months of repeated exposure before sensitive clients show symptoms.

As a nail technician, you are also at risk. Prolonged, repeated, or long-term exposures can cause anyone to become sensitive. This is usually caused by overexposure. Simply touching monomer liquid or UV gels does not cause sensitivities. It usually requires months of improper handling and overexposure. Some likely places for allergies to occur are:

- Between a technician's thumb and pointer finger.
- On the nail technician's wrist or palm or on the back of the hand.
- On the nail technician's face, especially the cheeks.
- On the client's eponychium, fingertips, or the sensitive tissues of the underlying nail bed.

If you examine the area where the problem occurs, you can usually determine the cause. For example, nail technicians often smooth wet brushes with their fingers. This is both prolonged and repeated contact! Eventually the area becomes sore and inflamed.

The same problem occurs when technicians lay their arms on the towels contaminated with UV gel, monomer liquid and polymer powder, or

> It also important to remember that a nail technician should not attempt to diagnose a skin disorder...

Did **You** Know...

The most important rule of being a good nail technician is: *Never touch any nail enhancement product to the skin—the client's or yours.*

filings. The palms are overexposed by picking up containers that have traces of monomer liquid and polymer powder on the outside. Small amounts of product on your hands are often transferred to the cheeks or face. Direct product contact with the skin is the cause of these facial irritations, not the vapors. Nail enhancement product vapors will not cause a skin allergy.

Touching a client's skin with any monomer liquid and polymer powder or UV gel has the same effect. This is the most common reason for client sensitivities. With each service the risk of sensitization increases. Sensitization is a greatly increased or exaggerated allergic sensitivity to products. It is extremely important that you always leave a tiny, free margin (approximately 1/16") between the product and the skin.

IMPROPER PRODUCT CONSISTENCY

The second most common reason for an allergy is improper product consistency. If too much monomer liquid is used, the result is an overly wet bead. Many technicians do not realize that the initiator, a special ingredient found in monomer liquids that is used to deliver a boost of energy needed to start a chemical reaction that joins the monomer liquid to the polymer powder, can only harden a certain amount of the monomer liquid. Wet beads are incorrectly balanced. Beads with too wet of a consistency will harden with some monomer liquid trapped inside. This extra monomer liquid eventually works its way down to the nail bed and may cause an allergic reaction. It is very important that only the polymer powders designed to work with the monomer liquids of your choice should be used. Using the wrong polymer powder with your monomer liquid may result in improper curing (hardening) leading to a service breakdown and an increased risk of adverse skin reactions.

Service breakdown and an increased risk of adverse skin reaction are also problems that can occur with UV gel nail enhancements. In fact, many things can cause UV gels to improperly cure, including:

- Applying product too thickly.
- Too short of a time under the light.
- Dirty lamps in the light unit.
- Old lamps that should be changed.
- Using a UV light unit not specifically designed for the chosen UV gel system.

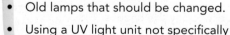

What is the difference between a UV lamp and a UV light unit?

A *UV lamp* (UV light bulb) is a special bulb that emits UV light to cure UV gel nail enhancements. There are a number of different lamps that are used to cure UV gels. There are 4-watt, 6-watt, 7-watt, 8-watt, and 9-watt lamps.

(handwritten note: now LED)

A *UV light unit* (UV light) is a specialized electronic device that powers and controls UV lamps to cure UV gel nail enhancements. Light units may look similar at first, but there are differences. The differences include the number of lamps in the unit, the distance the lamps are from the bottom of the unit, and the size of the unit. These differences will affect the curing power of the unit.

Remember that wattage is a measure of how much electricity the lamp consumes, much like miles per gallon tell you how much gasoline it will take to drive your car a certain distance. Miles per gallon will not tell you how fast the car can go, just like wattage does not indicate how much UV light a lamp will produce. For example, if a unit has 4 lamps in it and each lamp is 9 watts, then the light unit is called a 36-watt light unit. Likewise, if the light unit only has 3 lamps and each lamp is also 9 watts, then it is called a 27-watt light unit. Wattage does not indicate how much UV light a UV light unit will emit. This is why it is best to always select the UV light unit designed for the UV gel system of your choice.

UNDERCURING UV GEL ENHANCEMENTS

A third problem that can cause allergic reactions is undercuring the UV gel enhancements. Several thin coatings and long exposures lead to the best and most complete cure. UV gels are cured by a UV light unit and UV lamp inside the light unit (see sidebar). If the UV lamp is dirty or old, it does not give enough energy to fully cure the enhancement. Always use UV light units and lamps that are designed for the UV gel system you choose. There is no such thing as a UV light unit that works for all UV gel systems. If the incorrect UV light unit is used, service breakdown and adverse skin reactions become much more likely. Also, if the nail technician's arm, wrist, hands, or fingers are overexposed to dusts from undercured artificial nails, the potential for developing allergic reactions becomes more likely.

There are several other problems with UV gel services that can cause irritation or allergic reaction including:

- The gooey layer on top of UV gel enhancements must never come in contact with soft tissue. It is partially cured gel.

- Using extra-large or oversized brushes. Brushes that are too large do not save time—they cause skin exposure and may lead to allergic reactions.

- Mixing product lines or custom blending your own special mixture can also create chemical imbalances, which lead to allergic reactions. Do not take unnecessary risks. Always use products exactly as instructed and never mix your own products. If you do, do not be surprised when you or your clients develop skin problems.

It is estimated that skin disorders of the hands affect more than 30 percent of all nail technicians sometime during their careers. Skin problems and allergies force many good nail technicians to give up successful careers. No one should suffer from any work-related allergy or irritation.

ALLERGIC CONTACT DERMATITIS

Allergy-causing substances will damage the epidermis. When the skin is damaged by an allergy-causing substance, the immune system springs into action. It floods the tissue with water, trying to dilute the irritant. This is why swelling occurs.

The body is trying to stop things from getting any worse. The immune system also tells the blood to release chemicals, called histamines, that enlarge the vessels around the injury. Blood can then rush to the scene more quickly and help remove the allergy-causing substance.

You can see and feel all the extra blood under the skin. The entire area becomes red and warm, and may throb. It is the histamines that cause the itchy feeling that often accompanies allergic contact dermatitis. After everything calms down, the swelling will go away. The surrounding skin is often left damaged, scaly, cracked, and dry. Unfortunately, skin allergies often are permanent. If you can avoid repeated and/or prolonged contact with the allergy-causing substance, the symptoms may go away, but you may still have the allergy.

Remember, to avoid allergies, use the following precautions when working with monomer liquids and polymer powders:

- *Never* smooth the enhancement surface with more liquid monomer and polymer powder.

- *Never* use monomer liquid and polymer powder to clean up the edges, under the nail, or sidewalls.

- *Never* touch any monomer liquids and polymer powders, UV gels, or adhesives to the skin.

- *Never* touch the bristles of the brush with your fingers.

- *Never* mix your own special product blends.

- *Always* use a bead that has a medium consistency, never wet.

- *Always* follow the manufacturer's instructions exactly as they are printed!

CAUTION

Once a client becomes allergic, things will only get worse if you continue using the same techniques. It is best to discontinue use of the products in question until you figure out what is wrong. Medications and illness do not make clients sensitive to nail products. Only prolonged and repeated contact causes these allergies.

IRRITANT CONTACT DERMATITIS

Unlike allergies, irritant contact dermatitis can be temporary and the damage caused to you or your clients will usually reverse itself after exposure is discontinued. Corrosives are one exception. A corrosive, such as a high-pH callus softener or alphahydroxy acid peel, are types of irritants that can cause irreversible damage to living skin.

Surprisingly, tap water is a very common salon irritant. Hands that remain damp for long periods often become sore, cracked, and chapped. Avoiding the problem is simple. Always completely dry the hands. Regularly use moisturizing hand creams to compensate for loss of skin oils.

Frequent hand washing, especially in hard water, can further irritate and damage the skin. Do not wash your hands excessively. Washing your hands more than 10 or 15 times a day can cause them to feel dry or become irritated and damaged. Cleansers, detergents, and hand sanitizers can worsen the problem. They increase damage by stripping away sebum and other natural skin chemicals that protect the skin. Prolonged or repeated contact with many solvents will strip away skin oils, leaving the skin dry or damaged.

Sometimes it is difficult to determine the cause of the irritation. One way to identify the irritant is by observing the location of the reaction. Symptoms are always isolated to the contact area. The cause may be something that you may be doing to this part of the skin.

PROTECT YOURSELF

Take extreme care to keep brush handles, containers, and tabletops clean and free from product dusts and residues. Repeatedly handling and working with these items will cause overexposure if they are not kept clean. Enhancement products are not designed for skin contact!

> Many serious problems can be related to contact dermatitis.

Many serious problems can be related to contact dermatitis. Do all that you can to protect yourself and your clients so you can both enjoy nail enhancements for a long time to come!

✔ **LO6 Complete**

review questions

1. Define dermatology.

2. Briefly describe healthy skin.

3. Name the main divisions of the skin and the layers within each division.

4. List the three types of nerve fibers found in the skin.

5. Name the two types of glands contained within the skin and describe their functions.

6. What is collagen?

7. Explain the effect of overexposure to the sun on the skin.

8. What are the six important functions of the skin?

9. Why can't the skin be nourished with cosmetic products?

10. What is the one essential item that no person can live without and why is it essential to the skin and body?

11. List the factors that contribute to aging of the skin.

12. What is a skin lesion?

13. Name and describe at least five types of skin pigmentation disorders.

14. List at least six skin conditions and disorders that should be referred to a physician.

15. Name and describe the three forms of skin cancer.

16. Name the precautions that nail technicians can take to prevent allergic reactions to themselves and/or their clients.

8

nail structure and growth

✓ Learning Objectives

After you have completed this chapter, you will be able to:

1 **Describe the structure and composition of nails.**

2 **Discuss how nails grow.**

Key Terms

Page number indicates where in the chapter the term is used.

bed epithelium / 143

cuticle / 144

eponychium / 144

free edge / 143

hyponychium / 145

lateral nail fold / 145

ligament / 145

lunula / 143

matrix / 143

nail bed / 143

nail folds / 145

nail grooves / 145

nail plate / 143

nail unit / 143

natural nail / 142

onyx / 142

sidewall / 145

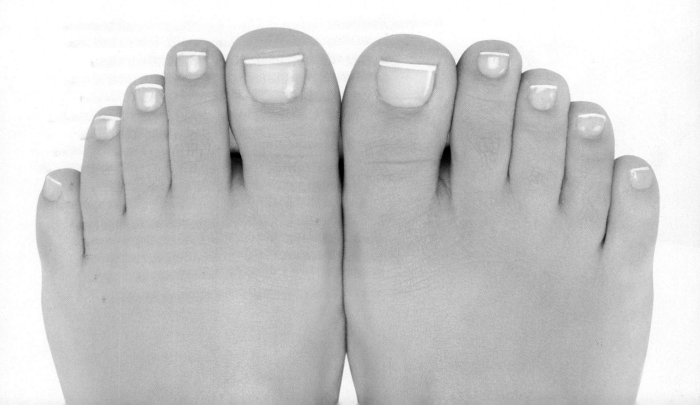

When people think of nail services, they immediately envision pleasurable manicures, pedicures, and nail enhancements that produce strong gorgeous nails. While your goal for nail school should be to learn how to expertly groom, strengthen, and beautify the nails, it is equally important to understand their physiology.

The natural nail is the hard protective plate located at the end of the finger or toe. It is an appendage of the skin and is part of the integumentary system. The nail plates protect the tips of the fingers and toes, and their appearance can reflect the general health of the body. To provide professional services and care for your clients, you must educate yourself about the natural nail's structure and growth.

The Natural Nail

The natural nail, which is technically referred to as onyx (AHN-iks), is composed mainly of keratin, the same fiber protein found in skin and hair. The keratin in natural nails is harder than the keratin in hair or skin.

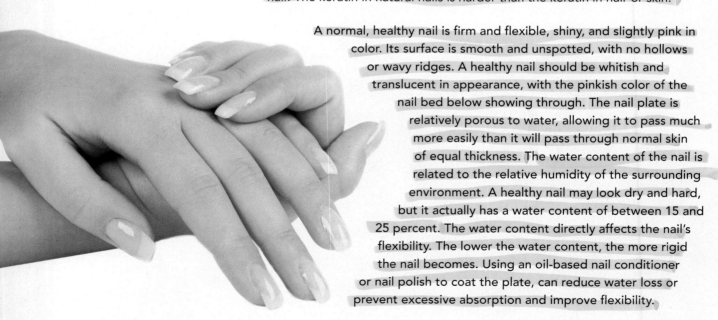

A normal, healthy nail is firm and flexible, shiny, and slightly pink in color. Its surface is smooth and unspotted, with no hollows or wavy ridges. A healthy nail should be whitish and translucent in appearance, with the pinkish color of the nail bed below showing through. The nail plate is relatively porous to water, allowing it to pass much more easily than it will pass through normal skin of equal thickness. The water content of the nail is related to the relative humidity of the surrounding environment. A healthy nail may look dry and hard, but it actually has a water content of between 15 and 25 percent. The water content directly affects the nail's flexibility. The lower the water content, the more rigid the nail becomes. Using an oil-based nail conditioner or nail polish to coat the plate, can reduce water loss or prevent excessive absorption and improve flexibility.

Nail Anatomy

The natural nail is divided into several major parts, including the nail bed, matrix, nail plate, cuticle, eponychium, hyponychium, specialized ligaments, and nail folds. Each of these parts forms the natural nail unit.

NAIL PLATE

The nail plate is the hardened keratin plate that sits on and slowly slides across the nail bed while it grows, and it is the most visible and functional part of the nail unit. The nail plate is formed by the matrix cells. The sole job of the matrix cells is to create nail plate cells. The nail plate may appear to be one solid piece, but it is actually constructed of about 100 layers of nail cells. The free edge is the part of the nail plate that extends over the tip of the finger or toe.

NAIL BED

The nail bed is the portion of living skin that supports the nail plate as it grows toward the free edge. Because it is richly supplied with blood vessels, the area under the nail plate has a pinkish appearance in the area that extends from the lunula to the area just before the free edge of the nail. The nail bed is supplied with many nerves, and is attached to the nail plate by a thin layer of tissue called the bed epithelium (ep-ih-THEE-lee-um). That bed epithelium helps guide the nail plate along the nail bed as it grows (**Figure 8-1**).

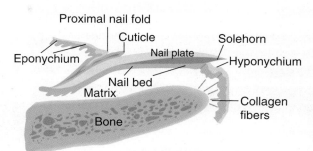

▲ FIGURE 8-1
Structure of the natural nail.

MATRIX

The matrix is the area where the nail plate cells are formed. It is composed of matrix cells that produce other cells that become the nail plate. The matrix area contains nerves, lymph, and blood vessels to nourish the matrix cells. As long as it is nourished and is kept in healthy condition, the matrix will continue to create new nail plate cells.

The matrix extends from under the nail fold at the base of the nail plate. The visible part of the matrix that extends from underneath the living skin is called the lunula (LOO-nuh-luh). It is the whitish, half-moon shape at the base of the nail. This appearance is caused by the reflection of light off the surface of the matrix. The lighter color of the lunula shows the true color of the matrix. Everyone has a lunula, but not all lunulas are visible. Some have a shorter lunula that remains hidden under the eponychium and cannot be seen.

Growth of the nails can be affected if an individual is in poor health, if there is a nail disorder or disease present, or if there has been an injury to the matrix.

Did **You** Know...

Sometimes the names used for professional nail products can create confusion. To avoid this problem, pay close attention to what the product is actually designed to do. For example, look at products marketed as *cuticle moisturizers*, *softeners*, or *conditioners*. The cuticle is dead skin on the nail plate, so why are there products designed to pamper, soften, and moisturize the cuticle? That does not make any sense! Cuticle moisturizers, softeners, or conditioners are *actually* designed for the *eponychium*, *lateral sidewalls*, and *hyponychium*—not the cuticle!

Cuticle removers are properly named and are just what they say they are. These professional products can quickly dissolve soft tissue and, when carefully applied to the nail plate, they speed removal of stubborn cuticle tissue.

CUTICLE

The cuticle (KYOO-tih-kul) is the dead, colorless tissue attached to the nail plate. The cuticle comes from the underside of the skin that lies above the natural nail plate. This tissue is incredibly sticky and difficult to remove from the nail plate. Its job is to seal the space between the natural nail plate and living skin above to prevent entry of foreign material and microorganisms and to help prevent injury and infection.

EPONYCHIUM

The eponychium (ep-oh-NIK-eeum) is the living skin at the base of the nail plate covering the matrix area. The eponychium is often confused with the cuticle. They are not the same. The cuticle is the *dead tissue* adhered to the nail plate; the eponychium is living tissue that grows up to the nail plate. The cuticle comes from the underside of this area, where it completely detaches from the eponychium and becomes strongly attached to the new growth of nail plate. It is pulled free to form a seal between the natural nail plate and the eponychium.

fyl

Many people cannot tell the difference between the cuticle and the eponychium, but it is easy when you use these simple checklists:

- Is the tissue adhering directly to the nail plate, but can be removed with gentle scraping?
- Is the tissue very thin and colorless, but is easily visible under close inspection?
- Is the tissue non-living and not directly attached to living skin?

If you answered *Yes* to *any* of the questions above, then this tissue is called the *cuticle*.

- Is the tissue any part of the skin that grows up to the base of the nail plate?
- Is the tissue any part of the skin that covers the nail matrix and lunula?
- If you cut deep enough into this tissue will it bleed?

If you answered *Yes* to *any* of the questions above, this tissue is called the *eponychium*.

Nail technicians are *permitted* to gently push back the eponychium, but are *prohibited* from cutting or trimming *any* part of the eponychium, since it is living skin. Cutting living skin is a practice that is outside the scope of nail technology and not allowed under any conditions or circumstances.

HYPONYCHIUM

The hyponychium (hy-poh-NIK-eeum) is the slightly thickened layer of skin that lies between the fingertip and the free edge of the nail plate. It forms a protective barrier that prevents microorganisms from invading and infecting the nail bed.

SPECIALIZED LIGAMENTS

A ligament (LIG-uh-munt) is a tough band of fibrous tissue that connects bones or holds an organ in place. Specialized ligaments attach the nail bed and matrix bed to the underlying bone. They are located at the base of the matrix and around the edges of the nail bed.

NAIL FOLDS

The nail folds are folds of normal skin that surround the nail plate. These folds form the nail grooves, the slits or furrows on the sides of the nail. The sidewall is also called the lateral nail fold.

✓ LO1 Complete

Nail Growth

The growth of the nail plate is affected by nutrition, exercise, and a person's general health. A normal nail grows forward from the matrix and extends over the tip of the finger. Normal, healthy nails can grow in a variety of shapes, depending on the shape of the matrix. The length, width, and curvature of the matrix determine the thickness, width, and curvature of the natural nail plate. For example, a longer matrix produces a thicker nail plate, and a highly curved matrix creates a highly curved free edge. So, nothing can make the nail plate grow thicker. This would require the size of the matrix to grow larger.

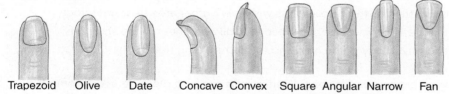

Trapezoid   Olive   Date   Concave   Convex   Square   Angular   Narrow   Fan

The average rate of nail growth in the normal adult is about 1/10" (3.7 mm) per month. Nails grow faster in the summer than they do in the winter. Children's nails grow more rapidly, while those of elderly persons grow at a slower rate. The nail of the middle finger grows fastest and the thumbnail grows the slowest. Nail growth rates increase dramatically during the last trimester of pregnancy because of hormonal changes in the body. The nail growth rate decreases dramatically after delivery and returns to normal, as do hormone levels in the body. It is a myth that this is caused by taking prenatal care vitamins; nail growth rates will accelerate whether or not a woman takes these vitamins. Although toenails grow more slowly than fingernails, they are thicker and harder because the toenail matrix is longer than the matrix found on fingernails (Figure 8-2).

Activity

Use a small magnifying glass and examine the cuticles and eponychiums of at least 10 friends or classmates. Observe how the thin cuticle tissue attaches to and rides on top of the nail plate as it emerges from under the eponychium at the base of the nail plate. Then examine the eponychium to see how these two differ in appearance. Identify which one can be removed and which should never be cut.

◀ ▼ **FIGURE 8-2**
Cross-section of the nail.

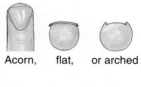

Acorn,   flat,   or arched

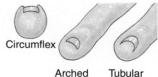

Circumflex

Arched   Tubular

NAIL MALFORMATION

If disease, injury, or infection occurs in the matrix, the shape or thickness of the nail plate can change. The natural nail will continue to grow as long as the matrix is healthy and undamaged. Ordinarily, replacement of the natural nail takes about four to six months. Toenails take nine months to one year to be fully replaced. Nails are not shed automatically or periodically, as is the case with hair.

✓ **LO2 Complete**

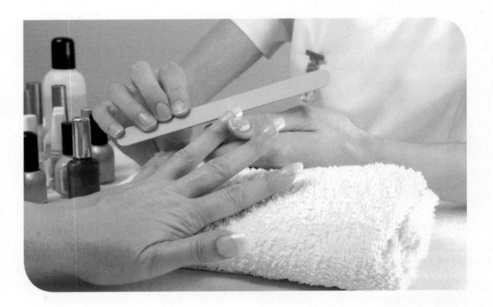

Know Your Nails

> Working on good, strong, healthy nails can be a pleasure.

Many nail professionals are interested in nails because of the creative opportunities they present. As with every other area of cosmetology, this creativity must be grounded in a full awareness of the structure and physiology of the nails and the surrounding tissue.

Working on good, strong, healthy nails can be a pleasure. As a licensed nail professional, you are only allowed to work on healthy nails and skin with no visible signs of disease or infection. Working on healthy nails will be the canvas on which your creativity and artistry can soar!

review questions

1. What is the technical term for the nail?

2. What protein is in the nail plate?

3. Describe the appearance of a normal, healthy nail.

4. Name the basic parts of the nail unit.

5. Explain the difference between the nail bed and the nail plate.

6. What part of the nail unit contains the nerve, lymph, and blood vessels?

7. Why are nail technicians not allowed to cut the skin around the base of the nail plate, even if the client requests it during the service?

9 nail diseases and disorders

chapter outline

▶ **Nail Disorders**
▶ **Nail Diseases**

☑ Learning Objectives

After you have completed this chapter, you will be able to:

1 List and describe the various disorders and irregularities of nails.

2 Recognize diseases of the nails that should not be treated in the salon.

Key Terms

Page number indicates where in the chapter the term is used.

> Nails are an interesting and surprising part of the human body.

To give clients professional and responsible service and care, you need to learn about not only the structure and growth of the nail as you did in Chapter 8, but you must also know when it is safe to work on a client. Nails are an interesting and surprising part of the human body. They are small mirrors of the general health of the entire body. You must be able to recognize conditions you may encounter while servicing clients. Some of these conditions are easily treated in the salon—hangnails, for instance, or camouflaging a bruise on the nail bed—but some are infectious and cannot be treated by salon professionals. Some of these conditions may signal mild to serious health problems that warrant the attention of a doctor and some conditions may be infectious. You will need to be able to spot these to protect yourself and your clients. Carefully studying this chapter will vastly improve your expertise in caring for nails. It will also help ensure that you are protecting your clients, rather than promoting the spread of disease.

A normal healthy nail is firm and flexible, and should be shiny and slightly pink in color, with more yellow tones in some races. Its surface should be smooth and unspotted, without any pits or splits. Certain health problems in the body can show up in the nails as visible disorders or poor nail growth.

Nail Disorders

A nail disorder is a condition caused by injury or disease. Most, if not all, of your clients have experienced one or more types of common nail disorder at some time in their lives. The technician should recognize normal and abnormal nail conditions, and understand what to do. You may be able to help your clients with nail disorders in one of two ways.

- You can tell clients that they may have a disorder and refer them to a physician, if required.
- You can cosmetically improve certain nail plate conditions if the problem is cosmetic and not a medical condition or disorder.

It is your professional responsibility and a requirement of your license to know which option to choose. A client whose nail or skin is infected, inflamed, broken, or swollen should not receive services. Instead, the client should be referred to a physician if you determine that is the appropriate recommendation, based on their condition and your training.

Bruised nails are a condition in which a blood clot forms under the nail plate, forming a dark purplish spot. These discolorations are usually due to small injuries to the nail bed. The dried blood absorbs into the bed epithelium on the underside of the nail plate and grows out with it. Treat this injured nail gently and advise your clients to be more careful with their nails if they want to avoid this problem in the future. Advise them to treat their nails like "jewels" and not "tools"! This condition can usually be covered with nail polish or camouflaged with an opaque nail enhancement.

Eggshell nails are noticeably thin, white nail plates that are much more flexible than normal. Eggshell nails are normally weaker and can curve over the free edge (Figure 9-1a and 9-1b). The condition is usually caused by improper diet, hereditary factors, internal disease, or medication. Be very careful when manicuring these nails because they are fragile and can break easily. Use the fine side of an abrasive board (240 grit or higher) to file them gently, but only if needed. It would be best not to file a nail plate of this type. A thin protective overlay of enhancement product can be helpful, but do not extend these nails beyond the free edge.

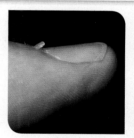

▲ FIGURE 9-1A

Eggshell nail, front view.

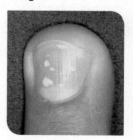

▲ FIGURE 9-1B

Eggshell nail, end view.

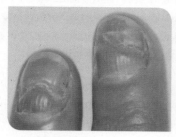

▲ FIGURE 9-2

Beau's lines.

Beau's lines are visible depressions running across the width of the natural nail plate (Figure 9-2). These usually result from major illness or injury that has traumatized the body, such as pneumonia, adverse drug reaction, surgery, heart failure, massive injury, or a long lasting high fever. Beau's lines occur because the matrix slows down in producing nail cells for an extended period of time, say a week or a month. This causes the nail plate to grow thinner for a period of time. The nail plate thickness usually returns to normal after the illness or condition is resolved.

Did You Know...

Clients cannot sign a waiver or verbally give a nail technician permission to disobey state or federal rules and regulations.

Hangnail or agnail (AG-nayl) is a condition in which the living skin around the nail plate splits and tears (Figure 9-3). Dryness of the skin or cutting this living tissue can result in hangnails. If there are no signs of infection or an open wound, advise the client that proper nail care, such as hot oil manicures, will aid in correcting the condition. Also, never cut the living skin around the natural nail plate, not even if it is dry and looks like it is not living tissue. Other than to carefully remove the thin layer of dead cuticle tissue on the nail plate, you should not cut skin anywhere on the hands or feet. Hangnails can be carefully trimmed, as long as the living skin is not cut or torn in the process. It is against state board regulations to intentionally cut or tear the client's skin and can lead to serious infections for which you and the salon may be legally liable. If not properly cared for, a hangnail can become infected. Clients with symptoms of infections in their fingers should be referred to a physician. Signs of infection are redness, pain, swelling, or pus.

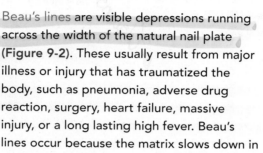

▲ FIGURE 9-3

Hangnail.

Leukonychia spots (loo-koh-NIK-ee-ah), or white spots, are a whitish discoloration of the nails, usually caused by injury to the nail matrix. They are not a symptom of any vitamin or mineral deficiency. Instead, they are results of minor damage to the matrix. It is a myth that these result from calcium or zinc deficiency (Figure 9-4). They appear frequently in the nails but do not indicate disease. As the nail continues to grow, the white spots eventually disappear.

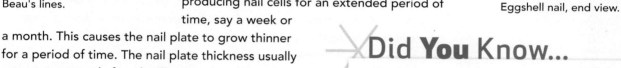

▲ FIGURE 9-4

Leukonychia spots. From R. Baran and E. Haneke, *The Nail in Differential Diagnosis* (2006) with permission from Informa Healthcare (London and New York).

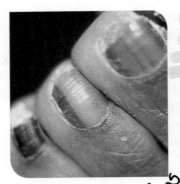

▲ FIGURE 9-5
Melanonychia.

Melanonychia (mel-uh-nuh-NIK-ee-uh) is darkening of the fingernails or toenails. It may be seen as a black band within the nail plate, extending from the base to the free edge. In some cases, it may affect the entire nail plate. A localized area of increased pigment cells (melanocytes), usually within the matrix, is responsible for this condition. As matrix cells form the nail plate, melanin is laid down within the plate by the melanocytes. This is a fairly common occurrence and considered normal in African Americans, but could be indicative of a disease condition in Caucasians (Figure 9-5).

or Asians

◀ FIGURE 9-6
Bitten nails.

Onychophagy (ahn-ih-koh-FAY-jee), or bitten nails, is the result of a habit that prompts the individual to chew the nail or the hardened, damaged skin surrounding the nail plate (Figure 9-6). Advise the client that frequent manicures and care of the hardened eponychium can often help to overcome this habit, while improving the health and appearance of the hands. Sometimes, the application of nail enhancements can beautify deformed nails and discourage the client from biting the nails. However, the bitten, damaged skin should not be treated by the nail professional and if the skin is broken or infected, no services can be provided until the area is healed.

Onychorrhexis (ahn-ih-koh-REK-sis) refers to split or brittle nails that also have a series of lengthwise ridges giving a rough appearance to the surface of the nail plate. This condition is usually caused by injury to the matrix, excessive use of cuticle removers, harsh cleaning agents, aggressive filing techniques, or hereditary causes. Nail services can be performed only if the nail is not split and exposing the nail bed. Nail enhancement product should never be applied if the nail bed is exposed. This condition may be corrected by softening the nails with a conditioning treatment, and discontinuing the use of harsh detergents, cleaners, or improper filing (Figure 9-7). These nail plates often lack sufficient moisture, so twice-daily treatments with a high-quality, penetrating nail oil can be very beneficial. Nail hardeners should always be avoided on brittle nails, since these products will increase their brittleness.

> Nail enhancement product should never be applied if the nail bed is exposed.

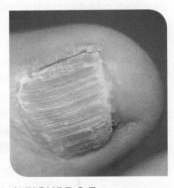

▲ FIGURE 9-7
Onychorrhexis.

Plicatured nail (plik-a-CHOORD) figuratively means "folded nail" (Figure 9-8), and is a type of highly curved nail plate often caused by injury to the matrix, but may be inherited. This condition often leads to ingrown nails.

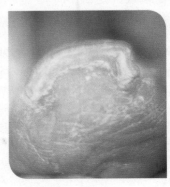

▲ FIGURE 9-8
Plicatured nail.

Nail pterygium (teh-RIJ-ee-um) is an abnormal condition that occurs when skin is stretched by the nail plate. This disorder is usually caused by serious injury, such as burns or an adverse skin reaction to chemical nail enhancement products. (**Figure 9-9**). The terms "cuticle" and "pterygium" do not designate the same thing, and they should never be used interchangeably. Nail pterygium is abnormal and is caused by damage to the eponychium or hyponychium.

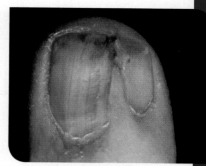

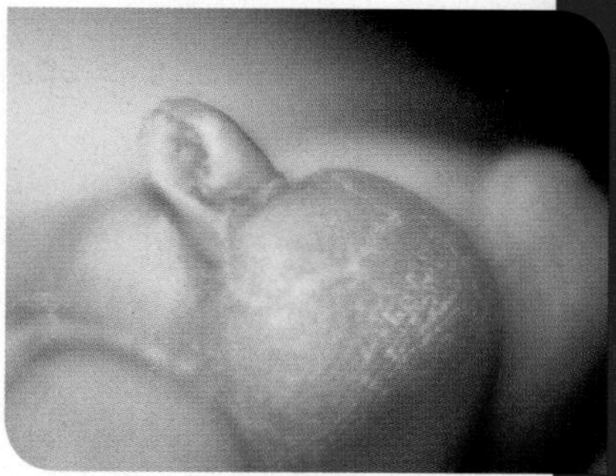

▲ **FIGURE 9-9**
Nail pterygium.

Do not treat nail pterygium and never push the extension of skin back with an instrument. Doing so will cause more injury to the tissues and will make the condition worse. The gentle massage of conditioning oils or creams into the affected area may be beneficial. If this condition becomes irritated, painful, or shows signs of infection, recommend that the client see a physician for examination and proper treatment if necessary.

Ridges running vertically down the length of the natural nail plate, are caused by uneven growth of the nails, usually the result of age. Older clients are more likely to have these ridges, and unless they become very deep and weaken the nail plate, they are perfectly normal. When manicuring a client with this condition, carefully buff the nail plate to minimize the appearance of these ridges. This helps to remove or minimize the ridges, but great care must be taken not to overly thin the nail plate, which could lead to nail plate weakness and additional damage. Ridge filler is less damaging to the natural nail plate, and can be used with colored polish to give a smooth appearance to the plate while keeping it strong and healthy.

Did You Know...

To learn more about the natural nail and understand more about infections, diseases, and disorders, be sure to read Nail Structure and Product Chemistry, second edition, by Douglas Schoon (Cengage Learning, 2005).

Splinter hemorrhages are caused by physical trauma or injury to the nail bed which damages the capillaries and allows small amounts of blood flow. As a result, the blood stains the bed epithelium, the tissue that forms "rails" to guide the nail plate along the nail bed during growth. This blood oxidizes and turns brown or black, giving the appearance of a small splinter underneath the nail plate. Splinter hemorrhages will always be positioned lengthwise in the direction of growth, in other words, pointing toward the front and back of the nail plate. The reason for this is in how the bed epithelium "rails" grow. Splinter hemorrhages are normal and the vast majority of the time are associated with some type of hard impact or other physical trauma to the fingernail or toenail.

INCREASED CURVATURE NAILS

Nails plates with a deep or sharp curvature at the free edge have this shape because of the matrix. The greater the curvature of the matrix, the greater the curvature of the free edge. Increased curvature can range from mild to severe pinching of the soft tissue at the free edge. In some cases, the free edge pinches the sidewalls into a deep curve. This is known as pincer nail or trumpet nail. The nail can also curl in upon itself (**Figure 9-10**) or may only be deformed only on one sidewall. In each of these cases, the natural nail plate should be carefully trimmed and filed. Extreme or unusual cases should be referred to a qualified medical doctor or podiatrist. A brief summary of nail disorders is found in **Table 9-1**.

▲ **FIGURE 9-10**
Pincer or trumpet nail.

TABLE 9-1 Overview of Nail Disorders

DISORDER	SIGNS OR SYMPTOMS
Discolored nails	Nails turn variety of colors; may indicate surface staining, a systemic disorder, poor blood circulation.
Bruised nails	Dark purplish spots, usually due to physical injury.
Ridged nails	Lengthwise, wavy ridges seen in normal aging.
Eggshell nails	Noticeably thin, white plate, more flexible than normal; usually caused by improper diet, hereditary factors, internal disease, or medication.
Beau's lines	Depressions running across the width of the nail plate; a result of serious illness or injury.
Hangnail	Living skin around the nail plate (often the eponychium) becomes split or torn.
Infected finger	Redness, pain, swelling, or pus; refer to physician.
Leukonychia spots	Whitish discoloration of the nails; usually caused by minor injury to the nail matrix. Not related to the body's health or vitamin deficiencies.
Melanonychia	Significant darkening of the fingernails or toenails.
Onychophagy	Bitten nails.
Onychorrhexis	Abnormal surface roughness on the nail plate.
Plicatured nails	Sharp bend in one corner of the nail plate creating increased curvature.
Nail pterygium	Abnormal stretching of skin around the nail plate; usually from serious injury or an allergic skin reaction.
Nail psoriasis	Nail surface pitting, roughness, onycholysis, and bed discolorations.
Pincer nails	A form of dramatically increased nail curvature.
Trumpet nails	A form of dramatically increased nail curvature.

✓ **LO1 Complete**

NAIL INFECTIONS: *harsh cleaning solutions*

Fungi (FUN-jy) (singular fungus, FUNG-gus) are parasites, which under some circumstances may cause infections of the feet and hands. Nail fungi are of concern to the nail salon because they are contagious and can be transmitted through contaminated implements. Fungi can spread from nail to nail on the client's feet, but it is much less likely that these pathogens will cause fingernail infections. Fungi infections prefer to grow in conditions where the skin is warm, moist, and dark, that is, on feet inside shoes. It is extremely unlikely that a nail technician could become infected from a client, but it is possible to transmit fungal infections from one client's foot or toe to another client.

With proper decontamination and disinfection practices the transmission of fungal infections can be very easily avoided. Clients with suspected nail fungal infection must be referred to a physician.

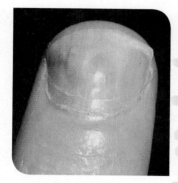

▲ FIGURE 9-11
Pseudomonas aeruginosa.

It Is Not a Mold!

In the past, discolorations of the nail plate (especially those between the plate and artificial enhancements) were incorrectly referred to as "molds." This term should not be used when referring to infections of the fingernails or toenails. The discoloration is usually a bacterial infection that is caused by several types of bacteria, such as *pseudomonas aeruginosa* or *staphylococcus aureus*. These naturally occurring skin bacteria can grow rapidly to cause an infection if conditions are correct for growth (**Figure 9-11**).

Bacterial infections are more likely the cause of infections on the hands, but can be found on the feet, as well. Bacteria do not need the same growing conditions as fungal organisms, and can thrive on fingernails just as easily as they can on the feet. Infection can be caused by the use of implements that are contaminated with large numbers of these bacteria. These infections are not a result of moisture trapped between the natural nail and artificial nail enhancements. This is a myth! Water does not cause infections. Infections are caused by large numbers of bacteria or fungal organisms on a surface. This is why proper cleansing and preparation of the natural nail plate, as well as cleaning and disinfection of implements, are so important. If these pathogens are not present, infections cannot occur. A typical bacterial infection on the nail plate can be identified in the early stages as a yellow-green spot that becomes darker in its advanced stages. The color usually changes from yellow to green to brown to black. Clients with these symptoms should be immediately referred to a physician for treatment. It is illegal for a nail professional to diagnosis or treat a nail infection. Do not remove the artificial nail unless directed to do so by the client's treating physician.

You should never provide any type of nail services to clients with a nail bacterial or fungal infection.

CAUTION *Large #*

Nail infection caused by bacteria and fungi can be easily avoided by following state board guidelines for proper cleaning and disinfection. Do not take shortcuts or omit any of the cleaning and disinfection procedures when performing an artificial nail service. Do not perform nail services for clients who are suspected of having an infection of any kind on their nails. If you repeatedly encounter nail infections on your clients' nails, you should re-examine *your* cleaning, disinfection, preparation, and application techniques. Completely disinfect all other metal and reusable implements, throw away single-use nail files, wash linens or replace with disposable towels, and thoroughly clean the table surface before and after the procedure (**Figure 9-12**).

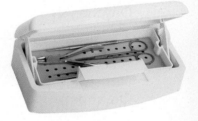

▲ FIGURE 9-12
Always practice strict cleaning protocol when working with nails.

Activity

Go to a library or use the Internet to research the "scope of practice" for medical doctors, dermatologists, and podiatrists. You should be familiar with what these professions do as well as the strict limitations placed on nail technicians' "scope of practice" so that you'll better understand what you *cannot* do.

Nail Diseases

There are several nail diseases that you may come across. A brief summary of nail diseases is found in **Table 9-2**. Any nail disease that shows signs of infection or inflammation (redness, pain, swelling, or pus) should not be diagnosed or treated in the salon. Medical examination is required for all nail diseases and any treatments will be determined by the physician.

TABLE 9-2 Overview of Nail Diseases

DISEASE	SIGNS OR SYMPTOMS
Onychia	Inflammation of the matrix and shedding of the nail.
Onychocryptosis	Ingrown nails.
Onycholysis	Separation of the nail plate and bed, often due to physical injury or allergic reactions.
Onychomadesis	Separation and falling off of a nail from the nail bed.
Onychomycosis	Fungal infection of the natural nail plate.
Paronychia	Bacterial inflammation of the tissues around the nail plate, causing pus, swelling, and redness.
Pyrogenic granuloma	Severe inflammation of the nail in which a lump of red tissue grows up from the nail bed to the nail plate.
Tinea pedis	Red itchy patches of skin on the bottom of feet and/or between the toes.

A person's occupation can cause a variety of nail infections. For instance, infections develop more readily in people who regularly place their hands in harsh cleaning solutions. Natural oils are removed from the skin by frequent exposure to soaps, solvents, and many other types of substances. The nail technician's hands are exposed daily to professional products. These products should be used according to manufacturer's instructions to ensure that they are being used correctly and safely. If those instructions or warnings tell you to avoid skin contact, you should take heed and follow such advice. If the manufacturer recommends that you wear gloves, make sure that you do so to protect your skin. Contact the product manufacturer if you are not sure how to use the product safely and obtain the MSDS.

> Product manufacturers can always provide you with additional information and guidance.

Product manufacturers can always provide you with additional information and guidance. Call them whenever you have any questions related to safe handling and proper use.

Onychosis (ahn-ih-KOH-sis) is any deformity or disease of the nails.

Onychia (uh-NIK-ee-uh) is an inflammation of the nail matrix followed by shedding of the natural nail plate. Any break in the skin surrounding the nail plate can allow pathogens to infect the matrix. Be careful to avoid injuring sensitive tissue, and make sure that all implements are properly cleaned and disinfected. Improperly cleaned and disinfected nail implements can cause this and other diseases, if an accidental injury occurs.

Onychocryptosis (ahn-ih-koh-krip-TOH-sis), or ingrown nails, can affect either the fingers or toes (Figure 9-13). In this condition, the nail grows into the sides of the tissue around the nail. The movements of walking can press the soft tissues up against the nail plate, contributing to the problem. If the tissue around the nail plate is not infected, or if the nail is not imbedded in the flesh, you can carefully trim the corner of the nail in a curved shape to relieve the pressure on the nail groove. However, if there is any redness, pain, swelling or irritation, you may not provide any services. Nail professionals are not allowed to service ingrown nails. Refer the client to a physician, if appropriate.

Onycholysis (ahn-ih-KAHL-ih-sis) is the lifting of the nail plate from the bed without shedding, usually beginning at the free edge and continuing toward the lunula area (Figure 9-14). This is usually the result of physical injury, trauma, or allergic reaction of the nail bed, and less often related to a health disorder. It often occurs when the natural nails are filed too aggressively, nail enhancements are improperly removed, or on the toenails when clients wear shoes without sufficient room for the toes. If there is no indication of an infection or open sores, a basic pedicure or manicure may be given. The nail plate should be short to avoid further injury, and the area underneath the nail plate should be kept clean and dry. If the trauma that caused the onycholysis is removed, the area will begin to slowly heal itself. Eventually, the nail plate will grow off the free edge and the hyponychium will reform the seal that provides a natural barrier against infection (Figure 9-15).

Onychomadesis (ahn-ih-koh-muh-DEE-sis) is the separation and falling off of a nail plate from the bed. It can affect fingernails and toenails (Figure 9-16). In most cases, the cause can be traced to a localized infection, injuries to the matrix, or a severe systemic illness. Drastic medical procedures such as chemotherapy may also be the cause.

Whatever the reason, once the problem is resolved, a new nail plate will eventually grow again. If onychomadesis is present, do not apply enhancements to the nail plate. If there is no indication of an infection or open sores, a basic manicure or pedicure service may be given.

Nail psoriasis often causes tiny pits or severe roughness on the surface of the nail plate. Sometimes these pits occur randomly, and sometimes they appear in evenly spaced rows. Nail psoriasis can also cause the surface of the plate to look like it has been filed with a coarse abrasive, or may create a ragged free edge, or both. (Figure 9-17).

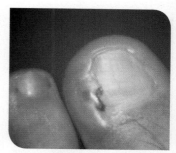
▲ FIGURE 9-13
Onychocryptosis.

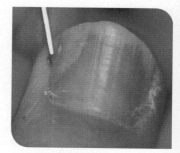
▲ FIGURE 9-14
Onycholysis.

▲ FIGURE 9-15
Onycholysis caused by trauma.

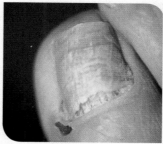
▲ FIGURE 9-16
Onychomadesis.

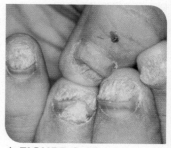
▲ FIGURE 9-17
Nail psoriasis.

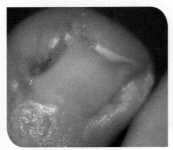

▲ FIGURE 9-18
Chronic paronychia.

▲ FIGURE 9-19
Paronychia.

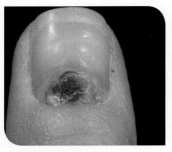

▲ FIGURE 9-20
Pyrogenic granuloma.

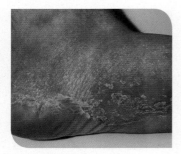

▲ FIGURE 9-21
Tinea pedis.

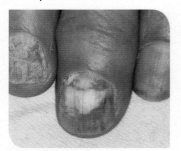

▲ FIGURE 9-22
Onychomycosis.

People with skin psoriasis often experience these nail disorders. Neither skin nor nail psoriasis are infectious diseases. Nail psoriasis can also affect the nail bed, causing it to develop yellowish to reddish spots underneath the nail plate, called salmon patches. Onycholysis is also much more prevalent in people with nail psoriasis. When all of these symptoms are present on the nail unit at the same time, nail psoriasis becomes a likely cause of the client's problem nails and they should be referred to a physician for diagnoses and treatment, if needed.

Paronychia (payr-uh-NIK-ee-uh) is a bacterial inflammation of the tissues surrounding the nail (Figure 9-18). Redness, pus, and swelling are usually seen in the skin fold adjacent to the nail plate.

Individuals who work with their hands in water, such as dishwashers and bartenders, or who must wash their hands continually, such as health care workers and food processors, are more susceptible, since their hands are often very dry or chapped from excessive exposure to water, detergents, and so on. This makes them much more likely to develop infections.

Toenails, because they spend a lot of time in a warm, moist environment, are often more susceptible to paronychia infections as well (Figure 9-19). Use moisturizing hand lotions to keep skin healthy, and keep feet clean and dry.

Pyrogenic granuloma (py-roh-JEN-ik gran-yoo-LOH-muh) is a severe inflammation of the nail in which a lump of red tissue grows up from the nail bed to the nail plate (Figure 9-20).

Tinea pedis is the medical term for fungal infections of the feet. These infections can occur on the bottoms of the feet and often appear as a red itchy rash in the spaces between the toes, most often between the fourth and fifth toe. There is sometimes a small degree of scaling of the skin. The client should be advised to wash their feet every day and dry them completely. This will make it difficult for the infection to live or grow. Advise clients to wear cotton socks and change them at least twice per day. They should also avoid wearing the same pair of shoes each day, since it can take up to 24 hours for a pair of shoes to completely dry. Over-the-counter antifungal powders can help keep feet dry and may help speed healing (Figure 9-21).

Onychomycosis (ahn-ihkoh- my-KOH-sis) is a fungal infection of the nail plate (Figure 9-22). A common form is whitish patches that can be scraped off the surface of the nail. Another common type of infection shows long whitish or pale yellowish streaks within the nail plate. A third common form causes the free edge of the nail to crumble and may even affect the entire plate. These types of infection often invade the free edge and spread toward the matrix.

✓ **LO2 Complete**

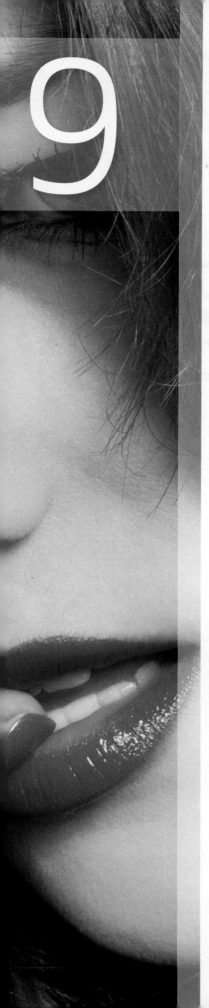

review questions

1. What conditions do fungal organisms favor for growth?

2. Name two common causes of onycholysis.

3. In what situation should a nail service not be performed?

4. What is *pseudomonas aeruginosa*? Why is it important to learn about it?

5. Name at least eight nail disorders and describe their appearance.

6. What is the most effective way to avoid transferring infections among your clients?

7. If a client develops a nail infection, can nail technicians offer treatment advice for this condition?

8. Can nail technicians treat an ingrown toenail if there is no sign of pus or discharge?

10

basics of chemistry

chapter outline

► Chemistry
► Matter
► Potential Hydrogen (pH)

✓ Learning Objectives

After you have completed this chapter, you will be able to:

1. Explain the difference between organic and inorganic chemistry.
2. Discuss the different forms of matter: elements, compounds, and mixtures.
3. Explain the difference between solutions, suspensions, and emulsions.
4. Explain pH and the pH scale.

Key Terms

Page number indicates where in the chapter the term is used.

acidic / 165

acids / 165

alkaline / 165

alkalis / 165

anion / 164

atoms / 157

cation / 164

chemical change / 159

chemical properties / 159

chemistry / 156

compound molecules / 158

element / 157

elemental molecule / 157

emulsifier / 161

emulsion / 161

exothermic reactions / 159

glycerin / 163

hydrophilic / 162

immiscible / 161

inorganic chemistry / 156

ion / 164

ionization / 164

lipophilic / 162

matter / 157

miscible / 161

molecule / 157

oil-in-water (O/W) emulsion / 162

organic chemistry / 156

pH / 164

pH scale / 165

physical change / 159

physical mixture / 160

physical properties / 159

pure substance / 159

silicones / 163

solute / 161

solution / 161

solvent / 161

surfactants / 162

suspensions / 161

volatile / 163

volatile organic compounds (VOCs) / 164

water-in-oil (W/O) emulsion / 163

"Nail services are not possible without the use of chemicals.

Nail services are not possible without the use of chemicals. To use professional products effectively and safely, all nail professionals need to have a basic understanding of chemistry. With this knowledge you can troubleshoot and solve common problems with nail services. This chapter provides you with the overview you need of basic chemistry.

Chemistry

Chemistry is the science that deals with the composition, structures, and properties of matter and how matter changes under different conditions.

Organic chemistry is the study of substances that contain the element carbon. All living things, or things that were once alive, whether they are plants or animals, contain carbon. Organic substances that contain both carbon and hydrogen can burn. Although the term "organic" is often misused to mean "natural" or "safe" because of its association with living things, not all organic substances are natural or healthy or safe.

You may be surprised to learn that poison ivy, gasoline, motor oil, plastics, synthetic fabrics, pesticides, and fertilizers are all organic substances. All nail enhancements, nail tips, and nail polishes are organic chemicals. Organic does not mean natural or healthy; it means that the material is based on carbon and hydrogen from either natural or synthetic sources.

Inorganic chemistry is the study of substances that do not contain carbon but may contain hydrogen. Most inorganic substances do not burn because they do not contain carbon. Inorganic substances are not, and never were, alive. Metals, minerals, glass, water, and air are inorganic substances. Titanium dioxide, a white pigment used to make white polymer powders and nail polish, is an example of an inorganic substance.

✓ LO1 Complete

Matter

Matter is any substance that occupies space and has mass (weight). All matter has physical and chemical properties, and exists in the form of a solid, liquid, or gas. All matter is made from chemicals, so everything made out of matter is a chemical. Matter has physical properties that you can touch, taste, smell, or see. In fact, everything you can see or touch is matter and therefore a chemical. The only exceptions are light and electricity. You can see visible light and light that electrical sparks create, but these are not made of matter. Light and electricity are forms of energy, and energy is not matter. Everything known to exist in the universe is either made of matter or energy, there are no exceptions to this rule.

Energy does not occupy space or have mass (weight). Energy is discussed in Chapter 12, Basics of Electricity. This chapter is dedicated to matter.

ELEMENTS

An element is the simplest form of chemical matter and cannot be broken down into a simpler substance without a loss of identity. There are 90 naturally occurring elements, each with its own distinctive physical and chemical properties. All matter in the universe is made up of these 90 different chemical elements. Each element is identified by a letter symbol, such as O for oxygen, C for carbon, H for hydrogen, N for nitrogen and S for sulfur. chemistry textbooks or by searching the Internet.

ATOMS

Atoms are the chemical particles from which all matter is composed, therefore all matter is made entirely of chemicals. Atoms are the structural units that make up the elements. Different elements are different from one another because the structure of their atoms is different. An atom is the smallest chemical particle of an element that retains the properties of that element. Atoms cannot be divided into simpler substances by ordinary chemical means.

MOLECULES

Just as words are made by combining letters, molecules are made by combining atoms. A molecule is a chemical combination of two or more atoms. For example, water is made from hydrogen and oxygen molecules. Carbon dioxide is made from carbon and oxygen.

Atmospheric oxygen makes up much of the air you breathe along with other chemical substances like nitrogen and water vapor. This type of oxygen is called an elemental molecule is a molecule containing two atoms of the element oxygen that are united chemically in definite proportions. It is written as O_2. Both water and air are made of 100 percent chemicals. Ozone is a very dangerous form of oxygen and a major component of smog; it contains three atoms of the element oxygen, and is written as O_3 (Figure 10-1).

▼ FIGURE 10-1

Elemental molecules contain atoms of the same element.

Atomic oxygen

Oxygen, O_2

Ozone, O_3

Sodium chloride, NaCl

Carbon dioxide, CO_2

Water, H_2O

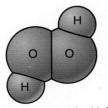

Hydrogen peroxide, H_2O_2

Compound molecules are chemical combinations of two or more atoms of different elements **(Figure 10-2)**. Sodium chloride (NaCl), or common table salt, is a chemical compound that contains one atom of the element sodium (Na) and one atom of the element chlorine (Cl).

STATES OF MATTER

All matter exists in one of three different physical forms:

1 Solid

2 Liquid

3 Gas

These three forms are called the states of matter. Matter assumes one of these states, depending on its temperature **(Figure 10-3)**.

Solid   Liquid   Gas

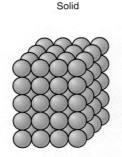 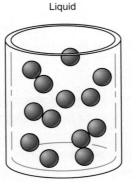 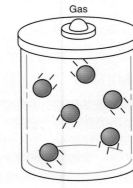

▲ FIGURE 10-3

Solids, liquids, and gases.

Like many other substances, water (H_2O) can exist in all three states of matter, depending on its temperature. For instance, when water freezes, it turns to ice. When ice melts, it turns to water. When water boils, it turns to steam vapor. When the steam cools, it turns back into water. The form of the water physically changes according to changes in the temperature, but it is still water (H_2O). It does not become a different chemical. It stays the same chemical, but in a different physical form. This is called a physical change (see Physical and Chemical Changes in this chapter).

The three different states of matter have the following distinct characteristics:

- Solids have a definite shape and volume. Ice is an example of a solid.
- Liquids have a definite volume, but not a definite shape. Water is an example of a liquid.
- Gases do not have a definite volume or shape and can never be liquid at normal temperatures and pressure. Propane is an example of a gas. It must be highly pressurized before it will turn into a liquid.
  - Vapor is a liquid that has evaporated into a gas-like state. Vapors can return to being a liquid when they cool to room temperatures, unlike gases. Steam is an example of a vapor. Vapors are not a unique state of matter; they are liquids that have undergone a physical change.

Every substance has unique properties that allow us to identify it.

PHYSICAL AND CHEMICAL PROPERTIES

Every substance has unique properties that allow us to identify it. The two different types of properties are physical and chemical.

Physical properties are those characteristics that can be determined without a chemical reaction and do not involve a chemical change. Physical properties include color, size, weight, hardness, and gloss.

Chemical properties are those characteristics that can only be determined by a chemical reaction and a chemical change in the substance. Chemical properties include the ability of iron to rust, wood to burn, or nail enhancements to harden.

Physical and Chemical Changes

Matter can be changed in two different ways. Physical forces cause physical changes and chemical reactions cause chemical changes.

A physical change is a change in the form, or physical properties of a substance, without a chemical reaction or the creation of a new substance. No chemical reactions are involved in physical change and no new chemicals are formed. Solid ice undergoes a physical change when it melts into liquid water and then converts into a vapor **(Figure 10-4)**. A physical change occurs when an abrasive file is used on the nail plate and both the nail plate and the file are changed, or when nail polish is taken off the nail with a remover solvent.

A chemical change is an alteration in the chemical composition or makeup of the substance. These changes are the result of a chemical reaction that creates a new substance or substances, usually by combining or subtracting certain elements. A chemical change results from chemical reactions that create new chemicals. These new chemical substances have new and different chemical and physical properties. **(Figure 10-5)**. An example of a chemical change is the polymerization (hardening) of nail products to create nail enhancements. Under certain circumstances chemical reactions can release a significant amount of heat. These types of chemical reactions are called exothermic (ek-soh-THUR-mik) reactions. An example of a nail product which undergoes exothermic reactions is a nail enhancement during polymerization. Exothermic reactions normally occur and, in general, clients cannot feel the heat being released. When properly applied, high-quality nail enhancement products should not create excessive amounts of heat nor should they make the client uncomfortable.

Pure Substances and Physical Mixtures

All matter can be classified as either a pure substance or a physical mixture (blend).

A pure substance is a chemical combination of matter, in definite (fixed) proportions. Pure substances have unique properties. All atoms, elements, elemental molecules, and compound molecules are pure substances. Water is a pure chemical substance that results from the combination of two atoms of the element hydrogen and one atom of the element oxygen, in definite

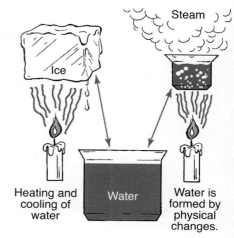

▲ FIGURE 10-4

Physical changes.

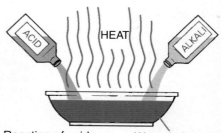

▲ FIGURE 10-5

Chemical changes.

Did **You** Know...

The sugar in grapes chemically converts into ethyl alcohol in wine when it is fermented in a wooden vat. This is an example of a chemical reaction.

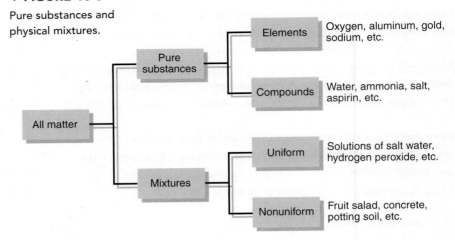

▼ FIGURE 10-6

Pure substances and physical mixtures.

proportions. Liquid water has different properties than hydrogen and oxygen gases. Most substances do not exist in a pure state. Air contains many substances including nitrogen, carbon dioxide, and water vapor.

A physical mixture is a physical combination of matter, in any proportions. The properties of a physical mixture are the combined properties of the substances in the mixture. Salt water is a physical mixture of salt and water, in any proportions. The properties of salt water are the properties contained in salt and in water. Salt water is salty and wet. Most of the products nail technicians use are physical mixtures (**Figure 10-6**). See **Table 10-1** which summarizes the differences between pure substances and physical mixtures.)

✓ **LO2 Complete**

❮ TABLE 10-1 How Pure Substances and Physical Mixtures Are United

PURE SUBSTANCES	PHYSICAL MIXTURES
United chemically	United physically
In definite (fixed) proportions	In any proportions
Have unique chemical and physical properties	Have combined chemical and physical properties.
Salt (NaCl) and water (H_2O)	Salt water is a physical mixture of salt (NaCl) and water (H_2O).

SOLUTIONS, SUSPENSIONS, AND EMULSIONS

Solutions, suspensions, and emulsions are all physical mixtures. The differences among solutions, suspensions, and emulsions are determined by the size of the particles and the solubility of the substances.

A solution is a stable uniform blend of two or more substances. The solute is the substance that is dissolved into solution. The solvent is the substance that dissolves the solute and makes the solution; it is the matrix that holds the solute. Water is known as a universal solvent because it has the ability to dissolve more substances than any other solvent. Liquids are either miscible or immiscible.

Miscible (MIS-uh-bul) liquids are mutually soluble, meaning that they can be mixed into stable solutions. Water and alcohol are examples of miscible liquids, as are polish remover and water.

Immiscible liquids are not capable of being mixed into stable solutions. Water and oil are examples of immiscible liquids.

Solutions contain small particles that are invisible to the naked eye. Solutions are usually transparent, although they may be colored. They do not separate when left still. Salt water is a solution of a solid dissolved in a liquid. Water is the solvent that dissolves the salt (solute) and holds it in solution.

Suspensions are unstable mixtures of undissolved particles floating in a liquid. Suspensions contain larger and less miscible particles than solutions. The particles are generally visible to the naked eye but not large enough to settle quickly to the bottom. Suspensions are not usually transparent and may be colored. Suspensions are unstable and separate over time which is why lotions and creams can separate in the bottle, as does the glitter in nail polish.

Oil and vinegar salad dressing is an example of a suspension, with tiny oil droplets suspended in the vinegar. The suspension will separate when left still and must be shaken well before using. Some lotions are suspensions and need to be shaken or mixed well before use. Calamine lotion and nail polish are examples of suspensions.

An emulsion is an unstable physical mixture of two or more substances that normally will not stay blended without a special ingredient called an emulsifier. An emulsifier brings two normally incompatible materials together and binds them into a uniform and fairly stable blend. Eventually, emulsions separate but usually very slowly over time. A properly formulated emulsion, stored under ideal conditions can be stable up to three years. Since this is not often the case, it is best to use all cosmetic products such as these within one year of purchase. Always refer to the product's instructions and cautions for specific details. **Table 10-2** offers a summary of the differences among solutions, suspensions, and emulsions.

Activity

Put a tablespoon of sugar in a cup of hot water. Cover it loosely with a paper towel and set it aside for a week. What happens when the water evaporates? What are the crystals that form inside the cup made from? Taste them to see whether your conclusions were right. When sugar dissolves in water is it a physical or chemical change? What about if you heated the sugar on an open flame? Would this cause a chemical or physical change?

TABLE 10-2 Solutions, Suspensions, and Emulsions

SOLUTIONS	SUSPENSIONS	EMULSIONS
Miscible	Slightly miscible	Immiscible
No surfactant	No surfactant	Surfactant
Small particles	Larger particles	Largest particles
Stable mixture	Unstable mixture	Limited stability
Usually clear	Usually cloudy	Usually a solid color
Solution of nail primer	Nail polish	Hand lotions

Surfactants (sur-FAK-tants) are substances that act as a bridge to allow oil and water to mix, or emulsify. The term surfactant is a contraction for "surface active agent." A surfactant molecule has two distinct parts (**Figure 10-7**).

Oil-loving tail

Water-loving head

▲ **FIGURE 10-7**

A surfactant molecule.

The head of the surfactant molecule is hydrophilic (hy-drah-FIL-ik), meaning water-loving, and the tail is lipophilic (ly-puh-FIL-ik), meaning oil-loving. Since "like dissolves like," the hydrophilic head dissolves in water and the lipophilic tail dissolves in oil. So a surfactant molecule mixes with and dissolves in both oil and water and temporarily joins them together to form an emulsion.

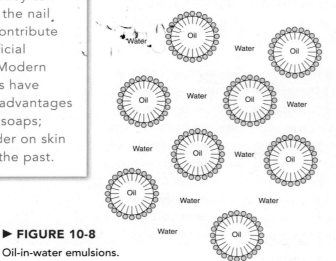

► **FIGURE 10-8**

Oil-in-water emulsions.

In an oil-in-water emulsion (O/W emulsion), oil droplets are emulsified in water. The droplets of oil are surrounded by surfactants with their lipophilic tails pointing in. Tiny oil droplets form the internal portion of an O/W emulsion because the oil is completely surrounded by water (**Figure 10-8**). Oil-in-water emulsions do not feel as greasy as water-in-oil emulsions because the oil is hidden and water forms the external portion of the emulsion.

Mayonnaise is an example of an oil-in-water emulsion of two immiscible liquids. Although oil and water are immiscible, the egg yolk in mayonnaise emulsifies the oil droplets and distributes them uniformly in the water. Without the egg yolk as an emulsifying agent, the oil and water would separate. Most of the emulsions used in a salon are oil-in-water. Lotions and creams are common examples.

Activity

Have you ever heard the saying, "Oil and water don't mix"? Pour some water into a glass, and then add a little cooking oil (or other oil). What happens? Stir the water briskly with a spoon, and then observe for a minute or two. What does the oil do?

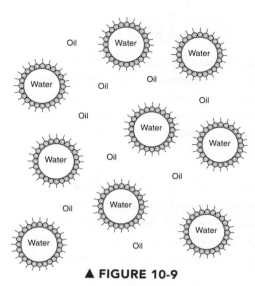

▲ **FIGURE 10-9**
Water-in-oil emulsions.

In a water-in-oil emulsion (W/O emulsion), water droplets are emulsified in oil. The droplets of water are surrounded by surfactants with their hydrophilic heads pointing in (Figure 10-9). Tiny droplets of water form the internal portion of a W/O emulsion because the water is completely surrounded by oil. Water-in-oil emulsions feel greasier than oil-in-water emulsions because the water is hidden and oil forms the external portion of the emulsion. Foot balms are an example. Since W/O emulsions are so oily, they are not often used in nail salon products.

✔ LO3 Complete

OTHER PHYSICAL MIXTURES

Ointments, pastes, pomades, and styling waxes are semisolid mixtures made with any combination of petrolatum (petroleum jelly), oil, and wax. Powders are a physical mixture of one or more types of solids. White and/or colored polymer powders are examples of mixtures of powders and pigments.

Common Product Ingredients

Some of the most common chemical ingredients used in salon products are described below.

Most people are familiar with volatile (VAHL-uh-tul) alcohols, those that evaporate easily, such as isopropyl alcohol (rubbing alcohol) and ethyl alcohol (alcoholic beverages). But there are many other types of alcohols, from free-flowing liquids to hard, waxy solids. Fatty alcohols, such as cetyl alcohol and cetearyl alcohol, are nonvolatile alcohol waxes that are used as skin conditioners.

— Contain Carbon

Glycerin (GLIS-ur-in) is a sweet, colorless, oily substance. It is used as a solvent and as a moisturizer in skin and body creams.

Silicones are a special type of oil used in nail polish dryers and as skin protectants. Silicones are less greasy than other oils and form a "breathable" film that does not cause comedones (blackheads). Silicones also impart a silky smooth feel on the skin and great shine to hair.

Volatile organic compounds (VOCs) are compounds that contain carbon (organic) and evaporate very quickly (volatile). For example, volatile organic solvents such as ethyl acetate and isopropyl alcohol are used in nail polish, base and top coats, and polish removers.

Potential Hydrogen (pH)

Although pH, the abbreviation used for potential hydrogen, is often discussed with regard to salon products, it is one of the least understood chemical properties. Notice that the term pH is written with a small p (which represents a quantity) and a capital H (which represents the hydrogen ion). Understanding what pH is and how it affects the skin and nails is essential to understanding all salon services.

WATER AND pH

Before you can understand pH, you need to first learn about ions. An ion (EYE-ahn) is an atom or molecule that carries an electrical charge. Ionization (eye-ahn-ih-ZAY-shun) causes an atom or molecule to split in two, creating a pair of ions with opposite electrical charges. An ion with a negative electrical charge is an anion (AN-eye-on). An ion with a positive electrical charge is a cation (KAT-eye-un).

In water, some of the water molecules (H_2O) naturally ionize into hydrogen ions and hydroxide ions. The pH scale measures these ions. The hydrogen ion (H+) is acidic, and the more hydrogen ions there are in a substance, the more acidic it will be. The hydroxide ion (OH–) is alkaline, and the more hydroxide ions the substance has, the more alkaline it will be. pH is only possible because of this ionization of water. Only products that contain water can have a pH.

► **FIGURE 10-10**

The ionization of water.

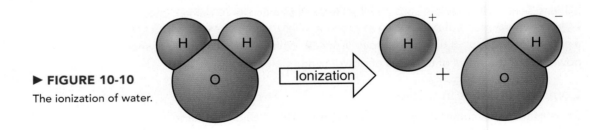

In pure water, each water molecule that ionizes produces one hydrogen ion and one hydroxide ion (**Figure 10-10**). Pure water has a neutral pH because it contains the same number of hydrogen ions as hydroxide ions. It is an equal balance of 50 percent acid and 50 percent alkaline. The pH of any substance is always a balance of both acidity and alkalinity. As acidity increases, alkalinity decreases. The opposite is also true; as alkalinity increases, acidity decreases. Even the strongest acid also contains some alkalinity (**Figure 10-11**). Pure water is 50% acidic and 50% alkaline.

▼ **FIGURE 10-11**

The pH scale.

Hair & skin
"Pure" rain (5.6)
Distilled water
Lemon juice
Vinegar
Baking soda
Ammonia

0 1 2 3 4 5 6 7 8 9 10 11 12 13 14

◄——— Acidic   Neutral   Alkaline ———►

THE pH SCALE

The pH scale measures the acidity and alkalinity of a substance. It has a range of 0 to 14. A pH of 7 indicates a neutral solution; a pH below 7 indicates an acidic solution; and a pH above 7 indicates an alkaline solution.

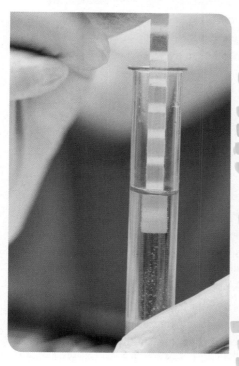

The term logarithm (LOG-ah-rhythm) means multiples of ten. Since the pH scale is a logarithmic scale, a change of one whole number represents a tenfold change in pH. That means that a pH of 8 is 10 times more alkaline than a pH of 7. A change of two whole numbers represents a change of 10 times 10, or a hundredfold change. That means that a pH of 9 is 100 times more alkaline than a pH of 7. A small change on the pH scale indicates a large change in the pH.

pH is always a balance of both acidity and alkalinity. Pure water has a pH of 7, which is an equal balance of acid and alkaline. Although a pH of 7 is neutral on the pH scale, it is not neutral compared to the hair and skin, which has an average pH of 5. Pure water, with a pH of 7, is 100 times more alkaline than a pH of 5. Pure water is 100 times more alkaline than your hair and skin. Pure water can cause the hair to swell as much as 20 percent and is drying to the skin.

ACIDS AND ALKALIS

All acids owe their chemical reactivity to the hydrogen ion (H+). Acids have a pH below 7.0 and turn litmus paper from blue to red. Alpha hydroxyl acids (AHA) are examples of acids found in salons. Citric acid is often used to help adjust the pH of a lotion or cream.

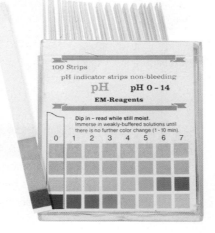

All alkalis (AL-kuh-lyz) owe their chemical reactivity to the hydroxide (OH–) ion. The terms "alkali" and "base" are interchangeable. Alkalis have a pH above 7.0 and turn litmus paper from red to blue. They feel slippery and soapy on the skin. Alkalis soften and swell the cuticle on the nail plate and callused skin.

Did You Know...

For a product to have a pH, it must contain water. Oils, waxes, nail polish, and nail monomers have no pH because they contain no water.

Sodium hydroxide, commonly known as lye, is a very strong alkali used in drain cleaners and callus softeners. These products must be used according to manufacturer's instructions. Avoid using callus removers since your license does not allow you to remove a callus. You may only smooth calluses with a gentle abrasive to make them more cosmetically attractive. High pH (greater than [>]12) callus softeners can be useful for softening the callus so that it can be smoothed more easily, but these products should be kept off living skin. Take special precautions while using these products to avoid skin contact surround the callus. After just a few minutes of skin contact, some products can cause injury, so prevent contact and carefully rinse all traces from the hands or feet. Excessive exposure can result in the feet becoming red and irritated, then quickly developing a painful skin burn. These types of products may be especially dangerous to get into the eyes, so always wear safety glasses to avoid eye contact. Consult the product's MSDS for more specific information on safe use.

> After just a few minutes of skin contact, some products can cause injury...

ACID-ALKALI NEUTRALIZATION REACTIONS

The same reaction that naturally ionizes water (H_2O) into hydrogen (H+) ions and hydroxide ions (OH−) also runs in reverse. When acids (H+) and alkalis (OH−) are mixed together in equal proportions, they neutralize each other to form water (H_2O) **(Figure 10-12)**. Liquid soaps are usually slightly acidic and can neutralize alkaline callus softener residues left on the skin after rinsing.

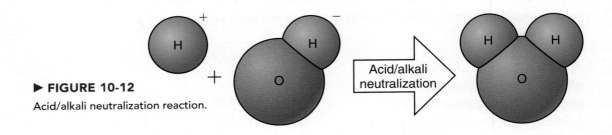

▶ **FIGURE 10-12**
Acid/alkali neutralization reaction.

✓ **LO4 Complete**

review questions

1. What is chemistry?

2. Why is a basic understanding of chemistry important?

3. What is the difference between organic and inorganic chemistry?

4. What are atoms?

5. What are elements?

6. What are the physical and chemical properties of matter? Give examples.

7. What is the difference between a physical and chemical change? Give examples.

8. Describe the three states of matter.

9. Explain elemental molecules, compound molecules, pure substances, and physical mixtures.

10. What is the difference between solutions, suspensions, and emulsions? Give examples.

11. Define pH and the pH scale.

11 nail product chemistry

SIMPLIFIED

chapter outline

- ▶ Understanding Chemicals
- ▶ Adhesion, Adhesives, and Primers
- ▶ A Clean Start
- ▶ Fingernail Coatings
- ▶ The Overexposure Principle

☑ Learning Objectives

After you have completed this chapter, you will be able to:

1. Understand the basic chemistry of nail salon products.
2. Explain adhesion and how adhesives work.
3. Identify the two main categories of nail coatings.
4. Describe the basic chemistry of all nail enhancements.
5. Describe the overexposure principle and its application to nail care products.

Key Terms

Page number indicates where in the chapter the term is used.

acrylics / 183

acrylates / 183

adhesion / 177

adhesive / 177

catalyst / 182

chemical / 176

coatings / 180

corrosive / 178

cross-linker / 182

cyanoacrylates / 183

evaporate / 176

gas / 176

methacrylates / 183

methyl methacrylate monomer (MMA) / 183

monomers / 181

oligomer / 182

overexposure / 186

overfiling / 179

plasticizers / 184

polymerization / 181

polymers / 181

primer / 177

simple polymer chains / 182

UV stabilizers / 184

vapor / 176

Almost everything you do depends on chemistry, and with a little chemical product knowledge, you can troubleshoot and solve common salon problems that may cause service breakdowns and problem nails for your clients. Chemical knowledge is the key to becoming a great nail professional. Even if you just want to "do nails," your success depends on having an understanding of chemicals and chemistry.

Understanding Chemicals

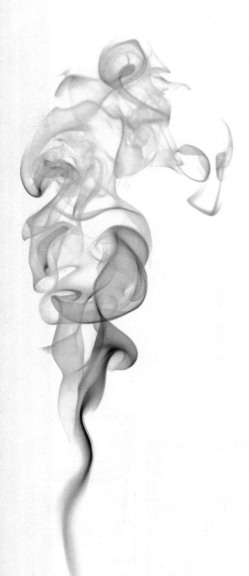

It is incorrect to think all chemicals are dangerous or toxic substances.

It is incorrect to think all chemicals are dangerous or toxic substances. Most chemicals are completely safe. Everything around you is made of chemicals. The walls, this book, food, vitamins, even oxygen is a chemical. In fact, everything you can see or touch, except light and electricity, is a chemical, a substance obtained by a chemical process or producing a chemical effect. Chemical molecules are like tiny tinker toys. They can be arranged and rearranged into an unlimited number of combinations. Petroleum oil can be chemically converted into vitamin C. Acetone can be changed into water or oxygen. Paper can be made into sugar. The possibilities are endless. In medieval times, alchemists searched in vain for ways to turn lead into gold. Today, it is possible to do so, but the process costs more than the value of the gold.

VAPORS AND GASES

Most people are very familiar with the definitions of solid and liquid. It is easy to see that something liquid is not a solid. However, since people cannot easily see the differences between gas and vapor, these terms are often confused. There is a very important difference between these two terms. It is very important that nail professionals understand proper terminology. All professions have a specific set of terms practitioners must be familiar with. As a nail professional, you should always strive to use the proper terminology.

Gases are very different from vapors. Vapors are formed when liquids evaporate into the air. Any substance that is liquid at room temperature will form vapors. The higher the temperature, the faster vapors will form. Also, vapors will turn back into liquids if they are cooled again. Water, alcohol, and acetone form vapors. All types of nail enhancement systems will form vapors. Monomer liquids (even odorless monomer), UV gels, wrap resins, and adhesives all form vapors, not gases or fumes.

Fumes are a mixture of soot-like particles and vapors. They usually result from burning substances, such as candles, incense, cigarettes, and gasoline in a car engine. They must not be confused with vapors, which are described above.

✓ LO1 Complete

Adhesion, Adhesives, and Primers

ADHESION

Adhesion is a force of nature that makes two surfaces stick together. Adhesion results when the molecules on one surface are attracted to the molecules on another surface. Paste sticks to paper because its molecules are attracted to paper molecules. Oils, waxes, and soil will contaminate a surface and block adhesion. This is why a clean, dry surface will provide better adhesion.

ADHESIVES

An adhesive is a chemical that causes two surfaces to stick together. Adhesives allow incompatible surfaces to be joined. Scotch® tape is a plastic that is coated with a sticky adhesive. Without the adhesive, the plastic film would not stick to paper. The sticky adhesive layer acts as a "go-between," and holds the tape to the paper. Adhesives are like a ship's anchor. One end of the anchor holds the ship, and the other end attaches to the ground.

There are many types of adhesives. Different adhesives are compatible with different surfaces.

PRIMER

A primer is a substance that improves adhesion. Nail polish base coats are primers. Why? Because the base coats make nail polish adhere better. Base coats act as the "go-between" or "anchor." They improve adhesion.

Other types of primers are sometimes required with nail enhancements. There are three basic types: acid-based, nonacid, and acid-free. These are especially useful if the client has oily skin. Most types of primers act like double-sided sticky tape (Figure 11-1). One side sticks well to the nail enhancement and the other side holds tightly to the nail plate. A common misconception is that nail primers "eat" or "etch" the nail. This is completely false.

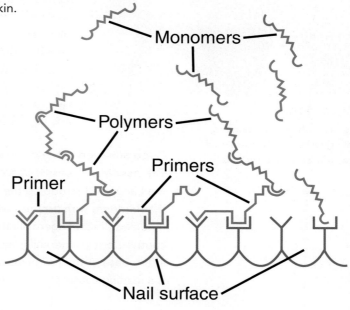

▶ **FIGURE 11-1**

Many primers act as "double-sided sticky tape" to anchor monomers firmly to the surface of the natural nail plate.

> **Nail clippings can soak for many years in any primer without dissolving.**

Nail clippings can soak for many years in any primer without dissolving. Still, nail primers must be used with caution. Some are very corrosive to soft tissue. A corrosive is a substance that can cause visible and possibly permanent skin damage. Nail primers, like most professional nail products, must never touch the skin! Acid-based primers are corrosive and can cause painful burns and scars to soft tissue. This is why corrosive primers must be kept in containers with child-resistant caps.

Even though primers will not damage or etch the nail plate, corrosive acid-based primers can burn the nail bed tissue. Overfiling the natural nail will excessively thin the nail, making it more porous. If too much primer is used, the nail plate can become overly saturated with it. Tiny amounts may reach the nail bed causing sensitivity and painful burns. It may also lead to separation of the nail plate from the bed. Use primer sparingly! One very thin coat is enough for most clients. If you find that you rely on two or more coats to prevent lifting, something is wrong! Check your nail preparation and application procedure for problems. Primer can become a crutch, covering up improper application or inadequate nail plate preparation. In the long run, it is better to get to the root of the problem and improve your technique rather than rely on excessive amounts of primer.

Not all primers are corrosive to skin. Noncorrosive primers, sometimes called *nonacid* or *acid-free* primers, do not contain methacrylic acid, the acid-base primer ingredient. Nonacid primers may actually contain other acids, while acid-free primers contain no acids and have a neutral pH. Both types are noncorrosive to skin and, therefore, will prevent burning of the soft tissue. They must be used with caution and skin contact must be avoided (**Figure 11-2**). Prolonged and repeated skin contact is caused by improper application. Over time, repeated contacts with the product may lead to an allergic reaction. If you never bring the product into contact with the skin, it is extremely unlikely the client will become allergic to the product. Product vapors do not cause skin allergies. These types of allergies are caused by repeated product skin contact. Thus, it is best to avoid all contact between nail enhancement products and soft tissues.

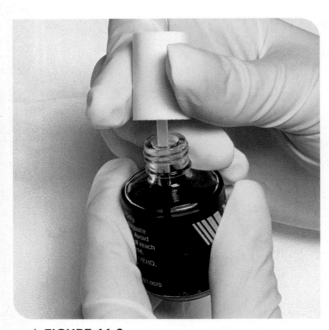

▲ FIGURE 11-2
Wear gloves when using primers, adhesives, wraps, monomer liquids, polymer powders, and UV gels.

A Clean Start

Good adhesion depends on proper technique and high-quality products. The best way to ensure success is to start with a clean, dry surface. Washing the hands and scrubbing the nail plate removes surface oils and contaminants that interfere with proper adhesion. Scrubbing also gets rid of the bacteria that cause most fingernail infections. Skipping this important step is a major contributor to fingernail infections and can lead to product lifting, mainly at the base of the nail plate near the eponychium. Improper nail preparation is a leading cause of most types of nail enhancement product lifting.

A nail dehydrator temporarily removes surface moisture from the nail plate.

Moisture on the surface of the plate can interfere with product adhesion, just as surface oils can. Some dehydrators remove both moisture and oil. But, within 30 minutes, the normal natural oils and moisture will begin to return to the nail plate. How is that information useful? It should suggest that for problem lifters, it might help to dehydrate only one hand at a time, very thoroughly, and after a good scrubbing.

It is a myth that nail enhancements and tips do not stick unless you "rough up the nail." This is absolutely false and very harmful to clients. Adhesion is best when the nail plate is clean and dry. Use only a medium/fine (240 grit) abrasive or buffer to remove only the surface shine. Avoid using heavy-grit abrasives, heavy-handed filing (too much downward pressure), and improper use of electric files. All of these can strip away layers of the natural nail plate. The thinner the nail plate, the weaker it will be. This is not what your clients pay for when they come to you for service. Thinner nail plates create a weaker foundation for nail enhancements. The thicker the nail plate, the better the foundation will be for these types of services. In other words, your clients will have better success wearing nail enhancements if you do not overfile the nail plate! This is extremely important to remember. How you treat the natural nail when applying nail enhancements nails can make or break your professional nail career. So, read the section below very carefully. Keeping the nail plate thick, strong, and healthy is the nail professional's first duty!

When nail enhancements are removed, clients can see the damage caused by heavy filing. They mistakenly blame primers and nail enhancements for what they see. Rough filing damages both the nail plate and underlying sensitive tissues of the nail bed. Do not be a nail professional who does this to customers or you might not be a nail professional for very long! Also, heavy abrasives and overfiling, excessively roughing up the nail plate, may cause the nail plate to lift and separate from the nail bed. Overfiling may cause potentially dangerous, excessive thinning of the nail plate, and once this occurs clients often develop infections under the nail plate. It must be avoided at all costs.

Overfiling the nail plate causes more problems for nail professionals than you might realize. Overfiling is one of the leading causes of nail enhancement service breakdown. It can lead to lifting, breaking, free-edge chipping, and free-edge product separation or "curling." It also can promote allergic reactions and may cause painful friction burns to the soft tissue of the nail bed.

Did **You** Know...

Nail enhancements are not designed to be taken off frequently (more than twice per year). Product removal is the most potentially damaging service that can be performed. Even when done carefully, complete removal can damage and dry the nail plate. It is best to leave the enhancements in place and only remove it when clients no longer want to wear them. Even removing them three or four times a year can be damaging. It is better for the nail tech to leave them in place and keep them properly maintained.

If you feel that you need to rough up the nail plate to get good adhesion, then something is wrong! Many nail professionals have great success without roughing up the nail plate. Why? The answer is simple: They properly spend more time and attention preparing the nail plates by removing all dead tissue from the side walls and cuticle area, as well as bacteria, oil, and moisture from the nail plate. They use correct application techniques and high-quality professional products. Lifting problems can usually be traced back to one of those key areas and usually most of these problems are caused by improper nail preparation.

LO2 Complete

Fingernail Coatings

As a nail professional, you must perform many tasks. The most important of these is to apply coatings to the nail plate. Coatings are products that cover the nail plate with a hardened film. Examples of typical coatings are nail polish, top coats, nail enhancements, and adhesives. The two main types of coatings include:

- Coatings that cure or polymerize (chemical reaction)
- Coatings that harden upon evaporation (physical reaction)

Nail polish and top coats are examples of coatings created by evaporation. Nail enhancements are examples of coatings created by chemical reactions.

Below is a brief overview of the chemistry behind these products. To learn more about the chemistry of your products and how to use them safely read **Milady's Nail Structure and Product Chemistry,** second edition, by Douglas Schoon. It is the most complete and authoritative book available on this subject.

MONOMERS AND POLYMERS

Creating a nail enhancement is a good example of a chemical reaction. Trillions of molecules must react to make just one sculptured nail. Durable and long-lasting coatings or nail enhancements are all created by chemical reactions. All monomer liquid and polymer powder nail enhancements, UV gels, wraps, and adhesives work in this fashion.

The molecules in the product join together in extremely long chains, each chain containing millions of molecules. These gigantic chains of molecules are called polymers (POL-uh-murs). Polymers can be liquids, but they are usually solid. The chemical reaction that makes polymers is called polymerization (puh-lim-uh-ruh-ZAY-shun). Sometimes the terms cure, curing, or hardening are used, but they all have the same meaning.

There are many different types of polymers. Teflon®, nylon, hair, and wood are polymers. Proteins are also polymers. Nail plates are made of a protein called keratin. So, nail plates are also polymers.

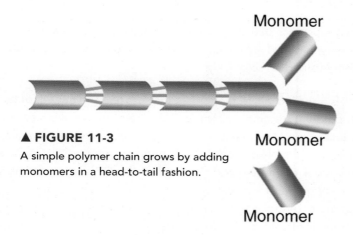

▲ FIGURE 11-3
A simple polymer chain grows by adding monomers in a head-to-tail fashion.

The individual molecules that join to make the polymer are called monomers (MON-uh-murs). In other words, monomers are the molecules that make up polymers. For example, amino acids are monomers that join together to make the polymer called keratin (**Figure 11-3**).

✓ LO3 Complete

UNDERSTANDING POLYMERIZATION

If you understand the simple basics of polymerization, you will be able to prevent many common salon problems. Monomer liquid and polymer powder nail enhancements, UV gels and wraps all seem very different, but they are actually quite similar. Each type of product is made from a different, but closely related monomer. Monomers are like track runners mingling around the starting line, patiently waiting for the race to begin. The race starts when the proper signal is given. Once given, the runners do not stop until they reach the finish line.

The same is true for monomer molecules. They are like the runners, waiting for something to trigger the polymerization. This is done by a special ingredient called an initiator. Initiator molecules energize! They carry extra energy. Each time an initiator touches a monomer, the initiator excites it with a boost of energy. But the monomer molecules do not like the extra energy and try to get rid of it. They do this by attaching themselves to the tail end of another monomer and passing the energy along. The second monomer uses the same trick to get rid of the energy.

As this game of tag continues, the chain of monomers gets longer and longer. A billion monomers can join in less than a second! Soon, the many growing monomer chains begin to get in each other's way. They become tangled and knotted, which explains why the product starts to thicken. Eventually, the chains are much too long and crowded to freely move around. The product has become a teeming mass of microscopic-sized strings. When this occurs, the surface is hard enough to file, but it will be several days before the chains reach their ultimate lengths. This explains why all nail enhancements become stronger during the first 48 hours.

A catalyst is a substance that speeds up a chemical reaction. Catalysts are found in every type of nail enhancement product and are the reason why nail enhancements harden so quickly.

An oligomer is a short chain of monomers that has had the growth of its chain halted before it became a polymer. Oligomers are useful because they can be joined quickly and easily into long chains to create polymers. In a sense, oligomers are like microwave dinners that are partially cooked so that they finish cooking more quickly in your kitchen. Oligomers are important ingredients in UV gels and are what give them their sticky consistency. Without oligomers, UV gel products might take 2 or 3 hours to harden into nail enhancements, instead of 2 or 3 minutes.

SIMPLE VERSUS CROSS-LINKING POLYMER CHAINS

Normally, the head of one monomer reacts with the tail of another, and so on. The result is a long chain of monomers attached head to tail. These are called simple polymer chains. Wraps and tip adhesives form this type of polymer. In these polymers, the tangled chains are easily unraveled by solvents, which helps explain why they are easily removed. Polymer chains can also be unraveled by force. Products with simple polymer chains are easily damaged by sharp impacts or heavy stresses. Dyes and stains can also get lodged between the tangled chains. Nail polishes, marker ink, foods, and many other things may cause unsightly stains on the surface.

To overcome these problems, UV gels and monomer liquid and polymer powder nail enhancements use small amounts of special monomers called cross-linkers. A cross-linker is a monomer that joins different polymer chains together. These cross-links are like rungs on a ladder. Cross-links create strong net-like polymers. The result is a single three-dimensional structure of great strength and flexibility known as a nail enhancement.

Activity

Polymers are everywhere in nature: hair, nails, even wood. Use the Internet or your local library and find five other useful, naturally occurring polymers not mentioned in the book. Can you find five? You should be able to since there are many thousands of examples! Explain how the five that you found are useful.

Nail plates and hair also contain cross-links, which make them tough, durable, and resilient. Besides increasing the strength of both natural nails and nail enhancements, cross-links make them more resistant to staining. Cross-links are also more resistant to solvents. This explains why cross-linked nail enhancements take longer to remove in acetone than products that are not cross-linked such as wraps and tip adhesives.

The differences between the various types of nail enhancement products are not as great as you might imagine. All nail enhancements and adhesives are based on a family of chemical ingredients called the acrylics. Yes, all of them are acrylics, even though most nail professionals use this term only in reference to monomer liquid and polymer powder systems. There are three main types of acrylics used to make all nail enhancements and glues. They are:

- Methacrylates
- Acrylates
- Cyanoacrylates

Methacrylates are used to make all monomer liquid and polymer powder systems and at least one type of UV gel. All other UV gels are based on another type of acrylic called acrylates. All nail adhesives (glues) and wraps are based on cyanoacrylates. Even though these three types of acrylics are closely related, they are different enough to create the unique properties that make these types of products useful to nail technicians. In other words, their physical properties may be very different, but the chemistry behind nail enhancement products and adhesives is very similar.

✓ LO4 Complete

Methyl methacrylate monomer (MMA), in wide use around the world for many applications, is a substance with continued use in some nail salons despite both US and international bans. Many nail technicians do not understand why they should not use MMA and wrongly believe that "toxicity" is the reason. This is untrue. When properly used, MMA is a safe substance that is in wide use around the world for many applications. MMA is the preferred bone repair cement for implantation into the body. MMA is not a carcinogen, is not absorbed into the blood to affect health, does not cause brain tumors, nor is it dangerous to inhale in the salon environment when proper ventilation is used. There are four main reasons that MMA monomer makes a poor ingredient for nail enhancement products and should never be used:

- MMA nail products do not adhere well to the nail plate without shredding the surface of the nail plate with a course abrasive or electric file which overly thins the nail plate, making it weaker.

- MMA creates nails that are rigid and difficult to break, so when jammed or caught, the overly filed or thinned natural nail plate will often break, instead of the MMA enhancement. This can cause serious nail damage.

- MMA is extremely difficult to remove and will not dissolve in product removers, so it is often pried off, creating still more damage. Since MMA products tend to discolor and become brittle more quickly than traditional products, they must be removed more often, and the difficult removal process often causes a lot of nail damage.

- The FDA and most state boards of cosmetology say not to use it! This is the most important reason. The FDA bases its prohibition on the large number of consumer complaints resulting from the use of MMA nail enhancements in the late 70s, and it continues to maintain this position today.

EVAPORATION COATINGS

Nail polishes, top coats, and base coats also form coatings. However, these products are entirely different. They do not polymerize. No chemical reactions occur, and they contain no monomers or oligomers. These products all work strictly by evaporation. The majority of the ingredients are volatile or quickly evaporating solvents. Special polymers are dissolved in these solvents. These polymers are not cross-linked polymers, so they dissolve easily. As the solvents evaporate, they leave behind a smooth polymer film. This film can hold pigments, which give it color. Artist paints and hair sprays work in the same fashion. These types of products also contain ingredients called plasticizers, which are used to keep the products flexible and UV stabilizers which control color stability and prevent sunlight from causing fading or discoloration. These types of ingredients are also found in nail enhancement products where they serve the same function. Of course, the strength of non–cross-linked polymers is much lower than cross-linked nail enhancement polymers. This is why polishes are prone to chipping and are so easily dissolved by removers. Now you can see for yourself the great difference between coatings that cure or polymerize and those that harden upon evaporation.

"BETTER FOR THE NAIL" CLAIMS

Some believe that certain types of nail enhancement products are "better" for the natural nail. Or that some are natural or organic and that others are not. This is absolutely false! All nail enhancements are made from organic substances. These are false claims designed to fool nail technicians. No one type of nail enhancement product is better for the nail plate than another.

What is better for the nail? That is easy to answer. The best thing for the natural nail is a highly skilled, educated, and conscientious nail professional. She is the natural nail's best friend. Good nail professionals protect the health of the nail plate and prevent natural nail damage and infection. The job of every nail professional is to nurture the nail plate and surrounding skin. When problems occur, they are usually caused by improper nail plate preparation, improper application or maintenance, or improper removal. It is wise to educate yourself about the products you are using and their proper application. Any nail enhancement product can be applied, worn, and removed safely. It is up to you to use your knowledge and skill to see that it happens. Educate your clients to maintain their nail enhancements routinely, so that they can help ensure that their nails will always be in perfect condition. For example, suggest professional products designed to penetrate the natural and enhanced nail to keep it flexible, that is, penetrating nail oils.

Did **You** Know...

Two common myths are that some UV gel nail enhancement products are made from sugar and that some types of polymer powders are edible. Both are false marketing claims. All UV gels are made from oligomers, not sugar. Also, no nail enhancement products are edible. They are cosmetics, not foods, and it is illegal to market them in this fashion.

PROTECT YOURSELF

Take extreme care to keep brush handles, containers, and table tops clean and free from product dusts and residues. Repeatedly handling these items will cause overexposure if the items are not kept clean. Nail enhancement products are not designed for skin contact! If you avoid contact, neither you nor your client will ever develop an allergic reaction. Many serious problems can be related to contact dermatitis. Do not fall into the trap of developing bad habits.

The Overexposure Principle

People usually think of toxic substances as dangerous poisons. You may hear the term "toxic" often, but should nail professionals try to avoid products that are toxic? The answer to this question may surprise you.

Paracelsus, a famous sixteenth-century physician, was the first to talk about poisons and toxins in a scientific way. What he said was so profound that scientists to this day quote him regularly. He said, "All substances are poisons; there is none that is not a poison. Only the dose differentiates a poison and a remedy." Paracelsus was right. He was the first to recognize that everything on Earth is toxic to some degree. There is nothing in the world that is completely non-toxic. In fact, the word "non-toxic" is a made-up marketing term that has no precise scientific meaning.

CAUTION

During the removal process of some nail enhancement products, your client's fingertips must soak in acetone. Place a clean terrycloth towel over the container. This helps to minimize the acetone vapors. Acetone is frequently used to remove nail polish and to dissolve nail enhancements and other coatings. It is one of the safest solvents used in nail salons. When used as a polish remover, acetone dissolves old polish (the solute). Acetone works quickly because it is a good solvent. However, it is highly flammable and must be used with appropriate caution. It should always be kept away from excessive heat, open flames, or other sources of ignitions.

For more information on the safety of acetone, see the **"Is Acetone Safe?"** section in **Nail Structure and Product Chemistry**, second edition, by Douglas Schoon (Cengage Learning, 2005).

To understand how to safely use and handle your products, get the manufacturer's Material Safety Data Sheet (MSDS) for important safety information that will help you protect yourself and your clients.

The *overexposure principle* is the modern-day expression of what Paracelsus learned. This important principle says that overexposure determines toxicity.

The next time someone tells you that a product is "nontoxic," think about what you have learned. Salt water is very toxic to drink. Still, you can safely swim in the ocean without fear of poisoning. Rubbing alcohol is also quite toxic. A tablespoonful could poison and kill a small child, but it is safe to use if kept out of reach of children. Toxicity does not make a substance automatically unsafe; instead it means that you must learn how to use it in a safe manner.

✓ LO5 Complete

Business Tip:

RETAIL As You Work

All services that you perform provide the perfect opportunity to sell nail care products to your clients. For example, during a hand massage, if the client comments that the lotion you are using feels good, selling it should be easy—just explain the lotion's important features and benefits, and then ask if they would like some for home use. Even if the client seems uninterested in the products that you are using, you can still sell other items.

Talk to your clients about the product you are using while applying it to their nails, hands, or feet, saying something like: "This is our latest high-shine top coat." or "This oil would be very beneficial for your dry nail plates." (or whatever else you think that they could benefit from). Feature the products you use while performing the service. At the end of the manicure, place the item in the client's hand and ask if you can add it to her or his ticket. This last step is crucial to close the sale. If you make a recommendation early in the appointment, but do not pursue it at the end, the client often forgets about it.

review questions

1. Can primers eat the nail plate? Explain your answer.

2. Define monomers.

3. What is one possible cause for an allergic reaction?

4. Give four reasons why MMA products should not be used in the nail salon.

5. _____ and/or _____ skin contact can cause a client to become allergic to products.

6. In your own words, explain what Paracelsus discovered about toxic substances. How can you use this knowledge to work safely?

7. To which family of ingredients do all UV gels, monomer liquid and polymer powder systems, wraps and adhesives belong?

12

basics of electricity

chapter outline

- ► Electricity
- ► Electrical Equipment Safety

☑ Learning Objectives

After you have completed this chapter, you will be able to:

1 Define the nature of electricity and the two types of electric current.

2 Define electrical measurements.

3 Understand the principles of electrical equipment safety.

Key Terms

Page number indicates where in the chapter the term is used.

alternating current (AC) / 191	**direct current (DC)** / 191	**milliampere (mA)** / 192
amp (ampere) (A) / 191	**electric current** / 190	**ohm (O)** / 192
catalyst / 192	**electricity** / 190	**rectifier** / 191
circuit breaker / 193	**fuse** / 193	**ultraviolet (UV) light** / 192
complete electrical circuit / 190	**grounding** / 193	**volt (voltage) (V)** / 191
conductor / 190	**insulator (or nonconductor)** / 190	**watt (W)** / 192
converter / 191	**kilowatt (K)** / 192	**wavelength** / 192

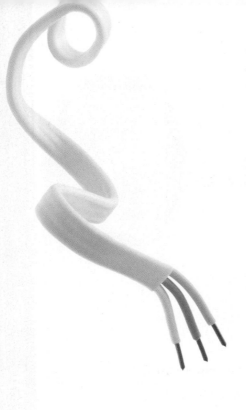

Even though you have decided to enter this field because you love to do nails, your career will heavily rely on the use of electricity. To use their products and electricity effectively and safely, all nail professionals need to have a basic working knowledge of their respective tools and how they are maintained.

Electricity

Just as this book has provided you with a very general overview of chemistry, it will do the same with electricity since this also plays an important role in your work. If you look out at lightning on a stormy night, what you are seeing is the effect of electricity. If you plug a poorly wired appliance into a socket and sparks fly out, you are also seeing the effects of electricity. You are not really "seeing" electricity, but its effects on the surrounding air. Electricity does not occupy space or mass (weight), so it is not matter. If it is not matter, then what is it? Electricity (ee-lek-TRIS-ih-tee) is the movement of particles around an atom that creates pure energy.

An electric current is the flow of electricity along a conductor. All substances can be classified as conductors or insulators (nonconductors), depending on the ease with which an electric current can be transmitted through them.

A conductor (kahn-DUK-tur) is any substance that conducts electricity. Most metals are good conductors. Copper is a particularly good conductor, and is used in electric wiring and electric motors. The ions in ordinary water make it a good conductor. This explains why you should not swim in a lake during an electrical storm.

An insulator (IN-suh-layt-ur) or nonconductor (nahn-kun-DUK-tur) is a substance that does not easily transmit electricity. Rubber, silk, wood, glass, and cement are good insulators. Electric wires are composed of twisted metal threads (conductor) covered with rubber (insulator). A complete electrical circuit (kahm-PLEET ee-LEK-trih-kul SUR-kit) is the path of electrical currents moving from the generating source through conductors and back to the generating source (Figure 12-1).

> ...your career will heavily rely on the use of electricity.

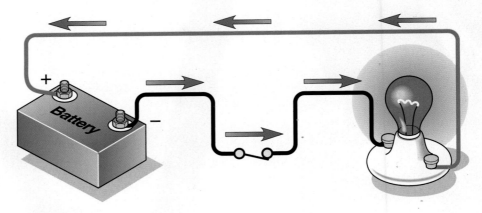

▲ FIGURE 12-1
A complete electrical circuit.

TYPES OF ELECTRIC CURRENT

There are two kinds of electric current.

1   Direct current (DC) (dy-REKT KUR-unt) is a constant, even-flowing current that travels in one direction only. Flashlights, cellular telephones, and cordless electric drills use the direct current produced by batteries. The battery in your car stores electrical energy. Without it, your car would not start in the morning. A converter (kun-VUR-tur) is an apparatus that changes direct current to alternating current. Some cars have converters that allow you to use appliances that would normally be plugged into an electrical wall outlet.

2   Alternating current (AC) (AWL-tur-nayt-ing KUR-rent) is a rapid and interrupted current, flowing first in one direction and then in the opposite direction. This change in direction happens 60 times per second. Electric files, table lamps, and paraffin heaters that plug into a wall outlet use alternating current. A rectifier (REK-ti-fy-ur) is an apparatus that changes alternating current to direct current. Cordless electric clippers and battery chargers use a rectifier to convert the AC current from an electrical wall outlet to DC current needed to recharge their DC batteries.

✓ LO1 Complete

ELECTRICAL MEASUREMENTS

The flow of an electric current can be compared to water flowing through a hose on a sink in the salon.

A volt (V) (VOLT), or voltage (VOL-tij), is the unit that measures the pressure or force that pushes the flow of electrons forward through a conductor, much like the water pressure that pushes electricity through a conductor (**Figure 12-2**). Without pressure, neither water nor electrons would flow. Car batteries are 12 volts. Normal wall sockets that power your hair dryer and curling iron are 121 volts. Most air conditioners and clothes dryers run on 220 volts. A higher voltage indicates more power.

An amp (A), (AMP) or ampere (AM-peer), is the unit that measures the strength of an electric current (the number of electrons flowing through a wire). Just as a water hose must be able to expand as the amount of water flowing through it increases, so a wire must expand with an increase in the amount of electrons (amps). A hair dryer rated at 12 amps must have a cord that is twice as thick as one rated at 5 amps; otherwise, the cord might overheat and start a fire. A higher amp rating indicates a greater number of electrons and a stronger current (**Figure 12-3**).

Low voltage   High voltage

▲ **FIGURE 12-2**
Volts measure the pressure or force that pushes electrons forward.

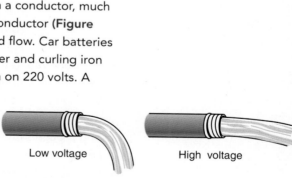

Low amperage   High amperage

▲ **FIGURE 12-3**
Amps measure the number of electrons flowing through the wire.

Wattage does not tell you how bright or powerful a light bulb is, only how much electricity it consumes during use. Some 9-watt UV bulbs create less UV light than certain 4-watt UV bulbs. You cannot judge a UV nail lamp by the wattage of its bulbs. When replacing bulbs in your UV lamp, the replacements should be the same wattage as the originals. Do not skimp and buy a cheaper replacement bulb or your service quality may suffer.

A milliampere (mA) (mil-ee-AM-peer) is one-thousandth of an ampere. The current for facial and scalp treatments is measured in milliamperes; an ampere current would be much too strong and would damage the skin or body.

An ohm (O) (OHM) is a unit that measures the resistance of an electric current. Current will not flow through a conductor unless the force (volts) is stronger than the resistance (ohms).

A watt (W) (WAHT) is a measurement of how much electric energy is being used in 1 second. A 40-watt light bulb uses 40 watts of energy per second.

A kilowatt (K) (KIL-uh-wat) is 1,000 watts. The electricity in your house is measured in kilowatts per hour (kwh). A 1,000-watt (1-kilowatt) appliance uses 1,000 watts of energy per second.

✓ **LO2 Complete**

People used to believe light traveled in straight *rays* but we now know that it oscillates in wave formations, hence the term *wavelengths*. The word *ray* still remains, but is considered antiquated and therefore should not be used in technical discussions.

LIGHT AND HEAT ENERGY

A catalyst (CAT-a-list), an action or substance that speeds up a reaction, and is used to make reactions happen more quickly. Some catalysts use heat as an energy source while others use light. Whatever the source, catalysts absorb energy like a battery. At the appropriate time, they can pass this energy to a light-sensitive initiator which in turn activates the chemical reaction like a fired gun before a race. For example, light-cured nail enhancements use ultraviolet (UV) light. Ultraviolet light (ul-truh-VY-uh-let LYT) is invisible light that has a short wavelength (giving it more energy), is less penetrating than visible light, causes chemical reactions to happen quicker, produces less heat than visible light, and kills germs. A wavelength (WAYV-lengk-th) is the distance between successive peaks of electromagnetic waves. All other nail enhancement products use heat energy during the curing process. You can see why it is important to protect UV curing products from light. Sunlight and even artificial room lights can chemically change while inside the container and become less effective. The same can happen when heat-curing monomers are put in a hot car trunk, a store window, or other warm area. The high heat may also cause discoloration or premature hardening while still in the original container.

Electrical Equipment Safety

When working with electricity, you must always be concerned with your own safety, as well as the safety

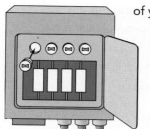

▲ FIGURE 12-4
Fuse box.

of your clients. All electrical equipment should be inspected regularly to determine whether it is in safe working order. Careless electrical connections and overloaded circuits can result in an electrical shock, a burn, or even a serious fire.

SAFETY DEVICES

A fuse (FYOOZ) is a special device that prevents excessive current from passing through a circuit. It is designed to blow out or melt when the wire becomes too hot from overloading the circuit with too much current, such as when too many appliances or faulty equipment are connected to an electricity source. To re-establish the circuit, disconnect the appliance, check all connections and insulation, and insert a new fuse (**Figure 12-4**).

A circuit breaker (SUR-kit BRAYK-ar) is a switch that automatically interrupts or shuts off an electric circuit at the first indication of overload. Circuit breakers have replaced fuses in modern electric circuits. They have all the safety features of fuses but do not require replacement, and can simply be reset. Your electric file has a circuit breaker located in the electric plug designed to protect you and your client in case of an overload or short circuit. When a circuit breaker shuts off, you should disconnect the appliance and check all connections and insulation before resetting (**Figure 12-5**).

GROUNDING

The principle of grounding (GROWND-ing), completing an electrical circuit and carrying the current safely away, is another important way of promoting electrical safety. All electrical appliances must have at least two electrical connections. The *live* connection supplies current to the circuit. The ground connection completes the circuit and carries the current safely away to the ground. If you look closely at electrical plugs with two rectangular prongs, you will see that one is slightly larger than the other. This guarantees that the plug can only be inserted one way, and protects you and your client from electrical shock in the event of a short circuit.

For added protection, some appliances have a third circular, electrical connection that provides an additional ground. This extra ground is designed to guarantee a safe path of electricity if the first ground fails, or is improperly connected. Appliances with a third circular ground offer the most protection for you and your client (**Figure 12-6**).

GUIDELINES FOR SAFE USE OF ELECTRICAL EQUIPMENT

Salon fires do occur. When they do, often it is due to electrical problems such as shorts or improper use of appliances, extension cords, or plugs. Pay close attention to the following, or you could show up to work one day and find the salon in ruin!

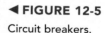

◄ FIGURE 12-5
Circuit breakers.

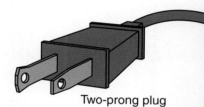
Two-prong plug

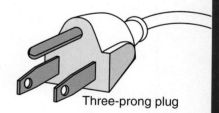
Three-prong plug

▲ FIGURE 12-6
Two-prong and three-prong plugs.

Careful attention to electrical safety helps to eliminate accidents and to ensure greater client satisfaction. The following reminders will help ensure the safe use of electricity.

- All the electrical appliances you use should be UL certified (**Figure 12-7**).
- Read all instructions carefully before using any piece of electrical equipment.
- Disconnect all appliances when not in use.
- Inspect all electrical equipment regularly.
- Keep all wires, plugs, and electrical equipment in good repair.
- Use only one plug for each outlet; overloading may cause the circuit breaker to pop (**Figure 12-8**).

▲ **FIGURE 12-7**

UL symbol as it appears on electrical devices.

▼ **FIGURE 12-8**

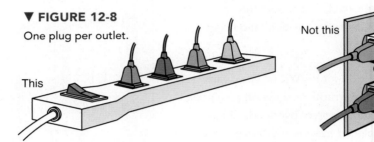

One plug per outlet.

This

Not this

- You and your client should avoid contact with water and metal surfaces when using electricity, and do not handle electrical equipment with wet hands.
- Do not leave your client unattended while connected to an electrical device.
- Keep electrical cords off the floor and away from people's feet; getting tangled in a cord could cause you or your client to trip.
- Do not attempt to clean around electric outlets while equipment is plugged in.
- Do not touch two metal objects at the same time if either is connected to an electric current.
- Do not step on or place objects on electrical cords.
- Do not allow electrical cords to become twisted; this can cause a short circuit.
- Disconnect appliances by pulling on the plug, not the cord.
- Do not attempt to repair electrical appliances unless you are qualified.

> Do not attempt to repair electrical appliances unless you are qualified.

✓ **LO3 Complete**

review questions

1. Define *electric* current.

2. Explain the difference between a conductor and an insulator or nonconductor.

3. Describe the two types of electric current and give examples of each.

4. Explain the difference between a volt and an amp.

5. Define *ohm*.

6. Define *watt* and *kilowatt*.

7. Explain the function of a fuse.

8. What is the purpose of a circuit breaker?

9. What is the purpose of grounding, and how is it accomplished?

10. List at least five steps to take for electrical safety.

Part3

NAIL CARE

13
manicuring

chapter outline

✓ Learning Objectives

After you have completed this chapter, you will be able to:

1. Identify the four types of nail implements and/or tools required to perform a manicure.

2. Explain the difference between reusable and disposable implements.

3. Name and describe the Three Part Procedure used in the performance of the basic manicure.

4. Describe the importance of hand washing in nail services.

5. Explain why a consultation is necessary each time a client has a service in the salon.

6. Name the five basic nail shapes for women.

7. Name the most popular nail shape for men.

8. List the types of massage movements most appropriate for a hand and arm massage.

9. Explain the difference between a basic manicure and a spa manicure.

10. Describe how aromatherapy is used in manicuring services.

11. Explain the use and benefits of paraffin wax in manicuring.

12. Name the correct cleaning and disinfection procedure for nail implements and tools.

13. Describe a proper setup for the manicuring table.

14. List the steps in the post-service procedure.

15. List the steps taken if there is an exposure incident in the salon.

16. List the steps in the basic manicure.

17. Describe the proper technique for the application of nail polish.

18. Describe the procedure for a paraffin wax hand treatment before a manicure.

Key Terms

Page number indicates where in the chapter the term is used.

aromatherapy / 223

dimethyl urea hardeners / 212

effleurage / 220

essential oils / 223

fine-grit abrasives / 208

friction / 220

implements / 200

lower-grit abrasive / 208

massage / 220

medium-grit abrasives / 208

metal pusher / 205

microtrauma / 205

Material Safety Data Sheet (MSDS) / 211

multi-use implements / 205

nail clippers / 206

nail creams / 210

nail oils / 210

nipper / 205

oval nail / 217

paraffin / 224

pointed nail / 217

protein hardener / 211

round nail / 217

Scope of Practice (SOP) / 200

service sets / 202

single-use implements / 205

square nail / 217

squoval nail / 217

wooden pusher / 206

Once you have learned the fundamental techniques in this chapter, you will be officially on your way to becoming a professional in the art of manicuring. Manicuring and pedicuring services are currently the fastest-growing services on salon and spa menus.

During your studies you will also be learning about the regulations concerning performing these services within your state. These regulations are very important to you, as a nail technician, and map out what is called your Scope of Practice (SOP), the list of services that you are legally allowed to perform in your specialty in your state; the SOP may or may not also state those services you cannot legally perform. Your instructor will provide these important guidelines for your adhering closely to your SOP in your state. Know that if you perform services outside these regulations concerning allowable services, you may lose your license. Also, if damages to a client occur while performing an illegal service, you are fully liable.

Nail Technology Tools

As a professional nail technician, it is important that you learn to work with the tools required for nail services and know all safety, sanitation, and disinfection procedures as stated in your state's regulations.

The four types of nail technology tools that you will incorporate into your services include:

1 Equipment

2 Implements

3 Materials

4 Professional cosmetic nail products

...many believe nitrile gloves are the best choice for nail services.

LO1 Complete

EQUIPMENT

Equipment includes all permanent tools used to perform nail services that are not implements.

Manicure Table

A standard manicuring table usually includes one or more drawers and shelves (with or without doors) for storing properly cleaned and disinfected implements and professional products **(Figure 13-1)**. The table can vary in length, but it is usually 36" to 48" long and the width is normally 16" to 21". The surface of the table must be cleaned and disinfected between clients so it must be a hard and impenetrable surface, such as Formica or glass, and be kept clear of clutter.

▼ **FIGURE 13-1**
Manicure table.

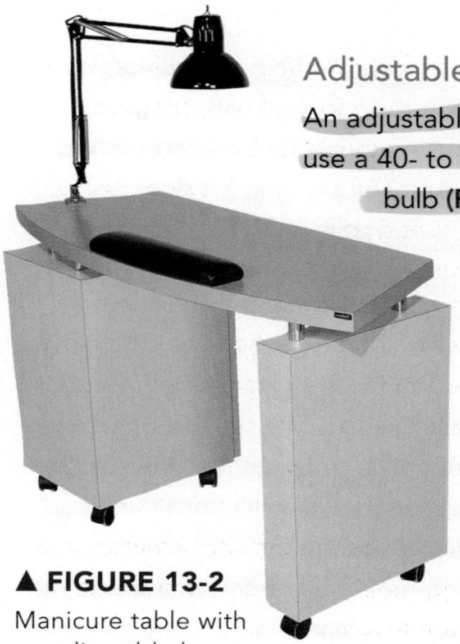

Adjustable Lamp

An adjustable lamp is attached to the table and should use a 40- to 60-watt incandescent bulb or a fluorescent bulb (Figure 13-2). Fluorescent bulbs are very popular because they emit a cooler light. Most people prefer true color fluorescent bulb lamps as they show the skin and polishes in their actual color. Fluorescent lights also do not heat up objects underneath the lamp as do high- watt incandescent bulbs. Higher temperatures caused by an incandescent bulb can increase the curing speed of some nail enhancement products.

▲ FIGURE 13-2
Manicure table with an adjustable lamp and arm cushion.

CAUTION

Do not touch or allow your client too close to your light source. Light bulbs, especially incandescent ones, can become very hot while in use and the possibility of a serious burn is very real.

Nail Technician's and Client Chairs

The nail technician's chair should be selected for ergonomics, comfort, durability, resistance to staining, and ease of cleaning. The most appropriate chair has wheels to allow the technician maneuverability, and hydraulics to allow adjustment up and down (Figure 13-3).

◀ FIGURE 13-3
Technician chair with wheels for maneuverability and hydraulics for height.

The client's chair must be durable and comfortable. For the comfort of clients, select a chair that has no or low arms on the sides, allowing it to be moved closer to the table. This will allow the client's arms to rest on the nail table and prevent the client and nail technician from needing to stretch forward. The chair should also have a supportive back so the client can sit comfortably and relax during the service.

Gloves

Gloves are Personal Protective Equipment (PPE) worn to protect the nail technician from exposure to microbes during services. The Occupational Safety and Health Act (OSHA) defines PPEs as "specialized clothing or equipment worn by an employee for protection against a hazard." The hazards this particular standard refers to are Bloodborne Pathogens (BBPs), pathogenic microorganisms that are present in human blood and other body fluids that can cause disease in humans. These pathogens include, but are not limited to, hepatitis B virus (HBV) and human immunodeficiency virus (HIV).

Currently, differences of opinion exist in the nail industry concerning whether gloves must be worn by service providers. Many say gloves should be worn throughout every service as occasionally nail technicians are exposed to blood. Others say it is only important when "there is exposure to blood," meaning a large amount of blood. The rulings from OSHA's Universal Precautions standard which was implemented in 1993 as an addition to the OSHA Act of 1970 provided the answer as per federal standards. Universal Precautions include gloves, masks, and eyewear. The Universal Precautions standard within OSHA reads: "Universal Precautions shall be observed to prevent occupational exposure to blood or other potentially infectious materials. Occupational

Did You Know...

Gloves are available in latex, vinyl, and nitrile materials. Know that some clients are allergic to latex and that vinyl gloves do not protect the wearer from many microbes. Also, latex gloves many times shred into pieces when used to apply some lotions. For that reason, many believe nitrile gloves are the best choice for nail services. They come in boxes of 100 and are available at beauty and medical supply stores.

Exposure includes any reasonably anticipated skin, eye, mucous membrane, or potential contact with blood or other potentially infectious materials that may result from the performance of an employee's duties." It does not say "exposure to a large amount of blood."

Remove gloves by inverting the cuffs and pulling them off inside out and then dispose of them into the trash. The glove taken off first is held in the hand with a glove still on it and then the glove taken off last is pulled over the first glove and they are disposed of together. If a manicure and pedicure are being performed on the same client, a new set is to be worn for each service. The technician is to perform hand washing after removing each set of gloves and before putting on a new set when two services are being performed together. Many beauty nail technicians use antimicrobial gel cleanser when cleaning the hands between sets of gloves during the same appointment.

> "Disinfectants must never be allowed to come in contact with the skin.

Fingerbowl

A fingerbowl is important for soaking the client's fingers in warm water to soften the skin and cuticle. It can be made from materials such as plastic, metal, glass, or even an attractive ceramic. It should be durable and easy to thoroughly clean and disinfect after use on each client (**Figure 13-4**).

▲ **FIGURE 13-4**
Soak fingertips to soften skin.

Disinfection Container

A disinfection container must be large enough to hold sufficient liquid disinfectant solution to completely immerse several service sets of implements. Containers that do not allow the entire implement, including handles, to be submerged are not acceptable for use in professional salons.

They come in a number of shapes, sizes, and materials and must have a lid to keep the disinfectant solution from becoming contaminated when not in use. Most containers are equipped with a tray, and lifting the tray by its handle allows the technician to remove the implements from the solution without contamination of the solution or implements. After the implements are removed from the disinfectant container, they must be rinsed and air- or towel- dried in accordance with the manufacturer's instructions and state regulations.

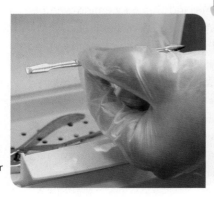

▶ **FIGURE 13-5**
Disinfection container with removable tray.

Disinfectants must never be allowed to come in contact with the skin. If your disinfectant container does not have a lift tray or basket, always remove the implements with tongs or tweezers and always wear gloves (**Figure 13-5**). It is important to wear gloves when removing and rinsing implements because gloves prevent your fingers from coming into contact with disinfectant solution.

All containers must be kept closed when not in use to prevent contamination and/or evaporation.

Client's Arm Cushion

An 8" to 12" cushion that can be cleaned with soap and water specially made for cushioning the client's arm is an option when performing nail services. It must be covered with a fresh, clean towel for each client. A clean towel that is folded or rolled to cushion size may also be used instead of a commercially purchased cushion.

Service Cushion (optional)

A foam cushion, higher in the middle, lower on the ends, can be placed between the client and the nail technician during a manicure; it is believed to provide more comfort during the service for both parties (**Figure 13-6**). It must be fully covered by a fresh, clean towel throughout each service.

Gauze and Cotton Wipe Container

This container holds absorbent cotton, lint-free wipes, or gauze squares for use during the services. This container must have a lid to protect the contents from dust and contaminants.

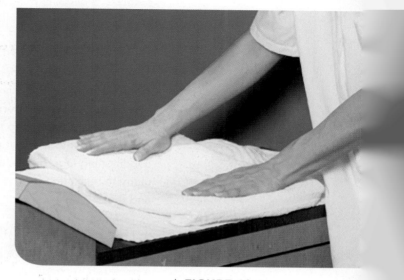

▲ **FIGURE 13-6**
Service cushion on nail table.

Trash Containers

A metal trash container with a self-closing lid that is operated by a foot pedal should be located next to your workstation (**Figure 13-7**). The trash container should be lined with a disposable trash bag and closed when not in use. It must be emptied at the end of each workday before you leave, and washed and disinfected often. A trash container with a self-closing lid is one of the best ways to prevent excessive odors and vapors in the salon.

▲ **FIGURE 13-7**
Metal trash can with a self-closing lid.

Supply Tray (Optional)

This sturdy tray holds cosmetics such as polishes, polish removers, and creams. It should be sturdy and easy to clean. Many technicians put every product they need for a service they perform on a tray and then lift the designated service's tray on and off a shelf in their station in one, efficient movement. This allows the tabletop to be clear and easy to disinfect after each service.

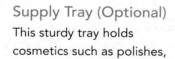

Did You Know...

Implements must be properly prepared or prepped with a thorough cleansing before being placed in the disinfectant solution. They must be scrubbed with warm water, liquid soap and a brush, then rinsed and patted dry before placing in the disinfectant liquid (**Figure 13-8**). Dirty or improperly prepared implements will not be disinfected in the solution.

▲ **FIGURE 13-8**
Scrub implements to prepare for disinfection.

Ultraviolet or Electric Nail Polish Dryer (Optional)

A nail polish dryer is designed to shorten the time necessary for the client's nail polish to dry. Electric dryers have heaters and fans that blow warm air onto the nail plates to speed evaporation of solvents from nail polishes, allowing them to harden more quickly. Light bulb–type nail polish dryers also create warmth to speed drying and work in the same fashion as electric dryers but without fans. Ultraviolet polish dryers are designed to cure polishes that contain an ingredient sensitive to the UVA wave length of the bulb in the dryer. Exposure to that wave length triggers cure (drying) of the polish.

Electric Hand/Foot Mitts (Optional)

These heated mitts are designed to add a special service to a manicure. A manicure in which these are used is a higher cost service, or it can be an add-on to a lower cost service. After the massage, conditioning lotion or even a mask is applied to the feet which are then placed in a plastic cover and inserted into the foot mitts. The warmth aids in penetration of the conditioning ingredients, adds to the comfort of the service, and provides ultimate relaxation for the client. Electric mitts are available for both hands and feet.

Terry Cloth Mitts (Optional)

These washable mitts are placed over a client's hands or feet after a penetrating conditioning product and a cover have been applied. These mitts are routinely used over paraffin to hold the heat in.

Paraffin Bath (Optional)

A paraffin tub has an automatic thermostat that will maintain the paraffin at the ideal temperature for application to the hands and feet. Paraffin is used for moisturization of the skin and can be added to manicures and pedicures for an extra charge **(Figure 13-9)**. Though there are many ways to apply paraffin from the bath, the traditional method is to dip the hands and feet into the paraffin in the bath. The paraffin coating covers the skin, holding the skin's natural moisture in the epidermal layers and thus promoting moisturization of the skin. This bath is often the first purchase for many salons and spas after their basic equipment. Check the regulations in your state concerning the use of paraffin in salons.

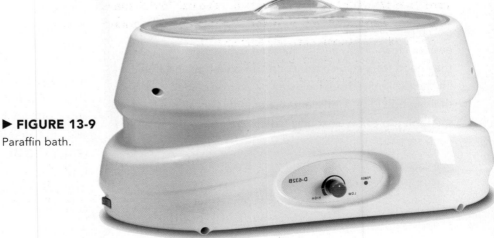

▶ **FIGURE 13-9**
Paraffin bath.

IMPLEMENTS

Implements are tools used to perform your services and are multiple use (reusable) or single use (disposable). Multi-use implements are generally stainless steel as they must be properly cleaned and disinfected prior to use on another client. Less expensive nickel-plated metal implements will corrode during disinfection. Single-use implements cannot be reused and must be thrown away after a single use. It is recommended that nail technicians have several clean and disinfected service sets of implements available for use at all times.

✓ LO2 Complete

Did **You** Know...

Many nail technicians separate their clean, disinfected implements into service sets (sets of all the clean and disinfected tools that will be used in a service). These sets can be wrapped in a clean towel and stored in a clean place, or they can be inserted into a sterile pouch before being autoclaved. At the start of each service, open the implements in front of the client so that they can see that the set has been disinfected prior to their arrival.

Multi-use Implements

Metal Pusher

The metal pusher, many times incorrectly called a cuticle pusher, is actually not to be used to push back the eponychium, but is designed to gently scrape cuticle tissue from the natural nail plate. Metal pushers must be stainless steel and used carefully to prevent damage to the nail, the nail matrix, or microscopic trauma or injury to the tissues. Improper use on the nail can cause grooving. Damage to the nail matrix can cause nail growth problems, and tiny unseen openings in the skin, called microtrauma, that can allow microbes entrance into the skin and can lead to infection.

If you have rough or sharp edges on your metal pusher, use an abrasive to smooth or remove them. This prevents digging into the nail plate or damaging the protective barriers created by the eponychium and cuticle.

Hold the metal pusher the way you hold a pencil with the flat end held at a 20-30 degree angle from the nail plate. The spoon end is used to carefully loosen and push back the dead cuticle tissue on the nail plate **(Figure 13-10)**.

▲ **FIGURE 13-10**
Metal pusher.

Nippers

A nipper is a stainless steel implement used to carefully trim away *dead* skin around the nails. It is never used to cut, rip, or tear live tissue as the live nail fold tissue is important to ward off microbes and prevent infection around the nail plate. Nippers must be cleaned and disinfected before use on every client, taking special care to open the hinges for cleaning and disinfecting.

Always maintain a sharp edge on your nippers to prevent accidental ripping and tearing into the live tissue.

It is important that you learn the correct use of nail nippers while in school. To use nippers, hold your thumb around one handle and three fingers around the other with the blades facing the nail plate. Your index finger is placed on the box joint to help control the blade and guide it properly **(Figure 13-11)**.

▲ **FIGURE 13-11**
Nippers.

Tweezers

Tweezers are multi-task implements for lifting small bits of debris from the nail plate, retrieving and placing nail art, removing implements from disinfectant solutions, and much more **(Figure 13-12).** They must be properly cleaned and disinfected before use on any client as they may come in contact with a client's skin or nails. They must be stainless steel to allow disinfection after use.

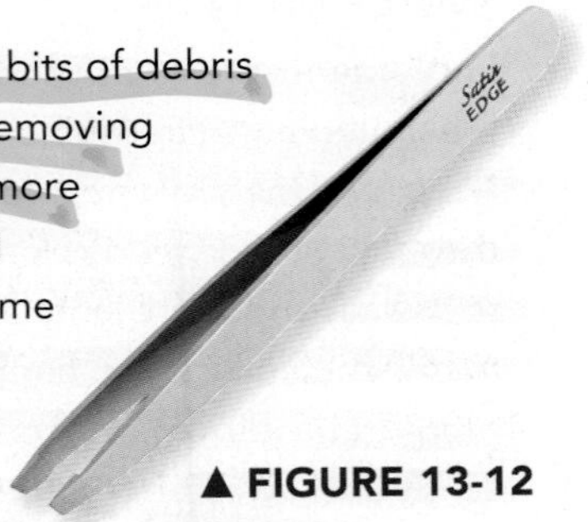

▲ FIGURE 13-12
Tweezers.

Did **You** Know...

A nail technician will need at least three sets of quality, stainless steel implements to always have a completely clean and disinfected set ready for each client. One set is in the disinfectant, one is being used, and another is ready for use. By always having a set of implements ready, your clients won't have to wait for the disinfection process if you run late. When the current client is finished, the implements in the disinfectant are removed, rinsed and dried or placed to air dry, the ones just used are prepared for disinfection, and the ones ready are used on the next client. Remember, it takes approximately 20 minutes to properly clean and disinfect implements after each use.

Nail Clippers

Nail clippers shorten the free edge quickly and efficiently. If your client's nails are too long, clipping them will save filing time in your service. Clip the nails from each side to prevent stress damage to the sides of the nail plates and then file to shape the nails. Nail clippers must be properly cleaned and disinfected before use on every client. These implements must be stainless steel to be properly disinfected.

Single-use Implements

Brushes and Applicators

Any brush or applicator that comes into contact with a client's nails or skin during a manicure or pedicure must be properly cleaned and disinfected before use on another client. If they cannot be properly cleaned and disinfected according to your state's regulations, they must be disposed of after a single use. Check with the manufacturer if you are unsure whether a brush or applicator can be properly cleansed and disinfected.

Wooden Pusher

The wooden pusher is used to remove cuticle tissue from the nail plate, to clean under the free edge of the nail, or to apply products. Hold the stick as you would a pencil with the tip at 20-30 degrees from the nail plate while pushing the cuticle free **(Figure 13-13).** It is a single-use implement and not intended for reuse or disinfection. Apply nail products by completely wrapping the end of the stick with a small piece of cotton and placing or dipping the product onto the cotton. If the cotton tip is dipped into product, enough must be retrieved for the entire application. If more product is needed, the cotton on your wooden pusher must be changed after each application to prevent contamination of the product. Using products that have spout lids can shorten time in the application. The spout must not touch the cotton tip, nail plate or the skin.

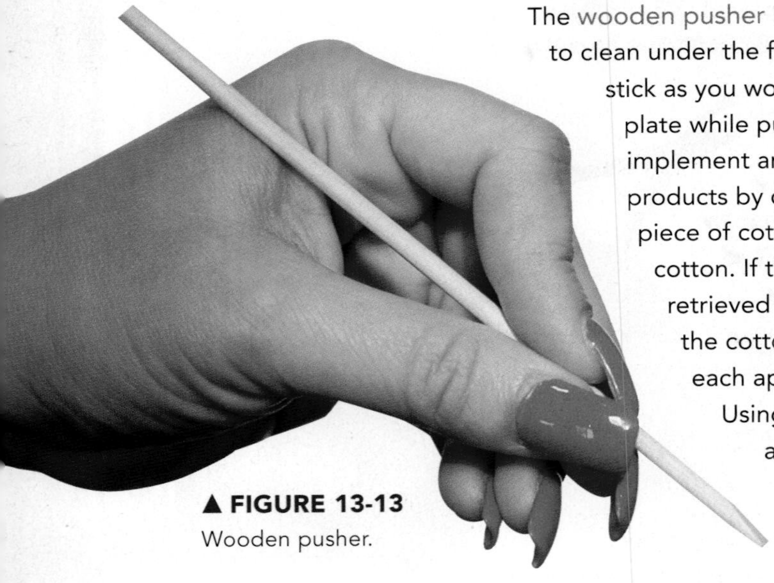

▲ FIGURE 13-13
Wooden pusher.

Nail Brush

This plastic implement is used in many ways during nail services **(Figure 13-14)**. It is used by the client when arriving at the salon while performing the hand washing procedure and by the technician to cleanse during hand washing between clients. It is used during the manicure to remove debris from the nail plate, and to scrub the implements before disinfection, a very important task.

It is recommended that you purchase inexpensive, readily available packages of disposable brushes to apply products that can support bacterial growth, one application for each brush. You dip enough product out of the container on your brush for your entire application, or pour the product into a clean dappen dish for use. The brush is disposed of after each use.

One exception to this rule would be brushes used in products that are not capable of harboring or supporting the growth of pathogenic microbes, such as alcohol, nail polish, monomers and polymers, UV gels, nail primers, dehydrators, and bleaches, among others. Since these products cannot harbor or support pathogen growth, these brushes do not need to be cleaned and disinfected between each use unless it touches a contaminated nail immediately before moving to another nail. Since nail technicians can only work on healthy nails, that should not happen. However, a brush used to apply penetrating nail oil to the nail plate would be considered contaminated if the brush is placed back into the product, since these products can become contaminated with bacteria and can support growth of pathogens. Disposable brushes or droppers should be used to apply oils to the nail plate or surrounding skin.

Did **You** Know...

It is the salon's choice as to whether nail brushes are reused or disposed of after a single use. To prevent cross-contamination, the brush must be clean and fresh for each client. It must be disinfected between services, thrown away after use, or sent home with the client. Many salons find a resource for inexpensive brushes so they can dispose of or send the used brushes home with the client. This eliminates the time and effort needed for disinfection and eliminates the need for a larger disinfection container and the counter space it would occupy. It also saves the increased cost of liquid for the brush disinfection process.

MATERIALS

Materials and supplies used during a manicure are designed to be single-use and must be replaced for each client. These items are considered to be not "reusable."

Abrasive Nail Files and Buffers

Abrasive nail files **(Figure 13-15)** and buffers **(Figure 13-16)** are available in many different types and grits, such as those with firm, rigid supporting cores or others with padded and very flexible cores. They are generally single-use only. Grits range from less than 180 to over 240 per centimeter. A rule of thumb is the lower the grit, the larger the abrasive particles on the file and the more

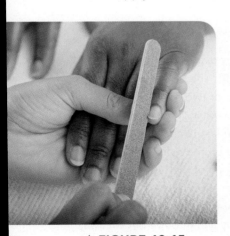

aggressive its action. Therefore, lower-grit abrasive files and buffers (less than 180 grit) are aggressive and will quickly reduce the thickness of any surface. Lower-grit files also produce deeper and more visible scratches on the surface than do higher-grit. Therefore, lower-grit files must be used with greater care and generally are not used on natural nails, since they can cause damage.

You must prep or edge your abrasive files before using them on a client to prevent harm of the client by the sharp edges. These files are stamped from a large sheet of prepared materials, leaving very sharp edges, and these sharp edges are not removed before the files are shipped. You are responsible for removing this damaging edge from every new file.

▲ FIGURE 13-17
Store disinfected implements in a covered container.

To prepare it for use, rub another (clean, unused) file across the edge to remove that sharp edge; this action is referred to as "file prepping." Many nail technicians prepare all their new files and then store them in a clean container. If this edge is not removed on new boards you may put that client at risk for cuts. Check the corners of buffers also as they may need to be prepped.

Medium-grit abrasives (180 to 240 grit) are used to smooth and refine surfaces and the 180 is used to shorten and shape natural nails. Fine-grit abrasives are in the category of 240 and higher grits. They are designed for buffing, polishing, and removing very fine scratches.

Abrasive boards and buffers typically have one, two, or three different grit surfaces, depending on type, use, and style. Some abrasive boards and buffers can be cleaned and disinfected. Check with the manufacturer to see if the abrasive of your choice can be disinfected. All abrasives must be cleaned and disinfected before reuse on another client. Check with your instructor as to whether your state allows abrasive boards that are able to be disinfected and buffers within the SOP. Abrasives that cannot survive the cleaning and disinfection process without being damaged are considered disposable and must be discarded after a single use.

Two-Way or Three-Way Buffer

The two- or three-way buffer abrasive technology replaces the chamois and creates a beautiful shine on nails **(Figure 13-18).** The buffer is shaped like a two-sided nail file, long and narrow, with one or two additional grit abrasives and a final shine surface. Begin with the lowest grit abrasive surface in the smoothing task; move to the larger grit, then last to the shining surface (usually no grit). The result is a glossy shine on the nails. This buffer is generally used on natural nails and in the final steps of the two-color application of monomer liquid and polymer powder nails, such as the French manicure look, for nails that will be worn with sheer or clear polish only.

Most two- or three-way buffers are single-use only and must be thrown away after each use. The salon or technician must find an inexpensive source for purchasing them or a reusable one if regulations in the state allow their use.

▲ FIGURE 13-18
Three-way buffer.

Single-use or Terrycloth Towels

Towels are an example of materials that do not require disinfection. Cloth towels must be washed between clients and paper towels must be thrown away after use. A fresh, clean terry cloth towel or a new disposable paper towel is used by the client after washing his or her hands. The best terry cloth towels for use in a personal service are white as they can be bleached during their washing between uses. Other clean towels are used to cover any surfaces that cannot be disinfected during each manicure including the work area. If spills occur on the table, other terry cloth or disposable towels must be used to wipe them from the surface.

Gauze, Cotton Balls, or Plastic-Backed Pads

Lint-free, plastic-backed, fiber or cotton pads are often used to remove nail polish. Plastic backing protects nail professionals' fingertips from overexposure to drying solvents and other chemicals **(Figure 13-19)**.

Gauze squares or cotton balls are also popular for removal of nail polish as they are inexpensive and perfectly designed for this and other application tasks. Gauze squares (2" x 2" or 4" x 4") have many uses in manicure services, from product removal to application. All these materials must be stored in a manner to prevent dust and debris from contaminating them.

■■ **Law**
□□

State Regulatory ALERT!

Reusing implements without properly cleaning and disinfecting them is against the law in every state. The inappropriate and illegal use of implements puts clients at risk of the transfer of infection.

▲ **FIGURE 13-19**
Materials used to remove polish and cleanse nail bed before polishing.

Plastic or Metal Spatulas

A single-use plastic or multi-use metal spatula must be used for removing products from their respective containers to prevent contamination of the products and the spread of disease. If a spatula comes into contact with your or the client's skin, it must be properly cleaned and disinfected before being used again, or replaced. Also, never use the same spatula to remove unlike products from different containers as the chemistry of the products may be altered.

PROFESSIONAL COSMETIC PRODUCTS

As a professional, you need to know how to properly use each nail product, what ingredients it contains, and what it does during use. You must also know how to properly store products and remove them from their containers in a sanitary manner. This section provides a basic understanding of several professional cosmetic nail products. For more detailed information on products and ingredients, see **Nail Structure & Product Chemistry, Second Edition, by Doug Schoon, Cengage Learning, 2005.**

Soap

Soap is used to clean the nail technician's and client's hands before a service begins. It acts as an infection control tool during this pre-service hand washing procedure by mechanically removing microbes and debris. It is known to remove over 90 percent of pathogenic microbes from the hands, if performed properly.

Liquid soaps **(Figure 13-20)** are recommended and preferred because bar soap harbors bacteria and can become a breeding ground for pathogenic (disease-producing) bacteria.

Polish Remover

Removers are used to dissolve and remove nail polish. There are two types of polish removers available: acetone and non-acetone. Acetone works more quickly and is a better solvent than non-acetone removers.

Non-acetone removers will not dissolve enhancement products as quickly as acetone, so they are preferred when removing nail polish from nail enhancements such as wraps. Both acetone and non-acetone polish removers can be used safely. As with all products, read and follow the manufacturer's instructions for use.

Nail Creams, Lotions, and Oils

These products are designed to soften dry skin around the nail plate and to increase the flexibility of natural nails. They are especially effective on nails that appear to be brittle or dry and are the #1 nail product that should be sold to manicure and pedicure clients. Nail creams are barrier products as they contain ingredients designed to seal the surface of the skin and hold in the subdermal moisture in the skin. Nail oils are designed to absorb into the nail plate to increase flexibility and into the surrounding skin to soften and moisturize. Typically, oils and lotions can penetrate the nail plate or skin and will have longer-lasting effects than creams, but all three can be highly effective and useful for clients, especially as daily-use home-care products.

Cuticle Removers

Cuticle removers are designed to loosen and dissolve dead tissue on the nail plate so this tissue can be more easily and thoroughly removed from the nail plate. These products typically contain 2 percent to 5 percent sodium or potassium hydroxide plus glycerin or other moisturizing ingredients to counteract the skin-drying effects of the remover. They must be used in strict accordance with the manufacturer's directions, and skin contact must be avoided where possible to counter the affects of the alkaline ingredients. Excessive exposure of the eponychium to cuticle removers can cause skin and eponychium dryness, as well as hangnails.

▼ FIGURE 13-20
Use pump bottles of soap at handwashing station.

Nail Bleach

These products are designed to apply to the nail plate and under the free edge of natural nails to remove yellow surface discoloration or stains (e.g., tobacco stains). Usually nail bleaches contain hydrogen peroxide or some other keratin-bleaching agent. Always use these products exactly as directed by the manufacturer to avoid damaging the natural nail plate or surrounding skin. Since nail bleaches can be corrosive to soft tissue, take care to limit skin contact.

Colored Polish, Enamel, Lacquer, or Varnish

Colored coatings applied to the natural nail plate are variously known as polish, enamel, lacquer, or varnish. All of these terms are actually marketing terms used to describe the same types of products containing similar ingredients.

Polish is a generic term describing any type of solvent-based colored film applied to the nail plate for the purpose of adding color or special visual effects (e.g., sparkles). It is usually applied in two coats over a base coat and followed by a top coat **(Figure 13-21)**.

Base Coat

The base coat creates a colorless layer on the natural nail and nail enhancement that improves adhesion of polish. It also prevents polish from imparting a yellowish staining or other discoloration to the natural nail plate as some nail plates are especially susceptible to stains from red or dark colors. Base coats are also important to use on nail enhancements under colored polish to prevent surface staining. These products usually rely on adhesives which aid in retaining polish for a longer time. Like nail polishes, base coats contain solvents designed to evaporate. After evaporation, a sticky, adhesion-promoting film is left behind on the surface of the nail plate to increase adhesion of the colored coating.

Nail Hardener

Nail hardeners are used to improve the surface hardness or durability of weak or thin nail plates. Some can also prevent splitting or peeling of the nail plate, if used properly. Hardeners can be applied before the base coat or after as top coat, according to the manufacturer's directions.

There are several basic types of nail hardeners:

Protein hardener is a combination of clear polish and protein, such as collagen. These provide a clear, hard coating on the surface of the nail, but do not change or affect the natural nail plate itself. Protein (collagen) has very large molecules that cannot be absorbed into the nail plate.

Did **You** Know...

Never shake your polish bottles. Shaking will cause air bubbles to form and make the polish application rough and appear irregular. Instead, gently roll the polish bottles between your palms to thoroughly mix.

▲ FIGURE 13-21
Polish, top coat, and base coat for manicure.

Other types of nail hardeners contain reinforcing fibers such as nylon that also cannot be absorbed into the nail plate. Therefore, the protection they provide comes from the coating itself. They are not therapeutic. These products can be used on any natural nail. Hardeners do not contain formaldehyde as believed before in the industry. The ingredient is actually methylene glycol, an ingredient that creates bridges or cross-links between the keratin strands that make up the natural nail, making the plate stiffer and more resistant to bending and breaking. Methylene glycol is also not irritating to the skin.

These products are useful for thin and weak nail plates, but should never be applied to nails that are already very hard, rigid and/or brittle. Methylene glycol hardeners can make brittle nails become so rigid that they may split and shatter. If signs of excessive brittleness or splitting, discoloration of the nail bed, development of ventral pterygium, or other signs of adverse nail and skin reactions occur, discontinue use. These products should be used as instructed by the manufacturer until the client's nails reach the desired goal, and then use should be discontinued until the product is needed again. Clients are generally instructed to apply the product daily over nail polish as a top coat, or under nail polish as a base coat when the polish is removed and reapplied. Clients must be instructed to follow manufacturer instructions.

Dimethyl urea hardeners use dimethyl urea (DMU) to also add cross-links to the natural nail plate, DMU does not cause adverse skin reactions. These hardeners do not work as quickly as hardeners containing methylene glycol, but they will not overharden nails as those may with over use.

⟩Did **You** Know...

Products sold to clients for their use at home are called retail products, and are packaged for that purpose. The reality is that in this industry they are home-care products, not retail products, because they are sold under professional recommendation and the client is given instruction on how to use them before taking them home. Home-care products, by law, must have usage directions and cautions listed on the bottles or boxes or have written instructions in the box, while professional products (usually bulk sizes) do not.

Top Coat

Top coats are applied over colored polish to prevent chipping and to add a shine to the finished nail. These products contain ingredients that create hard, shiny films after the solvent has evaporated. Typically the main ingredients are methacrylic or cellulose-type film formers.

Nail Polish Dryers

These products are designed to hasten the drying of nail polishes. They are typically applied with a dropper or a brush or are sprayed onto the surface of the polish. They promote rapid drying by pulling solvents from the nail polish, causing the colored film to form more quickly. These products can dramatically shorten drying time and will reduce the risk of the client smudging the recent polish application.

Hand Creams and Lotions

Hand creams and lotions add a finishing touch to a manicure. Since they soften and smooth the hands, they make the skin and finished manicure look as beautiful as possible. Hand creams are generally designed to be barriers on the skin to help the skin retain moisture or they contain penetrating ingredients to soften the skin or repair damage. Their purpose is to make the skin on the hands less prone to becoming dry or cracked. Lotion is generally more penetrating than creams and may treat lower levels of the epidermis. A treatment lotion can be used with warming mitts or paraffin dips to enhance penetration of the ingredients into the skin.

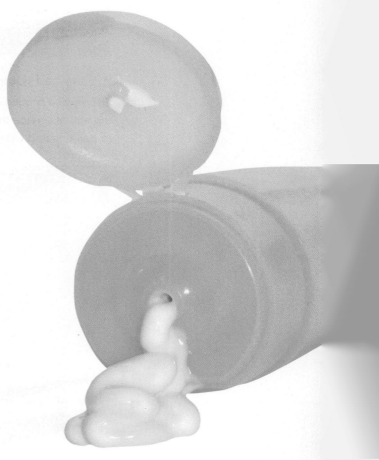

Nail Conditioners

Nail conditioners contain ingredients to reduce brittleness of the nail. They should be applied as directed by the manufacturer, but they are especially useful when applied at night before bedtime. They can be oils, lotions, or creams.

Sunscreens

These lotions contain ingredients that protect the skin from damage by the Ultra Violet rays (UVA) from the sun. UVA is known to cause age spots (hyperpigmentation) on the backs of the hands and damage to the DNA of the cells of the skin. Overexposure to the sun is known as a major cause of aging and skin cancer. Encourage your clients to purchase and use sunscreen on all their exposed skin.

CAUTION

All base coats, top coats, nail polishes, and hardeners are highly flammable.

The Basic Manicure

The basic manicure is the foundation of all nail technology services and it is vital that you know and recognize all of the components necessary for making the basic manicure service successful. The information you learn for the basic manicure will serve as your foundation for all of the other nail services you will perform in your career.

Work to get your basic manicure procedure to 45 minutes at the most, including polishing, before you leave your school environment and you will be more hirable and more successful in your career. Practice until you can perform the skills automatically, without considering what is next in the protocol and you will portray the confidence and professional aura that clients prefer in their nail technician.

Work to get your basic manicure procedure to 45 minutes at the most...

THREE-PART PROCEDURE

It is easier to keep track of what you are doing, to remain organized, and to give consistent service if you break your nail care procedures down into three individual parts. These three parts are: pre-service, actual service, and post-service.

A. Pre-Service Procedure

The pre-service procedure is an organized step-by-step plan for the cleaning and disinfecting of your tools, implements, and materials; for setting up the basic manicuring table; and for meeting, greeting, and escorting your client to your service area.

GO TO → **PROCEDURE 13-1 page 226**

B. Service Procedure

The service procedure is an organized, step-by-step plan for accomplishing the actual service the client has requested, such as a manicure, pedicure, or nail tips and wraps.

GO TO → **PROCEDURE 13-5 page 234**

C. Post-Service Procedure

The post-service procedure is an organized step-by-step plan for caring for your client after the procedure has been completed. It details helping your client through the scheduling and payment process of the salon and provides information for you on how to prepare for the next client.

PROCEDURE 13-2 page 230

✔ **LO3 Complete**

Hand Washing

To prevent the spread of communicable disease it is imperative to wash your hands before and after each client, and to have your clients wash their hands before they sit down at your cleaned and disinfected manicure table. The practice of hand washing before any procedure should be so well taught to your regular clients that they go directly to the washing station before coming to your station.

The nail brush, which is an integral part of the hand washing procedure, should be in a well-known storage place so clients can retrieve it easily and quickly. Mark the clean nail brush container well so the client will know where to retrieve the fresh brush. The client can bring the brush to the table or leave it in a marked dirty brush container.

To prevent cross-contamination, clients each must have a clean brush for scrubbing their hands. There are two choices for providing these brushes:

1 Clean and disinfect your brushes between clients. Many salons cleanse them at the end of the day, disinfect them, then rinse and dry them, and place them in a container marked Clean Brushes with convenient access by your clients.

2 Purchase them in bulk and give them to clients or throw them away after each service. Clients bring them to the chair for use during their manicure after they wash.

Did **You** Know...

Although the CDC states that hand sanitizers are appropriate for use, they also note that hand sanitizers are only for use when water is not available for hand washing. It is very important to remember that these products cannot and do not replace proper hand washing. Proper hand washing is a vital part of the service and it cannot be skipped or ignored. Clients must also properly wash their hands before and after the service, and you must properly wash your hands between each customer. Resort to using a hand sanitizer only when it's absolutely necessary!

PROCEDURE 13-3 page 231

✔ **LO4 Complete**

The Manicure Consultation

The consultation with the client before the manicure, or any other service, is an opportunity for getting to know one another and for the nail technician to understand what her client's expectations are. Do not rush through the consultation—it is an important part of the service!

If the client is new to the salon, he or she should already have filled out the information on the consultation form in the waiting room. Use this information to perform the client consultation. Look at the forms closely for important responses from the client and then record your observations after the service.

Always check the client's nails and skin to make sure that they are healthy and that the service you are providing is appropriate. Next, discuss the shape, color and length of nails that your client prefers. You must be careful not to diagnose a disease or disorder in any way. All information should then be recorded on the client service form. If there are no health issues observed, continue with the service.

Keep the following considerations in mind: shape of the hands, length of fingers, shape of the eponychium area, hobbies, recreational activities, and type of work. Generally it is recommended that the shape of the nail plate enhance the overall shape of the fingertips, fingers, and hands of the client.

(REVIEW STEPS OF THE CLIENT CONSULTATION, CHAPTER 4, Pages 43-45)

Basic Nail Shapes for Women

You should always discuss the final shape your client wants for her nails during the consultation and do your best to please her. Here are the five basic shapes that women most often prefer.

(SEE TABLE 13-1, BASIC NAIL SHAPES, PAGE 217.)

TABLE 13-1 Basic Nail Shapes

SHAPE	DEFINITION
 square	The square nail is completely straight across the free edge with no rounding at the outside edges.
 squoval	The squoval nail has a square free edge that is rounded off at the corner edges. If the nail extends only slightly past the fingertip this shape will be sturdy because there is no square edge to break off and any pressure on the tip will be reflected directly back to the nail plate, its strongest area. Clients who work with their hands—nurses, computer technicians, landscapers or office workers—will need shorter, squoval nails.
 round	The round nail should be slightly tapered and usually should extend just a bit past the fingertip.
 oval	The oval nail is a conservative nail shape that is thought to be attractive on most women's hands. It is similar to a squoval nail with even more rounded corners. Professional clients who have their hands on display (e.g., businesspeople, teachers, or salespeople) may want longer oval nails.
 pointed	The pointed nail is suited to thin hands with long fingers and narrow nail beds. The nail is tapered and longer than usual to emphasize and enhance the slender appearance of the hand. Know, however, that this nail shape may be weaker, may break more easily, and is more difficult to maintain than other nail shapes. Rarely are natural nails successful with this nail shape so they are usually enhancements. They are for fashion-conscious people who do not need the strongest, most durable shape of nail enhancements.

Choosing a Nail Color

Polishing is very important for the satisfaction of your clients and for the success of the service, and may help determine whether they return to you. It is the last step in a perfect manicure and a constant visual reminder of your work for your clients between visits. When your clients look at nails that are polished perfectly, they will admire your work and will likely return. If the polish is not applied perfectly, they will have a constant reminder for a week or more of a less-than-perfect manicure and may not return.

Did You Know...

When applying an iridescent or frosted polish, you must make sure the strokes are parallel to the sidewalls of the nail to avoid shadow lines in the polish.

GO TO **PROCEDURE 13-4** page 232

▲ FIGURE 13-22
Finished manicure.

Many clients will ask for help in choosing a polish color, or they will ask you, "Do you like this color?" When asked for help, suggest a shade that complements the client's skin tone by placing the hand on a white towel under your true-color light, then holding the potential polish colors over the skin on the top of the hand. It is best to allow the client to make the choices to ensure her satisfaction. If the manicure is for a special occasion, you might suggest the client pick a color that matches or coordinates with the clothing the client will be wearing, or represents the holiday, the event, or the season. Some clients will request nail art or other nail fashion enhancements that are popular at the time. Generally, darker shades are appropriate for fall and winter and lighter shades are better for spring and summer, though this is no longer a hard-and-fast fashion rule. Always have a wide variety of nail polish colors available and the appropriate colors for the French manicure polish techniques.

Applying Polish

The most successful nail polish application is achieved by using four coats. The first, the base coat, is followed by two coats of polish color and one application of top coat to give a protective seal. The application techniques are the same for all polishes, base coats, and top coats.

In addition to improved appearance, the purpose of using multiple layers of product when applying polish is to improve longevity and durability of the polish **(Figure 13-22)**. By building layer upon layer, you will improve adhesion and staying power.

Apply thin, even coats to create maximum smoothness and minimum drying time. When you have completed the polish application, the nail should look smooth, evenly polished, and shiny.

> **GO TO** ➤ **PROCEDURE 13-7 page 242**

A Man's Manicure Service

Since men are becoming more and more interested in their grooming regimens, many are seeking services offered by nail professionals. A man's manicure is executed using the same procedures as described previously for the basic manicure, though you omit the colored polish and/or buff the nails with a high-shine buffer **(Figure 13-23)**.

Did **You** Know...

Most times, unless the hands are in really poor shape, you can give men a longer massage since polish time is not a factor.

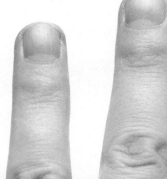

Most men tend to go longer between services and will need a little more work than women on their nails and skin. A citrus- or spice-scented hand cream is recommended, instead of a flowery scent, for the male client.

MEN'S NAIL SHAPES

Men usually prefer their nails shorter than women do. Round nails are the most common choice for male clients because of their natural appearance. Some men, however, prefer their nails really short, with only a small amount of free edge that is shaped according to the base of the nail plate. **(Figure 13-24).**

MEN'S MASSAGE

Most men love the massage portion of the manicure and want a longer one! Usually they will want a more firm effleurage than women, though that does not mean providing a deep, sports-type massage—since you are not trained to perform that massage. It just means more firm finger movements on the palm and longer, firmer slides in your effleurage movements **(Figure 13-25)**.

MEN'S BASIC COLOR: CLEAR

Men usually prefer buffed nails, clear gloss, or a dull, clear satin coating. This satin coating nail polish finish is designed especially to help men protect their nails without having nails that appear too polished or feminine **(Figure 13-26)**. Although a man may rarely want a shiny top coat or colored nail polish on his nails, you should always discuss his preferences during the client consultation.

You must prepare the nails for polish (remove oils and debris) carefully because peeling or chipping gloss is very annoying to men. Use a base coat under clear to encourage staying power; clear without a base tends to peel. Apply a thin base coat and then one thin coat of clear and a quick-drying top coat or just one coat of base and a satin clear.

Always ask for the next appointment and suggest having a pedicure with the manicure. Men love pedicures!

MARKETING TO MEN

Since most men are new to professional nail care, include a brief written description of what is included in the service and a rundown of the benefits on your service menu and your website. You may also want to distribute flyers that target men at local athletic gyms and stores, and other places where men gather. Gift certificates sold to your female clients for their boyfriends and husbands are great marketing tools.

To make men feel more at home in your chair, have men's magazines on hand and be careful that your decor is unisex. Staying open later or opening earlier on chosen days makes it easier for your male clients to schedule appointments.

▲ **FIGURE 13-23**
Buffing a client's nails.

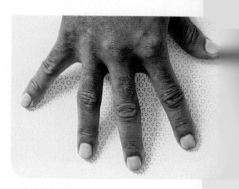

▲ **FIGURE 13-24**
Round nails—the nails most men choose.

▲ **FIGURE 13-25**
Beginning a massage.

▲ **FIGURE 13-26**
Most men prefer buffed nails, clear gloss, or a dull, clear coating.

Many salons and spas also have a weekly or biweekly men's night, with no women allowed, so male clients can come in without being among women.

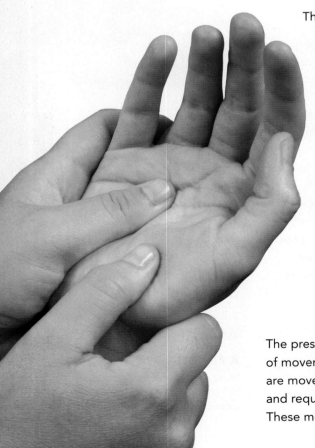

▪▪ Law
▪ □

State Regulatory ALERT!

In a few states a *cosmetology* license does not permit you to perform a hand or foot massage. Be guided by your instructor concerning your state's mandatory requirements and procedures for massage during nail services.

Massage

Massage is the manipulation of the soft tissues of the body. It is an ancient therapeutic treatment to promote circulation of the blood and lymph, relaxation of the muscles, and relief from pain, and has many other benefits. A hand and arm massage, a manicuring specialty, is a service that can be offered with all types of manicures. It is included in all spa manicures, and can be performed on most clients.

A massage is one of the client's highest priorities during the manicure and is, often, the most memorable part of the manicure. Most clients look forward to the soothing and relaxing effects. The massage manipulations should be executed with rhythmic, long, and smooth movements, always having one hand on the client's arm or hand during the procedure.

Hand and arm massages are optional during a basic manicure, but it is to the advantage of the nail professional to always incorporate this special, relaxing segment of a manicure as it has proven to be the favorite part of the service for many clients.

GENERAL MOVEMENTS

Massage generally is a series of movements performed on the human body that, in combination, produce relaxation or treatment.

The following massage movements are usually combined to complete a massage:

1 Effleurage (EF-loo-rahzh): a succession of strokes in which the hands glide over an area of the body with varying degrees of pressure or contact

2 Pétrissage or kneading: lifting, squeezing, and pressing the tissue

3 Tapotement: rapid tapping or striking motion of the hands against the skin

4 Vibration: continuous trembling or shaking movement applied by the hand without leaving contact with the skin

5 Friction: various strokes that manipulate or press one layer of tissue over another.

The pressure and manipulation of the tissues and muscles vary with each type of movement. However, you should keep in mind that pétrissage and friction are movements that massage therapists combine for therapeutic purposes and require in-depth training for their safe and comfortable application. These movements can be painful, even dangerous, when performed by

someone without the proper training. Also, remember that the purpose of massage in manicuring is the inducement of relaxation. For that reason, effleurage is the movement that should be perfected, varied, and expertly used in services. Effleurage is relaxing and calming and meets the overall purpose of massage in manicures and pedicures.

In the traditional manicure, the massage is performed after the basic manicure procedures, just before the polish application. After performing a massage, it is essential that the nail plate be thoroughly cleansed to ensure that it is free from any residue such as oil, cream, wax, or lotion. You can use alcohol or nail polish remover to cleanse the nail plate.

GO TO ➡ **PROCEDURE 13-6** page 238

✓ **LO8 Complete**

Spa Manicures

Spa manicures are fast becoming much-requested and desired salon services but require more advanced techniques than basic manicures. Nail professionals who advance their education and knowledge of spa manicures and their specialized techniques will not only make their clients happy, but they may find these manicures are very lucrative as well.

Spa manicures encompass not only extensive knowledge of nail care but skin care as well. Many spa manicures are exceptionally pampering, while others target specific results through the use of advanced skin-care-based methods. Most include a relaxing massage and all contain some form of exfoliation for not only polishing and smoothing the skin, but also for enhancing penetration of professional products.

Spa manicures designed for relaxation may have unique and distinctive names that describe the treatment. For example, "The Rose Garden Rejuvenation Manicure" may incorporate the use of rose oils in the products and rose petals for ambiance.

The results-oriented spa manicures, sometimes called "treatment manicures," many times have names that closely represent their purpose, such as "anti-aging manicure," which may incorporate the use of an alpha hydroxy acid–based product for exfoliation and skin rejuvenation, or "scrub manicure" to exfoliate callused skin. Many may have more imaginative names, such as "spot-be-gone," for lightening age spots. Treatment manicures require further training to produce safe and obvious results. To learn about this and other specialty manicures, see **Spa Manicuring for Salons and Spas** by **Janet McCormick, Cengage Learning.**

Business **Tip:**

A newly developed "dry manicure" eliminates the soak, using lotion and heated mitts to soften the skin and cuticles.

Many clients now define their cosmetic and service decisions around lifestyle choices such as preferring all-natural products (**Figure 13-27**). These clients will seek out spa manicures that meet their needs and they may ask about the products you are using. To answer, you must know whether your product lines make these claims and how to answer these questions.

fyi

Some clients may ask for products that are chemical-free. The truth is that no products are or can be chemical-free—even air and water contain chemicals!

When faced with clients who feel strongly about their beliefs and knowledge—whether their information is based on truth or not—know about your product line and its claims, and offer the information to them, if they want it so they can make an informed decision.

▲ **FIGURE 13-27**
"All-natural products" are products made from only natural resources.

The reality is that, despite what the product marketing implies, few all-natural products are commercially available and virtually none are chemical-free.

One alternative is to mix your own products from fresh ingredients. If you choose to create your own fresh products, you may want to make a small batch for each procedure or per day as they can spoil very quickly and you must have refrigeration in your salon.

Additional techniques that may be incorporated into a spa manicure consist of aromatic paraffin dips; hand masks; and warm, moist towel applications. When performing any advanced procedures which include any oils or cosmetics, always check with your client regarding aroma preferences and allergies.

✔ **LO9 Complete**

THEME MANICURES

Many salons and spas have developed services around themes. The entire service contains products that support the theme the salon has chosen, from lotions to oils to masks, and some salons even serve theme refreshments to clients during the service that supports the theme (**Figure 13-28**).

Examples might include the "Chocolate Wonder Manicure and Pedicure," or the "Pumpkin Fall Festival Manicure and Pedicure." The names and themes of these kinds of services are limited only by your imagination. Let yours go wild and have fun developing these well-received manicures and pedicures. Clients love them!

▲ **FIGURE 13-28**
Relaxed client during a spa manicure.

Aromatherapy

In the 1870s, Professor Rene' Maurice Gattefosse, a French scientist, discovered the therapeutic use of essential oils which are now inhaled or applied to the skin **(Figure 13-29)**. These oils are used in manicures, pedicures, and massages to induce such reactions as relaxation or invigoration, or to simply create a pleasant fragrance during the service. Many clients enjoy the various aromas, so when it is appropriate, incorporate aromatherapy into your nail services.

The practice of aromatherapy involves the use of highly concentrated, non-oily, and volatile essential oils that are extracted using various forms of distillation from seeds, bark, roots, leaves, wood, and/or resin. Each part of these resources produces a different aroma. For instance, the needles, resin, and wood of a Scotch pine tree each yields a different aroma and, therefore, a different response from the target person. The use of essential oils is limited only by the knowledge of the person controlling their application.

Performing aromatherapy requires study and expert use of the knowledge gained. The oils are very powerful and can produce actual changes in the client. In some countries, the oils are considered medicines and are only prescribed by physicians. Therefore, unless a nail technician is prepared to study these volatile oils in-depth, he or she should use blended oils, those that are already mixed and tested, and apply them only as directed.

▲ FIGURE 13-29
Essential oils are used in manicure products.

✓ **LO10 Complete**

Did **You** Know...

Blended oils are usually mixed to target a particular response from the client, such as relaxation or an increase in energy. These oils are safe and easy to use by persons who haven't studied aromatherapy in depth and are usually added into such products as massage lotion, body lotion, and masks. These aromas and products are designed to provide maximized results for clients and a greater enjoyment of services.

▲ FIGURE 13-30
Paraffin treatment is a luxury service, as well as a treatment for dry skin.

Paraffin Wax Treatment

Paraffin wax treatments are designed to trap moisture in the skin while the heat causes skin pores to open. Besides opening the pores, heat from the warm paraffin increases blood circulation. This is considered to be a luxurious add-on service and can be safely performed on most clients **(Figure 13-30)**. Be sure to examine the client's intake form during the client consultation

to identify any contraindications to wax or the heat involved in the service and discuss any additional precautions that should be taken for clients with any health factors or risks, such as diabetes or poor circulation.

Paraffin is a petroleum by-product that has excellent sealing properties (barrier qualities) to hold moisture in the skin. Special heating units melt solid wax into a gel-like liquid and maintain it at a temperature generally between 125 and 130°F. When using this treatment, only use the equipment that is designed specifically for this use. Never try to heat the wax in anything other than the proper equipment. This can be very dangerous and may result in painful skin burns or a fire.

If proper procedures are followed, paraffin will not adversely affect nail enhancements or natural nails. A paraffin wax treatment may be offered before a manicure, during a manicure, or as a stand-alone service. Be guided by your instructor and your state regulations because some states require the service to be performed before the manicure.

GO TO → **PROCEDURE 13-8** page 244

✓ **LO11 Complete**

BEFORE A MANICURE

Performing the paraffin wax treatment before beginning a manicure has advantages:

- It allows the client to have her nails polished immediately at the end of the manicure service.
- It is a way to pre-soften rough or callused skin.

Read and follow all operating instructions that come with your paraffin heating unit. Generally, you should avoid giving paraffin treatments to anyone who has impaired circulation or skin irritations such as cuts, burns, rashes, warts, or eczema. Senior citizens and chronically ill clients may be more sensitive to heat because of medications or thinning of the skin. In these cases, ask the clients to bring their physician's permission prior to having a paraffin treatment.

A patch test for heat tolerance can be performed on all clients the first time they have the service. Place a small patch of wax on the client's skin to see if the temperatures can be tolerated by these individuals.

DURING A MANICURE

Many salons and spas have developed manicures that include specialized and additional treatments such as masks and paraffin wax that are performed after the massage and before polishing.

Performing the paraffin wax treatment before beginning a manicure has advantages...

STAND-ALONE SERVICE

Many clients enjoy a paraffin treatment. This service can be on the menu with its own price, as clients like the way a paraffin treatment makes their skin feel. The heat provides pain relief for those with arthritis. And when the temperature is cold outside, many clients remember the warm feeling the paraffin provides and will book an appointment or drop in for a dip.

Nail Art

Many clients love the application of artistic designs on their nails (nail art). The techniques are fun to apply and are only limited by your imagination. Techniques range from freehand designs to complex nail art **(Figure 13-31)**, to simple glue-on, airbrushing **(Figure 13-32)**; 3D nail art **(Figure 13-33)**; and from portrait to modern design.

▲ **FIGURE 13-31**
Complex nail art (by Massimiliano Braga).

Only The Beginning

▲ **FIGURE 13-32**
Airbrush nail art (by Emilio's Airbrush Studio).

▲ **FIGURE 13-33**
3-D nail art (by Alisha Rimando Botero).

During your time in school it is important that you learn the basic procedures of nail technology, as well as the importance of proper cleaning, disinfection, and other skills necessary for ensuring client safety and enjoyment during nail procedures. You must make the commitment to continue to learn and grow as a nail technician if you want to remain competitive in today's marketplace. The "real world" requires you to perform at a very high level of expertise and you are expected to have a great deal of knowledge and skill, far beyond the basics.

Advanced techniques in manicuring may be learned from your instructor, through attending advanced nail care seminars, reading trade magazines, and attending beauty shows. Advanced skill and information books are available from Milady, an imprint of Cengage Learning, such as **Spa Manicuring for Salons and Spas** by Janet McCormick to enhance your knowledge of manicures and pedicures. Further, for an in-depth understanding of natural nail anatomy, disorders, and so forth, see **Nail Structure & Product Chemistry, second edition, by Douglas Schoon,** also published by Cengage Learning.

Business Tip:

It is important that you never stop learning about new innovations and continue to seek out information about your industry. Things change, and the wise nail technician studies and changes with the world to remain on the cutting edge.

A. CLEANING

1. It is important to wear gloves while performing this pre-service procedure to prevent possible contamination of the implements by your hands and to protect your hands from the powerful chemicals in the disinfectant solution.

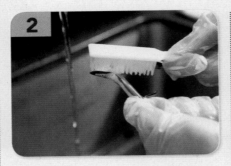

2. Rinse all implements with warm running water, and then thoroughly wash them with soap, a nail brush, and warm water. Brush grooved items, if necessary, and open hinged implements to scrub the area.

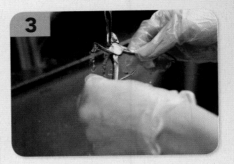

3. Rinse away all traces of soap with warm running water. The presence of soap in most disinfectants can cause them to become inactive. Soap is most easily rinsed off in warm, but not hot, water. Hotter water will not work any better. Dry implements thoroughly with a clean or disposable towel, or allow to air dry on a clean towel. Your implements are now properly cleaned and ready to be disinfected.

5. Remove implements, avoiding skin contact, and rinse and dry tools thoroughly.

4. It is extremely important that your implements be completely clean before placing them in the disinfectant solution. If they are not, your disinfectant may become contaminated and rendered ineffective. Before immersing cleaned implements, open any hinged implements to the open position. Immerse cleansed implements in an appropriate disinfection container holding an EPA-registered disinfectant for the required time (usually 10 minutes). If it is visibly dirty, the solution has been contaminated for quite a while and must be replaced immediately. Make sure to avoid skin contact with all disinfectants by using tongs or by wearing gloves.

6. Store disinfected implements in a clean, dry container until needed.

7. Remove gloves and thoroughly wash your hands with liquid soap, rinse, and dry with a clean fabric or disposable towel.

✓ **LO12** Complete

B. BASIC TABLE SETUP

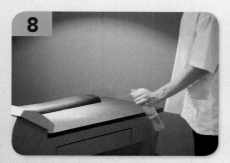

8. Clean and disinfect manicure table and drawer with an appropriate or approved disinfectant-cleanser.

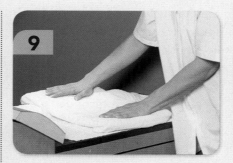

9. Wrap your client's arm cushion, if used, with a clean terrycloth or disposable towel. Place the cushion in the middle of the table so that one end of the towel extends toward the client and the other end extends in your direction.

10. Ensure that your disinfection container is filled with clean disinfectant solution at least 20 minutes before your first service of the day. Use any disinfectant solution approved by your state board regulations, but make sure that you use it exactly as directed by the manufacturer. Also make sure that you change the disinfectant every day or according the manufacturer's instructions. Put cleaned, multi-use implements into the disinfection container for the required time.

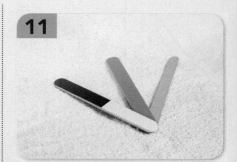

11. Place the abrasives and buffers of your choice on the table to your right (if left-handed, place on the left).

B. BASIC TABLE SETUP CONT.

12. Place the fingerbowl filled with warm water and the manicure brush in the middle of the table, toward the client. The fingerbowl should not be moved from one side to the other side of the manicure table. It should stay where you place it for the duration of your manicure.

13. Tape or clip a plastic bag that can be closed securely to the right side of the table (if left-handed, tape to the left side), if a metal trash receptacle with a self-closing lid is not available. This is used for depositing used materials during your manicure. These bags must be emptied after each client departs to prevent product vapors from escaping into the salon air.

14. Place polishes to the right if right-handed, to the left if left-handed.

✓ **LO13 Complete**

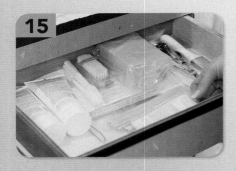

15. The drawer can be used to store the following items for immediate use: extra cotton or cotton balls in their original container or in a fresh plastic bag, abrasives, buffers, nail polish dryer, and other supplies. Never place used materials in your drawer. Only completely cleaned and disinfected implements stored in an sealed container (to protect them from dust and re-contamination) and extra materials or professional products should be placed in the drawer. Your drawer should always be organized and clean.

C. GREET CLIENT

16. Greet your client with a smile, introduce yourself if you've never met, and shake hands. If the client is new, ask her for the consultation card she filled out in the reception area.

17. Escort your client to the hand washing area and demonstrate the hand washing procedure for her on your own hands. Once you have completed the demonstration, hand your client a fresh nail brush to use and ask her to wash her hands.

18. Be sure that your towels look clean and are not worn. A towel with stains or holes definitely will affect how your client feels about her service. A dirty towel can tell a client either not to come back, or cause her to report your salon to the state board.

19. Show your client to your work table and make sure she is comfortable before beginning the service.

20. Discuss the information on the consultation card and determine a course of action for the service.

Post-Service Procedure

A. ADVISE CLIENTS AND PROMOTE PRODUCTS

1. Proper home maintenance will ensure that the client's nails look beautiful until he or she returns for another service (a week to ten days).

2. Depending on the service provided, there may be a number of retail products that you should recommend for the client to take home. This is the time to do so. Explain why they are important and how to use them.

B. SCHEDULE NEXT APPOINTMENT AND THANK CLIENT

3. Escort the client to the front desk to schedule the next appointment and to pay for the service. Set up date, time, and services and then write the information on your or the salon's appointment card and give it to the client.

4. Before you return to your station and the client leaves the salon, be sure to thank her for her business.

5. Record service information, products used, observations, and retail recommendations on the client service form.

C. PREPARE WORK AREA AND IMPLEMENTS FOR NEXT CLIENT

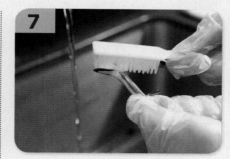

7. Follow steps for disinfecting implements in the Pre-Service Procedure. Reset work area with disinfected tools.

6. Remove your products and tools then clean your work area and properly dispose of all used materials.

✓ **LO14 Complete**

Proper Hand Washing

Hand washing is one of the most important procedures in your infection control efforts and is required in every state before beginning any service. The hand washing procedure should last a minimum of 20 seconds during rubbing of the hands, and for a minimum of 20 seconds during the brush cleansing of the nails on each hand.

1. Escort the client to the wash station. Before beginning any service, explain the salon or spa's hand washing policy and why it is performed.

2. Turn the water on, wet your hands, then pump soap from a pump container onto the palm of your hand. Rub your hands together, all over and vigorously, until a lather forms. Continue in this manner for about 20 seconds.

3. After your demonstration, hand the client a clean nail brush and instruct her to wash her hands as well. Choose a clean nail brush, wet it, pump soap on it, and brush your nails horizontally back and forth under the free edges. Change the direction of the brush to vertical and move the brush up and down along the nail folds of the fingernails. The process for brushing both hands should take about 60 seconds to finish. Rinse hands in running water.

4. Hand the client a clean towel for drying hands and inform her what to do with the towel. Dry hands using a clean cloth or paper towel, according to the salon policies for hand drying.

5. After drying, turn off the water with the towel and then dispose of the towel.

6. Escort the client to the table while explaining that hand washing should be performed before every service.

Handling an Exposure Incident During a Manicure

Should you accidentally cut a client, calmly take the following steps:

1. Immediately put on gloves unless you already have them on and inform your client of what has occurred. Apologize and proceed.

2. Apply slight pressure to the area with cotton to stop the bleeding and then clean with an antiseptic.

3. Apply an adhesive bandage to completely cover the wound.

4. Clean and disinfect the workstation, as necessary.

✓ **LO15 Complete**

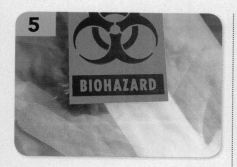

5. Discard all disposable contaminated objects such as wipes or cotton balls by double-bagging (placing the waste in a plastic bag and then in a trash bag). Use a biohazard sticker (red or orange), or a container for contaminated waste. Deposit sharp disposables in a sharps box.

6. Remember, before removing your gloves, all tools and implements that have come into contact with blood or body fluids must be thoroughly cleaned and completely immersed in an EPA-registered hospital disinfectant solution or 10 percent bleach solution for ten minutes. Because blood can carry pathogens, you should never touch an open sore or wound.

7. Wash your hands with soap and warm water before returning to the service.

Application **Tip:**

Always remember to use the Universal Precautions established by the Occupational Safety and Health Administration (OSHA) when handling items exposed to blood or body fluids **(see Chapter 5 Infection Control: Principles and Practices).** Be guided by your instructor for your state's mandatory requirements and procedures for disinfecting any implements that have come into contact with blood or body fluids.

Performing a Basic Manicure

IMPLEMENTS AND MATERIALS

You will need all of the basic materials on your manicuring table:

- Gloves
- Fingerbowl
- Disinfection Container
- Client's Arm Cushion
- Service Cushion
- Gauze and Cotton Wipe Container
- Trash Containers
- Supply Tray (Optional)
- Ultraviolet or Electric Nail Polish Dryer (Optional)

- Electric Hand/Foot Mitts (Optional)
- Terry Cloth Mitts (Optional)
- Wooden Pusher
- Abrasive Nail Files and Buffers
- Disposable or Terry Cloth Towels
- Polish Remover
- Nail Creams, Lotions, and Penetrating Nail Oils
- Cuticle Removers

- Nail Bleach
- Colored Polish, Enamel, Lacquer, or Varnish
- Base Coat
- Nail Hardener
- Top Coat
- Nail Polish Dryers
- Hand Creams and Lotions

PREPARATION

Refer to Procedure 13-1, Pre-Service Procedure.

PROCEDURE

1. Begin with your client's left hand, little finger. Saturate cotton ball, gauze pad, or plastic-backed cotton pad with polish remover. Hold the saturated cotton on each nail while you silently count to 10. The old polish will now come off easily from the nail plate with a stroking motion, moving toward the free edge. Use a confident, firm touch while removing the polish. If all polish is not removed, continue until all traces of polish are gone.

Complete removal of the former polish is important to client satisfaction. It may be necessary to wrap cotton around the tip of a wooden pusher and use it to clean polish away from the nail fold area. After removal, look closely at the nails to check for abnormalities that could have been hidden by the polish.

2. Using your abrasive board, shape the nails as you and the client have agreed. Start with the left hand, little finger, holding it between your thumb and index finger. Do not use less than a medium-grit (180) abrasive file to shape the natural nail. File from one side to the center of the free edge, then from the other side to the center of the free edge. Never use a sawing back and forth motion when filing the natural nail, as this can disrupt the nail plate layers and cause splitting and peeling. To lessen the chance of developing ingrown nails, do not file into the corners of the nails. File each hand from the little fingernail to the thumb.

> **CAUTION**
>
> Always file the nails in a manicure before they are soaked, as water will absorb into the nail plate and make it softer and more easily damaged during filing.

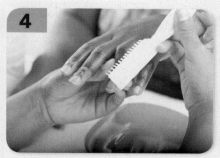

3. After filing the nails on the left hand, and before moving on to the right hand, place the fingertips of the left hand in the fingerbowl to soak and soften the eponychium (living skin on the posterior and sides of the nail) and cuticle (dead tissue adhered to the nail plate) while you file the nails on the right hand. When finished with filing of the right hand, remove the left hand from the soak and place the fingertips of the right hand in the fingerbowl.

4. Brushing the nails with a nail brush removes service debris from the nail surface. After filing the nails on the right hand, remove the left hand from the soak, holding it above the fingerbowl, brush the fingers with your wet nail brush to remove any debris from the fingertips. Use downward strokes, starting at the first knuckle and brushing toward the free edge.

5. Dry the hand with a towel designated as this client's service towel. As you dry, gently push back the eponychium with the towel. Now place the right hand in the soak.

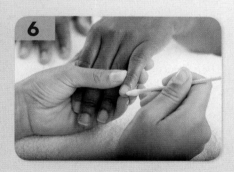

6. Use a cotton-tipped wooden or metal pusher or cotton swab to carefully apply cuticle remover to the cuticle on each nail plate of the left hand. Do not apply this type of product on living skin as it can cause dryness or irritation. Spread evenly on the nail plate. Cuticle removers soften skin by dissolving skin cells so are inappropriate for contact with the living skin of the eponychium. Typically, these products have a high pH (caustic) and are irritating to the skin.

Application **Tip:**

If the nails need to be shortened more than the depth of routine filing, they can be cut with nail clippers, clipping from the sides toward the center of the nails to prevent stress to the sides and possible splitting. This clipping will save time during the filing process. File the free edge after using the nail clipper to perfect the shaping.

Law

State Regulatory ALERT!

State regulations do not permit nail technicians to cut or nip living skin.

Application Tip:

To ensure stability of your hand holding the pusher, place a finger on another finger as a fulcrum (stabilizer) from the implement hand on a finger of the hand being worked on as a fulcrum (Figure 13-34).

FIGURE 13-34
Correct hold.

7

7. After allowing the product to set on the nail for the manufacturer's recommended length of time, the cuticle will be easily removed from the nail plate. Use your wooden pusher or the inside curve of a metal pusher to gently push and lift cuticle tissue off each nail plate of the left hand.

8

8. Use sharp nippers to remove any loosely hanging tags of dead skin (hangnails). Never rip or tear the cuticle tags or the living skin, since this may lead to infection.

9

9. Carefully clean under the free edge using a cotton swab or cotton-tipped wooden pusher. Take care to be gentle, as cleaning too aggressively in this area can break the hyponychium seal under the free edge and cause onycholysis. Remove the right hand from the fingerbowl, dry it, and set it aside.

10. Brush the left hand over the finger bowl one last time to remove bits of debris and traces of cuticle remover. (The client can be sent to the sink to wash the nail plate with their nail brush.) It is important all traces of cuticle remover are washed from the skin as remnants can lead to dryness and/or irritation. Then, instruct the client to rest the left hand on the table towel.

11. Repeat Steps 5 to 10 on the right hand.

12. If the client's nails are yellow, you can bleach them with a nail bleach product designed specifically for this purpose. Apply the bleaching agent to the yellowed nail with a cotton-tipped orangewood stick. Be careful not to apply bleach on your client's skin because it may cause irritation. Wear gloves while bleaching the nails.

Repeat the application if the nails are extremely yellow. You may need to bleach certain clients' nails several times during several services as all of the yellow stain or discoloration may not fade after a single service. If this is true, inform the client so he or she will not be disappointed in your work; suggest a series of treatments to address the problem. Surface stains are removed more easily than those that travel deep into the nail plate. Know that yellow discoloration that penetrates deep into the nail plate will never be completely removed by nail bleaches. The yellowing can be improved, however. These products work best for surface stains (e.g., tobacco). Inform the client if this is true for his or her nails.

13. Use a three-way or four-way buffer to smooth out surface scratches and give the natural nail a brilliant shine.

CAUTION

Excessive pressure or buffing too long with too low-grit abrasives on the nail plate can generate excessive and painful heat into the nail bed and can lead to onycholysis and possible infection. If your client is feeling heat or burning lighten the pressure, lower the speed of the buffing, and buff fewer times between raising the buffer from the surface.

14. Use a cotton-tipped wooden pusher, a cotton swab, or an eyedropper to apply nail oil to each nail plate. Start with the little finger, left hand, and massage oil into the nail plate and surrounding skin using a circular motion.

15. To remove any rough edges on the free edges, bevel (BEH-vel) the underside of the free edge. Hold a medium-grit abrasive board at a 45-degree angle to the underside of the nail and file with an upward stroke. This removes any rough edges or cuticle particles. A fine-grit abrasive board or buffer may also be preferred for weak nails.

16. Apply massage lotion or oil and follow massage procedure.

GO TO → **PROCEDURE 13-6 page 238**

17. After the massage, you must remove all traces of lotion or oil from the nail plate before polishing or the polish will not adhere well. Use a small piece of cotton saturated with alcohol or polish remover as though you were removing a stubborn, red nail polish. Do not forget to clean under the free edge of the nail plate to remove any remaining massage lotion. The cleaner you get the nail plate, the better the polish will adhere.

18. Most clients will have their polish already chosen before or during the consultation but if they do not, ask them to choose a color.

19. Always apply a base coat to keep polish from staining the nails and to help colored polish adhere to the nail plate. Nail strengthener/hardener is an option you may recommend for a treatment if the client's nail plates are thin and weak. Apply this before the base coat if the client requests this treatment.

GO TO → PROCEDURE **13-7** page 242

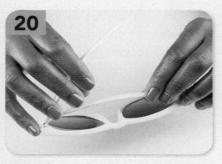

20. You've performed a beautiful, finished manicure.

POST-SERVICE

Refer to Procedure 13-2, Post-Service Procedure.

✓ **LO16 Complete**

Hand and Arm Massage

PROCEDURE **13-6**

IMPLEMENTS AND MATERIALS

In addition to the basic materials on your manicuring table, you will need the following supplies for the Hand and Arm Massage:

• Massage lotion, oil or cream

PREPARATION

Complete Procedure 13-5, Performing a Basic Manicure.

> **fyi** Before performing a hand and arm massage routine, make sure that you are sitting in a comfortable position and not stretching or leaning forward toward your customer. Your posture should be correct and relaxed, and your feet parallel and flat on the floor. Sitting or working in an uncomfortable or strained position can cause back, neck, and shoulder injuries.

PROCEDURE

1. Apply the massage lotion, oil, or cream and distribute to the client's arm. Enough should be applied to allow movement across the skin without resistance (skin drag). Skin drag is not comfortable for the client.

Be sure to hold the client's hand or arm loosely without too much restraint during the massage. A firm but gentle, slow, and rhythmic movement in a predictable routine are the key to a relaxing massage. Moving quickly sends the message to the client that you are hurrying to get the massage over and do not care about providing a good service.

Application **Tip:**

A firm but gentle, slow, and rhythmic movement in a predictable routine are the key to a relaxing massage. Moving quickly sends the message to the client that you are hurrying to get the massage over and do not care about providing a good service.

fyi

Before performing a service that includes a hand and/or arm massage consult the client's consultation or intake form. During the consultation acknowledge and discuss any medical condition your client listed that may be contraindicated for a massage. If they have not discussed massage with their physician, encourage them to do so before performing the service.

Many clients that have high blood pressure (hypertension), diabetes, or circulatory conditions, may still have hand and/or arm massage without concern, especially if their condition is being treated by a physician. Hand and/or arm massage is, however, contraindicated for clients with severe, uncontrolled hypertension. Avoid using vigorous or strong massage techniques on clients who have arthritis. Do not talk to your client during the massage except to ask once whether your touch should be more or less firm. Talking eliminates the relaxation therapy of the massage.

When making decisions about whether to perform a massage on a person who has a medical condition, be conservative. When in doubt, don't include massage as part of your service.

2. The following joint movements are usually performed at the start of the massage to relax the client.

Application **Tip:**

If more cream, oil, or lotion is needed during the massage, always leave one hand on the client's hand or arm and retrieve more product with the other. Having your product in a pump container facilitates this important massage technique.

3. At the beginning of the hand massage, place the client's elbow on a cushion covered with a clean towel or a rolled towel. With one hand, brace the client's arm in the wrist area with your non-dominant hand. With your other hand, hold the client's wrist and bend it back and forth slowly and gently but with a firm touch, 5 to 10 times, until you feel that the client has relaxed.

4. Lower the client's arm, brace the arm at the wrist with the left hand, and with your right hand (or dominant hand) start with the little finger, holding it at the base of the nail. Gently rotate fingers to form circles. Work toward the thumb, about three to five times on each finger.

5. Place the client's elbow on the cushion or towel near the center of the table and your elbows on the table at the sides of it. With your thumbs in the client's palm, rotate them in a circular movement in opposite directions. The circular movements should start from the bottom, center of the hand and move out, up, across the underside of the fingers, and back down to the bottom, center, in a smooth pattern of altering movements of each thumb over the palm. This pattern becomes rhythmic and relaxing. You can feel the client's hands relax as you perform these movements.

6a. Hold the client's hand gently at the wrist with your non-dominant hand and place the palm of your other hand on the back of the client's hand just behind the fingers. Press lightly and move towards the wrist, lift slightly, and move back to the original position and perform the movement. Perform the movement three to five times gently with the palm wrapped warmly around the back of the hand. It is important that enough massage cream, lotion, or oil is on the surface to reduce drag on the skin. Effleurage movements must be smooth and gentle, even predictable, to induce relaxation. After performing the relaxation movements, move to the following effleurage movements.

6b. Perform the transition movement and then move to the fingers. Now, holding the hand with your non-dominant hand, move to the finger tip. Hold each finger with your palm down and the thumb on one side of the finger, the inside of the knuckle of the index finger holding the other side. Gently move the finger back, sliding slowly towards the hand, then turn your hand over completely, moving the thumb to the other side of the finger, your palm up. Then return to the tip, gently pulling the finger. Turn the hand over, back to the original position, and push towards the back of the finger again. Repeat 3 to 5 times, then at the fingertip, move the thumb to under the fingertip, the arch of the index finger over the top of the nail plate, and gently squeeze and pull off the finger. Now, move to the next finger. Perform this movement on all fingers the same number of times, moving from small fingers to thumbs.

This concludes the hand massage usually performed in the Basic Manicure, though the last movement of the arm massage is also performed at the end of this massage. It is not if the massage is continuing on with an arm massage. Then, it is performed at the end of the arm massage.

7a. Now holding the wrist firmly but gently, glide your hand up the arm from wrist to elbow with your palm and fingers on the skin; be certain enough lotion is on the skin to allow a smooth glide of the hand. Cup your movement fingers around the arm, moving up with slight pressure on the skin with your fingers, thumb, and palm to induce relaxation, then move back to the wrist area with a lighter pressure on the skin. Perform this gliding several times. When finishing a movement each time at the top of the arm, rotate the hand to the underside of the arm while pulling the hand back towards you.

7b. Now move to the underarm and perform the same movement. When performing the movement on the underarm, press forward, then at the end release the pressure, gently rotate the hand to the top of the arm, and pull it lightly back toward the hand.

7c. Apply lotion on the palm of one of your hands, then apply to the elbow while holding the arm bent and up gently with the other (cupping the elbow). Glide the palm of the hand over and around the elbow to allow moisturization. Take care to be very gentle. Perform the movement for 10-20 seconds, gently and slowly. Take care not to hit the nerve in the elbow that often is referred to as "the funny bone" as it can be very be painful to the client.

7d. Last, holding the hand with your non-dominant hand, move to the finger tip, and with your thumb on top and pointer finger below, gently grab and pull the finger down to the tips.

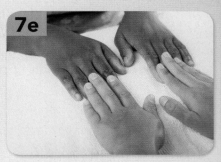

7e. After the finger pulls are performed, lay both of the client's hands palmdown on the table, cover them with your own hands, palmdown on them, and gently press them. Then, as your hands lay on the client's hand, gently, with a light-as-a-feather touch, pull your fingers from the back of the client's hands down the fingers and off the tips of the fingers. Perform two to three times. The client learns quickly this final movement, called "feathering off," is the end of the massage.

Application **Tip:**

Perform the movements several times slowly and rhythmically on this hand or arm and repeat as this is relaxing to the client. Perform the full massage on one arm—palm, back of hand, arm—repeating the gliding movements on each arm several times with transition movements between Now, move to the other hand/arm, starting over in the routine you have developed.

CAUTION

Take care not to press or move with pressure over the bones of the arms as this can be quite painful.

IMPLEMENTS AND MATERIALS

In addition to the basic materials on your manicuring table, you will need the following supplies for Polishing the Nails:

- Base coat
- Colored nail polish

PREPARATION

Complete Procedure 13-5, Performing a Basic Manicure.

PROCEDURE

1a. Be certain the client's nail plates are clean of oil and other debris.

1b. Before applying polish, ask your client to put on any jewelry and outerwear she may have taken off before the service and ask her to get car keys ready to avoid smudges to the freshly applied polish. Have the client pay for services also, to avoid later smudging the polish.

1c. Polish the client's dominant hand first, then place in a nail dryer while you polish the other hand. This will give the most-used, key-holding hand a head start in drying and reduce the likelihood of smudging.

2. Apply base coat to cover the entire nail plate of all nails, and be sure to use a thin coat.

3. When applying nail polish, remove the brush from the bottle and wipe the side of the brush away from you on the inside of the lip of the bottle to remove excess polish. You should have a bead of polish on the end of the other side of the brush large enough to apply one layer to the entire nail plate without having to re-dip the brush (unless the nail plate is unusually long or large). Hold the brush at approximately a 30-degree to 35-degree angle.Place the tip of the brush on the nail 1/8" away from the cuticle area in the center of the nail. Lightly press the brush onto the nail plate, producing a slight"fanning" of the brush and then push the it towards the eponychium to produce a rounded posterior edge to the polish Leave a small, rounded area of unpolished nail at the back of the nail. Pull the brush toward the free edge of the nail, down the center.

4. Move to each side of the nail and pull in even strokes towards the nail tip.

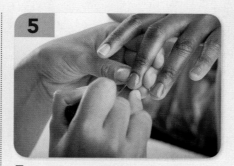

5. After finishing the first coat of each nail, move the brush back and forth on the very end of the free edge, barely touching, to apply color to it. Use the same technique for every nail while applying the first coat of color.

6. When you return to apply the second coat, do not fan the brush and do not reapply to the tip. Just start at the base of the polish curve and move towards the free edge.

7. Apply an ample coat of top coat to prevent chipping and to give nails a glossy, finished appearance. Be sure to coat the free edge of the nail with top coat as well.

LO17 Complete

8. If you use a polish-drying topcoat product, apply according to the manufacturer's instructions. After the application, ask the client to be seated at a separate table with her hands under a nail dryer or seat her comfortably away from your table. The drying time should be about ten minutes.

9. Beautifully polished nails.

Paraffin Wax Treatment

IMPLEMENTS AND MATERIALS

In addition to the basic materials on your manicuring table, you will need the following supplies for the Paraffin Wax Procedure:

- Moisturizing lotion or penetrating oil
- Paraffin bath and heating unit
- Plastic wrap
- Plastic, terry cloth or mitt, or warming (electric) mitts

PREPARATION

Refer to Procedure 13-1, Pre-Service Procedure.
Refer to Procedure 13-3, Hand Washing Procedure.

PERFORMING A PARAFFIN WAX TREATMENT BEFORE A MANICURE

1. Check the hands carefully for open wounds, diseases, or disorders. It is not appropriate to apply heat to clients with abnormal skin conditions. If it is safe to perform the procedure, ensure the client's hands are clean and continue with the service.

2. Apply moisturizing lotion or penetrating oil to client's hands and gently massage into the skin.

3. Test the temperature of the wax.

4. Prepare the client's hand for dipping into the paraffin by placing the palm facing down with the wrist slightly bent and the fingers straight and slightly apart.

5. Dip the first hand into the wax up to the wrist for about 3 seconds. Remove. Allow the wax to solidify some before dipping again.

6. Repeat the dip process three to five times to coat the skin.

7. Wrap the hands in plastic wrap or insert into plastic mitts designed for this purpose, then put them into terry cloth or warming (electric) mitts. Allow the paraffin to remain on the hands for approximately 5 to 10 minutes.

8. Repeat Steps 5 through 7 on the other hand.

9. To remove the paraffin, turn the plastic cover under at the wrist and peel away at the wrist, The wax will easily come off as you gently pull the cover down the hand to the fingertips. The paraffin removed from the hands will collect in the plastic cover of the hands.

10. Properly dispose of the used paraffin.

11. Begin the manicuring procedure. For many clients who opt to have a paraffin wax treatment before the manicure, soaking is not necessary because the paraffin treatment has already softened the skin sufficiently.

✓ **LO18 Complete**

PERFORMING A PARAFFIN WAX TREATMENT DURING A MANICURE

1. Perform the basic manicure up to the completion of the massage.

2. Apply a hydrating lotion on one hand and briefly rub it into the hand.

3. Apply the paraffin with your method of choice.

4. Cover the hand with a plastic bag or wrap, then a terry cloth or heated mitt.

5. Repeat Steps 1 through 4 on the other hand. Allow the client to relax for 5 to10 minutes.

6. Remove the paraffin mitt and rub in the remaining lotion.

7. Remove any remaining oils or lotions from the nail plate. Use alcohol or polish remover on a cotton-tipped wooden stick or a cotton ball. Do not allow the alcohol or polish remover on the skin or the benefits of the treatment will be lessened by the drying effects of these solvents.

8. Polish or clear coat nails, according to client's request.

PART **3**

PERFORMING A PARAFFIN WAX TREATMENT AS A STAND-ALONE SERVICE

For applying paraffin wax as a stand-alone service, the client must wash her hands, then you follow the same steps as in **Performing a Paraffin Wax Treatment Before a Manicure.**

POST-SERVICE

Refer to Procedure 13-2,
Post-Service Procedure.

Here's a **Tip:**

If a client is uncomfortable about dipping her hands into the wax bath, there are other ways to apply the wax that will allow it to perform well. Consider the methods below:

- Place about a half cup of paraffin in a plastic bag and insert the client's hand. Then move the wax around the hand, covering the surface.

- Wrap the hand with cheesecloth or paper towels that was dipped into the paraffin, Dip, then raise up the cloth or towel to allow them to drip. Now, press each piece close and around the hands. Next, cover with plastic mitts or plastic wrap.

- Spray paraffin on the hands then place in plastic mitts or plastic wrap.

- Purchase one-time-use commercial gloves that heat and have paraffin in them. Merely insert the hands and the paraffin heats to become a paraffin mitt.

Law

State Regulatory ALERT!

Once paraffin wax is used on a client it becomes contaminated and therefore should never be reused!

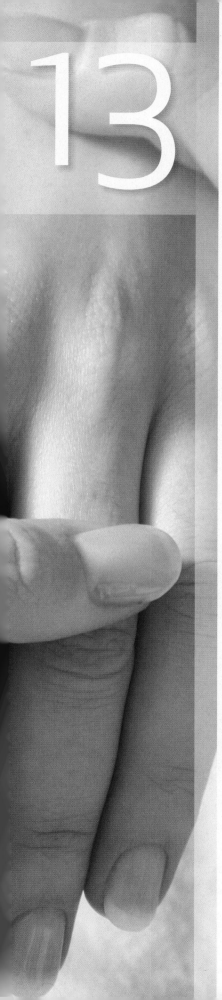

review questions

1. Name the four types of nail implements and/or tools required to perform a manicure.

2. What is the difference between reusable and disposable implements?

3. What is the Three Part Procedure and how is it used in the performance of the basic manicure?

4. Why is it important for both the nail technician and the client to wash their hands before nail services?

5. Is a consultation necessary each time a client has a service in the salon? Why?

6. Name the basic nail shapes for women.

7. What is the most popular nail shape for men?

8. Which massage movements are most appropriate for a hand and arm massage? Why?

9. What is the difference between a basic manicure and a spa manicure?

10. How is aromatherapy used in manicuring services?

11. Explain the use and benefits of paraffin wax treatments in manicuring.

12. List the correct steps for cleaning and disinfecting nail implements and tools.

13. What would be on the manicuring table if it were properly set up?

14. What are the steps in the post-service procedure?

15. What is an exposure incident? If an exposure incident occurs, what steps should be taken?

16. List the steps in the basic manicure.

17. How is nail polish applied properly?

18. What is the procedure for a paraffin wax hand treatment before a manicure?

14

pedicuring

After you have completed this chapter, you will be able to:

1. Identify and explain the equipment used when performing pedicures.

2. Identify and explain three materials used when performing pedicures.

3. Describe a callus softener and how it is best used.

4. Explain the differences between a basic pedicure and a spa pedicure.

5. Describe reflexology and its use in pedicuring.

6. Know why consistent cleaning and disinfection of pedicure baths must be performed.

7. Know and describe the steps involved in the proper cleaning and disinfecting of whirlpool foot spas and air jet basins.

8. List and perform the steps in the pedicure pre-service procedure.

9. Describe the proper tool and technique to use to reduce the instance of an ingrown toenail.

10. Demonstrate the proper procedures for a basic pedicure.

11. Demonstrate a foot and leg massage.

Key Terms

Page number indicates where in the chapter the term is used.

callus softener / 257

curette / 254

exfoliating scrubs / 256

foot files (paddles) / 254

foot soaks / 256

mask / 252

massage / 262

microtrauma / 261

nail rasp / 254

nipper / 255

pedicures / 250

reflexology / 263

toe separators / 255

toenail clippers / 253

Pedicures are cosmetic services performed on the feet by a licensed nail technician or cosmetologist and includes trimming, shaping the nails, exfoliating skin, and polishing toenails as well as a foot massage. Though this service has been in the beauty industry for decades and in the world of foot care since ancient times, it was rarely performed until as recently as the late 1980s.

Then, with the development of the spa industry and new, pampering equipment, techniques, and products, the service exploded onto service menus in the 1990s and became the fastest growing service in the industry. Now, for many clients, pedicures are a regular ritual in their personal care regimen. Pedicures are considered a standard service performed in salons by nail professionals and cosmetologists.

The information in this chapter will provide you with the skills you need to perform beautification and routine care on your clients' feet, toes, and toenails. Pedicures are now a basic part of good foot care and hygiene and are particularly important for clients who are joggers, dancers, and cosmetologists, or for anyone who spends a lot of time standing on his or her feet.

Pedicures are not merely "manicures on the feet." Although they are a similar basic service, they require specific skills; much more knowledge of chronic illnesses, diseases, and disorders; and additional precautions. Pedicures present more potential for damage to clients than a manicure does. Experts recommend that you become proficient in performing manicures before learning how to perform pedicures. Pedicures create loyalty in clients, are good income producers, and can be important preventive health services for many clients. In short, pedicure services, are for just about everyone. Once your clients experience the comfort, relaxation and value of a great pedicure, they will return for more. For these reasons, you would be wise to perfect your pedicures skills while you are in school.

> *Pedicures are now a basic part of good foot care and hygiene...*

Pedicure Tools

As in manicuring, in pedicuring it is important that you learn to work with the tools required for this service, and to incorporate all safety, cleansing, and disinfection procedures as stated in your state's regulations. They include the standard manicure tools plus a few that are specific to the pedicure service. Again, the four types of nail technology tools that you will incorporate into your services include:

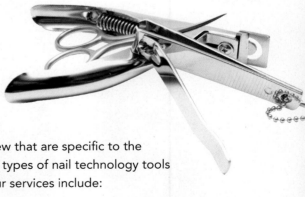

- Equipment
- Implements
- Materials
- Pedicure products

EQUIPMENT

Equipment includes all permanent tools used to perform nail services that are not implements. Some permanent equipment for performing pedicures is different from that used for manicures.

Pedicure Station

Pedicure stations include a comfortable chair with an armrest and footrest for the client, and an ergonomic chair for the nail professional. Designs vary according to several factors, such as the size of the area, the location of the water in the salon, and cost (**Figure 14-1, Figure 14-2, and Figure 14-3**).

▲ **FIGURE 14-1**
Comfortable chair and pedicure chair.

Pedicure Stool and Footrest

Pedicures can present many more challenges than manicures to the service provider in maintaining a healthy posture while performing the service. For that reason, the nail technician's pedicuring stool is usually low to make it ergonomically easier for the pedicurist to work on the client's feet. Some stools come with a built-in footrest for the client, or a separate footrest can be used. Your chair must be comfortable and allow ergonomically correct positioning (**Figure 14-4 and Figure 14-5**).

▲ **FIGURE 14-2**
turdy pedicure center ith removable foot bath nd adjustable footrest.

▲ **FIGURE 14-3**
Fully-plumbed station comes with many options.

The pedicure foot bath varies in design from the basic stainless steel basin to an automatic whirlpool that warms and massages the client. The soak bath is filled with comfortably warm water and a product to soak the client's feet. The bath must be large enough to completely immerse both of the client's feet comfortably.

Basin soak baths can be large stainless steel bowls or beautiful ceramic ones. Also, small transportable baths can be purchased from retail or beauty supply stores, or from industry manufacturers. They must be manually filled and emptied after each client's service (**Figure 14-6**).

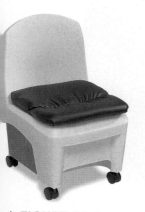

▲ **FIGURE 14-4**
Low pedicure chair with back support.

A step above the portable water baths is the more customized pedicure unit which has a removable foot bath and the technician's stool built in. These are more ergonomically designed for the nail technician than when she sits on the floor to perform the service. A portable pedicure unit includes a place for the foot bath and a storage area for supplies.

◄ **FIGURE 14-6**
Self-contained foot bath with hose.

▲ **FIGURE 14-5**
Pedicure chair with drawers and back support.

The next step up in cost and ease of use is the portable foot basin with built-in whirlpool-action (Figure 14-7). These baths add an extra touch to the service with the gentle massaging action of the whirlpool. The bath is filled from the sink through attachable hoses. After the service, the bath is drained by pumping the water back into the sink through the attached hoses. It has a built-in foot rest and the surrounding cabinet has areas for storage of pedicure supplies.

▲ FIGURE 14-7
Typical portable foot bath, usually with a whirlpool fan.

The ultimate pedicure foot bath is the fully plumbed pedicure chair, sometimes referred to as a "throne-design" chair. These units are not portable. They are permanently plumbed to both hot and cold water as well as to a drain. Most units have a built-in massage feature in the chair and a warmer which adds to the relaxation of the client. Recently, many throne-type chairs with a self-cleaning and disinfection cycle have become available.

Pedicure Carts

These carts are designed to keep supplies organized. There are many different designs available that include a hard surface for placement of your implements and in-service supplies as well as drawers and shelves for storage of implements, supplies, and pedicure products. Some units include a space for storage of the footbath. Most take up very little space and greatly aid in organization of the area. (Figure 14-8).

▲ FIGURE 14-8
Portable pedicure cart with drawers.

Electric Foot Mitts (Optional)

These heated mitts, similar to electric manicure mitts but shaped for the feet, are designed to add a special touch to a more-than-a-basic pedicure. A pedicure in which these are used is a higher cost service, or it can be an add-on to a lower cost service for an added cost. After a foot massage, a conditioning lotion or a mask is applied to the feet and then they are placed in a plastic wrap or cover. Finally, the feet are placed inside the warm foot mitts. A mask, also known as a masque, is a concentrated treatment product often composed of mineral clays, moisturizing agents, skin softeners, aromatherapy oils, botanical extracts and other beneficial ingredients to cleanse, exfoliate, tighten, tone, hydrate, and nourish the skin.

The warmth provided by the mitts aids in penetration of the conditioning ingredients of the mask, adds to the comfort and warmth of the service, and provides the ultimate relaxation of the client.

Terry Cloth Mitts (Optional)

These washable mitts, available for both hands and feet, are placed over a client's feet after a penetrating conditioning product and a cover have been applied. These are routinely used also over paraffin and a cover, as they hold in the heat provided by the paraffin to encourage conditioning of the feet or hands by the product.

Paraffin Bath (Optional)

Discussed in Chapter 13, paraffin is an especially wonderful treatment in a pedicure. **(Figure 14-9)**.

▲ FIGURE 14-9
Paraffin bath.

Though there are many ways to apply paraffin from the bath that many clients, salon and spa owners, and professionals prefer (discussed in **Chapter 13, Manicuring**), the traditional method is to dip and re-dip the hands and feet three to four times into the larger paraffin bath. The paraffin coating covers the skin, sealing the surface of the skin and promoting moisturization from products and masks and moisture within the lower layers of the skin. The paraffin bath also stimulates circulation and the deep heat it provides helps to reduce inflammation and promote circulation to the affected joints. Some unique health precautions for providing pedicures must be considered for clients who are chronically ill. Do not provide the paraffin wax treatment to clients with lesions or abrasions, impaired foot or leg circulation, or loss of feeling in their feet or legs or other diabetes-related problems. The skin of elderly clients may be more sensitive to heat or thinner so a pre-service wax patch test must be performed to check for client comfort in having the treatment.

✓ LO1 Complete

IMPLEMENTS

The implements mentioned in **Chapter 13, Manicuring**, are used in pedicures also. There are, however, implements that are specific for use in pedicures.

Below is a list of these implements:

Toenail Clippers

These toenail clippers are larger than fingernail clippers and are specifically designed for shortening toenails. Use only these professional toenail clippers made especially for cutting toenails. The jaws on toenail clippers are curved or straight. The best clippers for toenails have jaws which are straight and come to a point. Those with blunt points are difficult to use in the small corners of highly curved nail plates. For your client's safety, only use high-quality implements made specifically for performing professional pedicures. They will last longer and make your job easier.

Curettes

A curette is an implement with a small, scoop-shaped end that, if carefully used, allows for more efficient removal of debris from the nail folds, eponychium, and hyponychium areas. Curettes are ideal for use around the edges of the big toenail plate (**Figure 14-10**). A double-ended curette, which has a 0.06 inch (1.5 mm) diameter on one end and a 0.1 inch (2.5 mm) diameter on the other, is recommended. Some are made with a small hole, making the curette easier to clean after it has been used.

Curettes require gentle and careful maneuvers to prevent damage to the skin in the nail folds. It is never to be used to "cut out" any tissue or debris that is adhering to living tissues. Nail technicians must never use curettes with sharp edges as they can seriously injure clients. Only those with dull edges are safe and appropriate for use by cosmetologists or nail technicians.

Nail Rasp

The nail rasp is a metal file used in a specific fashion. Ask your instructor to demonstrate its use for you. It is designed to file in one direction with a filing surface of about 1/8-inch wide and about 3/4-inch long attached to a straight or angled metal handle (**Figure 14-11**). The angled rasp is recommended because it is easier to control under the free edge of the nail.

The rasp is placed under the nail, angling from the center of the nail out past the side free edge, then gently pulled toward the center to file free edges that might grow into the tissues, potentially causing an ingrown nail. The rasping process may be repeated to make sure there are no rough edges remaining along the free edge. Do not overfile.

As you become proficient in the use of a nail rasp you will find it to be an invaluable and time-saving implement. Properly used, it will add the professional finishing touch required in the care of the toenails that need it. Take special care with this tool and never use it on the top of the nail or past the hyponichium area of the side of the free edge as it can damage the skin and initiate infections. Never use it on nails that are already ingrown; refer these clients to a podiatrist.

Pedicure Nail Files

For toenails, a medium grit will work best, always finishing with the fine grit to seal the edges. Some nail technicians use metal files on toenails (**Figure 14-12**). Check with your instructor to find out whether metal files are legal in your state. Metal files must be cleansed and disinfected or sterilized after each use and before reuse.

Foot Files or Paddles

These large foot files or paddles are designed to smooth foot calluses (**Figure 14-13**). They come in many different grits and shapes. They must be properly cleaned and disinfected between each use or disposed of after a single use, if not able to be disinfected.

▼ **FIGURE 14-10**
Double-ended curette.

▲ **FIGURE 14-11**
Nail rasp.

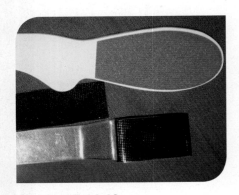

▲ **FIGURE 14-12**
Metal abrasive file.

▲ **FIGURE 14-13**
Foot files for reducing calluses.

In general, if an abrasive file cannot survive proper cleaning and disinfection procedures without being rendered unusable, it must be considered single-use or be given to the client for home use.

Many reasonably priced foot paddles are now available for purchase in bulk for single-use in pedicures. Foot paddles with disposable and replaceable abrasive surfaces are also available. The handles of these files must be cleaned and disinfected before re-use. Check with your instructor to find out whether these are legal for use in your state.

Nippers

A nipper is an implement used in manicures and pedicures to trim tags of dead skin. Because of the many precautions in performing pedicures, nail technicians must take great care to avoid cutting, tearing, or ripping living tissue with this implement. Do not use nippers on the feet of clients who have diabetes since the risk of infection, amputation, even death from accidental injury, is great. Also, avoid using nippers on clients with psoriasis since injury to the toenail unit can create new psoriasis lesions where the damage occurs.

MATERIALS

All materials mentioned in **Chapter 13, Manicuring**, also are used in pedicuring. In addition, a few unique materials are used in this service.

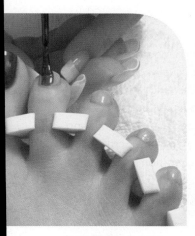

▲ **FIGURE 14-14**
Toe separators.

Toe Separators

Toe separators are made of foam rubber or cotton and used to keep toes apart while polishing the nails. Toe separators are important for performing a quality pedicure **(Figure 14-14)**. Since toe separators cannot be cleaned and disinfected, a new set must be used on each client and then thrown away.

Pedicure Slippers

Single-use paper or foam slippers are provided for those clients who have not worn open-toe shoes and want to avoid smudging their newly applied toenail polish. They are specially designed not to touch the nails while being worn.

Gloves

Nail technicians must wear gloves while performing pedicures because repeated exposure of their skin to pedicure water can cause extreme dryness and cracking on the hands. Gloves also protect the technician from exposure to pathogens that may be present on the feet or in the water. A new set of gloves is worn for each pedicure then thrown away. If the client or nail technician is allergic to latex, nitrile gloves should be worn. (See Chapter 13, Manicuring, for more information.)

✓ **LO2 Complete**

■■ Law

■ State Regulatory ALERT!

It is illegal for nail technicians to cut or dramatically reduce calluses on clients unless working under the direct supervision of a physician or podiatrist as an assistant. Cutting falls under the category of medical treatment, and is not a cosmetic service. It is considered outside the scope of practice of a nail technician in most states and will be determined so in the others in lawsuits. The technician may have to explain this truth to some clients who are accustomed to these illegal activities in other salons. Simply say, "I'm sorry, but cutting is a medical treatment and we are not allowed to use blades for that reason. We have good products and procedures to reduce calluses without dangerously cutting your skin."

CAUTION

It is especially dangerous to cut into and damage the skin on the feet of immuno-suppressed clients as the healing of their wounds is a slow process and sometimes even impossible. Do not trim cuticles, use metal pushers, or use sharp implements on clients who have any chronic illness. Even a tiny break in the skin that cannot be seen can cause infection, even amputation and death.

Professional Pedicure Products

Products for pedicure services include the products discussed in **Chapter 13, Manicuring**, plus others that are unique to pedicuring. These new product types are:

- Soaks
- Scrubs
- Masks
- Pedicure lotions and creams
- Callus softeners

FOOT SOAKS

Foot soaks are put into the water in the pedicure bath to soften the skin on the feet during the soak time. A good foot soak product is gentle but effective and thoroughly cleans and deodorizes the feet. It is better to use professionally formulated products as they are designed to properly cleanse without being overly harsh to the skin. Other ingredients may include moisturizing oils that contain aromatherapy qualities. The soak sets the stage for the rest of the pedicure, so be sure to use a high quality one to start your pedicure service on a good note.

EXFOLIATING SCRUBS

These gritty lotions are massaged on the foot and leg to remove dry, flaky skin and reduce calluses. They leave the skin feeling smoother and moisturized. Exfoliating scrubs are usually water-based lotions that contain an abrasive as the exfoliating agent. Sea sand, ground apricot kernels, pumice, quartz crystals, jojoba beads, and polypropylene beads are all exfoliating agents that may be found in pedicure scrubs. Scrubs also contain moisturizers which help to condition the skin. Nail technicians must wear gloves when using these products as repeated use will irritate the skin on the hands.

MASKS

Masks are concentrated treatment products often composed of mineral clays, moisturizing agents, skin softeners, aromatherapy oils, and beneficial extracts and other ingredients to cleanse exfoliate, tighten, tone, hydrate and nourish the skin. They are highly valued by clients. Masks are applied to the skin and left in place for five to ten minutes to allow penetration of beneficial ingredients. Menthol, mint, cucumber, and other ingredients are very popular in foot care masks.

FOOT LOTIONS OR CREAMS

Lotions and creams are important to condition and moisturize the skin of the feet, to soften calluses, and to provide slip for massage during the service. They are also formulated as home-care products to sell to clients after services for maintenance of the service or improvement of the skin. Nail technicians who work in a podiatry or medical office, however, will be

---

CAUTION

No additive that is added to the water during a pedicure soak kills pathogens and replaces your obligation to clean and disinfect the equipment and implements after the pedicure. Any chemical that is strong enough to adequately kill pathogens is not safe for contact with skin. Disinfectants must never be placed in the foot bath with your client's feet. They can be harmful to the skin.

Did **You** Know...

Avoid excessively abrasive scrubs since they may leave tiny, invisible scratches on clients' skin that can be portals of entry for pathogenic microorganisms. Portals of entry are openings in the skin caused by damage in a professional service.

introduced to treatment-level lotions and creams that are associated with the improvement of medical conditions of the feet. Whether you work in a salon, spa, or medical office, get to know your product line well in order to recommend products to aid the client in maintaining the benefits of your pedicure.

CALLUS SOFTENERS

These professional strength callus softener products are applied directly to the client's heels and over pressure point calluses and are left on for a short period of time, according to the manufacturers' directions, to soften and smooth thickened tissue (calluses). After the product softens the skin, it is more easily reduced and smoothed with files or paddles.

 LO3 Complete

About Pedicures

Pedicures have settled into the lifestyles of Americans to the extent that many go to their salon for pedicures more often than they have their hair cut. These clients are as choosy about their pedicure as they are about their haircuts. As with most beauty procedures, a pedicure is a service that must be practiced and perfected, and you must continually search for education and new ideas to keep up with the changes.

CHOOSING PEDICURE PRODUCTS

Many pedicure products are available, but the most synergistic ones (those designed to work well together) are developed in systems or lines by companies. They also are the fastest and easiest way to develop an optimal pedicure service. They are available from many manufacturers of professional nail and foot products. Before choosing any one line, check out a variety of product lines, compare them, and then decide for yourself which line is best for your clients.

Always check the quality of the company's educational support and its commitment to the nail technicians using its products. Find technicians who use the products and discuss the quality of the company's customer service and its shipping competence, and listen closely to their experiences. Then, look at your research and make the decision based on which company best meets your and your clients' needs.

When using a manufacturer's product line, follow its recommendations and suggested procedures because its methods have been tested and found to enhance the effectiveness of its product line.

CAUTION

Cuticle removers and callus softeners are potentially hazardous to the eyes. For that reason, safety glasses should be worn whenever using or pouring them. Be sure to wear gloves during their use. Used improperly, these products may cause severe irritation to the nail technician's eyes, hands and skin. Used correctly, they are safe and effective.

CAUTION

Remember that calluses protect the underlying skin from irritation and are there for a purpose. For example, joggers, waitresses, cosmetologists, nurses, teachers, and others are on their feet many hours a day. Calluses protect their feet in stress areas. Remove only enough to make the client comfortable. Calluses should be softened and smoothed, not excessively thinned or removed. Never use a blade on calluses as it is illegal and can cause debilitating infections in clients.

Educate your client about callus formation and the protective function calluses provide. Also discuss products for home use to help soften and condition callused areas between salon appointments.

SERVICE MENU

Tailor your foot care menu of services to meet the lifestyle and requests of your clientele. For example, younger clients will probably love nail art, while the older ones may not, but may enjoy paraffin wax treatments.

Shorter services are great menu expanders. Not all clients will want or need a full pedicure. Some clients may only want or need a professional nail trimming. Others may want a pampering massage appointment between their full pedicure services to relieve tension and stress. Some may only want a polish change. List these additional services on your menu with your full pedicures to provide options for your clients.

INTERACTION DURING THE SERVICE

During the procedure, discuss with your client the products that are needed to maintain the pedicure between salon visits. However, only talk to clients who wish to have a discussion. Never discuss personal issues. Those who want to drift off should be allowed the peace and tranquility they are seeking. If this is the case, discuss your product recommendations during polishing or when closing the service.

Remember, clients are often in the salon to relax and be pampered. Offer them refreshment and suggest they sit back and relax, then smile and start the service. There should be no distractions for you or the client during the pedicure. Clients purchase this service, aside from the foot care performed, because of the relaxation it provides. Distractions prevent this from happening.

To grow your clientele, you must encourage your clients to schedule regular, monthly pedicures. The accepted time between pedicure appointments is generally four weeks because of the slow growth of the toenails. Mention that their feet are in constant use and need routine maintenance. Remind them that proper foot care, through pedicuring, improves both personal appearance and basic foot comfort.

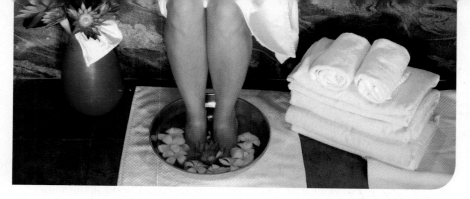

SCHEDULING

When scheduling a client for a pedicure over the telephone, warn female clients not to shave their legs within 48 hours prior to the pedicure. Why? Shaving the legs within this time frame before a pedicure increases the presence of tiny microscopic abrasions from the shaving that may allow portals of entry for pathogenic microbes and can increase the risk of stinging, irritation, or infection. This is an important infection control policy.

To help uphold the policy, post a tasteful sign with the same message in the pedicure area, and place it on your service menu and Web site where your pedicures are listed. Then, before you place your client's feet in the pedicure soak, ask her when she last shaved her legs—if it was within the last 48 hours, reschedule the appointment. It is the responsible thing to do.

Additionally as a customer service, when clients are scheduling an appointment for a pedicure suggest they wear open-toed shoes or sandals so that polish will not be ruined immediately following the service. Many spas provide single-use pedicure slippers for those who forget their sandals, but a reminder when scheduling is greatly appreciated since the appearance of their polish is a priority to these clients.

It's important to schedule the appointments for the proper length of time and for the technicians to stay on time. Clients dislike waiting for a nail technician who is running late. For that reason, learn the time that individual steps of the pedicure (toenail shortening, cuticle removal, massage, callus removal) should be allotted within the total time assigned on the menu for the service and then practice to meet those times. Knowing where you should be in a service at a specific time also helps you to stay on time for your next client. An example might be that you must be polishing 45–50 minutes after beginning a one-hour pedicure in order to be on time.

The basic pedicure in most salons does not include a leg massage; a spa pedicure usually does. It is a longer, more upscale and more expensive service, and therefore deserves that additional time. The basic pedicure may be 45 minutes, but the spa pedicure, with the added mask and leg massage, even a paraffin wax service, will be much longer, possibly even a half hour longer, depending upon the additional services and how luxurious they might be. Do not cram too much into a pedicure or it will not be relaxing for your client and you will not enjoy offering it. It may even cause you backaches.

Time your services appropriately and clients will believe they are receiving better services, and will be willing to pay what you deserve to receive.

There may also be times when a client will book a pedicure, but because of the condition of his or her feet, the client will need more time than was scheduled. If you are completing the client consultation and evaluating the client's feet, you know quite quickly if this is the case. You must tell this client that you will do the best you can in the time scheduled but he or she must schedule another pedicure very soon to get the feet into the excellent condition they will enjoy. Usually clients with problem feet know that this is the case and they shouldn't be surprised at the need for another appointment and further work. Do not work beyond your scheduled time.

By sticking to the appointment time allotted, you will not only be preserving your schedule, but you will also be protecting the client. If his or her feet are in bad shape, and you work as long as is necessary to get them in optimal condition in only one service, the client's feet may become irritated or painful. The best option is to sell the client home-care products to improve the condition of the feet and schedule him or her for another service in one to two week's time.

> Some improvements in the feet require more than one appointment...

SERIES PEDICURES

Some improvements in the feet require more than one appointment in services referred to as a series. A series example is callus reduction. When a client comes in with heavy calluses, never use a blade. Not only is its use dangerous and can potentially cause infection, but it is against the law in most states. It also stimulates heavier growth of calluses as the skin attempts to grow back quickly to protect the damaged skin.

To reduce calluses and to maintain their reduction, perform a safe amount of exfoliation during a pedicure with a scrub; apply the new, more effective callus reduction products on them; and use the foot paddle to remove a safe amount of callus. Explain the negatives for speedy removal of the calluses to the client and explain that weekly callus reduction appointments for four to six weeks will lower the calluses and allow them to then be maintained at the lower level with monthly pedicures.

The entire pedicure is not performed between the monthly pedicures during the series appointments; the appointment is merely a weekly treatment of a soak, application of the reduction product, a set time (usually five minutes) to allow for it to work, reasonable callus reduction, application of a lotion, and dismissal. It takes about a half hour and should be a less expensive service than an entire pedicure.

At the four-week appointment, a full pedicure is performed with treatments following again. Some clients will require more than the six weeks, and this should be explained when the series is suggested. The client can also be sold a glycolic or lactic acid hand and body lotion to use on the feet every other day, with the use of a lotion containing DMU daily to soften and prevent the scaly condition from returning. A foot paddle can also be sold to the client for use after showers between treatment appointments. Gloves must be worn during these services.

Another condition that can require weekly treatment is scaly feet. First, however, the client must be sent to a podiatrist to define whether the feet are fungal, resulting in a scaly condition on the feet. If everything is okay, the client can return weekly for three to six weeks for a foot exfoliation treatment with scrubs and the use of a callus reduction treatment, such as a mask, all over the feet for one to three minutes, no more. These treatments are designed so that the client will have beautiful feet when the series is finished. Home-care products must be recommended to maintain the condition.

SPA PEDICURE

The pedicure described in Procedure 14-3, The Basic Pedicure, is the basis from which all other pedicure services are designed. For example, in the basic pedicure, the massage is performed on the foot only, while in the upgrade to a spa pedicure, the massage is performed on the foot and the leg to the knee.

Another upgrade in the more expensive spa pedicure would be the use of a mask on the foot and/or leg, covering it, and allowing a relaxing set time for the effectiveness of the mask. A further upgrade would be the incorporation of special products such as the use of aromatherapy lotions, oils, paraffin, and other specialty products.

✔ LO**4** Complete

ELDERLY CLIENTS

Older people need proper foot care even more than younger people, on a regular basis, and year-round. Many elderly cannot reach their feet, cannot see them, or cannot squeeze the nail clippers to trim the nails. They need continual help in their foot care maintenance, especially since it can become a health issue for many. The nail technician who offers pedicure services for this segment of the population will be doing these individuals a great service and will find plenty of willing clients in need of their services.

Did **You** Know...

Most salons will have a protocol to follow when finishing services. Follow them closely for two reasons. First, a routine keeps things moving in the salon, and second, clients get used to the closing protocol and know what to expect. If your salon does not have a post-service protocol, or if you work alone, establish one. Clients are more comfortable with a familiar routine.

Many of these clients have health issues that require exceptionally gentle care. Never cut their tissues or push back the eponychium as even a microscopic opening, or microtrauma, can be fatal for these clients. Discuss health issues with them; do not perform pedicures on diabetics or on people with circulatory diseases without their physician's permission. Seek training in how to work with these clients so you will know how to work safely with them.

▲ FIGURE 14-15

Gel toe art.

PEDICURE PRICING

The salon or spa will probably already have a price list for services in place. If and when you find yourself in a position to price your services, a good rule of thumb is to determine the price of your basic pedicure first and then set your prices for your more upscale and luxurious pedicures by increasing the base price of the pedicure according to the value of the added treatments, products, and time it takes you to perform the additional services.

Another great way to upgrade your pedicure price is through nail art. Many clients enjoy adding a little something special to their normal pedicure polish, especially if they are not permitted to wear polish or art on their hands where they work. It is easy to get your clients addicted to toenail art by giving the first example free. Once they have it, and their friends comment, they will want it every time, and you will quickly see an increase in revenue with your existing clientele **(Figure 14-15)**. Toenail art is especially popular in sandal season and when wearing formal open footwear.

Many salons and spas have found that selling manicure and pedicure packages works very nicely for them. Selling manicures and pedicures together are like salt and pepper—although they are different, they go well together.

One great way to do this is to develop theme services for holidays and special events, such as Christmas, Valentine's Day, Mother's Day, prom, weddings, and birthday packages; market them, and you will see your clientele grow.

PEDICURE MASSAGE

According to post-visit client salon surveys, massage is the most enjoyed aspect of any nail service. This is especially true for pedicures. For that reason, spend time designing one you will enjoy giving and that your client will enjoy receiving.

The art of massage enjoys a rich history and may have been around since the beginning of time. The definition of massage according to the Merriam-Webster Dictionary, is "a method of manipulation of the body by rubbing, pinching, kneading, tapping." General body massage can be relaxing or for therapeutic purposes, however, massage given during manicures and pedicures definitely focuses on relaxation.

The number of massage styles and routines are as vast as the number of persons massaging. No matter what technique you use, perfect it so that it becomes second nature to you. During this part of the pedicure, be keenly aware of your client's health, meet any precautionary requirements, and offer a massage that relaxes the client but is not harmful to him or her.

 Until you receive permission from a physician, placating massages, such as a gentle, relaxing massage on the soles of the feet only can be provided to clients who have health precautions. Do not exert pressure and do not massage their legs. Inform the client that your massage will be even more enjoyable after permission for it is obtained.

As in manicures, the massage is predominantly effleurage. It is even truer for pedicures than manicures because of the circulatory issues that may be present in your clients. You must ask clients questions concerning their health during consultation. If they have a circulatory disease, high blood pressure, or other chronic diseases that affect their legs or feet, you must get permission from the client's physician before providing a full spa pedicure massage.

Most of us enjoy being touched, and the art of massage takes a pedicure to a higher level. It's special; many think it is more special than a massage on any other part of the body. Foot massage induces a high degree of relaxation and stimulates blood flow. Be aware of the areas of the feet and legs where the client most enjoys massage and put a greater emphasis in these areas.

Every nail technician has his or her own massage style and technique. No matter what you define as yours, perfect it so that it becomes second nature to you.

REFLEXOLOGY

Reflexology is a unique method of applying pressure with thumb and index fingers to the hands and feet, and demonstrates health benefits. This specialty massage of the soles of the feet is offered by many professionals and it can employ many of the principles of acupressure and acupuncture. It is considered a science by many technicians.

Reflexology is based on the principle that areas (reflexes) in the feet and hands correspond to all the organs, glands, and parts of the body. It is said that stimulating these reflexes or points can reflect positive energy and increase blood flow to these areas when pressed.

Professional, hands-on training is essential in reflexology for two reasons. First, there is a certain type of touch in reflexology that can be learned only through hands-on training. Clients who have experienced a reflexology treatment from a certified expert reflexologist know what that touch is and respond negatively to those who cannot deliver the same treatment because of minimal or no training. Second, an untrained professional may not be able to produce results for the client, who in turn, will see no reason for the additional cost or time.

If a salon truly wishes to offer reflexology services to its clients, it is best that the staff or professional receives authentic training and certification in the art of reflexology.

✓ **LO5 Complete**

ERGONOMICS

Performing pedicures can be a serious challenge to the health and well-being of a nail technician. Many develop serious and painful back conditions if they are careless about properly protecting themselves through ergonomics.

> Pay attention to your body's positioning and make sure you are working ergonomically.

Pay attention to your body's positioning and make sure you are working ergonomically. Always sit in a comfortable position, relaxed, and unstrained to reduce the risk of injury to your back, shoulders, arms, wrists, and hands. For example, avoid leaning forward or stretching to reach your client's feet. Take a minute to stretch before and after a pedicure to keep your body limber, in line, and more resistant to injury.

Although it is important to give your client the best possible service, it is also important to keep yourself healthy during the process and avoid injuries caused by strain or repeated motion.

THREE-PART PROCEDURE

As discussed in **Chapter 13, Manicuring**, it is easier to keep track of what you are doing, to remain organized, and to give consistent service, if you break your foot care procedures down into three individual parts. These three parts are: the pre-service procedure, the service procedure, and the post-service procedure.

A. Pre-service Procedure

The pre-service procedure is an organized step-by-step plan for the cleaning and disinfecting of your tools, implements, and materials; for setting up the basic pedicuring station; and for meeting, greeting, and escorting your client to your service area.

GO TO **PROCEDURE 14-1** page 269

B. Service Procedure

The service procedure is an organized, step-by-step plan for accomplishing the actual service the client has requested, such as a pedicure or foot massage.

GO TO **PROCEDURE 14-3** page 272

GO TO PROCEDURE 14-4 page 275

C. Post-service Procedure

The post-service procedure is an organized step-by-step plan for caring for your client after the procedure has been completed. It details helping your client through the scheduling and payment process of the salon and advises you how to prepare for the next client.

GO TO PROCEDURE 14-2 page 271

Disinfection

Disinfection of the pedicure bath has been both discussed and sensationalized in the media—and for good reason. There are specific criteria and steps that must be followed exactly to ensure proper disinfection and infection control. Improper, rushed, or careless cleaning of the pedicure bath may lead to health safety concerns for salon clients. It is the responsibility of the salon and the individual performing the procedure to ensure that proper disinfection occurs and that procedures are followed.

The following are recommended procedures developed by the Nail Manufacturer's Council (NMC), a group of representatives of companies that produce nail care products, and the International Nail Technicians Association (INTA), a group of professional nail technicians, for cleaning and disinfecting all types of pedicure equipment, including:

- whirlpool units
- air jet basins
- pipe-less and all non-whirlpool basins
- sinks
- bowls
- tubs

In addition, salons must always use an EPA-registered hospital disinfectant that the label claims is a broad spectrum bactericide, virucide, and fungicide. In addition, most states require salons record the time and date of each disinfecting procedure that is performed in a salon pedicure log or disinfection log for accountability purposes.

Salon teams are encouraged to incorporate the disinfection procedures (see procedures on the following pages) into their regular cleaning schedules, and to display the procedures in employee areas. Always check your state regulations concerning the required disinfection protocol.

WEB RESOURCES

For more information concerning disinfection and other important topics in the nail industry, go to http://www.probeauty.org/NMC. This site contains many informational brochures relevant to manicuring and pedicuring. They are published in several languages, including Vietnamese and Spanish, are written by the leading scientists and technical experts in the industry, and are reviewed by other industry leaders before publishing.

✓ LO6 Complete

DISINFECTION OF WHIRLPOOL FOOT SPAS AND AIR JET BASINS

After every client:

1 Drain all water from the basin.

2 Scrub all visible residue from the inside walls of the basin with a brush and liquid soap and water. Use a clean and disinfected brush with a handle. Brushes must be cleaned and disinfected after each use.

3 Rinse the basin with clean water.

4 Refill the basin with clean water and circulate the correct amount (according to the mixing instructions on the label) of the EPA-registered hospital disinfectant through the basin for ten minutes.

5 Drain, rinse, and wipe dry with a clean paper towel.

At the end of every day:

1 Remove the screen and any other removable parts. (A screwdriver may be necessary.)

2 Clean the screen and other removable parts and the area behind these with a brush and liquid soap and water to remove all visible residues and replace the properly cleaned screen and other removable parts.

3 Fill the basin with warm water and chelating detergent (cleansers designed for use in hard water) and circulate the chelating detergent through the system for five to ten minutes (following the manufacturer's instructions). If excessive foaming occurs, discontinue circulation and let soak for the remainder of the time, as instructed.

4 Drain the soapy solution and rinse the basin.

5 Refill the basin with clean water and circulate the correct amount (according to the mixing instructions on the label) of the EPA-registered hospital disinfectant through the basin for ten minutes.

6 Drain, rinse, and wipe dry with a clean paper towel.

7 Allow the basin to dry completely.

At least once each week:

1 Drain all water from the basin.

2 Remove the screen and any other removable parts. (A screwdriver may be necessary.)

3 Clean the screen and other removable parts and the area behind these with a brush and liquid soap and water to remove all visible residues and replace the properly cleaned screen and other removable parts.

4 Scrub all visible residue from the inside walls of the basin with a brush and liquid soap and water. Use a clean and disinfected brush with a handle. Brushes must be cleaned and disinfected after each use.

5 Fill the basin with clean water and circulate the correct amount (according to the mixing instructions on the label) of the EPA-registered hospital disinfectant through the basin.

6 Do not drain the disinfectant solution. Instead, turn the unit off and leave the disinfecting solution in the unit overnight.

7 In the morning, drain and rinse.

8 Refill the basin with clean water and flush the system.

DISINFECTION OF PIPE-LESS FOOT SPAS

For units with footplates, impellers, impeller assemblies, and propellers, after every client:

1 Drain all water from the basin.

2 Remove impeller, footplate, and any other removable components according to the manufacturer's instructions.

3 Thoroughly scrub impeller, footplate, and/or other components and the areas behind each with a liquid soap and a clean, disinfected brush to remove all visible residues, and then reinsert impeller, footplate, and/or other components.

4 Refill the basin with water and circulate the correct amount (according to the mixing instructions on the label) of the EPA-registered hospital disinfectant through the basin for ten minutes.

5 Drain, rinse, and wipe dry with a clean paper towel.

At the end of every day:

1 Fill the basin with warm water and chelating detergent and circulate the chelating detergent through the system for five to ten minutes (following manufacturer's instructions). If excessive foaming occurs, discontinue circulation and let soak for the remainder of the ten minutes.

2 Drain the soapy solution and rinse the basin.

3 Refill the basin with clean water and circulate the correct amount (according to the mixing instructions on the label) of the EPA-registered hospital disinfectant through the basin for ten minutes.

4 Drain, rinse, and wipe dry with a clean paper towel.

At least once each week:

1 Drain all water from the basin.

2 Remove impeller, footplate, and any other removable components according to the manufacturer's instructions.

3 Thoroughly scrub impeller, footplate, and/or other components and the areas behind each with a liquid soap and a clean, disinfected brush to remove all visible residues, and then reinsert impeller, footplate, and/or other components.

4 Refill the basin with water and circulate the correct amount (according to the mixing instructions on the label) of the EPA-registered hospital disinfectant through the basin for ten minutes.

5 Do not drain the disinfectant solution. Instead, turn the unit off and leave the disinfecting solution in the unit overnight.

6 In the morning, drain and rinse.

7 Refill the basin with clean water and flush the system.

Here's a Tip:

Think that you don't have 10 minutes between pedicures to disinfect? Try this. Before reaching for the massage lotion, place the client's feet to the side outside of the soak bath, clean the basin or foot spa, and fill with water and disinfectant solution. Or, if the client is experiencing a mask, place the client's feet to the side outside of the soak bath, clean the tub, refill it with water, and put in the disinfectant during the mask time. The disinfectant can remain in the basin while you complete the pedicure, meeting the time requirement for disinfection. This minimizes the procedure time, keeps you on schedule, and allows the client to see you disinfect the tub, which supports a claim that you consistently provide safe services.

DISINFECTION OF NON-WHIRLPOOL FOOT BASINS OR TUBS

This includes basins, tubs, footbaths, sinks and bowls—all non-electrical equipment that holds water for a client's feet during a pedicure service. After every client:

1 Drain all water from the foot basin or tub.

2 Clean all inside surfaces of the foot basin or tub to remove all visible residues with a clean, disinfected brush and liquid soap and water.

3 Rinse the basin or tub with clean water.

4 Refill the basin with clean water and the correct amount (according to the mixing instructions on the label) of the EPA-registered hospital disinfectant. Leave this disinfecting solution in the basin for ten minutes.

5 Drain, rinse, and wipe dry with a clean paper towel.

At the end of every day:

1 Drain all water from the foot basin or tub.

2 Clean all inside surfaces of the foot basin or tub to remove all visible residues with a brush and liquid soap and water.

3 Fill the basin or tub with water and the correct amount (according to the mixing instructions on the label) of the EPA-registered hospital disinfectant. Leave this disinfecting solution in the basin for ten minutes.

4 Drain, rinse, and wipe dry with a clean paper towel.

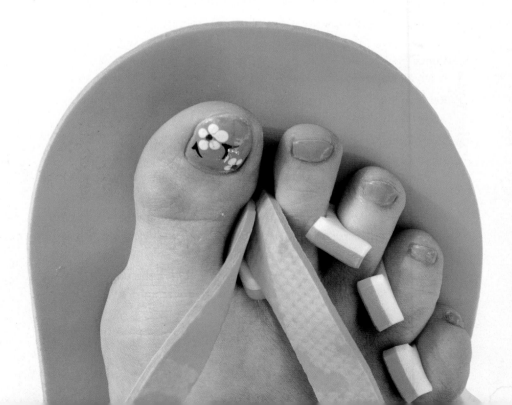

Your pedicure area should be convenient to or plumbed to water for filling the pedicure baths for your service.

A. CLEANING AND DISINFECTING

1. It is important to wear gloves while performing this pre-service to prevent possible contamination of the implements and to protect your hands from the powerful chemicals in the disinfectant solution.

2. Rinse all implements with warm running water and then thoroughly wash them with soap, a nail brush, and warm water. Brush grooved items, if necessary, and open hinged implements to scrub the area.

3. Rinse away all traces of soap with warm running water. The presence of soap in most disinfectants can cause them to become inactive. Soap is most easily rinsed off in warm, but not hot, water. Hotter water will not work any better. Dry implements thoroughly with a clean or single-use towel, or allow to air dry on a clean towel. Your implements are now properly cleaned and ready to be disinfected.

4. It is extremely important that your implements be completely clean before placing them in the disinfectant solution. If they are not, your disinfectant may become contaminated and rendered ineffective. Be sure to open any hinged implements to the open position before immersing. Immerse cleansed implements in an appropriate disinfection container holding an EPA-registered disinfectant that has been mixed and changed according to instructions for the required time (usually 10 minutes). Make sure to avoid skin contact with all disinfectants by using tongs or by wearing gloves.

5. Remove implements, avoiding skin contact, and rinse and dry tools thoroughly.

6. Store disinfected implements in a clean, dry container until needed.

7. Remove gloves and thoroughly wash your hands with liquid soap, rinse, and dry with a clean fabric or disposable towel.

B. BASIC TABLE SETUP

1. Your station should be set up to include a clean, comfortable, and ergonomically correct pedicuring stool/chair for the nail technician, a client chair, and a footrest for your client. Be certain the station has been cleaned and disinfected before proceeding further with setup.

2. The disinfected work surface of a manicure table or pedicure cart must be set up to hold your service implements and materials. A clean cloth or disposable towel is placed on the work surface as a service towel. Additional cloth towels are folded neatly and placed on your work surface or on shelves below for during your service.

B. BASIC TABLE SETUP CONTINUED

3. If the foot bath is portable and the client's feet will be on the floor when not in the bath, cover the floor with a plastic bag and then spread three terry cloth towels on the floor in front of the client's chair, one on top of the other for use during the pedicure. If it is a portable whirlpool tub, a pedicure cart with a footrest, or a plumbed chair, spread at least two towels over the footrest. The towels will present a clean surface under the feet to the client, be used to dry the feet after lifting them out of the soak, and for other purposes during the service.

4. Ensure that your disinfection container is filled with clean disinfectant solution at least 20 minutes before your first service of the day. Use any disinfectant solution approved by your state board regulations, but make sure that you use it exactly as directed by the manufacturer. Also make sure that you change the disinfectant every day or more frequently when the container is visibly contaminated with debris. Put all cleaned, multi-use implements into the disinfection container, and place the disinfection container so that you can easily access it.

5. Place the professional products that you will use during the service on the table or cart. Place the abrasives, buffers of your choice, and implements on a clean cloth or single-use towel beside the service towel.

6. Place polishes near your work area or have a setup to bring them to the client for choosing. Most large salons or spas have a central location for their polishes. If so, the client must pick out her polish before sitting down in the chair.

7. Tape or clip a plastic bag to the table if a metal trash receptacle with a self-closing lid is not available close by. Deposit used materials in it or in a wastebasket during your pedicure. The bags clipped or taped to the table must be closed and thrown away after each client.

8. The bath should be filled with warm water and the soak product. Always follow the manufacturer's directions. Always check the water temperature before seating your client, then again prior to placement of the client's feet into it. It must not exceed 104 degrees.

C. GREET CLIENT

1. Greet your client with a smile, introduce yourself if you have never met, and shake hands. If the client is new, ask for the consultation card or sheet filled out while in the reception area.

2. Ask your client to remove shoes and socks or hose and to roll pant legs to the knees. If you are in a salon or spa with a dressing room and robes, prepare the client as per the spa protocols.

3. Place the feet on the footrest and evaluate them for appropriateness of the service. If there is a break in the skin, swelling, or blisters, the pedicure cannot be performed. Ask the client if he or she has any chronic diseases and discuss their relevance to the service.

C. GREET CLIENT CONTINUED

Discuss the polish to be applied and recommend the appropriate service. Suggest home-care products and discuss how they are used as well as activities to improve the condition of the feet. You should always keep in mind your client's goals and expectations for the service. Record the client's responses and your observations on the client card.

 **LO8 Complete**

 **Law**

State Regulatory ALERT!

It is illegal to perform a pedicure on a client when any signs of infection or lesions are present. If you do, you are risking your client's health and your professional license!

Post-Service Procedure

A. ADVISE CLIENTS AND PROMOTE PRODUCTS

1. Advise your client about proper foot care. For example, remind the client that wearing poorly fitting shoes or very high heels can cause problems with the feet.

2. Suggest that your client purchase products to extend the service and to improve the condition of the feet. Instruct the client how to use the products. Products such as polish, foot lotions or creams, skin moisturizers, softeners, cooling gels, powders, and topcoat help to maintain the pedicure until their next service. Softening and exfoliating lotions can improve the texture of the skin and reduce the accumulation of calluses.

B. SCHEDULE NEXT APPOINTMENT AND THANK THE CLIENT

1. Escort the client to the front desk to schedule his or her next appointment and to pay for the service. Set up date, time, and services for your client's next appointment. Write the information on your business card and give it to the client.

2. Before you return to your station and the client leaves the salon, be sure to thank him or her for the business.

3. Record service information, observations, and product recommendations on the client service form.

C. PREPARE WORK AREA AND IMPLEMENTS FOR NEXT CLIENT

1. Remove your products and tools. Then clean your work area and properly dispose of all used materials.

2. Follow steps for disinfecting implements in the Pre-service Procedure. Reset work area with disinfected tools.

PART **3**

IMPLEMENTS AND MATERIALS

You will need all of the basic materials discussed in Chapter 13 as well as the following to perform the basic pedicure:

- Gloves
- Pedicure Basin or Foot Bath
- Electric Foot Mitts (Optional)
- Terry Cloth Mitts (Optional)
- Paraffin Bath (Optional)
- Toenail Clippers

- Curettes
- Nail Rasp
- Pedicure Nail Files
- Pedicure Paddle
- Nippers
- Toe Separators

- Pedicure Slippers
- Foot Soak
- Exfoliant
- Foot Lotions or Creams
- Callus Softeners

PREPARATION

Complete Procedure 14-1, Pre-service Procedure

PROCEDURE

1. Put on gloves. Check the temperature of the pedicure bath for safety. Place the client's feet in the bath and allow them to soak for 5 minutes to soften and clean the feet before beginning the pedicure.

2. Lift the client's foot you will be working with first from the bath. Using the towels on the footrest, the floor, or your lap, wrap the first towel around the foot and dry it thoroughly. Make sure you dry between the toes. Place the foot on the footrest or on a towel you have placed on your lap if you are using a basin or portable bath.

Application **Tip:**

The first foot you work on should not be the foot on the dominant side of the client as that foot usually needs more soaking and attention. It needs to soak those few extra minutes while you are working on the other foot. The dominant side of the body is determined by the side of the client's writing hand.

3. First remove polish from the little toe and move across the foot towards the big toe. Complete polish removal is important to a quality pedicure finish.

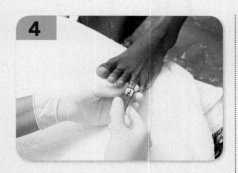

4. Carefully clip the toenails of the first foot straight across and even with the end of the toes. The big toenail is usually the most challenging to trim. Do not leave any rough edges or "hooks" that might create an opportunity for infections.

5. Carefully use the foot rasp, if needed. The rasp is narrow and will only file the nail in one direction. It can be used to remove, smooth, and round off any sharp points or edges on the sides of the free edges that might eventually cause infection. Do not probe with the rasp nor point the tip toward the hyponicium. Gently draw it along the side edge of that portion of the free edge that you have just trimmed, pulling it towards the center of the nail free edge. Small, short strokes with the file will accomplish the task.

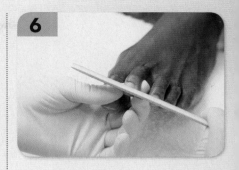

6. Carefully file the nails of the first foot with an appropriate single-use and prepped abrasive file. File them straight across, rounding them slightly at the corners. Smooth rough edges with the fine side of an abrasive file.

7. Apply callus remover and cuticle softener to the calluses and then wrap the foot in a towel and lay it aside. Remove the other foot from the water and perform Steps 2 through 7 on that foot.

8. Remove the first foot from the towel wrap; use a wooden pusher to gently remove any loose, dead tissue. Next, exfoliate the foot with a scrub to remove the dry or scaly skin. Use extra pressure on the heels and other areas where more calluses and dry skin build up. Next, use a foot file to smooth and reduce the thicker areas of calluses.

9. Place the first foot in the foot bath and rinse off the cuticle softener and callus remover completely. Then, lift the foot to above the water and brush the nails with a nail brush. Remove the foot and dry thoroughly. Wrap loosely in the towel.

10. Repeat Steps 8 and 9 on the other foot.

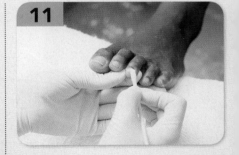

11. Use the single-use cotton-tipped wooden pusher or product dispenser to re-apply cuticle remover to the first foot. Begin with the little toe and work toward the big toe.

Application **Tip:**

Toe separators can be used to hold the toes apart while filing or applying cuticle remover. Always use new separators for every client.

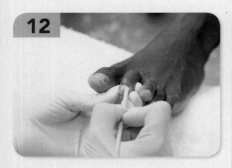

12. Carefully remove the cuticle tissue from the nail plate using a wooden or metal pusher, staying away from the eponychium and taking care not to break the seal between the nail plate and eponychium. Use a nipper to carefully remove any loose tags of dead skin, but don't cut, rip, or tear living skin, since this may lead to serious infections. Loosely re-wrap this foot unless Step 13 is necessary.

CAUTION

Take care not to clip the nails too short and not to break the seal of the hyponychium, an important protection of the toenail unit from infection.

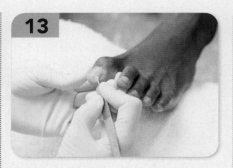

13. Next, if necessary, the curette is used on the first foot to gently push the soft tissue folds away from the walls of the lateral nail plate. This allows you to visually inspect the nail plate and the surrounding tissue. If there is extra buildup of debris between the nail plate and surrounding tissue it should be gently removed with the curette. To use this implement, place the rounded side of the spoon toward the sidewall of living skin. A gentle scooping motion is then used along the nail plate to remove any loose debris. Take care not to overdo it. Do not use this implement to dig into the soft tissues along the nail fold as injury may occur. If the tissue is inflamed (i.e., ingrown toenail), the client must be referred to a qualified medical doctor or podiatrist.

✔ LO**9** Complete

14. Dip your client's first foot into the foot bath. With the foot over the foot bath, brush it again with the nail brush to remove bits of debris. Dry the foot thoroughly. Wrap it in a towel and perform Steps 11 to 13 on the other foot. When finished, wrap that foot in the foot towel and set it aside while performing the following steps on the first foot.

Business Tip:

It is very easy to create a "specialty" pedicure by adding masks, paraffin treatments, or other special applications after the massage and before polishing.

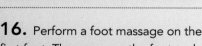

15. Apply lotion, cream, or oil to the first foot for skin conditioning and massage. Use a firm touch to avoid tickling your client's feet.

16. Perform a foot massage on the first foot. Then re-wrap the foot and place it on the towel on the floor.

GO TO **PROCEDURE 14-4 page 275**

17. Massage the second foot.

18. Remove traces of lotion, cream, or oil from the nails of both feet with polish remover.

19. Ask the client to put on the sandals he or she will wear home or provide single-use pedicure slippers. Insert the toe separators, if possible. Apply base coat to the nails on both feet, then two coats of color, and finally a topcoat. Apply polish drying product (optional) to prevent smudging of the polish. You may want to escort the client to a drying area and offer him or her refreshment.

20. Beautifully pedicured feet.

POST-SERVICE

Perform Procedure 14-2, Post-Service Procedure.

Foot and Leg Massage

These techniques and illustrations provide instruction for massage on the feet and legs. A massage for a basic pedicure will include only the foot while a spa pedicure will also include the leg massage, and may include the front of the knee.

IMPLEMENTS AND MATERIALS

You will need the following material to perform massage:

- Massage oil or lotion
- Gloves

PROCEDURE (FOOT MASSAGE)

1. Put on gloves. Rest the client's heel on a footrest or stool and suggest that your client relax. Grasp the leg gently just above the ankle and use your other hand to hold the foot just beneath the toes; rotate the entire foot in a circular motion.

2. Hold the foot and move the other hand to the dorsal surface of the foot. Place the base of your palm of that hand on top of the foot behind the toes. (Your fingers do not touch the skin; lift them away.) Slide up to the ankle area with gentle pressure of the palm and heel of your hand. Repeat 3 to 5 times in the middle, then on the sides of the dorsal surface of the foot. Ever so slightly lift the palm each time to return to the initial position of the slide after reaching the ankle.

3. Keep one hand in contact with the foot. Slide the other hand and place the thumb on the plantar surface of the foot with the fingers gently holding the dorsal side of the foot. Now, transition to the next movement, slide the other hand to the same position on the foot, opposite side. Move one thumb in a firm circular movement, moving from one side of the foot, across, above the heel, up the medial side (center side) of the foot to below the toes, across the ball of and back down the other side of the foot (distal side) to the original position. Now, move the thumb of the other hand across and up the outside of the foot, then down to its original position. The base of the thumbs through to the pad of the fingers should be in contact with the skin throughout the movement. Your nails must not touch the client's skin.

Application **Tip:**

Always apply enough lotion or oil to the foot to allow sufficient slide and no skin drag. If there is a need to apply more lotion during a massage, one hand remains on the foot or leg while the other hand reaches for a pump of the lotion or oil bottle for more product. Place your thumb over the pump then press down to deposit more product onto the fingers below the pump. Distribute the lotion and return to the massage.

4. Alternate the movements of the thumbs in a smooth, firm motion. Repeat several times. This is a very relaxing movement.

5. Perform the same thumb movement on the surface of the heels, rotating your thumbs in opposite directions. Repeat 3 to 5 times.

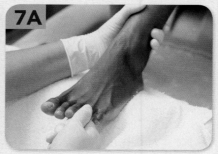

6. Place your one hand on top of the foot, cupping it, and make a fist with your other hand. The hand on top of the foot will press the foot towards you while your other hand twists into the instep of the foot. This helps stimulate blood flow and provides relaxation. Repeat 3 to 5 times. This is a friction movement. The bottom of the foot is the only place a friction movement is performed in manicure and pedicure services.

7A. Transition your hands then start with the little toe by placing the thumb on the top of the toe and arching the index finger underneath it. (Your palm is facing up.) Push the fingers and thumb in that position back to the base of the finger then rotate the thumb and finger in a circular, effleurage movement until the index is arched over the top of the finger with the thumb underneath. Pull the finger and thumb toward the end of the toes.

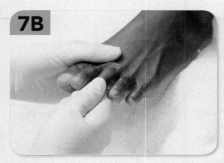

7B

7B. Hold the tip of the toe, starting with the little toe, and make a figure eight with each toe. Repeat 3 to 5 times on each toe and then transition to the next one. After the last movement on each toe, gently squeeze the tip once, then transition to the next one. You must have sufficient lotion for this to be comfortable and relaxing.

fyi

Before performing a service that includes a foot and/or leg massage, consult the client's consultation or intake form. During the consultation, acknowledge and discuss any medical condition your client listed that may be contraindicated for a foot and/or leg massage. Ask the client if they have discussed massage with their physician, and if they have not already done so, encourage them to seek their physician's advice as to whether or not a foot and/or leg massage is advisable before performing the service.

Many clients that have high blood pressure (hypertension), diabetes, or circulatory conditions, may still have foot and/or leg massage without concern, especially if their condition is being treated and carefully looked after by a physician. Foot and/or leg massage is, however, contraindicated for clients with severe, uncontrolled hypertension. For clients who have circulatory problems such as varicose veins, massaging the foot and/or leg may be harmful because it increases circulation. Ask for written permission from the client's physician before performing this massage.

If your client has sensitive or redness-prone skin, avoid vigorous or strong massage techniques. This is especially important for clients who have arthritis. Do not talk to your client during the massage except to ask once whether your touch should be more or less firm. Talking eliminates the relaxation therapy of the massage.

When making decisions about whether to perform a foot and/or leg massage on a person who has a medical condition, be conservative. When in doubt, don't include massage as part of your service.

8. Now, return your hands to the position described in #4, and repeat Steps 3 and 4.

9. Repeat all movements on each foot as many times as you wish, adding other movements that you like to perform, then move to the other leg/foot.

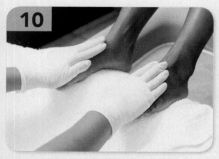

10. Every massage, whether pedicure or body massage, must end. To make the end special, to provide a signal for experienced clients that the massage is ending, and to provide a "release" from the client, feathering, a traditional release in massage was developed in many forms.. One designed for pedicures follows. At the end of the previous movement, in a smooth transition, place both of the client's feet onto the footrest, or on another stable surface, and move your palms to the top of the feet with your fingers toward the leg. Press your entire hands 3 times slowly onto the feet. (This should not be a hard press, just a firm push.) Maintain each press for 1–2 seconds. After the last press, lift your palms slightly, but maintain contact with the feet with your fingertips. Now, gently pull your hand toward the tips of the toes with a feather-light touch of your fingertips. (Do not allow your fingernails to touch the skin.) Pull completely off the end of the toes. Perform the final feather off movement only once, then allow the client to relax a minute or two before moving to the next step of the pedicure.

11. Once the massage of both feet is completed, you may move on in the pedicure procedure. If you are performing a luxury pedicure, do not perform the feather off movement; slide your hands to the leg and move on to the leg massage after Step 9.

✔ LO**11** Complete

Business **Tip**:

The basic pedicure does not include the leg massage, only the foot massage, for two reasons. The first reason is the time constraints. Most salons schedule less time for the basic procedure so the massage must be less. Second, the higher-cost pedicures must be more special to be perceived as worth a higher price, and the leg massage is one of the special additions.

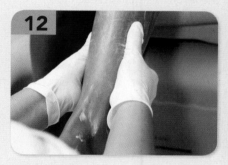

12. Place the foot on the footrest or stabilize it on your lap, then gently grasp the client's leg from behind the ankle. Perform effleurage movements from the ankle to below the knee on the front of the leg with the other hand. Move up the leg and then lightly return to the original location. Perform 5 to 7 repetitions, then move to the sides of the leg and perform an additional 5 to 7 repetitions.

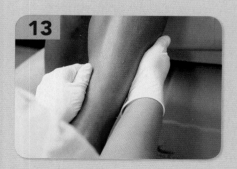

13. Slide to the back of the leg and perform effleurage movements up the back of the leg. Stroke up the leg, then, with less pressure, return to the original location; perform 5 to 7 times. Each pedicurist will design her own effleurage movements. They must be relaxing and in a routine used on every client.

Application **Tip:**

The most enjoyable massage is a rhythmic, slow slide with the fingers and palm connecting to the client as much as possible. Maintain a touch connection with the client throughout the massage, sliding the hands from one location to the next in a smooth transition.

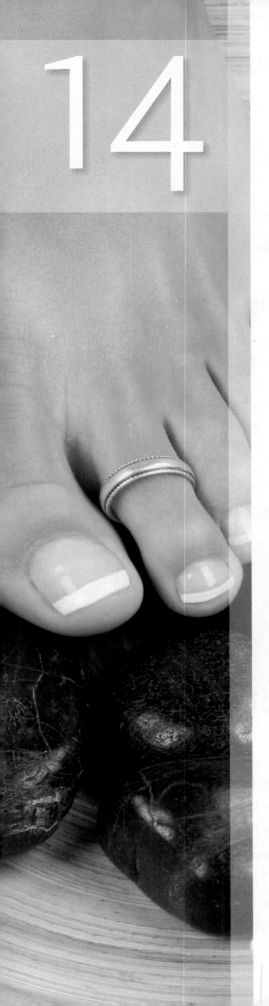

review questions

1. Name five pieces of equipment unique to pedicures.

2. Name three specialty materials used when performing pedicures.

3. What is a callus softener and how is it used?

4. What is the difference between a basic and a spa pedicure?

5. What is reflexology and how is it used in pedicuring?

6. Why is consistent cleaning and disinfection of pedicure baths so important?

7. What are the steps involved in the proper cleaning and disinfecting of whirlpool foot spas and air jet basins after each client?

8. What are the steps in the pedicure pre-service procedure?

9. What is the proper tool to use to reduce the instance of an ingrown toenail and how should it be used?

10. List and describe the proper procedures for a basic pedicure.

11. List and explain the procedure for a foot and leg massage.

15

electric
filing

chapter outline

☑ Learning Objectives

After you have completed this chapter, you will be able to:

1 Name the types of electric files most often used by nail professionals.

2 Define RPM.

3 Define torque.

4 Define tolerance.

5 Define variable speed.

6 Understand the need for bits to be concentric.

7 Determine which shank sizes cannot be used in professional electric files.

8 Identify the types of bits that have grits.

9 Explain how carbide bits differ from bits with grits.

10 Name which bits are one-use only.

11 Perform the practice technique for the cuticle area.

12 Understand the causes of excessive heat when nails are being filed.

13 Know the procedure for cleaning and disinfecting metal file bits.

Key Terms

Page number indicates where in the chapter the term is used.

bits / 286

concentric bits / 286

flutes / 287

grit / 287

maintenance / 294

microshattering / 298

revolutions per minute (RPM) / 284

rings of fire / 288

tolerance / 284

torque / 284

There are several types of electric files that are made specifically for nails.

Electric files are very safe when used by trained nail technicians and can provide many benefits besides speeding up the time spent on a service. With today's nail services, electric files are a necessary tool when offering nail enhancements and pedicures in the salon. In addition to speeding up your time—once you have perfected your skill—you can shape the nails more consistently, file in areas a hand file cannot, perform more precise maintenance procedures, and refine your work more easily. And the use of an electric file may help to alleviate the stress and pressure put on your hands and wrists, thus possibly reducing the incidence of carpel tunnel syndrome.

Electric file training can be found in many places:

- Private classes by independent educators
- Workshops
- Trade shows
- Industry electric file manufacturers

Many manufacturers and trade publications offer education on electric filing, plus there are tutorials and videos that can be found on the Internet.

Types of Electric Files

There are several types of electric files that are made specifically for nails. These machines have warranties from electric file manufacturers that support the nail industry. A professional nail technician should never purchase an electric file outside the nail industry, as these files may not have the high quality needed to be used on nails.

BELT-DRIVEN ELECTRIC FILES

A belt-driven electric file is a traditional, older style of dental machine that was originally used in salons in the 1970s and 1980s. These files have long belts on pulleys that attach to the motor. They are expensive and cumbersome on the manicuring table and not used much anymore.

MICROMOTOR MACHINES

Most professional electric filing machines are called micromotor machines. The motor is actually located inside the handpiece. The base box that sits on the manicuring table houses the transformer and the on/off and speed control switches. Smaller versions can have the same handpiece with the transformer attached to the cord instead of being inside. They are just as powerful as the bigger micromotor machines. You will want to try both types to determine which one you prefer.

Battery-Operated Micromotor Machines

Smaller versions of the micromotors are battery operated. You will have approximately two to six or more hours of battery usage before you must plug in the machine to recharge it. They are small, compact, and powerful, but some may have much less torque.

Hand-Held Micromotor Machines

Hand-held micromotors have their power source and handpiece combined. The result is a larger unit that may be more difficult to manage than a two-piece unit. Also, each micromotor manufacturer recommends its own method for changing bits. Be sure to read and follow the manufacturer's directions.

CRAFT AND HOBBY TOOLS

Electric files that are purchased at craft, hobby, and tool stores are not suitable for the professional salon industry because they are usually manufactured for use on glass, wood, and ceramics. The bits needed for these electric files have a different shank size (1/8") compared to the industry standard shank size of 1/32". Most of these machines have a tremendous amount of vibration that can damage the natural nail, microshatter the monomer and polymer products, and cause wrist damage to the nail technician **(Figure 15-1)**.

▲ FIGURE 15-1

Nail damage caused by improper use of electric files.

LO1 Complete

Choosing an Electric File

▲ FIGURE 15-2

An example of an electric file with bits.

When choosing an electric file, determine your needs and know how much you are willing to spend (**Figure 15-2**).

Before purchasing an electric file, you should understand a few basic terms that will be very helpful when you are deciding the features you want for your electric file.

POWER AND SPEED

Speed is defined in revolutions per minute, or RPM. This means the number of times the bit turns in a complete circle in one minute. Machines vary in RPM capacity, between 0 and 35,000. Think of RPM as a speedometer in a car. The motor works in the middle of the range from zero to the highest number. (You do not drive your car at the highest number on the speedometer.) Working in the middle range of its capacity prolongs the working life of the motor.

Average 3,000 to 30,000

TORQUE

Torque is the power in the machine or its ability to keep turning when applying pressure during filing. Machines vary in torque and RPM, so know your machine's capacity. More powerful machines have larger, better motors. This means higher torque, so you should work at lower speeds because these machines are stronger and can accomplish more at a lower speed. Less powerful machines have less powerful motors and plastic handpieces, so you will work at higher speeds and possibly use more pressure to shape the nails, which may cause heat. These lightweight, less powerful machines can do all of the same procedures as more powerful machines, but need to work at higher speeds to compensate. Your handpiece should not "bog down" or stop rotating when you apply pressure; if it does, then there is not enough torque. Again, the more expensive handpieces have better torque.

TOLERANCE

Tolerance is the tightness of the inside of the shank where the bit fits into the handpiece. If you have a bit that does not fit into the handpiece, it could be because of the tolerance. If the bit slips out while in use, the tolerance is too loose.

There are several features to consider when purchasing an electric file. Consider these:

- *RPMs.* Most techs use a range of 5,000 to 20,000 RPMs.
- *Handpiece.* The handpiece should weigh approximately 4 – 6 ounces, should be comfortable in your hand, and have virtually no vibration.
- *Size of machine.* Most electric files are table machines that are about 4" x 4" x 4". Some are smaller and have the power pack on the outside of the box.
- *Usage.* How much you plan on using the electric file will dictate how much you should spend. The more you use the machine, the higher quality you will need. A higher quality file will last longer, but be prepared to spend more to purchase it.
- *Warranty.* Most electric file manufacturers offer a limited warranty with the purchase.
- *Price.* The more money you spend, the better the machine. A higher quality file will last longer and have less vibration, but be prepared to spend more to purchase one. High-end machines can cost as much as $500.00, while less-expensive machines can be purchased for as little as $150.00.
- *Forward and reverse.* The only time that reverse is needed is for left-handed techs. Keep in mind that some bits do not cut when turning in reverse.
- *Keyless chuck for ease in changing bits.* Most machines have twist-lock or push chucks for ease in changing bits.
- *Foot pedal option.* Some machines offer a foot pedal option. You can plug in a foot pedal on the back of the file and override the speed controls on the front of the machine. The foot pedal works like the accelerator of a car or like the pedal of a sewing machine, that is, the more you press, the faster the bit turns, and when you reduce pressure, the bit slows down.
- *Closed casing handpiece.* Some handpieces have slots or openings that allow dust and debris to get inside the file; this can damage the motor. Closed casings can prolong the life of your machine; be sure to purchase a machine that does not have any open sections.
- *Variable speed dial.* This dial allows you to vary your speed by having a complete range of speed from lowest to highest instead of just the traditional high, medium, low speed options **(Figure 15-3)**.

✓ **LO5 Complete**

LIFE EXPECTANCY

How long should an electric file last? That depends on two things:

- *Usage.* The more you use your electric file, the greater the wear and tear on the machine.
- *Maintenance.* If you maintain and care for your electric file on a regular basis, it will be in good working order for many years. Check with the manufacturer for recommended handpiece cleaning, service, and replacement of cords.

Here's a Tip:

A great time for electric file maintenance is while you are on vacation, since most manufacturers can service and return your machine to you within a week to 10 days. On your last day of work, ship your handpiece to the manufacturer and leave a number for them to call you with a quote. Otherwise, your handpiece may not be serviced until they can reach you for repair approval. Once approved, your handpiece will be worked on and shipped right back. It is always a good idea to have a second handpiece you can use as backup. All manufacturers sell handpieces separately.

▲ **FIGURE 15-3**
The dial on a variable speed drill.

MAINTENANCE AND WARRANTIES

When you purchase your electric file, make sure to ask about the warranty. Do not purchase an electric file that does not have a warranty. Terms and conditions of the warranty will vary, but most manufacturers will fix or replace a malfunctioning electric file within one year of purchase at no cost to you.

Machines vary in price from $25 for battery-operated models to over $500 for high-end machines. Keep in mind that all machines can perform the same procedures, but some do it more easily than others do. Purchase the best electric file that you can afford. It is the most valuable tool you will use in professional nail services.

All About Bits

Electric file bits come in all different shapes, sizes, and styles. You should choose your bits based on how they work for you and the types of services you are performing. Be sure to always read and follow the manufacturer's instructions for using electric file bits.

Following are a few basic terms that will help you understand electric file bits and make it easier for you to choose your bits.

CONCENTRIC BITS

Concentric bits are balanced bits that do not wobble or vibrate. Some people refer to concentric bits as being centered. If you drop your bit while still in the handpiece, it may become bent, which will throw off the concentricity and render the bit unusable. If the concentricity is not perfect, the bit may actually be hitting the nail as it spins, causing damage and microshattering.

SURFACE SMOOTHNESS

Check to see whether the particles on the bit are larger in some areas, missing, or unevenly distributed. Bits with these kinds of surfaces will scratch the nail enhancement as you file, instead of refining it.

EDGES

Bits are cut with finished edges so that they are not sharp on the top. Feel the edges of the bit before using it. If these are sharp, dull the edges with a hand file with the bit spinning at a slow speed.

Here's a Tip:

An electric file should run smoothly without excessive vibration. Wobbling bits can harm the electric file or cause damage to the client's nails, and may cause the nail professional to develop a cumulative trauma disorder (CTD). Handpieces or bits that vibrate excessively increase the risk of injury to your hand and/or wrist. If your handpiece creates excessive vibration, it should be serviced immediately. Remember, repetitive motions of any type, including motions used while electric filing, can cause repetitive trauma disorders such as CTDs. If you develop symptoms related to any type of repetitive trauma disorder, you should consult with a physician for diagnosis and treatment.

GRITS

Grit is measured by the number of abrasive particles per square inch. In higher-numbered grits, the particles are smaller and therefore finer and more of them are needed to cover the square inch. The coarser the grit, the lower the grit number will be and the larger each individual piece of grit will be to cover the square inch. This holds true for all abrasive boards, blocks, buffers, and electric file bits.

SHANK

The industry standard shank size for electric files is 1/32". Electric files used for crafts are usually 1/8" and will not fit a professional electric file.

 **LO7 Complete**

TYPES OF BITS

There are many different styles of bits available in carbide, diamond, gold, silver, natural nail bits, and sanding bands. These bit styles are available in a variety of grits and shapes.

Diamond Bits

Diamond bits are made from either natural or synthetic diamond particles attached to the surfaces of metal bits. Diamond bits come in various grits, file the surface of the product, and can be used in a back-and-forth motion when the machine is in either the forward or reverse position.

Diamond bits vary significantly in quality and price, but all are capable of accomplishing the same procedures. Lower-quality bits cost less, but leave scratches on the surface of the product. If you use these because of budgetary constraints, simply follow with another, higher grit to smooth out the surface of the product.

Higher-quality diamond bits have more consistency in construction because each particle on every bit is cut the same size and shape and then adhered to a stainless steel blank bit **(Figure 15-4)**.

✓ **LO8 Complete**

Carbide Bits

Carbide bits are made of metal with flute-like cuts that shave the enhancement product instead of scratching it the way file, sand, and diamond bits do. Flutes are long, slender cuts or grooves found on a carbide bit. Carbide bits are measured by the number of flutes in each bit. They are categorized in the same way the grit scale measures the file: the larger and deeper the grooves, the coarser the bit. Shallower and more closely spaced grooves create a finer bit.

▼ **FIGURE 15-4**
Diamond bits.

CAUTION

Never use carbide bits on the natural nail!

▲ FIGURE 15-5

A carbide bit.

◀ FIGURE 15-6

Small and large barrel bits.

▲ FIGURE 15-7

Tapered barrel bits.

▲ FIGURE 15-8

A cuticle safety bit.

▲ FIGURE 15-9

A cone-shaped bit.

▲ FIGURE 15-10

A football-shaped bit.

There are three types of carbide bits: traditional, one-way and cross-cut. Traditional carbides must be used from right to left with the machine in forward rotation. If used in a back-and-forth motion, traditional carbides will work better in one direction than the other. One-way carbides can be used only in one direction and are usually made for right-handed nail technicians. With cross-cut carbides, the grooves are cut at the same angle and shave evenly when filing back and forth. Cross-cut carbides can be used to file in both directions and in a back-and-forth filing motion **(Figure 15-5)**.

Small and Large Barrel Bits

The circumference of the small barrel bit is less than that of the large barrel bit, but both are the standard length **(Figure 15-6)**. These bits are usually used to shorten the length and shape the surface of the nail. The flat top of the bit can be used to cut a new smile line, as well. These bits should not be used at the cuticle area as they can easily produce rings of fire damage to the nails. Rings of fire are grooves carved into the nail by filing with bits at the incorrect angle.

Tapered Barrel Bits

This shorter, cone-shaped bit is designed with a flat top and can be used to shape the top surface of the nail and to cut maintenance on small nails at a flat angle and at the cuticle and sidewalls (the areas on the sides of the nail plate that grow free of an attachment to the skin) as well as to prep the cuticle area product for a fill **(Figure 15-7)**.

Cuticle Safety Bits

This bit was designed for safe cuticle work **(Figure 15-8)**. It can be used for underneath the nail and for shaping. The shorter, tapered shape and round top of this bit allow the nail tech to get into the cuticle area and sidewalls to bevel the nail enhancement flush with the natural nail without causing damage or discomfort to the client. This bit is perfect for beveling the enhancement at the cuticle during the fill process.

Cone-Shaped Bits

This slim, long, tapered, and pointed bit can be used at the cuticle, underneath the nail, on top of the nail, and to prep the cuticle area for a fill. It comes in various sizes, depending upon the manufacturer **(Figure 15-9)**.

Football-Shaped Bits

The football-shaped bit also can be used for underneath the nails and the cuticle area. It does have a point on the top that can damage the hyponychium, so use it with care. This bit is perfect for finishing the underside surface of long curved nails **(Figure 15-10)**.

UNC Bits

The under-the-nail cleaner bit (UNC) is a small, pointed bit that can be used for tight spaces such as under the nail, sidewalls, and for making designer holes in nails. The point size varies from manufacturer to manufacturer (**Figure 15-11**).

▲ **FIGURE 15-11**
A UNC bit.

Bullet Bits

The bullet bit is a small, slender bit that is available in a flat-topped or round-tipped version and is similar to the UNC bit. Many nail techs use this bit in a fine diamond style to prep the natural nail at the cuticle area for nail enhancement work (**Figure 15-12**).

▲ **FIGURE 15-12**
A bullet bit.

Needle Bits

This pointed bit is usually as slim as the actual shank of a bit. It can be used at the cuticle; underneath the nails; in small, tight spaces; and for specialty design work (**Figure 15-13**).

▲ **FIGURE 15-13**
A needle bit.

Maintenance Bits

Bits used to perform the maintenance procedure are commonly marketed and referred to as backfill bits. The backfill bit was originally designed to trench (carve) out the growth at the smile line and to replace white tip powder. Backfill bits come in two sizes: small (1/4 the size of a barrel bit) and medium (1/2 the size of a barrel bit). They are available in inverted shapes for more ergonomic and precise cutting. Backfill bits are used to cut a new smile so you can replace the white tip product. It is generally used by angling the top edge of the bit and cutting into the nail across the smile line area. Larger backfill bits can be used flat to the tip to remove the white tip product (**Figure 15-14**).

▲ **FIGURE 15-14**
Maintenance bits.

French Fill Bits

A French fill bit was designed to use sideways to carve out a "V" into the smile line area during a maintenance procedure. Made in diamond style only, these bits come in several sizes (**Figure 15-15**).

▲ **FIGURE 15-15**
A french fill bit.

Natural Nail Discs

▲ **FIGURE 15-16**
A natural nail disc.

The natural nail disc has a diamond surface that is used flat on the tip of the natural nail to shorten and shape. The outer edge is made of metal or plastic and acts as a safety edge when you file (**Figure 15-16**).

Rubber Synthetic Natural Nail Bits

Rubber synthetic natural nail bits come in three different color grits (yellow, black, and green) and three different shapes (long barrel shape with a flat top and two different sizes with rounded tips). Use these bits to buff the surface of a natural nail smooth or to smooth the cuticle areas. You can push the cuticle back gently on a slow speed as you press down to remove any dead cuticle on the nail. These bits are perfect for difficult cuticle clean-up. Rubber bits wear down quickly and can be reshaped in between use with a clean hand file at a low speed (**Figure 15-17**).

▲ **FIGURE 15-17**
Rubber synthetic natural nail bits.

► **FIGURE 15-18**

A high shine bit.

High Shine Bits

High shine bits, sometimes called buffer bits, are usually made of natural chamois, cotton, or soft leather material. They are used on the nail with buffing cream to create a high shine. High shine bits are one-use-only bits, as they cannot be effectively disinfected (Figure 15-18).

Pedicure Bits

usually Made of Carbide

Pedicure bits are usually cone-shaped and made of diamond material. They work best for smoothing and contouring dry, callused skin. Most come with longer shanks. Some have hollow centers to ensure that they do not heat up too quickly. You also may find some pedicure bits with rounded edges on the top. These can be used along the sides of toenails on callused skin. Pedicure bits are used on a slow or medium speed. They should be used carefully in one direction only so as not to cause any discomfort to the client. This bit is also perfect for use on a man's hand calluses and for getting into difficult spots on the feet that a large foot file cannot (Figure 15-19).

▼ **FIGURE 15-19**

A pedicure bit.

PREPPER BITS

Diamond prepper bits are similar to a tapered barrel shape but slightly smaller. They come in various grits. It is recommended that you use a fine grit on a natural nail to prep it at the cuticle area for nail enhancement work (Figure 15-20).

▲ **FIGURE 15-20**

A prepper bit.

MANDRELS

Mandrels are the metal or rubber bits that are inserted into the handpiece. The sanding and arbor bands (below) are slipped over the mandrels (Figure 15-21).

◄ **FIGURE 15-21**

Mandrels.

▲ **FIGURE 15-22**

A sanding and arbor band.

SANDING AND ARBOR BANDS

These are one-use-only paper bits that slip onto a mandrel. These bits are made of file paper just like hand files and cannot be disinfected. Sanding bands generally are used for shortening and shaping the top surface of the nails, removing a gel sealant, and filing calluses on feet. Fine sanding bands are good for smoothing the surface of toenails in preparation for nail enhancements. These bits should not be used at the cuticle area as they can easily cause rings of fire damage to the nails (Figure 15-22).

✓ **LO10 Complete**

JEWELRY AND SPECIALTY BITS

A jewelry bit is a long, slender carbide bit that has been made for drilling a hole into the free edge of a nail enhancement to attach nail jewelry. Only use jewelry bits on the extended free edge of the nail and never over the nail bed. Other bits have a small carbide or diamond ball on the end that can be used to carve designs into the nail enhancement **(Figure 15-23)**.

▲ **FIGURE 15-23**
A jewelry and specialty bit.

BITS

Metal bits are cleaned and disinfected in the same way that you would clean and disinfect other multi-use tools and implements such as nippers and manicure tools. Never use a dirty bit!

Be sure to:

- Wash and disinfect each bit used on clients between every service.
- Remove a dirty bit from the handpiece of your electric file when the file is not being used.
- Replace the dirty bit with a blank as part of your clean-up in between every client.

The disinfection procedure for metal bits follows the same steps and cautions as the procedure for cleaning and disinfecting all multi-use (reusable) tools and implements.

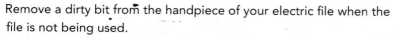

Did **You** Know...

Leaving a file bit in disinfection solution for more than 10 minutes at a time can cause it to rust.

CAUTION

Disinfectants must never be allowed to come in contact with the skin. If your disinfectant container does not have a lift tray or basket, always remove the implements with tongs or tweezers, and always wear gloves to prevent your fingers from coming into contact with disinfectant solution.

GO TO → **PROCEDURE 15-1 page 301**

ELECTRIC FILING TECHNIQUES

Before you use an electric file on a client, it is extremely important to get the proper education; then practice, practice, practice!

Glue a nail tip on a dowel or round clothes pin and hold the dowel as you would a client's finger. Practice on a bare tip (with no enhancement) until you have gained confidence in your abilities. You need to feel the gentle pressure you should use when filing on a bare tip before applying enhancement products.

Once you have gained some experience with the machine, apply an enhancement product and practice on a classmate or salon mate who can tell you about your technique and give you honest feedback. It is important that you are comfortable holding the handpiece; use the bits at the correct angle and speed so you do not injure the client. The more you work with your electric file, the more comfortable and skilled you will become.

▲ FIGURE 15-24
Use fulcrum finger for
proper balance and control.

PRACTICE TECHNIQUES

Hand Balancing/Fulcrum Finger

1 Sit up straight at your table with your feet flat on the floor.

2 Hold your handpiece like a pencil for comfort and control.

3 Place your forearms on the table to make sure your hands are stable.

4 Use a firm steady grip. Do not use too tight a grip as your hands may begin to cramp.

5 Balance your hands by using the pinky finger as the fulcrum finger (or, balance point). This occurs when you balance the tip of one pinky finger to the tip of the pinky finger on the other hand as you work. By doing this, you will take the negative pressure off the bit and displace it with the fulcrum finger. This will give you more control of the handpiece and bit as you work **(Figure 15-24)**.

TYPE OF FILING	SUGGESTED SPEED
Surface work	Fast
Maintenance	Medium
Cuticle work	Slow

Examine and Mark the Dial

Most electric files do not have an RPM chart on the variable speed dial, so it is up to you to dissect your dial and know where the best speeds are. You may want to mark the dial. For a 0 to 35,000 RPM machine, dissect your dial for slow, medium, and fast speeds.

Insert Bit

1 Insert a barrel bit or a sanding band into the handpiece, leaving a slight neck on the shank of the bit.

2 If it is a twist-lock chuck, lock the bit into place. If it is a push chuck, check the security of the bit.

Practice Bit Angles

1 With the machine off, practice:

- Holding the bit in the center of the nail and moving the file from right to left.

- Picking up the bit and returning it to the right side of the nail, then repeating this step.

- Holding the bit flat to the nail, making contact with the center of the bit.

2 Repeat the placements in #1 above, using the bottom of the bit on the bottom of the nail.

3 Repeat the placements in #1 above, using the top of the bit on the top (not cuticle) of the nail.

Turn On the Machine

1 Choose a low RPM after turning on the machine.

2 Make sure the file is in the forward position.

Practice Surface Work

1 Hold the bit flat to the nail so the center of the bit is making contact with the nail.

2 Start on the right side of the nail and work across to the left side.

3 Pick up the bit off the nail and return to the right side of the nail to begin again.

4 When you conquer this, try going back and forth. Remember to pick up the bit off the nail occasionally so you do not create heat.

5 Practice using the correct angles for bottom, center, and cuticle areas.

Practice Cuticle Work

1 Practice cuticle work with a safety bit or a rounded-top cone.

2 Place the bit at the cuticle area, holding the bit at a slight angle so that the top and at least 50 percent of the bit is making contact with the nail.

3 With the machine off, start on the right side and work toward the left side. Use your wrists and turn the nail to meet the bit.

4 On a very low speed, practice this technique and watch where dust appears on the bit so you know when you are making contact.

5 Watch from the side view as you work to make sure you are beveling the product at the correct angle so it is almost flush with the natural nail.

✔ LO11 Complete

Here's a Tip:

Watch the dust! This will tell you where you are making contact with the nail. Occasionally stop the electric file and use a nail brush to remove the dust before continuing.

IMPORTANT THINGS TO REMEMBER

1 Use the correct bit angle. When using an electric file, it is important to always keep the bit flat and parallel with the nail you are working on to avoid causing damage to the nail.

2 Avoid rings of fire. Rings of fire are caused by holding flat-tipped bits at the wrong angle, especially at the cuticle areas, which allows the edge of the bit to dig into the surface of the nail. This can cause damage to the natural nail (**Figure 15-25**).

3 Choose the correct speed. Be sure to use a safe working speed. Higher speeds allow you to use less pressure. If the bit grabs and wraps around the finger, this is an indication that your filing pressure is incorrect. If the speed of the electric file bogs down, the speed is too low.

▲ FIGURE 15-25
Rings of fire.

[handwritten note: Sometimes it is both services more time, more Mon.]

NAIL ENHANCEMENT MAINTENANCE

Maintenance is the term used for when a nail enhancement needs to be serviced after two or more weeks from the initial application of the nail enhancement product. The maintenance service actually accomplishes two goals: it allows the tech to apply the enhancement product onto the new growth of nail, commonly referred to as a *fill or a backfill,* and it allows the tech to structurally correct the nail to ensure its strength, shape and durability; this is commonly referred to as a rebalance.

To prepare nail enhancements for a maintenance service, use a medium-grit bit to smooth old product in the growth area of the nail. Keep the bit parallel to the nail and reduce the product down to the natural nail without touching the nail itself. Use a bit with a round-tipped safety edge for this procedure.

REMOVING LIFTED PRODUCT

Never trim or remove loose nail enhancement products with a pair of nippers. It causes the remaining product, which may not be loose, to pull away from the healthy nail causing damage to the nail plate. There are several bits that can be used to remove the lifted areas and loosen product safely when used at a safe angle.

CRACKS

Use a flat-tipped barrel, backfill bit, or bullet bit and place it sideways into the crack. Slowly bevel a trench with the body of the bit, exposing the crack so that new product can fill in the groove and reinforce that area.

CAUTION

Never use a sander on the natural nail or to remove cuticle tissue from the nail plate!

SHAPING THE TOP SURFACE

You may use a variety of bits—barrel bit, sanders, or a tapered barrel—to shape the top surface of the nail. Place the bit flat on the nail and go from one side to the other, picking up the bit to return to where you started. Repeat this step as you continue to work. Angle the bit so you use the bottom of the bit on the bottom of the nail and the center of the bit in the center of the nail. Angle it toward the cuticle (without touching the cuticle area) to bevel the cuticle area product. By angling the bit slightly as you work, you will contour the shape of the nail.

SHORTENING THE NAILS

Using a medium or coarse barrel bit, hold the bit to the tip of the nail at a 90-degree angle, making sure you have a firm grip. Use a faster RPM and quickly move back and forth on the outer surface to shorten the nail.

CUTICLE WORK

Use a round-tipped bit at the cuticle area, holding the bit flat to the nail, which will safely allow the angle of the bit to do the contouring of the cuticle product. Change the angle (east, north, or west) of how you hold the bit (keeping it flat to the nail) to get into the sidewalls of the cuticle area.

MAINTENANCE SERVICES FOR A TWO-COLOR FRENCH MANICURE

A backfill, the first aspect of the maintenance service, can be performed in a variety of ways. Some nail techs prefer to reduce the entire nail and apply a new layer of white product at the tip, while others prefer to simply thin the product at the growth area. Either can be done with any shaped, round-tipped bit. The purpose is to reshape the apex of the nail that offsets the balance when it has grown out, so it remains thin at the tip and cuticle areas. This provides strength in the center of the nail. Be careful not to touch the natural nail when filing; focus on the enhancement product as you reduce it at the cuticle area.

After you have prepped the nails for maintenance, remove the dust with a clean, dry, and disinfected nail brush. Use a medium or coarse barrel or cone or a safety bit on the tips to thin down the thickness from the stress area to the tip. Remove 75 percent of the product at an angle, not by cutting a new smile line. Use your bit back and forth, from side to side, so the tips of all nails are all thinned evenly. When you replace the product, the color and density should be consistent.

Backfill bits come in different sizes, a one-week, a two-week, a half-barrel, and an inverted backfill bit. They all can perform the same task—you should decide which one you prefer to use. Backfill also can be done with full-barrel bits, which are capable of cutting and removing the remainder of the tip product without your having to change bits because they are big enough to handle the work. Again, it is your preference.

GO TO ▶ PROCEDURE 17-5 page 352

SHAPING C-CURVES

Barrel-shaped or tapered bits, in any size, are best to use under the free edge to refine C-curves. Choose the size of the bit depending on the size of the underside of the C-curve you are refining.

FINISHING

Graduating grits is the key to finishing nails without leaving scratches. Graduate bits from coarser to finer, as with hand-held abrasives, and remove the dust each time, in between changing bits as you graduate. These will keep you from scratching the surface and give a smoother finish.

BUFFING OILS

Buffing oils can enhance your finish work by reducing heat and holding dust on the surface of the bit. Use buffing oils sparingly, as they can seep up the neck of the bit into the handpiece and cause damage. Rub the oil into the nails. After the buffing is complete, it is important to remove all the oil before polishing or using UV gel sealants for better adhesion.

Application Tip:

A good way to practice using the electric file when performing a two-color French application is to glue a tip to a wooden dowel, cut the length, and cover with pink- and white-colored monomer liquid and polymer powder. Practice cutting new smile lines until you have no more room, then break the used tip off and glue on another.

HIGH-SHINE BUFFING

After filing to a smooth finish, nail enhancements can be shined with a buffing bit and buffing cream. Lift the bit frequently and do not apply too much pressure; these bits can heat up quickly and burn your client. If your buffing does not produce a high gloss, then you did not file the nails smooth enough before buffing.

BUFFING CREAMS

Buffing creams enhance the shine when used with buffing bits. Most creams come with pumice and can be used with any style buffing bit. Apply the buffing cream to the nail and rub it in before you use the buffing bit. If you do not rub it in, it will fly off the nail when the bit spins! You also can apply the buffing cream to the bit first.

NATURAL NAIL WORK

You should never use a metal bit or sanding band on the natural nail plate unless you have experience in doing this procedure safely. You can use a natural nail rubber synthetic bit to prep the nail plate by pushing gently toward the cuticle. This procedure removes any dead cuticle on the nail plate safely.

You also can use a natural nail bit to smooth the surface of the natural nail plate. Use a slow speed and hold the bit flat to the nail.

Electric Files for Pedicures

Electric filing on foot calluses needs to be done when the foot is dry. You can perform the pedicure first or last. Just be sure the feet are soft and dry before you start work on the callus.

Apply a callus treatment, wait the recommended length of time, and use a terry towel to slough off the product and the skin it removes. Rinse and dry the foot well. Use your pedicure bit in one direction to remove any remaining callus. Using the bit slowly and going only in one direction will keep the bit from getting hot and causing discomfort to the client. Pedicure bits can be used anywhere on the foot where there is callus, including the skin on the sides of the toenails and under the toes.

> Electric filing on foot calluses needs to be done when the foot is dry.

Troubleshooting

REDUCING DUST

Because of the way that bits cut, different types of bits cause different sizes of dust particles. The smallest particles are caused by sanders or sleeves. The dust is finer and flies higher into the air and can enter your breathing zone. If you use sanders, you may want to wear an appropriate dust mask when filing. Diamond bits create slightly heavier particles that do not fly as high into the air and are not as likely to enter the breathing zone. Carbide bits shave the surface of the product and create heavier particles that are directed down toward the table and onto your hands. There is very little airborne dust when using carbide bits.

HEAT

Improper filing techniques, not the bits, cause heat when using an electric file. Heat is caused by pressing down too hard and leaving the bit on the nail too long when filing. Lift the bit off the nail frequently while working and adjust the speed slightly higher so you can use less pressure as you continue to file.

Heat can cause the client discomfort and can damage the natural nail. Electric filing should not hurt the client and if it does cause discomfort, adjust your procedures.

Keep in mind although diamond and sanding bits are appropriate to use, they require greater pressure when filing and do heat up slightly faster (because of the pressure) than a carbide bit. The carbide bit requires less pressure to shave the product because it is sharper. Natural material bits, such as a chamois, heat up faster also.

Causes of Heat

- Applying too much pressure during filing.
- Incorrect speed (RPM).
- Leaving the bit in the same place for too long while filing.
- Using sanders or sleeves. These generate more heat than metal bits.

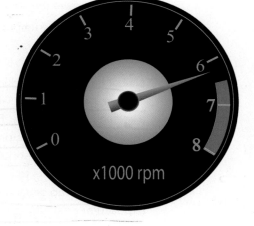

Solutions to Reduce Heat

- Adjust the speed of the machine (RPM).
- Apply less pressure during filing.
- Lift the bit frequently during filing.

GRABBING

Grabbing occurs when the bit grabs the skin around the nail during filing. Grabbing can be avoided by using the bit at the proper angle when working around sidewalls and the cuticle area and the correct speed when working on the surface of the nail. It is important to remember that bits have two sides; we tend to look at the side toward the center of the nail while filing. It is the other side that is on or near the skin that can grab and cut the skin. Bits turn clockwise, so it is a given that the bit will dig into the skin if it gets too close to the sides of the nail.

Causes of Grabbing

- Improper speed (RPMs).
- Improper pressure.

Solutions to Grabbing

- Keep the bit parallel to the nail.
- Angle the finger, not the bit, to file the sides of the nail and the cuticle area.
- Use bits with rounded ends such as safety style bits.

RINGS OF FIRE

Rings of fire are caused by holding flat-tipped bits at the wrong angle and allowing the edge of the bit to dig into the surface of the nail. This can cause damage to the natural nail and be very uncomfortable for a client.

Causes of Rings of Fire

- Wrong angle of the bit.
- Using a flat tipped bit at an angle at the cuticle area.

Solutions to Rings of Fire

- Keep the bit parallel to the nail as you work.
- Decrease the speed of your machine.
- Reduce the amount of pressure applied during filing.

PRODUCT BREAKDOWN

Nail enhancement products are like a jungle of vines that are densely packed. Trauma, heat, age, and vibration can cause the vines to snap. Products also can become brittle. Free edge separation can be caused by product breakdown, age of the product, and how hard the client is on his or her nails. A client who is not careful or gentle with their nail enhancements can cause their enhancements to loosen and lessen the adhesion of the product to the nail. To repair tip separation, you must remove the old product, prep the exposed natural nail again, and reapply primer and product.

As nail enhancements age with wear they can become brittle and develop tiny cracks. This is called microshattering, and it can be caused by aggressive filing with or without an electric file, though it is easier to cause microshattering with an electric file.

Potential Causes of Microshattering

- Improper speed of the machine during filing.
- Poor quality or bent bits.
- Using bits that are too coarse.
- Using low-quality and brittle nail enhancement products.
- Holding the handpiece at the wrong angle.
- Working too aggressively with the electric file.

Solutions to Microshattering

- Use a slower speed.
- Use proper filing techniques.
- Keep the bit parallel to the table during filing.
- Use correct application techniques.
- Make sure the bit is not bent.
- Use a finer grit bit.
- Use quality electric files according to manufacturer's instructions.

VIBRATION

High vibration is something to avoid when using an electric file. Vibration can create microshattering with enhancement products and can be harmful to the nail professional's hand, wrist, and arm. It also may lead to cumulative trauma disorders such as carpal tunnel syndrome. Choose a machine with the least vibration.

The best way to test the vibration of a machine is to hold the handpiece, turn on the power, and feel the vibration. If the vibration is high and it is uncomfortable just holding it for a minute or so, it will be a problem when you use the machine in the salon.

BENT BITS

Bits should be concentric and run true by spinning perfectly without wobbling in the shank of the handpiece. Manufacturers join the shanks and the heads of the bits so they become one part. If this is not done precisely, they may not be concentric. Other causes of wobbling can include inexpensive manufacturing or dropping the bit while it is in the handpiece, which nail techs tend to do frequently. When a bit is dropped it should be replaced, even if appears normal. When a bent bit is used on the nail it can cause damage to the nail or microshattering.

Safety Tips for Electric Filing

It is important that you understand and remember the following basic safety tips for electric filing. By doing so, you will ensure that your client has a good experience and that you produce beautiful results!

- Keep the bit parallel to the nail.
- Angle the client's hand and the handpiece.
- Compensate for pressure with speed. If you feel that you need to press harder, increase the speed of the machine and reduce the pressure you apply to the nail.
- Lift the bit frequently when filing to avoid causing heat build-up.
- Do not use bits in a heavy-handed or aggressive way.

- Keep the bit straight up (90-degree angle) and down when shortening the free edge to avoid skipping, which can cause the product to weaken and breakdown. Skipping occurs when the bit loses contact with the nail and skips or jumps across the nail because of a lack of control of the file.
- Keep a good grip and adjust your speed if this happens. Turn the client's hand, along with the bit, to file around the sidewalls and cuticle area.
- Keep your long hair tied back or put it up so that that it is not caught in the handpiece.
- Wear a dust mask during filing to avoid inhaling dust particles.
- Receive the proper education before using any machine or product.
- Wear eye protection when filing to avoid dust particles from getting into the eyes.
- Avoid repetitive motions that cause pain, swelling, or injury to the wrist, elbow, shoulder, arms, or back.

Continuing Education

A true nail professional will recognize the value of seeking advanced training on correctly and safely operating an electric file before using one on a client. An electric file is a safe tool in the hands of a skilled and knowledgeable professional.

Continuing education is valuable to every nail profession at all skill levels. Electric file training and certification is available in many locations, as well as through private, hands-on training from seasoned professionals. Remember to practice proper cleaning and disinfection at all times, keep a blank in the handpiece when it is not in use, and always use electric files safely. You will find that electric filing will enhance your work as well as save you time and money.

A. CLEANING AND DISINFECTING

1. It is important to wear gloves while performing this procedure to prevent possible contamination of the bits by your hands and to protect your hands from the powerful chemicals in the disinfectant solution.

2. Remove any nail enhancement debris from the bit with a clean, disinfected nail brush. If needed, soak the bit in acetone to soften any hardened monomer and polymer or soakable UV gel enhancement product or use a stiff or wire brush to remove residue. Keep in mind the continued use of a wire brush can dull the finish of your bits. Rinse all bits with warm running water, and then thoroughly wash them with soap, the nail brush, and warm water. Brush grooved bits, if necessary.

3. Rinse away all traces of soap with warm water. The presence of soap in most disinfectants can cause them to become less effective. Soap is most easily rinsed off in warm, but not hot, water. Hotter water will not work any better. Dry bits thoroughly with a clean or disposable towel, or allow to air dry on a clean towel. Your bits are now properly cleaned and ready to be disinfected.

4. It is extremely important that your bits be completely clean before placing them in the disinfectant solution. If they are not, your disinfectant may become contaminated and rendered ineffective. Immerse cleansed bits in an appropriate disinfection container holding an EPA-registered disinfectant for the required time (usually 10 minutes). If it is cloudy, the solution has been contaminated and must be replaced. Make sure to avoid skin contact with all disinfectants by using tongs or by wearing rubber gloves.

5. Remove bits, avoiding skin contact, and rinse and dry tools thoroughly.

6. Store disinfected bits in a clean, dry container until needed.

7. Remove gloves and thoroughly wash your hands with liquid soap, rinse, and dry with a clean fabric or disposable towel.

✓ **LO13 Complete**

Did **You** Know...

Acetone is not an EPA-recognized disinfectant. It can be used to remove any remaining enhancement product and debris from a bit before washing and disinfecting but should not be used as a disinfectant.

review questions

1. What types of electric files are most often used by nail professionals?

2. Can a craft or hobby tool be used on the nails?

3. Define RPM.

4. Define torque.

5. Define tolerance.

6. Define variable speed.

7. Why should bits be concentric?

8. What size shank cannot be used in professional electric files?

9. Which types of bits have grits?

10. How are carbide bits different from bits with grits?

11. What bits are one-use only?

12. Describe the practice technique for the cuticle area.

13. What causes clients to feel excessive heat when nails are being filed?

14. How do you clean and disinfect metal file bits?

16 nail tips and wraps

chapter outline

- ▶ Nail Tips
- ▶ Nail Wraps
- ▶ Nail Wrap Maintenance, Repair, And Removal
- ▶ Procedures

Learning Objectives

After you have completed this chapter, you will be able to:

1. Identify the supplies needed for nail tip application and explain why they are needed.

2. Name and describe the three types of nail tips available and describe the importance of correctly fitting nail tips.

3. List the types of fabrics used in nail wraps and how they are used.

4. Explain the benefits of using each type of fabric nail wrap.

5. Demonstrate the stop, rock, and hold method of applying nail tips.

6. Demonstrate the proper procedure and precautions to use in applying nail tips.

7. Demonstrate the proper removal of tips.

8. Demonstrate the proper procedures and precautions used in a fabric wrap application.

9. Describe the Two-Week Fabric Wrap Maintenance procedure.

10. Describe the Four-Week Fabric Wrap Maintenance procedure.

11. Demonstrate the proper procedure and precautions for fabric wrap removal.

Key Terms

Page number indicates where in the chapter the term is used.

acrylonitrile butadiene styrene (ABS) / 306

adhesive nail

enhancements / 309

cy-

a-

no-

acrylate / 308

fabric wrap / 308

fiberglass / 308

linen / 308

maintenance / 310

nail dehydrator / 306

nail tip adhesive / 307

nail tips / 306

nail wrap / 308

nail wrap resin / 308

overlay / 306

paper wrap / 308

position stop / 306

repair patch / 311

silk / 308

stress strip / 311

tip cutter / 306

wrap resin accelerator / 309

One of the most popular services that a nail professional can offer clients is the opportunity to wear beautiful nails in an almost endless variety of lengths and strengths. Regardless of whether a client is interested in wearing long, medium, or short nails, she may opt to have nail tips applied over her natural nails for strength and durability. Once a tip is applied, she will have an opportunity to choose from a variety of products that can be layered over the natural nail and the tip to further secure the strength of the nail and its beauty.

Nail Tips

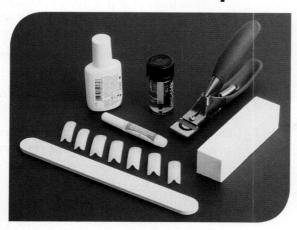

▲ FIGURE 16-1

Supplies needed for nail tip application.

Nail tips are plastic, pre-molded nails shaped from a tough polymer made from acrylonitrile butadiene styrene (ABS) plastic. They are adhered to the natural nail to add extra length and to serve as a support for nail enhancement products. Tips are combined with an overlay, a layer of any kind of nail enhancement product that is applied over the tip for added strength. Nail tips that do not have an overlay are not long-wearing and can break easily without the reinforcement of the overlay.

In addition to the basic materials on your manicuring table, you will need an abrasive board; buffer block; tip adhesive; tip cutter, an implement similar to a nail clipper, designed especially for use on nail tips; nail dehydrator, a substance used to remove surface moisture and tiny amounts of oil left on the natural nail plate; and a variety of nail tips for the nail tip application (Figure 16-1).

✓ LO1 Complete

> **fyi**
>
> Do not use fingernail or toenail clippers to cut tips. Cutting the tip with these types of clippers will weaken the tip and cause it to crack.

▲ FIGURE 16-2

Tips with a full well, a partial well, and well-less (no well at all).

Many nail tips have a shallow depression called a well that serves as the point of contact with the nail plate. The position stop, the point where the free edge of the natural nail meets the tip, is where the tip is adhered to the nail. There are various types of nail tips including: partial well, full well, and well-less (no well at all) (Figure 16-2).

Nail tips are available in many sizes, colors, and shapes so that it is easier to fit each client with precisely the right size and shape tip. Tips can be purchased in large containers of 100 to 500 pieces, as well as in various individual refill sizes. With such a wide assortment, it is easy to fit each client correctly. Make sure when fitting tips to your client that the tips you choose exactly cover the nail plate from sidewall to sidewall. Do not make the mistake of using a tip that is narrower than the nail plate. This can cause the tip to crack at the sides or split down the middle.

Rather than attempting to force a too-small tip onto the nail, it is better to use a slightly larger tip, and use an abrasive board to tailor the tip before you apply it. You can also trim and bevel the well area before applying the tip to the nail, which can save you blending time. Nail tips that are pre-beveled require much less filing on the natural nail after application. This also lessens the potential for damage to the natural nail.

✓ LO2 Complete

The bonding agent used to secure the nail tip to the natural nail is called nail tip adhesive. Adhesives can be purchased in either tubes or brush-on containers and are available in several different forms, depending on the thicknesses of the adhesive. For instance, "gel" adhesives, sometimes referred to as resin, are the thickest and require more time to dry than fast-setting thinner adhesives that dry in about five seconds.

Nail adhesives usually come in either a tube with a pointed applicator tip, a one-drop applicator, or as a brush-on. Use care when opening adhesive containers—always point the opening away from your face and not in the direction of your client. Nail professionals and their clients should always wear eye protection when using and handling nail tip adhesives. Even the smallest amount of adhesive in the eyes can be very dangerous and may cause serious injury.

Once the nail tips are applied, the contact area will need to be reduced with an abrasive, so that the tip blends in with the natural nail. With a perfect tip application, there should be no visible line where the natural nail stops and the tip begins.

GO TO → **PROCEDURE 16-3** page 315

GO TO → **PROCEDURE 16-4** page 318

Nail Wraps

Any method of securing a layer of fabric or paper on and around the nail tip to ensure its strength and durability is called a nail wrap. Nail wraps are one type of overlay that can be used over nail tips. Nail wraps are also used to repair or strengthen natural nails or to create nail extensions.

Nail wrap is a term used to describe any overlay that uses a nail wrap resin, used to coat and secure fabric wraps, to the natural nail and nail tip. Wrap resins are made from cyanoacrylate (adhesive) and are closely related to those used to create other types of nail enhancements.

Fabric wrap made of silk, linen, or fiberglass, is the most popular type of nail wrap because of their durability. Fabric wraps are cut to cover the surface of the natural nail and the nail tip and are laid onto a layer of wrap resin to build and strengthen the enhancement. Fabric wraps may be purchased in swatches, rolls, or in packages of pre-cut pieces, some with and some without adhesive backing.

The wrap material is the heart of a nail wrap system and gives this system its unique properties. Nail wraps can be used as an overlay to strengthen natural nails or to strengthen a nail tip application.

✔ **LO3 Complete**

Silk wraps are made from a thin natural material with a tight weave that becomes transparent when wrap resin is applied. A silk wrap is lightweight and has a smooth appearance when applied to the nail.

Linen wraps are made from a closely woven, heavy material. It is much thicker and bulkier than other types of wrap fabrics. Wrap adhesives do not penetrate linen as easily as silk or fiberglass. Because it is opaque, even after wrap resin is applied, a colored polish must be used to cover it completely. Linen is used because it is considered to be the strongest wrap fabric.

Fiberglass wraps are made from a very thin synthetic mesh with a loose weave. The loose weave makes it easy to use and allows the wrap resin to penetrate, which improves adhesion. Even though fiberglass is not as strong as linen or silk, it can create a durable nail enhancement.

Some clients and nail techs prefer to use a paper wrap. Paper was one of the very first materials used to create wraps. Paper wraps are temporary nail wraps made of very thin paper. They are quite simple to use, but do not have the strength and durability of fabric wraps. For this reason, paper wraps are considered a temporary service and need to be completely replaced each time your client comes in for maintenance.

✔ **LO4 Complete**

A wrap resin accelerator or activator acts as the dryer that speeds up the hardening process of the wrap resin or adhesive overlay. Activators come in several different forms: brush-on bottle, pump spray-on, and aerosol. Activator will dissipate in about two minutes after being applied, so be sure not to reapply additional wrap resin immediately or you may find that the activator causes the wrap resin to harden on the brush, tip of the bottle, or extender when it touches the nail. Activator also does not need to be applied after every layer of adhesive; this is an optional step and activator can be used as needed.

In addition to your chosen wrap material, you will need wrap resin and resin accelerator, nail buffer and file, small scissors, plastic, and tweezers to perform a nail wrap overlay **(Figure 16-3)**.

GO TO → **PROCEDURE 16-5 page 319**

▲ **FIGURE 16-3**
Supplies needed for nail wrap application.

fyi

To further strengthen a fabric wrap, some clients will enjoy a method professionals like to use called Dip Powder and Adhesive Enhancements. For this technique, a fine polymer powder is sprinkled or spooned onto the nail over a completed fabric wrap. Several layers of the dip powder can be applied. Any style of adhesive or resin can be used for this procedure. Usually, an activator is used to ensure drying.

Many clients who normally cannot wear monomer liquid and polymer powder nail enhancements on their nails because of skin sensitivity or allergy enjoy this service for the additional strength and wearability it provides them.

You may have heard about, or even tried using, a method of nail enhancement called No Light Gels. These were once used professionally, but now are popular as do-it-yourself kits for nail clients and are available for purchase in grocery and drug stores.

If you should encounter a client who may have used No Light Gels, you should know that the product's chemistry makes it more like adhesive nail enhancements than like the traditional UV gel products available. No Light Gels employ a thick adhesive that many companies and marketers mistakenly call a gel.

No Light Gels actually have the same chemical composition as wrap systems with wrap resin and can be used with a spray-on activator to harden or cure the adhesive.

Nail Wrap Maintenance, Repair, And Removal

Fabric wraps need regular maintenance to keep them looking fresh. In this section, you will learn how to maintain fabric wraps after two weeks and after four weeks. You also will learn how to repair cracks and to remove nail wraps when necessary.

NAIL WRAP MAINTENANCE

Nail wraps must have consistent maintenance, after the initial application. Maintenance is the term used for when a nail enhancement needs to be serviced after two or more weeks from the initial application of the nail enhancement product. The maintenance service actually accomplishes two goals: it allows the tech to apply the enhancement product onto the new growth of nail, commonly referred to as a fill or a backfill, and it allows the tech to structurally correct the nail to ensure its strength, shape and durability; this is commonly referred to as a rebalance.

Wrap maintenance can be done with either additional wrap resin, as in the Two-Week Fabric Maintenance or with fabric and resin, as in the Four-Week Fabric Maintenance. The maintenance is necessary for the nail's beauty and durability.

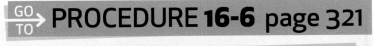

GO TO **PROCEDURE 16-6 page 321**

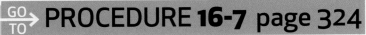

GO TO **PROCEDURE 16-7 page 324**

Business Tip:

HOST NAIL FASHION NIGHTS

Whoever coined the phrase "Seeing is believing"" must have known that people are more likely to purchase something familiar. To acquaint customers firsthand with the latest manicure looks, try hosting a nail fashion night. For a $10.00 to $16.00 admission fee, you can showcase the latest nail looks by giving each attendee a manicure—using the season's most popular fashion colors and hottest new products, of course. To top off the evening, offer each client a nail care fashion kit that includes trial-size products and a gift certificate for 10 to 15 percent off the next nail care purchase or service. Spending an entire night focused on the products creates a buzz about them and shows clients how to use them. The sample size gets them hooked and the gift certificate gives them an incentive to return to you.

FABRIC WRAP REPAIR

There will be circumstances when nail wraps will need to be repaired. In those cases, small pieces of fabric can be used to strengthen a weak point in the nail or to repair a break in the nail.

A stress strip is a strip of fabric cut to 1/8" in length and applied to the weak point of the nail during the Four-Week Fabric Wrap Maintenance, to repair or strengthen a weak point in a nail enhancement.

A repair patch is a piece of fabric cut to completely cover a crack or break in the nail. Use the Four-Week Fabric Wrap Maintenance Procedure to apply the repair patch.

GO TO → **PROCEDURE 16-7** page 324

FABRIC WRAP REMOVAL

There may be times when a client would like to have her nail wraps removed. When this occurs it is important to remove the wraps as carefully as possible so as not to damage the nail plate. Nail wraps are removed by immersing the entire enhancement into a small glass bowl filled with acetone. Wait for the nail wrap to melt away and then gently and carefully slide the softened wrap material away from the nail with a wooden pusher. Always suggest a manicure after removal of an enhancement to re-hydrate the natural nail and cuticle.

GO TO → **PROCEDURE 16-8** page 326

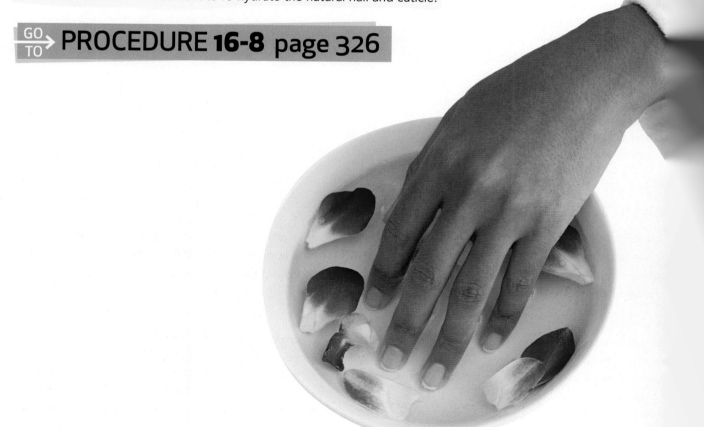

A. CLEANING

1. Put on a fresh pair of gloves while performing this pre-service to prevent possible contamination of the implements by your hands and to protect your hands from the powerful chemicals in the disinfectant solution.

2. Clean all tools and implements and any other reusable, nonelectrical item by first rinsing it in warm running water, and then thoroughly washing it with soap, a small, nylon brush, and warm water. Brush grooved items, if necessary, and open-hinged tools to scrub the area.

3. Rinse away all traces of soap with warm running water. The presence of soap in most disinfectants can cause them to become inactive. Dry items thoroughly with a clean or disposable towel, or allow to air dry on a clean towel. Your implements are now properly cleaned and ready to be disinfected.

4. Immerse cleaned implements in an appropriate disinfection container holding an EPA-registered disinfectant for the required time (usually 10 minutes). Before immersing cleaned implements open any hinged implements to the open position. If the disinfection solution is visibly dirty, the solution has been contaminated and must be replaced.

5. Remove implements, avoiding skin contact, and rinse and dry tools thoroughly.

6. Store disinfected implements in a clean, dry container until needed.

7. Remove gloves and thoroughly wash your hands with liquid soap, rinse, and dry with a clean fabric or disposable towel.

B. BASIC TABLE SETUP

1. Clean and disinfect manicure table and drawer with an appropriate or approved disinfectant cleanser.

2. Wrap your client's arm cushion, if used, with a clean terry cloth or disposable towel. Place the cushion in the middle of the table so that one end of the towel extends toward the client and the other end extends in your direction.

3. Ensure that your disinfection container is filled with clean disinfectant solution at least 20 minutes before your first service of the day. Use any disinfectant solution approved by your state board regulations, but make sure that you use it exactly as directed by the manufacturer. Also make sure that you change the disinfectant every day or according to the manufacturer's instructions. Put cleaned, multi-use implements into the disinfection container for the required time.

4. Place the professional products that you will use during the service (except polish) on the right side of the table behind your disinfection container if you are right-handed, or on the left side of the table if you are left-handed.

5. Place the abrasives and buffers of your choice on the table to your right if you are right-handed, or to your left if you are left-handed.

6. Tape or clip a plastic bag to the right side of the table if you are right-handed, or to the left side if you are left-handed, if a metal trash receptacle with a self-closing lid is not available. This is for depositing used materials during your service. These bags must be emptied after each client departs to prevent product vapors from escaping into the salon air.

7. Place polishes to the left if you are right-handed, or to the right if you are left-handed.

8. The drawer can be used to store the following items for immediate use: extra cotton or cotton balls in their original container or in a fresh plastic bag, abrasives, buffers, nail polish dryer, and other supplies. Never place used materials in your drawer. Only completely cleaned and disinfected implements stored in an sealed container (to protect them from dust and re-contamination) and extra materials or professional products should be placed in the drawer. Your drawer should always be organized and clean.

C. GREET CLIENT

1. Greet your client with a smile, introduce yourself if you've never met, and shake hands. If the client is new, ask her for the consultation card she filled out in the reception area.

2. Escort your client to the hand-washing area and demonstrate the hand-washing procedure for her on your own hands. Once you have completed the demonstration, hand your client a fresh nail brush to use and ask her to wash her hands.

GO TO → **PROCEDURE 13-3** page 231

3. Be sure that your towels look clean and are not worn. A towel with stains or holes definitely will affect how your client feels about her service. A dirty towel can tell a client either not to come back, or cause her to report your salon to the state board.

4. Show your client to your work table and make sure she is comfortable before beginning the service.

5. Discuss the information on the consultation card and determine a course of action for the service.

A. ADVISE CLIENTS AND PROMOTE PRODUCTS

1. Proper home maintenance will ensure that the client's nails look beautiful until he or she returns for another service (a week to ten days).

2. Depending on the service provided, there may be a number of retail products that you should recommend for the client to take home. This is the time to do so. Explain why they are important and how to use them.

B. SCHEDULE NEXT APPOINTMENT AND THANK CLIENT

1. Escort the client to the front desk to schedule the next appointment and to pay for the service. Set up date, time, and services and then write the information on your or the salon's appointment card and give it to the client.

2. Before you return to your station and the client leaves the salon, be sure to thank her for her business.

3. Record service information, products used, observations , and retail recommendations on the client service form.

C. PREPARE WORK AREA AND IMPLEMENTS FOR NEXT CLIENT

1. Remove your products and tools, then clean your work area and properly dispose of all used materials.

2. Follow steps for disinfecting implements in the Pre-Service Procedure. Reset work area with disinfected tools.

3. Advise the client about proper home maintenance for the service. Proper home maintenance will ensure that the nail service looks beautiful until your client returns for another service.

4. Depending on the service provided, there may be a number of retail products that you should recommend for the client to take home. This is the time to do so. Explain why they are important and how to use them.

D. SCHEDULE NEXT APPOINTMENT AND THANK CLIENT

1. Escort the client to the front desk to schedule the next appointment and to pay for the service. Set up date, time, and services for your client's next appointment. Write the information on your business card and give it to the client.

2. Before you return to your station and the client leaves the salon, be sure to thank her for her business.

3. Record service information, observations, and product recommendations on the client service form.

E. PREPARE WORK AREA AND IMPLEMENTS FOR NEXT CLIENT

1. Clean your work area. Remove your products and tools, then clean your work area and properly dispose of all used materials.

2. Follow steps for disinfecting implements in Procedure 16-1, Pre-Service Procedure. Reset work area with disinfected tools.

Nail Tip Application

IMPLEMENTS AND MATERIALS

In addition to the basic materials on your manicuring table, you will need the following supplies for the Nail Tip Application procedure:

- Nail tips
- Nail tip adhesive
- Abrasive boards
- Tip cutter
- Buffer block
- Nail dehydrator

PREPARATION

Refer to Procedure 16-1, **Pre-Service Procedure.**

PROCEDURE

1. Begin with your client's little finger on the left hand and remove existing nail polish, working toward the thumb. Then repeat on the right hand.

2. Gently push back the eponychium, using a wooden stick, pusher, or other suitable implement.

3. Carefully and gently remove the cuticle tissue from the nail plate, using a wooden stick, pusher, or other suitable implement.

4. Buff very lightly over the nail plate with a medium/fine abrasive (240 grit or higher) to remove the shine caused by natural oil and contaminants on the surface of the nail plate. Do not use a coarse abrasive, and be careful to avoid applying excessive pressure. The goal is to remove only the shine and as little nail plate thickness as possible. Remove the dust with a clean, dry nail brush by stroking from the cuticle area toward the free edge.

5. Apply nail dehydrator to remove surface moisture and tiny amounts of oil left on the natural nail plate. Be careful not to touch the natural nail with your fingers as any deposit of oils from your fingers could cause lifting of the overlay after it is applied.

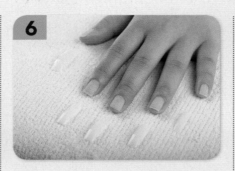

6. Take time to ensure that you are choosing properly sized tips for your client's nail plate before beginning to adhere them to the natural nail. Make sure that the tips you choose exactly cover the nail plate from sidewall to sidewall. Put all of the pre-tailored and pre-sized tips on a towel, in the order of finger position.

CAUTION

If you accidentally touch or contaminate the freshly prepped natural nail, you must clean it again and reapply nail dehydrator.

7. Place enough adhesive on the nail plate to cover the area where the tip will be placed, or apply the adhesive to the well of the tip. Do not apply too much—less is more when it comes to nail tip adhesives! Do not let adhesive run onto the skin. Apply adhesive from the middle of the nail plate to the free edge. You also can use a thin brush-on adhesive and cover the entire nail, then press the tip into it.

8. Slide the tips onto the client's natural nail and remember to stop, rock, and hold when applying tips. Find the stop against the free edge at a 45-degree angle. Rock the tip on slowly. Hold the tip in place for 5 to 10 seconds until the adhesive has dried. You may also apply the adhesive to the well area of the tip. This will ensure that there are fewer air bubbles trapped in the adhesive. This technique also works on well-less tips, followed by positioning on the nail plate and holding it in place for five to ten seconds until the adhesive hardens.

Application **Tip:**

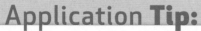

Consider using a well-less tip that requires no blending with the natural nail. Buff the surface of the nail tip gently once it is applied for better overlay adhesion.

Application **Tip:**

When applying a tip that has a well, be sure that the well butts up to the natural nail when adhering it to the nail.

✓ **LO5 Complete**

9. Trim the nail tip to desired length using a tip cutter.

Talking **Point:**

During the nail tip application procedure, discuss products such as polish, top coat, and hand lotion or cream that will help your client maintain the beauty and durability of her nails between salon visits.

10. If you applied tips with a well, you will still need additional blending to make them match with the surface of the natural nail plate. Take great care because this step can cause damage to the natural nail plate, if done improperly. Using a medium- to fine-grit file or buffing block file (180 grit or higher), carefully smooth the contact area down until it is flush with the natural nail. Make sure to keep your buffer (or board) flat to the nail as you blend the tip. Never hold the file at an angle because the edge of abrasive may gouge the nail plate and damage it. After you finish blending, remove the shine from the rest of the tip.

11. Use an abrasive to shape the new, longer nail.

12. Your nail tip application process is now complete. Although your client's tips blend with natural nails, tips should not be worn without an additional nail overlay such as wraps because tips will not be strong enough to wear alone.

13. Complete set of applied nail tips.

✓ **LO6 Complete**

POST-SERVICE

Complete Procedure 16-2, Post-Service Procedure.

IMPLEMENTS AND MATERIALS

In addition to the basic materials on your manicuring table, you will need the following supplies for the Nail Tip Removal procedure:

- Small glass bowl
- Tip remover solution or acetone
- Buffer block

PREPARATION

Refer to Procedure 16-1, **Pre-Service Procedure.**

PROCEDURE

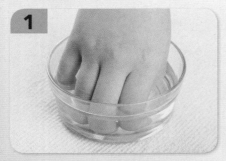

1. Place enough acetone in a small glass bowl to cover nails. Soak for a few minutes.

2. Use a pusher to slide off the softened nail tip. Be careful not to pry the nail tip off because you can damage the nail unit. If the nail tip is still too adhered to the nail, have the client soak that nail again for a few more minutes until the entire nail tip is easily removed.

3. Gently buff the natural nail with a fine buffer to remove any adhesive residue.

CAUTION

Never nip off the nail tip! This may lead to damage of the nail plate by pulling off layers of the natural nail and can break the seal of the remainder of the enhancement.

4. Reapply the nail tip if the client desires, as directed in Procedure 16-3 or if not, proceed with the desired service.

5. Finished look.

POST-SERVICE

Complete Procedure 16-2, Post-Service Procedure.

✓ **LO7 Complete**

IMPLEMENTS AND MATERIALS

In addition to the basic materials on your manicuring table, you will need the following supplies for the Nail Wrap Application procedure:

- Adhesive-backed Fabric
- Wrap Resin
- Wrap resin accelerator
- Small scissors
- Nail buffer
- Small piece of plastic
- Tweezers (optional)

PREPARATION

Refer to Procedure 16-1, **Pre-Service Procedure.**

PROCEDURE

1. Remove existing polish.

2. Push back the eponychium and remove the cuticle.

3. Lightly buff the nail plate with a medium/fine abrasive (240 grit) to remove shine caused by the oil found on the natural nail plate. Do not use a coarse file, and be careful not to apply very much pressure. Remove only the oily shine and avoid removing layers from the natural nail plate. Nail wraps can be performed over natural nails or over a set of nail tips. If you are using nail tips, you should use your abrasive to shape the free edges of the natural nails to match the shape of the nail tip to the stop point. Remove the dust with a clean dry disinfected nail brush.

4. Spray or wipe a nail dehydrator onto the nail plate. The dehydrator will remove moisture from the surface and will help improve adhesion. Wiping the dehydrator with a plastic-backed cotton pad on the nail plate has the added benefit of removing any remaining natural oil and helps ensure superior adhesion, even on clients with oily skin.

5. Apply nail tips, if desired. Refer to Procedure 16-3, Nail Tip Application.

6. Before removing the backing on the fabric, cut it to the approximate width and shape of the nail plate or nail tip.

7. Apply a layer of wrap resin over the entire surface of the nail and tip. Remember to keep the resin off the skin. Besides potentially damaging your client's skin, this could cause the wrap to lift or separate from the nail plate. Begin with the pinky finger of the left hand and apply the wrap resin to all 10 fingers. Once completed return to the fist finger and apply fabric wrap.

8. Remove the backing from the fabric, being careful to keep the dust and oils on your fingers from contaminating the adhesive side of the fabric, as this could prevent the fabric from adhering to the nail. Gently fit fabric over the nail plate covering the entire nail (you may also use a pair of tweezers to apply the fabric), if desired, and keeping it 1/16" away from the sidewalls and eponychium. Use a small piece of thick plastic to press the fabric on to the nail and to smooth it.

Application **Tip:**

Using a 6"× 4" piece of flexible plastic sheet—a sandwich baggie works great—to press fabric onto the nail plate will prevent the transfer of oil and debris from your fingers. Wrap resin will not easily penetrate fibers that are contaminated with oil, and those strands become visible in the clear coating. Thus, it is best not to touch them more than you must. Changing to an unused portion of the plastic for each finger is necessary.

9. Once the fabric is secure on the nail, use small scissors to trim fabric 1/16" away from sidewalls and the free edge. Trimming fabric slightly smaller than the nail plate prevents fabric from lifting and separating from the nail plate.

10. Draw a thin coat of wrap resin down the center of the nail using the extender tip or brush. Do not touch the skin. The wrap resin will penetrate the fabric and adhere to the nail surface. Use the plastic again to make sure that the wrap resin is evenly distributed and that there are no bubbles or areas of bare fabric. Once saturated with wrap resin, the wrap fabric or paper will appear almost invisible, with the exception of the linen fabric because is quite thick.

11. Wrap resin accelerator is a product specially designed to help any cyanoacrylate glue or wrap resin dry more quickly. Spray, brush, or drop on a wrap resin accelerator that is specifically designed to work with the product you are using. Use according to manufacturer's instructions. Keep the wrap resin accelerator off skin to prevent overexposure to the product.

12. Apply and spread a second coat of wrap resin and seal free edge to prevent lifting and tip separation.

13. Apply a second coat of wrap resin accelerator.

14. Use medium-fine abrasive (240 grit) to shape and refine the wrap nail.

15. Apply nail oil and buff to a high shine with a fine (350 grit or higher) buffer. Use the buffer to smooth out rough areas in the fabric. Do not buff excessively or for too long. Overbuffing can wear through the wrap and weaken it.

16. Apply hand lotion and massage the hand and arm.

17. Remove traces of oil. Use a small piece of cotton ball or plastic-backed pad and non-acetone polish remover to eliminate traces of oil from the nail so that the polish will adhere.

18. Polish the nails.

19. Finished look.

✓ **LO8 Complete**

POST-SERVICE

Complete Procedure 16-2, Post-Service Procedure.

Two-Week Fabric Wrap Maintenance

PROCEDURE **16-6**

IMPLEMENTS AND MATERIALS

In addition to the basic materials on your manicuring table, you will need the following supplies for the Two-Week Fabric Wrap Maintenance procedure:

- Wrap Resin
- Wrap Resin Accelerator
- Abrasive buffer or fileblock

PREPARATION

Refer to Procedure 16-1, **Pre-Service Procedure.**

PROCEDURE

1. Use a non-acetone polish remover to remove existing nail polish and to avoid damaging nail wraps. Acetone will break down the wrap resin too quickly.

2. Clean the natural nails.

3. Push back the eponychium.

4. Lightly buff the surface of the exposed nail plate to remove oily shine.

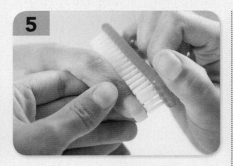

5. Remove the dust with a clean, dry nylon nail brush and apply nail dehydrator to nails with a cottontipped wooden pusher, cotton pad with a plastic backing, brush, or spray. Begin with the little finger on the left hand and work toward the thumb. Repeat on the right hand.

6. Apply a small amount of nail wrap resin to the area of new nail growth. Spread the wrap resin, taking care to avoid touching the skin.

7. Spray, brush, or drop on a wrap resin accelerator that is specifically designed to work with the product you are using. Follow the manufacturer's instructions. Keep the wrap resin accelerator off skin to prevent overexposure to the product.

8. Apply a second coat of wrap resin to the entire nail plate to strengthen and reseal the nail wrap.

9. Apply a second coat of wrap resin accelerator.

10. Use a medium-fine abrasive over the surface of the nail wrap to remove any high spots and/or other imperfections.

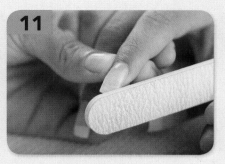

11. Apply nail oil and buff to a high shine with the fine buffer (350 grit or higher).

12. Apply hand lotion and massage the hand and arm.

13. Remove traces of oil. Use a small piece of cotton ball or plastic-backed pad and non-acetone polish remover to eliminate traces of oil from the nail so that the polish will adhere.

14. Polish the nails.

15. Finished look.

POST-SERVICE

Complete Procedure 16-2, Post-Service Procedure.

✓ LO**9** Complete

PART **3**

Four-Week Fabric Wrap Maintenance

IMPLEMENTS AND MATERIALS

In addition to the basic materials on your manicuring table, you will need the following supplies for the Four-Week Fabric Wrap Maintenance procedure:

- Wrap Resin
- Wrap Resin Accelerator
- Abrasive buffer or file
- Adhesive-backed Fabric

- Small scissors
- Small piece of plastic
- Tweezers (optional)

PREPARATION

Refer to Procedure 16-1, **Pre-Service Procedure.**

PROCEDURE

1. Use a non-acetone polish remover to remove existing nail polish and to avoid damaging nail wraps. Acetone will break down the wrap resin too quickly.

2. Clean the natural nails.

3. Push back the eponychium.

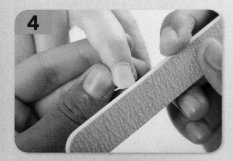

4. Lightly buff the nail plates with a medium-fine (240 grit) abrasive to remove the shine created by natural oils and to remove any small pieces of fabric that may have lifted since the last service. Buff the end of the wrap until smooth, without scratching or damaging the natural nail plate. Carefully refine the nail until there is no obvious line of demarcation between new growth and fabric wrap. Avoid damaging the natural nail with the abrasive. Do not file the natural nail surface.

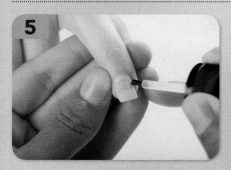

5. Remove the dust with a clean, dry nylon nail brush and apply nail dehydrator to nails with a cotton-tipped wooden pusher, cotton pad with a plastic backing, brush, or spray. Begin with the little finger on the left hand and work toward the thumb. Repeat on the right hand.

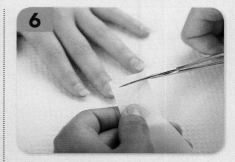

6. Cut a piece of fabric large enough to cover the new growth area and to slightly overlap the old wrap fabric.

7. Apply a small amount of wrap resin to the fill area and spread throughout the new growth area. Be careful to avoid touching the skin.

8. Gently fit the fabric over the new growth area and smooth.

9. Apply another small amount of wrap resin, again avoiding the skin.

10. Spray, brush, or drop on the wrap resin accelerator to dry the wrap resin more quickly. Follow the manufacturer's instructions.

11. Apply a second coat of wrap resin to the regrowth area.

12. Apply a second coat of wrap resin accelerator.

13. Apply a thin coat of nail wrap resin to the entire nail to strengthen and seal wrap.

14. Apply the wrap resin accelerator.

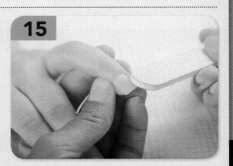

15. Use a medium-fine abrasive (240 grit) over the surface of the nail to remove any high spots or other imperfections. Carefully avoid the skin around the cuticle and sidewalls so that you do not cause cuts or damage.

PART **3**

16. Apply nail oil and buff to a high shine with a buffer.

17. Apply hand lotion and massage the hand and arm.

18. Use a small piece of cotton ball or plastic-backed pad and non-acetone polish remover to eliminate traces of oil from the nail so that the polish will adhere.

19. Professionally maintained nails.

POST-SERVICE

Complete Procedure 16-2, Post-Service Procedure.

✓ **LO10 Complete**

Fabric Wrap Removal

PROCEDURE **16-8**

IMPLEMENTS AND MATERIALS

In addition to the basic materials on your manicuring table, you will need the following supplies for the Fabric Wrap Removal procedure:

- Small glass bowl
- Acetone

PREPARATION

Refer to Procedure 16-1, **Pre-Service Procedure.**

PROCEDURE

1

1. Put enough acetone in a small glass bowl to cover the nail wrap. Immerse the client's fingertips in the bowl, making sure that the wraps are covered. Soak for a few minutes. The acetone should be approximately 1/2" above the nail wraps.

2

2. Use a pusher to slide softened wraps away from the nail plate.

3

3. Gently buff natural nails with a fine buffer (240 grit) to remove the wrap resin.

4

5. Proceed to the desired service.

6

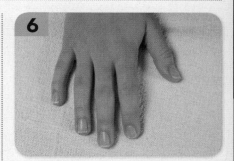

4. Condition the skin surrounding the nail plate with nail oils or lotions designed for this purpose.

6. Finished look.

POST-SERVICE

Complete Procedure 16-2, Post-Service Procedure.

 **LO11 Complete**

PART **3**

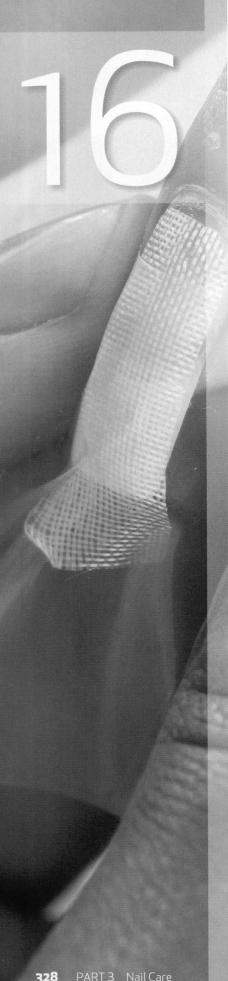

review questions

1. What are the supplies, in addition to your basic manicuring table, that you need for nail tip application?

2. What are the types of nail tips available and why is it important to properly fit them for your client?

3. What types of fabrics are used in nail wraps?

4. What are the benefits of using each of these types of fabric wraps?

5. Describe the stop, rock, and hold method of applying nail tips.

6. Describe the Nail Tip Application procedure.

7. Describe the Nail Tip Removal procedure.

8. Describe the Fabric Wrap Application procedure.

9. What is the main difference between performing the Two-Week Fabric Wrap Maintenance and the Four-Week Fabric Wrap Maintenance?

10. Describe how to remove fabric wraps and what to avoid.

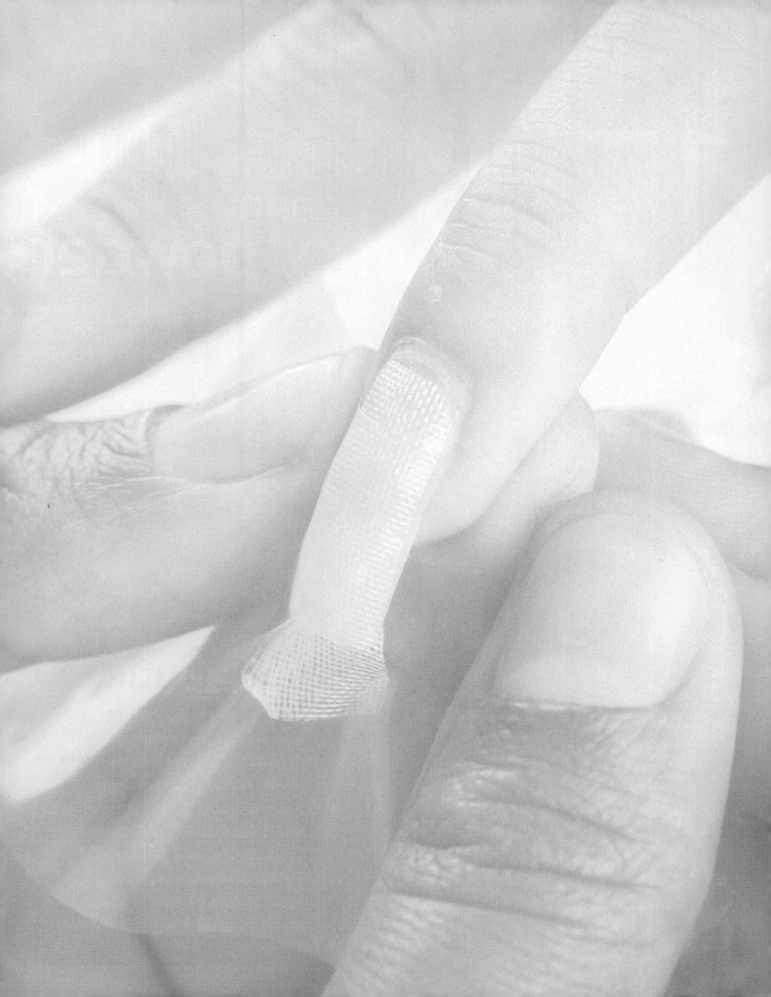

17

monomer liquid
and
polymer powder

NAIL ENHANCEMENTS

chapter outline

☑ Learning Objectives

After you have completed this chapter, you will be able to:

1 Explain monomer liquid and polymer powder nail enhancement chemistry and how it works.

2 Describe the apex, stress area, sidewall, and where they are located on the nail enhancement.

3 Demonstrate the proper procedures for applying one-color monomer liquid and polymer powder nail enhancements over tips and on natural nails.

4 Demonstrate the proper procedures for applying two-color monomer liquid and polymer powder nail enhancements using forms over nail tips and on natural nails.

5 Describe how to perform a one-color maintenance service on nail enhancements using monomer liquid and polymer powder.

6 Demonstrate how to perform crack repair procedures.

7 Implement the proper procedure for removing monomer liquid and polymer powder nail enhancements.

Key Terms

Page number indicates where in the chapter the term is used.

apex (arch) / 339

catalysts / 334

chain reaction / 334

initiators / 334

monomer liquid / 332

monomer liquid and polymer powder nail enhancements / 332

nail extension underside / 340

odorless monomer liquid and polymer powder products / 341

polymer / 332

polymer powder / 332

polymerization / 333

sidewall / 340

stress area / 340

Nail enhancements based on mixing together liquids and powders are commonly referred to as "acrylic" (a-KRYL-yk) nails. It might surprise you to discover the real definition of "acrylic," since for many years this word has actually been used incorrectly by the nail enhancement industry. The term "acrylic" actually refers to an entire family of thousands of different substances, all of which share important, closely related features. Acrylics are used to make a wide range of things including contact lenses, cements for mending broken bones, Plexiglas® windows, and even makeup and other cosmetics. Surprisingly, all nail enhancement products are based almost entirely on ingredients that come from the acrylic family. For example, the ingredients in two-part monomer liquid and polymer powder enhancement systems belong to a branch of the acrylic family called "methacrylates." In other words, "acrylic" is a very general term for a large group of ingredients. Monomer liquid and polymer powder nail enhancement products are based on methacrylates (METH-ah-cry-latz). You can see some similarity in the spelling of the terms, which indicates that they are from the same chemical family or group. To be as accurate and specific as possible, you will find that the two-part monomer liquid and polymer powder enhancement system in this book is referred to as monomer liquid and polymer powder, but please also keep in mind that other industry literature, product marketing, and the like may continue to use the word acrylic.

Today's monomer liquids and polymer powders come in many colors, including variations of basic pink, white, clear, and natural. These colors can be used alone or blended to create everything from customized shades of pink to match or enhance the color of your client's nail beds, to bold primaries or pastels that can be used to create a wide range of designs and patterns. With these powders you can create unique colors or designs that can be locked permanently in the nail enhancement. They offer a wonderful way to customize your services or to express your artistry and creativity. Monomer liquid and polymer powder overlays and nail enhancements can be created with a single color powder, if the client wears nail polish all the time. Or they can be created by using a pink or natural-colored powder over the nail bed or a natural or soft white powder to replicate a natural nail free edge. A stark white powder can be use to create the French manicure look. The finished nail enhancement can be polished with nail polish or buffed to a high-glossy shine for a more natural look. These types of services are extremely versatile and highly durable, which partially explains their great popularity.

Monomer Liquid and Polymer Powder Nail Enhancements

Monomer liquid and polymer powder nail enhancements are created by combining monomer (MON-oh-mehr) liquid and polymer (POL-i-mehr) powder; thus the names liquid and powder. *Mono* means *one* and *mer* stands for *units*, so a *monomer* is one unit called a *molecule*. *Poly* means *many*, so polymer means *many units* or many molecules linked together in a chain.

This is important to remember, since you will hear these terms many times throughout your career.

Monomer liquid and polymer powder products can be applied in three basic ways:

1 On the natural nail as a protective overlay,
2 Over a nail tip, and
3 On a form to create a nail extension.

A natural hair, pointed, round, or oval application brush is the best brush to use for applying these products. The brush is immersed in the monomer liquid. The natural hair bristles absorb and hold the monomer liquid like a reservoir. The tip of the brush is then touched to the surface of the dry polymer powder, and as the monomer liquid absorbs the polymer powder, a small bead of product forms. This small bead is then carefully placed on the nail surface and molded into shape with the brush.

The monomer liquid portion is usually one of three versions of monomer liquid used in the nail industry: ethyl methacrylate, methyl methacrylate, or odorless monomer liquid. All three often contain other monomers that are used as customizing additives. The industry standard is the ethyl methacrylate monomer liquid (EMA) and odorless monomer liquid. Methyl methacrylate (MMA) is not recommended for use on nails and is not legal according to the state board rules in some states.

It may seem strange that polymer powder is also made mostly from ethyl methacrylate monomer liquid. The polymer powder is made using a special chemical reaction called polymerization (POL-i-mehr-eh-za-shun). In this process, trillions of monomers are linked together to create long chains. These long chains create the tiny round beads of polymer powder used to create certain types of nail enhancements.

During the production of polymer powder, the powder forms into tiny round beads of slightly varying sizes. These are poured through a series of special screens that sort the beads by size. The ones that are the right size are separated and then mixed with other special additives and colorants. The final mixture is packaged and sold as polymer powder. It is a surprisingly high-tech process that requires very specific manufacturing equipment, lots of quality control, and scientific know-how to do it right.

Special additives are blended into both the liquid and powder. These additives ensure complete set or cure, maximum durability, color stability, and shelf-life, among other attributes. It is these "custom" additives that make products work and behave differently. The polymer powders are usually blended with pigments and colorants to create a wide range of shades, including pinks, whites, and milky translucent shades, as well as reds, blues, greens, purples, yellows, oranges, browns, and even jet black.

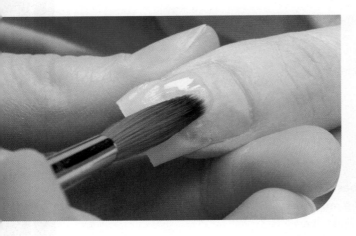

When liquid is picked up by a brush and mixed with the powder, the bead that forms on the end of the brush quickly begins to harden. It is then put into place with other beads and shaped into place as they harden. In order for this process to begin, the monomers and polymers require special additives called catalysts (KAT-a-lists), additives designed to speed up chemical reactions and initiators. Catalysts are added to the monomer iquid and used to control the set or curing time. In other words, when the monomer liquid and polymer powder are combined, the catalyst (in the liquid) helps control the set-up or hardening time. How? The catalyst energizes and activates the initiators.

The initiators start a chain reaction that leads to the creation of very long polymer chains. It is actually the initiators found in the powder that, when activated, will spring into action and start causing monomer molecules to permanently link together into these long polymer chains. This is another example of the polymerization process discussed above, except this time it is actually occurring on the fingernail. The polymerization process begins at the same time the liquid in the brush picks up powder from the container and forms a bead. Creating polymers can be thought of as a chain reaction, much like many dominos and set on their edges and lined up—tap the first domino, and it hits the next, and so on. This is how polymers form. Once the monomers join together to create a polymer, they do not detach from each other easily.

The initiator that is added to the polymer powder is called benzoyl peroxide (BPO). It is the same ingredient used in over-the-counter acne medicine, except that it has a different purpose in nail enhancement products. BPO is used to start the chain reaction that leads to curing (hardening) of the nail enhancement. There is much less BPO in nail powders than in acne treatments. Diverse nail enhancement products often use different amounts of BPO, since the polymer powders are designed to work specifically with a certain monomer liquid. Some monomer liquids require more BPO to properly cure than others. This is why it is very important to use the polymer powder that was designed for the monomer liquid that you are using. Using the wrong powder can create nail enhancements that are not properly cured and may lead to service breakdown or could increase the risk of your clients developing a skin irritation or sensitivity.

There are many monomer liquid and polymer powder systems available, and you will have to try many to find the product that fits best for you and your clients.

> ❝ There are many monomer liquid and polymer powder systems available...

✓ LO1 Complete

To learn more about how products work and how to troubleshoot problems, see *Nail Structure and Product Chemistry*, second edition, by Douglas Schoon (Cengage Learning, 2005).

Monomer Liquid and Polymer Powder Nail Enhancement Supplies

Just as every type of nail enhancement service requires specific tools, implements, equipment, and supplies, so do monomer liquid and polymer powder nail enhancements. Here is a list of those requirements (**Figure 17-1**). In addition to the supplies in your basic manicuring setup, you will need:

MONOMER LIQUID

The monomer liquid will be combined with polymer powder to form the sculptured nail. The amount of monomer liquid and polymer powder used to create a bead is called the *mix ratio*. A bead mix ratio can be best described as *dry*, *medium*, or *wet*. If equal amounts of liquid and powder are used to create the bead, it is called a *dry bead*. If twice as much liquid as powder is used to create the bead, it is called a *wet bead*. Halfway between these two is a *medium bead*, which contains one-and-a-half more liquid than powder. In general, medium beads are the ideal mix ratio for working with monomer liquids and polymer powders.

The mix ratio typically ensures proper set and maximum durability of the nail enhancement. For example, if too much flour is added when making cookies, the cookies will be dry and crumbly; too little flour will make the cookies soft and gooey. The same holds true for monomer liquids and polymer powders. If too much powder is picked up in the bead, the enhancement will cure incorrectly and may lead to brittleness and/or discoloration. If too little powder is used, the nail enhancement can become weak, and the risk of clients developing skin irritation and sensitivity may increase.

POLYMER POWDER

Polymer powder is available in white, clear, natural, pink, and many other colors. The color(s) you choose will depend on the nail enhancement method you are using.

▲ **FIGURE 17-1**
Supplies needed for monomer liquid and polymer powder nail enhancement applications.

Here's a Tip:

Monomer Liquid Bead Mix Ratio Guidelines

1 part monomer liquid
+ 1 part polymer powder
= dry bead

1-1/2 parts monomer liquid
+ 1 part polymer powder
= medium bead

2 parts monomer liquid
+ 1 part polymer powder
= wet bead

fyi Manufacturer's instructions for using monomer liquid and polymer powder nail enhancement products may differ slightly from the general guidelines presented in this chapter. You should always use products in accordance with the manufacturer's instructions. If you are in doubt about how to use the products, contact the manufacturer.

Always have your clients wash their hands thoroughly with a fingernail brush before any service. Hand sanitizers are an alternative when hand washing is not available, but they do not clean the hands. They cannot remove dirt or debris from hands and underneath the nails. They kill some of the bacteria on skin, but not all of it. Hand sanitizers do give clients peace of mind, though. Clients like to see nail professionals using hand sanitizers and many clients prefer to use them as well. Keep a high-quality, professional hand sanitizer at your station and offer some to your clients. Let them see you using it, and they will have a greater degree of confidence in the cleanliness of your services. Do not let hand sanitizers replace hand washing—there is no replacement for that.

CAUTION

Acid-based nail primers are very effective but can cause serious—and sometimes irreversible—damage to the skin and eyes. Never use acid-based nail primer or any other corrosive material without wearing protective gloves and safety eyewear.

NAIL DEHYDRATOR

Nail dehydrators remove surface moisture and tiny amounts of oil left on the natural nail plate, both of which can block adhesion. Nail dehydrator should be applied liberally to the natural nail plate only; skin contact should be avoided. This step is a great way to help prevent lifting of the nail enhancement prior to applying primer.

NAIL PRIMER

Many kinds of nail primers are available today. Acid-based nail primer (methacrylic acid) once was widely used to help adhere enhancements to the natural nail. Since this type of nail primer is corrosive to the skin and potentially dangerous to eyes, *acid-free* and *nonacid primers* were developed. These are the types of primers that are most often used today. These alternatives work as well as or better than acid-based nail primers, and they have the added advantage of not being corrosive to skin or eyes. Even so, all nail primer products must be used with caution, and skin contact must be avoided. Read the manufacturer's instructions and refer to the MSDS for safe handling recommendations and instructions. Acid-based nail primers must be used with caution and strictly in accordance with the manufacturer's instructions.

For nonacid and acid-free nail primers: using the applicator brush, insert brush into the nail primer. Wipe off excess from the brush. Using a slightly damp brush, completely cover the nail plate with the primer. Do not use too much product—it will run onto the skin and cause skin irritation or sensitivity. The brush should hold enough product to treat two or three nails. Be sure the entire nail plate is covered. Before dipping the brush back into the container, gently wipe the brush on a clean table towel so you do not contaminate the bottle with any debris the brush may have picked up. Be sure to read the label for the manufacturer's suggested application procedures and precautions.

ABRASIVES

Select a medium grit (180 to 240) for natural nail preparation and initial shaping. Choose a medium grit for smoothing and a fine buffer (350 grit or higher) for final buffing. A three-way buffer is used to create a high shine on the enhancement when no polish is worn. If you avoid putting the product on too thickly, a 180 grit is usually enough to shape the nail enhancement. Avoid using coarser (lower-grit) abrasives or aggressive techniques on freshly applied enhancement products, as they can damage the freshly created nail enhancement.

NAIL FORMS

Nail forms are placed under the free edge and used to extend the nail enhancements beyond the fingertip for additional length. Nail forms often are made of paper or

Mylar and coated with adhesive backs or are made of pre-shaped plastic or aluminum. Each of these forms is disposable, except the plastic and aluminum forms, which can be properly cleaned and disinfected.

NAIL TIPS

These are pre-formed nail extensions made from ABS or tenite acetate plastic and are available in a wide variety of shapes, styles, and colors, such as natural, white, and clear.

GO TO → **PROCEDURE 16-3 page 315**

DAPPEN DISH

The monomer liquid and polymer powder are each poured into a special holder called a *dappen dish*. These dishes must have narrow openings to minimize evaporation of the monomer liquid into the air. Do not use open-mouth jars or other containers with large openings. Those types of containers will dramatically increase evaporation of the liquid and can allow the product to be contaminated with dust and other debris. Dappen dishes must be covered with tightly-fitting lids when not in use.

Each time the brush is dipped into the dappen dish, the remaining monomer liquid is contaminated with small amounts of polymer powder. So never pour the unused portion of monomer liquid back into the original container. Empty the monomer liquid from your dappen dish after the service and wipe it clean with a disposable towel. To avoid skin irritation or sensitivity, do not contact skin with the monomer liquid during this process. Wipe the dish clean with acetone, if necessary, before storing in a dust-free location.

fyi The best way to dispose of small amounts of monomer liquid is to mix them with small amounts of the powder designed to cure them. (This is safe for amounts ranging from less than a half-ounce of monomer liquid to quarts or gallons.) They should never be disposed of in the trash or down the drain. Tiny amounts left in a dappen dish can be wiped out with a paper towel and disposed of in a metal trash can with a self-closing lid. Be sure to avoid contact with your skin during the process and have the trash disposed of several times during the day so that vapors do not evaporate and escape into the salon air.

NAIL BRUSH

The best brush for use with these types of procedures is composed of sable hair and is usually an oval or round style application brush. Odorless monomer liquid requires less liquid and a flat brush holds less liquid.

Synthetic and less expensive brushes do not pick up enough monomer liquid or do not release the liquid properly. Choose the brush shape and size with which you feel the most comfortable. Avoid overly large brushes (size 12 to 16), since they can hold excessive amounts of liquid and alter the mix ratio of the powder and liquid.

Having too much monomer liquid on your brush can increase the risk of accidentally touching the client's skin and may increase the risk of developing skin irritation or sensitivities.

SAFETY EYEWEAR

Safety eyewear should be used to protect eyes from flying objects or accidental splashes. There are many types and styles. You can get more information by searching the Internet or contacting a local optometrist, who can also help you with both nonprescription and prescription safety eyewear.

DUST MASKS

Dust masks are designed to be worn over the nose and mouth to prevent inhalation of excessive amounts of dust. They provide no protection from vapors.

PROTECTIVE GLOVES

Both disposable and multiuse varieties of protective gloves can be purchased. Several types of materials are used to make these gloves. For many nail salon–related applications, gloves made of *nitrile* polymer powder work best.

STORING MONOMER LIQUID AND POLYMER POWDER PRODUCTS

Store monomer liquid and polymer powder products in covered containers. Store all primers and liquids separate from each other in a cool, dark area. Do not store products near heat.

After a service, you must discard used materials. Never save used monomer liquid that has been removed from the original container. Use on one client only. To dispose of small amounts of leftover monomer liquid, carefully pour it into a very absorbent paper towel and then place it in a plastic bag. Avoid skin contact with the monomer liquid and never pour it directly into the plastic bag! Should skin contact occur, wash hands with liquid soap and water. After all used materials have been collected, seal them in a plastic bag and discard the bag in a closed waste receptacle. It is important to remove items soiled with enhancement products from your manicuring station after each client. This will help maintain the quality of the air in your salon. Dispose of these items according to local rules and regulations.

Here's a Tip:

Avoid wiping your brush too rapidly or hard against a table towel. This can press hairs against the sharp edge of the metal ferrule that holds the hairs in place and cut them off.

Monomer Liquid And Polymer Powder Nail Enhancement Maintenance, Crack Repair, and Removal

Regular maintenance helps prevent nail enhancements from lifting or cracking. If the nail enhancements are not regularly maintained, they have a greater tendency to lift, crack, or break, which increases the risk of the client developing an infection or having other problems.

When a nail technician has a client with a piece or section of the monomer liquid and polymer powder enhancement that has broken, lifted, or cracked, it is repaired by filing the area and adding monomer liquid and polymer powder to it. This is called a crack repair.

Proper maintenance must be performed every two to three weeks, depending on how fast the client's nails grow. Properly maintaining nails is a critical skill for you to learn, if you choose to offer nail enhancement services to your clients. Do not let clients go too long without having a proper maintenance service, or you will have many more repairs to perform when they return. Proper maintenance is both safe and gentle to the nail unit and will not result in injury or damage. In the maintenance service, the nail is thinned down, the apex of the nail is removed, and the entire nail enhancement is reduced in thickness.

GO TO → **PROCEDURE 17-5** page 352

GO → **PROCEDURE 17-6** page 356

AREAS OF CONCERN FOR BUILDING PROPERLY STRUCTURED NAIL ENHANCEMENTS

Nail enhancements should not only look good, but they should also remain strong and healthy while your client is wearing them. Several areas of the nail must be considered when the nail enhancement is being built to accomplish this. Paying particular attention to the following areas of the nail enhancement will help you to create the look your clients desire and also provide them with the best and longest-lasting nail enhancements.

The apex or arch is the area of the nail that has all of the strength. Having strength in the apex allows the base of the nail, sidewalls, and tip to be thin, yet leaves the nail strong enough to resist frequent chipping or breaking. The apex is usually oval-shaped and is located in the center of the nail. The high point is visible no matter where you view the nail.

> Nail enhancements should not only look good but they should also remain strong and healthy...

The stress area is where the natural nail grows beyond the finger and becomes the free edge. This area needs strength to support the extension.

The sidewall is the area on the side of the nail plate that grows free of its attachment to the nail fold and where the extension leaves the natural nail.

The nail extension underside is the actual underside of the nail extension. The nail extension underside can jut straight out or may dip depending on the nail style. Undersides should be even and match in length from nail to nail on all fingers. The tip should fit the nail and finger properly, and the underside of the nail extension should be smooth without any glitches.

The thickness of the nail enhancement should be rather thin if a client is to wear it comfortably while going about her day. The enhancement should graduate seamlessly from the cuticle area to end of the nail extension so you do not feel an edge. The sidewalls and tip's edge should be credit-card thin.

The C-curve of the nail enhancement depends on the C-curve of the natural nail. In the salon, a 35 percent C-curve is the average. The top surface and bottom side should match perfectly.

To make sure the lengths of the nail extension and enhancements are appropriate and even, be sure to measure the length of the index, middle, and ring fingers; these should be the same length. The thumb and pinkie fingers should also be in proportion and match.

✓ **LO2 Complete**

MONOMER LIQUID AND POLYMER POWDER NAIL ENHANCEMENT REMOVAL

There will be circumstances when your client feels that she wants to have her monomer liquid and polymer powder nail enhancements removed. Do not worry. The procedure is simple: soak the enhancements off of the nail using acetone or the manufacturer's suggested removal solution, remove the enhancement, and complete the service.

GO TO → **PROCEDURE 17-7 page 358**

Odorless Monomer Liquid and Polymer Powder Products

Odorless monomer liquid and polymer powder products do not necessarily have the same chemistry as all other monomer liquid and polymer powder products. Rather than use ethyl acrylic these products rely on monomers that have little odor. Even though these products are called *odorless*, they do have a slight odor. Generally, if a monomer liquid does not produce a strong enough odor that others in the salon can detect its presence, it is considered to be an *odorless product*. Those that create a slight odor in the salon are called *low odor*.

In general, odorless products must be used with a dry mix ratio (equal parts liquid and powder in bead). If used too wet, there is the risk of the client developing skin irritation or sensitivity. This mix ratio creates a snowy-appearing bead on your brush. After it is placed on the nail, it will slowly form into a firm glossy bead that will hold its shape until pressed and smoothed with the nail brush. Wipe your brush frequently to avoid the product sticking to the hairs. Never re-wet the brush with monomer liquid. This will change the mix ratio, which can lead to product discoloration, service breakdown, and increased risk of skin irritation and sensitivity. Without re-wetting your brush, use it to shape and smooth the surface to perfection.

Odorless products harden more slowly and create a tacky layer called the inhibition layer. Once the enhancement has hardened, this layer can be removed with alcohol, acetone, or a manufacturer-recommended product. It is always best to use a plastic-backed cotton pad to avoid skin contact with the inhibition layer, since repeated contact with this layer can lead to skin irritation and sensitivity. This layer also can be filed away, but avoid skin contact with these freshly filed particles.

Colored Polymer Powder Products

Polymer powders are now available in a wide range of colors that mimic almost every shade available in nail polish. Nail artistry with colored polymer powder is limited only by your imagination. Some nail professionals use colors to go beyond the traditional pink and white French manicure combinations and offer custom-blended colors to their clients. They maintain recipe cards so that they can reproduce customized nail enhancements that clients cannot get from anyone else. As with all customized techniques, clients are willing to pay a few dollars more for the special service.

A. CLEANING AND DISINFECTING

1. Put on a fresh pair of gloves while performing this pre-service to prevent possible contamination of the implements by your hands and to protect your hands from the powerful chemicals in the disinfectant solution.

2. Clean all tools and implements and any other reusable, nonelectrical item by first rinsing it in warm running water, and then thoroughly washing it with soap, a small, nylon brush, and warm water. Brush grooved items, if necessary, and open-hinged tools to scrub the area.

3. Rinse away all traces of soap with warm running water. The presence of soap in most disinfectants can cause them to become inactive. Dry items thoroughly with a clean or disposable towel, or allow to air dry on a clean towel. Your implements are now properly cleaned and ready to be disinfected.

4. Before immersing cleaned implements, open any hinged implements to the open position. Immerse cleaned implements in an appropriate disinfection container holding an EPA-registered disinfectant for the required time (usually 10 minutes). If the disinfection solution is visibly dirty, the solution has been contaminated and must be replaced.

5. Remove implements, avoiding skin contact, and rinse and dry tools thoroughly.

6. Store disinfected implements in a clean, dry container until needed.

7. Remove gloves and thoroughly wash your hands with liquid soap, rinse, and dry with a clean fabric or disposable towel.

B. BASIC TABLE SETUP

1. Clean and disinfect manicure table and drawer with an appropriate or approved disinfectant cleanser.

2. Wrap your client's arm cushion, if used, with a clean terry cloth or disposable towel. Place the cushion in the middle of the table so that one end of the towel extends toward the client and the other end extends in your direction.

3. Ensure that your disinfection container is filled with clean disinfectant solution at least 20 minutes before your first service of the day. Use any disinfectant solution approved by your state board regulations, but make sure that you use it exactly as directed by the manufacturer. Also make sure that you change the disinfectant every day or according to the manufacturer's instructions. Put cleaned, multi-use implements into the disinfection container for the required time.

4. Place the professional products that you will use during the service (except polish) on the right side of the table behind your disinfection container if you are right-handed, or on the left side of the table if you are left-handed.

B. BASIC TABLE SETUP CONTINUED

5. Place the abrasives and buffers of your choice on the table to your right if you are right-handed, or to your left if you are left-handed.

6. Tape or clip a plastic bag to the right side of the table if you are right-handed, or to the left side if you are left-handed, if a metal trash receptacle with a self-closing lid is not available. This is for depositing used materials during your service. These bags must be emptied after each client departs to prevent product vapors from escaping into the salon air.

7. Place polishes to the left if you are left-handed, or to the right if you are right-handed.

8. The drawer can be used to store the following items for immediate use: extra cotton or cotton balls in their original container or in a fresh plastic bag, abrasives, buffers, nail polish dryer, and other supplies. Never place used materials in your drawer. Only completely cleaned and disinfected implements stored in an sealed container (to protect them from dust and re-contamination) and extra materials or professional products should be placed in the drawer. Your drawer should always be organized and clean.

C. GREET CLIENT

1. Greet your client with a smile, introduce yourself if you've never met, and shake hands. If the client is new, ask her for the consultation card she filled out in the reception area

2. Escort your client to the hand-washing area and demonstrate the hand-washing procedure for her on your own hands. Once you have completed the demonstration, hand your client a fresh nail brush to use and ask her to wash her hands.

GO TO → **PROCEDURE 13-3** page 231

3. Be sure that your towels look clean and are not worn. A towel with stains or holes definitely will affect how your client feels about her service. A dirty towel can tell a client either not to come back, or cause her to report your salon to the state board.

4. Show your client to your work table and make sure she is comfortable before beginning the service.

5. Discuss the information on the consultation card and determine a course of action for the service.

PART **3**

A. ADVISE CLIENTS AND PROMOTE PRODUCTS

1. Proper home maintenance will ensure that the client's nails look beautiful until he or she returns for another service (a week to ten days).

2. Depending on the service provided, there may be a number of retail products that you should recommend for the client to take home. This is the time to do so. Explain why they are important and how to use them.

B. SCHEDULE NEXT APPOINTMENT AND THANK CLIENT

1. Escort the client to the front desk to schedule the next appointment and to pay for the service. Set up date, time, and services and then write the information on your or the salon's appointment card and give it to the client.

2. Before you return to your station and the client leaves the salon, be sure to thank her for her business.

3. Record service information, products used, observations, and retail recommendations on the client service form.

C. PREPARE WORK AREA AND IMPLEMENTS FOR NEXT CLIENT

1. Remove your products and tools, then clean your work area and properly dispose of all used materials.

2. Follow steps for disinfecting implements in the Pre-Service Procedure. Reset work area with disinfected tools.

One-Color Monomer Liquid and Polymer Powder Nail Enhancements Over Nail Tips Or Natural Nails

IMPLEMENTS AND MATERIALS

In addition to the basic materials on your manicuring table, you will need the following supplies for the One-Color Monomer Liquid and Polymer Powder Nail Enhancements over Nail Tips or Natural Nails procedure:

- Nail dehydrator
- Nail primer
- Monomer liquid
- Polymer powder
- Application brushes
- Dappen dishes
- Abrasives

PREPARATION

Refer to Procedure 17-1, Pre-Service Procedure.

PROCEDURE

1. Use a pusher to gently push back the eponychium, and if needed then apply cuticle remover. Use as directed by the manufacturer, and carefully remove cuticle tissue from the nail plate. Have the client wash and dry hands again to remove any oils form the cuticle remover.

2. Buff (gently) the nail plate with medium/fine abrasive (240 grit) to remove the shine caused by natural oil on the surface of the nail plate. Avoid over-filing of the nail plate. Remove the nail dust with a clean dry nail brush and do not touch the surface of the nails with your fingers as you may deposit oils from your fingertips, degrading the cleanliness of the nail.

3. Apply nail dehydrator to nails. Begin with the little finger on the left hand and work toward the thumb.

4. Apply tips, if your client wants them, as described in Procedure 16-3, Nail Tip Application in Chapter 16. Cut tips to desired length.

5. Apply nail primer and follow the manufacturer's directions. Allow nail primer to dry thoroughly. Acid-free primer will dry sticky and shiny. Never apply nail enhancement product over wet nail primer. This can cause product discoloration and service breakdown. Avoid overuse of nail primers. Apply primer to the natural nail, and avoid putting it on the nail tips unless instructed by the manufacturer of the nail primer.

CAUTION

Check your nail primer daily for clarity to ensure that it does not become contaminated with nail dust and other floating debris, which can dramatically reduce primer effectiveness. Never use nail primers that are visibly contaminated with floating debris. Wipe the primer brush on a clean, dust-free towel before replacing the brush in the bottle to avoid contamination.

6. Pour monomer liquid and polymer powder into separate dappen dishes.

7. Dip brush into the monomer liquid and wipe on the edge of the container to remove the excess.

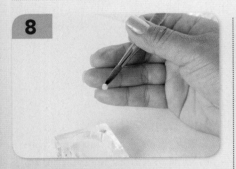

8. Dip the tip of the same brush into the polymer powder and rotate slightly. Pick up a bead of product—with a medium-to-dry consistency, not runny or wet—that is large enough for shaping the entire free edge extension. If it is too large to shape properly, two smaller beads may be easier.

9. Place the pink product bead in the center of the free edge of the tip or natural nail. Immediately wipe your brush on the table towel gently to remove any product left in the bristles and bring the brush back to a perfect point.

10. Use the middle portion of your sable brush to press and smooth the product to shape the enhancement's free edge. Do not "paint" the product onto the nail. Pressing and smoothing produces a more natural-looking nail. Keep sidewall lines parallel, and avoid widening the tip beyond the natural width of the nail plate.

11. Use a medium consistency and place the second bead on the nail plate below the first bead and next to the free edge line in the center of the nail. Immediately wipe your brush on the table towel gently to remove any product left in the bristles and bring the brush back to a perfect point.

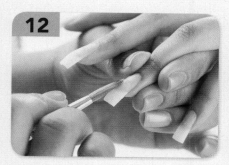

12. Press and smooth the product to sidewalls, making sure that the product is very thin around all edges. Leave a tiny free margin between the product placement and skin. Avoid placing the product too close to the skin or the product may lift away from the nail plate, and also may increase the chance of the client developing a skin irritation or sensitivity. Be sure to use a medium consistency mix that is not too wet.

13. Pick up smaller beads of pink polymer powder with your brush and place them at the base of the nail plate, leaving a tiny free margin between the product and the skin. Immediately wipe your brush on the table towel gently to remove any product left in the bristles and bring the brush back to a perfect point.

14. Use the brush to press and smooth beads over the entire nail plate. Glide the brush over the nail to smooth out imperfections.

15. Apply more product near eponychium, sidewall, and free edge if needed to complete the application, but be sure that the product in these areas remains thin for a natural-looking nail .

16. Use medium abrasive (180 to 240 grit) to shape the free edge and to remove imperfections. Then refine with medium-fine abrasive (240 grit).

17. Buff the nail enhancement with fine-grit buffer (350 grit or higher) until the entire surface is smooth. Use a high-shine buffer, if nail polish is to be worn.

18. Apply and rub nail oil into the surrounding skin and nail enhancement, and massage briefly to speed penetration.

19. Apply hand cream and massage the hand and arm.

20. Ask the client to either wash her hands with soap and water at the hand washing station or ask her to use the nail brush to clean nails over fingerbowl. Rinse with clean water to remove soap residue that may cause lifting. Dry thoroughly with a clean disposable towel.

21. Polish nail enhancements or apply a gel sealant..

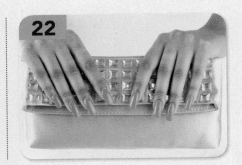

22. Finished look .

22

POST-SERVICE

Complete Procedure 17-2, Post-Service Procedure.

✓ **LO3 Complete**

Two-Color Monomer Liquid And Polymer Powder Nail Enhancements Using Forms

PROCEDURE **17-4**

IMPLEMENTS AND MATERIALS

In addition to the basic materials on your manicuring table, you will need the following supplies for the Two Color Monomer Liquid and Polymer Powder Nail Enhancements Using Forms procedure:

- Nail dehydrator
- Nail forms
- Nail primer
- Monomer liquid

- Polymer powder (pink and white)
- Application brushes
- Dappen dishes

PREPARATION

Refer to Procedure 17-1, Pre-Service Procedure.

PROCEDURE

1. Clean the nails and remove existing polish or gel sealant.

2. Push back the eponychium and remove the cuticle from the nail plate.

3. Remove oily shine from the natural nail surface with a medium/fine abrasive.

4. Apply nail dehydrator.

5. Position the nail forms. If you are using disposable forms, peel a nail form from its paper backing and, using the thumb and index finger of each of your hands, bend the form into an arch to fit the client's natural nail shape. Slide the form into place and press adhesive backing to the sides of the finger. Check to see that the form is snug under the free edge and level with the natural nail.

If you are using multiuse forms, slide the form into place, making sure the free edge is over the form and that it fits snugly. Be careful not to cut into the hyponychium under the free edge. Tighten the form around the finger by squeezing lightly.

6. Apply nail primer by touching the brush tip to the edge of the bottle's neck to release the excess primer back into the bottle. Using a light dotting action, dab the brush tip to the prepared natural nail only. One end of the primer molecule chemically bonds to the nail protein, the other end of the molecule is a methacrylate so it can bond to the monomer liquid as it cures. Always follow the manufacturer's directions. Allow the nail primer to dry thoroughly. Acid-free primer will dry to a shiny sticky surface. Never apply nail enhancement product over wet nail primer, since this can cause product discoloration and service breakdown. Avoid overuse of nail primers.

7. Pour monomer liquid and polymer powder into separate dappen dishes. With the two-color method you will need three dappen dishes—one for the white tip powder; one for the clear, natural, or pink powder; and one for the monomer liquid. You can work out of the monomer liquid and polymer powder containers, as well.

8. Saturate your application brush monomer liquid and wipe out the liquid completely. Dip the brush in the monomer liquid and wipe on the edge of the container to remove the excess so you can get the liquid you need to pick up the powder.

9. Dip the tip of the same brush into the white polymer powder and pick up a bead of product—it should have a dry-to-medium consistency, not runny or wet—that is large enough to cover the entire free-edge extension up to the edge of the smile line. If this is too large a bead to shape properly, using two smaller beads may be easier.

10. Place the white bead in the center of the nail form at the point where the free edge joins the nail form. Wipe your brush gently on a clean or disposable towel—do not use the table towel—to remove any remaining product and allow your bead to start to self-level and begin setting up. Working with a freshly applied bead of monomer liquid and polymer powder will be sticky; allowing it to set up a bit will give you a less sticky surface to work with. After the product has set up but still moves, use the tip of your application brush to wipe the smile line so it is crisp.

11. Shape the free edge.

12. Pick up a second bead of white powder, again with a medium consistency, and place it on the natural nail above the last bead, inside the free edge smile line and in the center of the nail. Wipe your brush gently on a clean or disposable towel—do not use the table towel—to remove any remaining product and allow your bead to start to self-level and begin setting up.

13. Shape the second bead of white powder.

Application **Tip:**

Do not touch the primed area of the nail with your application brush until you apply enhancement product on the area. The enhancement may become discolored where wet nail primer touches the product, and this can also lead to lifting.

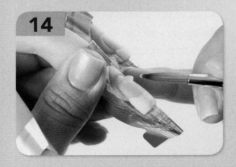

14. Pick up a small bead of pink polymer powder with your brush and place it at the cuticle area of the nail plate, leaving a tiny free margin between it and the skin. Use the brush to press and smooth these beads over the entire nail plate.
Glide the brush over the nail to smooth out imperfections. Enhancement product application near eponychium, sidewall, and free edge must be thin for a natural-looking nail.

15. Repeat Steps 5 through 14 on remaining nails.

Application **Tip:**

One of the most common mistakes made is applying product too thickly, especially near the base of the nail plate. Avoid this and you will save money and time.

16. When nail enhancements are thoroughly hardened, loosen forms and slide them off. Nail enhancements will harden enough to file and shape after several minutes; they should make a clicking sound when lightly tapped with a brush handle.

17. Use medium abrasive (180 to 240 grit) to shape and remove imperfections. Begin by shaping the tip's edge on all nails. Be sure to measure the length so they are consistent.

18. File the left side and right side of each nail.

19. File the underside of nail extensions on both sides of each nail.

20. Glide the abrasive over the nail with long sweeping strokes to further shape and perfect the enhancement surface. Thin the product near the base of all nail plates, free edges, and sidewalls.

21. Buff the nail enhancements.

22. Apply nail oil.

23. Apply hand cream and massage the hand and arm.

24. Clean the nail enhancements.

25. Polish the nail with a clear gloss polish or apply a gel sealant.

26. Finished look .

POST-SERVICE

Complete Procedure 17-2, Post-Service Procedure.

☑ LO**4** Complete

One-Color Monomer Liquid and Polymer Powder Maintenance

*This procedure may be completed using hand files/abrasives (as in steps 1 through 21)
or using an electric file (as in steps A through H).*

IMPLEMENTS AND MATERIALS

In addition to the basic materials on your manicuring table, you will need the following supplies for the Two Color
Monomer Liquid and Polymer Powder Nail Enhancements Using Forms procedure:

- Nail dehydrator
- Nail primer
- Monomer liquid
- Polymer powder
- Application brushes
- Dappen dishes

PREPARATION

Refer to Procedure 17-1, Pre-Service Procedure.

PROCEDURE

1. Remove the existing polish or gel sealant.

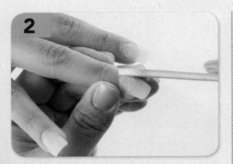

2. Using a medium-coarse abrasive (120 to 180 grit), carefully smooth down the ledge of the existing product until it is flush with the new growth of nail plate. Do not dig into or damage the natural nail plate with your abrasive.

3. Hold the medium abrasive (180 to 240 grit) flat and glide it over the entire nail enhancement to reshape, refine, and thin out the free edge until the white tip appears translucent. Take care not to damage the client's skin with the abrasive.

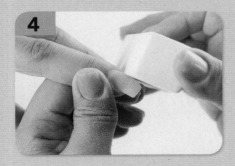

4. Use a fine-grit buffer (350 grit or higher) to buff the product, and smoothly blend it into new growth area without damaging the natural nail plate.

5. Use a medium-abrasive (180 to 240 grit) file to smooth out any areas of product that may be lifting or forming pockets. Do not file into the natural nail plate.

CAUTION

Do not use a nipper to clip away loose nail enhancement product. Nipping may perpetuate the lifting problem and can damage the nail plate. If lifting is excessive, soak off the enhancement and start fresh with a new nail application.

6. Clean the nail enhancements.

7. Remove the oily shine from the natural nail surface.

8. Apply nail dehydrator.

9. Apply nail primer and follow manufacturer's directions. Allow primer to dry thoroughly. Avoid applying nail enhancement product over wet primer, since this can cause product discoloration and service breakdown. Avoid overusing nail primer.

Application **Tip:**

After you have applied the dehydrator and the nail is dry, do not touch the nail plates again with your fingers or allow the client to rest her hands against her face. Touching the prepped nail plate—or getting makeup or moisturizer on it—can deposit oils and cause possible lifting.

10. Prepare monomer liquid and polymer powder.

11. Pick up one or more small beads of enhancement product and place at the natural nail area, the regrowth.

12. Use the brush to smooth these beads over the new growth area. Glide the brush over the nail to smooth out imperfections. Enhancement product application near the eponychium, sidewall areas, and free edge must be extremely thin for a natural-looking nail. Be sure to leave a tiny free margin between the nail enhancement product and skin for more small beads of powder and place them at the center of the nail plate.

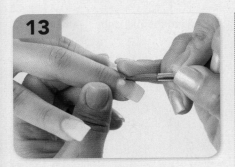

13. Pick up one or more small beads of enhancement product and place them at the center or apex of the nail.

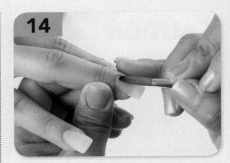

14. Use the brush to smooth these beads over the entire nail enhancement. Glide the brush over the nail to smooth out imperfections. Enhancement product application near the eponychium, sidewall areas, and free edge must be extremely thin for a natural-looking nail. Be sure to leave a tiny free margin between the nail enhancement product and skin for more small beads of powder and place them at the center of the nail plate.

15. Allow the nails to harden. Nails are hard when they make a clicking sound when lightly tapped with a brush handle. Once hardened, shape the nail enhancements with an abrasive board.

Application **Tip:**

Using a coarse-grit abrasive or sanding band will scratch and damage the nail plate and may cause rings of fire, which will not happen if you prep the nail plate properly.

ALTERNATIVE FOR STEP 15—PERFORMING A ONE-COLOR MONOMER LIQUID AND POLYMER POWDER MAINTENANCE USING AN ELECTRIC FILE

If you are performing the maintenance service using an electric file, follow the steps below.

15A. Follow Steps 1 and 2 above in this procedure.

15B. With a fine or medium barrel bit, shorten the lengths and contour the tops of all the nails. Remove any UV gel sealants you may have applied previously and any discoloration, and reshape and rebalance the entire top surface of all ten nails.

15C. With a rounded-top safety bit, bevel the cuticle area product flush with the natural nail. Be careful not to touch the natural nail with the bit. Use the safety bit flat to the nail to bevel and remove more product than normal. Beveling and removing more product will remove any lifting and ensure no fill lines. Remove the dust with a clean, dry sanitary nail brush.

15D. Dehydrate the natural nail with one coat of dehydrator and let dry. Once you have applied the dehydrator and before you return the brush to the bottle, wipe the brush on a clean paper towel. This will prevent any dust you may pick up on the nail plate from being deposited into the bottle and contaminating the dehydrator.

15E. Apply one coat of primer only to the exposed natural nail area on all the nails. Do not apply primer to the product already on the nails because it can cause yellowing. Be sure to not touch the surrounding skin and cuticles. If you are using an acid-free primer, only one coat is necessary, and it will appear wet with a shiny appearance when dry.

15F. Apply polymer powder to the growth area and pull it down over the entire nail plate. Allow the nails to harden. Nails are hard when they make a clicking sound when lightly tapped with a brush handle.

15G. File and shape the nails with a fine or medium barrel bit. Refine your cuticle work with a safety bit or cone and finish the nails.

15H. Go to Step 16 below and follow through to end of service.

16. Buff the nail enhancement.

17. Apply nail oil.

18. Apply hand cream and massage the hand and arm.

19. Clean the nail enhancements.

20. Apply nail polish or gel sealant.

21. Finished look.

POST-SERVICE

Complete Procedure 17-2, Post-Service Procedure.

✓ LO**5** Complete

Crack Repair For Monomer Liquid and Polymer Powder Nail Enhancements

IMPLEMENTS AND MATERIALS

In addition to the basic materials on your manicuring table, you will need the following supplies for the Crack Repair for Monomer Liquid and Polymer Powder Nail Enhancements procedure:

- Nail dehydrator
- Nail primer
- Nail forms
- Monomer liquid

- Polymer powder
- Application brushes
- Dappen dishes

PREPARATION

Refer to Procedure 17-1, Pre-Service Procedure.

PROCEDURE

1. Remove the existing polish or gel sealant.

2. File a V shape into the crack or file flush to remove crack. File more than just the crack for extra protection.

3. Apply nail dehydrator to any exposed natural nail in the crack.

4. Apply nail primer to any exposed natural nail in the crack.

5. If the crack needs support, apply a nail form.

6. Prepare monomer liquid and polymer powder.

7

7. Pick up one or more small beads of product, and apply them to the cracked area. If you are using the two-color system, be sure to use the correct color of polymer powder.

8

8. Press and smooth the enhancement product to fill the crack. Be careful not to let the product seep under the form.

9

9. Apply additional beads, if needed, to fill in the crack or reinforce the rest of the nail. Shape the enhancement and allow it to harden.

10

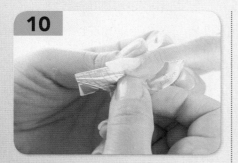

10. Remove the form, if used.

11. Reshape the nail enhancement using a medium abrasive (180 to 240 grit).

12. Use a fine abrasive (350 grit or higher) to buff and smooth the nail. Use a high-shine buffer, if desired.

13. Apply nail oil.

14. Apply hand cream and massage the hand and arm.

15. Clean the nail enhancements.

16. Apply nail polish or gel sealant.

17

17. Repaired nail.

POST-SERVICE

Complete Procedure 17-2, Post-Service Procedure.

LO6 Complete

PART **3**

IMPLEMENTS AND MATERIALS

In addition to the basic materials on your manicuring table, you will need the following supplies for the Monomer Liquid and Polymer Powder Nail Enhancements procedure:

- Metal or glass bowl
- Acetone

PREPARATION

Refer to Procedure 17-1, Pre-Service Procedure.

PROCEDURE

1. Fill the glass bowl with enough acetone or product remover to cover 1/2" higher than client's enhancements. Place the bowl inside another bowl of hot water to heat the acetone safely and speed up the removal procedure.

2. Soak the client's nail enhancements for 20 to 30 minutes, or as long as needed to remove the enhancement product. Refer to the manufacturer's directions and precautions for nail enhancement product removal.

3. Once or twice during the procedure, use a wooden or metal pusher to gently push off the softened enhancement. Repeat until all enhancements have been removed. Do not pry them off with nippers, as this will damage the natural nail plate. Avoid removing enhancements from the acetone or product remover, or they will quickly reharden, making them more difficult to remove. The key is to leave the nails in the acetone until they fall off and leave the natural nail free of product. Use a plastic-backed cotton pad to remove the remaining product.

4. Condition the skin and nails.

5. Lightly buff the nails to smooth any remaining ridges or residue.

6. Recommend that the client receive a basic manicure.

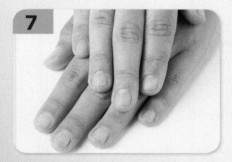

7. Finished look.

POST-SERVICE

Complete Procedure 17-2, Post-Service Procedure.

✓ **LO7 Complete**

fyi

Nail plates may appear to be thinner after enhancements have been removed. This is generally because there is more moisture in the natural nail plate, which makes them more flexible. It is not an indication that the nail plates have been weakened by the nail enhancement. This excess flexibility will be lost as the natural nails lose moisture over the next 24 hours, and the nail plates will seem to be more rigid and thick.

PART **3**

review questions

1. What is the chemistry behind monomer liquid and polymer powder nail enhancements and how does it work?

2. What are the definitions of apex, stress area, and sidewall, and where is their location on the nail enhancement?

3. What is the proper procedure for applying one-color monomer liquid and polymer powder nail enhancements over tips and on natural nails?

4. What is the proper procedure for applying two-color monomer liquid and polymer powder nail enhancements using forms?

5. What is the proper procedure for performing a one-color maintenance service on nail enhancements using monomer liquid and polymer powder?

6. How is a crack repair performed?

7. How are monomer liquid and polymer powder removed from the nail?

18 uv gels

chapter outline

☑ Learning Objectives

After you have completed this chapter, you will be able to:

1 Describe the chemistry and main ingredients of UV gels.

2 Describe when to use the one-color and two-color methods for applying UV gels.

3 Name and describe the types of UV gels used in current systems.

4 Identify the supplies needed for UV gel application.

5 Determine when to use UV gels.

6 Identify which type of UV gel is best suited for a service.

7 Discuss the differences between UV light units and UV lamps.

8 Describe how to apply one-color UV gel on tips and natural nails.

9 Describe how to apply UV gels over forms.

10 Describe how to maintain UV gel nail enhancements.

11 Explain how to correctly remove hard UV gels.

12 Explain how to correctly remove soft UV gels.

Key Terms

Page number indicates where in the chapter the term is used.

> ...new UV gel technologies have been developed recently...

This chapter introduces UV gels, a type of nail enhancement product that hardens when exposed to a UV light source, as an increasingly popular method for nail enhancement services.

Nail enhancements based on UV curing are not traditionally thought of as being methacrylates; however, they are very similar. Like wrap resins, adhesives, and monomer and polymer nail enhancements, UV gel enhancements rely on ingredients from the monomer and polymer chemical family. Their ingredients are part of a subcategory of this family called acrylates. Wrap resins are called cyanoacrylates, and monomer liquid/polymer powder nail enhancements are from the same category called methacrylates.

Although most UV gels are made from acrylates, new UV gel technologies have been developed recently that use methacrylates. Like wraps and monomer liquid and polymer powder nail enhancements, UV gels can also contain monomers, but they rely mostly on a related form called an oligomer. The term mono means one and poly means many. Oligo means few. An oligomer is a short chain of monomers that is not long enough to be considered a polymer and is often referred to as a pre-polymer. Nail enhancement monomers are liquids, while polymers are solids. Oligomers are in between. Oligomers are often thick, gel-like, and sticky.

Traditionally, UV gels rely on a special type of acrylate called a urethane acrylate, while newer UV gel systems may use urethane methacrylates by themselves or in combination with urethane acrylates. Urethane acrylate and urethane methacrylate are the main ingredients used to create UV gel nail enhancements. The term urethane refers to the type of starting material that is used to create the most common UV gel resins. The chemical family of urethanes is known for high abrasion resistance and durability.

UV gel resins react when exposed to the UV light that is recommended for the gel. A chemical called a photoinitiator creates the polymerization reaction to begin. The key thing to remember here is that it takes the combination of the resin, photoinitiator, and the proper curing lamp to cause the gel to cure. UV gel systems employ a single component resin compound that is cured to a solid material when exposed to a UV light source. UV gels typically do not use a powder that is incorporated into the gel resin. There are a few UV gels on the market that do incorporate a powder that is sprinkled into the gel, but the rest of the chapter will refer to gels as being the more common single component type.

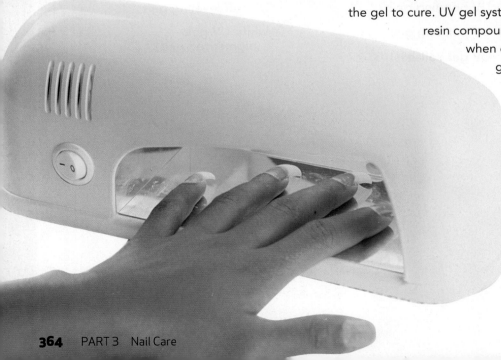

UV gels can be easy to apply, file, and maintain. They also have the advantage of having very little or no odor. Although they typically are not as hard as monomer and polymer nail enhancements, UV gels can create beautiful, long-lasting nail enhancements.

The UV gel application process differs from other types of nail enhancements. After the nail plate is properly prepared, each layer of product applied to the natural nail, nail tip, or form requires exposure to UV light to cure or harden. The UV light required for curing comes from a special lamp designed to emit the proper type and intensity of UV light.

LO1 Complete

UV Gels

There are many types of UV gels. Choosing the UV gel that is your favorite is as important as choosing the monomer and polymer system that you prefer. Some professionals favor a UV gel that is thick and will not level by itself. Other professionals like to use UV gels that self-level quickly. It is up to you to find the UV gel that you prefer to use and to learn how to use it well.

The different UV gels can be described as thin viscosity gels, medium viscosity gels, thick viscosity gels, and building or sculpting gels. Remember that viscosity is the measurement of the thickness or thinness of a liquid and effects how the fluid flows. Manufacturers have their market names for the UV gels that they make, but most UV gels fall under these general categories:

1 A clear resin used for the one-color method, for clients who wish to wear colored polish or uv gel polish over the enhancement.

2 Pink resin and white-pigmented resin used for the two-color method for clients who want the french or american manicure finish without using any nail lacquer. There are many processes for performing a two-color method over tips or natural nails. The process varies from one uv gel manufacturer to another, and even within the manufacturer's product lines. Consult with the uv gel manufacturer about the product before you perform a two-color method.

GO TO → **PROCEDURE 18-3** page 376

GO TO → **PROCEDURE 18-4** page 384

✔ **LO2 Complete**

TYPES OF UV GELS

UV bonding gels are used to increase adhesion to the natural nail plate, similar to monomer and polymer primers. UV bonding gels will vary in consistency and chemical components. This increased adhesion decreases the tendency for enhancements to separate from the natural nail. Some UV bonding gels contain certain chemicals that smell like monomer and polymer primers, while other UV bonding gels may not have a strong odor. UV gel manufacturers are constantly including new technology in the formulation of UV bonding gels. These technologies could make the use of odiferous chemicals obsolete. Some UV gel manufacturers use air-dry bonding systems. Just because the bonding product may not be cured in an ultraviolet light unit does not make it any less effective than a bonding system that is cured in a UV light unit.

UV building gels include any thick viscosity resin that allows the nail technician to build an arch and curve to the fingernail. UV building gels can be used with self-leveling UV gels and, if done correctly, this combination can reduce the amount of filing and shaping to contour the enhancement later in the service. There are UV building gels that have fiberglass strands compounded into the gel during the manufacturing process. These UV gels typically have hardness and durability properties that closely resemble monomer and polymer systems. They are very helpful when repairing a break or crack in a client's enhancement.

UV self-leveling gels are used to enhance the thickness of other gels while providing a smoother surface than some UV building gels. Professionals who are experienced in UV gel application often will choose to apply a UV building gel first during a service, then use a self-leveling UV gel during the second part of the service to reduce filing and contouring later.

White UV gels (pigmented gels) can be building gels or self-leveling gels that include color pigment. It is more common for the building style of pigmented gels to be used earlier during the service because these gels are used to create a two-color process similar to a two-color monomer and polymer process. Self-leveling pigmented UV gels are used near the final contouring procedure—either before or after the contouring—because these gels are applied much thinner than the pigmented building gels and normally require little if any filing. It is best to consult the manufacturer's instructions for their use.

UV gel polishes are an alternative to traditional nail lacquers. UV gel polishes do not dry as nail lacquers do; they cure in the UV light unit. When the UV gel polish is finished curing, a gloss gel can be applied over it to create a high lustrous shine. The end result is an enhancement that looks like it has been lacquered but does not have any solvent odor and will not become smudged the way a traditional nail lacquer might. UV gel polishes also may be used on natural nails, if your client prefers.

UV gloss gels also may be called sealing gels, finishing gels, or shine gels. These gels are used to create a high shine. UV gloss gels do not require buffing and can also be used over a monomer and polymer enhancement. There are two types of UV gloss gels: traditional gloss gels that cure with a sticky inhibition layer that requires cleaning, and tack-free gloss gels that cure to a high shine without the inhibition layer. An inhibition layer is a tacky surface left on the nail after a UV gel has cured. Choose the gloss gel that is best for you. Traditional UV gloss gels do not discolor after prolonged exposure to UV light, while tack-free gloss gels can discolor. Many UV gel manufacturers are developing tack-free gloss gels that do not discolor upon exposure to UV light. These advancements may make traditional UV gloss gels obsolete, but for now, traditional UV gloss gels still hold the market on non-yellowing performance.

UV gels are available in a wide array of colors. They are available in cream and frosted colors, and some even include glitter! These gels can be mixed together to create a few hundred more colors. UV gels provide a nail technician and client with a wide variety of colors and options for expressing their personality and creativity.

✓ LO3 Complete

After you have determined how each gel behaves on the fingernail, learn how to use the pink gels and white gels in the same fashion. Similar to clear gels, pink gels and white gels can be formulated in a variety of viscosities, colors, and opacities, the amount of pigment concentration in a gel making it difficult to see through. There are many different gels on the market and each of these gels can be combined to give any appearance that you and your client desire.

Activity

We have discussed how gels require a UV light source to cure properly. Gels will not cure if the light cannot penetrate through the gel. If the gel is pigmented, then the pigment can block the transmission of the UV light into the gel and decrease its curing potential.

Place some gel on a disposable form and spread it using a gel brush. Apply the gel so that you are able to see through it onto the surface of the form. Cure the gel in your UV lamp for the recommended period of time. Clean the surface of the gel to remove the sticky residue—the inhibition layer. Peel the gel from the form and examine the side of the gel that was against the form. If there is a layer of uncured gel, then the gel was applied too thickly. Reapply the gel thinner and repeat the curing and examination process.

Activity

Acquire samples of gels that are on the market by calling a few popular companies. When you receive the gels, place a small amount of gel on a plastic tip that you have adhered to a wooden stick. Study the gel as it moves over the tip. Try applying the gel in a different way (such as brushing a thin layer, then applying a ball of gel in the stress area) and observe the gel again. Repeat this procedure with all of the samples. The more you know about how the gels work, the easier it will be for you to apply the gels on your client.

UV Gel Supplies

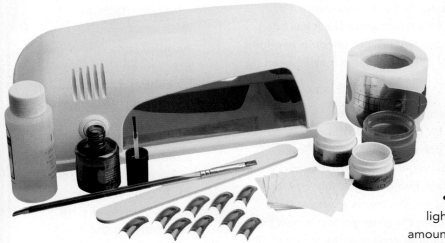

▲ FIGURE 18-1
Supplies needed for a UV gel service.

Just as every type of nail enhancement service requires specific tools, implements, equipment, and supplies, so do UV gel enhancements. Here is a list of those requirements (Figure 18-1). In addition to the supplies in your basic manicuring setup, you will need:

- *UV gel light unit.* Choose a UV gel light unit designed to produce the correct amount of UV light needed to properly cure UV gel nail enhancement products you use.

- *Brush.* Synthetic brushes with small, flat (or oval) bristles to hold and spread the UV gel.

- *UV gel primer or bonding gel.* Primers and bonding gels are designed specifically to improve adhesion of UV gels to the natural nail plate. Use UV gel primers as instructed by the manufacturer of the product that you are using.

- *UV gel.* This should include pigmented gel(s) for a one-color or two-color service. This also will include a gel that creates a gloss, depending upon the gel system that you choose.

- *Nail tips.* Use nail tips recommended for the UV gel nail enhancement systems.

- *Nail adhesive.* There are many types of nail adhesives for securing pre-formed nail tips to natural nails. Select a type and size best suited for your work.

- *Nail cleanser or primer.* Removes surface moisture and tiny amounts of oil left on the natural nail plate, both of which can block adhesion and help prevent lifting of the nail enhancements.

- *Abrasive files and buffers.* Select a medium abrasive (180 grit) for natural nail preparation. Choose a fine abrasive (240 grit) for smoothing, and a fine buffer (350 grit or higher) for finishing. UV gel manufacturers may have other recommendations for abrasives, so consult the manufacturer's guidelines for more information on their system.

- A *cleansing solution.* Cleansing solutions usually contain isopropanol. They may contain other solvents, as well. The cleansing solution you choose should be the one recommended by the manufacturer.

- Lint-free cleansing wipes.

✓ LO4 Complete

When To Use UV Gels

This may seem like a personal preference question, but it really is a question of logic. The general answer could be, "Anytime!" Gel technology has been able to create some very hard, durable, and tough UV gels. The new UV resin technology allows UV gel manufacturers to create tough, durable, and hard products that will perform as well as many of the monomer and polymer systems on the market. The answer could easily be, "Never," because there are customers that prefer to wear monomer liquid and polymer powder. It is what they know—they have been wearing them for years and refuse to change. Most clients will do what you recommend. If you wear and recommend monomer and polymer enhancements, that is what most of your clients will wear. If you wear and recommend UV gels, that will be their preference. You are the professional and, as such, you should recommend a system that you have used and feel will perform best for the client. There may be a situation when you use a system on your client and that system is not performing as the two of you would like. It may be best to try something else. Maybe a different gel resin or a change to monomer and polymer might be best. The answer to this question remains in your capable hands. It is also possible to use a monomer and polymer system for the fill or full-set, but combine that with a UV gloss gel to create the shine over the enhancement. Pigmented gels, such as UV gel polishes, may also be used over the monomer and polymer system, if that is what you prefer.

Choosing The Proper UV Gel

There are many gels to choose from to perform your service. Here are a few guidelines that will assist you in refining your choices:

- If the client has flat fingernails, more building will need to be done to create an arch and curve. This building will be easiest when done with a thicker UV building gel.
- If the client has fingernails that have an arch and curve, then a self-leveling gel may be the best option. Choose the self-leveling gel that you prefer—either a medium or thick viscosity gel.
- If your client returns to the salon often with her enhancements broken, then a gel that uses fiberglass may be best suited for the next service.

UV Light Units and Lamps

What is the difference between a UV lamp and a UV light unit?

A UV lamp (or UV light bulb) is a special bulb that emits UV light to cure UV gel nail enhancements. There are a number of different lamps that are used to cure UV gels. There are 4-watt, 6-watt, 7-watt, 8-watt, and 9-watt lamps.

A UV light unit (or UV light) is a specialized electronic device that powers and controls UV lamps to cure UV gel nail enhancements. Light units may look similar at first but there are differences. The differences include the number of lamps in the unit, the distance the lamps are from the bottom of the unit, and the size of the unit. They will affect the curing power of the unit.

Light units are typically called by the number of lamps inside the light unit multiplied by the wattage of the lamps that are used. Remember that unit wattage is a measure of how much electricity the lamp consumes, much like miles per gallon tell you how much gasoline it will take to drive your car a certain distance. Miles per gallon will not tell you how fast the car can go, just like wattage does not indicate how much UV light a lamp will produce. For example, if a unit has 4 lamps in it and each lamp is 9-watts, then the light unit is called a 36-watt light unit. Likewise, if the light unit only has 3 lamps and each lamp is also 9-watts, then it is called a 27-watt light unit. Wattage does not indicate how much UV light a UV light unit will emit **(Figure 18-2)**.

UV gel light units are designed to produce the correct amount of UV light needed to properly cure UV gel nail enhancement products. UV gels are usually packaged in small opaque pots or squeeze tubes to protect them from UV light. Even though UV light is invisible to the eye, it is found in sunlight and tanning lamps. Also, both true-color and full-spectrum lamps emit a significant amount of UV light. If the UV gel product is exposed to these types of ceiling or table lamps, the product's shelf-life may be shortened, causing the product to harden in its container.

▼ FIGURE 18-2
UV light unit.

Depending on their circuitry, different light units produce greatly differing amounts of UV light. This is referred to as the UV lamp intensity or concentration. The intensity will vary from one light unit to the next and is more important than rating a UV light unit based on the wattage of the lamp or the number of lamps in the unit. For these reasons, it is important to use the UV light unit that was designed for the selected UV gel product. Using the light unit that was specifically designed for the UV gel product will give you a much greater chance of success and fewer problems.

UV lamps will stay blue for years, but after a few months of use they may produce too little UV light to properly cure the enhancement. Typically, UV lamps must be changed two or three times per year, depending on the use of the UV light unit. If lamps are not changed regularly, service breakdown, skin irritation, and product sensitivity are more likely to occur as a result of inadequately cured gels.

The most common UV lamp that is on the market is a 9-watt. Other lamps are 4-watt lamps, 6-watt lamps, 7-watt lamps, and LED (light-emitting diode) lamps. While many of the UV gel systems use the 9-watt lamp, most of the gels can be cured in any manufacturer's 9-watt light unit. A gel that has been specifically designed to cure in a 9-watt light unit may not be able to be cured properly in a 4-watt light unit. The UV gel may become hard when cured in the 4-watt light unit, but it may not become as hard or cure to completion. If this is the case, the gel will crack, lift, and separate from the nail. It may not have a high shine and the client will not be pleased with the service. The result will be similar to a monomer and polymer system that has been applied with an incorrect mix-ratio between the liquid and the powder.

The light unit has as much to do with the proper curing of the UV gel as the lamp! Not all light units are the same. The differences between the structures of the light units will alter the curing potential of the unit. For example, if two light units are similar in every respect, but light unit A has been constructed with the UV lamps closer to the fingernails than light unit B, light unit A will have more curing potential than B. Thus, both lamps are not going to have the same results. Both light units are 9-watt and both have the same number of lamps in them, but light unit A is more powerful than light unit B.

Consult with the gel manufacturers to receive more detailed information on which light unit and lamp will properly cure their UV gels.

 **LO7 Complete**

UV Gel Polishes

UV gel polishes have become a popular service to complement gels, and all other enhancements services including natural nails. UV gel polishes are a relatively new system that evolved in 2000 with the emergence of new chemistries that became available to the beauty industry. The more popular UV gel polishes are highly pigmented, which gives these systems the appearance of a traditional solvent-based nail lacquer. Also, UV gel polishes are available in hundreds of shades, much the same as traditional nail polish, to suit every client.

Wearing UV gel polishes instead of traditional nail lacquers does bring some great advantages, however, they are removed differently than traditional nail polish is removed. One advantage of UV gel polishes is that they do not dry—they cure. Cured UV gel polish systems will not imprint or smudge if the client hits her hands while the nail lacquer is still drying. A second advantage is that the UV gel polish does not thicken over time because the solvent does not evaporate. Solvent evaporation is what makes nail lacquers thicken and dry more slowly after the bottle of nail polish has been opened for a few months.

To remove a UV gel polish, professionals typically file the polish off by hand, using an abrasive, or by using an electric file. There are some UV gel polishes now, however, that are removed by soaking the nails in a solution of acetone for five to ten minutes to soften them and allow the nail tech to easily scrape off the polish with a wooden stick.

UV gels can generate an uncomfortable amount of heat when used on some clients. The heat can be controlled by slowly inserting the hand into the UV lamp. This will help to slow the gel reaction and generate less heat. The heat is a result of the exothermic reaction of the gel as each bond of the polymer is created; the more bonds that are formed when the gel cures, the more heat that is generated. Likewise, the more bonds that are created when the gel polymerizes, the stronger the gel will be.

UV Gel Maintenance and Removal

UV gel enhancements must be maintained regularly, depending on how fast the client's nails grow.

UV GEL MAINTENANCE

Begin the maintenance using a medium abrasive file (180 grit) to thin and shape the enhancement. Be careful not to damage the natural nail plate with the abrasive. When you are performing the UV gel fill portion of the maintenance, follow the instructions in Procedure 18-6, UV Gel Maintenance.

Before filing the nail, be sure to clean the nail with the UV gel manufacturer's recommended cleanser or isopropanol (99 percent or better). This removes oils from the fingernail and results in better adhesion of the gel to the nail plate. It is important to remember that you must file with a lighter touch because it is usually easier to file UV gel enhancements than monomer and polymer enhancements.

GO TO → **PROCEDURE 18-6 page 387**

UV GEL REMOVAL

There are two generally accepted methods of removing gels. One method involves hard UV gels, which are typically defined as the traditional UV gels; they cannot be removed with acetone. The other method involves soft UV gels, which are removed fairly easily with acetone. It is important that you read and follow the manufacturer's directions before proceeding to remove UV gel nails.

GO TO → **PROCEDURE 18-8 page 391**

GO TO → **PROCEDURE 18-9 page 392**

For more interesting and useful information about UV gel enhancement products, see ***Nail Structure and Product Chemistry***, second edition, **by Douglas Schoon (Cengage Learning, 2005).**

Here's a Tip:

When providing enhancement services, ask whether the client would like the enhancements to be removed easily. If the client does want this type of service, use a soak-off UV gel as the base coat (following the manufacturer's recommendations on the UV gel's application), then perform the remainder of the service. Before the client leaves the salon, arrange a date for her to return to have the UV gels removed.

A. CLEANING AND DISINFECTING

1. It is important to wear gloves while performing this pre-service to prevent possible contamination of the implements by your hands and to protect your hands from the powerful chemicals in the disinfectant solution.

2. Rinse all implements with warm running water, and then thoroughly wash them with soap, a nail brush, and warm water. Brush grooved items, if necessary, and open hinged implements to scrub the area.

3. Rinse away all traces of soap with warm running water. The presence of soap in most disinfectants can cause them to become inactive. Soap is most easily rinsed off in warm, but not hot, water. Hotter water will not work any better. Dry implements thoroughly with a clean or disposable towel, or allow to air dry on a clean towel. Your implements are now properly cleaned and ready to be disinfected.

4. It is extremely important that your implements be completely clean before placing them in the disinfectant solution. If they are not, your disinfectant may become contaminated and rendered ineffective. Before immersing cleaned implements, open any hinged implements to the open position. Immerse cleansed implements in an appropriate disinfection container holding an EPA-registered disinfectant for the required time (usually 10 minutes). If it is visibly dirty, the solution has been contaminated and must be replaced. Make sure to avoid skin contact with all disinfectants by using tongs or by wearing gloves.

5. Remove implements, avoiding skin contact, and rinse and dry tools thoroughly.

6. Store disinfected implements in a clean, dry container until needed.

7. Remove gloves and thoroughly wash your hands with liquid soap, rinse, and dry with a clean fabric or disposable towel.

B. BASIC TABLE SETUP

1. Clean and disinfect manicure table and drawer with an appropriate or approved disinfectant clean.

2. Wrap your client's arm cushion, if used, with a clean terrycloth or disposable towel. Place the cushion in the middle of the table so that one end of the towel extends toward the client and the other end extends in your direction.

3. Ensure that your disinfection container is filled with clean disinfectant solution at least 20 minutes before your first service of the day. Use any disinfectant solution approved by your state board regulations, but make sure that you use it exactly as directed by the manufacturer. Also make sure that you change the disinfectant every day or when visibly contaminated with debris. Put all cleaned, multi-use implements into the disinfection container, and place the disinfection container to your right, if you are right-handed, or to your left, if you are left-handed.

4. Place the professional products that you will use during the service (except polish) on the right side of the table behind your disinfection container if you are right-handed, or on the left if you are left-handed.

B. BASIC TABLE SETUP CONTINUED

5. Place the abrasives and buffers of your choice on the table to your right if you are right-handed, or on the left if you are left-handed.

6. Place the fingerbowl and brush in the middle of the table, toward the client. The fingerbowl should not be moved from one side to the other side of the manicure table. It should stay where you place it for the duration of your service.

7. Tape or clip a plastic bag to the right side of table if you are right-handed, or to the left side of the table if you are left-handed, if a metal trash receptacle with a self-closing lid is not available. This is used for depositing used materials during your service. These bags must be emptied after each client departs to prevent product vapors from escaping into the salon air.

8. Place polishes to the left if you are right-handed, or on the right if you are left-handed.

9. The drawer can be used to store the following items for immediate use: extra cotton or cotton balls in their original container or in a fresh plastic bag, abrasives, buffers, nail polish dryer, and other supplies. Never place used materials in your drawer. Only completely cleaned and disinfected implements stored in an unsealed container (to protect them from dust and re-contamination) and extra materials or professional products should be placed in the drawer. Your drawer should always be organized and clean.

C. GREET CLIENT

1. Greet your client with a smile, introduce yourself if you've never met, and shake hands. If the client is new, ask her for the consultation card she filled out in the reception area.

2. Escort your client to the hand-washing area and demonstrate the hand washing procedure for her. Once completed, hand your client a fresh nail brush to use and ask her to wash her hands.

3. Hand your client a fresh towel for drying her hands. Be sure that your towels look clean and are not worn. A towel with stains or holes definitely will affect how your client feels about her service.

4. Escort the client to the table and seat her. Make sure your client is comfortable before beginning the service.

5. Perform a consultation before beginning the service. Discuss the information on the consultation card and determine a course of action for the service.

A. ADVISE CLIENTS AND PROMOTE PRODUCTS

1. Advise client about proper home maintenance for her service. Proper home maintenance will ensure that the nail service looks beautiful until your client returns for another service.

2. Depending on the service provided, there may be a number of retail products that you should recommend for the client to take home. This is the time to do so. Explain why they are important and how to use them.

B. SCHEDULE NEXT APPOINTMENT AND THANK CLIENT

1. Escort the client to the front desk to schedule next appointment and to pay for the service. Set up date, time, and services for your client's next appointment. Write the information on your business card and give it to the client.

2. Before you return to your station and the client leaves the salon, be sure to thank her for her business.

3. Record service information, observations, and product recommendations on the client service form.

C. PREPARE WORK AREA AND IMPLEMENTS FOR NEXT CLIENT

1. Remove your products and tools, then clean your work area and properly dispose of all used materials.

2. Follow steps for disinfecting implements in the Pre-Service Procedure. Reset work area with disinfected tools.

One-Color Method UV Gel on Tips or Natural Nails with UV Gel Polish

IMPLEMENTS AND MATERIALS

In addition to the basic materials on your manicuring table, you will need the following supplies:

- Nail tips
- UV gel for the application
- UV gel primer or bonding gel
- Brush
- UV gel light unit

- A cleansing solution
- Lint-free cleansing wipes
- Nail cleanser or primer
- UV gel polish

PREPARATION

Refer to Procedure 18-1, Pre-Service Procedure.

PROCEDURE

1. Clean the nails and remove existing polish. Begin with your client's little finger on the right hand and work toward the thumb. Repeat on the left hand. Ask the client to place her nails into a finger bowl with liquid soap. Use a nail brush to clean the nails over the fingerbowl. Thoroughly rinse with clean water to remove soap residues that can cause lifting.

2. Use a cotton-tipped wooden or metal pusher to gently push back eponychium, then apply cuticle remover to the nail plate. Use as directed by the manufacturer and carefully remove cuticle tissue from the nail plate.

3. Use a solvent-based cleanser per the manufacturer's recommendation. Remove any oils from the fingernail before abrading with a file. This increases the adhesive properties of the gel. Start with the little finger and work toward the thumb.

4. Lightly buff the nail plate with a medium (180 grit) abrasive, or the abrasive recommended by the gel manufacturer, to remove the shine on the surface of the nail plate.

5. Remove the dust from the nail surface per the manufacturer's recommendations.

6. If your client requires nail tips, apply them according to Procedure 16-3, Nail Tip Application, in Chapter 16. Be sure to shorten and shape the tip before the application of the UV gel. During the procedure, the UV gel overlaps the tip's edge to prevent lifting. During the filing process, the seal can be broken, allowing the UV gel to peel or lift. Be careful not to break this seal.

7. Follow the manufacturer's instructions for applying the bonding or priming material. Your success depends on your ability to properly prepare the nail plate for services and apply this bonding material. Using the applicator brush, insert the brush into the nail primer or bonding gel. Wipe off any excess from the brush, and, using a slightly damp brush, ensure that the nail plate is completely covered per the manufacturer's recommendations. Avoid using too much product to prevent running into the skin, which can increase the risks of developing skin irritation or sensitivity to the enhancement system.

8. Cure the bonding gel according to the manufacturer's directions.

9. Gently brush UV gel onto the fingernail surface, including the free edge. Leave a 3/16" gap around the cuticle and sidewall area of the fingernail. Keep the UV gel from touching the cuticle, eponychium, or sidewalls. When applying this gel, do not pat the gel as you would monomer and polymer material; instead gently brush or float the gel material onto the fingernail. Avoid introducing air into the gel as this will reduce the strength of the cured gel and may lead to bubbles and cracking. Apply to client's right hand from pinky to pointer.

Application **Tip:**

The procedure recommended for applying and curing UV gel varies from one manufacturer to another. Some systems recommend applying UV gel to four nails on one hand and curing, then repeating this procedure on the other hand before applying and curing UV gel on the thumbnails. Be sure to follow the instructions recommended by the manufacturer of the system that you are using.

10. Properly position the hand in the UV lamp for the required cure time as defined by the manufacturer. Always cure each layer of the UV gel for the time required by the manufacturer's instructions. Curing for too little time can result in service breakdown, skin irritation, and/or sensitivity. Improper positioning of the hands inside the lamp also can cause improper curing.

11. Repeat Steps 9 and 10 on the left hand, and then repeat the same steps for both thumbs.

12. Apply a small amount of UV gel (a self-leveling gel works best at this stage of the application) over the properly cured first layer. Carefully pull the UV gel across the first layer, and smooth it into place. Avoid patting the brush or pressing too hard as this will introduce air into the gel and decrease its strength. Brush the UV gel over and around the free edge to create a seal. Avoid touching the skin under the free edge to prevent skin irritation and sensitivity. Repeat this application process for the other four nails on the client's left hand.

13. Cure second UV gel (building or self-leveling gel) and properly position the hand in the UV lamp for the manufacturer's required cure time.

14. Repeat Steps 12 and 13 on the left hand, and then repeat the same steps for both thumbs.

15. Apply another layer of the second UV gel, if needed. Another layer of the second UV gel (building or self-leveling UV gel) will add thickness to the enhancement if additional thickness is desired and cure for the time required by the manufacturer.

16. Remove the inhibition layer by cleaning with the manufacturer's cleanser on a plastic-backed cotton pad to avoid skin contact. If the cleanser is not available, then alcohol, acetone, or another suitable remover could suffice; confirm with the gel manufacturer. Prolonged or repeated skin contact with the inhibition layer may cause skin irritation or sensitivity.

17. Using a medium or fine abrasive (180 or 240 grit), refine the surface contour. File carefully near the sidewalls and eponychium to avoid injuring the client's skin. Bevel down, stroking the file at a 45-degree angle from the top center dome to the free edge. Check the free edge thickness and even out imperfections with gentle strokes. Make certain that you avoid excessive filing of the gel on the sidewalls of the enhancements. Excessive filing may lead to the enhancement being too thin, which can result in cracking that begins at the sidewalls.

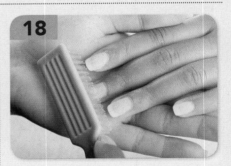

18. Remove dust and filings with a clean and disinfected nylon brush.

19. Remove any oils that may have been deposited on the fingernail during filing. This will decrease potential problems that may cause defects in the final coat of gel.

20. Apply a first, thin coat of UV gel polish over the entire surface of the enhancement in a brushing technique. Use ample pressure to ensure a smooth finished look to the application. Apply a small amount of the UV gel polish to the free edge of the fingernail to cap the end and create an even and consistent appearance.

21. Place the hand inside the UV light unit in the proper location and cure the first coat of UV gel polish for the recommended period of time.

22. Apply a second thin coat of UV gel polish over the entire surface of the enhancement in a brushing technique and apply a small amount of the UV gel polish to the free edge of the fingernail to cap the end and create an even and consistent appearance.

23. Cure second coat of UV gel polish.

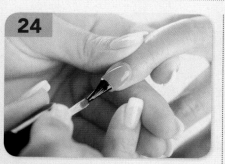

24. Apply gloss UV gel (sealer, gloss, or finisher gel) .

25. Cure the gloss gel.

26. Remove the inhibition layer, if required.

27. Apply nail oil.

28. Apply hand lotion and massage the hand and arm.

29. Clean the nail enhancements. Evaluate the work you just completed and make any necessary adjustments.

30. Finished look.

POST-SERVICE

Complete Procedure 17-2, Post-Service Procedure.

☑ **LO8 Complete**

Application **Tip:**

During the procedure, keep the brush and UV gel away from sunlight, UV gel lamps, and full-spectrum table lamps to prevent the gel from hardening. When the service is completed, store your application brush away from all sources of UV light. Do not leave your container of gel open and near a window or UV light unit. If the gel is exposed to these sources of UV light, it will cure and become polymerized in the container.

Two-Color Method UV Gel On Tips or Natural Nails

PROCEDURE **18-4**

IMPLEMENTS AND MATERIALS

In addition to the basic materials on your manicuring table, you will need the following supplies:

- Nail tips
- Pink UV gel and white UV gel
- UV gel primer or bonding gel
- Brush

- UV gel light unit
- A cleansing solution
- Lint-free cleansing wipes
- Nail cleanser or primer

PREPARATION

Refer to Procedure 18-1, Pre-Service Procedure.

PROCEDURE

1. Clean the nails and remove existing polish.

2. Push back the eponychium and remove the cuticle from the nail plate.

3. Clean and dehydrate the fingernail.

4. Prepare the nails.

5. Remove the dust from the nail surface.

6. Apply nail tips, if desired.

7. Apply primer or bonding gel.

8. Cure bonding resin, if required.

Application Tip:

It is important when using tips with UV Gels to size the tip so that the curve of the tip matches the curve of the nail. If the curves do not match and the tip is spread too flat, then the tips could crack lengthwise down the center. So, if you find a tip has cracked lengthwise down the center, you know that the curve of your tip was not matched to the curve of the fingernail.

9. Select the desired white gel to create the two-color process. Working from right to left on the hand, apply a coat of the white gel over the tip and along the sidewalls of the fingernail to create the smile line. Be sure to apply this layer of gel thin enough to have the gel cure completely through to the surface of the tip. If the gel does not cure completely through, it will lift from the surface of the tip and fingernail. If there is white UV gel where you do not want it to be, wipe the unwanted gel from the fingernail tip.

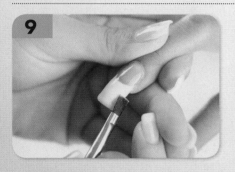

10. Using a lint-free nail wipe, pinch the bristles of the brush in the nail wipe so that the bristles form a squeegee-like surface. Do not use solvents to clean the bristles.

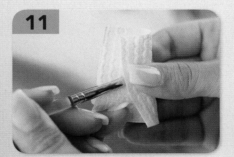

11. Using the tip of your clean application brush, wipe away any unwanted gel from the tip to create a crisp smile line. Repeat this process until you have the desired smile line. Make certain that all smile lines are uniform in appearance before curing the gel.

12. Cure the white gel in the UV lamp for the recommended time.

PART **3**

13. If the white gel does not have the same brightness on all fingers, repeat Steps 8, 9, and 10.

14. Gently brush a pink-tinted UV gel onto the fingernail surface including the free edge. Leave a 3/16" gap around the cuticle and the sidewall area of the fingernail. Keep the UV gel from touching the cuticle, eponychium, or sidewalls. When applying this gel, do not pat the gel as you would a monomer and polymer material. Gently brush or float the gel material onto the fingernail. Avoid introducing air into the gel as this will reduce the strength of the cured gel and may lead to cracking. Apply to client's right hand from pinky to pointer.

Application **Tip:**

It is very common for gel manufacturers to have many colored gels for the two-color method. These pigmented gels can vary in opacity and viscosity. You should follow the manufacturer's recommendations for applying the pigmented gel in a two-color method. Usually, the more opaque gels have thinner viscosities and are applied after the second coat of building gel. The less opaque pigmented gels are often thicker in viscosity and are applied before the first coat of building gel.

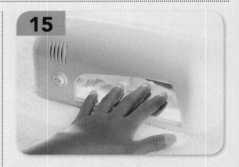

15. Cure the first coat of the UV gel (building gel).

16. Repeat Steps 14 and 15 on the left hand, and then repeat the same steps for both thumbs.

17. Apply a small amount of pink UV gel (a self-leveling gel works best at this stage of the application) over the properly cured first layer. Carefully pull the UV gel across the first layer, and smooth it into place. Avoid patting the brush or pressing too hard as this will introduce air into the gel and decrease its strength. Brush the UV gel over and around the free edge to create a seal. Avoid touching the skin under the free edge to prevent skin irritation and sensitivity. Repeat this application process for the other four nails on the client's right hand from pinky to pointer.

18. Cure the second UV gel (building or self-leveling gel).

19. Repeat Steps 17 and 18 on the left hand and then repeat the same steps for both thumbs.

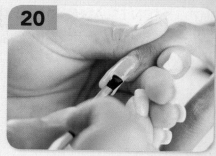

20. Another layer of the second UV gel will add thickness to the enhancement if additional thickness is desired.

21. Remove the inhibition layer.

22. Check the fingernail contours.

23. Remove dust.

24. Clean the fingernail.

25. Apply the gloss UV gel (sealer, gloss or finisher gel).

26. Remove the inhibition layer, if required.

27. Apply nail oil.

28. Apply hand lotion and massage the hand and arm.

29. Clean the nail enhancements. Evaluate the work you just completed and make any necessary adjustments.

30. Finished look.

POST-SERVICE

Complete Procedure 18-2, Post-Service Procedure.

UV Gel Over Forms

IMPLEMENTS AND MATERIALS

In addition to the basic materials on your manicuring table, you will need the following supplies:

- Nail forms
- UV gel
- UV gel primer or bonding gel
- Brush

- UV gel light unit
- A cleansing solution
- Lint-free cleansing wipes
- Nail cleanser or primer

PREPARATION

Refer to Procedure 18-1, Pre-Service Procedure.

1. Clean the nails and remove existing polish.

2. Push back the eponychium and remove the cuticle from the nail plate.

3. Clean and dehydrate the fingernail.

4. Remove shine from the natural nail surface.

5. Remove the dust from the nail surface.

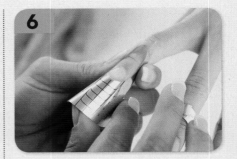

6. Fit forms onto all fingers (as described in Chapter 17). Remember to clean and disinfect multiuse forms, if disposable forms are not used. Clear plastic forms are sometimes used to allow UV light to penetrate from the underside for more complete curing of the free edge.

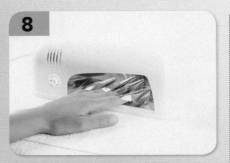

9. Repeat Steps 7 and 8 on the left hand and then repeat the same steps for both thumbs.

7. Apply the primer or bonding gel.

8. Cure the bonding gel, if required.

10. Apply the first coat of UV gel (building or self-leveling gel).

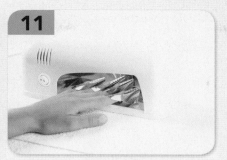

11. Properly position the hand and cure the UV gel for the required time.

12. Apply a second layer of the UV gel (building or self-leveling gel).

13. Properly position the hand and cure the UV gel for the required time.

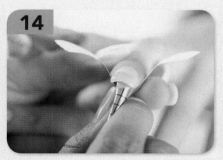

14. Remove nail forms by pinching the form just before the hyponychium of the finger and then gently pulling the form down and away from the finger.

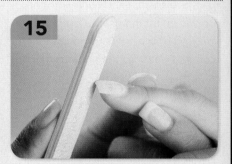

15. Use a medium or fine abrasive (180 or 240 grit) to shape the free edge of the enhancement.

16. Apply another layer of UV gel (building or self-leveling gel), if needed, over the entire enhancement.

17. Cure the UV gel (building or self-leveling gel).

18. Remove the inhibition layer.

PART **3**

19. Using a medium abrasive (180 or 240 grit), refine the surface contour. Be certain to file the enhancement to create an arch and curve into the enhancement in order to optimize the strength of the overlay and create an elegant beauty to the enhancement.

20. Remove the dust.

21. Apply the gloss UV gel (sealer, gloss, or finisher).

22. Cure the UV nail.

23. Remove the inhibition layer, if required.

24. Apply nail oil.

25. Apply hand lotion and massage the hand and arm.

26. Clean the nail enhancements. Evaluate the work you just completed and make any necessary adjustments.

27. Apply nail polish, if desired.

28. Finished look.

✓ LO**9** Complete

POST-SERVICE

Complete Procedure 18-2, Post-Service Procedure.

IMPLEMENTS AND MATERIALS

In addition to the basic materials on your manicuring table, you will need the following supplies:

- UV Gel
- UV gel primer or bonding gel
- Brush
- UV gel light unit

- A cleansing solution
- Lint-free cleansing wipes
- Nail cleanser or primer

PREPARATION

Refer to Procedure 18-1, Pre-Service Procedure.

PROCEDURE

1. Clean the nails and remove existing polish.

2. Push back the eponychium and remove the cuticle from the nail plate.

3. Clean and dehydrate the fingernail.

4. Lightly buff the natural nail regrowth with a medium (180 grit) abrasive or the abrasive recommended by the gel manufacturer to remove the shine on the surface of the natural nail plate.

5. Remove the dust from the nail surface.

6. Apply primer or bonding gel to the natural nail.

7. Cure the bonding resin.

8. Lightly brush the UV gel onto the nail from the natural nail regrowth to the free edge. Keep the UV gel from touching the cuticle, eponychium, or sidewalls. When applying this gel, do not pat the gel as you would a monomer and polymer material. Gently brush or float the gel material onto the fingernail. Avoid introducing air into the gel as this will reduce the strength of the cured gel and may lead to cracking. Apply the gel material to the client's right hand from pinky to pointer.

9. Cure the first UV gel.

10. Repeat Steps 8 and 9 on the other hand, then repeat the same steps for both thumbs.

11. Cure the UV gel.

12. Remove the inhibition layer.

Application **Tip:**

When removing the inhibition layer from the UV gel, avoid cleaning the nail in a manner that would put the gel onto the surface of the skin. Using your nail wipe, start at the top of the fingernail nearest the cuticle and wipe away from the cuticle to the free edge of the fingernail.

13. UV gel nails can be softer than monomer and polymers, so they can file very easily. Using a medium or fine abrasive (180 or 240 grit), refine the surface contour. File carefully near the sidewalls and eponychium to avoid injuring the client's skin. Bevel down, stroking the file at a 45-degree angle from the top center dome to the free edge. Check the free edge thickness and even out imperfections with gentle strokes with the abrasive. Make certain that you avoid excessive filling of the gel on the sidewalls of the enhancements. Excessive filing may lead to the enhancement being too thin which can result in cracking that begins at the sidewalls of the enhancement.

14. Remove the dust.

15. Clean the fingernail.

16. Apply the gloss UV gel (sealer, gloss, or finisher gel).

17. Cure the gloss gel.

18. Remove the inhibition layer, if required.

19. Apply the nail oil.

20. Apply hand lotion and massage the hand and arm.

21. Clean the nail enhancements. Evaluate the work you just completed and make any necessary adjustments.

22. Apply nail polish, if desired.

23. Finished look.

✔ **LO10 Complete**

POST-SERVICE

Complete Procedure 18-2, Post-Service Procedure.

UV Gel Over Monomer Liquid and Polymer Powder Nail Enhancements With UV Gel Polish

PROCEDURE **18-7**

IMPLEMENTS AND MATERIALS

In addition to the basic materials on your manicuring table, you will need the following supplies:

- UV Gel
- UV gel primer or bonding gel
- Brush
- UV gel light unit

- Lint-free cleansing wipes
- Nail cleanser or primer
- UV gel polish

PREPARATION

Refer to Procedure 18-1, Pre-Service Procedure.

---

1. Perform monomer liquid and polymer powder application described in chapter 17.

2. After the liquid and polymer enhancement has hardened sufficiently to allow it to be filed, contour, smooth, and shape the enhancement. Do not use any oils during this process. Using a buffing or cuticle oil will cause the UV gel to have deformities on its surface and will look undesirable.

3. Remove dust and filings with a cleaned and disinfected nylon brush.

4. Remove any oils that may have been deposited on the fingernail during filing.

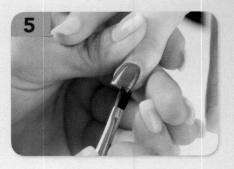

5. Apply a thin coat of UV gel polish over the entire surface of the enhancement in a brushing technique. Use ample pressure to ensure a smooth finished look to the application. Apply a small amount of the UV gel polish to the free edge of the fingernail to cap the end and create an even and consistent appearance.

6. Place the hand inside the UV light unit in the proper location and cure for the recommended period of time.

7. Apply a thin coat of UV gel polish over the entire surface of the enhancement in a brushing technique. Use ample pressure to ensure a smooth finished look to the application. Apply a small amount of the UV gel polish to the free edge of the fingernail to cap the end and create an even and consistent appearance.

8. Place the hand inside the UV light unit in the proper location and cure for the recommended period of time.

9. Apply a small amount of the third UV gel (sealer or finisher UV gel). Starting from the base of the nail plate, stroke toward the free edge, using polish-style strokes and covering the entire nail surface. Be sure not to contact the skin with the gel and to wrap this final layer under the natural nail's free edge to seal the coating and provide additional protection. Avoid touching the client's skin, as this will cause lifting.

10. Cure the gloss gel.

11. Remove the inhibition layer, if required.

12. Apply nail oil.

13. Apply hand lotion and massage the hand and arm.

14. Clean the nail enhancements. Evaluate the work you just completed and make any necessary adjustments.

15. Finished look.

POST-SERVICE

Complete Procedure 18-2, Post-Service Procedure.

UV Gel Removal—Hard Gel

PROCEDURE **18-8**

IMPLEMENTS AND MATERIALS

In addition to the basic materials on your manicuring table, you will need the following supplies:
- Polish remover
- Nail buffer

PREPARATION

Refer to Procedure 18-1, Pre-Service Procedure.

PROCEDURE

1. Remove polish.

2. Use a medium grit file (180 grit) to reduce the thickness of the enhancement on the fingernail. Take care not to file into the natural nail.

3. Use a nail buffer (280 grit) to smooth the enhancement for a more natural shine. Talk with the client about how to allow the rest of the enhancements to grow out and off of the fingernails.

PART **3**

4. Suggest natural nail manicures. Suggest that your client have natural nail manicures to ensure that the enhancements grow off correctly. Evaluate the work you just completed and make any necessary adjustments.

5. Finished look.

POST-SERVICE

Complete Procedure 18-2, Post-Service Procedure.

✓ **LO11 Complete**

UV Gel Removal—Soft Gel

IMPLEMENTS AND MATERIALS

In addition to the basic materials on your manicuring table, you will need the following supplies:

* UV gel remover
  (as recommended by the gel manufacturer)

PREPARATION

Refer to Procedure 18-1, Pre-Service Procedure.

PROCEDURE

1. Remove polish.

2. File the nail.

3. Deposit the soak-off solution in a finger bowl or other container so that the level of the remover is sufficient to completely immerse the fingernail enhancements in the solution.

4. Soak the client's fingernails in the solution for the manufacturer's recommended period of time.

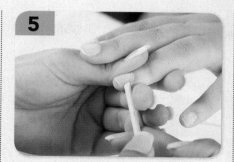

5. Use a wooden stick or stainless steel pusher to ease the gel off the fingernail.

6. Lightly buff the fingernail with a fine grit buffer (240 or 400 grit) to remove any remaining gel material from the fingernail area. Evaluate the work you just completed and make any necessary adjustments.

7. Clean the nail enhancements. Evaluate the work you just completed and make any necessary adjustments.

8. Finished look.

POST-SERVICE

Complete Procedure 18-2, Post-Service Procedure.

LO**12** Complete

review questions

1. Describe the chemistry and main ingredients of UV gels?

2. When would you use a one-color method of applying UV gels? When would you use a two-color method for applying UV gels?

3. What are the types of UV gels used in current systems?

4. What supplies are needed for UV gel application?

5. When should you use UV gels?

6. When should you use a building gel, a self-leveling gel or a UV gel that uses fiberglass?

7. What are the differences between UV light units and UV lamps?

8. List the steps to take when applying one-color UV gel on tips or natural nails.

9. Describe how UV gels are applied over forms.

10. Describe how to maintain UV gel nail enhancements.

11. Explain how to correctly remove hard UV gels.

12. Explain how to correctly remove soft UV gels.

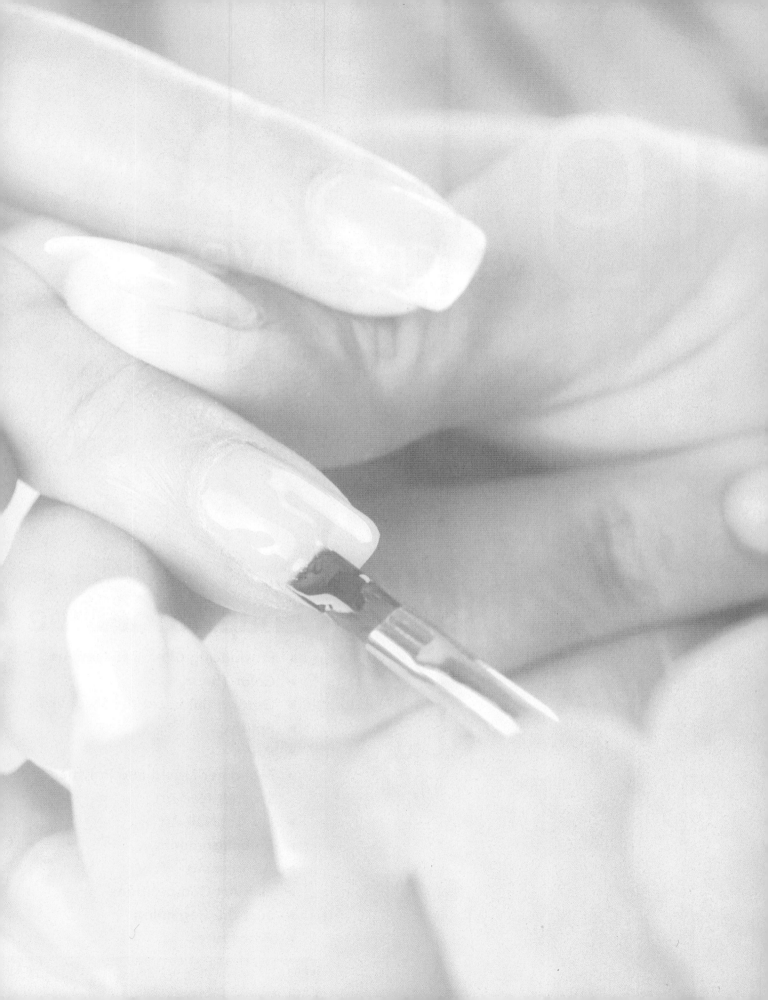

19

the creative touch

✓ Learning Objectives

After you have completed this chapter, you will be able to:

1 Describe the most effective ways to introduce nail art to clients.

2 List and describe the way color is classified on the color wheel.

3 Explain how nail polish can be used in the creation of nail art.

4 Describe nail art brushes and their uses.

5 Recognize the basic techniques used in handpainted nail art.

6 Know how to use monomer liquid and polymer powder to create 3-D nail art.

7 Describe the use of UV gel in the creation of an inlaid nail art design.

8 Understand what an embellishment is and when to use one.

9 Describe how an airbrush machine is used to create nail art.

10 Explain the benefits of nail art competition.

Key Terms

Page number indicates where in the chapter the term is used.

3-D art / 413

airbrush stencil / 409

analogous colors / 400

belly (brush) / 401

briefing / 413

color / 399

color blocking / 400

color fading / 400

color wheel / 399

competition kit / 412

complementary colors / 399

design sculpture / 414

fan brush / 401

fantasy art / 414

ferrule / 401

flash cure / 405

flat art / 413

flat brush / 401

French manicure / 400

French twist / 414

gravity-fed / 407

heel / 401

inlaid designs / 403

liner brush / 401

marbleizing / 400

mixed media / 414

nail art competitions / 410

position / 402

pressure / 402

primary colors / 399

pull / 402

round brush / 401

rules and guidelines / 410

secondary colors / 399

sink or sinking / 405

spotter brush (or detailer) / 401

striper brush / 402

stylus / 400

tertiary colors / 399

tip (or chisel edge) / 401

Nail art has become the most popular add-on service in the nail salon today. It has become the main focus for increasing revenue and expanding the service menu in salons across the globe. Many nail technicians even enter their work in nail art competitions for recognition, prestige, cash prizes, and the learning and networking opportunities associated with competing. With all the new techniques and art mediums introduced in the last 20 years, it's no wonder that nail art has lifted and expanded the nail industry and the imaginations of many!

Today, there are many nail art mediums with which you can choose to work, so no matter what your skill level or artistic preference, you can create an array of art on fingers and toes that clients will love.

Remember that most of the techniques shown in this chapter can be used with many different mediums or types of product. For example, you can create a French manicure look using monomer liquid and polymer powder, UV gel, polish, paint, crystals, or airbrushing. With just a little imagination and a lot of practice, you can create thousands of miniature works of art in minutes, and create many opportunities for increasing your income.

There are many nail art mediums you can choose to work with...

Introducing Clients to Nail Art

Introducing nail art to clients has never been easier. There are many beautiful ways to display the art samples; on tips in a glass case or frame, in a photo gallery or portfolio, and of course on your own nails. Once the client sees the artwork, it becomes a topic of conversation that will open the door to the introduction.

If you have displayed an array of the nail art, and the client becomes interested, ask her to show you which examples she likes best, so you can get an idea of the type or medium of art she is comfortable with. For example, she may only like flat or inlaid art as she doesn't care for things raised or hanging off her nails. A conservative client might only be comfortable with French manicures or a soft color graduation, while others may expect a new design at each visit.

With almost all clients one thing remains true; they will try something a little bolder on their toes than on their hands. So don't forget to offer art during pedicure services!

There are a few things to remember when introducing nail art to clients:
- Schedule ample time for these services and be sure to explain the time requirements. Some art services are relatively quick, while others can be time-consuming. This will keep you on schedule and give the client a realistic idea of the time and work required.
- Be sure that you have priced the nail art appropriately for the area and clientele. Always base the prices on the cost of materials, time investment, and the level of expertise. Be sure that the nail art services are priced competitively and be prepared to render artwork deserving of the fee.

- Have tools, implements, and supplies ready and easily accessible. Remember that nail art is usually an add-on service and can sometimes be a last-minute decision for a client. So be prepared: you may have to create the masterpiece in minutes!

Color Theory

Before you can expect to successfully produce appealing nail art, it is imperative that you have a working knowledge of colors and how they relate, blend, clash, and complement one another. In many art supply stores, you can easily obtain a laminated color guide called a color wheel (**Figure 19-1**). The color wheel illustrates and identifies the primary, secondary, tertiary, and complementary colors.

The light we see reflected from a surface is called color. Red nail polish appears that way because red light is reflecting off of its surface. We see black when no color is reflecting from a surface. Black nail polish absorbs light that hits its surface and none is reflected back to our eyes. Nail polish looks white when all colors are reflected. The color that we actually see depends on which colors are reflected and which are absorbed. Knowing the classifications of color will aid you in selecting shades for the artwork that are pleasing to the eye.

Primary colors are pure pigment colors that cannot be obtained from mixing any other colors together. They are the pure colors from which all other colors are made, and are often modified by adding varying amounts of black and white. Primary colors are red, yellow, and blue.

Secondary colors are the colors resulting from mixing equal parts of two primary colors together. They also sit opposite the primary colors on the color wheel, and are the complementary colors of the primary colors. Secondary colors are orange (1:1 red and yellow), green (1:1 yellow and blue), and violet (1:1 blue and red).

Tertiary colors are the colors directly resulting from mixing equal parts of one primary color and one of its nearest secondary colors. Tertiary colors are red-orange, red-violet, blue-violet, blue-green, yellow-green, and yellow-orange. Some also refer to tertiary colors as intermediate colors.

Complementary colors are those colors located directly opposite each other on the color wheel. When complementary colors are mixed together in equal parts they produce a neutral, muddy brown, and when mixed in unequal parts they produce a neutral color dominated by the color of the greatest amount. When these colors are applied side by side, they enhance each other, and thus make each other stand out.

▲ FIGURE 19-1

Learning the color wheel will help you choose color combinations.

Business Tip:

In the salon, time is money! It's important to make beautiful art, in a reasonable amount of time. So practice, practice, practice! Practicing the art will not only help you create more consistent and beautiful designs, but it also will help you increase speed.

Analogous colors are colors that are located beside each other on the color wheel. These colors blend well together, and are beautiful when fading one color into another.

 **LO2 Complete**

Getting The Look: Art Mediums

Nail art has never been easier to create. With so many art supplies and mediums available, it makes getting the perfect look easy and fun. During this section you will learn each medium available and how they can be used to create endless variations of designs.

Polish

Polish is one of the most common mediums of nail art used in the salon. When considering nail art, conservative clients will be more accepting of this medium as they are used to wearing polish. Polish is most commonly used to create nail art looks such as French manicures, color fades, color blocking, or marbleizing.

For a traditional French manicure look, as seen in Procedure 19-1, the nail bed is one color such as pink, peach, or beige (depending upon the client's skin tone), and the free edge of the nail is another color such as white. There are limitless variations to this traditional look just by changing or fading the color.

With color fading, or color graduation, one color fades into the other, and the meeting point is a combination of the two. You can achieve this by applying the product more thickly and opaquely and then using the product more thinly and translucently when meeting the other color (**Figure 19-2**). For example, if the top 1/3 of the nail is dark pink and the bottom 1/3 of the nail is light pink, then the middle 1/3 of the nail should be a combination of the two colors.

Color blocking is just as it sounds, blocks or sections of color on the nail. Achieve this look by polishing the entire nail with a base color, such as black, and then creating stripes or blocks with another color such as silver (**Figure 19-3**).

Marbleizing is a swirled effect created when you combine two or more colors while wet, and then mix them on the nail with a marbleizing tool known as a stylus (**Figure 19-4**). A stylus is a tool with a solid handle with a rounded ball tip on each end that can range in size. The rounded ball tips are excellent for swirling colors, dotting small circles of color, creating polka dots, eyes, bubbles, and much more. This marbleized effect can be done over the entire nail or just on a part of the nail for a unique nail art creation.

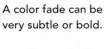

◄ **FIGURE 19-2**

A color fade can be very subtle or bold.

◄ **FIGURE 19-3**

Even simple nail art can give dramatic results.

► **FIGURE 19-4**

Art tools and embellishments can create an elaborate design.

THE FRENCH MANICURE

The French manicured look is one of the most popular nail art procedures in the salon today. You must master the technique and variations of it to stay competitive in the marketplace. Try various color combinations, fading techniques, and using embellishments to create looks clients will want to try **(Figures 19-5, 19-6, 19-7, and 19-8)**. The French manicured nail is always an up-charge in any salon and it's an easy way to create additional income.

> **GO TO** → **PROCEDURE 19-1 page 416**

✓ **LO3 Complete**

Paint

Hand painting is a very beautiful and often subtle art medium. You can create elaborate scenic views or just a tiny flower with paint and brush. Hand painting is very versatile and can be beautiful used alone or with another art medium.

BRUSHES

Brushes will be the most commonly used tools when painting nail art. Brushes come in many sizes, shapes, and qualities. There are a variety of brush types from very soft to very firm. Synthetic bristles are best used for water-based paints. Smaller-size brushes are usually the best choice for painting art on nails.

The very end of the bristles on a brush, farthest away from the handle, is referred to as either the tip or chisel edge, depending on the style of the brush. Round brushes, for example, have pointed tips, while flat brushes have a chiseled edge. The mid-section of the bristles is called the belly of the brush. This is the area of the brush that retains the most paint. The ferrule is the metal band around the brush that helps to hold the bristles in place. The area in which the bristles meet the ferrule is called the heel of the brush.

Here is a list of the most common brushes used for flat nail art **(Figure 19-9)**:

- A round brush is the most common and versatile style of brush and has a very good capacity for holding paint.
- A liner brush is a very good detail brush and is preferred for line work, outlining, and even lettering.
- A flat brush has a square tip with long bristles, which gives it added flexibility. This brush is useful for blending and shading.
- A fan brush is a flat brush with its bristles or hairs spread out like a fan. This brush is most commonly used for blending and special effects.
- A spotter brush or detailer is a short, round brush, having little belly and a very fine point at the tip. This brush offers maximum control for intricate, detailed work.

► **FIGURE 19-5**
Variations to the classic French give endless possibilities.

► **FIGURE 19-6**
Clean and classic with a little edge.

► **FIGURE 19-7**
Bridal white with a hint of glamour.

► **FIGURE 19-8**
Create more drama by adding embellishments.

▼ **FIGURE 19-9**
Some brushes used for nail art.

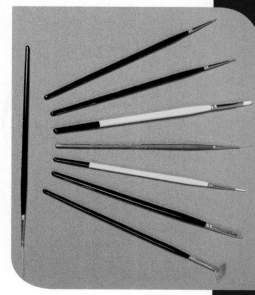

- A striper brush comes in various lengths. The striper brush is an extremely long, flat brush, having only a few fibers. It is incredibly efficient when creating long lines, striping effects, and animal prints.

✓ **LO4 Complete**

HANDPAINTED ART

Practicing the brush strokes will help you master the art of free-hand painting. Brush strokes are accomplished in a variety of ways, but there are three basic techniques to master: pressure, pull, and position.

The pressure refers to the amount of force that an artist applies to the brush while stroking. The more pressure applied, the larger the coverage area and the wider the stroke. As the amount of pressure is decreased, the width of the stroke decreases. Alleviating the pressure gradually, while pulling the brush across the paint surface, will taper the stripe and create a point where the brush tip lifts from the surface.

The second basic technique is the pull. The nail professional must learn to pull the brush, not push it. Pulling the brush across the paint surface creates a more fluid line or stroke. Pushing it will give a rough and spattered stroke that is more difficult to control.

The third basic technique is position. Position refers to how you hold the brush on the nail. For instance, the brush could be held in a straight up-and-down manner, with only the tip touching the paint surface (used for lettering, intricate details, and outlining), or it could be held flat and pulled across the surface (used when striping).

When you combine the pressure, pull, and position, you will be amazed at how many different design strokes you can create with only a few brushes. Some of the most versatile strokes include the "comma," "C," leaf, "S," ribbon, and teardrop **(Figure 19-10)**. Practice these strokes until you master each one. Practicing and gaining control of the paint, product, and brush will serve you when you try to duplicate a design.

> "Practicing the brush strokes will help you master the art of free-hand painting."

▶ **FIGURE 19-10**
Brush strokes to learn for hand painting nail art.

GO TO **PROCEDURE 19-2 page 417**

✓ **LO5 Complete**

THE NEXT STEP

Once you master the zebra stripes in Procedure 19-2, try to create a tiger stripe by painting or polishing the nail with gold, bronze, or copper, and then paint stripes with black paint. Other color variations are popular and fun during the spring and summer. Try any monochromatic paint scheme to create a fun and subtle look, such as a light pink on the entire nail and a darker shade of pink for the stripes. Or, try just stripping the nail with different colors **(Figure 19-11)** or nail edge, for a fun and "different" French manicure look!

You may want to take a hand painting class to get more tips and techniques for creating flowers and other more advanced designs **(Figure 19-12)**.

Monomer Liquid and Polymer Powder Nail Art

Monomer liquid and polymer powder can be used in a variety of ways to create unique nail art. This medium can be challenging to master, but it also has the most versatile results. Designs can be as simple as placing five small beads on a nail to create a three dimensional flower or fading six or seven colors as thin as paper to create a sunset backdrop for an inlaid design nail. Inlaid designs, designs inside a nail enhancement, are created when nail art is sandwiched between two layers of product while the nail enhancement is being formed.

Monomer liquid and polymer powder have come a long way from the traditional natural and clear polymer powders. There are a variety of colored and glittered powders to choose from on the market, as well as colored liquid drops to change the color of the monomer liquid.

When using monomer liquid and polymer powder for art, there are many brushes and tools available to mold the product into the desired shape. When first beginning to work in this medium, you can use the same brush you currently use to apply the monomer liquid and polymer powder to nail tips and overlays.

PRACTICING FOR MONOMER LIQUID AND POLYMER POWDER NAIL ART

Practice picking up beads of product; this will help you learn to control the product and determine drying time. When creating 3-D designs, where you want the design to stand up and have crisp clear lines, you will want to use a very dry bead of monomer liquid and polymer powder. When wanting to fade colors together, you will want to use a very wet bead of monomer liquid and polymer powder.

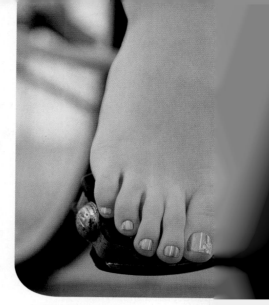

▲ **FIGURE 19-11**
Stripes look great on toenails.

▲ **FIGURE 19-12**
Master control of your brush and paint.

To practice, pick up a tiny bead of monomer liquid and polymer powder and dab off excess liquid on to a lint-free towel. You do not want the liquid to continue to saturate the bead. The perfect bead should be smooth, round, and shiny (**Figure 19-13**).

 **LO6 Complete**

Practice picking up beads and placing them on nail forms, thin monomer liquid and polymer powder sheets, and polished nail tips to learn product control on different surfaces. You can create a very thin sheet of clear monomer liquid and polymer powder to practice on by applying a large bead of product to a nail form, piece of foil, or a sheet of wax paper. Press the bead out so it is very thin and allow a few minutes to dry. Use this platform to practice the art on. It will give you some experience with how the product will react when placing wet monomer liquid and polymer powder on top of dried monomer liquid and polymer powder nail enhancements. Try picking up the exact same size bead ten times and placing the beads beside each other to learn product control and consistency (**Figure 19-14**).

Now, try this same practice technique with different sizes of beads and press them down with the brush until they are semi-flat. How large do they get? This exercise will help you to keep control over the size of the design and give you some experience with how the product behaves. Mastering this important step will help you to create very clean and crisp designs with monomer liquid and polymer powder.

Monomer liquid and polymer powder nail art can be used over polish or any other hardened nail enhancement surface. Monomer liquid and polymer powder art does not hold well on a clean natural nail unless you prep and prime the nail to receive a monomer liquid and polymer powder overlay.

When applying 3-D art over nail polish, you will want the polish to be dried for at least three minutes before applying the art. You can add a topcoat to the polished nail before you add the art if you would like the art to look matte when complete, or you may also add the monomer liquid and polymer powder straight to the polish color, and then seal the entire nail and art at once with a shiny topcoat, leaving the entire nail and art with a glossy finish.

If you are working on a surface that can be easily ruined with acetone, you will want to be careful not to touch the surface of the nail with the monomer liquid and polymer powder brush too often or you may damage it; when working on top of a polished nail, you can ruin the polish if you stroke the surface too many times with a brush wet with monomer liquid.

 **GO TO ▶ PROCEDURE 19-3 page 419**

▲ **FIGURE 19-13**
The perfect bead should be smooth, round, and shiny.

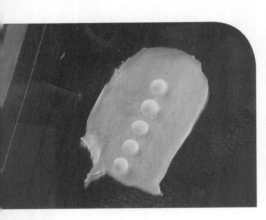

▲ **FIGURE 19-14**
Practice picking up the same size beads.

THE NEXT STEP

Keep practicing this simple flower design until you are able to complete it perfectly. Then, the next step in working with monomer liquid and polymer powder will be to add creative variations to your 3-D designs by adding several flowers on the same nail, adding embellishments, and even trying an inlaid design (**Figure 19-15** and **Figure 19-16**). Once you master the basic techniques, you are only limited by the imagination!

 **fyi**

When inlaying flowers in the nail, use the same technique as in the 3-D flower design except pick up smaller beads and flatten them out so that the size of the flower remains the same, but the flower design will be much thinner. This allows for a layer of clear monomer liquid and polymer powder to cover the design without the nail being too thick.

▲ **FIGURE 19-15**
Monomer liquid, colored polymer powders, and an electric file were used to create this look.

▲ **FIGURE 19-16**
An intricate design sculpture with 3-D flowers.

UV Gel Nail Art

UV gel can be used to create beautiful nail enhancements and can also be a very lucrative nail art medium. There are many colored UV gels on the market today and by using some simple techniques you can create an array of inlaid art that your clients will love. Inlaid art is art sandwiched between two layers of enhancement products. The finished art is inside the nail. The surface of the nail is smooth and the nail structure is not compromised by the art inside. It's also fun to add embellishments, such as glitter or confetti to clear UV gel, and this technique can be used to overlay any nail enhancement.

 ✔ **LO7 Complete**

PRACTICING FOR UV GEL NAIL ART

At first you might find working with UV gel to create nail art a bit difficult because it has a honey-like consistency, and it takes some practice to get used to. Practice by laying a long string of colored UV gel across a nail tip. Try to lay it so that it is the same width and consistency from one edge to another. Before the line starts to sink, flash cure the gel by putting it under the UV light for 5 to 10 seconds. Sinking happens when the product settles and flattens out. If you try to get any thickness with UV gels, you must flash cure the product quickly after application. Try doing the same with small dots of product. Practice keeping the dots the same size and consistency and flash curing the product before it sinks.

 **GO TO** **PROCEDURE 19-4 page 420**

THE NEXT STEP

When you feel comfortable working with UV gel art on hands, you can start practicing on toes! UV gel overlays on toes (**Figure 19-17**) are becoming a very popular service in the salon. Use the same UV gel application techniques for toes as you would on the hands as demonstrated in Chapter 18, and charge the same too! This technique is great, as the toenail surface and shape appear perfect after application, and the UV gel color and/or art last longer than traditional polish. It's also a great way to build loyalty—you now have a loyal client coming every two to three weeks for her toe enhancement maintenance.

Embellishments

Embellishments are the easiest and fastest nail art medium. Embellishments consist of any element that can be applied to the nail as art. Crystals, rhinestones, stripping tape, foils, feathers, crushed shells, gems, confetti, stickers, decals, beads, etc. are considered some common forms of embellishments used in the salon today.

Embellishments can be used either inside a nail when creating an inlaid design or on top of the nail for a 3-D effect. When using embellishments, there is no special preparation needed for the nail or for the surface they will be applied to. If applying on the surface of the nail, it's best to ensure that any other product, such as polish, is dry before applying the embellishment. You may use a resin, tip adhesive, or a topcoat to secure the embellishment in place if it does not have its own adhesive backing. Use a wooden stick with a small dab of topcoat on the end or a pair of tweezers to pick up the embellishment. Seal the nail with sealer or topcoat if it is required, or if you prefer a shiny finish on the embellishment.

When using embellishments inside the nail, make sure the embellishments are very thin. These work best when they do not have adhesive. Apply the embellishment to the nail plate, tip extension, or sculpted extension with a small bead of the product you are using such as monomer liquid and polymer powder or UV gel. Then overlay the embellishment with the same product, thus embedding the embellishment inside the nail.

GO TO → **PROCEDURE 19-4 page 420**

✓ **LO8 Complete**

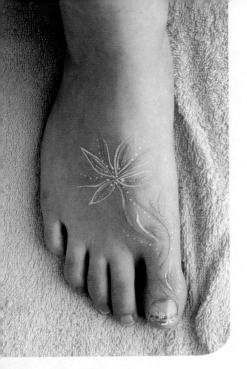

▲ **FIGURE 19-17**

Gel toes are a great way to create more income.

"Embellishments are the easiest and fastest nail art medium."

THE NEXT STEP

Embellishments are too easy and fun not to experiment and play with! Try mixing them to create works of art on the nail and inside the nail. Adding embellishments to other art mediums creates a very elaborate design while the time it takes to accomplish this type of nail art is kept to a minimum (**Figure 19-18**).

GO TO **PROCEDURE 19-5** page 423

Airbrushing

Airbrushing gives a look all its own that is hard to duplicate with any other art medium. This unique form of painting allows for color combinations, color fading, and designs that create endless options for clients wanting flat art. However, the supplies needed for airbrushing are some of the most expensive investments in all the nail art categories.

All airbrushes work on the same principle; they combine air and paint to form an atomized spray, which releases extremely tiny droplets that are spray-painted onto the nails. The ideal airbrush systems for nail art are designed for gravity-fed paint, which uses gravity to pull the paint into the airbrush. All airbrush machines consist of three basic parts; the handle, air hose, and compressor. It is common for these pieces to be sold separately.

The handle is where the paint is fed and released and is the part you will hold in your hand when working. The handle consists of the fluid nozzle, needle, cap, trigger, and paint well or cup. At the tip or end of the airbrush handle, there is a small cone-shaped fluid nozzle that a tapered needle fits into. When the trigger is pressed and the needle is drawn back, the airbrush begins to release paint. The farther the needle is drawn back, the more paint is allowed to come through the opening. When you are not using the airbrush you may want to use the cap to protect the needle.

This type of airbrush usually has a well or small color cup for holding the paint. A well, also called a reservoir, is a hole in the top of the airbrush, where drops of paint are placed. If the airbrush has a color cup, it may be located on top of the airbrush or it may be attached to the side of the airbrush for holding paint.

The air hose attaches to the handle and will connect to the compressor. There may be a pressure gauge located on the compressor or you may have to purchase this separately. Most nail professionals work at a pressure between 25 and 35 lbs per square inch (psi). When the compressed air reaches the air hose, moisture can accumulate. This moisture will form water droplets that can eventually be spit out from the airbrush. You may want to purchase a moisture trap to prevent this from happening.

▼ **FIGURE 19-18**

Designs get dramatic when embellishments are added.

Now that you are ready to try airbrushing on tips, you can really have some fun! Follow these steps for practice:

- Use double-sided tape to attach five nail tips to a paper towel keeping them about two to three inches apart.

- Apply basecoat to nail tips and let them dry.

- Load airbrush with paint. Drop the paint color into the well or color cup and start spraying onto the surface next to the nails. When the airbrush paint is spraying correctly, direct the spray at the nail.

- Apply one dry, powdery layer of color to all five nail tips. Usually three passes of the airbrush across each nail tip will build up a light color coating.

- Start with the first nail tip and repeat the procedure on each nail tip until you have reached the desired airbrushed nail color.

- Apply an ample amount of topcoat or sealer when the paint has dried. Float the brush across the surface; do not touch the nail with the bristles of the brush or it may scratch or smear the paint.

PRACTICING WITH AIRBRUSHING

When you begin airbrushing you will want to set up the products and create a cleaning area for the airbrush off to the side of the work area. This may consist of a bowl or jar lined with absorbent material like paper towels. You will use this container to spray out left-over paint and clean the handle after each color is used. You will need many hours of practice before working on clients to get comfortable with the airbrush and how it works, but don't be discouraged by this. Airbrushing is fun and is a very artistic form of nail art.

Begin practicing on absorbent paper or paper towels to become familiar with how the airbrush operates. Start spraying onto the paper approximately 2" to 3" from the surface of the paper. Move your whole arm up and down, diagonally, and side to side in order to move the airbrush spray around on the surface. Develop even color with no lines by moving back and forth over the same area a few times. If you are seeing streaks or lines on the paper and not a smooth even box of color, the airbrush is either too close to the paper or you are releasing too much paint at one time. Practice this technique until you can achieve an even coating of color on the paper with no streaks.

Then try spraying a consistent row of dots. When the dot appears where you expect it to, you have learned how to properly aim the airbrush. Now try to draw lines. To draw crisp lines, you must have the airbrush nozzle very close to the paper. The farther you pull the airbrush away from the paper, the wider and softer the line will become.

After experimenting with dots and lines, draw a grid on the paper by drawing horizontal and vertical lines overlapping each other. This will create rows of boxes. Place a dot in each of the boxes **(Figure 19-19)**. When you can master these techniques on a paper towel, you are ready to practice on nail tips.

✔ LO**9** Complete

To clean the airbrush of paint, you will want to remove the color cup (if applicable) and finish spraying all the paint from the handle into the cleaning container. Once all the color is gone and only air is coming out of the tip, add a couple of drops of water or airbrush cleaner to the well and continue to spray until all of the water comes out and only air is coming out of the tip. You can now put the handle away or add another color.

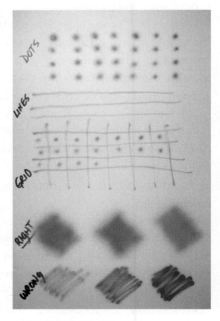

▲ **FIGURE 19-19**
Practice techniques on paper before moving to nail tips.

When you have successfully completed applying the airbrushed nail color to 10 nail tips, you are ready to move on to practicing color fading or color graduations.

TIPS FOR PREPARING THE NAIL FOR ART

Airbrushing can be done over most art mediums to accentuate or enhance other art. Airbrushing is commonly used alone or as the base for other nail art mediums such as embellishments or 3-D art. If airbrushing on top of another art medium, ensure the other product is dry before starting. If you are using airbrush artwork directly on clean nails, ensure they are free of any oils or other contaminants that may be left from the nail service. You will always want to cover the working area with paper towels or other lint-free absorbent towels to catch the overspray.

GO TO → **PROCEDURE 19-6** page 423

F☀CUS ON...

When first learning, most people are impatient and want to see the color rig away. If you are too close to the nail tip or release paint too quickly on the nail surface, the paint will puddle and begin to run off the nail. When correctl applied, airbrush paint appears dull and has a powdery look. If the airbrush pair is shiny or appears as droplets, wipe th nail tip off with a water-dampened pap towel or cotton pad and try again. Focu on keeping the passes light and the co thin! Move on to the next nail and after five or ten nails go back to the first to darken the color instead of trying to ge the achieved color or look all at once.

THE NEXT STEP

After mastering the color fade you may want to try fading three or more colors or creating distinct designs. To create designs or specific shapes when airbrushing you can use a commercially prepared airbrush stencil, a pre-cut sheet of clear, thin plastic with a sticky backing that is cut by a machine into various shapes or designs. You can also use any variety of paper, lace, mesh, fabric, or other material as a stencil to create a unique look when airbrushing designs.

To achieve an airbrushed design with a pre-cut stencil, remove the stencil from the sheet and remove the plastic shape from the inside. Place the sticky stencil on the nail and use the same spray techniques you have learned until the stencil shape is filled in. Remove the stencil once the image has dried to see the completed design (**Figure 19-20**).

There are hundreds of pre-cut stencils available, or you can create a custom shape or designs with sheets of un-cut mask paper and cut it yourself using a mask knife. For customizing stencils, place the mask paper on a glass plate or mat, and carefully cut the design out with the mask knife. Use the full edge of the knife, not just the point of the blade, or you will have an uneven and jagged cut.

Airbrushing can be very fun and creative. There are so many amazing techniques and looks you can achieve using an airbrush for nail art. While the instructions given here are for learning the basics of using the airbrush machine, there are plenty of continuing education classes or videos available. If you are serious about mastering the art of airbrushing you can contact a manufacturer that produces airbrush paints specifically for nails and check for hands-on classes available.

▲ **FIGURE 19-20**
Beautiful, faded airbrush design.

Nail Art Competitions

Nail competitions are very popular and prestigious events in the nail industry. In these competitions, nail technicians from around the globe compete to prove their skills to the industry and themselves. Creating beautiful nail enhancements is an art form unto itself, but nail art competitions are an open forum where there are no limits on the imagination. Nail art competitions create opportunities for licensed professionals or nail students to compete in a specified category where the art and theme of the nails are part of the judging criteria.

ABOUT COMPETITIONS

There are many rules and guidelines when competing, including time frames, models, presentation requirements, themes, products allowed, etc., and you will need to know this information before deciding to enter. These rules and guidelines are provided for each competition so that one understands what the competition allows and does not allow. You can request a copy of the rules and guidelines from the competition director, or you may be able to find this information on the competition or show Web site.

There are also experience categories in many competitions today. There are novice and veteran competitions as well as student and professional categories, and sometimes levels of competition experience are a factor in entering a category. There are masters' competitions that are by invitation only, or a national championship or title is required to enter. In any instance, you will need to know what the levels of experience are, and which you qualify for when entering.

After finding out the rules, guidelines, and location of the competition you want to enter, you will need to register and pay an entry fee. The registration form will be available on the Web site or will be included in the rules and guidelines package. You will want to take into consideration all costs associated with the competition such as flights, hotels, meals, entry fees, model expenses, and supplies used and needed, before deciding to enter.

There are also on-line and photo competitions which are a reasonably stress-free way to try your hand at competing. These types of competitions will have rules and guidelines as well that you will need to research. When researching these types of competitions it is wise to find the winners and/or submissions from previous years to see what the judges are looking for.

WHY COMPETE?

Nail art competitions can provide an amazing opportunity for learning, traveling, attending trade shows, and networking. For example, competing in a nail art competition at a trade show gets you to a trade show! Trade shows are a vital part of the industry and an important platform for nail professionals to gain knowledge and continuing education. Nail manufacturers showcase the latest and greatest in product advancements at these events. Attending these shows is a commitment to your profession and clients.

WEB RESOURCES

Nail art competitions are held all over the world and are mostly hosted at beauty shows. You can look at trade magazines and their Web sites to find listings of beauty shows and or nail competitions for the year. Look for information at:

Nails Magazine @
http://www.nailsmag.com

NailPro Magazine @
http://www.nailpro.com

Scratch Magazine @
http://www.
scratchmagazine.co.uk

Beautytech.com Calendar @
http://www.beautytech.com

While you will want to watch all the demonstrations and touch all the new products available, being involved in a competition will put you in a greater learning situation. Putting your nail art on display for your peers will give you invaluable feedback on where you need to improve and where you stand in comparison to the highest standards of the industry.

Talking to other competitors and seeing their work will inspire and motivate you to improve and try new techniques you have never even considered. Networking with peers will keep you on the cutting edge of trends and give you the tools and knowledge you need to keep excelling in the art and your business. New art and new techniques lead to developing new services on the menu. New services create new dollars. New dollars result in a long-lasting career!

While entering a competition is exciting and the experience invaluable, when you win, you are treated to even more rewards. Winning not only gives you press coverage in the trade magazines, a nice trophy to put in the salon, and usually a nice cash prize, it gives you credibility. Clients love to brag about their award-winning nail technician. Manufacturers and magazines also recruit competitors. Winning competitions can lead to other lucrative opportunities.

In the end, inspiration leads to motivation. Attending a show or competing in an event surrounded by other top talent will inspire you to try something new and become better. Being motivated in your career will ensure the drive toward success.

LO10 Complete

BECOMING A COMPETITOR

As mentioned previously, there are rules and guidelines you must abide by when in a competition. In some art competitions the final look may be completed before the competition even begins and the rules and guidelines will explain whether it is to be presented in a box or other display case, or if it is to be presented on a model.

If the artwork is presented in a box, you have unlimited hours of creativity ahead! There will be rules and regulations about the size and dimensions of the nails and products allowed, but the amount of time spent to create the vision will be up to you.

If a model is required, you will usually have a scheduled amount of time to complete the art on the competition floor. In this case the masterpiece is limited by the allotted time, so you must practice the art to increase the speed.

To prepare for this kind of competition, regardless of how the art is to be presented, you will need to begin by making a list of all the products you will need, and take them with you. Creating a competition kit will mean listing every product you will or might use and packing it to take to the competition. You will need to think of everything, including lamps, bulbs, extension cords, etc. This kit might be a small backpack or a large wheeled suitcase, depending on the competition.

Regardless of which competition you enter or how the final look is presented, there will be endless hours of practice and creativity ahead. Practicing art is not only trying to create something spectacular and intricate, it is about the fastest way to create it! Use these steps to assist you in preparing for the competition.

1 *Theme.* Sometimes there is a theme for the competition and the artwork must reflect this, so be sure you know what the theme is and are comfortable with it.

2 *Give yourself time to prepare.* You will need to save for the expenses, book time off from work, find a model that can be available for practice time and for the day of the competition. So, give yourself weeks or months to prepare!

3 *Draw it out.* Always sketch out the idea for the finished nail art on paper and list the supplies and tools you will need.

4 *Time yourself.* While you create the look or the main pieces of the look, keep track of the time it takes to complete the work. This will give you practice and give you an idea of the time it really takes!

5 *Keep improving.* After the first rendering, create a new sketch and a new list of products you will need that will help you to create the art better and faster. Sometimes you will have to decrease the design because of time restraints or increase the design to create a more intricate look.

6 *Be methodical.* If you are duplicating a piece of art on every nail, create those pieces all at once. For example, if you are making roses on all the nails, create them all at once before making the leaves. Produce the art like a factory worker. This will increase speed and, more importantly, consistency in the final look.

7 *Practice with the model.* If the competition is timed on a model, practice on the model two or more times before the competition.

8 *Keep practicing!* In any instance the artwork will need to be perfected over and over again before it is ready to be entered in a competition. Plastic nail tips are always available for practicing.

9 *Pack everything you need.* When packing the competition kit, refer to the sketch and the supplies list to ensure you have everything you will need.

10 *Get a good night's sleep before the competition.* You want to be well rested and alert on the big day and you can only do that if you get a good, full night of sleep the evening before.

> ...there are rules and guidelines you must abide by when in a competition.

11 *Eat before the competition begins*. You may think you are too nervous for breakfast the morning of the competition, but you should have a good and nutritious meal before you enter the competition arena. Nutritious food will provide the fuel and the energy needed to carry you through the competition.

12 *Arrive early*. Give yourself ample time to find the venue, set up, relax, and focus before the competition briefing. The briefing usually occurs 15 to 30 minutes before the start of the competition; the competition director or head judge will review the rules and guidelines to ensure everyone understands them and is able to comply. This is also the time when you may be told the criteria on which the nails will be judged. Listen and ask questions if you have any.

CATEGORIES OF NAIL ART COMPETITION

Flat art is a nail art category that includes all free-hand painting techniques that are flat, not raised (**Figure 19-21**). Embellishments and stencils are usually not allowed in this category. The art may be pre-done and presented in a box, or done on a model with a full set of nail enhancements on, in a timed competition. Nails are usually judged on degree of difficulty, color, and precision of details.

▲ FIGURE 19-21
Maps theme created for a nail art competition.

3-D art describes any art that protrudes from the nail (**Figure 19-22**). In these competitions most embellishments are allowed and most other artwork is created from forming monomer liquid and polymer powder, as this medium is easiest to work with in making 3-D art. Rules usually state limitations on dimensions of the art protruding from the nail. This art may be pre-done and presented in a box, or done on a model with a full set of nail enhancements on, in a timed competition. Nails are usually judged on degree of difficulty, color, and precision of details.

◄ FIGURE 19-22
Native American themed 3-D art.

▲ FIGURE 19-23

Design sculpture using monomer liquid and polymer powder.

▲ FIGURE 19-24

French twist created with white, glitter, pink and clear monomer liquid and polymer powder.

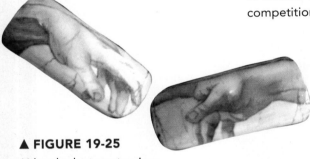

▲ FIGURE 19-25

Airbrushed art masterpiece with precision details.

Design sculpture nails are sculptured nail enhancements that have inlaid designs. These nails are produced using either monomer liquid and polymer powder or UV gel products **(Figure 19-23)**. This work is usually produced on the competition floor on a model with both hands free of product. The final look will have freehand artwork inlaid in all ten nails. All nails must be smooth and structurally correct. Nails are usually judged on theme, color, structure, and degree of artistic difficulty.

French twist is becoming a common art category **(Figure 19-24)**. In this competition you produce ten nails on a model with both hands free of product in a timed competition. You can create the look with nail tips or by sculpting the product on nail forms. You may use pink, white, clear, and glittered products to produce a unique twist on the French look. Nails are usually judged on creativity, structure, and precision of detail.

Airbrushed art may be pre-done and presented in a box, or done on a model with a full set of nail enhancements on, in a timed competition **(Figure 19-25)**. Nails are usually judged on degree of difficulty, color, and precision of details.

Mixed media is a category that allows many artistic freedoms **(Figure 19-26)**. The term mixed media is a description used for nail art when more than one nail art medium is used to create a design. In most competitions the final look is submitted in a box or display case. You can usually use any art medium to create the look. Sometimes the rules state you must use at least three different art mediums or art techniques to enter. There are usually guidelines on the size of the artwork or the distance of art pieces from the nail. The nails are usually judged on degree of difficulty, theme, color, and precision of details. This tiny masterpiece can usually be submitted to more than one competition as long as it has not won first place in a previous competition.

Fantasy art competitions allow the most artistic freedoms **(Figures 19-27 through 19-31)**. All art mediums are allowed and the only limitation is the imagination. Anything from running waterfalls in a forest of monomer liquid and polymer powder trees, to tiny electric lanterns in a small monomer liquid and polymer powder village can be seen on the competition floor. The art is usually displayed on a model that is dressed from head

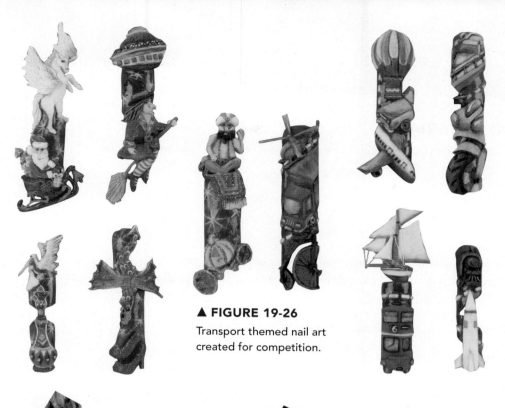

▲ FIGURE 19-26
Transport themed nail art created for competition.

FIGURE 19-27
Fantasy art #1.

► FIGURE 19-28
Fantasy art #2.

► FIGURE 19-29
Fantasy art #3.

◄ FIGURE 19-30
Fantasy art #4.

to toe in the theme of the art. Most competitors spend between 50 to 300 hours to produce these detailed works of art. Some competitors work 6 months to a year to produce a fantasy nail art display. This masterpiece can usually be submitted to more than one competition as long as it has not won first place in a previous competition.

Just the Beginning

Becoming interested in and entering the first nail art competition is only the beginning of a career that could be full of unimaginable artistic and creative freedom, traveling, learning, and meeting people who may become lifelong friends and mentors. Give yourself the opportunity to explore and research nail competitions, and if you're serious about trying one, take the step and do it. A world of fun, creativity, and opportunity awaits you!

► FIGURE 19-31
Fantasy art #5.

The French Manicure Using Polish

IMPLEMENTS AND MATERIALS

In addition to the basic materials on your manicuring table, you will need the following supplies:

- White polish
- Sheer pink, peach, or beige polish
- Basecoat
- Glossy topcoat

PREPARATION

Prepare the nail the same way you would for polish. You may be starting with a manicured natural nail or a nail enhancement, but either way the nail should be clean and free of oil and dust.

1. Apply basecoat to all nails.

2. Apply one coat of sheer pink polish to all nails.

3. Start with the little finger and hold the lateral edges of the finger, pulling the skin down on both sides to expose the entire free edge.

4. Take the white polish brush with polish on one side and start at the left edge of the nail slightly higher than where you want the smile line to be. Gently pull the brush down, creating the arc of the smile line. When creating the French manicure look, try to get all of the white tip areas the same width and degree of smile line on every nail.

5. Without removing the brush from the nail, lay the brush across the edge of the nail at a 45 degree angle and drag it along the edge of the nail while you rotate the finger with the holding hand.

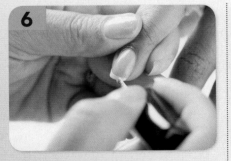

6. When you get toward the right edge, tilt the brush up to create the arc of the smile line. Finishing the line in one movement will keep the smile line smooth and crisp.

7. Seal the tip. With a tiny bit of white polish, polish the edge of the nail to seal it.

8. Repeat Steps 4 through 7 on all nails.

9. Apply topcoat.

10. Finished look.

Application **Tip:**

To soften the look of a traditional French manicure, apply the white polish onto the tip first and then apply the sheer pink over the entire nail. This will soften the dramatic white line and create a more subtle French manicure.

Animal Print Design Using Paint

PROCEDURE **19-2**

IMPLEMENTS AND MATERIALS

In addition to the basic materials on the manicuring table, you will need the following supplies:

- Paint (white, black)
- White polish (optional)
- Brushes (polish, striper)
- Topcoat

PREPARATION

- You most likely will paint your design over the top of polish or another art medium. Wait until the polish or other product is completely dry before you begin the handpainted art.
- Prepare the nail just as you would for polish; be sure the nail is clean and free of oil and dust.

PROCEDURE

1

1. Paint or polish the entire nail white. Allow it to dry.

2

2. Using the striper brush, load the lower three-quarters of the brush with black paint. Touch the tip of the brush to the left side lower edge of the nail and lay the belly of the brush on the nail.

3

3. Pull the brush across the nail toward the center in a slightly wavy motion, lifting it away from the nail near the center.

4

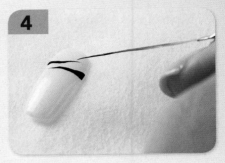

4. Leaving space between strokes, do the same technique on the opposite side and slightly pass the center.

5

5. Repeat Steps 2 through 4 until you reach the top of the nail. Try not to make the stripes perfect or meet in the middle; this creates a more realistic look. It also looks great to leave a large gap and create a short stripe in the center of the nail instead of always starting at one side or the other.

6

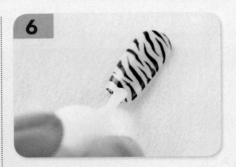

6. Apply topcoat.

✳fyi The more paint you put on the very tip of the brush, the wider the beginning of the stroke will be.

3-D Flower Using Monomer Liquid and Polymer Powder

IMPLEMENTS AND MATERIALS

In addition to the basic materials on the manicuring table, you will need the following supplies:

- Colored, white, or glitter polymer powders
- Monomer liquid
- Dappen dish
- Lint-free absorbent wipes for your brush
- Monomer liquid and polymer powder brushes such as a #8 or #4 flat oval

PROCEDURE

1. Envision a circle on the nail where the flower will be and divide the circle in half.

2. Place a dry bead down on the nail so that it is inside the edge of the circle.

3. Place the tip of the brush towards the center of the bead and gently press down to enlarge it; this will begin the design with the opening of the first petal. Lean the brush back and gently pull the brush so that it floats across the top of the monomer liquid and polymer powder bead to stretch the petal to the edge of the circle.

4. Repeat Steps 2 and 3 to make two more petals, making sure all three petals only consume half of the circle. This will ensure you leave enough space for the other two petals.

5. After adding petals four and five, create a very dry, tiny bead for the middle of the flower, or you may place a crystal or other embellishment in the center.

6. Leave the flower matte or apply topcoat for a finished look.

Application Tip:

For balance when adding connecting flowers or leaves, always place the center of the new piece between two petals of the main flower.

IMPLEMENTS AND MATERIALS

In addition to the basic materials on the manicuring table, you will need the following supplies:

- Colored and clear UV gels
- Silver glitter
- UV gel light unit
- Synthetic brush for gel

- Gel cleanser
- UV gel topcoat
- Flat or thin embellishments
- Medium grit abrasive boards and buffers

PREPARATION

Prepare the nails for UV gel and apply a set of clear tips, as described in Chapter 18. You can also create art or UV gel overlays on top of other nail enhancement surfaces, but you should not put UV gel over polish.

PROCEDURE

1. Apply a thin layer of clear UV gel over the entire nail and tip and cure for two minutes or longer according to manufacturer directions. Be sure not to get the UV gel on the eponychium or surrounding skin.

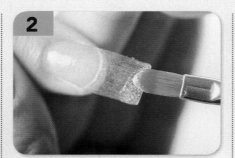

2. Pick up a very small bead of clear UV gel and dip it into the silver glitter, and then place the bead at the end of the nail tip. Smear the bead from side to side until the very edge is covered.

3. Brush the UV gel back to blend the glitter towards the nail bed. This will give the glitter a faded look. Cure for two minutes or longer according to manufacturer directions for the product.

4. Pick up a tiny bead of clear UV gel and a piece of confetti and place on the nail in the desired position.

5. Repeat Step 4 with all the embellishments until you have the entire nail decorated. Cure for two minutes or longer according to manufacturer directions for the product.

Application **Tip:**

To speed up the process when creating inlaid design nails, perform each step on all ten nails before you go to the next step. For example, do the glitter bead on all ten nails. Then apply all the pink hearts, then purple stars, etc. Then overlay four nails and cure those while you are overlaying the other hand. This process will also create consistency in the design.

6. Pick up a large bead of UV gel and overlay the entire nail. Be sure to seal the tip. Cure for two minutes or longer according to manufacturer directions for the product.

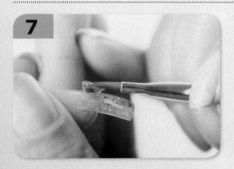

7. Pick up a medium size bead of UV gel and place it on the apex area. Remember to look at the nail from all angles to ensure that the nail has the correct structure and shape. Cure for two minutes or longer according to manufacturer directions for the product.

8. Remove the inhibition layer with a gel cleanser and file the shape and surface. Remember to be careful when filing inlaid design nails, as you want to be sure not to file through the product and file into the design. Do not file or buff the surface with anything finer than a 180 grit abrasive.

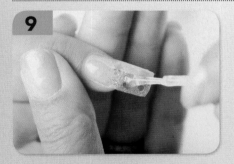

9. Apply UV gel topcoat according to manufacturer's directions.

10. Finished look.

Application **Tip:**

When creating an inlaid design nail you want to remember to keep the product very thin and choose thin embellishments. To create your design, you may need to use four or more layers of product, so keep it thin!

IMPLEMENTS AND MATERIALS

In addition to the basic materials on the manicuring table, you will need the following supplies:

- Wood stick
- Topcoat
- Brush-on adhesive

- Tweezers
- Embellishments (crystals of varying sizes, beads)

PREPARATION

Ensure the polish and topcoat are dry before proceeding.

PROCEDURE

1. Choose the embellishments and lay them on the table with the foil side down.

2. Apply a small amount of nail adhesive to the area where the crystals and beads will be laid. Apply the adhesive in small areas at a time so it does not dry before the embellishment is applied.

3. Place the larger crystals first using tweezers.

4. Add more adhesive where needed.

5. Pick up the smaller crystals with tweezers or a wood stick dipped in topcoat, and place them near the larger crystals.

6. Add more adhesive where needed.

7. Pick up the beads with a wood stick dipped in topcoat, and place them next to the smaller crystals, around larger crystals, or in any gaps or spaces to fill in the design.

8. Allow the adhesive to dry completely.

9. Apply topcoat to the nail around the crystal artwork and slightly covering the beads.

10. Finished look.

Application **Tip:**

When using an assortment of embellishments, lay them all out on a small paper towel instead of trying to grab one tiny piece of each from their original jar or grouping. This will save a lot of time and frustration. When you finish you can create a small container with the remaining assortment to use when the client comes back for maintenance or to repeat this design in the future.

Two-Color Fade or Color Graduation Using an Airbrush

PROCEDURE **19-6**

IMPLEMENTS AND MATERIALS

In addition to the basic materials on the manicuring table, you will need the following supplies:

- Airbrush machine
- Airbrush paint
- Extra color cups, if applicable
- Airbrush cleaner in a squirt bottle

- Topcoat or sealer and basecoat
- Cotton and paper towels
- Water, alcohol, polish remover, and cuticle oil
- Wood stick

PREPARATION

Apply basecoat to all ten nails and let them dry.

PROCEDURE

1. Load the airbrush. Put the paint into the unit and place your thumb on the client's finger just above the cuticle area. Most of the over-spray will land on your thumb and will reduce cleanup on the client.

2. Start the spray on the paper towel and when the spray is correct, direct the spray towards the nail.

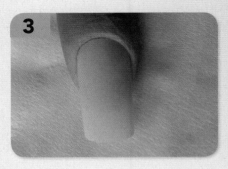

3. You may want to coat the nail with white paint first if you are using light colors, as this will give your colors a brighter appearance in the finished look.

4. Apply the first coat of color, spraying back and forth over the free edge of the nail, adding a few passes toward the center of the nail to create a soft edge for the second color to overlap.

5. Repeat on all nails.

6. Return to the first nail and continue to apply light, thin coats of paint until you have reached the desired color or opacity.

7. Clean the airbrush to remove the first color paint.

Application **Tip:**

The color fade or graduation is a popular nail art service and is easily achieved with an airbrush. With this technique, the colors you choose are the key to success. A conservative client might prefer subtle, soft hues of similar colors, while an outgoing client might choose bold colors that strongly contrast. This technique may be used as the background for another design or stand on its own as a unique, customized service.

8. Airbrush the second color starting at the cuticle area of the nail and moving down. When the colors overlap, they should fade together and begin to form a beautiful transition shade.

9. Repeat on all nails, and then return to the first nail and continue to spray the second color at the cuticle area of each nail until the desired color or opacity is achieved.

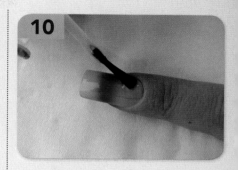

10. When the paint is dry, apply an ample amount of sealer or topcoat, being sure to seal all the edges.

11. Allow the client's nails to dry for three to five minutes.

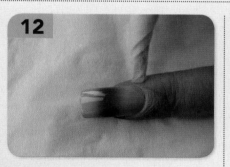

12. Remove over-spray from the client's skin by using a wood stick wrapped in cotton or a paper towel, and saturated with water or alcohol.

13. Repeat step 12 using polish remover if any paint remains, and repeat with cuticle oil if the skin is dry.

14. Apply a second layer of topcoat or sealer for maximum durability, if desired.

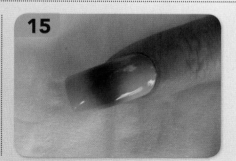

15. Finished look.

Application **Tip:**

You can assist in drying the airbrush paint when needed by spraying clean air over the nail after the handle is free of paint.

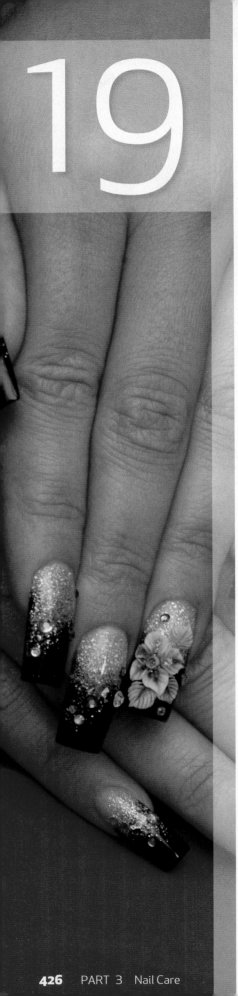

review questions

1. What are the most effective ways to introduce nail art to clients?

2. What are the classifications of color on the color wheel and what do they mean?

3. What techniques, using nail polish, can be used to create interesting nail art?

4. Name three types of brushes used to paint flat nail art and describe their use.

5. List and describe the basic techniques used in handpainted nail art.

6. Explain the use of dry and wet monomer liquid and polymer powder beads in the creation of nail art.

7. How is UV gel used and applied when creating an inlaid nail art design?

8. List four types of embellishments and how they are used.

9. What is the best airbrush system to use for nail art?

10. What is the most common air pressure reading used by nail professionals when airbrushing?

11. Name at least five benefits of participating in nail art competitions.

Part4

BUSINESS SKILLS

20

seeking
employment

☑ Learning Objectives

After you have completed this chapter, you will be able to:

1. Understand the process of passing your state licensing examination and securing the required credentials for nail technology.

2. Start networking and preparing to find a job by using the Inventory of Personal Characteristics and Inventory of Technical Skills forms.

3. Describe the different types of salon business categories.

4. Write a cover letter, develop a resume, and prepare an employment portfolio.

5. Know how to explore the job market, research potential employers, and understand the legal aspects of employment.

Key Terms

Page number indicates where in the chapter the term is used.

cover letter / 441

deductive reasoning / 434

employment portfolio / 444

networking / 446

resume / 441

test-wise / 432

transferable skills / 444

work ethic / 438

▲ FIGURE 20-1
There often are more jobs available for nail technology professionals than there are people to fill them.

There are plenty of great jobs out there for energetic, hardworking, talented people. If you look at the top professionals in the field, you will find they were not born successful; they achieved success through self-motivation, energy, persistence, mentoring, and a supportive network of people. Like you, these practitioners began their careers by enrolling in nail technology school. They were the ones who used their time wisely, planned for the future, went the extra mile, and drew on a reservoir of self-confidence to meet any challenge. They owe their success to no one but themselves because they created it. If you want to enjoy this same success, you must prepare for the opportunities that await you.

No matter what changes occur in the economy, there often are more jobs available for nail technology professionals than there are people to fill them. This is a tremendous advantage for you. By thoroughly researching the job market in your chosen area, you will be on your way to getting your first job (**Figure 20-1**)!

Preparing For Licensure

Before you can obtain a position as a nail technician, you must first secure the required credentials and pass your state licensing examination. Many factors will affect how well you perform during that licensing examination and on tests in general. They include your physical and psychological state; your memory; time management; and the skills you have developed in reading, math, writing, note taking, test taking, and general learning.

Of all the factors that will affect your test performance, the most important is your mastery of course content. Even if you feel that you have truly learned the material, though, it is still very beneficial to have strong test-taking skills.

PREPARING FOR THE WRITTEN EXAM

Being test-wise means having a complete and thorough knowledge of the subject matter and understanding the strategies for successfully taking tests. A test-wise student begins to prepare for taking a test by practicing good study habits and time management that are an important part of effective studying. These habits include:

- Having a planned, realistic study schedule.
- Reading content carefully, and become an active studier.
- Keeping well-organized notebooks and handouts.
- Developing a vocabulary list.
- Taking effective notes during class.
- Clarifying information by listening and asking questions.
- Reviewing past quizzes and tests.
- Obtaining and using practice tests.

> A test-wise student begins to prepare for taking a test by practicing good study habits...

In addition, here are some other, more holistic (having to do with the whole you), hints to keep in mind:

- Make yourself mentally ready, and develop a positive attitude toward taking the test.
- Maintain good physical, emotional, and spiritual health, including diet and eating habits.
- Get plenty of rest the night before the test.
- Dress comfortably.
- Anticipate some anxiety (feeling concerned about the test results may actually help you do better).
- Avoid cramming the night before an examination.
- Create an orderly plan of action and follow it.

ON TEST DAY

After you have taken all the necessary steps to prepare for your test, there are a number of strategies you can adopt on the day of the actual exam that may be helpful (**Figure 20-2**).

1 Start your day on a positive note. Relax and try to slow down physically.

2 If possible, review the material lightly the day of the exam.

3 Arrive early with a self-confident attitude; be alert, calm, and ready for the challenge. Note: Some exams may be administered at your school and some may be given in alternate locations. Always know exactly where you are going and how to get there before the day of the exam.

▲ **FIGURE 20-2**
Candidates taking the licensing examination.

4 Read all written directions, and listen carefully to all verbal directions before beginning. For the practical portion of the exam, bring extra supplies and alternate tools, implements, and equipment.

5 If there are things you do not understand, do not hesitate to ask the examiner questions.

6 Quickly look over the entire test before beginning.

7 Budget your time to ensure that you have plenty of opportunity to complete the test; do not spend too much time on any one question.

8 Wear a watch so that you can monitor the time, and be aware of how much time is allocated for the examination before beginning.

9   Begin work as soon as possible, and mark the answers in the test booklet carefully but quickly.

10   Answer the easiest questions first in order to save time for the more difficult ones. Quickly scanning all the questions first may give you an idea about which questions are more difficult.

11   Mark the questions you skip so that you can find them again later.

12   Read and review each question carefully to make sure that you know exactly what the question is asking and that you understand all parts of the question.

13   Answer as many questions as possible. If you are unsure about some questions, guess or estimate. Use scrap paper for personal note-taking, if allowed.

14   Look over the test when you are done to be sure that you have read all questions correctly and have answered as many as possible.

15   Make changes to answers only if there is a good reason to do so. Often, your first answer is correct.

16   Check the test booklet carefully before turning it in (for instance, you might have forgotten to put your name on it!).

DEDUCTIVE REASONING

Another technique that students should learn to use for better test results is called deductive reasoning. It is the process of reaching logical conclusions by employing logical reasoning.

...the process of reaching logical conclusions by employing logical reasoning.

Some strategies associated with deductive reasoning are:
- Eliminate options known to be incorrect. The more answers you can eliminate as incorrect, the better your chances of identifying the correct one.
- Watch for key words or terms. Keep an eye out for such words and phrases as usually, commonly, in most instances, never, and always.
- Study the stem (the question or problem). It will often provide a clue to the correct answer. Look for a match between the stem and one of the choices.
- Watch for grammatical clues. For instance, if the last word in a stem is "an," the answer must begin with a vowel rather than a consonant.
- Look for similar or related questions. They also may provide clues.

In answering essay questions, watch for words such as compare, contrast, discuss, evaluate, analyze, define, or describe and develop your answer accordingly. In reading tests that contain long paragraphs followed by several questions, read the questions first. This will help identify the important elements in the paragraph.

UNDERSTANDING WRITTEN TEST FORMATS

There are a few additional tips that all test-wise learners should know, especially with respect to the state licensing examination. Keep in mind, of course, that the most important strategy of test taking is knowing your material. With that in mind, consider the following tips on the various types of question formats.

True/False

- Watch for qualifying words (all, most, some, none, always, usually, sometimes, never, little, no, equal, less, good, bad). Absolutes (all, none, always, never) are generally not true.
- For a statement to be true, the entire statement must be true.
- Long statements are more likely to be true than short statements. It takes more detail to provide truthful, factual information.

Multiple Choice

- Read the entire question carefully, including all the choices.
- Look for the best answer; more than one choice may be true.
- Eliminate incorrect answers by crossing them out (if taking the test on the test form).
- When two choices are close or similar, one of them is probably right.
- When two choices are identical, both must be wrong.
- When two choices are opposites, one is probably wrong and one is probably correct, depending on the number of other choices.
- Pay special attention to words such as not, except, and but.
- The answer to one question may be in the stem of another.

Matching

- Read all items in each list before beginning.
- Check off items from the brief response list to eliminate choices.

Essays

- Organize your answer according to the cue words in the question.
- Think carefully and outline your answer before you begin writing.
- Make sure that what you write is complete, accurate, relevant to the question, well organized, and clear.

Remember that even though you may understand test formats and effective test-taking strategies, this does not take the place of having a complete understanding of the material on which you are being tested. To be successful at taking tests, you must follow the rules of effective studying and be thoroughly knowledgeable of the exam content for both the written and the practical examination.

To be better prepared for the practical portion of the examination, which is hands-on, the new graduate should follow these tips:

- Practice the correct skills required in the test as often as you can.
- Participate in mock licensing examinations, including the timing of the examination criteria.

- Familiarize yourself with the content contained in the examination bulletins sent by the licensing agency.

- Make certain that all equipment and implements are cleaned, disinfected, and properly stored before the exam.

- If allowed by the regulatory or licensing agency, observe other practical examinations before taking your exam.

- If possible, locate the examination site the day before the exam to ensure that you are on time for the exam.

- As with any exam, listen carefully to the examiner's instructions and follow them explicitly.

- Focus on your own knowledge; do not allow yourself to be concerned with what other test candidates are doing.

- Follow all sanitation and safety procedures throughout the entire examination.

PRACTICAL EXAM

Although every state will have different testing requirements, you most likely will be required to take a practical exam, as well as a theory or written exam. After you have successfully passed the theory or written exam, you will receive an appointment to take the practical exam.

The practical exam tests your skills at performing the services you were taught in school. You should find a trustworthy and serious person to act as your hand model. Your hand model must be willing to schedule some practice time for you, so you can prepare for the exam. Check your state's regulations about the various procedures you will be required to perform for the practical exam.

Be sure to read all of the materials you receive from your licensing agency about the practical exam, know and follow the directions as they are outlined, and know where the exam will take place before the day of the exam. You will eliminate a lot of unnecessary stress by having the materials and supplies you need and becoming familiar with the location of the exam.

LO1 Complete

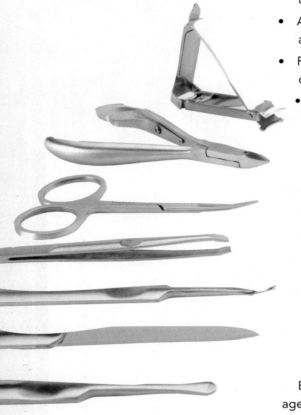

Preparing for Employment

When you chose to enter the field of nail technology, your primary goal was to find a good job after being licensed. Now you need to reaffirm that goal by reviewing a number of important questions.

- What do you really want out of a career in nail technology?

- What areas within the nail industry are the most interesting to you?

- What are your strongest practical skills and in what ways do you wish to use them?

- What personal qualities will help you have a successful career?

You will eliminate a lot of unnecessary stress by having the materials and supplies you need...

One way that you can answer these questions is to make a photocopy of, and then complete, the Inventory of Personal Characteristics and Inventory of Technical Skills form (Figure 20-3). After you have completed the inventory form and identified the areas that need further attention, you can determine where to focus the remainder of your training. You should also have a better idea of the type of establishment that would best suit you for eventual employment.

▼ FIGURE 20-3

Inventory of Personal Characteristics and Inventory of Technical Skills form.

INVENTORY OF PERSONAL CHARACTERISTICS

PERSONAL CHARACTERISTICS	EXC.	GOOD	AVG.	POOR	PLAN FOR IMPROVEMENT
Posture, Deportment, Poise					
Image, Grooming, Personal Hygiene					
Etiquette, Manners, Courtesy					
Communications Skills					
Personality, Attitude					
Goals, Self-Motivation					
Personal Habits, Procrastination					
Responsibility					
Self-esteem, Self Confidence					
Integrity, Honesty					
Dependability, Loyalty					

INVENTORY OF TECHNICAL SKILLS

TECHNICAL SKILLS	EXC.	GOOD	AVG.	POOR	PLAN FOR IMPROVEMENT
Manicures, Hand/Arm Massage					
Pedicures, Foot Massage					
Polish Applications					
Hand Filing, Electric Filing					
Nail Tip and Nail Form Applications					
Fabric Wrap Application					
UV Gel Application					
Monomer Liquid and Polymer Powder Nail Enhancements Application					
Nail Art					
Paraffin Wax Treatments					

After analyzing the above responses, would you hire yourself as an employee in your nail salon? Why or why not?

State short-term goals that you hope to accomplish in 6 to 12 months:

State long-term goals that you hope to accomplish in 1 to 5 years:

Ask yourself: Do you want to work in a big city or small town? Are you compatible with a sophisticated, exclusive salon or a trendy salon? Which clientele are you able to communicate with more effectively? Do you want to start out slowly and carefully or do you want to jump in and throw everything into your career from the starting gate? Will you be in this industry throughout your working career or is this just a stopover? Will you only work a 30 or 40 hour week or will you go the extra mile when opportunities are available? How ambitious are you and how many risks are you willing to take? Will you split your time up between freelancing in the entertainment industry while working in a salon?

▲ FIGURE 20-4
Your school counselor can help you find employment.

During your training, you may have the opportunity to network with various industry professionals who are invited to be guest speakers. Be prepared to ask them questions about what they like most and least about their current positions. Ask them for any tips they might have that will assist you in your search for the right establishment. In addition, be sure to take advantage of your institution's in-house placement assistance program and postings on the school bulletin boards when you begin your employment search (**Figure 20-4**).

Your willingness to work smart and hard is a key ingredient to your success. The commitment you make now in terms of time and effort will pay off later in the workplace, where your energy will be appreciated, rewarded, and valued. Having enthusiasm for getting the job done can be contagious, and when everyone works hard, everyone benefits. You can begin to develop this enthusiasm by establishing good work habits as a student.

✓ **LO2 Complete**

Activity

For one week, keep a daily record of your performance in the following areas and ask a few of your fellow students to provide feedback.

- Positive attitude
- Professional appearance
- Punctuality
- Regular class and clinic attendance
- Diligent practice of newly learned techniques
- Interpersonal skills
- Teamwork
- Helping others

HOW TO GET THE JOB YOU WANT

There are several key personal characteristics that will help you get the position you want and help you keep it. These characteristics include:

- Motivation. This means having the drive to take the necessary action to achieve a goal. Although motivation can come from external sources—parental or peer pressure, for instance—the best kind of motivation is internal.

- Integrity. When you have integrity, you are committed to a strong code of moral and artistic values. Integrity is the compass that keeps you on course over the long haul of your career.

- Good technical and communication skills. While you may be better in either technical or communication skills, you must develop both to reach the level of success you desire.

- Strong work ethic. In the beauty business, having a strong work ethic means taking pride in your work, and committing yourself to consistently doing a good job for your clients, employer, and salon team.

- Enthusiasm. Try never to lose your eagerness to learn, grow, and expand your skills and knowledge.

A SALON SURVEY

In the United States alone, there are nearly 313,000 professional salons. These salons employ more than 1,604,000 active beauty industry professionals. (To check for updates, go to http://www.naccas.gov) This year, like every year, thousands of beauty and nail technology school graduates will find their first position in one of the types of salons described below.

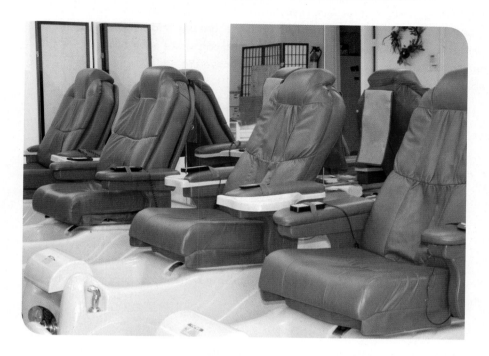

Small Independent Salons

Owned by an individual or two or more partners, this kind of operation makes up the majority of professional nail salons. The average independent salon has three manicure tables and pedicure stations, but many have as many as 10 nail techs working there regularly. Usually, the owners are nail technicians who maintain their own clientele while managing the business. There are nearly as many different kinds of independent salons as there are owners. Their image, decor, services, prices, and clientele all reflect the owner's experience and taste. Depending on the owner's willingness to help a newcomer learn and grow, a beginning nail technician can learn a great deal in an independent salon while also earning a good living.

Independent Salon Chains

These are usually chains of five or more salons that are owned by one individual or two or more partners. Independent salon chains range from basic nail salons, to full-service salons and day spas, and offer everything from low-priced to very high-priced services.

In large high-end salons, nail technicians can advance to specialized positions such as department manager or education director. Some larger salons also employ education directors, trainers, and in-house educators. Nail technicians are often hired to manage particular or multiple locations.

> These salons employ more than 1,604,000 active beauty industry professionals.

Large National Salon Chains

These companies operate salons throughout the country, and even internationally. They can be budget or value priced, nails-only or full-service, mid-price or high-end. Some salon chains operate within department store chains. Management and marketing professionals at the corporate headquarters make all the decisions for each salon, such as size, decor, hours, services, prices, advertising, and profit targets. Many newly licensed professionals seek their first jobs in national chain salons because of the secure pay and benefits, additional paid training, management opportunities, and corporate advertising. Since the chains are large and widespread, employees have the added advantage of being able to transfer from one location to another.

Franchise Salons

Another form of chain salon organization, the franchise salon, has a national name with a consistent image and business formula throughout the chain. Franchises are owned by individuals who pay a fee to use the name; these individuals then receive a business plan and can take advantage of national marketing campaigns. Such decisions as size, location, decor, and prices are determined in advance by the parent company. Franchises can be owned by nail technicians and investors who seek a return on their investment. Franchise salons often offer employees the same benefits as corporate-owned chain salons.

Basic Value-Priced Operations

Value-priced nail salons are often located in busy shopping center strips that have lower rents and that are anchored by a supermarket or other large business. These outlets depend on a high volume of walk-in traffic. They hire recent nail tech graduates and generally pay them by the hour, sometimes adding commission-style bonuses if an individual's sales pass a certain level. Manicures are usually priced below $15, and nail technicians need to perform basic nail services quickly and effectively. This type of nail salon provides novice nail techs with a wide range of experience and an opportunity to build their client base.

Mid-Priced Full-Service Salons

These salons offer a complete menu of hair, nail, skin, and waxing services and sell plenty of retail products. Successful mid-priced salons promote their most profitable services and often offer service and retail packages to entice clients. They also run strong marketing programs to encourage client returns and referrals. These salons train their professional salon team to be as productive and profitable as possible. If you are inclined to give more time to each client during the consultation, you may like working in a full-service salon. Here you will have the opportunity to build a relationship with clients that may extend over time.

High-End Salons or Day Spas

This type of business employs well-trained beauty professionals and salon assistants who offer higher-priced services that are filled with luxurious extras, such as a paraffin wax treatment, as part of the spa manicures and pedicures. Most high-end salons are located in upscale sections of the city; others may be located in elegant mansions, high-rent office and retail towers, or luxury hotels and resorts. Clients expect a high level of personal service, and such salons hire practitioners whose technical expertise, personal appearance, and communication skills meet their high standards (**Figure 20-5**).

Booth Rental Establishments

Booth renting (also called station or chair rental) is possibly the least expensive way of owning one's own business. Nail technicians now have the opportunity to rent a one-station salon suite housed independently or within a beauty salon/spa or shopping center or plaza. For a detailed discussion of booth rental, see Chapter 22.

 **LO3 Complete**

▲ **FIGURE 20-5**
High-end salon.

Resume and Employment Portfolio Development

A resume is a written summary of a person's education and work experience. It tells potential employers at a glance what your achievements and accomplishments are. Here are some basic guidelines to follow when preparing your professional resume.

- Keep it simple. Ideally your resume should be one, easy-to-read page.
- Always include a cover letter. A cover letter is a letter of introduction that highlights your goals, skills, and accomplishments. If you do not know how to write a cover letter, there are several resources available to help you. For example, you can find books at some school and public libraries or in bookstores.
- Print them on good quality bond paper that is white, buff, or gray.
- Include your name, address, phone number, and email address on both the resume and your cover letter.
- List recent and relevant work experience.
- List relevant education and the name of the institution from which you graduated, as well as relevant courses attended.
- List your abilities and accomplishments.
- Focus on information that is relevant to the position you are seeking.

The average time that a potential employer will spend scanning your resume before deciding whether to grant you an interview is about 20 seconds. That means you must market yourself in such a manner that the reader will want to meet you. Focus on your achievements and accomplishments.

Accomplishment statements should always show how you have achieved and/or surpassed the basic duties and responsibilities of your current position. You might ask yourself the following types of questions to help you develop accomplishment statements that will make you interesting to potential employers:

- How many regular clients do I serve?
- How many clients do I serve weekly?
- How many more clients do I serve now as compared to six months ago?
- What was my service ticket average?
- What was my client retention rate?
- What percentage of my client revenue came from retailing?
- What percentage of client revenue came from nail enhancement services or UV gels?

There is no better time for you to achieve significant accomplishments than while you are in school. Even though your experience may be minimal, you must still present evidence of your skills and accomplishments. This may seem a difficult task at this early stage in your working career, but by closely examining your training performance, extracurricular activities, and the full- or part-time jobs you have held, you should be able to create a good resume. For example, here are some questions to consider when preparing your resume and cover letter:

- Did you receive any honors during your course of training?
- Were you ever selected "student of the month"?
- Did you receive special recognition for your attendance or academic progress?
- Did you win any nail technology-related competitions while in school?
- What was your attendance average while in school?
- Did you work with the student body to organize any fundraisers? What were the results?

Answers to these types of questions may indicate your people skills, personal work habits, and personal commitment to success (Figure 20-6).

Since you have not yet completed your training, you still have the opportunity to make some of the examples listed above become a reality before you graduate. Positive developments of this nature while you are still in school can do much to improve your resume.

Marie Luster

333 Full Circle | Anytown, USA 11111 | (813) 555-1234

OBJECTIVE

To be a full service Nail Specialist and Nail Artist

ACCOMPLISHMENTS/ABILITIES

ACADEMICS
Achieved honor roll in theoretical requirements and excellent ratings in practical requirements; exceeded the number of practical skills required for graduation.

SALES
Named "Student of the Month" for best attendance, best attitude, highest retail sales, and most clients served; Increased nail services to 30 percent of my clinic volume by graduation. Achieved a client ticket average comparable to $30.00 in the local salon market.

Increased retail sales by 18 percent during part-time employment at local beauty supply and salon.

CLIENT RETENTION
Developed and retained a personal client base of over 25 individuals of all ages, both male and female.

IMAGE CONSULTING
Certified as an Image Consultant.

ADMINISTRATION
Supervised a student nail team which developed a business plan for opening a three station, full service nail salon; project earned an "A" and was recognized for thoroughness, accuracy, and creativity. As President of the student council, organized fund raising activities including makeovers, bake sales, and yard sales which generated enough funds to send 10 students to a national trade show.

APPRENTICESHIP
Trained one day weekly at a busy, full-service salon for 12 weeks in a student/recent graduate apprentice program.

SPECIAL PROJECTS
Reorganized school nail room for more efficiency and client comfort. Organized the school dispensary which increased inventory control and streamlined operations within the clinic.

Catalogued the school's library of texts, reference books, videos and other periodicals by category and updated the library inventory list.

EXPERIENCE

NAILS BEAUTY CENTER	Fall 2009	Training as an apprentice in all phases of nail care and nail art
NAIL COSMETICS INC.	Summer 2009	Marketing & retail sales of beauty products, nail products and cosmetics
J.M.O SALON	2008-2009	Salon public relations, marketing & special events coordinator

EDUCATION

Diploma of Nail Technology, Nail Technology College, 2009

B.A. in Mass Communications, Central State University (OH), 2007

▲ **FIGURE 20-6**
Achievement-oriented resume.

TIPS FOR PREPARING A RESUME

Keep these tips in mind when creating and preparing your resume. Stay positive and focused on the facts and your sincere desire to get that job!

- Make it easy to read. Use concise, clear sentences and avoid flowery language.

- Know your audience. Use vocabulary and language that will be understood by your potential employer.

- Keep it short. A one-page resume is customary.

- Stress accomplishments. Emphasize past accomplishments and the skills you used to achieve them.

- Focus on career goals. Highlight information that is relevant to your career goals and the position you are seeking.

- Emphasize transferable skills. Transferable skills are the skills you have mastered at other jobs that can be put to use in a new position.

- Use action verbs. Begin accomplishment statements with action verbs such as achieved, coordinated, developed, increased, maintained, and strengthened.

- Make it neat. A poorly structured, badly typed resume does not reflect well on you.

- Avoid salary references. Don't state your salary history or reason for leaving your former employment.

- Be honest and truthful. You might feel tempted to stretch the facts a bit about your experience or skill level, but remaining honest and truthful about the information on your resume is the best and most ethical way to go.

- Include professional references. Use only professional references on your resume and make sure you give potential employers the person's title, place of employment, and telephone number.

- Be realistic. Remember that you are just starting out in a field that should hold wonderful and fulfilling experiences. Be realistic about what you can accomplish.

Review the achievement-oriented resume in this chapter. It is a great example of a resume developed for a recent graduate of a nail technology course.

▲ FIGURE 20-7

An employment portfolio.

EMPLOYMENT PORTFOLIO

As you prepare to work in the field of nail technology, an employment portfolio can be extremely useful. An employment portfolio is a collection of photographs and documents that reflect a person's skills, accomplishments, and abilities in a chosen career field. Art stores and office supply stores offer many options for presenting your portfolio (**Figure 20-7**).

While the actual contents of the portfolio will vary from graduate to graduate, there are certain items that have a place in any portfolio. A powerful portfolio includes:

- Diplomas, including high school, college, and nail school
- Awards and achievements received while a nail technology student
- Current resume, focusing on accomplishments
- Letters of reference from former employers and mentors
- Summary of continuing education and/or copies of training certificates
- Statement of membership in industry and other professional organizations
- Statement of relevant civic affiliations and/or community activities
- Before-and-after photographs of services that you have performed on clients or models
- Brief statement about why you have chosen a career in the nail profession
- Any other information that you regard as relevant

...an employment portfolio can be extremely useful.

Once you have assembled your portfolio, ask yourself whether it accurately portrays you and your career skills. If it does not, identify what needs to be changed. If you are not sure, ask a neutral party (someone in the nail industry would be best) for feedback about how to make it more interesting and accurate. The portfolio, like the resume, should be prepared in a way that projects professionalism.

- All summaries and letters should be typed. Do not handwrite anything.
- For ease of use, you may want to separate sections such as Salon Work and Competition Nails with tabs.
- When writing about why you chose a career in nail technology, you may wish to include a statement that explains what you love about your new career, a description of your philosophy about the importance of teamwork, how you see yourself as a contributing team member, and a description of methods you would use to increase service and retail revenue.

LO4 Complete

Preparing for a Job Interview

You have gone to nail school, graduated, passed your written and practical exam, received your license, prepared your resume and portfolio, and, finally, you are ready to go on job interviews! Congratulations, you are almost there—getting your first job in the nail profession. To help prepare for the interviews, you will want to do some additional research so you can present a knowledgeable, confident persona to potential employers.

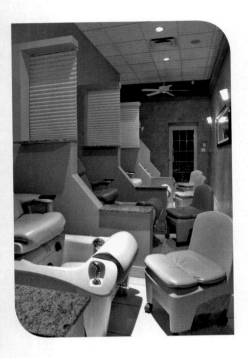

TARGETING THE ESTABLISHMENT

One of the most important steps in the process of job hunting is narrowing your search. Here are some points to keep in mind about targeting potential employers:

- You may work in many jobs before your dream job becomes available. Be genuinely happy and grateful for the jobs you will have throughout your career. Remain positive and learn all that you can from each experience and use that information to improve yourself and your skills.

- Do not wait until graduation to begin your search. If you do, you may be tempted to take the first offer you receive, instead of carefully investigating all possibilities before making a decision. When you prepare in advance you will have time to evaluate the pros and cons of each opportunity,

- Locate a salon that serves the type of clients you wish to serve. Finding a good fit with the clients and staff is critical from the outset of your career.

- Make a list of area salons or establishments. The Internet and yellow pages will be among your best sources for this kind of information. If you are considering relocating to another area, your local library will probably have out-of-state phone directories to help you compile your list. You may also access http://www.anywho.com on the Internet for a complete listing of businesses throughout the United States.

- Follow newspapers, television, and radio for salon advertising. Get a feel for what market each salon is targeting.

FIELD RESEARCH

A great way to find out about jobs is to actually get out there and use your eyes, ears, and any other sense that can help you gather information. A highly effective technique that you should learn is called networking.

Networking is establishing contacts that may eventually lead to a job and that help you gain valuable information about the workings of various establishments. If possible, make contact with salons while you are still a student. You might even make contact as a salon customer yourself. When you are ready to network, your first contact should be by telephone, and you should follow these guidelines:

1 Use your best telephone manner. Speak with confidence and self-assurance.

2 Ask to speak to the owner, manager, or personnel director.

3 State your name and explain that you are preparing to graduate from school in your chosen field.

4 Explain that you are researching the local salon market for potential positions and that you need just a few minutes to ask a few questions.

5 If the person is receptive to your phone call, ask whether the salon is in need of any new nail technicians and how many the salon currently employs.

6 Ask if you can make an appointment to visit the salon to observe sometime during the next few weeks. If the salon representative is agreeable, make an appointment and confirm it with an e-mail, formal business letter, or handwritten note on high-quality paper **(Figure 20-8)**.

While some nail professionals may be reluctant to make time for this kind of networking initially, remain positive and flexible. Offer to meet whenever the owner's schedule permits or ask whether you can meet with the salon managers instead.

THE SALON VISIT

When you visit the salon, take along a checklist to ensure that you observe all the key areas that might ultimately affect your decision making. The checklist will be similar to the one used for field trips you probably have taken to area salons while in school. Keep the checklist on file for future reference so that you can make informed comparisons between establishments **(Figure 20-9)**.

After your visit, always remember to write a brief note thanking the salon representative for his or her time **(Figure 20-10)**. Even if you did not like the salon, or would never consider working there, it is important to send a thank-you note **(Figure 20-11)**.

Never burn your bridges. Rather, build a network of contacts that have a favorable opinion of you.

ARRANGING THE EMPLOYMENT INTERVIEW

After you have graduated and completed the first two steps in the process of securing employment—targeting and observing salons—you are ready to pursue employment. The next step is to contact the establishments that you are most interested in by sending them a resume with a cover letter requesting an interview.

Mark your calendar for a time when it would be suitable to make a follow-up call to this letter. A week is generally sufficient. When you call, try to schedule an interview appointment. Keep in mind that some salons may not have openings and may not be granting interviews. When this is the case, be polite and ask them to keep your resume on file should an opening arise in the future. Be sure to thank them for their time and consideration.

INTERVIEW PREPARATION

When preparing for an interview, make sure that you have all the necessary information and materials in place. Use the Preparing for the Interview Checklist as a guide **(Figure 20-12)**. Also be sure to have the following information at the ready:

Marie Luster   333 Full Circle | Any town, USA 11111 | (813) 555-1234

DATE

Dear Ms. (or Mr.) _____,

I appreciate the time you spent with me on the telephone earlier today and I am looking forward to meeting with you and visiting your salon next Tuesday at 11:00 a.m. I am eager to observe your salon and staff at work.

If you should need to reach me before that time for any reason, my cellular phone number(s) is _____.

Thank you again for our scheduled appointment on Tuesday.

Sincerely,

(Your Name)

▲ **FIGURE 20-8**

Sample appointment confirmation note.

SALON VISIT CHECKLIST

When you visit a nail salon, full service salon or spa observe the following areas and rate them from 1 to 5, with 5 considered being the best.

_____ **SALON IMAGE:** Is the salon's image consistent and appropriate for your interests? Is the image pleasing and inviting? What is the decor and arrangement? (If you are not comfortable or if you find it unattractive, it is likely that clients will also.)

_____ **PROFESSIONALISM:** Do the employees present the appropriate professional appearance and behavior? Do they give their clients the appropriate levels of attention and personal service or do they act as if work is their time to socialize?

_____ **MANAGEMENT:** Does the salon show signs of being well managed? Is the phone answered promptly with professional telephone skills? Is the mood of the salon positive? Does everyone appear to work as a team?

_____ **CLIENT SERVICE:** Are clients greeted promptly and warmly when they enter the salon? Are they kept informed of the status of their appointment? Are they offered a magazine or beverage while they wait? Is there a comfortable reception area?

_____ **PRICES:** Compare price for value. Are clients getting their money's worth? Do they pay the same price in one salon but get better service and attention in another? If possible, take home salon brochures and price lists.

_____ **RETAIL:** Is there a well-stocked retail display offering clients a variety of product lines and a range of prices? Do the nail technicians and receptionist (if applicable) promote retail sales?

_____ **IN-SALON MARKETING:** Are there posters or promotions throughout the salon? If so, are they tasteful and of good quality?

_____ **SERVICES:** Make a list of all services offered by each salon and the product lines they carry. This will help you decide what earning potential nail techs have in each salon.

SALON NAME: _____

SALON MANAGER: _____

▲ **FIGURE 20-9**
Salon Visit Checklist form.

Marie Luster   333 Full Circle | Any town, USA 11111 | (813) 555-1234

DATE

Dear Ms. (or Mr.) _____,

I appreciate having had the opportunity to observe your salon/spa in operation last Tuesday. Thank you for the time you and your staff gave me. I was impressed by the efficient and courteous manner in which your nail technicians served their clients. The atmosphere was pleasant and the mood was positive.

Should you ever have an opening for a professional with my skills and training in nail care and nail art, I would welcome the opportunity to apply. You can contact me at the address and phone number listed above.

I hope we will meet again soon.

Sincerely,

(Your Name)

▲ **FIGURE 20-10**

Sample thank you note.

Marie Luster   333 Full Circle | Any town, USA 11111 | (813) 555-1234

DATE

Dear Ms. (or Mr.) _____,

I appreciate having had the opportunity to observe your salon in operation last Tuesday. I know how busy you and all your staff are and want to thank you for the time that you gave me. I realize that it can be somewhat disruptive to have visitors observing your activities. I hope my presence didn't interfere with the flow of your operations too much.

I certainly appreciate the courtesies that were extended to me by you and your staff. I wish you and your salon continued success.

Sincerely,

(Your Name)

▲ **FIGURE 20-11**

Thank you note to a salon at which you do not expect to seek employment.

PREPARING FOR THE INTERVIEW CHECKLIST

RESUME COMPOSITION

1. Does it present your abilities and what you have accomplished in your jobs and training?

2. Does it make the reader want to ask, "How did you accomplish that?"

3. Does it highlight accomplishments rather than detailing duties and responsibilities?

4. Is it easy to read, short, and does it stress past accomplishments and skills?

5. Does it focus on information that's relevant to your own career goals?

6. Is it complete and professionally prepared?

PORTFOLIO CHECKLIST

- [ ] Diploma, secondary, and post-secondary
- [ ] Awards and achievements while in school
- [ ] Current resume focusing on accomplishments
- [ ] Letters of reference from former employers
- [ ] List of, or certificates from, trade shows attended while in training.
- [ ] Statement of professional affiliations (memberships in nail technology organizations, etc.)
- [ ] Statement of civic affiliations and/or activities.
- [ ] Before and after photographs of technical skills services you have performed.
- [ ] Any other relevant information

Ask yourself: Does my portfolio portray me and my career skills in the manner that I wish to be perceived? If not, what needs to be changed?

GENERAL INFORMATION

- Describe specific methods or procedures you will employ in the salon to build your clientele.

- Describe how you feel about retail sales in the salon and give specific methods you would use in the salon to generate sales.

- State why you feel consumer protection and safety is so important in the field of nail technology.

- After careful thought, explain what you love about your new career. Describe your passion for nail technology.

▲ **FIGURE 20-12**

Preparing for the Interview Checklist form.

1 *Identification.*

- Social Security number
- Driver's license number
- Names, addresses, and phone numbers of former employers
- Name and phone number of the nearest relative not living with you

2 *Interview wardrobe.*

Your appearance is crucial, especially since you are applying for a position in the image and beauty industry **(Figure 20-13)**. It is recommended that you obtain one or two interview outfits. You may be asked to return for a second interview; you will need a different outfit for the second interview. Consider the following points:

- Is the outfit appropriate for the position?
- Is it both fashionable and flattering to your shape and personality?
- Are your accessories both fashionable and functional (e.g., not noisy or so large that they interfere with erforming services)?
- Are your nails groomed and do they say something positive about your abilities as a nail technician? Always keep your nails in pristine shape. Beautiful nails advertise your excellent skills and help an interviewer imagine the potential in you.
- Is your hairstyle current? Does it flatter your face and your overall style?
- Is your make-up current? Does it flatter your face and your overall style?
- For men, are you clean shaven or is your beard properly trimmed?
- Is your perfume or cologne subtle?
- Do you have an appropriate handbag or briefcase? Never carry both.

▲ **FIGURE 20-13**
Dressed for an interview.

3 *Supporting materials.*

- Resume and cover letter. Even if you have already sent one, take another copy of each with you.
- Facts and figures. Bring any additional class certificates or award certificates you may have received, and be sure to have plenty of copies of reference pages ready.
- Employment portfolio.

4 *Answers to anticipated questions.*

Certain questions are typically asked during an interview. It would be a good idea to reflect on your answers ahead of time. You might even consider role-playing an interview situation with friends, family, or fellow students. Typical questions include the following:

> **Talking Point:**
>
> If you have not visited the salon before interviewing, ask the person who calls or contacts you to set up the appointment and ask whether the salon has a Web site. From checking out their Web site you will be able to get an idea about the type of salon you will be doing business in and with. Ask the questions: "Do you have a Web site or a MySpace page that advertises your salon? Is your salon on Facebook or Twitter?"

- What did you like best about your training?
- Are you punctual and regular in attendance?
- Will your school director or instructor confirm this?
- What skills do you feel are your strongest?
- What areas do you consider to be less strong?
- Are you a team player? Please explain.
- Do you consider yourself flexible? Please explain.
- What are your career goals?
- What days and hours are you available for work?
- Do you have your own transportation?
- Are there any obstacles that would prevent you from keeping your commitment to full-time employment?
- What value do you believe you would bring to this salon and this position?
- Who is the most interesting person you have met in your work and/or education experience? Why?
- How would you handle a problem client?
- How do you feel about retailing?
- Would you be willing to attend our company training program?
- How would you provide excellent customer service to your clients?
- What consultation questions would you ask a client?
- What steps do you take to build your business and ensure that clients return to see you?

5   *Be prepared to perform a service.*

Some salons require applicants to perform a mini or full nail service as part of the interview. Be sure to confirm whether this is a requirement. If it is, make sure that your hand model is appropriately dressed and properly prepared for the experience. In some cases, the salon may provide hand models for interviewing purposes.

THE INTERVIEW

On the day of the interview, try to make sure that nothing occurs that will keep you from completing the interview successfully. There are certain behaviors you should practice in connection with the interview itself.

- Always be on time or—better yet—early. If you are unsure of the location, find it the day before so there will be no reason for delays. New technology allows us to use navigation systems from your car and/or cellular phone or go to a maps Web site for directions.
- Project a warm, friendly smile. Smiling is the universal language.
- Walk, sit, and stand with good posture.
- Be polite and courteous.
- Do not sit until asked to do so, or until it is obvious that you are expected to do so.

- Never smoke or chew gum, even if either is offered to you. Do not come to an interview with a cup of coffee, a soft drink, snacks, or anything else to eat or drink.

- Never lean on or touch the interviewer's desk. Some people do not like their personal space invaded without an invitation.

- Try to project a positive first impression by appearing as confident and relaxed as you can (**Figure 20-14**).

- Speak clearly. The interviewer must be able to hear and understand you.

- Answer questions honestly. Think the question and answer through carefully. Do not speak before you are ready, and not for more than two minutes at a time.

- Never criticize former employers.

- Always remember to thank the interviewer at the end of the interview.

▲ **FIGURE 20-14**
Interview in progress.

Activity

Find a partner among your fellow students and role-play the employment interview. Each of you can take turns as the applicant and the employer. After each session, have a brief discussion regarding how it went, that is, what worked and what didn't work. Discuss how the process could be further improved. Bear in mind that a role-play activity will never predict exactly what will occur in a real interview. However, the process will help you to be better prepared for that important event in your employment search.

Another critical part of the interview comes when you are invited to ask the interviewer questions of your own. You should think about those questions ahead of time and refer to your list of questions in the supporting materials. Doing so will show that you are organized and prepared. Some questions that you might consider are:

- Is there a job description that reflects duties and responsibilities? May I review it?

- Is there a salon manual and/or a policies and procedures statement?

- How frequently does the salon advertise?

- What are the salon's top three nail services?

- What products are used? Some nail salons may use products that you have been trained to use and some may not, so you will want to have the time to prepare yourself and to get information on unfamiliar lines or brands. Ask whether the salon provides training on the products they use or whether you are required to get training on your own.

- How long does a nail technician typically work here?

- Are employees encouraged to grow in skills and responsibility? How so?

- Does the salon offer continuing education opportunities?

- Is there room for advancement?

- If so, what are the requirements for promotion? Would a promotion include a pay raise?

- What benefits does the salon offer, such as paid vacations, personal days, and medical insurance?

- What is the form of compensation?

- When will the position be filled?

- Should I follow up with you regarding your decision, or will you contact me?

- May I have a tour of the salon and the nail department?

Do not feel that you have to ask all of your questions. The point is to create as much of a dialogue as possible. Be aware of the interviewer's reactions and be sensitive to when you may have asked enough questions. By obtaining the answers to at least some of your questions, you can compare the information you have gathered about other salons, and then choose the one that offers the best package of income and career development.

Remember to write a thank-you note. It should simply thank the interviewer for the time she or he spent with you. Close with a positive statement that you want the job (if you do). If the interviewer's decision comes down to two or three possibilities, the one expressing the most desire may be offered the position. Also, if the interviewer suggests that you call to learn about the employment decision, then definitely do so.

fyi

Many people find it difficult to afford the two or three outfits needed to project a confident and professional image. Fortunately, several nonprofit organizations have been formed to address this need. These organizations receive donations of clean, beautiful clothes in good condition from individuals and manufacturers. These donations are passed along to women who need them. You may obtain a referral from a social service agency. For more information, visit Wardrobe for Opportunity at http://www.wardrobe.org, and Dress for Success at http://www.dressforsuccess.org.

Did **You** Know...

Legal Questions

Are you over the age of 18?

Are you able to perform this job?

Are you authorized to work in the United States?

In which languages are you fluent?

LEGAL ASPECTS OF THE EMPLOYMENT INTERVIEW

Over the years, a number of issues have arisen about questions that may or may not be included in an employment application or interview, including race/ethnicity, sexual orientation, religion, and national origin. Generally, you should not be asked any questions in the following categories:

- Age or date of birth. It is permissible to ask the age of an applicant younger than 18. Age should not be relevant in most hiring decisions; date-of-birth questions prior to employment are improper.

- Disabilities or physical traits. The Americans with Disabilities Act prohibits general inquiries about health problems, disabilities, and medical conditions.

- Citizenship. Employers are not allowed to discriminate because an applicant is not a U.S. citizen. Upon request, you must be able to provide proof that you are legally in the U.S. and are allowed to work.

Potential employers may ask you questions regarding the use of drugs or tobacco. In fact, the employer may obtain an applicant's agreement to be bound by the employer's drug and smoking policies and to submit to drug testing.

THE EMPLOYMENT APPLICATION

Any time that you are applying for any position, you will be required to complete an application, even if your resume already contains much of the requested information. Your resume and the qualifications list you have prepared prior to the interview will assist you in completing the application quickly and accurately.

✓ **LO5 Complete**

Finding a Salon That is Right for You

You are ready to set out on your exciting new career as a professional nail technician. The right way to proceed is by learning important study and test-taking skills early and applying them throughout your program.

Think ahead to your employment opportunities and use your time in school to develop a record of interesting, noteworthy activities that will make your resume exciting. When you compile a history that shows how you have achieved your goals, your confidence will build and your ambitions will grow.

Always take one step at a time. Be sure to take the helpful preliminary steps that are discussed in this book when preparing for employment.

Develop a dynamic portfolio. Keep your materials, information, and questions organized to ensure a high-impact interview.

After you are employed, take the necessary steps to learn all that you can about your new position and the establishment where you are working. Read all you can about the industry. Attend trade shows and take advantage of continuing education. Become an active participant in making this great industry even better! See Chapter 21 to learn some great strategies for ensuring your career success.

Activity

Get ready for the application process by filling out some sample employment application forms! Search online for sample application forms or locate a career counseling center at the nearest community college or university and use their sample forms.

Try these Web sites for sample application forms:

http://www.quintcareers.com/

employment_application.pdf

http://jobsearch.about.com/od/

jobappsamples/a/printableapp.htm

http://www.samplewords.com/

professional-job-application-form.html

When filling out a practice application, make your information as detailed as possible. Review your application, then ask your fellow classmates or instructor to review it and give you feedback. The career counseling center in your area may have resume counselors who might be willing to assist you in preparing for employment. Also, check with the center for free classes they may offer in employment preparation.

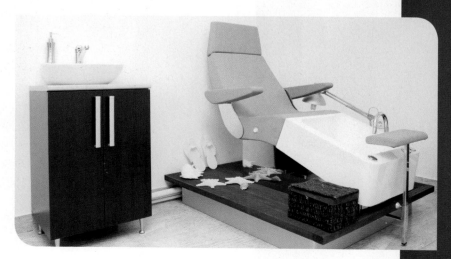

review questions

1. What habits and characteristics does a test-wise student have?

2. What is deductive reasoning?

3. What are the four most common testing formats?

4. List and describe the different types of salon businesses available to nail techs.

5. What is a resume?

6. What is an employment portfolio?

7. List the items that should be included in your employment portfolio.

8. What are some questions that you should never be asked when interviewing for a job?

21 on the job

chapter outline

✓ Learning Objectives

After you have completed this chapter, you will be able to:

1 **Describe the characteristics necessary to thrive in a service profession.**

2 **Understand the importance of and how to use a job description.**

3 **Understand the most common ways that nail technicians are compensated.**

4 **Manage a personal budget.**

5 **Suggest ticket upgrades or upsell services to salon clients.**

6 **Effectively market nail services to expand client base.**

7 **Understand the importance of rebooking appointments with clients.**

Key Terms

Page number indicates where in the chapter the term is used.

client base / 467

commission / 467

job description / 465

retailing / 471

**ticket upgrading
or up-selling services** / 471

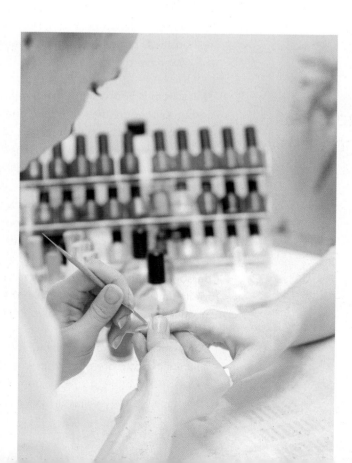

► **FIGURE 21-1**

Nail technician successfully transitioning from school to work.

Congratulations! You have worked hard and conducted yourself professionally while in school, passed your state's licensing exam, and may have been offered your first job in the field. Now, more than ever, you need to prioritize your goals and commit to personal rules of conduct and behavior. These goals and rules should guide you throughout your career. If you let them do so, you can always expect to have work and enjoy all the freedom that your chosen profession can offer (**Figure 21-1**).

Moving from School to Work

Making the transition from school to work can be difficult. While you may be thrilled to work, working for a paycheck or independently operating your own nail business brings with it a number of duties and responsibilities that you may not have thought about.

Nail school is a forgiving environment. You are given the chance to do a certain procedure over and over again until you get it right. Making and fixing mistakes is an accepted part of the process, and your instructors and mentors are there to help you. Schedules can be adjusted, if possible, and you are given some leeway in juggling your personal life with the demands of your schooling and career. When you become the employee of a salon or an independent operation, you will be expected to put the needs of the business and its clients ahead of your own. This means that you must always be on time for your scheduled shifts and be prepared to perform whatever services or functions are required, regardless of what is happening in your personal life. If someone comes to you with tickets for a concert on Saturday, for instance, you cannot just take the day off. To do so would definitely inconvenience your clients, who might even decide not to return to the salon.

Don't get into a habit of mixing your business and personal lives. To have balance in both, pre-plan your schedule and use your time management skills!

> Making the transition from school to work can be difficult.

Out in the Real World

Many students believe they should be rewarded with a high-paying job and be able to do only the kinds of services they wish to do, as soon as they graduate from school. Welcome to the world of nail technology! While working, you may be asked to do work or perform services that are not your first choice. The good news, however, is when you are working in the real world, you are learning every moment, and there is no substitute for that kind of experience.

The important thing is to be honest with yourself as you evaluate your skills to determine the type of position that is right for you. If you need help and direction in sorting out the different issues about the workplaces you are considering, ask your instructor and mentors for advice.

 Network with mentors, nail professionals, educators, and classmates; ask questions, take advice, listen, and consider all your options! By doing this, you will open yourself to knowledge, resources, and terrific nail industry information.

THRIVING IN A SERVICE PROFESSION

The first thing to remember when you are in a service business is that your work revolves around serving your clients. Some people have a hard time with the idea of customer service, because they feel that it is demeaning in some way. While it is true that there will always be some clients who do not treat people with respect, the majority of people you encounter will truly value the work you do for them. They will look forward to seeing you and will show their appreciation for your hard work with their loyalty. Never let anyone's negativity change your overall outlook.

Here are some points that will help guide you as you serve your clients.

- *Put others first.* You will have to quickly get used to putting your own feelings or desires aside and to putting the needs of the business and the client first. This means doing what is expected of you, unless you are physically unable to do so.

- *Be true to your word.* Choose your words carefully and honestly. Be someone who can be counted on to tell the truth and to do what you say you will do.

- *Be punctual.* Scheduling is central to the nail business. Getting to work on time is respectful to your clients. If you are late for appointments, coworkers will have to handle your clients; clients can become angered and switch salons if they have to wait for their techs or services too often.

- *Be grateful.* Remember that it is an honor to have a job that will provide you and your family with financial stability. If you become unhappy in any salon environment, move on before you start acting out in an ungrateful, disrespectful manner. This situation may also provide you an opportunity to take your career to the next level.

- *Be a problem solver.* No job or situation comes without its share of problems. Be someone who recognizes problems promptly and finds ways to resolve them constructively and quickly.

- *Be respectful.* Although you may not like or agree with someone, show respect for yourself and others, including salon managers and owners.

- *Be a lifelong learner.* A valued nail professional is one who intends to keep on learning. Thinking that you will never need to learn anything more after you are out of school is immature and limiting. Your career might go in all kinds of interesting directions, depending on what new things you learn. This applies to everything in your life. Besides learning new technical skills, you should continue gaining more insight into your own behavior, how to better deal with people, and how to improve your business skills.

✓ LO1 Complete

▲ FIGURE 21-2

Pitch in and be a team player by helping a teammate.

SALON TEAMWORK

Working requires that you practice and perfect your people skills. A salon is very much a business environment. Know your duties, as outlined in your job description, and commit to becoming a great teammate. To become a good team player, you should do the following things:

- *Strive to help.* Be concerned not only with your own success, but also with the success of others. Stay a little later, or come in a little earlier, to help out a teammate.

- *Pitch in.* Be willing to help with whatever needs to be done in the salon—from folding towels to making appointments—when you are not busy servicing clients **(Figure 21-2)**.

- *Share your knowledge.* Be willing to share what you know, especially to those who show a strong interest in learning or who are new to the nail and salon business. This will make you a respected member of any team.

- *Remain positive.* Given the stress of a typical salon, there will be lots of opportunities for you to become negative or to have conflicts with your teammates. Resist all temptations to give in to gossip.

- *Become a relationship builder.* Just as there are different kinds of people in the world, there are different types of relationships within the world of business. You do not have to be someone's best friend to build a good working relationship with that person. Make a point to connect with other nail technicians that have similar and common career goals.

- *Be willing to resolve conflicts.* The most difficult part of being in a relationship is when conflict arises. A real teammate is someone who knows that conflict and tension are bad for the people who are in it, those who are around it, and the salon. Conflict is also a natural part of life. If you can work constructively toward resolving conflict, you will always be a valued member of the team.

- *No one starts at the top.* Keep in mind that beginners almost always start out lower in the pecking order. How fast you are able to move up in the business will be determined by your attitude and your work ethic.

- *Be loyal.* Loyalty is vital to the workings of a salon. Nail technicians should be loyal to the salon and its management, and salon management should be loyal to the staff and clients. Ideally, clients will be loyal to the nail technician and the salon. Staff meetings are a good way to help build team loyalty. As you work on all the team-building characteristics, you will start to feel a strong sense of loyalty building up within you (**Figure 21-3**).

▲ **FIGURE 21-3**
Staff meetings are a good way to help build team loyalty.

THE JOB DESCRIPTION

When you accept a job, you will be expected to behave appropriately, perform services asked of you, and conduct your business professionally. To do this to the best of your abilities, you should be given a job description, a document that outlines all the duties and responsibilities of a particular position. Many nail salons have a pre-printed job description that they can give you. If you find yourself at a salon that does not use job descriptions, you may want to write one for yourself. You can then present this to your salon manager for review to ensure that both of you have a good understanding of what is expected of you.

After you have your job description, be sure you understand it. While reading it over, make notes and jot down any questions you want to ask your manager. When you assume your new position, you are agreeing to do everything that is listed in the job description. If you are unclear about something, or need more information, it is your responsibility to ask!

F☀CUS ON... **Be a Good Teammate**

While each individual may be concerned with getting ahead and being successful, a good teammate knows that no one can be successful alone.

You will be truly successful if your entire salon is successful!

In crafting a job description, the best salons cover their bases. They make sure to outline not only the duties and responsibilities of the job, but also the attitudes that they expect you to have and the opportunities that are available to you. **Figure 21-4** shows some highlights from a well-written nail specialist apprentice job description. This is just one example. Job descriptions come in all sizes and shapes and feature a variety of requirements, benefits, and incentives.

✓ **LO2 Complete**

Job Description: Nail Specialist Apprentice

Every apprentice must have a nail technology license as well as the determination to learn and grow on the job. As an assistant you must be willing to cooperate with coworkers in a team environment, which is most conductive to learning and to good morale among all employees. You must display a friendly yet professional attitude toward coworkers and clients alike.

Excellent time management is essential to the operation of a successful salon. An apprentice should be aware of clients who are early and late or nail technicians who are running ahead or behind in their schedule. You should be prepared to assist in those situations and to change your routine if necessary. Keep the receptionist and nail technicians informed about clients who have entered the salon. Be prepared to stay up to an hour late when necessary. Keep in mind always that everyone needs to work together to get the job done.

The responsibilities of an apprentice include:

1. Greeting clients by offering them a beverage, hanging up coats, and informing the receptionist and nail technicians that they have arrived.
2. Consultations for nail services and nail retail.
3. Assisting nail technicians in services that require extra help.
4. Cleaning and disinfecting stations and work areas.
5. Keeping the nail stations and inventory well stocked with appropriate products.
6. Notifying the nail salon manager about items and supplies that need to be reordered.
7. Making sure the pedicure stations are drained, cleaned, disinfected and free of debris.
8. Keeping the nail display is neat and clean.
9. Keeping the retail area neat and well stocked.
10. Keeping the bathroom and dressing room neat, clean, and stocked.
11. Performing housekeeping duties such as: emptying trash receptacles, cleaning up dust on floors, keeping the lunch room and dispensary neat and clean, helping with laundry, and dusting shelves.
12. Making fresh coffee when necessary.
13. Training new assistants.

Continuing Education

Your position as apprentice is the first step toward becoming a successful nail technician. In the beginning, your training will focus on the duties of an apprentice. Once you have mastered those, your training will focus on the skills you will need as a nail technician.

As part of your continuing education in this nail salon you will be required to:
• attend all salon classes
• attend our special Sunday Seminars

Advancement

You will need to acquire all professional tools necessary for training at twelve weeks (implements, nail brushes, hand files/electric file, nail art, etc.) Upon successful completion of all required classes and seminars and your demonstration of the necessary skills and attitudes, you will have the opportunity to advance to the position of nail technician. This advancement will always depend upon your performance as an apprentice as well as the approval of management.

Remember: how quickly you achieve your goals in this nail salon is up to you!

▲ **FIGURE 21-4**

Example of a nail specialist apprentice job description.

COMPENSATION PLANS

When you assess a job offer, your first concern will probably be the issue of compensation, or what you will actually get paid for your work.

Compensation varies from one salon to another. There are, however, three standard methods of compensation that you are likely to encounter: salary, commission, and salary plus commission.

Salary

Being paid an hourly rate is a way for a new nail professional to start out, since that person will most likely not have an established clientele for a while. An hourly rate is generally offered to new nail techs and is usually based on the minimum wage. Some salons offer an hourly wage that is slightly higher than the minimum wage to encourage new nail technicians to take the job and stick with it. Sometimes, nail techs may be paid an hourly wage for up to six months. When the nail tech has established a client base, customers who are loyal to a particular nail technician, the way they are compensated may change. Regular taxes will be taken out of earnings.

Remember: If you are offered a set salary each week, in lieu of an hourly rate, it must be equal to at least minimum wage, and you are entitled to overtime pay if you work more than 40 hours per week.

Commission

A commission, a percentage of the revenue that the salon takes in from sales earmarked for the practitioner, is usually offered to nail technicians after they have built up a loyal clientele. A commission payment structure is different from an hourly wage in that any money you are paid is a direct result of the total amount of service dollars you generate for the salon. Commissions are paid based on percentages of your total service dollars and can range anywhere from 45 to 70 percent, depending on your length of time at the salon, your performance level, and the benefits that are part of your employment package. For example, at the end of the week, when you add up all the services that you have performed, your total is $1,000. If you are at the 50 percent commission level, then you would be paid $500 (before taxes). With a commission payment structure, the salon usually provides all of the products you will need to perform the nail services. You are responsible for providing your personal tools, such as nail brushes, files, electric drills, and sometimes nail art supplies. In this instance, you may be able to negotiate a commission percentage for yourself that includes your tool, implement, and equipment expenses.

Salary Plus Commissions

A salary-plus-commission structure is another way to be compensated in the salon business. It basically means that you receive both a salary and a commission. This kind of structure is often used to motivate nail technicians to perform more services, thereby increasing their productivity. For example, imagine that you earn an hourly wage that is equal to $300 per week, and you perform about $600 worth of services every week. Your salon manager may offer you an additional 25 percent commission on any services you

> **" A salary-plus-commission structure is another way to be compensated...you receive both a salary and a commission.**

Here's a Tip:

Accepting a commission-paying position in a salon can have its positives and negatives for new nail pros. If you have think you have enough clients to work on commission and can make enough of a paycheck to pay your expenses, then go ahead and give it a try. It could be a great way to work into better commission scales or even booth renting.

If you don't think you can make enough money being paid solely on a commission basis, then take a job in a salon that is willing to pay you an hourly wage until you build your client base. After you have honed your nail service skills and built a solid client base, you can consider working on commission.

▲ FIGURE 21-5
Retail sales boost your income.

perform over your usual $600 per week. Perhaps you will receive a straight hourly wage, but you can receive as much as a 15 percent commission on all the retail products you sell. You can see how this kind of structure quickly leads to significantly increased compensation (**Figure 21-5**).

Tips

When you receive satisfactory service at a hotel or restaurant, you are likely to leave your server a tip. It has become customary for salon clients to acknowledge beauty professionals in this way, too. Some salons have a tipping policy; others have a no-tipping policy. This is determined by what the salon feels is appropriate for its clientele.

The usual amount to tip is 15 percent of the total service ticket. For example, if a customer spends $50, then the tip might be 15 percent of that, or $7.50. Tips are income in addition to your regular compensation. They must be recorded daily and reported on your income tax return. Reporting tips will be beneficial to you if you wish to take out a mortgage or another type of loan and want your income to appear as strong as it really is. An earnest and ethical professional will want to keep accurate records and to honestly report all of their earnings to maintain integrity with their commitment to the profession.

DECIDING ON APPROPRIATE COMPENSATION

As you can see, there are a number of ways to structure compensation for a nail professional. You will probably have the opportunity to try each of these methods at different points in your career. When deciding whether a certain compensation method is appropriate for you, it is important to be aware of what your monthly expenses are and to have a personal financial budget in place. We will address budget issues later in this chapter.

Did **You** Know...

Nail technicians can increase their chances of building a solid and loyal clientele more quickly if they:

- Live in a large city or choose areas within their cities that have lots of potential clients.
- Select a location where the competition for nail clients is less saturated.
- Have advanced training, skills, and certifications.
- Have and use their artistic abilities.
- Employ marketing and publicity strategies.
- Concentrate on an unusual niche within the nail business (teens, for example).

EMPLOYEE EVALUATION

The best way to keep tabs on your progress is to ask for feedback from your clients, salon manager, and key coworkers. Most likely, your salon will have a structure in place for evaluations. Commonly, evaluations are scheduled 90 days after hiring and then once per year after that. But you should feel free to ask for help and feedback any time you need it. This feedback can help you improve your technical abilities, as well as your customer service skills.

Ask your mentor, a seasoned coworker, or salon manager to sit in on one of your client consultations, and to make note of areas where you can improve. Ask this person to observe your technical skills and to point out ways you can perform your work more quickly and more efficiently. Have a trusted coworker watch and evaluate your skills for selling retail products. All of these evaluations will benefit your learning process enormously.

Find a Role Model

One of the best ways to improve your performance is to model your behavior after someone who is having the kind of success that you wish to have. Watch other nail technicians in your salon and in the industry. You will easily be able to identify who is really good and who is just coasting along. Focus on the skills of the ones who are really good. What do they do? How do they treat their clients? How do they treat the salon staff and manager? How do they book their appointments? How do they handle their continuing education? How do they select which products to use? What is their attitude toward their work? How do they handle crisis and conflicts?

Go to these professionals for advice. Ask for a few minutes of their time, but be willing to wait for it because it may not be easy to find time to talk during the day. If you are having a problem, explain your situation, and ask whether they can help you. Be prepared to listen and not to argue your points. Remember that you asked for help, even when what they are saying is not what you want to hear. Thank them for their help and reflect on the advice you have been given. A little help and direction from a skilled, experienced nail tech can go a long way toward helping you achieve your goals.

Managing Your Money

Although a career in the beauty industry is very artistic and creative, it is also a career that requires financial understanding and planning. Too many nail professionals live for the moment and do not plan for their futures.

In a corporate structure, the human resources department of the corporation handles a great deal of the employee's financial planning for them. For example, health and dental insurance, retirement accounts, savings accounts, and many other items may be automatically deducted and paid out of the employee's salary. Most nail technicians must research and plan for all of those things on their own. This may seem difficult, but it is a small price to pay for the kind of freedom, financial reward, and job satisfaction that a career in nail technology can offer. And the good news is that managing money is something everyone can learn to do.

F✹CUS ON... **Building Your Efficiency**

Some professionals believe that the more time they spend with their clients performing services, the better the service will be. Not so! Your client should be in the salon only as long as is necessary for you to adequately complete a service.

Be aware of how much time it takes you to perform your various services and then schedule accordingly. As you become more and more experienced, you should see a reduction in the amount of time it takes you to perform these services. That means clients wait less, you can increase your number of services, and the increase in services naturally increases your income.

MEETING FINANCIAL RESPONSIBILITIES

In addition to making money, responsible adults are also concerned with meeting their financial responsibilities, paying back their debts, and planning for the future. Throughout your life and your career, you will undoubtedly incur debt in the form of car loans, home and business mortgages, or student loans. Not paying back your loans is called defaulting, and it can have serious consequences regarding your personal and professional credit. The best way to meet all of your financial responsibilities is to know precisely what you owe and what you earn, so that you can make informed decisions about where your money goes.

Personal Budget

It is amazing how many people work hard and earn very good salaries, but never take the time to create a personal budget. Many people are afraid of the word budget because they think that it will be too restrictive on their spending, or they have to be mathematical geniuses in order to work with a budget. Thankfully, neither of these fears is rooted in reality.

You can create a personal budget that ranges from being extremely simple to extremely complex. It all depends on your needs. At the beginning of your career, a simple budget should be sufficient. To get started, take a look at **(Figure 21-6)**, the Personal Budget Worksheet. It lists the standard monthly expenses that most people have to budget. It also includes school loan repayment, savings, and payments into an individual retirement account (IRA).

Keeping track of where your money goes is one step toward making sure that you always have enough. It also helps you to plan ahead and save for bigger expenses such as a vacation, your own home, or even your own business. All in all, sticking to a budget is a good practice to follow faithfully for the rest of your life.

Personal Budget Worksheet

A. Expenses

1. My monthly rent (or share of the rent) is $_____
2. My monthly car payment is   _____
3. My monthly car insurance payment is   _____
4. My monthly auto fuel/upkeep expenses are   _____
5. My monthly electric bill is   _____
6. My monthly gas bill is   _____
7. My monthly health insurance payment is   _____
8. My monthly entertainment expense is   _____
9. My monthly bank fees are   _____
10. My monthly grocery expense is   _____
11. My monthly dry cleaning expense is   _____
12. My monthly personal grooming expense is   _____
13. My monthly prescription/medical expense is   _____
14. My monthly telephone is   _____
15. My monthly student loan payment is   _____
16. My IRA payment is   _____
17. My savings account deposit is   _____
18. Other expenses: _____

                  TOTAL EXPENSES $_____

B. Income

1. My monthly take-home pay is   _____
2. My monthly income from tips is   _____
3. Other income: _____

                  TOTAL INCOME $_____

C. Balance

   Total Income (B)   _____
   Minus Total Expenses (A)   _____

                  BALANCE $_____

▲ **FIGURE 21-6**
Personal Budget Worksheet.

Giving Yourself a Raise

After you have taken time to create, use, and work with your personal budget, you may want to look at ways in which you can generate greater income for yourself. You might automatically jump to the most obvious sources, such as asking your employer for a raise or asking for a higher percentage of commission. While these tactics are certainly valid, you will also want to think about other ways to increase your income, such as the following:

- Spending less money. Although it may be difficult to reduce your spending, it is certainly one way to increase the amount of money that is left over at the end of the month. These dollars can be invested or saved.

- Increasing service prices. It will probably take some time before you are in a position to increase your service prices. After you have fully mastered all the services that you are performing and you have a loyal client base, there is nothing wrong with increasing your prices every year or two, as long as you do so by a reasonable amount. Do a little research to determine what your supply and product expenses are and increase your fees accordingly.

- Another reason for increasing your service prices can be that your clientele has grown and you have become busier. As your service sales goals are increased and met and maintained for a specified period of time, you may find it necessary to raise your service prices.

Seek Professional Advice

Just as you will want your clients to seek your advice and services for their nail care needs, sometimes it is important for you to seek the advice of experts, especially when it comes to your finances. You can research and interview financial planners who will be able to give you advice on reducing your credit card debt, on how to invest your money, and on retirement options. You can speak to the officers at your local bank or credit union who may be able to suggest different types of accounts that offer you greater returns or flexibility with your money, depending on what you need.

When seeking advice from other professionals, be sure not to take anyone's advice without carefully considering whether the advice makes sense for your particular situation and needs. Before you buy into anything, be an informed consumer about other people's goods and services.

✓ LO4 Complete

Discover the Selling You

Another area that touches on the issue of you and money is selling. As a nail professional, you will have enormous opportunities to sell retail products and upgrade service tickets. Ticket upgrading, or upselling services, is the practice of recommending and selling additional services to clients that may be performed by you or other practitioners licensed in a different field. Retailing is the act of recommending and selling quality products to clients for at-home nail care (Figure 21-7). Retailing is good for clients because they will have the appropriate products needed for at-home maintenance and care of their nails. It is also good for nail technicians and salons because it increases their revenue.

Ticket upgrading or upselling services and product retailing can make all the difference in your economic picture. The following dialogue is an example of ticket upgrading. In this scene, Marie, the nail technician, suggests additional services to Brandi, her client, who has just had her nails done for a wedding she will be attending that evening.

Activity

Go through the budget worksheet on page 470 and fill in the amounts that apply to your current living and financial situation. If you are unsure of the amount of an expense, put in the amount you have averaged over the past three months or give it your best guess. For your income, you may need to have three or four months of employment history to answer, but fill in what you can.

- How do your expenses compare to your income?
- What is your balance after all your expenses are paid?
- Were there any surprises for you in this exercise?
- Do you think that keeping a budget is a good way to manage money?
- Do you know of any other methods people use to manage money?

Here's a Tip:

Increasing your service prices in $3.00 increments is a great way to increase your income each week, without it costing clients so much that they consider not using your services any longer.

► **FIGURE 21-7**

Sell quality nail products to clients.

Read the script yourself and change the words to make them fit your personality. Then try it the next time you feel that an additional service could help one of your clients.

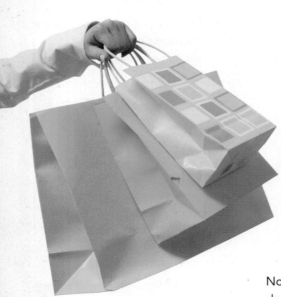

Marie: I'm really glad you like your new nail color. It will be perfect with the dress you described. Don't you just love formal weddings?

Brandi: Yes! To tell you the truth, I don't get dressed up very often, and putting the look together was harder than I thought it would be.

Marie: You will look great! Are you all set with your nail products and makeup for tonight, Brandi? It would be a shame to have a beautiful new dress and gorgeous nails, and then have to worry about your makeup.

Brandi: Well, actually, I was sort of wondering about that. I'm wearing this long black dress and I'm not really sure what the best look is for the occasion. Got any ideas?

Marie: Well, as you know, my specialty is nail care, but we have an excellent makeup artist right here. Shall I get her for you?

Brandi: Definitely. That sounds terrific!

Marie: You know, since this is such an important occasion, you may want to consider having Stephanie, one of our hairstylists, do your hair. That will ensure that your total look is the best it can be.

Brandi: I think that's a great idea. Thanks for the suggestion!

Now, that was a great example of a nail tech upselling services for other departments within the salon. If the salon is truly committed to the upselling strategy for increasing its sales and revenues, then hairstylists and makeup artists in other parts of the salon are upselling their clients by suggesting they try the salon's nail services.

✓ **LO5 Complete**

PRINCIPLES OF SELLING

Some nail technicians shy away from sales. They think that it is scary, being pushy, or beneath them. A close look at how selling works can set your mind at ease. Not only can you become very good at selling after you understand the principles behind it, but you can also feel good about providing your clients with a valuable service.

To be successful in sales, you need ambition, determination, and a good personality. The first step in selling is to sell yourself. Clients must like and trust you before they will purchase nail services or nail care items.

Remember, every client who enters the salon is a potential purchaser of additional services or merchandise. Recognizing the client's needs and preferences lays the foundation for successful selling.

To become a proficient salesperson, you must be able to apply the following principles of selling:

- Be familiar with the merits and benefits of the various services and products that you are trying to sell, and recommend only those that the client really needs.

- Adapt your approach and technique to meet the needs and personality of each client. Some clients may prefer a soft sell that involves informing them about the product, without stressing that they purchase it. Others are comfortable with a hard-sell approach that focuses emphatically on why a client should buy the product.

- Be self-confident when recommending products for sale. You become confident by knowing about the products you are selling and by believing that they are as good as you say they are.

- Generate interest and desire in the customer by asking questions that determine a need.

- Never misrepresent your services or products. Making unrealistic claims will only lead to your client's disappointment, and will make it unlikely that you will ever be able to sell to that client again.

- Do not underestimate the client's intelligence or knowledge of her own nail care regimen or particular needs.

- To sell a product or service, deliver your sales talk in a relaxed, friendly manner and, if possible, demonstrate use **(Figure 21-8)**.

- Recognize the right psychological moment to close any sale. After the client has offered to buy, quit selling. Do not oversell, except to praise the client for the purchase and to assure the client that she will be happy with it.

THE PSYCHOLOGY OF SELLING

Most people have reasons for doing what they do, and when you are selling something, it is your job to figure out the reasons that might motivate a person to buy. When dealing with salon clients, you will find that their motives for buying salon products vary widely. Some may be concerned with issues of looking better. Some are seeking personal satisfaction and

Here's a Tip:

Wondering what it takes to successfully sell retail products to nail clients? In a nutshell, it takes:

- Reasonable expectations for selling products in a month's time.
- An incentive program that rewards everyone—the salon, the nail tech, and the client!
- A positive attitude. No one wants to buy products from a person who is not genuinely happy to be at the salon.
- Smart promotional pricing and/or some kind of added value for the client who is making the purchase.
- Eye-catching displays.

▲ FIGURE 21-8
Demonstrate a product's benefits.

want to feel better about themselves. Others need to solve a problem that is bothersome and want to spend less time maintaining their nails.

The standard retail sales commission for nail technicians is 10 percent of their total retail sales per week.

Sometimes, a client may inquire about a product or service, but may still be undecided or doubtful. In this type of situation, you can help the decision along by offering honest and sincere advice. When you discuss a nail service with a client, address the results and benefits of that service. Always keep in mind that the best interests of the client should be your first consideration. You will need to know exactly what your client's needs are, and you need to have a clear idea as to how those needs can be fulfilled. Refer to the sample dialogues in this section—one involves ticket upgrading and the other involves retailing, both of which demonstrate effective selling techniques.

Here are a few tips on how to get the conversation started about retailing products:

- Ask clients what products they are using for home maintenance of their nails, hands, and feet.
- Place products in the clients' hands whenever possible, or have them in view (Figure 21-9).
- Advise clients about how recommended services will benefit them (stronger nails, longer-lasting nail polish, for instance).
- Keep retail areas clean, well lit, and appealing.
- Inform clients about any promotions and sales that are going on.
- Be informed about the merits of using professional products and explain to clients why they perform better than a generic or store brand.

▲ FIGURE 21-9
Place the retail product in the client's hands whenever possible.

While you realize that retailing products is a service to your clients, you may not be sure how to go about it. Imagine the following scenes and see how Cassandra, the nail technician, highlights the benefits and features of a product to her client, Ms. Jewell. Note that price is not necessarily the bottom line.

Ms. Jewell: I just love the way you do my nails. How do you always make my cuticles and hands look like they're in such good shape?

Cassandra: I always use a penetrating cuticle oil on your cuticles, Ms. Jewell. It's a wonderful product and one you should be using on your cuticles every day. I also use the lotion made by the same company.

Ms. Jewell: Is that the lotion you use with the great lavender scent?

Cassandra: I love that light lavender scent too. It's a really great moisturizing lotion that we swear by—it's fabulous for treating dry and even chapped skin. I use it on my pedicure clients too, and it soothes that dry, rough skin that can accumulate on feet, especially in dry winter weather. Do you use any lotion at home after your shower or after having your hands in water?

Ms. Jewell: Yes, I do. I picked up something in the grocery store one day. But it's runny, not thick like your lotion.

Cassandra: Oh, well, our lotion is very rich and emollient because it has been especially formulated to stay on your hands and feet and moisturize them throughout the day.

Ms. Jewell: Yeah, well, nothing really makes much of a difference in this weather.

Cassandra: Well, I can tell you that I have several clients who are using this lotion at home, and every one of them comes back in and raves about how much better their skin feels and how their dry flaky skin has gone away!

Ms. Jewell: Really?

Cassandra: Yes. You may want to give it a try yourself and see how it works for you. It's available at the front when you check out. I'll grab you a bottle of lotion and the cuticle oil product, so you can look at them while I finish up your service.

Ms. Jewell: Great!

Activity

Pick a partner from class and role-play the dynamics of a sales situation. Take turns being the customer and the nail technician. Evaluate each other on how you did, with suggestions about where you can improve. Then try this exercise with someone else, as no two customers are the same.

Keeping Current Clients and Expanding Your Client Base

After you have mastered the basics of good service, take a look at some marketing techniques that will keep your clients coming back to you for services. These are only a few suggestions; there are many others that may work for you. The best way to decide which techniques are most effective is to try several.

- Birthday cards. Ask clients for their birthday information (just the month and day, not the year) on the client consultation card, and then use it as a tool to get them into the salon again. About one month before the client's birthday, send a card with a special offer. Make it valid only during the birthday month.

- Provide consistently good service. It seems basic enough, but it is amazing how many professionals work hard to get clients, and then lose them because they rush through a service and leave clients feeling dissatisfied. Providing good-quality service must always be your first concern.

- Be reliable. Always be reliable, courteous, thoughtful, and punctual. Be at the salon when you say you will be there, and do not keep clients waiting. **(Refer to Chapter 4 for tips on how to handle the unavoidable times when you are running late.)** Give your clients the nail length and shape they ask for, not something else. Recommend a retail product only when you have tried it yourself, and you know what it can and cannot do.

Take a look at marketing techniques that will keep your clients coming back to you...

- Be respectful. When you treat others with respect, you become worthy of respect yourself. Being respectful means that you do not gossip or make fun of anyone or anything. Negative energy brings everyone down, especially you.

- Be positive. Become one of those people who always sees the glass as half full. Look for the positive in every situation. No one enjoys being around a person who is always unhappy.

- Be professional. Sometimes, a client may try to make your relationship more personal than it ought to be. It is in your best interest—and your client's best interest—not to cross that line. Remember that your job is to be the client's nail technician, not a psychiatrist, a marriage counselor, or a buddy.

- Use business card referrals. Make up a special business card with your information on it, but leave room for a client to put her name on it as well. If your client is clearly pleased with your work, give her several cards. Ask her to put her name on them and to refer her friends and associates to you. For every card you receive from a new customer with her name on it, give her 10 percent off her next salon service or a complementary service added to her next appointment. This gives the client lots of motivation to recommend you to others, which, in turn, helps build your clientele (**Figure 21-10**).

- Cross-market with local businesses. Another terrific way to build business is to work with other businesses in your area. Look for clothing stores, florists, gift shops, and other small businesses near your salon. Offer to have a card swap and commit to referring your clients to them when they are in the market for goods or services that your neighbors can provide, if they will do the same for you. This is a great way to build a feeling of community among local vendors and to reach new clients you may not be able to otherwise.

- Public speaking. Make yourself available to speak to local women's groups, the PTA, organizations for young men and women, and anywhere else that will put you in front of people in your community who are all potential clients. Put together a short program (20 to 30 minutes) in which, for example, you might discuss professional appearance with emphasis in your chosen field and other grooming tips for people looking for jobs or who are already employed.

▲ **FIGURE 21-10**
Referral cards help build a client base.

✓ LO**6** Complete

REBOOKING CLIENTS

The best time to think about getting your client back into the salon is while she is still in your salon. It may seem a little difficult to assure your client that you are concerned with her satisfaction on this visit while you are talking about her next visit, but, in fact, the two go together. The best way to encourage your client to book another appointment before she leaves is to simply talk with her, ask questions, and listen carefully to her answers.

During the time that you are working on a client's nails, for instance, talk about the condition of her nails, nail grooming habits at home, and the benefits of regular or special salon maintenance services. You might raise these issues in a number of ways.

- "Mrs. Evelyn, when I did your fill today, I noticed that your nail enhancements need to be completely replaced. Shall I book a full set for your next visit?"

- "Your son is getting married next month? How wonderful. Have you thought about having a deluxe pedicure service so your feet will look as beautiful as the rest of you in that new dress you told me about? I can set up an appointment for the day before the wedding."

Again, you will want to listen carefully to what your clients are telling you during their visit, because they will often give the careful listener many good clues as to what is happening in their lives. That will open the door to discussing their next appointment. Rebooking clients before they leave the salon will ensure that they receive the care they need when they need it, and that your appointment book remains filled.

 **LO7 Complete**

On Your Way

Your first job in the nail industry will most likely be the most difficult. Getting started in this business means being on a big learning curve for awhile. Be patient with yourself as you transition from the school you to the professional you. Always remember that in your work life, as in everything else you do, practice makes perfect. You will not know everything you need to know at the start, but be confident in the fact that you are graduating from nail school with a solid knowledge base. Make use of the many generous and experienced professionals you will encounter, and let them teach you the tricks of the trade. Make the commitment to perfecting your technical and customer service skills.

Above all, always be willing to learn and to discuss customer service and technical skills with the salon team. If you let the concepts that you have learned in this book be your guide, you will enjoy your life and reap the amazing benefits of a career in nail technology **(Figure 21-11)**.

F✹CUS ON... **Retailing**

For quick reference, keep these five points in mind when selling:

1 Establish rapport with the client.

2 Determine the client's needs.

3 Recommend products or services based on the client's needs.

4 Emphasize benefits.

5 Close the sale.

Here's a Tip:

There are plenty of books and Web articles that give great strategies for building a client base and keeping those clients coming back to you. Look into these and make a list of the suggestions that seem like a good fit for you, your client base, and your salon. Then, choose one strategy to try every two to three months, and see how well it worked for you. If it helped you to accomplish your goal of getting and keeping new clients, then put a star next to it and save the idea to use again, when the time is right!

◀ **FIGURE 21-11**
Discuss customer service and technical skills with the salon team.

review questions

1. List the characteristics necessary to thrive in a service profession.

2. What is a job description and why is it important?

3. List three common ways that nail technicians are compensated.

4. Why is it important to manage your money and what method can you use to do so?

5. List the ways that nail techs can increase their income.

6. What is ticket upgrading or upselling services?

7. How is retailing good for clients, nail technicians, and salons?

8. List five strategies that will help to expand your client base.

9. Why is it so important to rebook clients before they leave the salon?

22

the salon
business

chapter outline

After you have completed this chapter, you will be able to:

1. Identify two options for going into business for yourself.
2. Understand the responsibilities of a booth renter.
3. List the basic factors to be considered when opening a salon.
4. Distinguish the types of salon ownership.
5. Identify the information that should be included in a business plan.
6. Understand the importance of recordkeeping.
7. Recognize the elements of successful salon operations.
8. Explain why selling services and products is a vital aspect of a salon's success.

Key Terms

Page number indicates where in the chapter the term is used.

booth rental / 482	**corporation** / 486	**personnel** / 493
business plan / 487	**goals** / 484	**retail supplies** / 492
capital / 486	**mission statement** / 484	**sole proprietorship** / 486
consumption supplies / 492	**partnership** / 486	**vision statement** / 484

As you become more proficient in your craft and your ability to manage yourself and others, you may decide to become an independent booth renter, or even a salon owner. While this may seem like an easy thing to do, being a successful business person requires experience, a genuine love of people and solid business management skills. To become a successful entrepreneur, you will need to commit to always being a student of business. You will also have to learn how to attract nail technicians, beauty professionals and clients to your business, while maintaining their loyalty over long periods of time. Remember: The better prepared you are, the greater your chances of success.

Entire books have been written on each of the topics touched on in this chapter, so be prepared to read and research your business idea extensively before making any final decisions. The following information is only meant to be a general overview of the salon business.

Going into Business for Yourself

If you reach a point in your life when you feel that you are ready to become your own boss, you will have two main options to consider: **(1)** renting a booth in an existing salon, or **(2)** owning your own salon. Both options have their pros and cons **(Figure 22-1)**.

BOOTH RENTAL

Booth rental is popular in salons all over the United States. Many people see booth rental or renting a station in a salon (also known as chair rental) as a more desirable alternative to owning a salon.

In a booth rental arrangement, a nail technician generally:

- Rents a station or workspace in a salon from the salon owner.
- Is solely responsible for her own clientele, furniture, telephone, advertising, towels, insurance, laundry, supplies, record-keeping, accounting, and business management.
- Pays the salon owner a flat fee for use of the booth on a daily, weekly, biweekly, or monthly basis. In some cases, a renter may pay a yearly fee for booth rental.
- Sets up her own hours of operation.
- Becomes her own boss for a very small amount of money.
- Maintains expenses that are fairly low.

▲ FIGURE 22-1

Nail salon owner preparing for a grand opening.

Booth rental is a desirable situation for many professionals who have a large, steady clientele and do not have to rely on the salon to keep busy. Although it may sound like the clear choice, booth renting has its share of obligations, such as:

- Keeping records for income tax purposes and other legal reasons
- Paying all taxes, including higher Social Security (double that of an employee)
- Carrying adequate malpractice insurance and health insurance
- Compliance with all IRS obligations for independent contractors. Go to http://www.irs.gov and search for "independent contractors."
- Using your own telephone and booking system
- Collecting all service fees, whether they are paid in cash or via a credit card
- Creating all professional materials, including business cards and a service menu
- Purchasing of all supplies, including back-bar and retail
- Maintaining inventory
- Managing the purchase of products and supplies
- Budgeting for advertising, or offering incentives to ensure a steady influx of new clients
- Paying for all education
- Working in an independent atmosphere where teamwork usually does not exist, and salon standards are interpreted on an individual basis

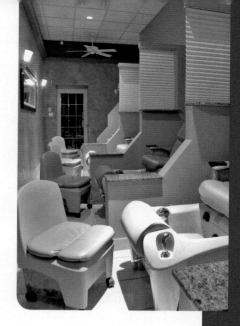

As a booth renter, you will not enjoy the same benefits as an employee of a salon would, such as paid days off or vacation time. Remember, when you are not working, you do not get paid. Perhaps most importantly, you must continually attract new clients and maintain the ones you have, which means working the hours they need you to be available.

✔ LO2 Complete

OPENING YOUR OWN SALON

Opening your own salon is a huge undertaking, financially, physically and mentally, as you face challenges that are complex and unfamiliar to you. You'll need to decide what products to use and carry, what types of marketing and promotions you will employ, and the best method and philosophy for running the business. You may also need to hire additional staff members before you can open the doors.

Regardless of the type of salon you hope to open, there are some basic factors that you should consider carefully.

Did **You** Know...

Currently, booth rental is legal in every state except Pennsylvania, where there is a law prohibiting it, and in New Jersey, where the state board does not recognize booth rental as an acceptable method of doing business.

Create a Vision and Mission Statement for the Business with Goals

A vision statement is a long-term picture of what the business is to become and what it will look like when it gets there. A mission statement is a description of the key strategic influences of the business such as the market it will serve, the kinds of services it will offer, and the quality of those services.

Goals are a set of benchmarks that, once achieved, help you to realize your mission and your vision. You can set both short-term goals and long-term goals for your business.

Create a Business Timeline

While initially you will be concerned with the first two aspects of the timeline, once your business is successful you will need to think about the others as well.

- *Year 1.* It could take a year or more to determine and complete all of the aspects of starting the business.
- *Years 2 to 5.* This time period is for tending to the business, its clientele, and employees, and for growing and expanding the business so it is profitable.
- *Years 5 to 10.* This time period can be for adding additional locations, expanding the scope of the business (adding spa services around your current services), constructing a larger space, or anything else your clients need and want.
- *Years 11 to 20.* In this time period you may want to move from being a working technician into a more full-time manager of the overall business and begin planning for your eventual retirement.
- *Over 20 years.* This may be the perfect time to consider selling your successful business or changing it in some way, such as taking on a junior partner and training him or her to take over the day-to-day operations of the business so you can have time away from the business to explore interests or hobbies.

> You can set both short-term goals and long-term goals for your business.

Determine Business Feasibility

Determining whether or not the business you envision is feasible means figuring out what is practical to do or offer. For example, do you have a special skill or talent that can help you set your business apart from other nail businesses in your area? Does the town or space in which you are planning to locate the business offer you the appropriate type of clientele for the products and services you want to offer? Based on what you envision for the business, how much money will you need to open the business, and is it or can it be available to you?

Choose a Business Name

The name you select for your business explains what it is and can also identify characteristics that set your business apart from competitors in the marketplace. The name you select for your business will also influence how clients and potential clients perceive the business; it will create a picture of your business in their minds, and, once there, it can be very difficult to change if you are not satisfied with the position your business is in.

◄ **FIGURE 22-2**
Location of the nail salon should have good visibility and high traffic.

Choose a Location

You will want to base your businesses location on your primary clientele and their needs. Select a location that has good visibility, high traffic, easy access, sufficient parking, and handicap access (**Figure 22-2**).

There are entire books written about business operations and starting your own business. Check http://www.milady.com for great and specific resources.

TYPES OF SALON OWNERSHIP

A salon business can be owned and operated in many different ways. Before deciding which of the following may be best for your situation and goals, you should seek the advice of an attorney and a tax specialist or accountant.

▲ FIGURE 22-3
Two independent owners meet
to discuss a partnership.

Sole Proprietorship

A sole proprietorship is a business that is owned and operated
by one person, although the owner may have employees. The sole
proprietor is the owner and, most often, the manager of the business.
She determines policies and has the last say in decision-making.
She also assumes responsibility for all expenses, receives the profits,
and bears all losses.

Partnership

A partnership is a business structure in which two or more people
share ownership, although not necessarily equally; management
and responsibilities of the business and its operation may be given
to one or more people. Partnerships form for many reasons and
not all partners will necessarily own an equal share in the business.
One reason for going into a partnership arrangement is to have
more money for investment; another is to have help running your
operation. Partners pool their skills and talents, making it easier to
share work, responsibilities, and decision-making **(Figure 22-3)**.

When you open your own business, you should
consult with an attorney and an accountant
before filing any documents to legalize your
business. Your attorney will advise you of the legal
documents and obligations that you will take on
as a business owner and your accountant can
inform you of the ways in which your business may
be registered for tax purposes.

Corporation

A corporation is a business that is owned by three or more people
called stockholders. It is a distinct legal entity separate from the
individuals who own it, which may allow business owners to protect
their personal assets. Corporations raise capital, money needed to
start a business, by issuing stock certificates or shares to stockholders
(people or companies that purchase shares) who have an ownership
interest in the company. The more stock they own, the bigger that
interest becomes. A business owner can be the sole stockholder or
shareholder, or the business may have many stockholders. Corporations
do require some corporate formalities, such as director and stockholder
meetings, to maintain a corporate status. Corporations cost more
to set up and run than a sole proprietorship or partnership, because
there are the initial formation fees, filing fees, and annual state fees.
Employees pay income tax on the salary that they draw, not on the
total profits of the business, and a stockholder of a corporation is
required to pay unemployment insurance taxes on his or her salary,
whereas a sole proprietor or partner is not.

✓ **LO4 Complete**

BUSINESS PLAN

Regardless of the type of salon you plan to own, it is imperative to have a thorough and well-researched business plan, a written plan of a business as it is seen in the present and envisioned in the future, to follow throughout the entire process of starting your own business. Many books, classes, DVDs, and Web sites offer much more detailed information than can be provided here, but below is a sampling of the kind of information and material that should be included in a business plan:

1 *Executive summary.* Summarizes your plan and states your objectives.

2 *Vision statement.* A long-term picture of what the business is to become and what it will look like when it gets there.

3 *Mission statement.* A description of the key strategic influences of the business such as the market it will serve, the kinds of services it will offer, and the quality of those services.

4 *Organizational plan.* Outlines employee and management levels and also describes how the business will run administratively.

5 *Marketing plan.* Outlines all of the research obtained regarding the clients your business will target and their needs, wants, and habits.

6 *Financial documents.* Includes the projected financial statements, actual (historical) statements, and financial statement analysis.

7 *Supporting documents.* Includes owner's resume, personal financial information, legal contracts, and any other agreements, etc.

8 *Salon policies.* Even small salons and booth renters should have policies that they adhere to. These ensure that all clients and employees are treated fairly and consistently.

✓ LO5 Complete

PURCHASING AN ESTABLISHED SALON

Purchasing an established salon could be an excellent opportunity, but, as with anything else, you have to look at all sides of the picture. Here are some things to consider and, when necessary, to discuss with an attorney before purchasing a nail business (**Figure 22-4**):

- Be sure an existing business has an organizational plan and operating system in place.

- Check the business's performance and reputation.

- Determine why it is for sale.

Did **You** Know...

Your accountant may suggest that your business become an S Corporation (Small Business Corporation), which is a business elected for S Corporation Status through the IRS. This status allows the taxation of the company to be similar to a partnership or sole proprietorship as opposed to paying taxes based on a corporate tax structure. Or your accountant may suggest that your business become registered as an LLC, (Limited Liability Company) which is a type of business ownership combining several features of corporation and partnership structures; owners of an LLC have the liability protection of a corporation. An LLC exists as a separate entity much like a corporation. Members cannot be held personally liable for debts unless they have signed a personal guarantee.

▲ **FIGURE 22-4**

A potential nail salon owner should meet with an attorney before purchasing a nail business.

- Study the business and research its market.

- Learn about the competition, the surrounding neighborhood, the local business community, and the current customer base.

- Determine the profitability and purchase price.

- Obtain an appraisal of the value of the building, equipment, furniture, fixtures, inventory, and personnel.

- Obtain a written purchase and sale agreement to avoid any misunderstandings between the contracting parties.

- Complete signed statement of inventory, fixtures, and the like, indicating the value of each article.

- If there is a transfer of a note, mortgage, lease, or bill of sale, you should initiate an investigation to determine whether there are defaults on the payment of debts or any other liabilities you may be responsible for as a result of buying the business.

- Obtain use of the salon's name and reputation for a definite period of time.

- Receive disclosure of any and all information regarding the salon's clientele and its purchasing and service habits.

- Obtain a non-compete agreement stating that the seller will not work or establish a new salon within a specified distance from the present location.

DRAWING UP A LEASE

Owning your own business does not mean that you own the building that houses your business; however, some people do. When renting or leasing space, you must have an agreement between yourself and the building's owner that has been well thought out and well written. The lease should specify clearly who owns what and who is responsible for which repairs and expenses. You should also secure the following:

- Exemption of fixtures or appliances that might be attached to the salon so that they can be removed without violating the lease.

- Agreement about necessary renovations and repairs, such as painting, plumbing, fixtures, and electrical installation.

- Option from the landlord that allows you to assign the lease to another person. In this way, obligations for the payment of rent are kept separate from the responsibilities of operating the business, should you decide to bring in another person or owner.

> Owning your own business does not mean that you own the building...

PROTECTING YOUR BUSINESS

- Ensure that your business has adequate locks, fire alarm system, and burglar alarm system.

- Purchase liability, fire, malpractice, and burglary insurance, and do not allow these policies to lapse while you intend to remain in business.

- Become thoroughly familiar with all laws governing cosmetology and nail technology and with the health and safety codes of your city and state.

- Keep accurate records of the number of employees, their salaries, lengths of employment, and Social Security numbers as required by various state and federal laws that monitor the social welfare of workers.

- Know the law. Ignorance of the law is no excuse for violating it. Always check with your regulatory agency if you have any questions about a law or regulation.

▲ **FIGURE 22-5**
Experienced nail educator provides helpful tips to a novice technician.

BUSINESS OPERATIONS

Whether you are an owner or a manager, there are laws and codes that you will need to be aware of and to obtain in order to run your business.

- Securing a business license. Contact your local Business Licenses Bureau or the city or county's clerk's office to legalize your business.

- Know the regulations and laws that your business will need to comply with.

- Obtain a seller's permit. You may need a seller's permit to collect sales tax when selling retail products in your salon.

In addition to knowing about the legal aspects of operating your business, there are also certain people and management skills that you must develop to successfully run a salon, such as:

- An excellent business sense: aptitude, good judgment, and diplomacy.

- Knowledge of sound business principles.

Because it takes time to develop these skills, you would be wise to establish a circle of contacts—business owners, including some salon owners—that can give you advice along the way. Consider joining a local entrepreneurs group, or your city's Chamber of Commerce, to extend the reach of your networking.

Smooth business management depends on the following factors:

- Sufficient investment capital.

- Efficiency of management.

- Good business procedures.

- Cooperation between management and employees.

- Trained and experienced salon personnel (**Figure 22-5**).

- Excellent customer service.

- Proper pricing of services (**Figure 22-6**).

NAILS by bernadette

NATURAL NAILS

$20 Manicure		$30 Spa Manicure
$35 Pedicure		$55 Spa Pedicure
$50 Manicure & Pedicure Combo		$75 Spa Manicure & Pedicure Combo

FULL SETS & MAINTENANCE: MONOMER & POLYMER, UV GELS & WRAPS

$45-65 Full Sets	starting at $65 Pink & White Full Sets
$25-40 Maintenance	$45-55 Pink & White Maintenance

price varies per color

Specialty full sets with colored Monomer & Polymer
Specialty maintenance with colored Monomer & Polymer

NAIL ART

price varies upon consulation

Free-Hand designs include acrylic paints in assorted colors, glitters, assorted rhinestones, floral nail designs etc.

Also available: Airbrush designs with stencils
2-D and 3-D nail art
Inlayed designs

▲ **FIGURE 22-6**
Example of a nail salon service menu and price list.

Selecting Insurance

Most small businesses buy a business owners policy (BOP) which includes property, liability, criminal coverage, and various specialty coverages that may be needed by the business.

Workers' compensation provides benefits to people injured at work, such as:

- Hospital and medical care and vocational rehabilitation, when necessary.
- Lost income during the time the employee is out of work and under medical care.
- Benefits if an employee is permanently disabled or dies.

In exchange for benefits, the employee usually forfeits the right to sue their employer for negligence and damage for any covered injury.

> Buying life insurance is a wise choice for business owners...

Buying life insurance is a wise choice for business owners since it will help you make provisions for your business and your beneficiaries. Health insurance plans are made available through trade associations and insurance companies specializing in small businesses. This may make it easier and less costly for your business to have health insurance for yourself and for your employees.

Allocation of Money

As a business owner, you must always know where your money is being spent. A good accountant and an accounting system are indispensable. The figures in **Table 22-1** serve as a guideline, but may vary depending on locality.

THE IMPORTANCE OF RECORD-KEEPING

Good business operations require a simple and efficient record system. Proper business records are necessary to meet the requirements of local, state, and federal laws regarding taxes and employees. Records are of value only if they are correct, concise, and complete. Proper bookkeeping methods include keeping an accurate record of all income and expenses. Income is usually classified as receipts from services and retail sales. Expenses include rent, utilities, insurance, salaries, advertising, equipment, and repairs. Retain check stubs, canceled checks, receipts, and invoices. A professional accountant or a full-charge bookkeeper is recommended to help keep records accurate. A full-charge bookkeeper is someone who is trained to do everything from recording sales and doing payroll to generating a profit-and-loss statement.

Purchase and Inventory Records

An area that should be closely monitored is the purchase of inventory and supplies. Purchase records help maintain a perpetual inventory, which prevents overstocking or shortage of needed supplies, and also alerts you to any incidents of petty theft by employees. These records also help establish the net worth of the business at the end of the year.

TABLE 22-1 Financial Benchmarks for Salons in the United States

REVENUE	% INCOME
Service Sales	88.00%
Retail Sales	12.00%
Total Revenue	100.00%

VARIABLE COSTS	
Retail Products (50% of retail sales)	6.00%
Professional Products (5.5% of service sales)	4.84%
Wages - Producers (45% of service sales + 10% of retail sales)	42.56%
Payroll Taxes - Producers (10% of Producer Wages)	4.26%
Merchant Fees	2.25%
Total Variable Costs	**59.91%**

GROSS PROFIT	**40.09%**

FIXED EXPENSES	
Advertising / Promotion	1.10%
Bank Fees	0.10%
Computer Expense	0.10%
Depreciation / Amortization	1.25%
Education	1.00%
Employee Benefits	1.40%
Insurance	1.10%
Interest	0.50%
Meals, Entertainment, Travel	0.50%
Office Supplies	0.70%
Payroll Service	0.40%
Professional (Acct'g & Legal)	1.00%
Rent / CAM's	6.00%
Repairs & Maintenance	1.00%
Salaries - Non Producers	10.00%
Payroll Taxes - Non Producers	1.00%
Supplies	1.00%
Business Fees / Taxes (non Income)	0.10%
Telephone	0.65%
Utilities	0.65%
Other Expenses	2.00%
Total Fixed Expenses	**31.55%**

NET INCOME (Before Income Taxes)	8.54%

Courtesy of Kopsa Otte CPA's & Advisors.

Keep a running inventory of all supplies, and classify them according to their use and retail value. Those to be used in the daily business operation are consumption supplies **(Figure 22-7)**. Those to be sold to clients are retail supplies.

Service Records

Always keep service records or client consultation cards that describe treatments given, and merchandise sold to each client. Either a card file system or software program will serve this purpose. All service records should include the name and address of the client, the date of each purchase or service, the amount charged, products used, and results obtained. Clients' preferences and tastes should also be noted. For more information on filling out these cards and for an example of a client consultation card, **see Chapter 4**.

✓ **LO6 Complete**

Operating a Successful Salon

The only way to guarantee that you will stay in business and have a prosperous salon is to take excellent care of your clients. Clients visiting your salon should feel completely satisfied with the services you offer them and always look forward to their next visit. To accomplish this, your salon must be physically attractive, well organized, smoothly run, and, above all, sparkling clean. The important five elements of a successful salon are planning the salon's layout, hiring skilled and educated personnel, properly managing the front desk, efficiently using the telephone, and effectively advertising salon services.

PLANNING THE SALON'S LAYOUT

One of the most exciting opportunities ahead of you is planning and constructing the best physical layout for the type of nail salon you envision. Maximum efficiency should be the primary concern.

However, if you are opening a high-end, full-service salon or luxurious day spa where clients expect the quality of the service to match the environment, you will want to plan for more room in the waiting area **(Figure 22-8)**. You may, in fact, choose to have several areas in which clients can lounge between services and enjoy beverages or light snacks. Some upscale salons feature small coffee bars that lend an air of sophistication to the environment. Others offer quiet, private areas where clients can pursue business activities such as phone work or laptop activities between services. The retail area should be spacious, inviting, and well lit. Your retail area may be any size that is appropriate for the number of products that the salon carries.

Layout is crucial to the smooth operation of a salon. After you have decided the type of salon that you wish to run, seek the advice of an architect with plenty of experience in designing salons. For renovations, a professional equipment and furniture supplier will be able to help you (**Figure 22-9**).

▲ **FIGURE 22-8**
Beautifully remodeled reception area.

▲ **FIGURE 22-9**
Typical layout of a nail salon.

PERSONNEL

The size of your nail salon will determine the size of your staff, also referred to as personnel. Large nail salons and nail spas require nail technicians, receptionists, and management specialists, and can include a variety of other specialty consultants. Smaller salons have some combination of these personnel who perform more than one type of service. The success of a salon depends on the quality of the work done by the staff.

When interviewing potential employees, consider the following:
- Level of skill. What is their educational background? When was the last time they attended an educational event?
- Personal grooming. Do they look like you would want their advice about personal grooming?
- Image as it relates to the salon. Are they too progressive or too conservative for your environment?
- Overall attitude. Do they seem more negative than positive in their responses to your questions?
- Communication skills. Are they able to understand your questions? Can you understand their responses?

Making good hiring decisions is crucial; undoing bad hiring decisions is painful to all involved, and can be more complicated than you might expect.

Activity

What would your dream salon look like? Try your hand at designing a salon that would attract the kinds of clients you want, offer the services you would like to specialize in, and provide an efficient, comfortable working environment for nail technician professionals.

Draw pictures, use magazine clippings, or try a combination of both. Pay attention to practical requirements, but feel free to dream a little too. Skylights? Fountains? An employee exercise room? You name it. It's your dream (**Figure 22-10**)!

▲ FIGURE 22-10
Could this be your dream salon?

Payroll and Employee Benefits

To have a successful business, one in which everyone feels appreciated and is happy to work hard and service clients, you must be willing to share your success with your staff whenever it is financially feasible to do so. You can do this in a number of ways.

- Make it your top priority to meet your payroll obligations. In the allotment of funds, this comes first.

- Whenever possible, offer hardworking and loyal employees as many benefits as possible. Either cover the cost of the benefits, or at least make them available to employees and allow them to decide if they can cover the cost themselves.

- Provide staff members with a schedule of employee evaluations. Make it clear what is expected of them if they are to receive pay increases.

- Create and stay with a tipping policy. It is a good idea both for your employees and your clients to know exactly what is expected.

- Put your entire compensation structure or plan in writing and discuss it with employees. The more they understand how the compensation plan works, the easier it will be for them to understand what goals or milestones they may have to achieve in order to increase their salary.

- Create incentives by giving your staff opportunities to earn more money, prizes, or tickets to educational events and trade shows.

Create salon policies and stick to them. Everyone in the salon should be governed by the same rules, including you!

Managing Personnel

As a new salon owner, one of your most difficult tasks will be to manage your staff. But this can also be very rewarding. If you are good at managing others, you can make a positive impact on their lives, and their ability to earn a living. If managing people does not come naturally, do not despair. People can learn how to manage other people, just as they learn how to drive a car or do nail services. Keep in mind that managing others is a serious job. Whether it comes naturally to you or not, it takes time to become comfortable with the role.

There are many great books, both in and out of the professional salon industry that you can use as resources for managing employees and staff. Spend an afternoon online or at your local bookstore researching the topic and purchasing a variety of products that will educate and inform you. Once you have a broad base of information, you will be able to select a technique or style that best suits your personality and that of your salon.

THE FRONT DESK

Most salon owners believe that the quality and pricing of the services are the most important elements of running a successful salon. Certainly these are crucial, but too often the front desk—the operations center—is overlooked. The best salons employ professional receptionists to handle the job of scheduling appointments and greeting clients.

The Reception Area

First impressions count, and since the reception area is the first thing clients see, it needs to be attractive, appealing, and comfortable. This is your salon's nerve center, where your receptionist will sit, retail merchandise will be on display, and the phone system is located. Make sure that the reception area is stocked with business cards and a prominently displayed price list that shows at a glance what your clients should expect to pay for various services.

The Receptionist

Second only in importance to your nail technicians is your receptionist. A well-trained receptionist is the quarterback of the salon, and will be the first person the client sees on arrival. The receptionist should be pleasant, greeting each client with a smile, and addressing her by name. Efficient, friendly service fosters goodwill, confidence, and satisfaction.

In addition to filling the crucial role of greeter, the receptionist handles other important functions, including answering the phone, booking appointments, informing nail techs that a client has arrived, preparing the daily appointment information for the staff, and recommending other services to the client. The receptionist should have a thorough knowledge of all retail products carried by the salon so that she can also serve as a salesperson and information source for clients (**Figure 22-11**).

During slow periods, it is customary for the receptionist to perform certain other duties and activities, such as straightening up the reception area and maintaining inventory and daily reports. The receptionist should also reserve these slow times for making any necessary personal calls, or otherwise being away from the front desk.

Booking Appointments

One of the most important duties the receptionist has is booking appointments. This must be done with care, as services are sold in terms of time on the appointment page. Appointments must be scheduled to make the most efficient use of everyone's time. Under ideal circumstances, a client should not have to wait for a service, and a nail tech should not have to wait for the next client.

Booking appointments may be the main job of the receptionist, but when she is not available, the salon owner or manager, or any of the nail technicians, can help with scheduling. Therefore, it is important

▲ FIGURE 22-11
A good receptionist is key to a salon's success.

▲ FIGURE 22-12
Computerized appointment system.

for each person in the salon to understand how to book an appointment and how much time is needed for each service. Regardless of who actually makes the appointment, anyone who answers the phone or deals with clients must have a pleasant voice and personality.

In addition, the receptionist must have the following qualities:
- Professional and stylish appearance.
- Knowledge of the various services offered.
- Unlimited patience with both clients and salon personnel.

Appointment Book

The appointment book helps nail technicians arrange time to suit their clients' needs. It should accurately reflect what is taking place in the salon at any given time. In most salons, the receptionist prepares the appointment schedule for staff members; in smaller salons, each person may prepare her own schedule. The appointment book may be an actual hardcopy book that is located on the reception desk, or it may be a computerized appointment book that is easily accessed through the salon's computer system (**Figure 22-12**).

USING THE TELEPHONE IN THE SALON

An important part of the business is handled over the telephone. Good telephone habits and techniques make it possible for the salon owner and nail technicians to increase business and improve relationships with clients and suppliers. With each call, a gracious, appropriate response will help build the salon's reputation.

Good Planning

Because it can be noisy, business calls to clients and suppliers should be made at a quiet time of the day or from a telephone placed in a quieter area of the salon.

When using the telephone, you should:
- Have a pleasant telephone voice, speak clearly, and use correct grammar. A smile in your voice counts for a lot.
- Show interest and concern when talking with a client or a supplier.
- Be polite, respectful, and courteous to all, even though some people may test the limits of your patience.
- Be tactful. Do not say anything to irritate the person on the other end of the line.

Incoming Telephone Calls

Incoming phone calls are the lifeline of a salon. Clients usually call ahead for appointments with a preferred technician, or they might call to cancel or reschedule an appointment. The person answering the phone should develop the necessary telephone skills to handle these calls. In addition, some guidelines for answering the telephone are discussed below.

When you answer the phone, say, "Good morning [afternoon or evening], Milady Salon. May I help you?" or "Thank you for calling Milady Salon. This is

Jane speaking. How may I help you?" Some salons require that you give your name to the caller. The first words you say tell the caller something about your personality. Let callers know that you are glad to hear from them.

Answer the phone promptly. On a system with more than one line, if a call comes in while you are talking on another line, ask to put the person on hold, answer the second call, and ask that person to hold while you complete the first call. Take calls in the order in which they are received. If you do not have the information requested by a caller, either put the caller on hold while you get the information, or offer to call the person back with the information as soon as you have it.

Do not talk with a client standing nearby while you are speaking with someone on the phone. You are doing a disservice to both clients.

Booking Appointments by Phone

When booking appointments, take down the client's first and last name, phone number, and service booked. Many salons call the client to confirm the appointment one or two days before it is scheduled.

You should be familiar with all the services and products available in the salon and their costs, as well as which nail professionals perform specific services. Be fair when making assignments. Try not to schedule six appointments for one tech and only two for another.

> Incoming calls are the lifeline of a salon.

However, if someone calls to ask for an appointment with a particular nail technician on a particular day and time, every effort should be made to accommodate the client's request. If the nail technician is not available when the client requests, there are several ways to handle the situation:

- Suggest other times that the nail technician is available.

- If the client cannot come in at any of those times, suggest another nail technician provide the service for this visit.

- If the client is unwilling to try another nail technician, offer to call the client if there is a cancellation at the desired time.

Handling Complaints by Telephone

Handling complaints, particularly over the phone, is a difficult task. The caller is probably upset and short-tempered. Respond with self-control, tact, and courtesy, no matter how trying the circumstances. Only then will the caller be made to feel that she has been treated fairly.

The tone of your voice must be sympathetic and reassuring. Your manner of speaking should convince the caller that you are really concerned about the complaint. Do not interrupt the caller. After hearing the complaint in full, try to resolve the situation quickly and effectively.

▲ FIGURE 22-13
Customer satisfaction
is the best advertising.

ADVERTISING

A new salon owner will want to get the business up and running as soon as possible to start earning some revenue and begin to pay off debts. One of the first things the new salon owner should consider is how to advertise the salon. It is important to understand the many aspects of advertising.

Advertising includes all activities that promote the salon favorably, from a newspaper ad to radio spots, to a charity event, such as a fashion show that the salon participates in. Advertising must attract and hold the attention of readers, listeners, or viewers to create a desire for a service or product.

A satisfied client is the very best form of advertising, because she will refer your salon to friends and family. So make your clients happy **(Figure 22-13)**!

If you have some experience developing ads, you may decide to do your own advertising. If you need help, you can hire a small local agency or ask a local newspaper or radio station to help you produce the ad. As a general rule, an advertising budget should not exceed three percent of your gross income. Plan well in advance for holidays and special yearly events such as proms, New Year's Eve, or the wedding season.

Here are some advertising venues that may prove fruitful for you.
- Newspaper ads and coupons, or coupon books.
  In-salon signage/advertising **(Figure 22-14)**.
- Direct mail to mailing lists and your current salon client list.
- Classified advertising in the local phone book or yellow pages directory.
- Email newsletters and discount offers to all clients who have agreed to receive such mailings. Always include an unsubscribe link.
- Web site offerings.
- Giveaways and promotional items such as nail files, key chains, refrigerator magnets, or calendars.
- Window displays that feature and attract attention to the salon and your retail products.
- Radio advertising.
- Television advertising.
- Community outreach by volunteering at women's and men's clubs, church functions, political gatherings, charitable affairs, and on TV and radio talk shows.
- Client referrals.
- Contacting clients who have not been in the salon for a while.

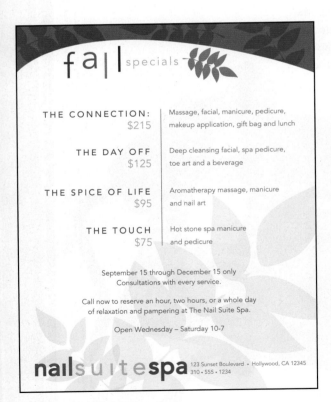

▲ FIGURE 22-14
In-salon signage advertising nail services.

- Telemarketing to tell your customers about products and services. (You need permission in advance to do this.)
- Videos in the salon to promote your salon, salon services, and products.

Selling in the Salon

An important aspect of the salon's financial success revolves around the sale of additional salon services and take-home or maintenance products. Whether you own or manage a large salon with several employees, or you are a booth renter with only yourself to worry about, adding services or retail sales to your service ticket means additional revenue. Nail professionals, in general, seem to feel uncomfortable about selling products or additional services. It is important to work at overcoming this feeling. When nail technicians are reluctant to sell, it is often because they do not want to seem pushy or aggressive. Remember that you are a beauty industry professional and you are making customer care your top priority. You will play a major role in the lives of your customer, and are very valuable to them because you offer good advice (**Figure 22-15**).

▲ **FIGURE 22-15**
Selling nail products benefits everyone.

review questions

1. Name and describe the two most common options for going into business for yourself.

2. What responsibilities does a booth renter assume? What are the disadvantages of booth renting?

3. List at least three of the basic factors that potential salon owners should consider before opening their business.

4. How many types of salon ownership are there? Describe each.

5. List and describe the categories of information that should be included in a business plan.

6. Why is it important to keep good records? What type of records should be kept?

7. List and describe the five elements of a successful salon.

8. Why is selling services and products such a vital aspect of a salon's success?

Glossary

3-D art Any art that protrudes from the nail.

abductor Muscles that separate the fingers and toes.

abductor hallucis Muscle of the foot that moves the toes and helps maintain balance while walking and standing.

ABS See **acrylonitrile butadiene styrene**.

acid A solution that has a pH below 7.0 and turns litmus paper from blue to red.

acidic See **acid**.

acne Skin disorder characterized by chronic inflammation of the sebaceous glands from retained secretions and *Propionibacterium acnes (p. acnes)* bacteria.

acne papule a pimple; small circumscribed elevation on the skin that contains no fluid but may develop pus.

acquired immunity Immunity that the body develops after overcoming a disease through inoculation (such as flu vaccinations) or through exposure to natural allergens, such as pollen, cat dander, and ragweed.

acquired immunodeficiency syndrome Abbreviated as *AIDS*; a disease caused by the HIV virus, which breaks down the body's immune system.

acrylates A specialized acrylic monomer (cross-linking) that has good adhesion to the natural nail plate and polymerizes in minutes. Used to make UV gels.

acrylic The name for an entire family of chemicals used to make all types of nail enhancements and adhesives, including wraps, glues, UV gels, and liquid/powder systems.

acrylonitrile butadiene styrene Abbreviated as *ABS*; a common thermoplastic used to make light, rigid, molded nail tips.

adductor Muscle at the base of each finger that draws the fingers together.

adhesion Chemical reaction resulting in two surfaces sticking together.

adhesive Agent that causes two surfaces to stick together.

adhesive nail enhancement A nail enhancement that is strengthened using nail adhesive.

adipose tissue See **subcutaneous tissue**.

adrenal glands glands that control metabolic processes of the body, including the fight-or-flight response.

AIDS See **acquired immunodeficiency syndrome**.

airbrush stencil A pre-cut sheet of clear, thin plastic with a sticky backing that is cut by a machine into various shapes or designs. Any variety of paper, lace, mesh, fabric or other material can be used as a stencil.

albinism Congenital leukoderma, or absence of melanin pigment of the body, including the hair, skin, and eyes.

alkali A solution that has a pH above 7.0 and turns litmus paper from red to blue.

alkaline See **alkali**.

allergic contact dermatitis Skin that becomes allergic to an ingredient in a product; often caused by prolonged or repeated contact.

allergy Reaction due to extreme sensitivity to certain foods, chemicals, or other normally harmless substances.

alternating current Abbreviated as *AC*; rapid and interrupted current, flowing first in one direction and then in the opposite direction, changing directions sixty times per second.

amp Also known as *ampere*; unit that measures the strength of an electric current (the number of electrons flowing through a wire);

ampere See **amp**.

anabolism Constructive metabolism; the process of building up larger molecules from smaller ones.

analogous colors Colors that are located beside each other on the color wheel.

anatomy Study of human body structure that can be seen with the naked eye, and what the body is made up of; the science of the structure of organisms or of their parts.

anhidrosis Deficiency in perspiration, often a result of fever or certain skin diseases.

anion An ion with a negative electrical charge.

anterior tibial artery See *popliteal artery*.

anterior tibial nerve See *deep peroneal nerve*.

antiseptics Chemical germicides formulated for use on the skin, registered and regulated by the FDA.

aorta The largest artery in the body.

apex Also known as *arch*; the area of the nail that has all of the strength; usually oval-shaped and is located in the center of the nail.

aromatherapy Involves the use of highly concentrated, non-oily, and volatile essential oils to induce such reactions as relaxation or invigoration or simply to create a pleasant fragrance during the service.

arrector pili muscle Tiny, involuntary muscle in the base of the hair follicle that causes "goose bumps".

arteries Thick-walled muscular and flexible tubes that carry oxygenated blood from the heart to the capillaries.

asymptomatic Showing no symptoms or signs of infection.

atom The smallest particle of an element that still retains the properties of that element.

atrium One of the two upper chambers of the heart, through which blood is pumped to the ventricles.

autonomic nervous system Abbreviated as *ANS*; the part of the nervous system that controls the involuntary muscles; regulates the action of the smooth muscles, glands, blood vessels, and heart.

axon and axon terminal The extension of a neuron by which impulses are sent away from the body to other neurons, glands, or muscles.

bacilli (singular: bacillus) Short rod-shaped bacteria.

bacteria (singular: bacterium) Also known as *microbes* or *germs*; one-celled microorganisms with both plant and animal characteristics. Some are harmful, some are harmless.

bactericidal Capable of destroying bacteria.

basal cell carcinoma Most common and least severe type of skin cancer; often characterized by light or pearly nodules.

basal cell layer Also known as the *stratum germinativum*; the bottom, live layer of the epidermis, where cell divides and begin the keratinization process.

Beau's lines Visible depressions running across the width of the natural nail plate.

bed epithelium Thin layer of tissue between the nail plate and the nail bed.

belly (brush) The midsection of the brush bristles; the area of the brush that retains the most paint.

belly (muscle) Middle part of a muscle.

bicep Muscle producing the contour of the front and inner side of the upper arm; it lifts the forearm and flexes the elbow.

bicuspid valve See *mitral valve*.

bit Filing tool that inserts into the handpiece that actually does the filing.

blood Nutritive fluid circulating through the circulatory system (heart, veins, arteries, and capillaries) to supply oxygen and nutrients to cells and tissues, and to remove carbon dioxide and waste from them.

blood spill See *exposure incident*.

blood vascular system Group of structures (heart, arteries, veins, and capillaries) that distributes blood throughout the body.

bloodborne pathogens Disease-causing microorganisms carried in the body by blood or body fluids.

body systems Groups of bodily organs acting together to perform one or more functions. The human body is composed of 11 major systems.

booth rental Also known as *chair rental*; renting a booth or station in a salon.

brain Part of the central nervous system contained in the cranium; largest and most complex nerve tissue; controls sensation, muscles, gland activity, and the power to think and feel emotions.

briefing Usually fifteen to thirty minutes before the start of the competition during which the competition director or head judge will review the rules and guidelines to ensure everyone understands and is able to comply.

bromhidrosis Foul-smelling perspiration, usually noticeable in the armpits or on the feet.

bruised nail Condition in which a blood clot forms under the nail plate, forming a dark purplish spot, usually due to physical injury.

bulla (plural: bullae) Large blister containing a watery fluid; similar to a vesicle but larger.

business plan Written plan of a business, as it is seen in the present and envisioned in the future.

callus See *keratoma*.

callus softeners Help to soften and smooth calluses, especially on heels and over pressure points.

capillary Tiny, thin-walled blood vessel that connects the smaller arteries to the veins.

capital Money needed to start a business.

cardiac muscle The involuntary muscle that is the heart. This type of muscle is not found in any other part of the body.

cardiovascular system See *circulatory system*.

carpus The wrist; flexible joint composed of a group of eight small, irregular bones held together by ligaments.

catabolism The phase of metabolism that involves the breaking down of complex

compounds within the cells into smaller ones. This process releases energy that has been stored.

catalysts Substances that speed up chemical reactions.

cation An ion with a positive electrical charge.

cell membrane Cell part that encloses the protoplasm and permits soluble substances to enter and leave the cell.

cells Basic unit of all living things from bacterial to plants and animals, including human beings; minute mass of protoplasm capable of performing all the fundamental functions of life.

central nervous system Consists of the brain, spinal cord, spinal nerves, and cranial nerves.

chain reaction Also known as a *polymerization reaction*; process that joins together monomers to create very long polymer chains.

chelating detergents Detergents that contain chelating agents to prevent hard tap water from reducing the effectiveness of the cleanser.

chelating soaps Soaps that contain chelating agents to prevent hard tap water from reducing the effectiveness of the cleanser.

chemical A substance obtained by a chemical process or producing a chemical effect.

chemical change A change in the chemical and physical properties of a substance by a chemical reaction that creates a new substance or substances.

chemical properties Those characteristics that can only be determined by a chemical reaction and a chemical change in the substance.

chemistry Science that deals with the composition, structures, and properties of matter, and how matter changes under different conditions.

chloasma Condition characterized by increased pigmentation on the skin from dark spots that are not elevated.

cicatrix See *scar*.

cilia Also know as *flagella*; slender, hairlike extensions used by bacilli and spirilla for locomotion.

circuit breaker Switch that automatically interrupts or shuts off an electric circuit at the first indication of overload.

circulatory system Also known as the *cardiovascular* or *vascular system*; system that controls the steady circulation of the blood through the body by means of the heart and blood vessels.

clarify To make clear.

clean A mechanical process (scrubbing) using soap and water or detergent and water to remove dirt, debris and many disease-causing germs. Cleaning also removes invisible debris that interferes with disinfection.

client base Customers who are loyal to a particular nail technician.

client consultation Verbal communication with a client to determine the desired result of a service.

client consultation form A questionnaire used to gather information about a client's needs, history and preferences; filled out before the client's first service is performed at the salon.

coatings Products, including nail polish, top coats, artificial nail enhancements, and adhesives, that cover the nail plate with a hard film.

cocci Round-shaped bacteria that appear singly (alone) or in groups (staphylococci; streptococci; diplococci).

collagen Fibrous protein that gives the skin form and strength.

color The light seen reflected from a surface.

color blocking Creating blocks or sections of color on the nail.

color fading Also known as *color graduation*; when one color fades into the other, and the meeting point is a combination of the two.

color wheel A color guide that illustrates and identifies the primary, secondary, tertiary, and complementary colors.

comedo (plural: comedones) Hair follicle filled with keratin and sebum. When the sebum of the comedo is exposed to the environment, it oxidizes and turns black (blackheads); when the follicle is closed and not exposed to the environment, comedones are a white or cream color (whiteheads).

commission Percentage of revenue that a salon takes in from sales earmarked for the nail technician.

common peroneal nerve A division of the sciatic nerve that extends from behind the knee to wind around the head of the fibula to the front of the leg where it divides into two branches.

communication The act of accurately sharing information between two people or groups of people so that it is effectively understood.

competition kit A kit you must take with you of all products you will use or might use in the competition.

complementary colors Colors located directly opposite each other on the color wheel.

complete electrical circuit The path of an electric current, from the generating source, through conductors, and back to its original source.

compound molecules Combinations of two or more atoms of different elements united together chemically.

concentric bits Balanced bits that do not wobble or vibrate.

conductor Any substance that conducts electricity.

connective tissue Fibrous tissue that binds together, protects, and supports the various parts of the body. Examples of connective tissue are bone, cartilage, ligaments, tendons, fascia, and fat or adipose tissue.

consumption supplies Supplies used in daily business operations.

contact dermatitis An eruptive skin infection caused by touching certain substances to the skin; may be short-term or long-term.

contagious disease Also known as communicable disease; disease that is spread by contact from one person to another person.

contamination The presence, or the reasonably anticipated presence, of blood or other potentially infectious materials on an item's surface, or visible debris/residues such as dust, hair, skin, etc.

converter Apparatus that changes direct current to alternating current.

corium See *dermis*.

corporation Business whose ownership is shared by three or more people, called stockholders.

corrosive A substance capable of seriously damaging skin, eyes, or other soft tissues on contact. Some corrosives have delayed action (minutes); others affect the skin almost instantly.

cosmetology The art and science of beautifying and improving the skin, nails, and hair; and the study of cosmetics and their applications.

cover letter Letter of introduction that highlights your goals, skills, and accomplishments.

cross-linker Monomer that joins together different polymer chains.

crust Dead cells that form over a wound or blemish while it is healing; an accumulation of sebum and pus, sometimes mixed with epidermal material.

cure Harden through exposure to UV light.

curette Small, spoon-shaped instrument used for cleaning debris from the edges of the nail plate.

cuticle The dead, colorless tissue attached to the nail plate.

cutis See *dermis*.

cyanoacrylate A specialized acrylic monomer (non-crosslinking) that has excellent adhesion to the natural nail plate and polymerizes in seconds, used to make wraps and nail adhesives.

cyst Closed, abnormally developed sac, containing fluid, semifluid, or morbid matter above or below the skin.

cytoplasm The protoplasm of a cell, except that which is in the nucleus; the watery fluid that cells need for growth, reproduction, and self-repair.

decontamination The removal of blood or potentially infectious materials on an item's surface an the removal of visible debris or residue such as dust, hair, skin, etc.

deductive reasoning Process of reaching logical conclusions by employing logical reasoning.

deep peroneal nerve Also known as the *anterior tibial nerve*; extends down the front of the leg, behind the muscles. It supplies impulses to these muscles and also to the muscles and skin on the top of the foot and adjacent sides of the first and second toes.

deltoid Large, triangular muscle covering the shoulder joint that allows the arm to extend outward and to the side of the body.

dendrites Tree-like branching of nerve fibers extending from a nerve cell; short nerve fibers that carry impulses toward the cell and receive impulses from other neurons.

derma See *dermis*.

dermatitis Abnormal inflammatory condition of the skin.

dermatologist Physician engaged in the practice of treating the skin, its structures, functions, and diseases.

dermatology Medical branch of science that deals with the study of skin and its nature, structure, functions, diseases, and treatments.

dermis Also known as the *derma, corium, cutis,* or *true skin*; underlying or inner layer of the skin.

design sculpture Nail enhancements that have inlaid designs and are produced using either monomer liquid and polymer powder or UV gel products.

diagnose See *diagnosis*.

diagnosis Determination of the nature of a disease from its symptoms and/or diagnostic tests.

diaphragm Muscular wall that separates the thorax from the abdominal region and helps control breathing.

digestive enzymes Chemicals that changes certain types of food into a form that can be used by the body.

digestive system The mouth, stomach, intestines, and salivary and gastric glands that change food into nutrients and wastes.

digit See *phalanges*.

digital nerve Nerve that, with its branches, supplies the fingers and toes.

dimethyl urea hardener A hardener that adds cross-links to the natural nail plate, but unlike those containing formaldehyde, DMU does not cause adverse skin reactions.

diplococci Spherical bacteria that grow in pairs and cause diseases such as pneumonia.

direct current Abbreviated as *DC*; constant, even-flowing current that travels in one direction.

direct transmission Transmission of blood or body fluids from or to the client through touching (including handshaking), kissing, coughing, sneezing, and talking.

disease Abnormal condition of all or part of the body, organ, or mind that makes it incapable of carrying on normal function.

disinfectants Chemical products that destroy all bacteria, fungi, and viruses (but not spores) on surfaces.

disinfection The process that eliminates most, but not necessarily all, microorganisms on non-living surfaces. This process is not effective against bacterial spores.

disposable See *single-use*.

disposable implements Implements that cannot be reused and must be thrown away after a single use.

dorsal A nerve that extends up from the toes and foot, just under the skin, supplying impulses to toes and foot, as well as the muscles and skin of the leg, where it is called the superficial peroneal nerve or the musculocutaneous nerve.

dorsal nerve Also known as *dorsal cutaneous nerve*; See *dorsal*.

dorsalis pedis artery See *popliteal artery*.

eczema Inflammatory, painful itching disease of the skin, acute or chronic in nature, presenting many forms of dry or moist lesions.

efferent nerves See *motor nerves*.

efficacy The effectiveness with which a disinfecting solution kills specific organisms when used according to the label instructions.

effleurage A succession of strokes by gliding the hands over an area of the body with varying degrees of pressure or contact.

eggshell nail Noticeably thin, white nail plate that is more flexible than normal.

elastin Protein base similar to collagen which forms elastic tissue.

electric current Flow of electricity along a conductor.

electricity The movement of particles around an atom that creates pure energy.

element The simplest form of matter, which cannot be broken down into a simpler substance without a loss of identity.

elemental molecules Chemical combinations of atoms of the same element.

employee evaluation A periodic assessment of an employee's skills, attitudes, and behaviors and how they are used and perceived in the salon setting.

employment portfolio Collection of photographs and documents that reflect a person's skills, accomplishments, and abilities in a chosen career field.

emulsion An unstable mixture of two or more immiscible substances united with the aid of a binder or emulsifier.

emulsifier Brings two normally incompatible materials together and binds them into a uniform and fairly stable blend; eventually separate but usually very slowly over time.

endocrine (ductless) glands Organs (such as the thyroid or pituitary glands) that release hormonal secretions directly into the bloodstream.

endocrine system Group of specialized glands that affect the growth, development, sexual activities, and health of the entire body.

epidermis Outermost layer of the skin.

epithelial tissue Protective covering on body surfaces, such as the skin, mucous membranes, tissue inside the mouth, the lining of the heart, digestive and respiratory organs, and glands.

eponychium Living skin at the base of the nail plate and covering the matrix area.

ergonomics the study of how a workplace and tools should be designed for maximum comfort, safety, efficiency, and productivity.

essential oils Oils extracted using various forms of distillation from seeds, bark, roots, leaves, wood, and/or resin.

esthetician Specialist in the cleansing, preservation of health, and beautification of the skin and body; one who gives therapeutic facial treatments.

ethics Principles of good character, proper conduct, and moral judgment, expressed through personality, human relation skills, and professional image.

evaporate Change from liquid to vapor form.

excoriation Skin sore or abrasion produced by scratching or scraping.

excretory system Group of organs including the kidneys, liver, skin, large intestine, and lungs that purify the body by the elimination of waste matter.

exfoliating scrubs Water-based lotions that contain a mild gritty-like abrasive and moisturizers to help in removing dry, flaky skin and reducing calluses.

exhalation The act of breathing outward, expelling carbon dioxide from the lungs.

exocrine glands Also known as *duct glands*; organs that produce a substance that travels through small tube-like ducts, such as the sudoriferous (sweat) glands and the sebaceous (oil) glands.

exothermic reactions Chemical reactions which produce heat.

exposure incident Contact with non-intact (broken) skin, blood, body fluid, or other potentially infectious materials that is the result of the performance of an employee's duties (previously called *blood spill*).

extensor Muscle that straightens the wrist, hand, and fingers to form a straight line.

extensor digitorum brevis Muscle of the foot that moves the toes and helps maintain balance while walking and standing.

extensor digitorum longus Muscle that bends the foot up and extends the toes.

eyes Body organs that control the body's vision.

fabric wrap Nail wrap made of silk, linen, or fiberglass.

fan brush Flat brush where the bristles or hairs are spread out like a fan. This brush is most commonly used for blending and special effects.

fantasy art Nail art category or competition where all art mediums are allowed and the only limitation is the imagination.

femur A heavy, long bone that forms the leg above the knee.

ferrule The metal band around the brush that helps to hold the bristles in place.

fiberglass Very thin synthetic mesh with a loose weave.

fibula The smaller of the two bones that form the leg below the knee. The fibula may be visualized as a bump on the little-toe side of the ankle.

fine-grit abrasives 240 grit and higher abrasives designed for buffing, polishing, and removing very fine scratches.

fissure Crack in the skin that penetrates the dermis, such as chapped hands or lips.

flagella (singular: flagellum) Slender, hairlike extensions used by bacilli and spirilla for locomotion.

flash cure Placing wet UV gel product under the UV light for five to ten seconds.

flat art A nail art category that includes all free-hand painting techniques that are flat, not raised.

flat brush A brush with a square tip with long bristles, which gives it added flexibility. This brush is useful for blending and shading.

flexor Extensor muscle of the wrist, involved in flexing the wrist.

flexor digitorum brevis Muscle of the foot that moves the toes and help maintain balance while walking and standing.

flute Long, slender cut or groove found on carbide bits.

foot file Also known as *foot paddle*; large abrasive file used to smooth and reduce thicker areas of callus.

foot soaks Products containing gentle soaps, moisturizers, and so on that are used in a pedicure bath to cleanse and soften the skin.

free edge Part of the nail plate that extends over the tip of the finger or toe.

French manicure Nail art technique where the nail bed is one color, usually pink, peach, or beige (depending upon the client's skin tone), and the free edge of the nail is another color, usually white.

French twist A competition where you may use pink, white, clear, and glittered products to produce a unique twist on the French manicure look.

friction In massage, various strokes that manipulate or press one layer of tissue over another.

fulcrum finger Also known as *balance point*; balancing the tip of one pinky finger with the tip of the pinky finger on the other hand as you work.

fungi (singular: fungus) Microscopic plant parasites, including molds, mildews, and yeasts.

fungicidal Capable of destroying fungi.

fuse Special device that prevents excessive current from passing through a circuit.

game plan The conscious act of planning your life rather than just letting things happen.

gas A state of matter different from liquid or solid. Gases are not formed by evaporation of liquids, as are vapors. Gases must not be confused with vapors or fumes.

gastrocnemius Muscle that is attached to the lower rear surface of the heel and pulls the foot down.

germs See *bacteria*.

gland Specialized organ that removes certain constituents from the blood to convert them into new substances.

glycerin Sweet, colorless, oily substance used as a moisturizing ingredient in cosmetic products.

goals A set of benchmarks that, once achieved, help you to realize your mission and your vision.

goal setting Identifying short-term and long-term goals to help you decide what you want to achieve in your life.

gravity-fed Airbrush system designed to pull the paint into the airbrush using gravity.

grit Number of abrasive particles per square inch.

grounding To complete an electrical circuit and carry the current safely away.

hangnail or agnail Condition in which the eponychium or other living tissue surrounding the nail plate becomes split or torn.

hard UV gels Also known as traditional UV gels; gels that cannot be removed with acetone.

heart Muscular cone-shaped organ that keeps the blood moving within the circulatory system.

heel Point at which the bristles of the brush meet the ferrule.

hematoma A collection of blood that is trapped underneath the nail. This blood usually results in pain and pressure on the nail bed. This excess blood may need draining by a physician.

hemoglobin Coloring matter of the blood; a complex iron protein in red blood cells that binds to oxygen.

hepatitis A bloodborne virus that causes disease affecting the liver.

histamine Chemicals released in the blood that enlarge the vessels around an injury so that blood can speed removal of any allergy-causing substance.

histology Also known as *microscopic anatomy*; the study of tiny structures found in tissues;

HIV See *human immunodeficiency virus*.

hormone Secretion, such as insulin, adrenalin, and estrogen, produced by one of the endocrine glands and carried by the bloodstream or body fluid to another part of the body to stimulate a specific activity.

hospital disinfectants Effective for cleaning blood and body fluids in hospitals and on nonporous surfaces in the salon, thus controlling the spread of disease.

human immunodeficiency virus Abbreviated as *HIV*; virus that can cause AIDS.

humerus Uppermost and largest bone in the arm, extending from the elbow to the shoulder.

hydrophilic Water-loving.

hyperhidrosis Excessive sweating, caused by heat or general body weakness.

hypertrophy Abnormal growth of the skin.

hyponychium Slightly thickened layer of skin that lies between the fingertip and free edge of the nail plate. It forms a protective barrier that prevents microorganisms from invading and infecting the nail bed.

immiscible Not capable of being mixed.

immunity The ability of the body to destroy and resist infection. Immunity against disease can be either natural or acquired and is a sign of good health.

implements Tools used to perform nail services that are multiple use (re-useable) or disposable.

indirect transmission Transmission of blood or body fluids through contact with an intermediate contaminated object such as a razor, extractor, nipper, or an environmental surface.

infection The invasion of body tissues by pathogens.

infectious Infection that can be spread from one person to another person or from one infected body part to another.

infectious disease Disease caused by pathogenic (harmful) microorganisms that enter the body. An infectious disease may or may not spread from one person to another person.

inflammation Condition in which a part of the body reacts to protect itself from injury, irritation, or infection, characterized by redness, heat, pain, and swelling.

inhalation The breathing in of air.

inhibition layer Tacky surface left on the nail once a UV gel has cured.

initiators Substance that starts the chain reaction that leads to the creation of very long polymer chains.

inlaid designs Designs inside a nail enhancement that are created when nail art is sandwiched between two layers of product while the nail enhancement is being formed.

inorganic chemistry The study of substances that do not contain carbon, but may contain hydrogen.

insertion Part of the muscle at the more movable attachment to the skeleton.

insulator Also known as *nonconductor*; a material that does not transmit electricity easily.

integumentary system The skin and its accessory organs, such as the oil and sweat glands, sensory receptors, hair, and nails.

interstitial fluid Blood plasma found in the spaces between tissues.

intestines A body organ that, along with the stomach, digests food.

ion An atom or molecule that carries an electrical charge.

ionization The separation of an atom or molecule into positive and negative ions.

irritant contact dermatitis Skin infection caused when the skin becomes irritated by a substance.

job description Document that outlines the duties and responsibilities of a particular position.

joint Connection between two or more bones of the skeleton.

keloid Thick scar resulting from excessive growth of fibrous tissue.

keratin Fiber protein found in nails, skin and hair. The keratin in natural nails is harder than the keratin in hair or skin.

keratoma Also known as *callus*; acquired, superficial, thickened patch of epidermis caused by pressure or friction on the hands and feet.

kidneys Body organs that excrete water and waste products.

kilowatt 1,000 watts.

lateral nail fold See *sidewall*.

latissimus dorsi Large, flat, triangular muscle covering the lower back.

lentigenes Technical term for freckles.

lesion Mark on the skin; certain lesions could indicate an injury or damage that changes the structure of tissues or organs. There are three types of skin lesions: primary, secondary, and tertiary.

leukocytes See *white blood cells*.

leukoderma Skin disorder characterized by light abnormal patches; caused by a burn or congenital disease that destroys the pigment-producing cells.

leukonychia spot Whitish discoloration of the nails, usually caused by injury to the matrix area; white spot.

ligament A tough band of fibrous tissue that connects bones or holds an organ in place.

linen Closely woven, heavy material used for nail wraps.

liner brush A detail brush preferred for line work, outlining, and lettering.

lipophilic Oil-loving.

liver organ that removes waste created by digestion.

local infection An infection such as a pimple or abscess, that is confined to a particular part of the body and is indicated by a lesion containing pus.

lower-grit abrasives Boards and buffers less than 180 grit that quickly reduce the thickness of any surface.

lungs Organs of respiration; spongy tissues composed of microscopic cells in which inhaled air is exchanged for carbon dioxide during one breathing cycle.

lunula Whitish, half-moon shape at the base of the nail plate, caused by the reflection of light off the surface of the matrix.

lymph Clear fluid that circulates in the lymph spaces (lymphatics) of the body; carries waste and impurities away from the cells.

lymphatic/immune system Body system made up of lymph, lymph nodes, the thymus gland, the spleen, and lymph vessels. Protects the body from disease by developing immunities and destroying disease-causing microorganisms, as well as draining the tissue spaces of excess interstitial fluids to the blood. It carries waste and impurities away from the cells.

lymph capillaries Blind end tubes that are the origin of lymphatic vessels.

lymph nodes Special structures found inside the lymphatic vessels that filter lymph.

macule (plural: maculae) Spot or discoloration on the skin, such as a freckle. Macules are neither raised or sunken.

maintenance Term used for when a nail enhancement needs to be serviced after two or more weeks from the initial application of the nail enhancement product. The maintenance service allows the professional to apply the enhancement product onto the new growth of nail, commonly referred to as a *fill* or a *backfill*, and it allows the professional to structurally correct the nail to ensure its strength, shape, and durability; this is commonly referred to as a *rebalance*.

malignant melanoma Most serious form of skin cancer, often characterized by black or dark brown patches on the skin that may appear uneven in texture, jagged, or raised.

marbleizer Also known as *stylus*; a tool with wooden handles and a rounded ball tip that can range in size and is excellent for dotting small circles of color on a nail.

marbleizing A swirled effect when you combine two or more colors together when wet and mix them on the nail with a marbleizing tool known as a stylus.

mask Also known as a *masque*; a concentrated treatment product often composed of mineral clays, moisturizing agents, skin softeners, aromatherapy oils, botanical extracts and other beneficial ingredients to cleanse, exfoliate, tighten, tone, hydrate, and nourish the skin.

massage the manipulation of the soft tissues of the body

Material Safety Data Sheet Abbreviated as *MSDS*; contains safety information about products compiled by a manufacturer, including the names of hazardous ingredients, safe handling and use procedures, precautions to reduce the risk of accidental harm or overexposure, and flammability warnings.

matrix Area where the nail plate cells are formed; this area is composed of matrix cells that make up the nail plate.

matter Any substance that occupies space and has mass (weight).

median nerve Nerve, with its branches, that supplies the arm and hand.

medium-grit abrasives 180 to 240 grit abrasives that are used to smooth and refine surfaces and shorten natural nails.

melanin Tiny grains of pigment (coloring matter) deposited into cells in the layer of the epidermis and papillary layers of the dermis. There are two types of melanin: pheomelanin, which is red to yellow in color, and eumelanin, which is dark brown to black.

melanocytes Melanin-forming cells.

melanonychia Significant darkening of the fingernails or toenails; may be seen as a black band under or within the nail plate, extending from the base to the free edge.

metabolism Chemical process that takes place in living organisms through which the cells are nourished and carry out their activities.

metacarpus Bones of the palm of the hand; parts of the hand containing five bones between the carpus and phalanges.

metal pusher A reusable implement, made of stainless steel; used to push back the eponychium, but can also be used to gently scrape cuticle tissue from the natural nail plate.

metatarsal One of three subdivisions of the foot comprised of five bones, which are long and slender, like the metacarpal bones of the hand, which help make up the foot. The other two subdivisions are the tarsal and phalanges. All three subdivisions comprise 26 bones.

methacrylate A type of acrylic monomer (cross-linking) that has very good adhesion to the natural nail plate and polymerizes in minutes; used to make all liquid/powder systems and at least one type of UV gel.

Methicillin-resistant *staphylococcus aureus* Abbreviated as *MRSA*; staph infection occurring most frequently among persons with weakened immune systems or in people having undergone medical procedures; highly resistant to certain antibiotics.

methyl methacrylate monomer Abbreviated as *MMA*; a substance in wide use around the world for many applications, such as bone repair cement for implantation into the body.

microbes/germs Nonscientific synonyms for disease-producing bacteria.

microorganism Any organism of microscopic or submicroscopic size.

microshattering Tiny cracks in nail enhancements as they age with wear and become brittle; can also be caused by aggressive filing with or without an electric file,

microtrauma The act of causing tiny unseen openings in the skin that may allow entry by pathogenic microbes.

mildew A type of fungus that affects plants or grows on inanimate objects, but does not cause human infections in the salon.

miliaria rubra Prickly heat; acute inflammatory disorder of the sweat glands, characterized by the eruption of small red vesicles and accompanied by burning, itching skin.

milliampere Abbreviated as *mA*; one-thousandth of an ampere.

miscible Capable of being mixed with another liquid in any proportion without separating.

mission statement A description of the key strategic influences of the business, such as the market it will serve, the kinds of services it will offer, and the quality of those services.

mitosis Cells dividing into two new cells (daughter cells); the usual process of cell reproduction of human tissue.

mitral valve Also known as bicuspid valve; the valve between the left atrium and the left ventricle of the heart.

mixed media Description used for nail art when more than one nail art medium is used to create the design.

mole Small, brownish spot or blemish on the skin, ranging in color from pale tan to brown or bluish black.

molecule Two or more atoms joined chemically.

monomer One unit called a molecule.

monomer liquid Chemical liquid mixed with polymer powder to form the sculptured nail enhancement.

monomer liquid and polymer powder nail enhancements Enhancements created by combining monomer liquid and polymer powder.

motility Self-movement.

motor nerve fibers Fibers of the motor nerves that are distributed to the arrector pili muscles attached to hair follicles. Motor nerves carry impulses from the brain to the muscles.

motor nerves Also known as *efferent nerves*; nerves that carry impulses from the brain to the muscles.

MRSA See **methicillin-resistant staphylococcus aureus**

MSDS See **Material Safety Data Sheet**.

multi-use Reusable, items that can be cleaned, disinfected, and used on more than one person, even if the item is accidentally exposed to blood or body fluid.

muscular system Body system that covers, shapes, and supports the skeleton tissue; contracts and moves various parts of the body.

muscular tissue Tissue that contracts and moves various parts of the body.

Mycobacterium fortuitum furunculosis a microscopic germ that normally exists in tap water in small numbers.

myology Study of the nature, structure, function, and diseases of the muscles.

nail art competitions Opportunities for licensed professionals or nail students to compete in a specified category where the art and theme of the nails are part of the judging criteria.

nail bed Portion of the living skin that supports the nail plate as it grows toward the free edge.

nail clippers A reusable implement used to shorten the nail plate quickly and efficiently.

nail creams Barrier products that contain ingredients designed to seal the surface and hold in the subdermal moisture in the skin.

nail dehydrator A substance used to remove surface moisture and tiny amounts of oil left on the natural nail plate.

nail disorder Condition caused by an injury or disease of the nail unit.

nail extension underside the actual underside of the nail extension; is usually smooth.

nail folds The folds of normal skin that surround the nail plate.

nail groove Slit or furrow on the sides of the nail.

nail oils Designed to absorb into the nail plate to increase flexibility and into the surrounding skin to soften.

nail plate Hardened keratin plate that sits on and slowly slides across the nail bed while it grows and it is the most visible and functional part of the nail unit.

nail psoriasis A non-infectious condition that affects the surface of the natural nail plate, causing it to appear rough and pitted, as well as causing reddish color spots on the nail bed and onycholysis.

nail pterygium Abnormal condition that occurs when the skin is stretched by the nail plate; usually caused by serious injury or allergic reaction.

nail rasp Metal file with an edge that can file the nail plate in only one direction.

nail technology The art and science of beautifying and improving the nails and skin of the hands and feet.

nail tips Plastic, pre-molded nails shaped from a tough polymer made from ABS plastic.

nail tip adhesive The bonding agent used to secure the nail tip to the natural nail.

nail unit All the anatomical parts of the fingernail necessary to produce the natural nail plate.

nail wrap A method of securing a layer of fabric or paper on and around the nail tip to ensure its strength and durability.

nail wrap resin Wrap resins are used to coat and secure fabric wraps. Wrap resins are made from cyanoacrylate and are closely related to those used to create other types of nail enhancements.

natural immunity Immunity that is partly inherited and partly developed through healthy living.

natural nail The hard protective plate that is located at the end of the finger or toe.

nerve Whitish cord made up of bundles of nerve fibers held together by connective tissue through which impulses are transmitted.

nerve tissue Tissue that carries messages to and from the brain and controls and coordinates all body functions.

nervous system Body system composed of the brain, spinal cord, and nerves; controls and coordinates all other systems inside and outside of the body and makes them work harmoniously and efficiently.

networking Establishing contacts that may eventually lead to a job and that help you gain valuable information about the workings of various establishments.

neurology Science of the structure, function, and pathology of the nervous system.

neuron Nerve cell; primary structural unit of the nervous system, consisting of cell body, nucleus, dendrites, and axon.

nevus Small or large malformation of the skin due to abnormal pigmentation or dilated capillaries; commonly known as a birthmark.

nipper A stainless steel implement used to carefully trim away dead skin around the nails.

nonpathogenic harmless organisms that may perform useful functions and are safe to come in contact with since they do not cause disease or harm.

nonstriated muscle See *smooth muscle*.

nucleus Dense, active protoplasm found in the center of the cell; plays an important part in cell reproduction and metabolism.

occupational disease Illness resulting from conditions associated with employment, such as prolonged and repeated overexposure to certain products or ingredients.

odorless monomer liquid and polymer powder products Nail enhancement product that has a very low odor.

ohm Unit that measures the resistance of an electric current.

oil-in-water emulsion Abbreviated as *O/W*; oil droplets emulsified in water.

oligomer Short chain of monomers that is not long enough to be considered a polymer.

-ology Suffix meaning study of (e.g., technology).

one-color method When only one color of nail enhancement product is applied over the entire surface of the nail.

onychia Inflammation of the matrix of the nail with shedding of the nail.

onychocryptosis Ingrown nail; nail grows into the living tissue around the nail.

onycholysis Separation of the nail plate from the nail bed, often caused by injury or allergic reactions.

onychomadesis The separation and falling off of a nail from the nail bed; can occur on fingernails and toenails.

onychomycosis Fungal infection of the natural nail plate.

onychophagy Bitten nails.

onychorrhexis Split or brittle nails that also have a series of lengthwise ridges giving a rough appearance to the surface of the nail plate.

onychosis Any deformity or disease of the natural nails.

onyx Technical term for nail of the fingers or toes.

opacities The amount of pigment concentration in a gel making it difficult to see through.

organs In plants and animals, structures composed of specialized tissues designed to perform specific functions.

organic chemistry The study of substances that contain carbon.

origin Part of the muscle that does not move; attached to the skeleton and usually part of a skeletal muscle.

os Bone.

osteology The study of anatomy, structure, and function of the bones.

oval nail A conservative nail shape that is thought to be attractive on most women's hands. It is similar to a squoval nail with even more rounded corners.

ovaries The female glands that function in sexual reproduction, as well as determining female sexual characteristics.

overexposure Prolonged, repeated, or long-term exposure that can cause sensitivity.

overfiling Excessively roughing up the nail plate.

overlay A layer of any kind of nail enhancement product that is applied over the natural nail or nail and tip application for added strength.

pancreas Organ that secretes enzyme-producing cells responsible for digesting carbohydrates, proteins, and fats.

paper wrap Temporary nail wrap made of very thin paper. Not nearly as strong as fabric wraps.

papillary layer Outer layer of the dermis, directly beneath the epidermis.

papule Pimple; small circumscribed elevation on the skin that contains no fluid but may develop pus.

paraffin A petroleum by-product that has excellent sealing properties (barrier qualities) to hold moisture in the skin.

parasite An organism that grows, feeds, and shelters on or in another organism (referred to as the host), while contributing nothing to the survival of that organism. Parasites must have a host to survive.

parasitic disease Disease caused by parasites, such as lice, mites, and ringworm.

parathyroid glands Glands that regulate blood calcium and phosphorus levels so that the nervous and muscular systems can function properly.

paronychia Bacterial inflammation of the tissues surrounding the nail; pus, redness and swelling are usually present.

partnership Business structure in which two or more people share ownership, although not necessarily equally; management and responsibilities of the business and its operations may be given to one or more people.

patella Also known as the *accessory bone*; forms the knee cap joint.

pathogenic Causing disease; may cause harmful conditions or infections in humans.

pathogenic disease Disease produced by organisms, including bacteria, virus, fungi, and parasites.

pectoralis major and pectoralis minor Muscles of the chest that assist the swinging movements of the arm.

pedicure A cosmetic service performed on the feet by a licensed nail technician or cosmetologist and includes trimming, shaping, exfoliating skin and polishing toenails as well as foot massage.

perfectionism An unhealthy compulsion to do things perfectly.

pericardium Double-layered membranous sac enclosing the heart.

peripheral nervous system System of nerves that connects the peripheral (outer) parts of the body to the central nervous system; it has both sensory and motor nerves.

peroneus brevis Muscle that originates on the lower surface of the fibula. It bends the foot down and out.

peroneus longus Muscle that covers the outer side of the calf and inverts the foot and turns it outward.

personal hygiene Daily maintenance of cleanliness by practicing good sanitary habits.

personnel Employees; staff.

pH See *potential hydrogen*.

pH scale Measures the acidity and alkalinity of a substance; ranges from 0 to 14.

phalanges Also known a *digits*; bones of the fingers or toes (singular: phalanx).

phenolic disinfectant A form of formaldehyde, a tuberculocidal disinfectant.

photoinitiator A chemical which in combination with resins and the proper curing lamp causes UV gels to cure.

physical change A change in the form or physical properties of a substance without the formation of a new substance.

physical mixture A physical combination of matter in any proportions.

physical presentation Person's physical posture, walk, and movements.

physical properties Those characteristics that can be determined without a chemical reaction and that do not cause a chemical change in the substance.

physiology Study of the functions and activities performed by the body's structures.

pincer nails Increased crosswise curvature throughout the nail plate caused by an increased curvature of the matrix.

pineal gland A gland of the endocrine system; plays a major role in sexual development, sleep, and metabolism.

pituitary gland A gland of the endocrine system; affects almost every physiologic process of the body: growth, blood pressure, contractions during childbirth, breast milk production, sex organ functions in both women and men, thyroid gland function, the conversion of food into energy (metabolism).

plasma Fluid part of the blood that carries food and other useful substances to the cells.

plasticizers Ingredients used to keep nail enhancement products flexible.

platelet Blood cell that aids in the forming of clots.

plicatured nail Also known as *folded nail*; a type of highly curved nail plate often caused by injury to the matrix, but may be inherited.

pointed nail Suited to thin hands with long fingers and narrow nail beds. The nail is tapered and longer than usual to emphasize and enhance the slender appearance of the hand.

polymer Substance formed by combining many small molecules (monomers) or oligomers, usually in extremely long, chain-like structure.

polymer powder Powder in white, clear, pink, and many other colors that is combined with monomer liquid to form the nail enhancement.

polymerization Also known as curing or hardening; chemical reaction that creates polymers.

popliteal artery Divides into two separate arteries known as the anterior tibial and the posterior tibial. The anterior tibial goes to the foot and becomes the dorsalis pedis, which supplies the foot with blood.

porous means that an item that is made or constructed of a material which has pores or openings. Some porous items can be safely cleaned, disinfected, and used on more than one client.

position The way that a brush is held to create nail art; the brush can be positioned straight up-and-down or laid flat and pulled across the nail surface.

position stop The point where the free edge of the natural nail meets the tip.

posterior tibial artery See *popliteal artery*.

potential hydrogen Abbreviated as *pH*; a measure of the acidity or alkalinity of a substance.

pressure Amount of force that an artist applies to a brush while in the stroke motion when applying nail art.

primary colors Pure pigment colors that cannot be obtained from mixing together other colors.

primer Substance that improves adhesion.

prioritize To make a list of tasks that need to be done in the order of most important to least important.

procrastination Putting off until tomorrow what you can do today.

professional image Impression projected by a person engaged in any profession, consisting of outward appearance and conduct exhibited in the workplace.

pronator Muscle that turns the hand inward so that the palm faces downward.

protein hardeners A combination of clear polish and protein, such as collagen.

protoplasm Colorless jelly-like substance found inside cells, in which food elements such as protein, fats, carbohydrates, mineral salts, and water are present.

pseudomonas aeruginosa One of several common bacteria that can cause nail infection.

psoriasis Skin disease characterized by red patches covered with silver-white scales, usually found on the scalp, elbows, knees, chest, and lower back, and rarely on the face.

pull The technique of pulling a liner or other brush across the surface of the nail to create a fluid line.

pulmonary circulation Blood circulation from heart to lungs to be purified, then back to the heart again.

pure substance A chemical combination of matter in definite (fixed) proportions.

pus A fluid created by tissue inflammation; a sign of a bacterial infection.

pustule Inflamed pimple containing pus.

pyrogenic granuloma Severe inflammation of the nail in which a lump of red tissue grows up from the nail bed to the nail plate.

quaternary ammonium compounds Also known as *quats*, these disinfectants are very effective when used properly in the salon.

radial artery Artery that supplies blood to the thumb side of the arm and the back of the hand; supplies the muscles of the skin, hands, fingers, wrist, elbow, and forearm.

radial nerve With its branches, supplies the thumb side of the arm and back of the hand.

radius Smaller bone in the forearm (lower arm) on the same side as the thumb.

rebalance Term often used to refer to the maintenance of a nail enhancement.

rectifier Apparatus that changes alternating current to direct current.

red blood cells Blood cells that carry oxygen from the lungs to the body cells and transport carbon dioxide from the cells back to the lungs.

reflective listening Listening to the client and then repeating, in your own words, what you think the client is telling you.

reflex Automatic reaction to a stimulus that involves the movement of an impulse from a sensory receptor along the sensory nerve to the spinal cord. A responsive impulse is sent along a motor neuron to a muscle, causing a reaction (e.g., the quick removal of the hand from a hot object). Reflexes do not have to be learned; they are automatic.

reflexology A unique method of applying pressure with thumb and fingers to the hands and feet; has demonstrated health benefits.

repair patch Piece of fabric cut to completely cover a crack or break in the nail. Use Procedure 16-7, Four-Week Fabric Wrap Maintenance, to apply the repair patch.

reproductive system Body system responsible for processes by which plants and animals produce offspring.

respiration Act of breathing; the exchange of carbon dioxide and oxygen in the lungs and within each cell.

respiratory system Body system consisting of the lungs and air passages; enables breathing, supplying the body with oxygen and eliminating carbon dioxide as a waste product.

resume Written summary of a person's education and work experience.

retail supplies Supplies sold to clients.

retailing Act of recommending and selling quality products to clients for at-home nail care.

reticular layer Deeper layer of the dermis that supplies the skin with oxygen and nutrients; contains fat cells, blood vessels, sweat glands, hair follicles, lymph vessels, arrector pili muscles, oil glands, nerve endings, and hair follicles.

reusable See *multi-use*.

reusable implements Implements that are generally stainless steel as they must be properly cleaned and disinfected prior to use on another client.

revolutions per minute Abbreviated as *RPM*; number of times a bit turns in a complete circle in one minute.

ridges Vertical lines running the length of the natural nail plate, usually related to normal aging.

rings of fire Grooves carved into the nail caused by filing with bits at the incorrect angle.

round brush Most common and versatile style of brush with a very good capacity for holding paint.

round nail A slightly tapered nail, usually extending just a bit past the fingertip.

rules and guidelines Information provided for each competition so that one understands what the competition allows and does not allow.

saphenous nerve Supplies impulses to the skin of the inner side of the leg and foot.

sanitation or sanitizing A chemical process for reducing the number of disease-causing germs on cleaned surfaces to a safe level.

scabies Contagious skin disease that is caused by the itch mite, which burrows under the skin.

scale Any thin plate of epidermal flakes, dry or oily, such as abnormal or excessive dandruff.

scar Also known as *cicatrix*; light-colored, slightly raised mark on the skin formed after an injury or lesion of the skin has healed.

scope of practice The list of services that you are legally allowed to perform in your specialty in your state.

sebaceous gland Oil gland of the skin connected to hair follicles. Sebum is the fatty or oily secretion of the sebaceous gland.

secondary colors Colors resulting from mixing equal parts of two primary colors; the positions opposite to the primary colors on a color wheel.

secretory coil A tube-like duct that is part of the sudoriferous gland. It ends at the surface of the skin to form the sweat pore.

secretory nerve fibers Fibers that are distributed to the sweat and oil glands. Secretory nerves, which are part of the autonomic nervous system, regulate the excretion of perspiration from the seat glands and control the flow of sebum to the surface of the skin.

sensitization Greatly increased or exaggerated allergic sensitivity to products.

sensory nerve Also known as *afferent nerves*; nerve that carries impulses or messages from the sense organs to the brain, where sensations of touch, cold, heat, sight, hearing, taste, smell, pain, and pressure are experienced.

sensory nerve fibers Sensory receptors that send messages to the brain. These react to heat, cold, touch, pressure, and pain.

serratus anterior Muscle of the chest that assists in breathing and in raising the arm.

service sets Sets of all the tools that will be used in a service.

sidewall The area on the side of the nail plate that grows free of its attachment to the nail fold and where the extension leaves the natural nail.

silicones Special types of oil used in nail polish dryers and skin protectants.

silk A strong, glossy, tightly woven natural fiber used for nail wrapping that becomes transparent when wrap resin is applied.

simple polymer chain Result of long chain of monomers that are attached from head to tail.

single-use Disposable; an item that cannot be used more than once, either because it cannot be properly cleaned and all visible residue removed or because cleaning and disinfecting damages or contaminates it.

sink Also known as *sinking*; the settling and flattening out of a UV gel or other product while working.

skeletal system Physical foundation of the body, comprised of 206 bones that vary in size and shape and are connected by movable and immovable joints.

skin Major organ that is the external protective coating that covers the body.

skin tag Small brown or flesh-colored outgrowth of the skin.

smooth muscle Also known as *involuntary* or *nonstriated muscle*; muscle that functions automatically, without conscious will.

sodium hypochlorite Common household bleach; disinfectant for salon use.

soft UV gels gels removed by soaking in acetone.

sole proprietor Owner and manager of a business.

soleus Muscle that originates at the upper portion of the fibula and bends the foot down.

solute The substance that is dissolved in a solution.

solution A stable uniform blend of two or more mixable substances.

solvent The substance that dissolves the solute in a solution.

spinal cord Portion of the central nervous system that originates in the brain, extends down to the lower extremity of the trunk, and is protected by the spinal column.

spirilla Spiral or corkscrew-shaped bacteria.

splinter hemorrhage Caused by physical trauma or injury to the nail bed, which damages the capillaries and allows small amounts of blood flow.

spotter brush Also known as *detailer*; a short, round brush, having little belly and a very fine point at the tip. This brush offers maximum control for intricate detailed work.

squamous cell carcinoma Type of skin cancer more serious than basal cell carcinoma, often characterized by scaly red papules or nodules.

square nail A nail completely straight across the free edge with no rounding at the outside edges.

squoval nail A nail with a square free edge that is rounded off at the corner edges.

stain Abnormal brown or wine-colored skin discoloration with a circular and irregular shape.

staphylococci Pus-forming bacteria that grow in clusters like bunches of grapes.

sterilization The process that completely destroys all microbial life, including spores.

stomach Major body organ that, along with the intestines, digests food.

stratum corneum Also known as the *horny layer*; outer layer of the epidermis.

stratum germinativum Also known as the *basal layer*; deepest, live layer of the epidermis that produces new epidermal skin cells and is responsible for growth.

stratum granulosum Granular layer of the epidermis.

stratum lucidum Clear, transparent layer of the epidermis under the stratum corneum.

stratum spinosum The spiny layer just above the basal cell layer.

streptococci Pus-forming bacteria arranged in curved lines resembling a string of beads.

stress A force or system of forces exerted on the body that result in strain and/or injury.

stress area The part of the nail enhancement where the natural nail grows beyond the finger and becomes the free edge. This area needs strength to support the nail extension.

stress strip Strip of fabric cut to 1/8″ in length and applied to the weak point of the nail during Procedure 16-7, Four-Week Fabric Wrap Maintenance, to repair or strengthen a weak point in a nail enhancement.

striated muscle Also known as *skeletal muscle*; this is muscle that is voluntarily or consciously controlled.

striper brush An extremely long, flat brush having only a few fibers. It is incredibly efficient when creating long lines, striping effects, and animal prints.

stylus Tool with a solid handle and a rounded ball tip on each end that can range in size. An excellent tool for marbleizing or dotting small circles of color on a nail.

subcutaneous tissue Also known as *adipose* or *subcutis tissue*; fatty layer found below the dermis that gives smoothness and contour to the body; contains fats for use as energy, and also acts as a protective cushion for the outer skin.

subcutis tissue See *subcutaneous tissue*.

sudoriferous glands Sweat glands of the skin.

superficial peroneal nerve Also known as the *musculo-cutaneous nerve*; extends down the leg, just under the skin, supplying impulses to the muscles and the skin of the leg, as well as to the skin and toes on the top of the foot.

supinator Muscle of the forearm that rotates the radius outward and the palm upward.

sural nerve Supplies impulses to the skin on the outer side and back of the foot and leg.

surfactants Surface active agents; substances that act as a bridge to allow oil and water to mix or emulsify.

suspension An unstable mixture of undissolved particles in a liquid.

sweat glands See *sudoriferous glands*.

system Comprised of a group of bodily organs acting together to perform one or more functions.

systemic circulation Also known as *general circulation*; circulation of blood from the heart throughout the body and back again to the heart.

systemic disease Disease that affects the body as a whole, often due to underfunctioning or overfunctioning of internal glands/organs. This disease is carried through the blood stream or lymphatic system.

tactile corpuscles Small epidermal structures with nerve endings that are sensitive to touch and pressure.

talus Also know as the *ankle bone* of the foot; one of three bones that comprise the ankle joint. The other two bones are the tibia and fibula.

tan Change in pigmentation of skin caused by exposure to the sun or ultraviolet light

tarsal One of three subdivisions of the foot comprised of seven bones (talus, calcaneous, navicular, three cuneiform bones, and the cuboid). The other two subdivisions are the metatarsal and the phalanges. All three subdivisions comprise 26 bones.

telangiectasia Dilation of surface blood vessels.

tertiary colors Colors resulting from mixing equal parts of one primary color and one of its nearest secondary colors.

test-wise Having a complete and thorough knowledge of the subject matter and understanding the strategies for taking tests successfully.

testes The male glands that function in sexual reproduction, as well as determining male sexual characteristics.

thorax The chest; elastic, bony cage that serves as a protective framework for the heart, lungs, and other internal organs.

thyroid gland Controls how quickly the body burns energy (metabolism), makes proteins, and controls how sensitive the body should be to other hormones.

tibia The larger of the two bones that form the leg below the knee. The tibia may be visualized as a bump on the big-toe side of the ankle.

tibial nerve A division of the sciatic nerve that passes behind the knee. It subdivides and supplies impulses to the knee, the muscles of the calf, the skin of the leg, and the sole, heel, and underside of the toes.

tibialis anterior Muscle that covers the front of the shin. It bends the foot upward and inward.

ticket upgrading or upselling services Practice of recommending and selling additional services to clients that may be performed by you or other practitioners licensed in a different field.

tinea pedis Medical term for fungal infections of the feet.

tip Also known as *chisel edge*; very end of the bristles, farthest away from the handle.

tip cutter Implement similar to a nail clipper, designed especially for use on nail tips.

tissue Collection of similar cells that perform a particular function.

toe separators Foam rubber or cotton disposable implements used to keep toes apart while polishing the nails. A new set must be used on each client and then thrown away.

toenail clippers Professional instruments with curved or straight jaws used for cutting toenails.

tolerance The tightness of the inside of the shank where the bit fits into the handpiece.

torque Power of a machine or its ability to keep turning when applying pressure during filing.

toxins Any of various poisonous substances, produced by some microorganisms (bacteria and viruses).

transferable skills Skills mastered at other jobs that can be put to use in a new position.

trapezius Muscle that covers the back of the neck and upper and middle region of the back; rotates and controls swinging movements of the arm.

tricep Large muscle that covers the entire back of the upper arm and extends the forearm.

tricuspid valve Heart valve which prevents backflow between the right atrium and right ventricle.

true skin See *dermis*.

trumpet nail Disorder in which the edges of the nail plate curl around to form the shape of a trumpet or sharp cone at the free edge.

tubercle Abnormal rounded, solid lump above, within, or under the skin, larger than a papule.

tuberculocidal disinfectants Proven to kill the bacteria that can cause tuberculosis.

tuberculosis A disease caused by a bacterium that is only transmitted through coughing.

tumor A swelling; abnormal cell mass resulting from excessive multiplication of cells, varying in size, shape, and color.

two-color method Two different colors of gel are applied to the surface of the nail, in different places, as in a French manicure.

ulcer Open lesion on the skin or mucous membrane of the body, accompanied by pus and loss of skin depth.

ulna Inner and larger bone of the forearm (lower arm), attached to the wrist and located on the side of the little finger.

ulnar artery Artery that supplies blood to the muscle of the little finger side of the arm and palm of the hand.

ulnar nerve Nerve, with its branches, that affects the little finger side of the arm and palm of the hand.

ultraviolet light Abbreviated as *UV light*; invisible and has short wavelengths (therefore contains more energy); is less penetrating than visible light, kills germs, and causes chemical reactions to happen more quickly.

unit wattage Measure of how much electricity a light bulb consumes.

Universal Precautions A set of guidelines published by OSHA that require the employer and the employee to assume that all human blood and body fluids are infectious for bloodborne pathogens.

urethane acrylate or urethane methacrylate Main ingredients used to create UV gel nail enhancements.

UV bonding gels Gels that increase adhesion to the natural nail plate.

UV building gels Thick viscosity adhesive gels that are used to build an arch and curve to the fingernail.

UV gel Type of nail enhancement product that hardens when exposed to an ultraviolet (UV) light source.

UV gel polishes An alternative to traditional nail lacquers. UV gel polishes do not dry as a nail lacquer does; they cure in the UV light unit.

UV gloss gels Sealing gels, finishing gels, or shine gels. These gels are used to finish the nails and to create a glossy shine.

UV lamp Also known as the *UV light bulb*; special bulb that emits UV light to cure UV gel nail enhancements.

UV light unit Also known as the *UV light*; specialized electronic device that powers and controls UV lamps to cure UV gel nail enhancements.

UV self-leveling gels A group of gels that is used to enhance the thickness of other gels while providing a smoother surface than some UV building gels.

UV stabilizers Ingredients which control color stability and prevent sunlight from causing fading or discoloration.

valve Structure that temporarily closes a passage or permits blood flow in one direction only.

vapor What is formed when liquids evaporate into the air.

vascular system See *circulatory system*.

vein Thin-walled blood vessel that is less elastic than an artery; veins contain cup-like valves to prevent backflow and carry blood containing waste products from the capillaries back to the heart and lungs for cleaning and to pick up oxygen.

ventricle One of the two lower chambers of the heart.

verruca Technical term for wart; hypertrophy of the papillae and epidermis.

vesicle Small blister or sac containing clear fluid, lying within or just beneath the epidermis.

virucidal Capable of destroying viruses.

virus (plural: viruses) A parasitic submicroscopic particle that infects and resides in cells of biological organisms. A virus is capable of replication only through taking over the host cell's reproduction function.

vision statement A long-term picture of what the business is to become and what it will look like when it gets there.

Vitamin A Aids in the health, function, and repair of skin cells; improves the skin's elasticity and thickness.

Vitamin C Needed for proper repair of the skin and various tissues; promotes the production of collagen in the skin's dermal tissues, keeping the skin healthy and firm.

Vitamin D Promotes healthy and rapid healing of the skin; enables the body to properly absorb and use calcium, the element needed for proper bone development and maintenance.

Vitamin E Helps fight against, and protect the skin from the harmful effects of the sunlight.

vitiligo Milky-white spots (leukoderma) of the skin. Vitiligo is hereditary and may be related to thyroid conditions.

volatile Easily evaporating.

volatile organic compounds Abbreviated as *VOCs*; compounds containing carbon (organic) and evaporate very quickly (volatile) and easily.

volt Unit that measures the flow of electrons forward through a conductor.

water-in-oil emulsion Abbreviated as *W/O*; Water droplets emulsified in oil.

watt Abbreviated as *W*; unit that measures how much electric energy is being used in one second.

wavelength Distance between successive peaks of electromagnetic waves.

wheal Itchy, swollen lesion that lasts only a few hours, caused by a blow, the bite of an insect, urticaria, or the sting of a nettle.

white blood cells Also known as *white corpuscles* or *leukocytes*; blood cells that perform the function of destroying disease-causing microorganisms.

white corpuscles See *white blood cells*.

white UV gels Also known as *pigmented gels*; building gels, used early in the service, or self-leveling gels, used near the final contouring procedure.

wooden pusher A wooden stick used to remove cuticle tissue from the nail plate (by gently pushing), to clean under the free edge of the nail, or to apply products.

work ethic Taking pride in your work, and committing yourself to consistently doing a good job for your clients, employer, and salon team.

wrap resin accelerator A product specially designed to help adhesives dry more quickly.

Index

moisture trap, airbrush, 407
"molds," 149
molecules, 163–164
moles, 130, 131–132
money management, 469–470
monomer liquid nail enhancements
    crack repair, 356–357
    nail art, 403–405, 413, 419
    odorless, 341
    overview, 332–335
    procedures, 345–359, 419
    proper maintenance of, 339–340
    removal of, 358–359
    storage of, 338
    supplies for, 335–338
    UV gel over, 389–391
monomers, 181–182
motility, 65
motivation, 17
motor nerve fibers, 119
motor nerves, 103
multiple choice exam questions, 435
multi-use implements, 76–77, 205–206
muscle tissue, 95
muscular system, 98–102
musculo cutaneous nerve, 104
Mycobacterium fortuitum furuncolosis, 62
myology, 99

N

nail anatomy, 143–144
    nail bed, 143
    nail folds, 145, 234
    nail plate, 143, 359
    nail unit, 143
nail extension underside, 340
Nail Manufacturer's Council (NMC), 265
nail pterygium, 153, 212
Nail Structure and Product Chemistry (Schoon), 153, 185, 209, 225
nail technology, defined, 4
narrow nails, 145f
natural immunity, 70
natural nail, 142–145, 296
natural nail bits, 289, 296
natural nail discs, 289
natural/organic products, 184, 222
neck problems, 32
needle bits, 289
Nefertiti, Queen, 4
nerves, 103
nerve tissue, 95
nervous system, 102–105

networking, 411, 446, 463
neurology, 102
neurons, 103
nevus, 130
nippers, 205, 236, 255, 294
nitrile gloves, 201
no-fragrance policies, 30
No Light Gels, 309
non-acetone polish removers, 210
nonconductor, 190
nonpathogenic bacteria, 63
nonstriated muscles, 99
"non-toxic" substances, 185–186
non-whirlpool foot basins/tubs, 87, 268
no-tipping policies, 468
nucleus, 93

O

occupational diseases, 67
Occupational Safety and Health Act (OSHA), 60, 201, 233
ohms (O), 192
oil-based conditioner/polish, 142
oil glands, 120–121
oil-in-water (O/W) emulsion, 168
oils, 210, 221, 237, 322
oligomers, 364
oligometer, 182
olive nails, 145f
one-color monomer liquid/polymer powder, 345–348, 352–354
one-color UV gel method, 365, 376–380
onychia, 157
onychocryptosis, 157
onycholysis, 157, 237
onychomadesis, 157
onychomycosis, 158
onychophagy, 152
onychorrhexis, 152
onychosis, 157
onyx, 142
opacities, 367
organic chemistry, 162
organic/natural products, 184, 222
organizational plan, 487
organs and body systems, 95–96
origin (muscle), 99
os, 96
osteology, 96
oval nails, 217
ovaries, 110
overexposure, 133, 185–186, 213
overfiling, 179
overlay, 306
overtime, 467
ownership, types of, 485–486

P

paddles, 254–255, 261
painted nail art, 401–403, 417–421
pancreas, 109
paper wraps, 308
papillary layer, 118
papules, 128
Paracelsus, 185
paraffin treatments, 204, 213, 223–225, 244–246, 253
paraformaldehyde, 75
parasites, 64, 70
parasitic diseases, 67
parathyroid glands, 109
paronychia, 158
partial well tips, 306
partnership, 486
patella, 98
pathogenic bacteria, 63–65, 67, 70
payroll, 494
pectoralis major/minor, 100
pedicure bits, 290, 296
pedicure cart, 252
pedicure nail files, 254
pedicures
    defined, 250
    marketing to men, 219
    materials, 255
    performing, 257–258, 272–275
    pricing, 262
    products, 256–258
    scheduling, 259–261
    spa, 261
    tools for, 250
pedicure spas, 78
pedicure station, 251
pedicure stool and footrest, 251
perfectionism, 16
performance evaluation form, 56
perfume, 30
pericardium, 105
peripheral nervous system (PNS), 102
peroneus brevis, 101
peroneus longus, 101
personal budget, 470
personal budget worksheet, 470
personal hygiene and grooming, 28–31
personality development, 23–24
personal matters, 50
Personal Protective Equipment (PPE), 201–202
personnel, salon, 493–496
petrissage, 220
pH (potential hydrogen), 170–172
phalanges, 97–98